Historic Documents
of 2015

SAGE was founded in 1965 by Sara Miller McCune to support the dissemination of usable knowledge by publishing innovative and high-quality research and teaching content. Today, we publish over 900 journals, including those of more than 400 learned societies, more than 800 new books per year, and a growing range of library products including archives, data, case studies, reports, and video. SAGE remains majority-owned by our founder, and after Sara's lifetime will become owned by a charitable trust that secures our continued independence.

Los Angeles | London | New Delhi | Singapore | Washington DC | Melbourne

Historic Documents
of 2015

Heather Kerrigan, Editor

FOR INFORMATION:

CQ Press
An Imprint of SAGE Publications, Inc.
2455 Teller Road
Thousand Oaks, California 91320
E-mail: order@sagepub.com

SAGE Publications Ltd.
1 Oliver's Yard
55 City Road
London, EC1Y 1SP
United Kingdom

SAGE Publications India Pvt. Ltd.
B 1/I 1 Mohan Cooperative Industrial Area
Mathura Road, New Delhi 110 044
India

SAGE Publications Asia-Pacific Pte. Ltd.
3 Church Street
#10-04 Samsung Hub
Singapore 049483

SAGE Editor: Laura Notton
Editor: Heather Kerrigan
Contributors: Rebecca Adams,
                Brian Beary, Anastazia
                Clouting, Melissa
                Feinberg, Sarah Gall,
                Linda Fecteau Grimm,
                Heather Kerrigan
Editorial Assistant: Jordan Enobakhare
Production Editor: David C. Felts
Copy Editor: Deanna Noga
Typesetter: C&M Digitals (P) Ltd.
Proofreader: Lawrence W. Baker
Indexer: Joan Shapiro
Cover Designer: Michael Dubowe
Marketing Manager: Leah Watson

Cover image: AP Images /Yorgos Karahalis

"Award Ceremony Speech." December 10, 2015. © The Nobel Foundation 2015. Used with permission.

"Government congratulates Wits on discovery of new hominin species." September 10, 2015. © 2011 - Current, Department: Science & Technology, Republic of South Africa. All rights reserved.

"Irreversible damage to overheated batteries in the Solar Impulse airplane pushes the second half of Round-the-World solar flight to April 2016." July 15, 2015. Used with permission of Solar Impulse.

"NAACP Applauds South Carolina State Legislature for Voting to Remove Confederate Battle Flag." July 9, 2015. Used with permission.

"Prime Minister Justin Trudeau's Open Letter to Canadians." November 4, 2015. Office of the Prime Minister of Canada. © Her Majesty the Queen in Right of Canada, 2016.

"Record-breaking solar flight reaches Hawaii after 5 nights and days airborne without fuel. Unlimited endurance is now proven thanks to clean technology." July 3, 2015. Used with permission of Solar Impulse.

"Remarks by Deputy President Cyril Ramaphosa on the occasion of the announcement of the discovery of a new species." September 10, 2015. © 2011 - Current, Department: Science & Technology, Republic of South Africa. All rights reserved.

"Resolution: NAACP Ends Boycott of South Carolina." July 11, 2015. Used with permission.

"Speech at the International Conference on Nepal's Reconstruction 2015—Takehiko Nakao." June 25, 2015. This article was first published by the Asian Development Bank (www.abd.org).

"Statement by AFL-CIO President Richard Trumka: Stop the Fast Track to Lower Wages." April 16, 2015. Used with permission.

"Statement by the Prime Minister of Canada Following the Swearing-in of the 29th Ministry." November 4, 2015. Office of the Prime Minister of Canada. © Her Majesty the Queen in Right of Canada, 2016.

"Statement by the Prime Minister of Canada on the Arrival of Syrian Refugees." December 11, 2015. Office of the Prime Minister of Canada. © Her Majesty the Queen in Right of Canada, 2016.

"Swiss explorers Bertrand Piccard and Andre Borschberg launch their attempt at flying Round-The-World in a solar-powered airplane. Their experimental aircraft, Solar Impulse 2 took-off this morning from Abu Dhabi." March 9, 2015. Used with permission of Solar Impulse.

"USW Opposes Fast Track Bill: It's Time for a New Trade Policy, Not More of the Same." April 16, 2015. Used with permission.

Printed in United States of America

ISBN 978-1-5063-3351-9

This book is printed on acid-free paper.

16 17 18 19 20 10 9 8 7 6 5 4 3 2 1

Contents

JANUARY

FEBRUARY

MARCH

APRIL

and a statement by the president on December 3, 2015, following the San Bernardino, California, mass shooting.

JULY

AUGUST

SEPTEMBER

OCTOBER

DECEMBER

Thematic Table of Contents

AMERICAN LIFE

BUSINESS, THE ECONOMY, AND LABOR

ENERGY, ENVIRONMENT, SCIENCE, TECHNOLOGY, AND TRANSPORTATION

GOVERNMENT AND POLITICS

HEALTH AND SOCIAL SERVICES

INTERNATIONAL AFFAIRS

AFRICA

INTERNATIONAL AFFAIRS
ASIA

INTERNATIONAL AFFAIRS
CANADA

INTERNATIONAL AFFAIRS
EUROPE

INTERNATIONAL AFFAIRS
LATIN AMERICA AND THE CARIBBEAN

INTERNATIONAL AFFAIRS
MIDDLE EAST

INTERNATIONAL AFFAIRS
GLOBAL ISSUES

NATIONAL SECURITY AND TERRORISM

RIGHTS, RESPONSIBILITIES, AND JUSTICE

List of Document Sources

CONGRESS

EXECUTIVE DEPARTMENTS, AGENCIES, FEDERAL OFFICES, AND COMMISSIONS

INTERNATIONAL GOVERNMENTAL ORGANIZATIONS

INTERNATIONAL NONGOVERNMENTAL ORGANIZATIONS

JUDICIARY

NONGOVERNMENTAL ORGANIZATIONS

NON-U.S. GOVERNMENTS

U.S. STATE AND LOCAL GOVERNMENTS

WHITE HOUSE AND THE PRESIDENT

Preface

Restored diplomatic U.S.–Cuba relations, the Iran nuclear deal, the global fight against ISIL, the Justice Dept.'s report on police brutality and discrimination in Ferguson, Missouri, economic strife in Greece and China, historic milestones in space science and exploration, the discovery of a new humanoid species in South Africa, the European migrant and refugee crisis, and landmark Supreme Court rulings legalizing same-sex marriage nationwide and upholding the Affordable Care Act subsidies are just a few of the topics of national and international significance chosen for discussion in *Historic Documents of 2015*. This edition marks the forty-third volume of a CQ Press project that began with *Historic Documents of 1972*. This series allows students, librarians, journalists, scholars, and others to research and understand the most important domestic and foreign issues and events of the year through primary source documents. To aid research, many of the lengthy documents written for specialized audiences have been excerpted to highlight the most important sections. The official statements, news conferences, speeches, special studies, and court decisions presented here should be of lasting public and academic interest.

Historic Documents of 2015 opens with an "Overview of 2015," a sweeping narrative of the key events and issues of the year that provides context for the documents that follow. The balance of the book is organized chronologically, with each article comprising an introduction entitled "Document in Context" and one or more related documents on a specific event, issue, or topic. Often an event is not limited to a particular day. Consequently, readers will find that some events include multiple documents that may span several months. Their placement in the book corresponds to the date of the first document included for that event. The event introductions provide context and an account of further developments during the year. A thematic table of contents (page xvii) and a list of documents organized by source (page xxi) follow the standard table of contents and assist readers in locating events and documents.

As events, issues, and consequences become more complex and far-reaching, these introductions and documents yield important information and deepen understanding about the world's increasing interconnectedness. As memories of current events fade, these selections will continue to further understanding of the events and issues that have shaped the lives of people around the world.

How to Use This Book

Each of the seventy entries in this edition consists of two parts: a comprehensive introduction followed by one or more primary source documents. The articles are arranged in chronological order by month. Articles with multiple documents are placed according to the date of the first document. There are several ways to find events and documents of interest:

By date: If the approximate date of an event or document is known, browse through the titles for that month in the table of contents. Alternatively, browse the tables of contents that appear at the beginning of each month's articles.

By theme: To find a particular topic or subject area, browse the thematic table of contents.

By document type or source: To find a particular type of document or document source, such as the White House or Congress, review the list of document sources.

By index: The index allows researchers to locate references to specific events or documents as well as entries on the same or related subjects.

An online edition of this volume, as well as an archive going back to 1972, is available and offers advance search and browse functionality.

Each article begins with an introduction. This feature provides historical and intellectual contexts for the documents that follow. Documents are reproduced with the original spelling, capitalization, and punctuation of the original or official copy. Ellipsis points indicate textual omissions (unless they were present in the documents themselves indicating pauses in speech), and brackets are used for editorial insertions within documents for text clarification. The excerpting of Supreme Court opinions has been done somewhat differently from other documents. In-text references and citations to laws and other cases have been removed when not part of a sentence to improve the readability of opinions. In those documents, readers will find ellipses used only when sections of narrative text have been removed.

Full citations appear at the end of each document. If a document is not available on the Internet, this too is noted. For further reading on a particular topic consult the "Other Historic Documents of Interest" section at the end of each article. These sections provide cross-references for related articles in this edition of *Historic Documents* as well as in previous editions. References to articles from past volumes include the year and page number for easy retrieval.

Overview of 2015

In the United States, 2015 was characterized by a breakdown in race relations, the build-up to the 2016 presidential election, and debates about religious freedom. Racial tensions were at the forefront of a number of events and issues throughout the year, ranging from a church shooting to the removal of the Confederate flag from South Carolina statehouse grounds to excessive use of police force that disproportionately affects minority communities. The issue gained steam late in the year after a series of attacks in Paris perpetrated by the Islamic State of Iraq and the Levant (ISIL) increased national dialogue about whether the United States should accept Syrian—and more specifically, Muslim—refugees.

Although the election to replace President Barack Obama would not take place until November 2016, Republican and Democratic candidates began throwing their hats in the ring for the nomination in earnest at the start of the year. By August, the Republicans had held their first debate, which featured a slate of seventeen candidates. Democrats followed shortly thereafter in October, with five candidates taking the stage. The debates highlighted the stark differences between the parties, and, at times, the splintering of the Republican Party.

The Supreme Court also issued a number of high-profile decisions, including a ruling to uphold the federal tax subsidies offered to eligible Americans under the Affordable Care Act (ACA), and a ruling to uphold the fundamental right of same-sex couples to marry. Similarly, lower courts faced fractious issues including Texas's voter identification law, which was upheld, and the refusal of a Kentucky clerk of courts to issue marriage licenses in light of the Supreme Court ruling. The clerk was temporarily jailed and her office ordered to issue license on her behalf.

Internationally, two main topics dominated the year: ISIL's ongoing global attacks and the further crumbling of Greece's economy. Until 2015, ISIL attacks had primarily targeted areas in Iraq and Syria, but in November the group evidenced its growing strength when it carried out major attacks in Beirut and Paris, resulting in nearly 200 deaths. The attack in Paris had a resounding impact as the city of Brussels went on lockdown, European Union (EU) leaders questioned how open their borders should be, and American politicians spoke out about whether the United States should continue to allow Middle Eastern refugees to enter the country on expedited visas. In Greece, the nation defaulted on its loan payment to the EU and the International Monetary Fund (IMF), which further weakened both the Greek and eurozone economies. Despite its unpopularity with the public, Greek leaders were able to secure a third bailout package in return for revising its internal economic policies. The near failure of Greece to accept assistance raised the issue of whether the eurozone could continue to withstand the existence of failing economies in its union.

DOMESTIC ISSUES

Civil Liberties in the Balance

Tensions between preserving Americans' religious freedoms and protecting their civil liberties fueled controversies in several states. In March, Indiana governor Mike Pence signed into law the Religious Freedom Restoration Act (RFRA), a measure he said would protect Indiana's citizens from being compelled by the state to provide services for same-sex weddings or similar events. The state immediately drew criticism from national organizations and businesses who argued that the law could provide legal cover to companies that chose to discriminate against the lesbian, gay, bisexual, and transgender (LGBT) community. Facing tremendous pressure, the Indiana legislature passed, and Governor Pence quickly signed, a second bill that clarified the RFRA's language but did not specifically extend antidiscrimination protections to the LGBT community. In Arkansas, Governor Asa Hutchinson faced similar pressure to veto a religious freedom bill passed by the state legislature in late March, and, following developments in Indiana, asked lawmakers to send him a less controversial bill, which he signed into law in April.

This issue resurfaced following the U.S. Supreme Court's ruling that same-sex couples have the right to marry, and thousands of same-sex couples began to seek marriage licenses. Kim Davis, a county clerk in Kentucky, stopped issuing marriage licenses entirely to avoid granting licenses to same-sex applicants. She claimed that issuing such licenses would be a violation of her religious faith. The American Civil Liberties Union (ACLU) of Kentucky filed suit against Davis on behalf of four couples who had been denied licenses, with a federal judge ruling that Davis was "free to disagree" with the Supreme Court's decision but was not excused from complying with it. Miller continued to deny same-sex couples marriage licenses and ultimately spent five days in jail for contempt of court.

In the case of *ACLU v. Clapper*, the U.S. Court of Appeals for the Second Circuit ruled that the National Security Administration's (NSA) collection of Americans' bulk telephone metadata "exceeds the scope of what Congress has authorized" under the Patriot Act. The NSA's top secret surveillance program had been revealed by former NSA contractor Edward Snowden in 2013 through several leaks to the press, igniting a firestorm of criticism from privacy rights advocates and civil libertarians who hailed the Second Circuit's ruling as a major victory. However, Congress allowed the challenged provisions of the Patriot Act to lapse weeks later and replaced them with the USA Freedom Act, which gave the NSA six months to end its bulk metadata collection and shift to a more narrowly targeted program for collecting call records as needed.

Obama Continues His Legacy; Election Season Heats Up

President Barack Obama faced legal challenges to a series of executive actions announced in fall 2014 to defer deportations of illegal immigrants living in the United States who met certain criteria. This included a Texas-led lawsuit involving twenty-six states that argued the deferred action programs did not follow federal rulemaking requirements and would either force the states to provide services to illegal immigrants or change their laws in order to avoid doing so. Two federal courts ruled that the president had exceeded his authority by using the programs to grant benefits without congressional approval and that states would indeed incur harmful costs to implement the programs. The administration subsequently appealed the case to the Supreme Court.

Also in 2014, Obama had called for the reclassification of all broadband services as utilities, and the debate surrounding network neutrality continued in early 2015 following the Federal Communications Commission's (FCC) approval of a new Open Internet Order that applied to both fixed and mobile broadband services. The order reclassified broadband Internet as a telecommunications service, though exempted it from some regulations that govern other utilities, such as rate regulations and state and local taxes. The order also prohibited providers from blocking access to or impairing Internet traffic for legal content, applications, and non-harmful devices, and prevented them from creating so-called fast lanes that favor select Internet traffic. While praised by open Internet advocates, the order prompted several telecommunications and Internet service providers to file lawsuits against the FCC, claiming the rules were arbitrary and exceeded the commission's regulatory authority.

President Obama also collaborated with Republican congressional leadership to pass a bill re-instating "fast-track" authority, which allows a president to negotiate trade agreements without the threat of congressional filibuster or amendments, to help facilitate ongoing Trans-Pacific Partnership (TPP) negotiations. The House and Senate also approved a related bill to continue funding education and retraining for American workers whose jobs were sent overseas as a result of international trade agreements—an acknowledgment of some lawmakers' concerns that free trade agreements harm the U.S. workforce. The final version of the TPP was agreed to and released in October. As written, the agreement would remove more than 18,000 tariffs on U.S. exports to the twelve participating nations, most of which are located in the Pacific Rim.

After Obama spent much of his presidency softening relations with Cuba, Secretary of State John Kerry led a team of diplomats in a series of negotiations with Cuban officials aimed at normalizing relations between the two nations. In January, the United States lifted some economic sanctions and announced that Americans would be able to travel to Cuba for select purposes for the first time since diplomatic ties had been severed in 1961. In May, Cuba was removed from the State Sponsors of Terrorism List, and in July, the U.S. embassy in Havana and the Cuban embassy in Washington, D.C., reopened. While polls indicated a majority of Americans supported resuming diplomatic relations with Cuba, congressional leadership remains largely opposed to normalizing relations and is unlikely to lift all economic sanctions until Cuba extends greater democratic freedoms to its citizens.

By early fall, the 2016 presidential campaign was in full swing, with the Republican and Democratic parties holding their first candidate debates in August and October, respectively. The emergence of wealthy real estate developer Donald Trump as the clear Republican frontrunner and his brash, colorful style dominated campaign coverage at the expense of his opponents' poll numbers. On the Democratic side, former secretary of state and presumed nominee Hillary Clinton sought to fight off an unexpectedly strong challenge from Bernie Sanders, the Independent U.S. senator from Vermont. The field had narrowed to twelve Republican and three Democratic candidates by the end of the year, with a total of eight contentious debates setting the stage for the first presidential primaries in early 2016.

RACE RELATIONS

Race relations remained at the forefront of domestic issues in 2015 amid new evidence and allegations of racial discrimination by law enforcement in several states. In March, the Department of Justice released two reports detailing its findings from an investigation

xxxvi OVERVIEW OF 2015

into the 2014 shooting and killing of unarmed African American teenager Michael Brown by police in Ferguson, Missouri. While one report explained that the department's findings did not support filing federal charges against the police officer involved in the tragic incident, the other was intensely critical of law enforcement practices in Ferguson, pointing to extensive evidence of a long-standing pattern of unlawful conduct and racial bias in the police department and court system. The report found that police routinely stopped and handcuffed residents without probable cause, arrested people for questioning police tactics, and used excessive and dangerous force, and that all of these practices were disproportionally applied to the African American population. Ferguson officials responded by making significant law enforcement staffing changes and began working with the Department of Justice on system reforms.

The outpouring of grief and anger resulting from Brown's death was further fueled by similar incidents in other states in 2014 and 2015. In Cleveland, Ohio, twelve-year-old Tamir Rice was shot and killed by police after they saw him playing with a toy gun. In North Charleston, South Carolina, Walter Scott was killed following a routine traffic stop. And in Baltimore, Maryland, violent protests erupted after Freddie Gray was killed while in police custody. These deaths further eroded trust and relationships between police departments and African American communities and prompted new calls for reforms to ensure greater accountability in law enforcement. Protestors gathered in cities across the country, occupying public buildings, disrupting transportation, and interrupting presidential campaign events to call for change.

Then on June 17, Dylann Roof opened fire on a prayer meeting at Emanuel African Methodist Episcopal Church in Charleston, killing nine and injuring one. All of the victims were African Americans. Unconfirmed reports suggested that Roof had committed the shootings for racial reasons, and officials discovered a manifesto and several photos on Roof's computer that featured the Confederate flag and indicated his support for the white supremacist movement. The Department of Justice later indicted Roof on thirty-three federal hate crimes and weapons charges, for which he could face the death penalty.

Partly because of the photos that surfaced, the Confederate flag quickly became a rallying cry for those who saw it as a symbol of a time in South Carolina's history that should not be celebrated. In the days following the shooting, South Carolina governor Nikki Haley, Senators Lindsey Graham, R-S.C., and Tim Scott, R-S.C., and former Governor Mark Sanford joined together to call upon state lawmakers to remove the Confederate flag from the statehouse grounds, where it had flown since 1961. In a watershed moment for the South, the state legislature voted in July to remove the Confederate flag, earning praise from Governor Haley and prompting the NAACP to end its fifteen-year economic boycott of the state. Several other southern states subsequently took similar measures to remove Confederate flags and related imagery from their capitol buildings and state license plates.

U.S. Supreme Court Decisions

The Supreme Court heard several emotionally charged cases during its 2014–2015 term, including *Obergefell v. Hodges*, in which the Court ruled 5–4 that same-sex couples have the same constitutionally protected right to marry as opposite-sex couples. The decision came two years after the Court overturned the Defense of Marriage Act, a law specifically denying federal marriage benefits to legally married same-sex couples, and meant that all states must now allow same-sex couples to marry.

On June 25, the Court issued its third major ruling on the ACA since the bill's passage in 2010. *King v. Burwell* centered on a challenge to the ACA's provision of tax credits and subsidies to low-income Americans to help make insurance purchased on a health care exchange more affordable. The challengers argued that ACA language limited these assistance programs to people living in one of the sixteen states that had created their own insurance exchange and did not extend assistance to those living in the remaining thirty-four states that rely on the federal exchange. The Court ruled 6–3 that the subsidies applied to both the state and federal exchanges and that removing such a central part of the ACA's architecture could well collapse the entire health care structure.

Also in June, the Court ruled on an Environmental Protection Agency (EPA) regulation designed to limit toxic mercury emissions from coal-fired power plants. Industry groups and twenty-three states challenged the rule in *Michigan v. EPA*, arguing that its implementation would impose punishing costs on utilities and that the agency had not adequately considered these costs when it developed the rule. The Court ruled 5–4 to strike down the EPA's regulation, even though most power companies had already made changes necessary to comply with the new rule by the time the case was heard.

On the final day before its summer recess, the Court issued its ruling in *Glossip v. Gross*, a case brought by three death row inmates in Oklahoma who argued that the combination of drugs the state uses in lethal injections made it unacceptably likely that they would suffer extreme pain before they died—a violation of the Eighth Amendment's ban on cruel and unusual punishment. The Court upheld the state's use of the drugs in a 5–4 ruling, stating that the inmates had failed to prove that the state's execution protocol entails substantial risk for severe pain.

FOREIGN AFFAIRS

Economic Challenges in Europe

The Greek economy was among the hardest hit by the 2008–2009 global economic downturn. By 2015, the nation had accepted two bailouts from the EU and IMF. On June 30, unable to reach an agreement with the EU and IMF on a third bailout package and extension of its repayment terms, Greece failed to make a required payment to the IMF and officially defaulted on its debt. Eurozone leaders scrambled to find a solution, fearing the weakening of the economic union if Greece was forced to exit. In a move strongly criticized by eurozone leaders, the Greek government of Prime Minister Alexis Tsipras decided to put the most recent bailout proposal offered by the EU and IMF before voters. In the run-up to the July vote, the government encouraged the public to reject the package as a show of force against the eurozone. Ultimately, the referendum to accept the EU-IMF bailout package failed by a vote of 61 percent to 39 percent.

Buoyed by their referendum victory, Greek leaders returned to negotiations in late July. A proposal was drafted that would keep Greece in the eurozone and provide the nation with access to €86 billion in bailout funds in return for the Greek government instituting economic reforms. The new package, officially announced in August, also adjusted Greek GDP targets from a primary deficit of 0.25 percent to a primary surplus of 3.5 percent in 2018, and gave the nation additional flexibility in repaying its debts. Greece would be responsible for decreasing public pensions, allowing increased investment in labor and product markets, and instituting additional measures to fight tax evasion.

Ongoing protests in Greece against the austerity measures imposed under the EU/IMF package led the prime minister to call for snap elections to give voters another opportunity to express their opinion about the deal. Surprisingly, the prime minister and his party won resounding victories in September, with polls suggesting that while Greeks disapproved of the reforms, they felt the prime minister had done well holding out for the best possible deal he could negotiate.

Ongoing ISIL Attacks

ISIL's rise is rooted in the fall of the regime of Saddam Hussein in 2003, but the group began gaining power when Syria's government crumbled during the Arab Spring uprisings of 2011. The United States became directly involved in combatting ISIL in August 2014 when President Obama authorized airstrikes against the terrorist organization in an effort to defend troops and protect U.S. interests in Iraq. The nation carried out thousands of airstrikes with its coalition partners in late 2014 and through 2015. In early 2015, President Obama asked Congress to approve an ISIL-specific Authorization of the Use of Military Force (AUMF) that would outline U.S. goals and strategies that could be used to target ISIL. Until that point, the president had been carrying out operations against ISIL under a 2001 AUMF that then-President George W. Bush used to launch military efforts in Afghanistan following the September 11 terrorist attacks. The president was unable to garner enough support in Congress for an ISIL-specific AUMF, because Democrats believed it had the potential to allow ground forces to be deployed, while Republicans did not believe the AUMF proposed by President Obama gave the United States enough options in the fight against the terrorist group.

The international community also continued to struggle to find a way to respond to the group's increasing power and land grabs, and by 2015, the terrorist organization had begun ramping up attacks outside of Syria and Iraq. On November 12, two suicide bombings hit a suburb outside of Beirut, which killed an estimated forty-three individuals. The attack was the deadliest since Lebanon's civil war ended in 1990. The following evening, a series of coordinated attacks took place around Paris, including suicide bombings at the national sports stadium and shootings at cafes, restaurants, and a concert venue in the city center. A total of 130 were killed during the November 13 attacks, which French president François Hollande characterized as an act of war.

In response to the attacks in Paris, France increased its airstrikes against ISIL in Syria, and a number of other Western nations, including the United States, followed suit. The traditionally fluid EU instituted temporary border controls when it was learned that all of the attackers held EU passports. In Brussels, the government announced a citywide lockdown while it attempted to find one of the masterminds behind the attack who was thought to be hiding in the city. For four days, schools, public transit, restaurants, and shops were shuttered as security forces combed the streets and carried out raids around the city.

Parisian investigators also announced that some of the attackers had likely entered Europe during the Syrian refugee influx. While EU leaders, including German chancellor Angela Merkel, said that their nations would continue to welcome and resettle refugees, across the Atlantic, U.S. governors began issuing statements indicating that they would not accept refuges in their own states. The debate became heated, with Republican presidential contender Trump insinuating that Muslims should not be allowed into the United States—whether they were legal citizens or not—until the government had an opportunity to determine if they had links to ISIL or any other terrorist organization.

Syrian Conflict Continues

The civil war in Syria entered its fifth year in 2015, with little evidence that President Bashar al-Assad would relinquish his power either to opposition groups or a transitional government. Syrian citizens continued to be attacked by government security forces and rebel groups alike, and fled their homes in droves. By the end of 2015, the United Nations (UN) estimated that 11 million Syrians were displaced because of the violence, 4.5 million of whom had left Syria and settled primarily in Jordan, Turkey, Lebanon, and various nations in Europe. An estimated 200,000 had been killed since the fighting began. The efforts of the UN and other humanitarian organizations to provide much-needed assistance were largely hampered by both the Assad regime and rebel groups that refused to allow aid workers into some parts of the nation.

The UN continued to work with its member states, and particularly countries near Syria, to find a peaceful resolution to the conflict. Late in the year, the UN opened discussions about the possible development of a roadmap that would set deadlines in 2016 and 2017 for Assad and opposition leaders to meet and discuss a political transition and new elections. Although the UN Security Council adopted a resolution advocating for such talks, by the end of the year, neither Syrian leaders nor opposition forces had expressed an interest in moving forward with the plan.

Violence and Instability in Africa

Al Qaeda–affiliated terrorist organizations carried out a number of attacks in Africa in 2015, with two of the largest taking place in Kenya and Mali. On April 2 in Kenya, al-Shabaab militants entered Garissa University and killed 142 students, marking the deadliest attack in Kenya since 1998. Christians were specifically targeted because, according to al-Shabaab, the Christian-dominated government in Kenya had perpetrated crimes against Somalia when it sent troops into the country beginning in 2011. In response to the attacks, the Kenyan government renewed efforts to root out terrorists in the region and stop their spread.

Seven months later, on November 20, gunmen operating under the auspices of al Mourabitoun and al Qaeda in the Islamic Maghreb took 170 hostages at the Radisson Blu hotel in the Malian capital of Bamako. The nation has lacked a stable government for years, giving rise to terrorist organizations and rebel groups operating within its borders. In June 2015, however, international partners had managed to secure a peace accord between the temporary government and rebel groups. A number of those staying in the hotel on the day of the attack were monitoring the accord's progress. More than two-dozen were killed in the siege, which was believed to be carried out to undermine the ongoing attempts to secure peace in the region.

Burundi, which has a long history of instability and violent conflict and is Africa's poorest country, faced an attempted coup that quickly failed but was followed by a largely unpopular president, Pierre Nkurunziza, being reelected. He quickly consolidated his power and began silencing his critics. A number of anti-government protesters were reportedly killed.

In Nigeria, a new president was elected on campaign promises to defeat Boko Haram, a terrorist organization that was responsible for the deaths and abductions of thousands of Nigerians. The Nigerian military was successful in freeing a number of hostages during the year; however, the new government was unable to make any headway toward fully pushing the group out of the country.

Refugee Crises Reach Devastating Heights

Growing instability in the Middle East and Northern Africa led to a dramatic rise in the number of refugees fleeing their homes in 2015, many of them bound for Europe. The migrant crisis gained nationwide attention in April when an estimated 800 migrants drowned while traveling by boat from Libya to Italy. Despite the dangers, hundreds of thousands of refugees continued to attempt the dangerous Mediterranean crossing. A majority of these migrants ended up in Greece, Italy, and Hungary, where the countries, unable to process and assist the massive influx of migrants, established crowded refugee camps and border fences that left refugees in a virtual no man's land.

European leaders established a response plan focused primarily on using military force to combat human traffickers who were leaving refugees stranded and using unsafe vessels to illegally transport migrants onto European shores. However, as the year wore on, it became increasingly clear that the EU would need to develop a plan to better assist those countries within its borders that were bearing the brunt of the refugee situation, including Germany, the United Kingdom, France, and Sweden. By the end of 2015, an estimated one million refugees had entered the EU.

In June, the UN High Commissioner for Refugees released its annual report on displaced persons around the world, which indicated that 2015 was a record year for the number of refugees, asylum seekers, and those displaced within their own countries. The largest number of refugees in 2015 landed in Europe, with Germany and Sweden receiving the highest number of asylum seekers. The increasing number of displaced persons was largely driven by fifteen specific conflicts in Africa, Asia, Europe, and the Middle East. A number of these conflicts, such as those in Afghanistan, Syria, and Somalia, were also preventing displaced persons from returning home.

Iran Nuclear Deal Finally Passed

A major breakthrough occurred in the P5+1 negotiations over Iran's nuclear program in 2015, following two years of delays in replacing the temporary Joint Plan of Action (JPA) that required the nation to reduce its nuclear activities. Negotiators from China, France, Germany, Iran, Russia, the United Kingdom, and the United States met in March 2015 to outline a final tentative agreement that included limits on Iran's nuclear program for ten years in return for the lifting of some economic sanctions. The final agreement was signed on July 15, 2015, and it permitted Iran to continue enriching uranium while placing limits on its stockpile and also allowed the country to continue some nuclear research and development activities. Iran agreed to allow international inspectors to review its nuclear facilities. The agreement was endorsed by the UN Security Council and all previous resolutions against Iran were terminated. The United States and EU followed suit by lifting some of its sanctions against Iran.

Reaction to the agreement was mixed. In the United States, criticism was led by congressional Republicans, who stated that they would attempt to pass a resolution to disapprove of the JPA, and Republican presidential candidates, who claimed that the deal was dangerous and gave Iran a free pass to continue nuclear development nearly unchecked. Democrats, in contrast, saw the agreement as the difference between diplomacy and war and felt that the United States and its collaborators in the negotiation had secured the best possible deal. Congress was unable to pass a resolution by a set deadline of September 17 to stop the agreement from taking effect, and on October 18, the Iranian parliament approved the plan.

Climate Change Summit Reaches Consensus

From November 30 to December 12, representatives from 195 countries met in Paris for the 21st Conference of the Parties to the United Nations Framework Convention on Climate Change (COP21) and the 11th Meeting of the Parties to the 1997 Kyoto Protocol (CMP11). The goal of these meetings was to develop an international climate change agreement that could replace the 1997 Kyoto Protocol, which was set to expire in 2020. Negotiations on such an agreement began one year earlier, when nations began meeting to establish compromises that would frame the discussion and were invited to submit their own individual roadmaps for reducing greenhouse gas emissions. Pledges submitted prior to the conference included a promise by the United States to cut emissions by 26 to 28 percent by 2025, as compared to 2005 levels and China's decision to peak its emission levels in 2030. By the time the COP21/CMP11 was set to begin, some 146 countries had submitted pledges.

On December 12, it was announced that the group had adopted the Paris Agreement, which committed nations to maintaining global temperature increases of 2°C (with strong encouragement that nations should work toward a goal of limiting temperature increases to no more than 1.5°C) and to become carbon neutral by the second half of the century. The Paris Agreement did not have any binding authority pertaining to the amount of emissions each nation would be required to cut. Instead, the group intended to hold nations to their earlier greenhouse gas reduction promises. There was a legally binding provision, however, that all participating nations review their pledges every five years starting in 2020 and another requiring reporting of emissions levels and reductions starting in 2023. There was no enforcement mechanism added to the agreement to encourage adherence to these provisions. Delegates believed that by not binding nations to a specific carbon emission reduction goal, the agreement would be more easily ratified. It will enter into force once fifty-five countries sign on.

—Heather Kerrigan and Linda Fecteau Grimm

January

Treaty on Eurasian Economic Union Takes Effect

JANUARY 1, 2015

A new chapter in Eurasian history began on January 1, 2015, with the entry into force of an intergovernmental treaty that commits five former republics of the Soviet Union to integrate their economies to form a single market. In setting up the Eurasian Economic Union (EEU), Belarus, Kazakhstan, and Russia (Armenia joined on January 2, 2015, and Kyrgyzstan joined on August 12, 2015) put in place an institutional structure that resembles the model of regional economic integration that the European Union (EU) has pioneered since the 1950s. But in contrast with the EU, the EEU's focus is strictly economic; democracy consolidation is not one of its goals. Indeed, the EEU treaty stresses that the individual political setup of each member country must be respected.

Belarus, Kazakhstan, and Russia are authoritarian states with poor human rights records, while Armenia and Kyrgyzstan rank slightly higher for political freedoms. Comprising more than 80 percent of the EEU's economy, Russia is by far the most powerful country in the bloc, which has led skeptics to claim that Russia's autocratic president Vladimir Putin sees the EEU as a vehicle for reincarnating the Soviet Union. But both Putin and the EEU refute this allegation. Russia's neighbors and trading partners are watching the EEU's evolution with great interest. Some have moved to conclude trade agreements with the bloc, while others, notably the EU, are keeping their distance.

EUROPEAN UNION'S ECONOMIC INTEGRATION SEEN AS EEU ROLE MODEL

The thousand-page EEU treaty was signed on May 29, 2014, in Astana, Kazakhstan, by Belarus, Kazakhstan, and Russia. Armenia signed an EEU accession treaty on October 10, 2014, and Kyrgyzstan did so on December 23, 2014, days before the treaty became effective. The EEU describes itself as "an international organization for regional economic integration" whose goals are to "raise the living standards" of its citizens and "raise the competitiveness" of the bloc. The members are committed to upholding the principles of "sovereign equality and territorial integrity; based on the respect to the specifics of the Member-States' political order." This wording is a clear signal that the EEU's remit is economic, not political, union—unlike its EU neighbors, where the goal is both political and economic integration. For the time being, there has been no move to form a single currency or enter into a mutual defense pact.

However, the EEU is modeling itself on the EU in certain ways, in particular by championing the "four freedoms": free movement of goods, services, capital, and labor. The EEU has established permanent institutions charged with carrying out its mission. A Supreme Council comprised of heads of state plus an intergovernmental council made up of prime ministers sets the organization's policy priorities. In addition, there is the

Moscow-based Eurasian Economic Commission (EEC) that is tasked with developing proposals to implement agreed upon policies. The organization has a court based in Minsk, Belarus, to ensure that the members adhere to the agreed rules. The five EEU members have a combined population of 182 million and a gross domestic product (GDP) of about $ 4 trillion, placing them in the second tier in the global economy alongside India and Japan but still well below the first tier including China, the EU, and the United States.

The treaty is specific in spelling out the common policies that the EEU should develop and includes some concrete timelines for when these processes should be completed. For instance, a common market for oil, gas, and electricity should be in place by 2025. Oil and gas are the main commodities produced by the bloc, with Russia as the dominant producer. The deadline for adopting a common policy on pharmaceuticals and medical devices is 2016. In the financial services sector, the goal is to have an EEU-wide regulator operating by 2025. As for the free movement of workers, the treaty says that as of January 1, 2015, no work permits are needed to gain employment in other EEU member states and educational degrees obtained in one member state should automatically be recognized by the others. In other policy fields, ambitions are more modest. In agriculture and macroeconomics, for example, the goal is greater policy coordination rather than full harmonization, while in transportation the goal is "step-by-step" liberalization. For social security, there is "a possibility to apply national treatment" along with a commitment to count pensions accumulated in other EEU members.

Emergence Out of Post-Soviet Chaos

For seven decades these five EEU members, along with ten other Central Asian and Eastern European nations, were part of the Soviet Union. At its zenith in the 1950s, the communist-led Soviet Union was one of the world's two superpowers, vying with the United States for domination after World War II. The Soviets generally lagged behind the United States economically, however, and fell further behind in the 1970s due to political and economic stagnation. Oil and gas wealth generated by the Soviet Union allowed it to develop into a military superpower and extend dominance over Central and Eastern Europe, and most countries in that region became military allies under the 1955 Warsaw Pact. But by the late 1980s, oil prices had plummeted and the Soviet bloc was becoming bankrupt. In 1989, the Soviet Union's Warsaw Pact allies realigned themselves with Western Europe and the United States, essentially ending the Cold War. In 1991, the Soviet Union dissolved into fifteen independent countries.

This sudden demise was a shock for all the countries involved, but especially for Russia because its status as a global superpower ended virtually overnight. An effort to replace the Soviet Union with a more loosely structured Commonwealth of Independent States (CIS) largely failed because the CIS members devoted most of their energies to solidifying their newly gained independence. However, as early as 1994, the leader of one CIS member recognized the value to be gained by reintegrating these once unified economies. President Nursultan Nazarbayev of Kazakhstan, a geographically large, pro-trade nation on Russia's southerly border, unveiled his vision of regional integration in a speech given at Lomonosov Moscow State University. In 1995, Belarus, Kazakhstan, and Russia agreed to form a customs union, meaning there would be no tariffs imposed on each other's goods and a common tariff imposed on goods imported from other countries.

The pace of integration was initially slow, and the customs union did not become operational until 2010. An important milestone was reached in 2012, when a Common Economic Space came into being, which aimed to build on the customs union by establishing the free movement of labor, services, and capital as well as the free circulation of goods. Pivotal to the success of this initiative was the EEC, an executive body responsible for drawing up the raft of technical regulations necessary to make the project a reality. The EEC started work in February 2012.

Clash with the EU Develops

In 2013, it became apparent that the EEU was emerging as a potential rival trading bloc to the EU. Situated to the west of the Eurasian countries, the EU by this time had grown from a free trade area of six Western European countries founded in the 1950s into a single market of 500 million people, twenty-eight countries, and a common foreign policy and currency. The EU rapidly grew in 2004 and 2007 by absorbing ten former communist countries of Central and Eastern Europe, including the Baltic nations Estonia, Latvia, and Lithuania, which once were part of the Soviet Union. Gripped by enlargement fatigue, the EU put the brakes on further expanding full membership eastward. Instead, under its Eastern Partnership policy launched in 2009, the EU shifted course by seeking to secure comprehensive free trade agreements with six ex-Soviet countries: Armenia, Azerbaijan, Belarus, Georgia, Moldova, and Ukraine.

By summer 2013, agreements with Armenia, Moldova, and Ukraine were ready to be finalized when Russian president Putin indicated that he viewed these EU trade deals as a threat both to Russia and the EEU. Putin pressured Armenia and Ukraine to ditch the EU deals and join the EEU instead. He succeeded with Armenia, a small, poor country heavily reliant on Russia for trade and security assistance. In September 2013, Armenia'n president Serzh Sargsyan suddenly announced that he was abandoning the EU free trade deal in favor of EEU membership. Putin nearly succeeded in Ukraine, too. In November 2013, he persuaded Ukraine president Viktor Yanukovych to cancel the EU deal. However, that move triggered a pro-EU backlash within Ukraine against Yanukovych, which culminated in his deposition in spring 2014, by a strongly pro-EU government that rushed to conclude the EU trade deal. Meanwhile, Ukraine's independence began to crumble after Putin orchestrated Russia's annexation of Ukraine's province of Crimea in February 2014 and backed armed separatists in eastern Ukraine, helping them establish rebel enclaves bordering Russia.

The government of the Caucasus nation of Georgia, which, during a war in 2008, had severed diplomatic ties with Russia over Russia's support for Georgia's separatist enclaves of Abkhazia and South Ossetia, also proceeded with its EU trade deal, which precluded it from joining the EEU. So, too, did the government of Moldova, a small country nestled between EU member state Romania and Ukraine. Meanwhile, the small, poor ex-Soviet bloc country Kyrgyzstan, situated in Central Asia, opted to join the Russian-backed EEU. With membership negotiations quickly concluded, the EEU grew from three to five members in early 2015.

Future of EEU Closely Tied to Russia's Status

Detractors of the EEU allege that it is a plot by Putin to re-exert Russian dominance over Eurasia. But supporters say it is a legitimate attempt to integrate the economies of the region by removing trade barriers. They note that Russia, despite its economic dominance, has the same voting weight in the EEU institutions as all the other members and that the EEU court has been quick to sanction Russia when it fails to respect EEU treaty provisions. Empowered with the authority to sign international agreements, the EEU hopes to conclude free trade deals with a variety of countries, including Iran, Israel, and Vietnam. It has also made overtures to the EU, but, because of the ongoing crisis in Ukraine that had led the EU to impose trade sanctions against Russia, any such plans are on ice for now.

Thus, the EEU is up and running, but its future is uncertain. In 2015, the Russian economy went into deep recession due to falling oil prices coupled with the negative effects of sanctions from the EU, Russia's primary trading partner. The countries that joined the EEU with the hope that their membership would foment greater economic growth now face a scenario where it could potentially have the exact opposite effect. Meanwhile, relations between Belarus and Russia are tense, partly because Belarus has not been targeted by the EU sanctions and so is acting as a transfer point for some sanctioned goods into Russia, thus creating a black market, which angers Russia. Whereas before the Ukraine crisis there had been speculation that EEU membership would expand further, prospective members seem to have been scared off in this adverse economic and political climate.

—Brian Beary

The following is the text of a release from the Eurasian Economic Commission on January 1, 2015, regarding the effective date of the Treaty on the Eurasian Economic Union.

Eurasian Economic Union Treaty Becomes Effective

January 1, 2015

January 1, the Treaty on the Eurasian Economic Union EAEU has become effective. The Treaty confirms the creation of an economic union that provides for free movement of goods, services, capital and labor and pursues coordinated, harmonized and single policy in the sectors determined by the document and international agreements within the Union.

The Treaty on the EAEU was signed by the Presidents of the Republic of Belarus, the Republic of Kazakhstan and the Russian Federation on May 29, 2014, in Astana. Apart from the three states, the Union members will also include the Republic of Armenia that signed Treaty on Accession to the Union on October 10, 2014 and the Kyrgyz Republic that signed similar Treaty on December 23, 2014.

The Eurasian Economic Union is an international organization for regional economic integration. It has international legal personality.

The Union is to create an environment for a stable development of the Member-States' economies in order to raise the living standards of their population, as well as to comprehensively upgrade and raise the competitiveness of and cooperation between the national economies in the conditions of the global economy.

The EAEU operates within the competence granted by the Member-States subject to the Treaty on the Union, based on the respect to the established principles of international law, including the principles of Member-States' sovereign equality and territorial integrity; based on the respect to the specifics of the Member-States' political order; based on the promotion of mutually beneficial cooperation, equal rights and the Parties' national interests; based on application of the principles of market economy and fair competition.

Governance of the Union is entrusted to the Supreme Eurasian Economic Council (SEEC) comprised of the Heads of the Member-States. The SEEC sessions are held at least once a year. The SEEC structure is formed by the Intergovernmental Council at the level of the Heads of the Governments, the Eurasian Economic Commission and the Court of the Union.

FOR REFERENCE:

Union bodies:

The Supreme Council is the EAEU supreme authority composed by the Presidents of the Union's Member-States.

The Intergovernmental Council is a Union body in charge of strategically important issues of the development of the Eurasian economic integration remained with no consensus when discussed in the Commission Council.

The Court of the EAEU is the Union's court of justice that ensures that the Member-States and the Union's bodies uniformly implement the Treaty on the EAEU and other international agreements within the Union.

The Eurasian Economic Commission is the Union's permanent supranational regulatory body formed by the Commission Council and Commission Board. The Commission's key tasks are to create environment for the Union's operation and development, as well as to develop proposals for economic integration within the EAEU.

The Commission Council includes the Prime-Ministers of the Union's Member-States.

The EEC Board is comprised of its Chairman and Ministers.

Key functional novelties of the Treaty on the EEU as compared to the stages of the CU and SES:

The Treaty on the EAEU secured the Member-States' agreement to pursue a coordinated energy policy and form common energy markets (electric energy, gas, oil and oil products) based on common principles. The document contemplates that such task will be implemented in several stages and completed by 2025: formation of single market of electric power is planned to be completed by 2019, and single market of hydrocarbons—by 2025.

The Treaty on the EAEU determines regulatory treatment of the turnover of pharmaceuticals and medical devices. By January 1, 2016, single market of pharmaceuticals and single market of medical devices (devices for medical purposes and medical equipment) will be created within the Union.

The Treaty establishes new long-term priorities of transport policy in the territory of the Eurasian Economic Union. The parties agreed on a step-by-step liberalization of transport carriages in the territory of the will-be Union, which pertains primarily to motor and railroad transport.

An agreement has been reached on the formation and implementation of a coordinated agricultural policy. It is not insignificant that policies in other areas of integration interaction, including application of sanitary, phytosanitary and veterinary measures to agricultural products, will be pursued in view of the goals, tasks and areas of the coordinated agricultural policy.

The Eurasian Economic Union operation would be unimaginable unless a coordinated macroeconomic policy were pursued, which provides for development and implementation of the Union Member-States' joint activities to achieve a balanced economic development. Subject to the Treaty, key areas of the coordinated macroeconomic policy include formation of single principles of the Union Member-States operation, their efficient interaction and development of common principles and benchmarks to predict the Parties' social and economic development.

To ensure coordinated regulation of financial markets, based on a step-by-step harmonization of the legislations, the EAEU Member-States agreed to establish by 2025 a single supranational body for financial market regulation.

The Treaty on the EAEU presupposes that, as of January 1, 2015, single services market will start operating in a number of sectors determined by the Union Member-States. National treatment will be the basis, i.e. the state will have to adopt full-fledged national treatment of service providers and partner-countries—there can be no restrictions. Later on, the Parties will seek to expand the sectors as much as possible. In particular, by way of a step-by-step reduction of deletions and restrictions, which will undoubtedly strengthen the Eurasian integration project.

Subject to the Treaty on the EAEU, the single services market within the Union shall operate in the sectors approved by the Supreme Council based on the coordinated proposals from the Member-States and the Commission. Based on the Treaty, Decision of the Supreme Eurasian Economic Council dated December 23, 2014 confirmed the lists of services sectors wherein the single market will start operating as of January 1, 2015. At the moment, following the proposals of Belarus, Kazakhstan and Russia, the list of services may include over 40 services sectors (construction services, wholesale/retail trade services, agricultural services, including sowing, processing and crop harvesting, etc.). The list of sectors wherein the rules of the single services market should be followed is subject to a step-by-step and coordinated expansion. In the services sectors where the single services market does not operate, providers and receivers of services are subject to national treatment and most favored nation treatment, and no quantitative or investment restrictions shall be applied thereto.

As of January 1, 2015, single labor market will start operating in the territories of Armenia, Belarus, Kazakhstan and Russia; the freedom of movement of labor will be exercised. The citizens of these states will work in equal conditions: workers from the EAEU Member-States won't need work permits to work within the Union. Once the common labor market is created, the EAEU citizens will be able to experience directly the benefits of the Eurasian Economic Union. Education degrees will be mutually recognized automatically, starting off January 1, 2015. Taxes on incomes of individuals, the EAEU citizens, will be paid according to the domestic resident rate as of the first days of employment. The EAEU Member-States' citizens will no longer have to fill in migration cards when crossing internal borders between the EAEU countries, unless they exceed a 30 day period of stay from the day of entry. Besides, workers and their family members will be relieved of the obligation to get registered with law enforcement authorities for a period not exceeding 30 days.

Another most important novelty of the Treaty on the EAEU is a possibility to apply national treatment to the citizens of all the four countries in what regards social security, including health care. In each EAEU country all health-care services provided by the state will be equally accessible for all the citizens of the Union countries. (Primarily, free ambulance services are meant).

Regarding pensions, the Treaty on the EAEU contains a commitment to solve the issue of pensions export and crediting of total seniority accumulated in another Union country. At the moment, the EEC, jointly with the Parties, elaborates an Agreement on pension coverage that will become effective after 2015.

SOURCE: Eurasian Economic Commission. "The Treaty on the Eurasian Economic Union is Effective." January 1, 2015. www.eurasiancommission.org/en/nae/news/Pages/01-01-2015-1.aspx.

OTHER HISTORIC DOCUMENTS OF INTEREST

FROM PREVIOUS *HISTORIC DOCUMENTS*

- Russian President on the State of Russia's Economy, *2014*, p. 627
- International Leaders Announce Sanctions Against Russia, *2014*, p. 375
- Crimea Votes to Secede from Ukraine, *2014*, p. 83
- Georgian, Russian, and U.S. Officials on the Conflict in South Ossetia, *2008*, p. 346

French President Responds to Attack on *Charlie Hebdo* Headquarters

JANUARY 7 AND 9, 2015

In the late morning of Wednesday, January 7, 2015, two gunmen stormed into the Paris offices of the French satirical magazine *Charlie Hebdo*, killing twelve in what was claimed to be an attack to avenge the Prophet Muhammad. Outrage came from around the world, particularly from media organizations decrying the idea that journalists would be targeted for their coverage of an issue. The pair responsible for the shooting was killed by police after a standoff on January 9, and shortly thereafter the terrorist organization al Qaeda in the Arabian Peninsula claimed responsibility for the attack. The January 7 attack would be the first of many experienced across France in 2015, the most deadly of which occurred in November when 130 were killed.

CHARLIE HEBDO DRAWS CRITICISM

In 1970, the French weekly satirical publication *Hara-Kiri* was banned by the government after running a cover image cartoon featuring both the death of Charles de Gaulle and a nightclub fire that killed 146 with the biting headline "Tragic Ball at Colombey, one dead." In an effort to resurrect the banned publication, the editorial staff changed the name to *Charlie Hebdo*. The far-left satirical magazine ceased publication between 1981 and 1992 but was later revived by its former editors. Throughout its history, the magazine has been attacked for its provocative coverage of political, religious, and pop culture issues. In 2006, then-French president Jacques Chirac criticized the magazine for printing a cartoon of the Prophet Muhammad, crying, with the caption "It's hard being loved by jerks." The Grand Mosque of Paris, in cooperation with the Muslim World League, and the Union of French Islamic Organisations sued then-editor Philippe Val for what it considered the ridicule of Muslims. Ultimately, Val was acquitted by the court under the argument that two of the three cartoons cited in the case were primarily about Muslim terrorists, and the third followed the tradition of French satire and should be viewed in the context of the magazine's primary content.

In November 2011, the magazine circulated the cover of its upcoming edition on social media featuring a cartoon of Muhammad and the caption "100 lashes of the whip if you don't die laughing." For the issue, the magazine was renamed *Charia Hebdo* (Sharia Hebdo) and Muhammad was listed as the editor-in-chief. In response, the magazine's office was firebombed. Then-editor Stéphane Charbonnier said the attack may have been carried out by "idiots who betray their own religion."

Most notably, in 2012, the magazine published a series of cartoons featuring Muhammad nude. The issue was released just one day after a number of attacks on U.S. embassies in the Middle East, many of which were thought to be linked to the anti-Islamic film *Innocence of Muslims*. The attacks resulted in the deaths of four Americans in

Benghazi, Libya, including Ambassador Christopher Stevens. In response to the *Charlie Hebdo* cartoons and attacks, the French government temporarily closed some twenty embassies around the world in fear of retaliation.

GUNMEN STORM *CHARLIE HEBDO* OFFICE

Shortly after 11:00 a.m. Paris local time, gunmen entered downtown Paris building Number 6 Rue Nicolas-Appert in search of the *Charlie Hebdo* editorial offices. After realizing that they were at the wrong address, the gunmen, brothers Chérif and Saïd Kouachi, advanced to Number 10 Rue Nicolas-Appert where they asked a security officer for directions to the *Charlie Hebdo* offices, killing him afterward. Once they made their way to the second floor, the gunmen forced *Charlie Hebdo* cartoonist Corinne Rey to enter her security code to open the office doors. She escaped unharmed. The gunmen then proceeded into an editorial meeting and began calling out the names of their targets. According to Paris prosecutor François Molins, the gunmen repeatedly yelled out "Allahu akbar" (God is great) and told the staff that they were there to avenge the Prophet Muhammad. In the editorial meeting, the terrorists killed editor-in-chief Charbonnier, his bodyguard (Charbonnier was provided with security after receiving many prior threats), four cartoonists, three other editorial staff, and one visitor. Eleven others were wounded. The attack lasted just minutes, and a number of staff survived the execution-style massacre by hiding under their desks or escaping to the building's roof. Others reported being told by the gunmen that they were spared because they were women.

The gunmen fled outside where their exit was temporarily blocked by a police car. In three separate instances during their getaway, the gunmen encountered and clashed with police, at one point executing a police officer. After evading police, the gunmen dumped their car and hijacked another. When police located the abandoned car, they found Molotov cocktails and jihadist flags inside.

MANHUNT CONTINUES OUTSIDE PARIS

By Thursday, police across the country searched for the two attackers. In Montrouge, an area outside Paris, a female police officer was shot and killed by two people who witnesses said were dressed similarly to the *Charlie Hebdo* attackers, as shown in photographs on national media. Initially, investigators did not believe the shooting was connected to the attack in Paris but quickly backtracked and said that the two events were linked. Later that same day, a gas station attendant northeast of Paris reported that the brothers had stolen gas and food before driving off in a vehicle that matched the description of the stolen getaway car.

By Friday, police had located the brothers twenty-two miles outside of Paris at a printing firm in Dammartin-en-Goële, where they had one hostage. Police attempted to negotiate with the brothers for eight hours before they finally exited the building and were immediately shot by police. At the same time, police separately negotiated the release of nineteen hostages at a kosher grocery store in Paris. During negotiations, Amedy Coulibaly—who police later learned was the primary suspect in the Montrouge shooting and with the Kouachi brothers coordinated the *Charlie Hebdo* attack—demanded the release of the Kouachi brothers, unaware that they were already dead, before police charged and killed him. Ultimately, Coulibaly and four of the hostages were killed, while another fifteen survived. Hayat Boumeddiene, Coulibaly's accomplice and widow, escaped and fled Europe. Her whereabouts are currently unknown, but she is believed to be in Islamic State of Iraq and the Levant (ISIL)-controlled territory.

AL QAEDA IN THE ARABIAN PENINSULA CLAIMS RESPONSIBILITY

On Friday evening, January 9, al Qaeda in the Arabian Peninsula claimed responsibility for orchestrating the attack, one of the deadliest in postwar France. In an eleven-minute video, Nasr al-Ansi called the Kouachi brothers "heroes of Islam" and promised more "tragedies and terror" until the "insults" against Muhammad stop. The group told its followers to use the attack as a rallying cry. The Taliban in Afghanistan, al-Shabaab, ISIL, and Boko Haram all praised the attack. Other radical Islamists around the world supported and praised the attackers. Yaqub Qureishi, the leader of the Bahujan Samaj Party in India, offered $8 million to the attackers, and a group of Filipino Muslims held a rally in which they characterized the massacre as a "moral lesson for the world to respect any kind of religion, especially the religion of Islam."

Others in the Muslim world sought to distance themselves from the attack. The League of Arab States released a condemnation of the attack, as did the Organisation of Islamic Cooperation. Hamas said that "differences of opinion and thought cannot justify murder," while the leader of Hezbollah said that the attack was a greater insult against Islam than the cartoons themselves. Perhaps the most poignant outcry against the attacks came from Malek Merabet, a Muslim and the brother of a police officer killed during the manhunt: "My brother was Muslim and he was killed by two terrorists, by two false Muslims."

RIFT WITH MUSLIM COMMUNITY GROWS; "JE SUIS CHARLIE"

In a show of solidarity with those killed, the phrase "Je suis Charlie" (I am Charlie) went viral on social media and became the global rallying cry of those who sought to support free speech and expression. French president François Hollande tweeted his support for media outlets across his nation, saying that "no barbaric act will ever extinguish the freedom of the press." In a statement, Hollande said, "These men, this woman, died because of their vision of France, namely freedom . . . the Republic equals culture, creation, it equals pluralism and democracy. That is what the assassins were targeting." More than three million rallied across Paris in the days following the attack. At the start of a march in Paris, forty world leaders, including president François Hollande, German chancellor Angela Merkel, Israeli prime minister Benjamin Netanyahu, British prime minister David Cameron, and Palestinian President Mahmoud Abbas, linked arms in a show of solidarity.

Western news outlets differed in how they covered the attack; some reprinted *Charlie Hebdo* cartoons of Muhammad, while others proceeded without the images. Those organizations that chose not to reprint the cartoons drew heavy criticism from both the public and other media outlets. The BBC reversed an internal policy and printed a *Charlie Hebdo* cover depicting Muhammad and said it would continue to review its policies that forbid such practice. The outcry was far from universal, however. Salah-Aldeen Khadr, an editor and producer at Al Jazeera English, wrote in an e-mail to staff, "Defending freedom of expression in the face of oppression is one thing; insisting on the right to be obnoxious and offensive just because you can is infantile."

The attack came at a time of distrust of the Muslim population in France and Islamic terrorism. Military personnel had been on a heightened state of alert in the month leading up to the massacre after a handful of attacks around the country, including one in Dijon and Nantes in which twenty-three were injured when a vehicle, carrying men shouting Islamic rallying cries, drove into crowds. Five years earlier, France's parliament passed a law banning women from wearing a full face veil in public, a tradition common among Muslims. The law was taken to Europe's highest human rights court and upheld, sparking uproar among the Muslim community.

Muslim leaders in France expressed outrage at the attack. "We are shocked and surprised that something like this could happen in the center of Paris," said Dalil Boubakeur, the rector of the Grand Mosque in Paris. "We strongly condemn these acts, and we expect the authorities to take the most appropriate measures." Still, in the week after the *Charlie Hebdo* attack, more than fifty anti-Muslim attacks were reported around France, including shootings and mosque grenade attacks.

CHARLIE HEBDO CONTINUES PUBLICATION

Seven weeks after the attack, *Charlie Hebdo* continued its normal publication with the strong support of the French government and media organizations around the world. The French government pledged $1.2 million to keep *Charlie Hebdo*'s voice from being silenced, and the magazine received additional donations from media groups in the millions of dollars. Traditionally the magazine had a print run of 60,000 copies with approximately 30,000 sold, but following the attack the first print run was nearly eight million. *Charlie Hebdo*'s editorial staff announced that all profits from the issue would be donated to the victims' families. The cover image of the February 24 edition depicted the Prophet Muhammad holding a "Je suis Charlie" sign with the caption "all is forgiven."

ATTACKS ACROSS FRANCE CONTINUE

Between January 7 and 9, five attacks took place in Île-de-France—the Paris region—including the *Charlie Hebdo* headquarters shooting and the attack on a kosher grocery store. In total, twenty were killed, including three attackers. On June 26, a French Muslim beheaded his employer and injured two others when he drove his vehicle into gas cylinders in southeastern France. Less than two months later, a man opened fire on a train en route from Amsterdam to Paris. Passengers, including American soldiers, stopped the attacker, who injured four.

The deadliest of the 2015 attacks took place on the evening of November 13. The attacks began in the Paris suburb of Saint-Denis at Stade de France, the national sports stadium, where a soccer match was taking place. There, one person was killed during a series of three suicide bombings. President Hollande, who was in attendance at the game, was evacuated but asked that the match be continued, believing that the safety of fans would be better guaranteed inside the stadium. At approximately 9:20 p.m., shooters attacked a café and adjacent restaurant in the center of Paris. Twenty minutes later, a third team of attackers opened fire inside the Bataclan Theater, where an estimated 1,500 were in attendance at an Eagles of Death Metal concert. The siege lasted for 20 minutes, after which upward of sixty hostages were taken before police were able to gain control of the situation.

A total of 130 people were killed in the November attacks—eighty-nine at the Bataclan Theater alone—and an estimated 100 were in critical condition. Seven of the nine attackers were killed either by suicide bomb or police fire. The attacks were the deadliest in

France since World War II. They prompted hundreds of raids across the country and in nearby Belgium to find those who had helped coordinate the shootings and suicide bombings and also led to enhanced border controls in the traditionally fluid European Union. ISIL claimed responsibility for the attacks, stating that they were carried out in retaliation for French airstrikes in Syria and Iraq. Hollande called the attacks "acts of war" and promised to "step up [French] operations in Syria."

—Heather Kerrigan

Following is the text of two addresses delivered by French president François Hollande on January 7 and 9, 2015, following the Charlie Hebdo *attacks.*

DOCUMENT

President Hollande Addresses Charlie Hebdo *Attacks*

January 7, 2015

My dear compatriots,

Today, France was attacked at its very heart in Paris, at the offices of a newspaper. This extremely violent shooting killed 12 people and injured several others; highly talented cartoonists, courageous columnists were killed. Their impertinence and independence influenced generations and generations of French people. I want to tell them that we will continue to defend this message, this message of freedom, in their name.

This cowardly attack also killed two police officers, the very ones who were responsible for protecting *Charlie Hebdo* and its editorial staff who have been threatened for years by obscurantism and who defended the freedom of expression.

These men, this woman, died because of their vision of France, namely freedom. I would like, on your behalf, to express our wholehearted gratitude to the families, to those affected, to the injured, to the friends, to all those who were deeply hurt today by this cowardly murder. They are now our heroes and that's why I have decided that tomorrow will be a day of national mourning. There will be a moment of silence at 12:00 p.m. in all government offices and I encourage everyone to join in. Flags will be flown at half-mast for three days.

Today it is the Republic as a whole that has been attacked. The Republic equals freedom of expression; the Republic equals culture, creation, it equals pluralism and democracy. That is what the assassins were targeting. It equals the ideal of justice and peace that France promotes everywhere on the international stage, and the message of peace and tolerance that we defend—as do our soldiers—in the fight against terrorism and fundamentalism.

France has received messages of solidarity and fraternity from countries around the globe, and we must take their full measure. Our response must be commensurate with the crime committed against us, first by seeking the perpetrators of this act of infamy, and then by making sure they are arrested, tried and punished very severely. And everything will be done to apprehend them. The investigation is now moving forward under the authority of the Ministry of Justice.

We must also protect all public spaces. The government has implemented what is known as the Vigipirate Plan on "attack" level, which means that security forces will be deployed wherever there is the hint of a threat.

Finally, we ourselves must be mindful of the fact that our best weapon is our unity: the unity of all our fellow citizens in this difficult moment. Nothing can divide us, nothing must pit us against one another, nothing must separate us. Tomorrow I will convene the Presidents of both assemblies as well as the political forces represented in Parliament to demonstrate our common resolve.

France is great when she is capable of rising to the test, rising to a level that has always enabled her to overcome hardships. Freedom will always be stronger than barbarity. France has always vanquished her enemies when she has stood united and remained true to her values. That is what I ask you to do: to join together, all of you, in every way possible; that must be our response. Let us join together at this difficult moment, and we shall win, because we are fully capable of believing in our destiny, and nothing can weaken our resolve.

Let us join together.

Vive la République et vive la France!

Source: Embassy of France in the United States. "Statement by Mr. François Hollande, President of the Republic, at the Elysee Palace." January 7, 2015. http://ambafrance-us.org/spip.php?article6408.

President Hollande Speaks to the Nation Regarding Terrorist Attacks

January 9, 2015

My dear compatriots,

France has been attacked for three consecutive days: on Wednesday, with the attack against *Charlie Hebdo*, which killed 12 people and seriously injured several others; on Thursday, with the murder of a municipal police woman and the assault of an employee in Montrouge; and today with two hostage sieges, one of which was in Paris, in Porte de Vincennes, which killed four people.

France faced up to the situation. First, I would like to express my wholehearted solidarity with the families, the victims, and the injured. France faced up to the situation; she overcame an ordeal that was a tragedy for the nation, but she had a duty to do so.

The murderers have been taken out of harm's way thanks to a two-fold intervention: one in Dammartin-en-Goële, in a warehouse and the other in Porte de Vincennes, at a Kosher store. I want to pay tribute to the courage, bravery and effectiveness of the gendarmes, the police officers, and all those who took part in these operations. I would like to tell them that we are proud; we are proud of them because when the order was given, they launched the attack simultaneously, and achieved the same result. They did so to save the lives of the hostages. They did so to neutralize the terrorists, those who had committed murders.

But even though she is aware that she has faced up to this situation and her security forces are composed of men and women who are capable of bravery and courage, France knows that there will be more threats targeted against her.

I call on you to remain vigilant, united and mobilized. Vigilance must be demonstrated, first and foremost, by the State. The Prime Minister and I have further stepped up the protection of our public places so that we may live quietly, without being subject to threats or dangers. But we must be alert.

I call on you to remain united, because—as I previously told the French people— it's our best weapon. We must show our determination to fight against anything that could divide us, and to be merciless when it comes to racism and anti-Semitism. For it was an appalling act of anti-Semitism that was committed today at that kosher store.

Not being divided means we must not paint people with a broad brush, we must reject facile thinking and eschew exaggeration. Those who committed these terrorist acts, those terrorists, those fanatics, have nothing to do with the Muslim religion.

Finally, we must mobilize our efforts. We must be able to respond to attacks by force, when we have no choice, but also through solidarity.

We must show just how effective solidarity is. We are a free nation that does not give in to pressure, that is not afraid, because we have an ideal that is greater than we are and we are able to defend it wherever peace is threatened. Once more I want to pay tribute to our soldiers who make it possible for us to shoulder our responsibilities with respect to terrorism.

Many leaders from around the world have expressed their solidarity with us. Several have told me that they will attend the mass demonstration on Sunday. I will be with them, and I call on all French people to stand up, this Sunday, for the values of democracy, freedom and pluralism that are so important to us all, and which Europe, in a way, represents.

I promise you that we will emerge even stronger from this ordeal.

Vive la République et vive la France.

SOURCE: Embassy of France in the United States. "Address by the President of the Republic François Hollande." January 9, 2015. http://ambafrance-us.org/spip.php?article6408.

OTHER HISTORIC DOCUMENTS OF INTEREST

FROM THIS VOLUME

FROM PREVIOUS *HISTORIC DOCUMENTS*

G10 Ambassadors, United Nations, and Houthi Leadership Respond to Overthrow of Yemen's Government

JANUARY 19 AND 26, APRIL 14, AND MAY 6, 2015

On the heels of a shaky, mid-2014 ceasefire agreement, Houthi rebels seized control of Yemen's central city of Sana'a, forced the resignation of the prime minister and his cabinet, and dissolved parliament before putting in place its own caretaker government. The Houthi government faced stiff resistance from outside forces, and in July, Saudi Arabia aided the government in exile in regaining some of its power.

FUEL SUBSIDIES FEED CENTRAL GOVERNMENT TAKEOVER

In mid-2014, public discontent with Yemen's central government was high. The body had been forced by the International Monetary Fund to drastically slash fuel subsides and increase oil prices in order to qualify for financial assistance. Because half of the population lives on less than $2 per day, the fuel subsidies had long provided much-needed relief. The Houthis, a rebel movement operating primarily in the northern part of the country, had been in conflict with the central government for decades and acted on this discontent by calling for protests against the government with the ultimate intent to seize Yemen's capital city of Sana'a.

On September 18, Houthi rebels moved into Sana'a, evacuated military headquarters, and took over the offices of the state-run television station. Within three days, the group had taken control of a majority of the central city, and faced little resistance from armed forces. Prime Minister Mohammed Basindawa resigned on September 21, stating that such action would help pave the way for a United Nations–brokered peace agreement. The day of Basindawa's resignation, the Peace and National Partnership Agreement was signed by the Houthis, Yemeni president Abdu Rabbu Mansour Hadi, and representatives from the nation's major political parties. The agreement called for an immediate ceasefire and required the formation of a technocratic government. Hadi was given three days to appoint a prime minister and a month to establish a caretaker government.

Hadi's initial choice for prime minister, his chief of staff, was pressured by the Houthis not to accept the seat, which was instead given to Khaled Bahah on October 13, 2014. The new government was seated on November 9, but the Houthis refused to participate, arguing that they had not been consulted on the development of the cabinet. Further, the Houthis declined to sign an annex to the peace agreement stipulating that all conflicts be worked out through dialogue so that the ceasefire could be maintained. Houthi leadership publicly stated that the decision was based on the fact that the annex had not been included in the initial agreement, but speculation swirled that in fact the group was using this stalemate as a reason to remain in the capital.

Peace Agreement Fails

Throughout late 2014 and into early 2015, the Houthis continued to subvert the power of the caretaker government. On January 17, 2015, Houthi rebels abducted Hadi's chief of staff, reportedly in retaliation for the draft constitution that Hadi had appointed a committee to develop and with which the Houthis did not agree. On January 20, Houthi fighters took control of the presidential palace and placed Hadi under house arrest. That day, Houthi leader Abdel Malik al-Houthi appeared on national television and declared that the group would use "all necessary measures" if Hadi did not make the political changes the group had demanded, including the reformation of the committee charged with writing the nation's draft constitution.

On January 21, Hadi gave in to Houthi demands and agreed to reduce his powers and give the Houthis a greater role in the government. Hadi's concessions also resulted in the release of his chief of staff. A member of the Houthi political council told the United Kingdom's *Guardian* newspaper that the "deal specifies a two week grace period to implement the core of what was agreed upon and we will be watching up close to see whether the government is serious or not this time." Ultimately, instead of following through with the agreement, Hadi and his cabinet resigned en masse on January 22.

On January 31, the Houthis began holding talks with one key political faction, the General People's Congress, headed by former Yemeni president Ali Abdullah Saleh, in an attempt to end the ongoing political crisis. United Nations envoy Jamal Benomar assisted in the negotiations. The discussions initially intended to include representatives from the separatist Southern Movement, but they chose to pull out of the talks, which they characterized as "pointless." The Houthis initially proposed the creation of a six-member presidential council with three representatives from the north of the country and three from the south, which would guide the development of a new government. Leaders from Yemen's political parties wanted assurance from the Houthis that the agreement would also include Hadi's release and the reinstatement of parliament for the purposes of calling a new election.

Houthi leadership gave the negotiations three days to reach an agreement. If unable to do so, Houthi member Ibrahim Abdulla Jaber said that "the committee has assigned the revolutionary leadership to act on its behalf to take the immediate and necessary actions to restore the state's authority during this transitional period."

Houthis Take Control of Government

Without any resolution from the three-day negotiations, the Houthis announced that beginning on February 6, the House of Representatives would be dissolved and the Houthis would be solely in control of the government. The rebel group indicated that it would establish a Revolutionary Committee that would hold power for two years and be responsible for the formation of a new parliament. Al-Houthi named himself acting president.

Demonstrations sprung up against the Houthi coup, primarily in the southern portion of the country, and attracted tens of thousands, many of whom called for the creation of an independent southern state. Western governments, including the United States, and international organizations such as the United Nations and Group of 10 Ambassadors refused to accept the newly established Houthi government as the rightful leaders of Yemen. In a statement, the G10 Ambassadors said they "reject the use of violence by those who seek to overturn Yemen's political transition for their own interests, and fully support President Hadi as the legitimately-mandated President." Houthi leadership continued to reject the idea that their takeover of the government had been a coup and said that they remained prepared to negotiate on the formation of a new government with any Yemeni political parties and international bodies.

On February February 10, the United States temporarily evacuated and closed its embassy in Sana'a, saying, "The United States remains firmly committed to supporting all Yemenis who continue to work toward a peaceful, prosperous and unified Yemen." France, Saudi Arabia, and the United Kingdom quickly followed suit. The embassies were eventually reopened in June.

New Attempts at Negotiation

International concern continued to rise over the ongoing power vacuum in Yemen. The nation is home to al Qaeda in the Arabian Peninsula, and although the Houthis do not align themselves with the terrorist organization, Yemen's government has long allowed the United States and its allies to conduct airstrikes against al Qaeda leaders in its territory.

On February 20, UN envoy Benomar announced that the Houthis had reached an initial agreement with other major political factions in Yemen to reinstate the House of Representatives and develop a new constitution. The agreement also created a "people's transitional council" made up of traditionally unrepresented factions, including the southern portion of the nation as well as women and young people. This council would work with the House of Representatives to govern the nation. Benomar called the initial agreement "an important breakthrough that paves the way towards a comprehensive agreement."

Hadi Regains Control in Exile

Two days after the agreement was reached, Hadi escaped his house arrest and fled to Aden in southern Yemen where he rescinded his resignation as president. Hadi and his government went to Saudi Arabia where they called on the Gulf Cooperation Council to use military force to protect Yemen's government from the Houthis. In the spring, Saudi Arabia formed an allied group and launched airstrikes against the Houthis while the Hadi government operated in exile.

As the fighting raged, the United Nations alternately called on the Houthis to accept a Security Council resolution that would remove the Houthis from the land they had seized and restore the Hadi government, and they also requested that Hadi's government agree to a ceasefire that would see the end of Arab coalition airstrikes on Houthi targets. In July, Hadi's spokesperson Rajeh Badi announced that the Yemeni government was prepared to accept a truce so long as its guarantees were met. These guarantees included the release of those being held by the Houthis, and Houthi withdrawal from the areas it had seized, including the capital. At the time of the announcement, an estimated 3,000 had been killed in the fighting and more than a million displaced.

In late September, the Hadi government was able to return to Aden, where it operated out of a hotel. The building was attacked in early-October by Houthi rebels;

however, no government officials were killed. By the end of the year, the United Nations was unable to encourage the Houthi rebels to agree to either the April Security Council resolution or the July truce.

—Heather Kerrigan

Following are two documents released by the U.S. Embassy in Yemen—a statement released on January 19, 2015, from the Group of 10 Ambassadors expressing concern about the Houthi takeover of Yemen's government and—a statement by the G10 Ambassadors on the ongoing violence in Sana'a released on January 26, 2015; the text of an April 14, 2015, United Nations Security Council meeting on the ongoing violence in Yemen; and a statement given by the Houthis on May 6, 2015.

G10 Ambassadors Respond to Houthi Takeover

January 19, 2015

The Group of Ten Ambassadors are deeply concerned about the situation in Sana'a. We call on all parties to take steps to implement an immediate and enduring ceasefire. The GCC Initiative, the National Dialogue Outcomes and the Peace and National Partnership Agreement all provide mechanisms for addressing disputes, which are endorsed by Yemen's political components. We reject the use of violence by those who seek to overturn Yemen's political transition for their own interests, and fully support President Hadi as the legitimately-mandated President, Prime Minister Bahah and the Government of Yemen.

The Group of Ten Ambassadors note that Ansar Allah, have claimed responsibility, through the so-called revolutionary committees, for abducting Dr. Ahmed bin Mubarak, the Secretary of the National Dialogue Secretariat and the Head of the President's Office. And we call on Ansar Allah to ensure Dr. bin Mubarak's safe and swift release.

The Group of Ten Ambassadors welcome the formation of the Presidential Committee seeking to end the tension in Marib and al-Jawf in line with the Peace and National Partnership Agreement and call for the implementation of the Agreement's outstanding provisions, and we continue to follow events in Marib and Taiz with concern.

The Group of Ten Ambassadors welcomes the preparation by the Constitutional Drafting Committee of a draft constitution, which has now passed to the National Body for consideration and public consultation. We believe it is essential that the political components represented on the National Body work swiftly, with commitment and co-operation to complete this crucial task. We continue to follow with interest the preparations of the Supreme Commission for Elections and the Referendum, and look forward to a referendum and elections in the coming months. It will only be possible to complete these critical tasks if there is greater peace and security in Yemen.

Source: Embassy of the United States Sana'a Yemen. "G10 Statement." January 19, 2015. http://yemen.usembassy.gov/pr011915.html.

G10 Ambassadors Respond to Ongoing Violence in Yemen

January 26, 2015

Members of the international community in Sana'a are profoundly concerned by recent developments in Yemen. The use of violence to achieve political means or overturn legitimate institutions is unacceptable. The President and government resigned in response to the pressures it had been under from spoilers seeking to derail the transition process.

The people of Yemen have suffered enough and they continue to face significant humanitarian and security challenges, including armed militias operating outside the framework of the state, illegal checkpoints and the threat from Al Qaeda in the Arabian Peninsula. Those who have brought the country in recent weeks to this situation should be accountable to the Yemeni people, more than half of whom live below the poverty line, and who will be hardest hit by recent events.

The continuation of the peaceful and legitimate political process must be the goal of all Yemenis with transparency and a clear timetable and based on the outcomes of the National Dialogue Conference, the Peace and National Partnership Agreement and the remaining tasks of the Gulf Cooperation Council Initiative, including a constitution, referendum and elections. We note that abducting or holding any Ministers or government officials under effective house arrest is entirely illegitimate.

We call on all parties to refrain from violence and to work together peacefully towards a brighter future for Yemen.

G10 and co-signed by Germany, Japan, Netherlands and Spain

SOURCE: Embassy of the United States Sana'a Yemen. "G10 and International Partners' Statement on Recent Developments in Yemen." January 26, 2015. http://yemen.usembassy.gov/pr012615.html.

UN Security Council Adopts Resolution on Yemeni Violence

April 14, 2015

ALSO IMPOSES SANCTIONS ON KEY FIGURES IN MILITIA OPERATIONS

Imposing sanctions on individuals it said were undermining the stability of Yemen, the Security Council today demanded that all parties in the embattled country, in particular the Houthis, immediately and unconditionally end violence and refrain from further unilateral actions that threatened the political transition.

Adopting resolution 2216 (2015) by 14 affirmative votes to none against, with one abstention (Russian Federation), the Council also demanded that the Houthis withdraw from all areas seized during the latest conflict, relinquish arms seized from military and security institutions, cease all actions falling exclusively within the authority of the legitimate Government of Yemen and fully implement previous Council resolutions.

Acting under chapter VII of Charter, the body also called upon the Houthis to refrain from any provocations or threats to neighbouring States, release the Minister for Defence, all political prisoners and individuals under house arrest or arbitrarily detained, and end the recruitment of children.

Imposing sanctions, including a general assets freeze, travel ban and arms embargo, on Abdulmalik al-Houthi, who it called the Houthi leader, and Ahmed Ali Abdullah Saleh, son of the president who stepped down in 2011, the resolution called upon all Yemeni parties to abide by the Gulf Cooperation Council and other initiatives and to resume the United Nations-brokered political transition.

Reaffirming the need for all parties to ensure the safety of civilians, the Council called on parties to facilitate the evacuation by concerned States and international organizations of their civilians and personnel from Yemen. The resolution requested the Secretary-General to report on the implementation of the resolution within 10 days.

Explaining his delegation's decision to abstain, the representative of the Russian Federation said the text failed to take into account proposals his country had made, refused to call on all sides to halt fire and lacked clarity on a humanitarian pause. There were inappropriate references to sanctions, he added, stating that resolution must not result in an escalation of the crisis.

The representative of Jordan, Council President for April, said, however, that the adoption of the resolution under Chapter VII was a clear and firm signal to the Houthis and all those supporting them to comply with their obligations. Stressing the regional ramifications of the escalating conflict, she stated that the Council was prepared to consider any additional measures required.

The Council had for months demanded that the parties in Yemen proceed with the agreed upon political transition, the representative of the United States recalled. In response, however, the Houthis had intensified their military actions, threatening the country's and region's security. For that reason, she strongly supported the resolution, which provided a general asset freeze and travel ban on spoilers.

Also welcoming the adoption, the representative of Yemen described it as a tangible demonstration of the seriousness of the international community's support for his people's effort to restore peace, rule of law and democracy. He said that while the Yemeni Government and other parties were finalizing a comprehensive peace framework, opposition forces had mounted a coup d'état, threatening the social fabric and cohesion of the Yemeini people. He applauded the response of the Gulf Cooperation Council to the crisis as consistent with the imperative of preserving Yemen's Constitution and rebuffing Iran's designs.

While also voting in favour of the text, the representative of Venezuela expressed concern at what he called the lack of inclusion and transparency in the deliberations, maintaining that the views of non-permanent members were side-lined.

Also speaking today were the representatives of the United Kingdom, Spain, China, Malaysia, Chile, Lithuania, France, New Zealand, Chad, Nigeria and Angola.

The meeting began at 10:05 a.m. and ended at 11 a.m.

Statements

MARK LYALL GRANT (<u>United Kingdom</u>), supporting Saudi-led military action at the request of Yemeni President Hadi, said that, ultimately, an inclusive political process would have to be reached. A political solution was also the best way to fight extremism and promote humanitarian relief. The resolution just adopted was aimed at ensuring that everyone engaged in the United Nations-negotiated process in good faith. It was right to increase political pressure against individuals who did not do so, he added. The security and stability of Yemen was in the interest of the world; the United Kingdom would use all tools in its disposal towards that end.

VITALY CHURKIN (Russian Federation) said his delegation had abstained because the resolution was not fully in line with what was required by the crisis in Yemen. The text failed to take into account proposals his country had made and to call on all sides to halt fire, did not provide for due reflection on consequences and lacked clarity on a humanitarian pause. There were also inappropriate references to sanctions, he added, stating that the resolution must not result in an escalation of the crisis. He stressed that there was no alternative to a political solution and action by the Council must be engendered from already-existing documents.

SAMANTHA POWER (United States) said the Council had for months demanded that the parties in Yemen proceed with the agreed-upon political transition. In response, however, the Houthis had intensified military action, threatening the country's and the region's security. The United States strongly supported the resolution, which provided a general asset freeze and travel ban on spoilers. The resolution also recognized the costs of the rapidly deteriorating humanitarian crisis. A consensus agreement of all political parties was the only way forward; the United Nations must continue its efforts in that light.

ROMÁN OYARZUN MARCHESI (Spain) said that the Council, through the resolution, had made its resolve clear to all parties. He underscored the need for an inclusive dialogue based on political consensus towards resolving the crisis, leading to a democratic transition led by the Yemeni people themselves. Such dialogue, he stressed, could be successful only if the armed conflict ended. While expressing strong support for the resolution, he underscored the need for the Council to ensure greater transparency and inclusiveness in its consultations.

LIU JIEYI (China) said the resolution reiterated the international community's support for the unity, sovereignty and territorial integrity of Yemen and its commitment to ensure that differences were resolved in a peaceful manner through dialogue. It was extremely important to restore stability in Yemen and the wider region, he added, stressing that there was no military solution. All parties must work towards achieving a prompt ceasefire and restoring stability and order through an inclusive political transition led by the Yemeni people. China hoped all parties would abide by all relevant resolutions, including those on humanitarian issues and on the evacuation and protection of diplomatic personnel and installations.

SITI HAJJAR ADNIN (Malaysia) said that the Council had been compelled to adopt another resolution on Yemen because of the deteriorating situation. She emphasized that the political transition hinged on the political will of the parties themselves. Strongly condemning spoilers of the peace process, she said their pursuit of narrow political interests had betrayed the hopes and aspirations of the Yemeni people. The blatant attack by the Houthis on the presidential palace was unacceptable and the Council had the duty and responsibility to press all parties to return to the negotiating table. Malaysia was deeply concerned at the worsening humanitarian situation and the difficulties in providing relief assistance to the most vulnerable. All parties to the conflict must protect civilians from the violence.

CRISTIÁN BARROS MELET (Chile) said that, despite different interpretations of the situation in Yemen, there was firm agreement on the disastrous effects the violence had on civilians. Expressing satisfaction at the final text that emerged from consultations on the resolution, he stressed that the humanitarian situation would not improve without a ceasefire and an inclusive political settlement. He regretted the fact that the resolution did not include references to the deadly violence committed against children and to attacks on hospitals and schools, saying they were dimensions the Council could not overlook. He called on Council members to make the negotiating process more transparent, in the effort of making resolutions more effective.

RAFAEL DARÍO RAMÍREZ CARREÑO (Venezuela) said he voted in favour of the text because the Council had the primary role vis-à-vis the crisis in Yemen. There was no alternative to a political solution; all parties must support efforts towards that end and diligently observe international human rights and humanitarian law and facilitate assistance to those in need. As the only ones who benefited from the current conflict were terrorist and extremist groups, it was essential to return to dialogue. He expressed concern at the lack of inclusion and transparency in Council deliberations, stating that non-permanent members were put on the side-lines. He urged an end to such practices.

RAIMONDA MURMOKAITĖ (Lithuania) said all parties should re-launch the transition process in Yemen, incorporating the outcomes of national dialogue conference. "The humanitarian situation is dire," she added, pointing out that 16 million people were in need of humanitarian assistance. A solution could be found and violence was not the answer. The arms embargo against the spoilers of peace, including Houthi leaders, would send a strong signal that the use of violence in defiance of Council resolutions would not be tolerated. The Council must now ensure that sanctions were fully implemented by all. The United Nations role remained vital in a return to stability, if that was still possible.

FRANÇOIS DELATTRE (France) noting that his country was a co-sponsor of today's resolution, said that the text dealt with the root causes of tensions in Yemen, which were political. Condemning the Houthi militia, he called on it to act in line with Council resolutions, as well as other negotiations being held under the United Nations aegis. The Houthis were jeopardizing the country's stability. "We have tirelessly indicated to spoilers the Council's determination to bring pressure to bear upon them," he stated. That message must now be put into practice, he maintained, adding that sanctions in this case were a means to realizing a political goal. He supported dialogue to establish a national unity Government, calling on the United Nations to help re-start inter-Yemeni dialogue, and he called for compliance with international humanitarian law, as well as unimpeded access to those in need. In addition, he supported ongoing efforts to bolster Yemen's legitimate presidency; firmness as regards spoilers; resumption of the political transition through an inclusive agreement; and combating terrorists. He called on the Yemeni parties, regional players and influential countries to cooperate along those lines.

JIM MCLAY (New Zealand) said it was important that the Council send a clear signal on the urgent need to end hostilities in Yemen and return to the political process agreed previously by the Council. In that light, he welcomed the fact that the resolution imposed measures for non-compliance. "This time the parties must listen", he stated. He also supported the call for resumed political dialogue, which, he noted, was in the best interests of all parties. Expressing deep concern about the humanitarian situation, he called for parties involved in military operations to comply with international humanitarian and human rights law. Absent a political solution, the humanitarian situation would continue to deteriorate, he warned. All parties should facilitate delivery of humanitarian assistance.

MAHAMAT ZENE CHERIF (Chad) said the situation in Yemen was extremely worrisome on the security and humanitarian fronts. He had voted for the resolution as it addressed the conflict's root causes. He was hoping to see the international community pool its efforts with those of the Gulf Cooperation Council to prevent Yemen's total collapse. He endorsed the Gulf Council's efforts to re-establish peace in Yemen, underscoring the need for robust international mobilization to stop the conflict's escalation and to promote United Nations-led negotiations in line resolution 2201 (2015). The Security Council must send strong and firm message to all parties, notably the Houthis, to immediately stop the violence and comply with the transition process, he stated, adding that it was unacceptable for an armed militia to use violence to jeopardize the constitutional order. All parties were obliged to comply with international humanitarian law and to not target civilian infrastructure.

KAYODE LARO (Nigeria) urged all parties in Yemen to abide by the Gulf Cooperation Council Initiative and other relevant road maps to ensure that all communities could live in peace and harmony. He expressed hope that the resolution just adopted would make an important contribution in that direction.

JULIO HELDER DE MOURA LUCAS (Angola) said the resolution had been necessitated by the Houthis' actions, which jeopardized what seemed to be a promising political transition in Yemen. Praising Jordan and the Gulf Cooperation Council for their contributions to drafting the resolution, he expressed growing concern at the number and scale of attacks by terrorists. All parties needed to resume negotiations at the earliest to reach a political solution, he stressed.

DINA KAWAR (Jordan) said the irresponsible practices of the Houthis and those who supported them had led the Council to name those who threatened peace and stability in Yemen and impose sanctions. The adoption of the resolution under Chapter VII of Charter was a clear and firm signal to them; a return to peace and stability in Yemen required unconditional implementation of the measures. Pointing to the regional ramifications of the escalating conflict, she stressed that the Council was prepared to consider any additional action that was required. She urged all parties to attend the peace conference scheduled to be held in Riyadh, Saudi Arabia. Noting that the resolution called for the evacuation of nationals from other countries and international organizations, she added that a humanitarian pause should be put in place when at an appropriate time and in consultation with the Yemeni Government.

KHALED HUSSEIN MOHAMED ALYEMANY (Yemen) said the resolution was a tangible demonstration of the seriousness of the international community in supporting the Yemini people's effort to restore peace, rule of law and democracy. He recalled the Council's "historic" visit to Yemen in January during which it underscored its commitment to the Gulf Cooperation Council Initiative and other agreed frameworks. While the Yemeni Government and other parties were finalizing a comprehensive peace framework, however, opposition forces mounted what he called a coup d'état against the

Constitution that had continued through manipulation by Iran, threatening the social fabric and cohesion of the Yemeni people. The "putschists" attempted to undermine and even attack the President, who was forced to seek refuge in a neighbouring country to preserve the unity of the country. The response of the Gulf countries was in consonance with the imperative of preserving the constitution and rebuffing Iran's designs. Yemen, he stressed, would remain ever grateful to Saudi Arabia and other Gulf countries. Yemenis had risen in unified defence, given the urgency of mitigating the suffering of the people.

Resolution

The full text of resolution 2216 (2015) reads as follows:

"*Security Council,*

"*Recalling* its resolutions 2014 (2011), 2051 (2012), 2140 (2014), 2201 (2015), and 2204 (2015) and presidential statements of 15 February 2013, 29 August 2014, and 22 March 2015,

"*Noting* the letter dated 24 March 2015 from the Permanent Representative of Yemen, to the United Nations, transmitting a letter from the President of Yemen, in which he informed the President of the Security Council that 'he has requested from the Cooperation Council for the Arab States of the Gulf and the League of Arab States to immediately provide support, by all necessary means and measures, including military intervention, to protect Yemen and its people from the continuing aggression by the Houthis', and *noting* the letter dated 26 March 2015 from the Permanent Representative of the State of Qatar, S/2015/217, transmitting a letter from the Representatives of the Kingdom of Bahrain, the State of Kuwait, the State of Qatar, the Kingdom of Saudi Arabia and the United Arab Emirates,

"*Recalling* the resolution of Summit XXVI of the League of Arab States on the developments in Yemen, stressing inter alia the necessity to resume Yemen's political transition process with the participation of all Yemeni parties in accordance with the Gulf Cooperation Council Initiative and its Implementation Mechanism and the outcomes of the comprehensive National Dialogue conference,

"*Reaffirming* its strong commitment to the unity, sovereignty, independence and territorial integrity of Yemen, and its commitment to stand by the people of Yemen,

"*Condemning* the growing number of and scale of the attacks by Al-Qaida in the Arabian peninsula (AQAP),

"*Expressing* concern at the ability of AQAP to benefit from the deterioration of the political and security situation in Yemen, mindful that any acts of terrorism are criminal and unjustifiable regardless of their motivation, whenever, wherever and by whomsoever committed,

"*Reiterating* its support for the efforts of the Gulf Cooperation Council in assisting the political transition in Yemen and *commending* its engagement in this regard,

"*Reaffirming* its support for the legitimacy of the President of Yemen, Abdo Rabbo Mansour Hadi, and *reiterating its call* to all parties and Member States to refrain from taking any actions that undermine the unity, sovereignty, independence and territorial integrity of Yemen, and the legitimacy of the President of Yemen,

"*Expressing* grave alarm at the significant and rapid deterioration of the humanitarian situation in Yemen, and emphasizing that the humanitarian situation will continue to deteriorate in the absence of a political solution,

"*Recalling* that arbitrary denial of humanitarian access and depriving civilians of objects indispensable to their survival, including wilfully [sic] impeding relief supply and access, may constitute a violation of international humanitarian law,

"*Emphasizing* the need for the return to the implementation of the Gulf Cooperation Council Initiative and its Implementation Mechanism and the outcomes of the comprehensive National Dialogue conference, including drafting a new constitution, electoral reform, the holding of a referendum on the draft constitution and timely general elections, to avoid further deterioration of the humanitarian and security situation in Yemen,

"*Reaffirming* its full support for, and commitment to, the efforts of the United Nations and the Special Adviser of the Secretary-General on Yemen, in particular to the UN-brokered negotiations, and its support for the efforts of the Group of Ambassadors in Sana'a,

"*Alarmed* at the military escalation by the Houthis in many parts of Yemen including in the Governorates of Ta'iz, Marib, AlJauf, Albayda, their advance towards Aden, and their seizure of arms, including missile systems, from Yemen's military and security institutions,

"*Condemning* in the strongest terms the ongoing unilateral actions taken by the Houthis, and their failure to implement the demands in resolution 2201 (2015) to immediately and unconditionally withdraw their forces from Government institutions, including in the capital Sana'a, normalize the security situation in the capital and other provinces, relinquish government and security institutions, and safely release all individuals under house arrest or arbitrarily detained, and *reiterating* its call on all non-State actors to withdraw from government institutions across Yemen and to refrain from any attempts to take over such institutions,

"*Deploring* any attempt by the Houthis to take actions that are exclusively within the authority of the legitimate Government of Yemen, and noting that such actions are unacceptable,

"*Expressing* alarm that such actions taken by the Houthis undermine the political transition process in Yemen, and jeopardize the security, stability, sovereignty and unity of Yemen,

"*Noting with concern* the destabilizing actions taken by the former President of Yemen, Ali Abdullah Saleh, including supporting the Houthis' actions, which continue to undermine the peace, security and stability of Yemen,

"*Welcoming* the intention of the Gulf Cooperation Council to convene a conference in Riyadh, upon the request of the President of Yemen, with the participation of all Yemeni parties to further support the political transition in Yemen, and to complement and support the UN-brokered negotiations,

"*Recalling* its resolution 2117 (2013) and expressing grave concern at the threat to peace and security in Yemen arising from the illicit transfer, destabilising accumulation and misuse of small arms and light weapons,

"*Recognizing* that the continuing deterioration of the security situation and escalation of violence in Yemen poses an increasing and serious threat to neighbouring States and *reaffirming its determination* that the situation in Yemen constitutes a threat to international peace and security,

"*Acting* under Chapter VII of the Charter of the United Nations,

"1. *Demands* that all Yemeni parties, in particular the Houthis, fully implement resolution 2201 (2015), *refrain* from further unilateral actions that could undermine the political transition in Yemen, and *further demands* that the Houthis immediately and unconditionally:

(a) end the use of violence;

(b) withdraw their forces from all areas they have seized, including the capital Sana'a;

(c) relinquish all additional arms seized from military and security institutions, including missile systems;

(d) cease all actions that are exclusively within the authority of the legitimate Government of Yemen;

(e) refrain from any provocation or threats to neighbouring States, including through acquiring surface-surface missiles, and stockpiling weapons in any bordering territory of a neighbouring State;

(f) safely release Major-General Mahmoud al-Subaihi, the Minister of Defence of Yemen, all political prisoners, and all individuals under house arrest or arbitrarily detained; and

(g) end the recruitment and use of children and release all children from their ranks;

"2. *Requests* the Secretary-General to report on the implementation of this resolution and resolution 2201 (2015), in particular paragraph 1 of this resolution, in 10 days from the adoption of this resolution; and in case of further non-implementation, *expresses* its intent to consider designating additional individuals and entities who are engaged in or providing support for acts that threaten the peace, security or stability of Yemen, to be subject to the measures imposed by paragraphs 11 and 15 of resolution 2140 (2014);

"3. *Decides* that the individuals listed in Annex I of this resolution shall be subject to the measures imposed by paragraphs 11 and 15 of resolution 2140 (2014);

"4. *Reiterates* the importance of the implementation of all measures imposed by resolution 2140 (2014), as extended in resolution 2204 (2015);

"5. *Calls* upon all Yemeni parties, in particular the Houthis, to abide by the Gulf Cooperation Council Initiative and its Implementation Mechanism, the outcomes of the comprehensive National Dialogue conference, and the relevant Security Council resolutions and to resume and accelerate inclusive United Nations–brokered negotiations, including on issues relating to governance, to continue the political transition in order to reach a consensus solution and *stresses* the importance of full implementation of agreements reached and commitments made towards that goal and *calls* on the parties, in this regard, to agree on the conditions leading to an expeditious cessation of violence, in accordance with the United Nations Charter and relevant Security Council resolutions, including this resolution and resolution 2201 (2015);

"6. *Demands* that all Yemeni parties adhere to resolving their differences through dialogue and consultation, reject acts of violence to achieve political goals, and refrain from provocation and all unilateral actions to undermine the political transition and *stresses* that all parties should take concrete steps to agree and implement a consensus-based political solution to Yemen's crisis in accordance with the Gulf Cooperation Council Initiative and its Implementation Mechanism and the outcomes of the comprehensive National Dialogue conference;

"7. *Urges* all Yemeni parties to respond positively to the request of the President of Yemen to attend a conference in Riyadh, under the auspices of the Gulf Cooperation Council, to further support the political transition in Yemen, and to complement and support the UN-brokered negotiations;

"8. *Calls on* all parties to comply with their obligations under international law, including applicable international humanitarian law and human rights law;

"9. *Reaffirms*, consistent with international humanitarian law, the need for all parties to ensure the safety of civilians, including those receiving assistance, as well as the need to ensure the security of humanitarian personnel and United Nations and its associated personnel, and *urges* all parties to facilitate the delivery of humanitarian assistance, as well as rapid, safe and unhindered access for humanitarian actors to reach people in need of humanitarian assistance, including medical assistance;

"10. *Calls on* all parties to facilitate the evacuation by concerned States and international organizations of their civilians and personnel from Yemen and commends steps already taken in this regard;

"11. *Reaffirms* the principle of the inviolability of diplomatic and consular premises and the obligations of host Governments, including under the 1961 Vienna Convention on Diplomatic Relations and under the 1963 Vienna Convention on Consular Relations, to take all appropriate steps to protect diplomatic and consular premises against any intrusion or damage, and to prevent any disturbance of the peace of these missions or impairment of their dignity;

"12. *Requests* the Secretary-General to intensify his efforts in order to facilitate the delivery of humanitarian assistance and evacuation, including the establishment of humanitarian pauses, as appropriate, in coordination with the Government of Yemen, and *calls on* Yemeni parties to cooperate with the Secretary-General to deliver humanitarian aid to those in need;

"13. *Further requests* the Secretary-General to intensify his good offices role in order to enable a resumption of a peaceful, inclusive, orderly and Yemeni-led political transition process that meets the legitimate demands and aspirations of the Yemeni people, including women, for peaceful change and meaningful political, economic and social reform, as set out in the Gulf Cooperation Council Initiative and Implementation Mechanism and the outcomes of the comprehensive National Dialogue conference, and *stresses* the importance of the United Nations' close coordination with international partners, in particular the Gulf Cooperation Council, Group of Ambassadors in Sana'a, and other actors, in order to contribute to a successful transition;

Arms Embargo

"14. *Decides* that all Member States shall immediately take the necessary measures to prevent the direct or indirect supply, sale or transfer to, or for the benefit of Ali Abdullah Saleh, Abdullah Yahya al Hakim, Abd al-Khaliq al-Huthi, and the individuals and entities designated by the Committee established pursuant to paragraph 19 of resolution 2140 (2014) (hereinafter referred to as 'the Committee') pursuant to paragraph 20 (d) of this resolution, the individuals and entities listed in Annex I of this resolution, and those acting on their behalf or at their direction in Yemen, from or through their territories or by their nationals, or using their flag vessels or aircraft, of arms and related materiel of all types, including weapons and ammunition, military vehicles and equipment, paramilitary equipment, and spare parts for the aforementioned, and technical assistance, training, financial or other assistance, related to military activities or the provision, maintenance or use of any arms and related materiel, including the provision of armed mercenary personnel whether or not originating in their territories;

"15. *Calls upon* Member States, in particular States neighbouring Yemen, to inspect, in accordance with their national authorities and legislation and consistent with international law, in particular the law of the sea and relevant international civil aviation agreements, all cargo to Yemen, in their territory, including seaports and airports, if the State concerned has information that provides reasonable grounds to believe the cargo contains items the supply, sale or transfer of which is prohibited by paragraph 14 of this resolution for the purpose of ensuring strict implementation of those provisions;

"16. *Decides* to authorize all Member States to, and that all Member States shall, upon discovery of items the supply, sale, or transfer of which is prohibited by paragraph 14 of this resolution, seize and dispose (such as through destruction, rendering inoperable, storage or transferring to a State other than the originating or destination States for disposal) of such items and *decides* further that all Member States shall cooperate in such efforts;

"17. *Requires* any Member State when it undertakes an inspection pursuant to paragraph 15 of this resolution, to submit promptly an initial written report to the Committee containing, in particular, explanation of the grounds for the inspections, the results of such inspections, and whether or not cooperation was provided, and, if prohibited items for supply, sale, or transfer are found, *further* requires such Member States to submit to the Committee within 30 days a subsequent written report containing relevant details on the inspection, seizure, and disposal, and relevant details of the transfer, including a description of the items, their origin and intended destination, if this information is not in the initial report;

Additional Designation Criteria

"18. *Reaffirms* the designation criteria set out in paragraph 17 of resolution 2140 (2014), the measures imposed by paragraph 11 and 15 of the same and *stresses* the importance of their full implementation;

"19. *Reaffirms* paragraph 18 of resolution 2140 (2014), and *underscores* that acts that threaten the peace, security, or stability of Yemen may also include the violations of the arms embargo imposed by paragraph 14 or obstructing the delivery of humanitarian assistance to Yemen or access to, or distribution of, humanitarian assistance in Yemen;

Mandate of the Sanctions Committee

"20. *Decides* that the Committee established pursuant to paragraph 19 of resolution 2140 (2014) shall also undertake the following tasks:

(a) monitoring implementation of the measures imposed in paragraph 14 of this resolution;

(b) seeking from all States whatever information it may consider useful regarding the actions taken by them to implement effectively the measures imposed by paragraph 14 above;

(c) examining and taking appropriate action on information regarding alleged non-compliance with the measures contained by this resolution;

(d) designating as may be necessary additional individuals and entities subject to the measures imposed by paragraph 14 above;

Mandate of the Panel of Experts

"21. *Decides* that the mandate of the Panel of Experts established pursuant to paragraph 21 of resolution 2140 (2014) and renewed by resolution 2204 (2015) shall also include monitoring implementation of the measures imposed by paragraph 14;

"22. *Requests* the Secretary-General, having due regard for the increased mandate of the Panel of Experts, to increase the Panel to five members, and make the necessary financial and security arrangements to support the work of the Panel;

"23. *Calls upon* the Panel of Experts to cooperate actively with other Panels or Groups of Experts established by the Security Council, including the 1267 Monitoring Team, as relevant to the implementation of their mandate;

Commitment to review

"24. *Reaffirms* its readiness to take further measures in case of non-implementation by any Yemeni party of this resolution and resolution 2201 (2015);

"25. *Decides* to remain actively seized of the matter.

ANNEX

"1. Abdulmalik al-Houthi

"Abdul Malik al Houthi is a leader of a group that has engaged in acts that threaten the peace, security, or stability of Yemen.

"In September 2014, Houthi forces captured Sanaa and in January 2015 they attempted to unilaterally replace the legitimate government of Yemen with an illegitimate governing authority that the Houthis dominated. Al-Houthi assumed the leadership of Yemen's Houthi movement in 2004 after the death of his brother, Hussein Badredden al-Houthi. As leader of the group, al-Houthi has repeatedly threatened Yemeni authorities with further unrest if they do not respond to his demands and detained President Hadi, Prime Minister, and key cabinet members. Hadi subsequently escaped to Aden. The Houthis then launched another offensive towards Aden assisted by military units loyal to former president Saleh and his son, Ahmed Ali Saleh.

"2. Ahmed Ali Abdullah Saleh

"Ahmed Ali Saleh has engaged in acts that threaten the peace, security, and stability of Yemen.

"Ahmed Ali Saleh has been working to undermine President Hadi's authority, thwart Hadi's attempts to reform the military, and hinder Yemen's peaceful transition to democracy. Saleh played a key role in facilitating the Houthi military expansion. As of mid-February 2013, Ahmed Ali Saleh had issued thousands of new rifles to Republican Guard brigades and unidentified tribal shaykhs. The weapons were originally procured in 2010 and reserved to purchase the loyalties of the recipients for political gain at a later date.

"After Saleh's father, former Republic of Yemen President Ali Abdullah Saleh, stepped down as President of Yemen in 2011, Ahmed Ali Saleh retained his post as commander of Yemen's Republican Guard. A little over a year later, Saleh was dismissed by President Hadi but he retained significant influence within the Yemeni military, even after he was removed from command. Ali Abdullah Saleh was designated by the UN under United Nations Security Council resolution 2140 in November 2014."

SOURCE: United Nations. "Security Council Demands End to Yemen Violence, Adopting Resolution 2216 (2015), with Russian Federation Abstaining." April 14, 2015. www.un.org/press/en/2015/sc11859 .doc.htm. © (2015) United Nations. Reprinted with the permission of the United Nations.

DOCUMENT   *Houthis Respond to Attacks in Yemen*

May 6, 2015

The Army and People's Committees regain control of the city Al-Tawahi

The Army and People's Committees managed today to regain full control of the city Al-Tawahi in Aden government and defeating the elements of the so-called Al-Qaeda and their associates from the city.

The official spokesman for Ansar Allah Mohamed Abdel Salam posted on Facebook: "This victory came despite continuous Saudi American aggression supporting (Al-Qaeda) through intense and unprecedented aerial bombardment around the clock," stressing that the army and people's committees were able to thwart achieving any progress to members of (Al-Qaeda) on the ground because they do not have any right to their aggression on Yemeni people and do not have any legitimacy in support of al-Qaeda elements to control the Yemeni people and their institutions to become the focus of conflict benefiting those murderers of inside agents and abroad criminals.

Abdul Salam pointed out that the Saudi American aggression on Yemen seeks to compensate their utter failure in its aggression and siege on Yemen by committing massacres and brutal bombing of civilians and residential neighborhoods, as happened in the city of Saada and some of its districts and in the city of Zamar, where 51 martyrs fell during the last twenty four hours, mostly women, children and entire families.

Abdul Salam greeted the army, security forces and people's committees on the heroic attitudes that they bring in various fronts confronting Al-Qaeda elements, whether in Marib or in Aden, despite military, financial and logistical support and aerial bombardment continued by the U.S. Saudi aggression, he also greeted the dear and generous people of Yemen, who stood and still standing in support of the army, security forces and people's committees by various types of support including financial, moral and communal support, and also confronting the brutal aggression on Yemen and the oppressive siege.

The spokesman of Ansar Allah pointed to the facts on the ground that revealed the mislead lying media channels that have remained throughout the last period announcing Al-Qaeda control over Aden airport to clear today that the battle has passed the airport by several kilometers. Despite the bitterness of truth to them and to their lies, they seek another aspect which is shedding crocodile tears for disastrous humanitarian situation in Yemen, forgetting that the U.S.–Saudi alliance is the one who imposes a comprehensive siege on the whole Yemeni people.

SOURCE: Houthi Media. "The Army and People's Committees Regain Control of the City Al-Tawahi." May 6, 2015. Translated from Arabic by SAGE Publishing. www.ansarollah.com/?p=858.

OTHER HISTORIC DOCUMENTS OF INTEREST

FROM PREVIOUS *HISTORIC DOCUMENTS*

State of the Union Address and Republican Response

JANUARY 20, 2015

In his sixth State of the Union address, President Barack Obama faced, for the first time, a newly elected Republican majority in both the House and Senate. The president primarily focused on the economy and advancement of the middle class in his annual address, which also touched on foreign relations, including the fight against the Islamic State of Iraq and the Levant (ISIL) and the ongoing negotiations with Iran over its nuclear program. Unlike his 2014 State of the Union, the president issued no threats to take executive action if Congress failed to make progress on his proposals. However, he still made it clear that he was still firmly in charge of the direction of the government. After noting that he had "no more campaigns to run," he added, "I know, because I won both of them."

Sen. Joni Ernst, R-Iowa, a first-term senator, was chosen by Republican Congressional leadership to deliver the party's official response to the president's speech. She used her time to hit back at the president's claims that his policies had been successful in turning around the economy and encouraging job growth. Four other Republicans delivered their own responses, hinting at disconnect and infighting within the party.

MIDDLE CLASS ECONOMICS

In characterizing the economy at the start of his address, the president said, "The shadow of crisis has passed ... Tonight, we turn the page." Traditionally, the president has shied away from appearing too confident on the economy, but in early 2015, he had a number of issues to celebrate, including an unemployment rate at 5.6 percent and gasoline prices near $2 per gallon in many parts of the country, both of which helped drive his approval ratings into the high 40s. The economic outlook began to improve for Americans as well.

But there were still a number of concerns, including a struggling middle-class and stagnant wages. "Will we accept an economy where only a few of us do spectacularly well? Or will we commit ourselves to an economy that generates rising incomes and chances for everyone who makes the effort?" the president asked in his speech, which was heavy on proposals to continue building the middle class. "That's what middle-class economics is: the idea that this country does better when everyone gets their fair shot, everyone does their fair share, everyone plays by the same set of rules." At the top of the president's to-do list were two years of free universal community college for those qualified, an increase in the national minimum wage, a reduction in student loan payments, and paid sick leave for all Americans. To pay for these programs, the president proposed raising the top tier tax rate on capital gains from 23.8 percent to 28 percent and extending that tax to include inherited wealth. According to the White House, these taxes would not impact the majority of Americans, but rather would be paid primarily by the top 1 percent of income earners.

Nearly every domestic program proposed by the president—the minimum wage increase, free community college, decreased student loan payments, and paid sick leave—would require Congressional approval, and nearly all these issues were nonstarters in the Republican-led Congress, not to mention the fact that Congress had already blocked a number of these issues in preceding years. Minimum wage, for example, was blocked by Senate Republicans in 2014, forcing the states to take the lead on raising the minimum wage within their own borders.

DOMESTIC ISSUES

The president hinted many times in his speech at the need for greater bipartisanship, especially in relation to domestic challenges. He said, "There are a lot of good people here, on both sides of the aisle. And many of you have told me that this isn't what you signed up for—arguing past each other on cable shows, the constant fundraising, always looking over your shoulder at how the base will react to every decision. . . . Imagine if we did something different." He went on to add that "a better politics isn't one where Democrats abandon their agenda or Republicans simply embrace mine. A better politics is one where we appeal to each other's basic decency instead of our basest fears." The president was particularly critical of the Republicans in Congress who made talking points out of a number of programs they had tried to roll back, including Obamacare and Wall Street regulations. "At every step, we were told our goals were misguided or too ambitious, that we would crush jobs and explode deficits," Obama said. But instead, according to the president, the nation experienced new economic growth and lower health care inflation. When Republicans failed to clap for this statement, the president responded with, "This is good news, people."

The Keystone XL pipeline, which would carry oil from Canada's tar sands to the Gulf Coast, has been a frequent talking point for Republicans who blame the president for unnecessary delays on approval of a project that could create thousands of jobs. Republicans in the Senate began working on a bill in early January to start the project under the threat of a presidential veto. Obama has repeatedly said that he is unsure whether the project merits American investment and has also expressed concern about the potential climate impacts. In his address, the president said the nation should shift its focus away from "a single oil pipeline" and onto a broad infrastructure plan "that could create more than 30 times as many jobs per year."

During his speech, the president also called for a reform of the tax code, a plan for which the White House had released a few days prior. The president noted that he wants to raise capital gains taxes on the wealthiest investors; close the tax loophole on inherited assets to ensure the wealthiest Americans are no longer able to pass on inheritances tax-free; and increase taxes on large, highly leveraged financial institutions. The increase in taxes on the wealthy would be coupled with additional tax credits for middle-class families. "Let's close the loopholes that lead to inequality by allowing the top 1 percent to avoid paying taxes on their accumulated wealth. We can use that money to help more families pay for childcare and send their kids to college," the president said. The issue was unlikely to go anywhere in the Republican-controlled Congress. Brendan Buck, the spokesperson for House Ways and Means chairman Paul Ryan, R-Wisc., said, "This is not a serious proposal," adding, "[w]e lift families up and grow the economy with a simpler, flatter tax code, not big tax increases to pay for more Washington spending."

Foreign Affairs

Cuba and Iran made up a bulk of the president's foreign policy points during his January speech. Following the December announcement that the United States and Cuba would reopen their borders to one another, resume diplomatic ties, and reestablish their embassies, in speaking before Congress the president found himself on the defensive because Republicans have characterized the agreement as a free pass to a dictatorship that has long used human rights violations to remain in power. In his speech, the president called on Congress to lift the embargo on Cuba. "When what you're doing doesn't work for fifty years, it's time to try something new," the president said.

On Iran, the president spoke about the P5+1 negotiations aimed at encouraging the Middle Eastern nation to end its program to build nuclear weapons, noting that while the group has failed to meet a handful of deadlines, the talks appear on track to produce a "comprehensive agreement that prevents a nuclear-armed Iran" in the coming months. Obama again told Congress that he would veto any bill that came to his desk containing new sanctions against Iran, saying that they would derail the negotiations.

Obama used his State of the Union address to tell Congress and the American public that he intended to submit a proposal for an Authorization of the Use of Military Force (AUMF) for action against ISIL. Such a plan would be used to continue the work being done to "degrade and ultimately destroy this terrorist group" but would not allow the United States to get "dragged into another ground war." To date, American action against ISIL has been authorized under President George W. Bush's 2001 AUMF, which was originally approved for action in Afghanistan.

In a nod to bipartisanship, the president called for fast-track approval of two trade deals—the Trans Pacific Partnership and the Transatlantic Trade and Investment Partnership. Republicans have strongly supported the measures, whereas some Democrats have been wary of how the deals might impact American manufacturers and labor unions. Still, the president argued that "95 percent of the world's customers live outside our borders, and we can't close ourselves off from those opportunities."

Sen. Ernst Delivers Republican Response

There were a total of five responses to the president's State of the Union address. The tea party response was delivered by Rep. Curt Clawson, R-Fla., who, according to the Tea Party Express, was its first victory for the 2014 cycle. Sen. Rand Paul, R-Ky., released a prerecorded speech on YouTube, during which he said Democrats were pushing "more of the same" economic policies "that have allowed the poor to get poorer and the rich to get richer." Sen. Ted Cruz, R-Texas, a favorite of the tea party, live-streamed his response.

The official response to the State of the Union was delivered by Sen. Ernst, the junior senator from Iowa who had been elected just one month earlier to a seat that had been in Democratic hands for three decades. Her speech marked the first time a first-year senator had ever delivered the Republican response. Frequently, Ernst drew on her Iowa roots to characterize herself as a leader who understood the economic challenges facing many Americans. "We were raised to live simply, not to waste," she said. "It was a lesson my mother taught me every rainy morning. You see, growing up, I had only one good pair of shoes. So on rainy school days, my mom would slip plastic bread bags over them to keep them dry. But I was never embarrassed, because the school bus would be filled with rows and rows of young Iowans with bread bags slipped over their feet."

In her speech, Ernst sought to categorize Obama's presidency as one of turmoil and economic hardship for individuals across the country. "For many of us, the sting of the economy and the frustration with Washington's dysfunction weren't things we had to read about. We felt them every day," she said, while adding that "the new Republican Congress also understands how difficult these past six years have been." Ernst said the newly seated Republican majority in both the House and Senate would fight for job creation for the middle class as well as tax and trade reform. Drawing on a bipartisan tone, she said that "the president has already expressed some support for these kinds of ideas."

During her ten-minute speech, Ernst also spoke about national security, an issue on which her colleagues consider her well-versed, having served in the Iraq War and as a lieutenant colonel in the Iowa National Guard. She called for a "comprehensive plan" to defeat terrorists abroad, including ISIL.

Sen. Ernst's speech was delivered in Spanish by Rep. Carlos Curbelo, R-Fla., and contained a notable difference. Whereas Ernst did not speak about immigration, Curbelo dedicated an entire paragraph to the hot-button issue, saying, "We should . . . work through the appropriate channels to create permanent solutions for our immigration system."

—Heather Kerrigan

Following is the full text of President Barack Obama's State of the Union address, delivered on January 20, 2015; and the complete text of Sen. Joni Ernst's Republican response to the State of the Union address, also on January 20, 2015.

DOCUMENT   *State of the Union Address*

January 20, 2015

The President. Mr. Speaker, Mr. Vice President, Members of Congress, my fellow Americans: We are 15 years into this new century. Fifteen years that dawned with terror touching our shores, that unfolded with a new generation fighting two long and costly wars, that saw a vicious recession spread across our Nation and the world. It has been and still is a hard time for many.

But tonight we turn the page. Tonight, after a breakthrough year for America, our economy is growing and creating jobs at the fastest pace since 1999. Our unemployment rate is now lower than it was before the financial crisis. More of our kids are graduating than ever before. More of our people are insured than ever before. And we are as free from the grip of foreign oil as we've been in almost 30 years.

Tonight, for the first time since 9/11, our combat mission in Afghanistan is over. Six years ago, nearly 180,000 American troops served in Iraq and Afghanistan. Today, fewer than 15,000 remain. And we salute the courage and sacrifice of every man and woman in this 9/11 generation who has served to keep us safe. We are humbled and grateful for your service.

America, for all that we have endured, for all the grit and hard work required to come back, for all the tasks that lie ahead, know this: The shadow of crisis has passed, and the State of the Union is strong.

At this moment—with a growing economy, shrinking deficits, bustling industry, booming energy production—we have risen from recession freer to write our own future than any other nation on Earth. It's now up to us to choose who we want to be over the next 15 years and for decades to come.

Will we accept an economy where only a few of us do spectacularly well? Or will we commit ourselves to an economy that generates rising incomes and chances for everyone who makes the effort?

Will we approach the world fearful and reactive, dragged into costly conflicts that strain our military and set back our standing? Or will we lead wisely, using all elements of our power to defeat new threats and protect our planet?

Will we allow ourselves to be sorted into factions and turned against one another? Or will we recapture the sense of common purpose that has always propelled America forward?

In 2 weeks, I will send this Congress a budget filled with ideas that are practical, not partisan. And in the months ahead, I'll crisscross the country making a case for those ideas. So tonight I want to focus less on a checklist of proposals and focus more on the values at stake in the choices before us.

It begins with our economy. Seven years ago, Rebekah and Ben Erler of Minneapolis were newlyweds. [Laughter] She waited tables. He worked construction. Their first child Jack was on the way. They were young and in love in America. And it doesn't get much better than that. "If only we had known," Rebekah wrote to me last spring, "what was about to happen to the housing and construction market."

As the crisis worsened, Ben's business dried up, so he took what jobs he could find, even if they kept him on the road for long stretches of time. Rebekah took out student loans and enrolled in community college and retrained for a new career. They sacrificed for each other. And slowly, it paid off. They bought their first home. They had a second son Henry. Rebekah got a better job and then a raise. Ben is back in construction and home for dinner every night.

"It is amazing," Rebekah wrote, "what you can bounce back from when you have to. . . . We are a strong, tight-knit family who has made it through some very, very hard times." We are a strong, tight-knit family who has made it through some very, very hard times.

America, Rebekah and Ben's story is our story. They represent the millions who have worked hard and scrimped and sacrificed and retooled. You are the reason that I ran for this office. You are the people I was thinking of 6 years ago today, in the darkest months of the crisis, when I stood on the steps of this Capitol and promised we would rebuild our economy on a new foundation. And it has been your resilience, your effort that has made it possible for our country to emerge stronger.

We believed we could reverse the tide of outsourcing and draw new jobs to our shores. And over the past 5 years, our businesses have created more than 11 million new jobs.

We believed we could reduce our dependence on foreign oil and protect our planet. And today, America is number one in oil and gas. America is number one in wind power. Every 3 weeks, we bring online as much solar power as we did in all of 2008. And thanks to lower gas prices and higher fuel standards, the typical family this year should save about $750 at the pump.

We believed we could prepare our kids for a more competitive world. And today, our younger students have earned the highest math and reading scores on record. Our high school graduation rate has hit an all-time high. More Americans finish college than ever before.

We believed that sensible regulations could prevent another crisis, shield families from ruin, and encourage fair competition. Today, we have new tools to stop taxpayer-funded bailouts and a new consumer watchdog to protect us from predatory lending and abusive credit card practices. And in the past year alone, about 10 million uninsured Americans finally gained the security of health coverage.

At every step, we were told our goals were misguided or too ambitious, that we would crush jobs and explode deficits. Instead, we've seen the fastest economic growth in over a decade, our deficits cut by two-thirds, a stock market that has doubled, and health care inflation at its lowest rate in 50 years. This is good news, people. *[Laughter]*

So the verdict is clear. Middle class economics works. Expanding opportunity works. And these policies will continue to work as long as politics don't get in the way. We can't slow down businesses or put our economy at risk with Government shutdowns or fiscal showdowns. We can't put the security of families at risk by taking away their health insurance or unraveling the new rules on Wall Street or refighting past battles on immigration when we've got to fix a broken system. And if a bill comes to my desk that tries to do any of these things, I will veto it. It will have earned my veto.

Today, thanks to a growing economy, the recovery is touching more and more lives. Wages are finally starting to rise again. We know that more small-business owners plan to raise their employees' pay than at any time since 2007. But here's the thing: Those of us here tonight, we need to set our sights higher than just making sure Government doesn't screw things up—*[laughter]*—that Government doesn't halt the progress we're making. We need to do more than just do no harm. Tonight, together, let's do more to restore the link between hard work and growing opportunity for every American.

Because families like Rebekah's still need our help. She and Ben are working as hard as ever, but they've had to forego vacations and a new car so that they can pay off student loans and save for retirement. Friday night pizza, that's a big splurge. Basic childcare for Jack and Henry costs more than their mortgage and almost as much as a year at the University of Minnesota. Like millions of hard-working Americans, Rebekah isn't asking for a handout, but she is asking that we look for more ways to help families get ahead.

And in fact, at every moment of economic change throughout our history, this country has taken bold action to adapt to new circumstances and to make sure everyone gets a fair shot. We set up worker protections, Social Security, Medicare, Medicaid to protect ourselves from the harshest adversity. We gave our citizens schools and colleges, infrastructure and the Internet, tools they needed to go as far as their efforts and their dreams will take them.

That's what middle class economics is: the idea that this country does best when everyone gets their fair shot, everyone does their fair share, everyone plays by the same set of rules. We don't just want everyone to share in America's success, we want everyone to contribute to our success.

So what does middle class economics require in our time? First, middle class economics means helping working families feel more secure in a world of constant change. That means helping folks afford childcare, college, health care, a home, retirement. And my budget will address each of these issues, lowering the taxes of working families and putting thousands of dollars back into their pockets each year.

Here's one example. During World War II, when men like my grandfather went off to war, having women like my grandmother in the workforce was a national security priority, so this country provided universal childcare. In today's economy, when having both parents in the workforce is an economic necessity for many families, we need affordable, high-quality childcare more than ever.

It's not a nice-to-have, it's a must-have. So it's time we stop treating childcare as a side issue, or as a women's issue, and treat it like the national economic priority that it is for all of us. And that's why my plan will make quality childcare more available and more afford-able for every middle class and low-income family with young children in America, by creating more slots and a new tax cut of up to $3,000 per child, per year.

Here's another example. Today, we are the only advanced country on Earth that doesn't guarantee paid sick leave or paid maternity leave to our workers. Forty-three mil-lion workers have no paid sick leave—43 million. Think about that. And that forces too many parents to make the gut-wrenching choice between a paycheck and a sick kid at home. So I'll be taking new action to help States adopt paid leave laws of their own. And since paid sick leave won where it was on the ballot last November, let's put it to a vote right here in Washington. Send me a bill that gives every worker in America the oppor-tunity to earn 7 days of paid sick leave. It's the right thing to do. *[Applause]* It's the right thing to do.

Of course, nothing helps families make ends meet like higher wages. That's why this Congress still needs to pass a law that makes sure a woman is paid the same as a man for doing the same work. I mean, it's 2015. *[Laughter]* It's time. We still need to make sure employees get the overtime they've earned. And to everyone in this Congress who still refuses to raise the minimum wage, I say this: If you truly believe you could work full time and support a family on less than $15,000 a year, try it. If not, vote to give millions of the hardest working people in America a raise.

Now, these ideas won't make everybody rich, won't relieve every hardship. That's not the job of government. To give working families a fair shot, we still need more employers to see beyond next quarter's earnings and recognize that investing in their workforce is in their company's long-term interest. We still need laws that strengthen rather than weaken unions, and give American workers a voice.

But you know, things like childcare and sick leave and equal pay, things like lower mortgage premiums and a higher minimum wage—these ideas will make a meaningful difference in the lives of millions of families. That's a fact. And that's what all of us, Republicans and Democrats alike, were sent here to do.

Now, second, to make sure folks keep earning higher wages down the road, we have to do more to help Americans upgrade their skills. America thrived in the 20th century because we made high school free, sent a generation of GIs to college, trained the best workforce in the world. We were ahead of the curve. But other countries caught on. And in a 21st-century economy that rewards knowledge like never before, we need to up our game. We need to do more.

By the end of this decade, two in three job openings will require some higher education—two in three. And yet we still live in a country where too many bright, striv-ing Americans are priced out of the education they need. It's not fair to them, and it's sure not smart for our future. And that's why I'm sending this Congress a bold new plan to lower the cost of community college to zero.

Keep in mind, 40 percent of our college students choose community college. Some are young and starting out. Some are older and looking for a better job. Some are veterans and single parents trying to transition back into the job market. Whoever you are, this plan is your chance to graduate ready for the new economy without a load of debt. Understand, you've got to earn it. You've got to keep your grades up and graduate on time.

Tennessee, a State with Republican leadership, and Chicago, a city with Democratic leadership, are showing that free community college is possible. I want to spread that idea all across America so that 2 years of college becomes as free and universal in America as high school is today. Let's stay ahead of the curve. And I want to work with this Congress to make sure those already burdened with student loans can reduce their monthly payments so that student debt doesn't derail anyone's dreams.

Thanks to Vice President Biden's great work to update our job training system, we're connecting community colleges with local employers to train workers to fill high-paying jobs like coding and nursing and robotics. Tonight I'm also asking more businesses to follow the lead of companies like CVS and UPS and offer more educational benefits and paid apprenticeships, opportunities that give workers the chance to earn higher paying jobs even if they don't have a higher education.

And as a new generation of veterans comes home, we owe them every opportunity to live the American Dream they helped defend. Already, we've made strides towards ensuring that every veteran has access to the highest quality care. We're slashing the backlog that had too many veterans waiting years to get the benefits they need. And we're making it easier for vets to translate their training and experience into civilian jobs. And Joining Forces, the national campaign launched by Michelle and Jill Biden—*[applause]*—thank you, Michelle; thank you, Jill—has helped nearly 700,000 veterans and military spouses get a new job. So to every CEO in America, let me repeat: If you want somebody who's going to get the job done and done right, hire a veteran.

Finally, as we better train our workers, we need the new economy to keep churning out high-wage jobs for our workers to fill. Since 2010, America has put more people back to work than Europe, Japan, and all advanced economies combined.

Our manufacturers have added almost 800,000 new jobs. Some of our bedrock sectors, like our auto industry, are booming. But there are also millions of Americans who work in jobs that didn't even exist 10 or 20 years ago, jobs at companies like Google and eBay and Tesla.

So no one knows for certain which industries will generate the jobs of the future. But we do know we want them here in America. We know that. And that's why the third part of middle class economics is all about building the most competitive economy anywhere, the place where businesses want to locate and hire.

Twenty-first century businesses need 21st-century infrastructure: modern ports and stronger bridges, faster trains and the fastest Internet. Democrats and Republicans used to agree on this. So let's set our sights higher than a single oil pipeline. Let's pass a bipartisan infrastructure plan that could create more than 30 times as many jobs per year and make this country stronger for decades to come. Let's do it. Let's get it done. *[Applause]* Let's get it done.

Twenty-first century businesses, including small businesses, need to sell more American products overseas. Today, our businesses export more than ever, and exporters tend to pay their workers higher wages. But as we speak, China wants to write the rules for the world's fastest growing region. That would put our workers and our businesses at a disadvantage. Why would we let that happen? We should write those rules. We should level the playing field. And that's why I'm asking both parties to give me trade promotion authority to protect American workers, with strong new trade deals from Asia to Europe that aren't just free, but are also fair. It's the right thing to do.

Look, I'm the first one to admit that past trade deals haven't always lived up to the hype, and that's why we've gone after countries that break the rules at our expense. But

95 percent of the world's customers live outside our borders. We can't close ourselves off from those opportunities. More than half of manufacturing executives have said they're actively looking to bring jobs back from China. So let's give them one more reason to get it done.

Twenty-first century businesses will rely on American science and technology, research and development. I want the country that eliminated polio and mapped the human genome to lead a new era of medicine, one that delivers the right treatment at the right time.

In some patients with cystic fibrosis, this approach has reversed a disease once thought unstoppable. So tonight I'm launching a new precision medicine initiative to bring us closer to curing diseases like cancer and diabetes and to give all of us access to the personalized information we need to keep ourselves and our families healthier. We can do this.

I intend to protect a free and open Internet, extend its reach to every classroom and every community and help folks build the fastest networks so that the next generation of digital innovators and entrepreneurs have the platform to keep reshaping our world. I want Americans to win the race for the kinds of discoveries that unleash new jobs: converting sunlight into liquid fuel; creating revolutionary prosthetics so that a veteran who gave his arms for his country can play catch with his kids again; pushing out into the solar system not just to visit, but to stay. Last month, we launched a new spacecraft as part of a reenergized space program that will send American astronauts to Mars. And in 2 months, to prepare us for those missions, Scott Kelly will begin a year-long stay in space. So good luck, Captain. Make sure to Instagram it. We're proud of you.

Now, the truth is, when it comes to issues like infrastructure and basic research, I know there's bipartisan support in this Chamber. Members of both parties have told me so. Where we too often run onto the rocks is how to pay for these investments. As Americans, we don't mind paying our fair share of taxes as long as everybody else does too. But for far too long, lobbyists have rigged the Tax Code with loopholes that let some corporations pay nothing while others pay full freight. They've riddled it with giveaways that the super-rich don't need, while denying a break to middle class families who do.

This year, we have an opportunity to change that. Let's close loopholes so we stop rewarding companies that keep profits abroad and reward those that invest here in America. Let's use those savings to rebuild our infrastructure and to make it more attractive for companies to bring jobs home. Let's simplify the system and let a small-business owner file based on her actual bank statement, instead of the number of accountants she can afford. And let's close the loopholes that lead to inequality by allowing the top 1 percent to avoid paying taxes on their accumulated wealth. We can use that money to help more families pay for childcare and send their kids to college. We need a Tax Code that truly helps working Americans trying to get a leg up in the new economy, and we can achieve that together. [Applause] We can achieve it together.

Helping hard-working families make ends meet, giving them the tools they need for good-paying jobs in this new economy, maintaining the conditions of growth and competitiveness—this is where America needs to go. I believe it's where the American people want to go. It will make our economy stronger a year from now, 15 years from now, and deep into the century ahead.

Of course, if there's one thing this new century has taught us, it's that we cannot separate our work here at home from challenges beyond our shores. My first duty as Commander in Chief is to defend the United States of America. In doing so, the question is not whether America leads in the world, but how. When we make rash decisions, reacting to the headlines instead of using our heads, when the first response to a challenge is to send in our military, then we risk getting drawn into unnecessary conflicts and neglect the broader strategy we need for a safer, more prosperous world. That's what our enemies want us to do.

I believe in a smarter kind of American leadership. We lead best when we combine military power with strong diplomacy, when we leverage our power with coalition building, when we don't let our fears blind us to the opportunities that this new century presents. That's exactly what we're doing right now. And around the globe, it is making a difference.

First, we stand united with people around the world who have been targeted by terrorists, from a school in Pakistan to the streets of Paris. We will continue to hunt down terrorists and dismantle their networks, and we reserve the right to act unilaterally, as we have done relentlessly since I took office, to take out terrorists who pose a direct threat to us and our allies. At the same time, we've learned some costly lessons over the last 13 years. Instead of Americans patrolling the valleys of Afghanistan, we've trained their security forces, who have now taken the lead, and we've honored our troops' sacrifice by supporting that country's first democratic transition. Instead of sending large ground forces overseas, we're partnering with nations from South Asia to North Africa to deny safe haven to terrorists who threaten America.

In Iraq and Syria, American leadership—including our military power—is stopping ISIL's advance. Instead of getting dragged into another ground war in the Middle East, we are leading a broad coalition, including Arab nations, to degrade and ultimately destroy this terrorist group. We're also supporting a moderate opposition in Syria that can help us in this effort and assisting people everywhere who stand up to the bankrupt ideology of violent extremism.

Now, this effort will take time. It will require focus. But we will succeed. And tonight I call on this Congress to show the world that we are united in this mission by passing a resolution to authorize the use of force against ISIL. We need that authority.

Second, we're demonstrating the power of American strength and diplomacy. We're upholding the principle that bigger nations can't bully the small, by opposing Russian aggression and supporting Ukraine's democracy and reassuring our NATO allies.

Last year, as we were doing the hard work of imposing sanctions along with our allies, as we were reinforcing our presence with frontline states, Mr. Putin's aggression, it was suggested, was a masterful display of strategy and strength. That's what I heard from some folks. [Laughter] Well, today, it is America that stands strong and united with our allies, while Russia is isolated with its economy in tatters. That's how America leads: not with bluster, but with persistent, steady resolve.

In Cuba, we are ending a policy that was long past its expiration date. When what you're doing doesn't work for 50 years, it's time to try something new. [Laughter] And our shift in Cuba policy has the potential to end a legacy of mistrust in our hemisphere. It removes a phony excuse for restrictions in Cuba. It stands up for democratic values and extends the hand of friendship to the Cuban people. And this year, Congress should begin the work of ending the embargo.

As His Holiness Pope Francis has said, diplomacy is the work of "small steps." And these small steps have added up to new hope for the future in Cuba. And after years in prison, we are overjoyed that Alan Gross is back where he belongs. Welcome home, Alan. We're glad you're here.

Our diplomacy is at work with respect to Iran, where, for the first time in a decade, we've halted the progress of its nuclear program and reduced its stockpile of nuclear material.

Between now and this spring, we have a chance to negotiate a comprehensive agreement that prevents a nuclear-armed Iran, secures America and our allies, including Israel, while avoiding yet another Middle East conflict. There are no guarantees that negotiations will succeed, and I keep all options on the table to prevent a nuclear Iran.

But new sanctions passed by this Congress, at this moment in time, will all but guarantee that diplomacy fails: alienating America from its allies, making it harder to maintain sanctions, and ensuring that Iran starts up its nuclear program again. It doesn't make sense. And that's why I will veto any new sanctions bill that threatens to undo this progress. The American people expect us only to go to war as a last resort, and I intend to stay true to that wisdom. Third, we're looking beyond the issues that have consumed us in the past to shape the coming century. No foreign nation, no hacker, should be able to shut down our networks, steal our trade secrets, or invade the privacy of American families, especially our kids. So we're making sure our Government integrates intelligence to combat cyber threats, just as we have done to combat terrorism.

And tonight I urge this Congress to finally pass the legislation we need to better meet the evolving threat of cyberattacks, combat identity theft, and protect our children's information. That should be a bipartisan effort. If we don't act, we'll leave our Nation and our economy vulnerable. If we do, we can continue to protect the technologies that have unleashed untold opportunities for people around the globe.

In West Africa, our troops, our scientists, our doctors, our nurses, our health care workers are rolling back Ebola, saving countless lives and stopping the spread of disease. I could not be prouder of them, and I thank this Congress for your bipartisan support of their efforts. But the job is not yet done, and the world needs to use this lesson to build a more effective global effort to prevent the spread of future pandemics, invest in smart development, and eradicate extreme poverty.

In the Asia-Pacific, we are modernizing alliances while making sure that other nations play by the rules: in how they trade, how they resolve maritime disputes, how they participate in meeting common international challenges like nonproliferation and disaster relief. And no challenge—no challenge—poses a greater threat to future generations than climate change.

Two thousand fourteen was the planet's warmest year on record. Now, 1 year doesn't make a trend, but this does: 14 of the 15 warmest years on record have all fallen in the first 15 years of this century.

Now, I've heard some folks try to dodge the evidence by saying they're not scientists, that we don't have enough information to act. Well, I'm not a scientist, either. But you know what, I know a lot of really good scientists—[laughter]—at NASA and at NOAA and at our major universities. And the best scientists in the world are all telling us that our activities are changing the climate, and if we don't act forcefully, we'll continue to see rising oceans, longer, hotter heat waves, dangerous droughts and floods, and massive disruptions that can trigger greater migration and conflict and hunger around the globe. The Pentagon says that climate change poses immediate risks to our national security. We should act like it.

And that's why, over the past 6 years, we've done more than ever to combat climate change, from the way we produce energy to the way we use it. That's why we've set aside more public lands and waters than any administration in history. And that's why I will not let this Congress endanger the health of our children by turning back the clock on our efforts. I am determined to make sure that American leadership drives international action.

In Beijing, we made a historic announcement: The United States will double the pace at which we cut carbon pollution. And China committed, for the first time, to limiting their emissions. And because the world's two largest economies came together, other nations are now stepping up and offering hope that this year the world will finally reach an agreement to protect the one planet we've got.

And there's one last pillar of our leadership, and that's the example of our values. As Americans, we respect human dignity, even when we're threatened, which is why I have prohibited torture and worked to make sure our use of new technology like drones is properly constrained. It's why we speak out against the deplorable anti-Semitism that has resurfaced in certain parts of the world. It's why we continue to reject offensive stereotypes of Muslims, the vast majority of whom share our commitment to peace. That's why we defend free speech and advocate for political prisoners and condemn the persecution of women or religious minorities or people who are lesbian, gay, bisexual, or transgender. We do these things not only because they are the right thing to do, but because ultimately, they will make us safer.

As Americans, we have a profound commitment to justice. So it makes no sense to spend $3 million per prisoner to keep open a prison that the world condemns and terrorists use to recruit. Since I've been President, we've worked responsibly to cut the population of Gitmo in half. Now it is time to finish the job. And I will not relent in my determination to shut it down. It is not who we are. It's time to close Gitmo.

As Americans, we cherish our civil liberties, and we need to uphold that commitment if we want maximum cooperation from other countries and industry in our fight against terrorist networks. So while some have moved on from the debates over our surveillance programs, I have not. As promised, our intelligence agencies have worked hard, with the recommendations of privacy advocates, to increase transparency and build more safeguards against potential abuse. And next month, we'll issue a report on how we're keeping our promise to keep our country safe while strengthening privacy.

Looking to the future instead of the past, making sure we match our power with diplomacy and use force wisely, building coalitions to meet new challenges and opportunities, leading always with the example of our values—that's what makes us exceptional. That's what keeps us strong. That's why we have to keep striving to hold ourselves to the highest of standards: our own.

You know, just over a decade ago, I gave a speech in Boston where I said there wasn't a liberal America or a conservative America, a Black America or a White America, but a United States of America. I said this because I had seen it in my own life, in a nation that gave someone like me a chance; because I grew up in Hawaii, a melting pot of races and customs; because I made Illinois my home, a State of small towns, rich farmland, one of the world's great cities, a microcosm of the country where Democrats and Republicans and Independents, good people of every ethnicity and every faith, share certain bedrock values.

Over the past 6 years, the pundits have pointed out more than once that my Presidency hasn't delivered on this vision. How ironic, they say, that our politics seems more divided than ever. It's held up as proof not just of my own flaws—of which there are many—but also as proof that the vision itself is misguided, naive, that there are too many people in this town who actually benefit from partisanship and gridlock for us to ever do anything about it.

I know how tempting such cynicism may be. But I still think the cynics are wrong. I still believe that we are one people. I still believe that together, we can do great things, even when the odds are long.

I believe this because over and over in my 6 years in office, I have seen America at its best. I've seen the hopeful faces of young graduates from New York to California and our newest officers at West Point, Annapolis, Colorado Springs, New London. I've mourned with grieving families in Tucson and Newtown, in Boston, in West, Texas, and West Virginia. I've watched Americans beat back adversity from the Gulf Coast to the Great Plains, from Midwest assembly lines to the Mid-Atlantic seaboard. I've seen something like gay marriage go from a wedge issue used to drive us apart to a story of freedom across our country, a civil right now legal in States that 7 in 10 Americans call home.

So I know the good and optimistic and big-hearted generosity of the American people who every day live the idea that we are our brother's keeper and our sister's keeper. And I know they expect those of us who serve here to set a better example.

So the question for those of us here tonight is how we, all of us, can better reflect America's hopes. I've served in Congress with many of you. I know many of you well. There are a lot of good people here on both sides of the aisle. And many of you have told me that this isn't what you signed up for: arguing past each other on cable shows, the constant fundraising, always looking over your shoulder at how the base will react to every decision.

Imagine if we broke out of these tired old patterns. Imagine if we did something different. Understand, a better politics isn't one where Democrats abandon their agenda or Republicans simply embrace mine. A better politics is one where we appeal to each other's basic decency instead of our basest fears. A better politics is one where we debate without demonizing each other, where we talk issues and values and principles and facts rather than "gotcha" moments or trivial gaffes or fake controversies that have nothing to do with people's daily lives.

A politics—a better politics is one where we spend less time drowning in dark money for ads that pull us into the gutter and spend more time lifting young people up with a sense of purpose and possibility, asking them to join in the great mission of building America.

If we're going to have arguments, let's have arguments, but let's make them debates worthy of this body and worthy of this country. We still may not agree on a woman's right to choose, but surely we can agree it's a good thing that teen pregnancies and abortions are nearing all-time lows and that every woman should have access to the health care that she needs.

Yes, passions still fly on immigration, but surely we can all see something of ourselves in the striving young student and agree that no one benefits when a hard-working mom is snatched from her child and that it's possible to shape a law that upholds our tradition as a nation of laws and a nation of immigrants. I've talked to Republicans and Democrats about that. That's something that we can share.

We may go at it in campaign season, but surely we can agree that the right to vote is sacred, that it's being denied to too many, and that on this 50th anniversary of the great march from Selma to Montgomery and the passage of the Voting Rights Act, we can come together, Democrats and Republicans, to make voting easier for every single American.

We may have different takes on the events of Ferguson and New York. But surely we can understand a father who fears his son can't walk home without being harassed. And surely we can understand the wife who won't rest until the police officer she married walks through the front door at the end of his shift. And surely we can agree that it's a good thing that for the first time in 40 years, the crime rate and the incarceration rate have come down together, and use that as a starting point for Democrats and Republicans, community leaders and law enforcement, to reform America's criminal justice system so that it protects and serves all of us.

That's a better politics. That's how we start rebuilding trust. That's how we move this country forward. That's what the American people want. And that's what they deserve.

I have no more campaigns to run.

[At this point, some audience members applauded.]

My only agenda—*[laughter].*

Audience member. [Inaudible]

The President. I know because I won both of them. *[Laughter]* My only agenda for the next 2 years is the same as the one I've had since the day I swore an oath on the steps of this Capitol: to do what I believe is best for America. If you share the broad vision I outlined tonight, I ask you to join me in the work at hand. If you disagree with parts of it, I hope you'll at least work with me where you do agree. And I commit to every Republican here tonight that I will not only seek out your ideas, I will seek to work with you to make this country stronger.

Because I want this Chamber, I want this city to reflect the truth: that for all our blind spots and shortcomings, we are a people with the strength and generosity of spirit to bridge divides, to unite in common effort, to help our neighbors, whether down the street or on the other side of the world.

I want our actions to tell every child in every neighborhood, your life matters, and we are committed to improving your life chances, as committed as we are to working on behalf of our own kids. I want future generations to know that we are a people who see our differences as a great gift, that we're a people who value the dignity and worth of every citizen: man and woman, young and old, Black and White, Latino, Asian, immigrant, Native American, gay, straight, Americans with mental illness or physical disability. Everybody matters. I want them to grow up in a country that shows the world what we still know to be true: that we are still more than a collection of red States and blue States, that we are the United States of America.

I want them to grow up in a country where a young mom can sit down and write a letter to her President with a story that sums up these past 6 years: "It's amazing what you can bounce back from when you have to. . . . We are a strong, tight-knit family who's made it through some very, very hard times."

My fellow Americans, we too are a strong, tight-knit family. We too have made it through some hard times. Fifteen years into this new century, we have picked ourselves up, dusted ourselves off, and begun again the work of remaking America. We have laid a new foundation. A brighter future is ours to write. Let's begin this new chapter together, and let's start the work right now.

Thank you. God bless you. God bless this country we love. Thank you.

SOURCE: Executive Office of the President. "Address Before a Joint Session of the Congress on the State of the Union." January 20, 2015. *Compilation of Presidential Documents* 2015, no. 00036 (January 20, 2015). www.gpo.gov/fdsys/pkg/DCPD-201500036/pdf/DCPD-201500036.pdf.

Republican Response to the State of the Union Address

January 20, 2015

Good evening.

I'm Joni Ernst. As a mother, a soldier, and a newly elected senator from the great State of Iowa, I am proud to speak with you tonight.

A few moments ago, we heard the President lay out his vision for the year to come. Even if we may not always agree, it's important to hear different points of view in this great country. We appreciate the President sharing his.

"Tonight though, rather than respond to a speech, I'd like to talk about your priorities. I'd like to have a conversation about the new Republican Congress you just elected, and how we plan to make Washington focus on your concerns again.

We heard the message you sent in November—loud and clear. And now we're getting to work to change the direction Washington has been taking our country.

The new Republican Congress also understands how difficult these past six years have been. For many of us, the sting of the economy and the frustration with Washington's dysfunction weren't things we had to read about. We felt them every day.

We felt them in Red Oak—the little town in southwestern Iowa where I grew up, and am still proud to call home today.

As a young girl, I plowed the fields of our family farm. I worked construction with my dad. To save for college, I worked the morning biscuit line at Hardees.

We were raised to live simply, not to waste. It was a lesson my mother taught me every rainy morning.

You see, growing up, I had only one good pair of shoes. So on rainy school days, my mom would slip plastic bread bags over them to keep them dry.

But I was never embarrassed. Because the school bus would be filled with rows and rows of young Iowans with bread bags slipped over their feet.

Our parents may not have had much, but they worked hard for what they did have.

These days though, many families feel like they're working harder and harder, with less and less to show for it.

Not just in Red Oak, but across the country.

We see our neighbors agonize over stagnant wages and lost jobs. We see the hurt caused by canceled healthcare plans and higher monthly insurance bills. We see too many moms and dads put their own dreams on hold while growing more fearful about the kind of future they'll be able to leave to their children.

Americans have been hurting, but when we demanded solutions, too often Washington responded with the same stale mindset that led to failed policies like Obamacare. It's a mindset that gave us political talking points, not serious solutions.

That's why the new Republican majority you elected started by reforming Congress to make it function again. And now, we're working hard to pass the kind of serious job-creation ideas you deserve.

One you've probably heard about is the Keystone jobs bill. President Obama has been delaying this bipartisan infrastructure project for years, even though many members of his party, unions, and a strong majority of Americans support it. The President's own State

Department has said Keystone's construction could support thousands of jobs and pump billions into our economy, and do it with minimal environmental impact.

We worked with Democrats to pass this bill through the House. We're doing the same now in the Senate.

President Obama will soon have a decision to make: will he sign the bill, or block good American jobs?

There's a lot we can achieve if we work together.

Let's tear down trade barriers in places like Europe and the Pacific. Let's sell more of what we make and grow in America over there so we can boost manufacturing, wages, and jobs right here, at home.

Let's simplify America's outdated and loophole-ridden tax code. Republicans think tax filing should be easier for you, not just the well-connected. So let's iron out loopholes to lower rates—and create jobs, not pay for more government spending.

The President has already expressed some support for these kinds of ideas. We're calling on him now to cooperate to pass them.

You'll see a lot of serious work in this new Congress.

Some of it will occur where I stand tonight, in the Armed Services Committee room. This is where I'll join committee colleagues—Republicans and Democrats—to discuss ways to support our exceptional military and its mission. This is where we'll debate strategies to confront terrorism and the threats posed by Al Qaeda, ISIL, and those radicalized by them.

We know threats like these can't just be wished away. We've been reminded of terrorism's reach both at home and abroad; most recently in France and Nigeria, but also in places like Canada and Australia. Our hearts go out to all the innocent victims of terrorism and their loved ones. We can only imagine the depth of their grief.

For two decades, I've proudly worn our nation's uniform: today, as a Lt. Colonel in the Iowa Army National Guard. While deployed overseas with some of America's finest men and women, I've seen just how dangerous these kinds of threats can be.

The forces of violence and oppression don't care about the innocent. We need a comprehensive plan to defeat them.

We must also honor America's veterans. These men and women have sacrificed so much in defense of our freedoms, and our way of life. They deserve nothing less than the benefits they were promised and a quality of care we can be all be proud of.

These are important issues the new Congress plans to address.

We'll also keep fighting to repeal and replace a health care law that's hurt so many hardworking families.

We'll work to correct executive overreach.

We'll propose ideas that aim to cut wasteful spending and balance the budget—with meaningful reforms, not higher taxes like the President has proposed.

We'll advance solutions to prevent the kind of cyberattacks we've seen recently.

We'll work to confront Iran's nuclear ambitions.

And we'll defend life, because protecting our most vulnerable is an important measure of any society.

Congress is back to work on your behalf, ready to make Washington focus on your concerns again.

We know America faces big challenges. But history has shown there's nothing our nation, and our people, can't accomplish.

Just look at my parents and grandparents.

They had very little to call their own except the sweat on their brow and the dirt on their hands. But they worked, they sacrificed, and they dreamed big dreams for their children and grandchildren.

And because they did, an ordinary Iowan like me has had some truly extraordinary opportunities because they showed me that you don't need to come from wealth or privilege to make a difference. You just need the freedom to dream big, and a whole lot of hard work.

The new Republican Congress you elected is working to make Washington understand that too. And with a little cooperation from the President, we can get Washington working again.

Thank you for allowing me to speak with you tonight.

May God bless this great country of ours, the brave Americans serving in uniform on our behalf, and you, the hardworking men and women who make the United States of America the greatest nation the world has ever known.

SOURCE: Office of the Speaker of the House. "FULL TEXT: Sen. Joni Ernst Delivers the Republican Address to the Nation." January 20, 2015.
www.speaker.gov/press-release/embargoed-full-text-sen-joni-ernst-delivers-republican-address-nation.

OTHER HISTORIC DOCUMENTS OF INTEREST

FROM THIS VOLUME

FROM PREVIOUS *HISTORIC DOCUMENTS*

February

Congressional Authorization Sought for Military Action against ISIL

FEBRUARY 11, 2015

Six months after beginning airstrikes against the Islamic State of Iraq and the Levant (ISIL), President Barack Obama appealed to Congress for authorization to extend the use of military force against ISIL to three years. Passage by Congress would have marked the first war authorization since 2002 when the Iraq War was launched; however, by late spring it appeared unlikely that the president's proposal could garner the 218 votes required for passage. By the end of the year, the proposal remained and no viable alternative had been introduced.

U.S. Begins Operations against ISIL

On August 7, 2014, in a nationally televised address, President Obama told the nation that he had authorized airstrikes against ISIL in an effort to protect U.S. interests in Iraq and defend troops delivering humanitarian assistance to refugees. Airstrikes began the following day, led by Air Force and Navy fighters, and included unmanned drones. The president continued to hold that he would not send ground troops into the country and did not have any intention of committing the United States to another long-term conflict in the Middle East. The action against ISIL involved a coalition of nearly sixty international partners.

By late September 2014, the president said in a *60 Minutes* interview that the United States had underestimated ISIL's power and overestimated the Iraqi military's ability to respond to the threat. Republicans were critical of the president's approach and did not believe it could succeed long-term. In December, Congress appropriated funds in its 2015 defense authorization to help combat ISIL. By February 2015, there were approximately 3,000 American troops operating primarily in Iraq and Syria training and advising local troops in the fight against ISIL, and more than 2,000 airstrikes had been carried out by coalition forces against ISIL targets.

Obama Seeks Congressional Authorization

To better define America's mission against ISIL, President Obama sought an Authorization of the Use of Military Force (AUMF) in early 2015. To date, he had been conducting operations against ISIL under the 2001 AUMF that first allowed then-President George W. Bush to launch military efforts in Afghanistan following the September 11 terrorist attacks. Although this statute provided the president with the authority to continue operations against ISIL, he had long stated that he wanted a bipartisan consensus on the efforts, as well as a clearly defined plan of action against the terrorist group.

President Obama first made his authorization request during his 2015 State of the Union Address on January 20. Speaking about current operations against ISIL, the president said, "Instead of getting dragged into another ground war in the Middle East, we are leading a broad coalition, including Arab nations, to degrade and ultimately destroy this terrorist group." Noting the importance of the U.S. role in the action against ISIL, the president said he would "call on this Congress to show the world that we are united in this mission by passing a resolution to authorize the use of force against ISIL."

On February 11, the president sent his authorization request to Congress and subsequently addressed the American public in a televised address to explain what the AUMF would and would not support. The authorization requested the power for the president to use military force against "ISIL or associated persons or forces" but would not, however, allow for the approval of "enduring offensive ground combat operations." Instead, the president sought approval "in other more limited circumstances" such as rescue operations, intelligence gathering, and special operations. In his televised address, the president said the new authorization would allow him to order Special Forces troops to take action in specific circumstances. "For example," the president said, "if we had actionable intelligence about a gathering of ISIL leaders, and our partners didn't have the capacity to get there, I would be prepared to order our Special Forces to take action." There was no geographic range stipulated in the request, meaning the troops deployed to fight ISIL and any "closely related successor entity in hostilities against the United States or its coalition partners" could potentially operate outside of Iraq and Syria.

In addition to requesting authority to act against ISIL, the president's authorization also sought to repeal the AUMF that in 2002 allowed the administration of President Bush to start the Iraq War. The 2001 authorization would remain in place, but the president wrote to Congress that he remained "committed to working with the Congress and the American people to refine, and ultimately repeal, the 2001 AUMF." He added, "Enacting an AUMF that is specific to the threat posed by ISIL could serve as a model for how we can work together to tailor the authorities granted by the 2001 AUMF."

Obama asked Congress to authorize actions against ISIL for three years, extending beyond his presidency; however, he was not seeking open-ended engagement as were those in Iraq and Afghanistan. But the president cautioned that the three years was "not a timetable. It is not announcing that the mission is completed at any given period. What it is saying is that Congress should revisit the issue at the beginning of the next President's term." He added that it was possible the mission against ISIL would be completed by then, but that the next president should have the authority to take the necessary action depending on the circumstances at that time.

Congressional Debate over Authorization

The president's request met with mixed reactions in Congress. Both Democrats and Republicans expressed weariness about involving the United States in new military actions, following more than a decade of combat in Iraq and Afghanistan, but they still welcomed the proposal. "The president's request for authorization for the use of military force is an important first step in demonstrating the commitment from both the executive and Congress to defeat this organization, but there is clearly more work left to be done," said House Majority Whip Steve Scalise, R-La. Sen. John Thune, R-S.D., the third ranking Republican in the Senate, said the request was noteworthy because "everybody realizes it's important enough that the Congress be heard" regarding involvement in the fight against

ISIL. But he added, "The president will probably lose a lot of people on the left; there are probably some Republicans who don't think it goes far enough." House Majority Leader Kevin McCarthy, R-Calif., for example, said he would not support "efforts that impose undue restrictions on the U.S. military and make it harder to win."

Democrats primarily believed that the president's proposal was too vague. According to Chris Van Hollen, D-Md., the draft "provides overly-broad, fresh authority for the deployment of U.S. ground forces in combat operations in Iraq, Syria, and any other countries in which ISIL or its affiliates may be operating," while also leaving a "blank check authority granted to the Executive in the 2001 AUMF."

While Democratic and Republican leadership in both houses of Congress worked with their respective conferences to either revise the legislation or secure approval, the White House pushed for passage. In an accompanying letter to Congress, the president encouraged both parties to work with the White House to approve the authorization to help stop the threat posed by ISIL. "If left unchecked," the president wrote, "ISIL will pose a threat beyond the Middle East, including to the United States homeland."

Congress Declines Passage, Offers No Alternative

Despite public support for Congressional involvement in the authorization of ongoing actions against ISIL, in April, Republican House leadership said that they had been unable to secure the 218 votes necessary for passage of the president's AUMF. Overall, Republicans felt that the request was too constraining, while Democrats felt that the country should shy away from another war authorization. Republicans held firm to the need for an AUMF but still desired a more robust proposal that would spell out the strategy for defeating ISIL. For the time being, Congressional Republicans found that leaving in place the current AUMF provided the president more power than his 2015 proposal, which reinforced their belief that any AUMF for the ISIL conflict should more broadly provide flexibility to deal with the situation as it continues to evolve.

Throughout the spring and summer, members of Congress continued to force action on an AUMF. In June, a measure was brought to the House floor that would force the president to remove all U.S. troops who had been sent to Iraq or Syria since August 7, 2014, for the purpose of fighting ISIL by December 2015. Under the bill, those troops would be allowed to remain in place if Congress authorized an AUMF. The bill failed 139–288. The Senate took a similar tact. There, Sen. Tim Kaine, D-Va., attempted to pass an AUMF by attaching it as an amendment to an unrelated State Department bill. Kaine called it "inexcusable that Congress has let 10 months of war go by without authorizing the U.S. mission against ISIL." Kaine withdrew the amendment while it was still in committee, with promises from the chair that the issue would be taken up at a future meeting.

—Heather Kerrigan

Following is the text of the remarks made by President Barack Obama on February 11, 2015, in an address to the nation on his request for an Authorization of the Use of Military Force (AUMF) for ongoing actions against ISIL; the text of the president's AUMF proposal released on February 11, 2015; and the text of the president's letter attached to his AUMF proposal sent to Congress also on February 11, 2015.

President Obama Addresses the Nation on AUMF Request

February 11, 2015

Good afternoon. Today, as part of an international coalition of some 60 nations, including Arab countries, our men and women in uniform continue the fight against ISIL in Iraq and in Syria.

More than 2,000 coalition airstrikes have pounded these terrorists. We're disrupting their command and control and supply lines, making it harder for them to move. We're destroying their fighting positions, their tanks, their vehicles, their barracks, their training camps, and the oil and gas facilities and infrastructure that fund their operations. We're taking out their commanders, their fighters, and their leaders.

In Iraq, local forces have largely held the line and, in some places, have pushed ISIL back. In Syria, ISIL failed in its major push to take the town of Kobani, losing countless fighters in the process, fighters who will never again threaten innocent civilians. And we've seen reports of sinking morale among ISIL fighters as they realize the futility of their cause.

Now, make no mistake, this is a difficult mission, and it will remain difficult for some time. It's going to take time to dislodge these terrorists, especially from urban areas. But our coalition is on the offensive, ISIL is on the defensive, and ISIL is going to lose. Its barbaric murders of so many people, including American hostages, are a desperate and revolting attempt to strike fear in the hearts of people it can never possibly win over by its ideas or its ideology, because it offers nothing but misery and death and destruction. And with vile groups like this, there is only one option: With our allies and partners, we are going to degrade and ultimately destroy this terrorist group.

And when I announced our strategy against ISIL in September, I said that we are strongest as a nation when the President and Congress work together. Today my administration submitted a draft resolution to Congress to authorize the use of force against ISIL. I want to be very clear about what it does and what it does not do.

This resolution reflects our core objective to destroy ISIL. It supports the comprehensive strategy that we've been pursuing with our allies and our partners: a systemic and sustained campaign of airstrikes against ISIL in Iraq and Syria; support and training for local forces on the ground, including the moderate Syrian opposition; preventing ISIL attacks in the region and beyond, including by foreign terrorist fighters who try to threaten our countries; regional and international support for an inclusive Iraqi Government that unites the Iraqi people and strengthens Iraqi forces against ISIL; humanitarian assistance for the innocent civilians of Iraq and Syria, who are suffering so terribly under ISIL's reign of horror.

I want to thank Vice President Biden, Secretaries Kerry and Hagel, and General Marty Dempsey for their leadership in advancing our strategy. Even as we meet this challenge in Iraq and Syria, we all agree that one of our weapons against terrorists like ISIL—a critical part of our strategy—is the values we live here at home. One of the best antidotes to the hateful ideologies that try to recruit and radicalize people to violent extremism is our own example as diverse and tolerant societies that welcome the contributions of all people, including people of all faiths.

The resolution we've submitted today does not call for the deployment of U.S. ground combat forces to Iraq or Syria. It is not the authorization of another ground war, like Afghanistan or Iraq. The 2,600 American troops in Iraq today largely serve on bases, and yes, they face the risks that come with service in any dangerous environment. But they do not have a combat mission. They are focused on training Iraqi forces, including Kurdish forces.

As I've said before, I'm convinced that the United States should not get dragged back into another prolonged ground war in the Middle East. That's not in our national security interest, and it's not necessary for us to defeat ISIL. Local forces on the ground that know their countries best are best positioned to take the ground fight to ISIL, and that's what they're doing.

At the same time, this resolution strikes the necessary balance by giving us the flexibility we need for unforeseen circumstances. For example, if we had actionable intelligence about a gathering of ISIL leaders, and our partners didn't have the capacity to get them, I would be prepared to order our Special Forces to take action, because I will not allow these terrorists to have a safe haven. So we need flexibility, but we also have to be careful and deliberate. And there is no heavier decision than asking our men and women in uniform to risk their lives on our behalf. As Commander in Chief, I will only send our troops into harm's way when it is absolutely necessary for our national security.

Finally, this resolution repeals the 2002 authorization of force for the invasion of Iraq and limits this new authorization to 3 years. I do not believe America's interests are served by endless war or by remaining on a perpetual war footing. As a nation, we need to ask the difficult and necessary questions about when, why, and how we use military force. After all, it is our troops who bear the costs of our decisions, and we owe them a clear strategy and the support they need to get the job done. So this resolution will give our Armed Forces and our coalition the continuity we need for the next 3 years.

It is not a timetable. It is not announcing that the mission is completed at any given period. What it is saying is that Congress should revisit the issue at the beginning of the next President's term. It's conceivable that the mission is completed earlier. It's conceivable that after deliberation, debate, and evaluation, that there are additional tasks to be carried out in this area. And the people's representatives, with a new President, should be able to have that discussion.

In closing, I want to say that in crafting this resolution we have consulted with, and listened to, both Republicans and Democrats in Congress. We have made a sincere effort to address difficult issues that we've discussed together. In the days and weeks ahead, we'll continue to work closely with leaders and Members of Congress on both sides of the aisle. I believe this resolution can grow even stronger with the thoughtful and dignified debate that this moment demands. I'm optimistic that it can win strong bipartisan support and that we can show our troops and the world that Americans are united in this mission.

Now, today, our men and women in uniform continue the fight against ISIL, and we salute them for their courageous service. We pray for their safety. We stand with their families who miss them and who are sacrificing here at home. But know this: Our coalition is strong, our cause is just, and our mission will succeed. And long after the terrorists we face today are destroyed and forgotten, America will continue to stand free and tall and strong. May God bless our troops, and may God bless the United States of America. Thank you very much, everybody.

SOURCE: Executive Office of the President. "Remarks on Proposed Legislation Submitted to the Congress to Authorize the Use of Military Force Against the Islamic State of Iraq and the Levant (ISIL) Terrorist Organization." February 11, 2015. *Compilation of Presidential Documents* 2015, no. 00092 (February 11, 2015). www.gpo.gov/fdsys/pkg/DCPD-201500092/pdf/DCPD-201500092.pdf.

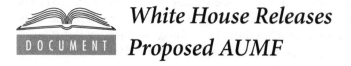

White House Releases Proposed AUMF

February 11, 2015

JOINT RESOLUTION

To authorize the limited use of the United States Armed Forces against the Islamic State of Iraq and the Levant.

***

Whereas the terrorist organization that has referred to itself as the Islamic State of Iraq and the Levant and various other names (in this resolution referred to as "ISIL") poses a grave threat to the people and territorial integrity of Iraq and Syria, regional stability, and the national security interests of the United States and its allies and partners;

Whereas ISIL holds significant territory in Iraq and Syria and has stated its intention to seize more territory and demonstrated the capability to do so;

Whereas ISIL leaders have stated that they intend to conduct terrorist attacks internationally, including against the United States, its citizens, and interests;

Whereas ISIL has committed despicable acts of violence and mass executions against Muslims, regardless of sect, who do not subscribe to ISIL's depraved, violent, and oppressive ideology;

Whereas ISIL has threatened genocide and committed vicious acts of violence against religious and ethnic minority groups, including Iraqi Christian, Yezidi, and Turkmen populations;

Whereas ISIL has targeted innocent women and girls with horrific acts of violence, including abduction, enslavement, torture, rape, and forced marriage;

Whereas ISIL is responsible for the deaths of innocent United States citizens, including James Foley, Steven Sotloff, Abdul-Rahman Peter Kassig, and Kayla Mueller;

Whereas the United States is working with regional and global allies and partners to degrade and defeat ISIL, to cut off its funding, to stop the flow of foreign fighters to its ranks, and to support local communities as they reject ISIL;

Whereas the announcement of the anti-ISIL Coalition on September 5, 2014, during the NATO Summit in Wales, stated that ISIL poses a serious threat and should be countered by a broad international coalition;

Whereas the United States calls on its allies and partners, particularly in the Middle East and North Africa, that have not already done so to join and participate in the anti-ISIL Coalition;

Whereas the United States has taken military action against ISIL in accordance with its inherent right of individual and collective self-defense;

Whereas President Obama has repeatedly expressed his commitment to working with Congress to pass a bipartisan authorization for the use of military force for the anti-ISIL military campaign; and

Whereas President Obama has made clear that in this campaign it is more effective to use our unique capabilities in support of partners on the ground instead of large-scale deployments of U.S. ground forces: Now, therefore, be it

Resolved by the Senate and House of Representatives of the United States of America in Congress assembled, That

SECTION 1. SHORT TITLE.

This joint resolution may be cited as the "Authorization for Use of Military Force against the Islamic State of Iraq and the Levant."

SEC. 2. AUTHORIZATION FOR USE OF UNITED STATES ARMED FORCES.

(a) AUTHORIZATION.—The President is authorized, subject to the limitations in subsection (c), to use the Armed Forces of the United States as the President determines to be necessary and appropriate against ISIL or associated persons or forces as defined in section 5.

(b) WAR POWERS RESOLUTION REQUIREMENTS.—

(1) SPECIFIC STATUTORY AUTHORIZATION.—Consistent with section 8(a)(1) of the War Powers Resolution (50 U.S.C. 1547(a)(1)), Congress declares that this section is intended to constitute specific statutory authorization within the meaning of section 5(b) of the War Powers Resolution (50 U.S.C. 1544(b)).

(2) APPLICABILITY OF OTHER REQUIREMENTS.—Nothing in this resolution supersedes any requirement of the War Powers Resolution (50 U.S.C. 1541 et seq.).

(c) LIMITATIONS.—

The authority granted in subsection (a) does not authorize the use of the United States Armed Forces in enduring offensive ground combat operations.

SEC. 3. DURATION OF THIS AUTHORIZATION.

This authorization for the use of military force shall terminate three years after the date of the enactment of this joint resolution, unless reauthorized.

SEC. 4. REPORTS.

The President shall report to Congress at least once every six months on specific actions taken pursuant to this authorization.

SEC. 5. ASSOCIATED PERSONS OR FORCES DEFINED.

In this joint resolution, the term "associated persons or forces" means individuals and organizations fighting for, on behalf of, or alongside ISIL or any closely-related successor entity in hostilities against the United States or its coalition partners.

SEC. 6. REPEAL OF AUTHORIZATION FOR USE OF MILITARY FORCE AGAINST IRAQ.

The Authorization for Use of Military Force Against Iraq Resolution of 2002 (Public Law 107–243; 116 Stat. 1498; 50 U.S.C. 1541 note) is hereby repealed.

SOURCE: The White House. "Joint Resolution." February 11, 2015. www.whitehouse.gov/sites/default/files/docs/aumf_02112015.pdf.

President Obama Requests AUMF From Congress

February 11, 2015

To the Congress of the United States:

The so-called Islamic State of Iraq and the Levant (ISIL) poses a threat to the people and stability of Iraq, Syria, and the broader Middle East, and to U.S. national security. It threatens American personnel and facilities located in the region and is responsible for the deaths of U.S. citizens James Foley, Steven Sotloff, Abdul-Rahman Peter Kassig, and Kayla Mueller. If left unchecked, ISIL will pose a threat beyond the Middle East, including to the United States homeland.

I have directed a comprehensive and sustained strategy to degrade and defeat ISIL. As part of this strategy, U.S. military forces are conducting a systematic campaign of airstrikes against ISIL in Iraq and Syria. Although existing statutes provide me with the authority I need to take these actions, I have repeatedly expressed my commitment to working with the Congress to pass a bipartisan authorization for the use of military force (AUMF) against ISIL. Consistent with this commitment, I am submitting a draft AUMF that would authorize the continued use of military force to degrade and defeat ISIL.

My Administration's draft AUMF would not authorize long-term, large-scale ground combat operations like those our Nation conducted in Iraq and Afghanistan. Local forces, rather than U.S. military forces, should be deployed to conduct such operations. The authorization I propose would provide the flexibility to conduct ground combat operations in other, more limited circumstances, such as rescue operations involving U.S. or coalition personnel or the use of special operations forces to take military action against ISIL leadership. It would also authorize the use of U.S. forces in situations where ground combat operations are not expected or intended, such as intelligence collection and sharing, missions to enable kinetic strikes, or the provision of operational planning and other forms of advice and assistance to partner forces.

Although my proposed AUMF does not address the 2001 AUMF, I remain committed to working with the Congress and the American people to refine, and ultimately repeal, the 2001 AUMF. Enacting an AUMF that is specific to the threat posed by ISIL could serve as a model for how we can work together to tailor the authorities granted by the 2001 AUMF.

I can think of no better way for the Congress to join me in supporting our Nation's security than by enacting this legislation, which would show the world we are united in our resolve to counter the threat posed by ISIL.

BARACK OBAMA
The White House,
February 11, 2015.

SOURCE: Executive Office of the President. "Message to the Congress on Submitting Proposed Legislation to Authorize the Use of Military Force Against the Islamic State of Iraq and the Levant (ISIL) Terrorist Organization." February 11, 2015. *Compilation of Presidential Documents* 2015, no. 00093 (February 11, 2015). www.gpo.gov/fdsys/pkg/DCPD-201500093/pdf/DCPD-201500093.pdf.

OTHER HISTORIC DOCUMENTS OF INTEREST

FROM THIS VOLUME

FROM PREVIOUS *HISTORIC DOCUMENTS*

FCC Votes on Internet
Service Regulation

FEBRUARY 26, 2015

The contentious debate over net neutrality in the United States spilled over into the early months of 2015 as the Federal Communications Commission (FCC) considered public comments gathered in response to its 2014 Notice of Proposed Rulemaking (NPRM) on how best to protect and promote an open Internet. Net neutrality is the principle that that all Internet data is treated the same, and broadband providers should not block or slow access to certain websites or content—even if that content is slowing down their networks—or impose fees for faster services. Consumer advocates and others argued that new FCC regulations are necessary to ensure free and fair access to the Internet, though providers dismissed such rules as superfluous given industry commitments to keep the Internet open and existing laws that protect consumers and marketplace competition. In February 2015, the FCC issued a new Open Internet Order that established stronger regulations than those suggested in the NPRM, earning high praise from open Internet advocates but also spurring a host of legal challenges from telecommunications companies and major Internet service providers (ISPs) that claimed the rules were arbitrary and beyond the agency's regulatory authority.

Verizon v. FCC

The public debate over net neutrality regulations ignited in January 2014, following the U.S. Court of Appeals for the District of Columbia Circuit's ruling in the case of *Verizon v. FCC*. The case centered on the FCC's Open Internet Order of 2010, which sought to address the agency's concerns that broadband providers had both the ability and the incentive to limit the open nature of the Internet for business gains after Comcast asserted that it had the right to slow its customers' access to a file-sharing website. The order prevented broadband providers from blocking lawful content and services; prohibited unreasonable discrimination against lawful network traffic; and required broadband providers to disclose their network management practices, performance characteristics, and terms of use to the FCC. The agency argued that consumers pay ISPs for a service and, consequently, it would be unlawful not to provide that service, particularly if in doing so the ISPs violated the order. Verizon sued the FCC in January 2011, claiming that the agency did not have the authority to issue such orders.

In its ruling, the appeals court found that portions of the FCC's net neutrality rules contradicted the agency's earlier decision that broadband was an "information service" and, therefore, largely outside of its regulatory authority. However, the court did uphold the FCC's authority in other areas and the agency's determination that rules protecting an open Internet were needed. Specifically, the court upheld the FCC's authority under Section 706 of the Telecommunications Act of 1996, which requires the agency to determine whether "advanced telecommunications capability [i.e., broadband or high-speed access] is being deployed to all Americans in a reasonable and timely fashion." If it is not, the FCC can "take immediate action to accelerate deployment of such capability by removing barriers to infrastructure investment and by promoting competition in the telecommunications market." FCC chairman Tom Wheeler subsequently announced that the agency would not appeal the ruling but would seek to reinstate open Internet rules that could achieve the goals of the 2010 order while following the legal roadmap laid out by the court.

On May 15, 2014, the FCC issued a NPRM seeking public comment on how best to protect and promote an open Internet. It included several initial proposed rules as well as a series of questions for the public to respond to, such as whether "paid prioritization"—in which ISPs can charge higher rates to companies that want faster connection speeds—should be banned. These so-called "fast lanes" were a major issue for consumer groups and open Internet advocates who worried that this would separate Internet users into "haves" and "have nots." The NPRM also sought to explore proposals to reclassify broadband providers as "common carriers," much like utility companies, which would give the FCC greater authority in a number of areas: regulation of ISPs under Title II of the Communications Act of 1934, another highly contentious issue; enhancement of the FCC's initial transparency rule—the only component of the 2010 order not vacated by the court—to require tailored disclosures from broadband providers including the nature of network congestion that impacts consumers' use of online service; revival of the agency's "no blocking" rule; and establishment of a new process for resolving Internet access-related disputes.

The NPRM's release initiated a four-month-long public comment period that lasted through September 15, as well as an intense flurry of lobbying by companies, advocacy groups, and grassroots campaigns. The agency received roughly four million comments, an overwhelming majority of which supported a reclassification of broadband providers as common carriers. President Barack Obama also weighed in, unveiling his own net neutrality plan on November 10, 2014, and calling for the FCC to reclassify all elements of broadband services as utilities.

Open Internet Order 2015

On February 26, 2015, the FCC announced that by a 3–2 vote it had officially adopted a new Open Internet Order. For the first time, the rules would apply to both fixed and mobile broadband alike to ensure that the FCC's regulations accounted for advances in mobile technology and wireless access. The order did include reclassification of broadband Internet as a telecommunications service under Title II of the Communications Act, though the agency was careful to note that despite this reclassification, another twenty-seven of the title's provisions and more than 700 regulations adopted under the title would not apply to broadband. For example, broadband providers would not be subject to utility-style rate regulations and broadband service would remain exempt from state and local taxation under the Internet Freedom Act. This selective approach was meant to address industry concerns that reclassification would expose them to rate and other burdensome regulations that would hinder investment and growth, as well as concerns that the Communications Act was seriously outdated and thus should not be applied to modern technology.

The order outlined three "bright line rules" that echoed the FCC's 2010 order by prohibiting broadband providers from blocking access to legal content, applications, or nonharmful devices; impairing or degrading lawful Internet traffic on the basis of content, applications, or nonharmful devices; and creating fast lanes that favor some lawful Internet traffic over other lawful traffic. In addition, the order established a standard for future ISP conduct to allow the FCC some latitude to address issues that emerge as new practices are developed, stating that providers cannot "unreasonably interfere with or unreasonably disadvantage" both the ability of consumers to select, access, and use the lawful content, applications, services, or devices of their choosing, and the ability of edge providers (content and application providers such as YouTube, Facebook, and Netflix) to make lawful content, applications, services, or devices available to consumers. It also established a standard for "reasonable network management" and said that any such practice must be primarily used for and tailored to achieve a legitimate network management purpose, not a business purpose. To help ensure transparency, the order further required that broadband providers disclose promotional rates, fees, surcharges, and data caps in a consistent format as well as any network management practices that could affect customers' service. It gave the FCC the authority to hear complaints and take enforcement action on issues surrounding the exchange of traffic between mass-market broadband providers and other networks and services as well.

Chairman Wheeler and Commissioners Jessica Rosenworcel and Mignon Clyburn voted to approve the new rules, with Commissioners Ajit Pai and Michael O'Rielly dissenting. Wheeler hailed the vote as a victory of the democratic process, emphasizing the public's role in helping shape the rules. "I am incredibly proud of the process the Commission has run in developing today's historic open Internet protections," he said. "The American people reasonably expect and deserve an Internet that is fast, fair, and open. Today they get what they deserve: strong, enforceable rules that will ensure the Internet remains open, now and in the future." Clyburn thanked Chairman Wheeler for working with her office to improve the order—having requested several changes to the rules just days before the vote—and offered her support for the package: "I believe it provides the strong protections we need and balances the concerns raised by stakeholders, large and small." Pai and O'Rielly were both highly critical of the order in their statements. Pai said the order "seizes unilateral authority to regulate Internet conduct, to direct where Internet service providers make their investments, and to determine what service plans will be available to the American public," adding that it was "a radical departure from the bipartisan, market-oriented policies that have served us so well for the last two decades." O'Rielly claimed the FCC was attempting "to usurp the authority of Congress by re-writing the Communications Act to suit its own 'values' and political ends," and argued that the agency had not provided sufficient notice or time for commenting on its NPRM. In fact, O'Rielly and Pai had requested that the FCC "immediately release the 332-page Internet regulation plan publicly and allow the American people a reasonable period of not less than 30 days to carefully study it," but their request was denied.

REACTION TO THE NEW RULES

Reaction to the order was expectedly mixed, with consumer groups, free speech advocates, and open Internet supporters applauding the vote. "This is a victory for free speech, plain and simple," said American Civil Liberties Union (ACLU) legislative counsel Gabe Rottman. "The FCC has a critical role to play in protecting citizens' ability to see what they want and say what they want online, without interference. Title II provides the firmest possible foundation for such protections." Michael Beckerman, president of the Internet Association, which represents companies including Google and Facebook, called the vote "a welcome step in our effort to create strong, enforceable net neutrality rules."

Industry groups, however, argued that the FCC overstepped its authority and that the new rules were unnecessary. "The FCC's decision to impose obsolete telephone-era regulations on the high-speed Internet is one giant step backwards for America's broadband networks and everyone who depends upon them," read a statement from Broadband America, a group representing major ISPs. "These 'Title II' rules go far beyond protecting the Open Internet, launching a costly and destructive era of government micromanagement that will discourage private investment in new networks and slow down the breakneck innovation that is the soul of the Internet today." The group also called on Congress to intervene, though Senate Commerce Committee chairman John Thune, R-S.D., indicated that Republicans, while highly critical of the NPRM, were unlikely to pass a bill that would undo the order. "We're not going to get a signed bill that doesn't have Democrats' support. This is an issue that needs to have bipartisan support," he said. Thune began circulating legislation in January that, while including some of the order's key rules, would prohibit the FCC from issuing such regulations, but he pulled it from consideration the week of the FCC vote due to lack of support.

Lack of congressional interest in challenging the rules did not prevent others from attempting to do so, even before the order took effect. On March 23, USTelecom, an organization representing large Internet providers, and Alamo Broadband, a Texas-based Internet provider, both filed separate lawsuits against the FCC. Then on April 14, AT&T, the National Cable & Telecommunications Association, CTIA-The Wireless Association, and the American Cable Association each filed a lawsuit challenging the rules. Broadly, their complaints argued that the new rules were arbitrary and contrary to existing laws and procedures. While the cases are still pending, the U.S. Court of Appeals for the District of Columbia Circuit did provide the FCC with a partial victory on June 11, rejecting a request from USTelecom to partly suspend implementation of the rules while they are being challenged in court. The court ruled that the group had "not satisfied the stringent requirements" needed to justify the stay, including proving irreparable harm from the rules' implementation.

—Linda Fecteau Grimm

Following is the Introduction and Executive Summary of the Federal Communications Commission (FCC) Open Internet Order, adopted on February 26, 2015, and released on March 12, 2015; a press release from the FCC issued on February 26 detailing the new Internet rules; and statements by Chairman Wheeler and Commissioners Clyburn, Rosenworcel, Pai, and O'Rielly, all released on February 26, 2015, in response to the new Internet rules.

FCC Open Internet Order

February 26, 2015

[Footnotes have been omitted.]

I. INTRODUCTION

1. The open Internet drives the American economy and serves, every day, as a critical tool for America's citizens to conduct commerce, communicate, educate, entertain, and engage in the world around them. The benefits of an open Internet are undisputed. But it must remain open: open for commerce, innovation, and speech; open for consumers and for the innovation created by applications developers and content companies; and open for expansion and investment by America's broadband providers. For over a decade, the Commission has been committed to protecting and promoting an open Internet.

2. Four years ago, the Commission adopted open Internet rules to protect and promote the "virtuous cycle" that drives innovation and investment on the Internet—both at the "edges" of the network, as well as in the network itself. In the years that those rules were in place, significant investment and groundbreaking innovation continued to define the broadband marketplace. For example, according to US Telecom, broadband providers invested $212 billion in the three years following adoption of the rules—from 2011 to 2013—more than in any three year period since 2002.

3. Likewise, innovation at the edge moves forward unabated. For example, 2010 was the first year that the majority of Netflix customers received their video content via online streaming rather than via DVDs in red envelopes. Today, Netflix sends the most peak downstream traffic in North America of any company. Other innovative service providers have experienced extraordinary growth—Etsy reports that it has grown from $314 million in merchandise sales in 2010 to $1.35 billion in merchandise sales in 2013. And, just as importantly, new kinds of innovative businesses are busy being born. In the video space alone, in just the last sixth months, CBS and HBO have announced new plans for streaming their content free of cable subscriptions; DISH has launched a new package of channels that includes ESPN, and Sony is not far behind; and Discovery Communications founder John Hendricks has announced a new over-the-top service providing bandwidth-intensive programming. This year, Amazon took home two Golden Globes for its new series "Transparent."

4. The lesson of this period, and the overwhelming consensus on the record, is that carefully-tailored rules to protect Internet openness will allow investment and innovation to continue to flourish. Consistent with that experience and the record built in this proceeding, today we adopt carefully-tailored rules that would prevent specific practices we know are harmful to Internet openness—blocking, throttling, and paid prioritization—as well as a strong standard of conduct designed to prevent the deployment of new practices that would harm Internet openness. We also enhance our transparency rule to ensure that consumers are fully informed as to whether the services they purchase are delivering what they expect.

5. Carefully-tailored rules need a strong legal foundation to survive and thrive. Today, we provide that foundation by grounding our open Internet rules in multiple sources of

legal authority—including both section 706 of the Telecommunications Act and Title II of the Communications Act. Moreover, we concurrently exercise the Commission's forbearance authority to forbear from application of 27 provisions of Title II of the Communications Act, and over 700 Commission rules and regulations. This is a Title II tailored for the 21st century, and consistent with the "light-touch" regulatory framework that has facilitated the tremendous investment and innovation on the Internet. We expressly eschew the future use of prescriptive, industry-wide rate regulation. Under this approach, consumers can continue to enjoy unfettered access to the Internet over their fixed and mobile broadband connections, innovators can continue to enjoy the benefits of a platform that affords them unprecedented access to hundreds of millions of consumers across the country and around the world, and network operators can continue to reap the benefits of their investments.

6. Informed by the views of nearly 4 million commenters, our staff-led roundtables, numerous *ex parte* presentations, meetings with individual Commissioners and staff, and more, our decision today—once and for all—puts into place strong, sustainable rules, grounded in multiple sources of our legal authority, to ensure that Americans reap the economic, social, and civic benefits of an open Internet today and into the future.

II. EXECUTIVE SUMMARY

7. The benefits of rules and policies protecting an open Internet date back over a decade and must continue. Just over a year ago, the D.C. Circuit in *Verizon v. FCC* struck down the Commission's 2010 conduct rules against blocking and unreasonable discrimination. But the *Verizon* court upheld the Commission's finding that Internet openness drives a "virtuous cycle" in which innovations at the edges of the network enhance consumer demand, leading to expanded investments in broadband infrastructure that, in turn, spark new innovations at the edge. The *Verizon* court further affirmed the Commission's conclusion that "broadband providers represent a threat to Internet openness and could act in ways that would ultimately inhibit the speed and extent of future broadband deployment."

8. Threats to Internet openness remain today. The record reflects that broadband providers hold all the tools necessary to deceive consumers, degrade content, or disfavor the content that they don't like. The 2010 rules helped to deter such conduct while they were in effect. But, as Verizon frankly told the court at oral argument, but for the 2010 rules, it would be exploring agreements to charge certain content providers for priority service. Indeed, the wireless industry had a well-established record of trying to keep applications within a carrier-controlled "walled garden" in the early days of mobile applications. That specific practice ended when Internet Protocol (IP) created the opportunity to leap the wall. But the Commission has continued to hear concerns about other broadband provider practices involving blocking or degrading third-party applications.

9. Emerging Internet trends since 2010 give us more, not less, cause for concern about such threats. First, mobile broadband networks have massively expanded since 2010. They are faster, more broadly deployed, more widely used, and more technologically advanced. At the end of 2010, there were about 70,000 devices in the U.S. that had LTE wireless connections. Today, there are more than 127 million. We welcome this tremendous investment and innovation in the mobile marketplace. With carefully-tailored rules in place, that investment can continue to flourish and consumers can continue to enjoy unfettered access to the Internet over their mobile broadband connections. Indeed, mobile broadband is becoming an increasingly important pathway to the Internet independent of any fixed broadband connections consumers may have,

given that mobile broadband is not a full substitute for fixed broadband connections. And consumers must be protected, for example from mobile commercial practices masquerading as "reasonable network management." Second, and critically, the growth of online streaming video services has spurred further evolution of the Internet. Currently, video is the dominant form of traffic on the Internet. These video services directly confront the video businesses of the very companies that supply them broadband access to their customers.

10. The Commission, in its May *Notice of Proposed Rulemaking*, asked a fundamental question: "What is the right public policy to ensure that the Internet remains open?" It proposed to enhance the transparency rule, and follow the *Verizon* court's blueprint by relying on section 706 to adopt a no-blocking rule and a requirement that broadband providers engage in "commercially reasonable" practices. The Commission also asked about whether it should adopt other bright-line rules or different standards using other sources of Commission authority, including Title II. And if Title II were to apply, the Commission asked about how it should exercise its authority to forbear from Title II obligations. It asked whether mobile services should also be classified under Title II.

11. Three overarching objectives have guided us in answering these questions, based on the vast record before the Commission: America needs more broadband, better broadband, and open broadband networks. These goals are mutually reinforcing, not mutually exclusive. Without an open Internet, there would be less broadband investment and deployment. And, as discussed further below, all three are furthered through the open Internet rules and balanced regulatory framework we adopt today.

12. In enacting the Administrative Procedure Act (APA), Congress instructed expert agencies conducting rulemaking proceedings to "give interested persons an opportunity to participate in the rule making through submission of written data, views, or arguments." It is public comment that cements an agency's expertise. As was explained in the seminal report that led to the enactment of the APA:

> *The reason for [an administrative agency's] existence is that it is expected to bring to its task greater familiarity with the subject than legislators, dealing with many subjects, can have. But its knowledge is rarely complete, and it must always learn the frequently clashing viewpoints of those whom its regulations will affect.*

13. Congress could not have imagined when it enacted the APA almost seventy years ago that the day would come when nearly 4 million Americans would exercise their right to comment on a proposed rulemaking. But that is what has happened in this proceeding and it is a good thing. The Commission has listened and it has learned. Its expertise has been strengthened. Public input has "improve[d] the quality of agency rulemaking by ensuring that agency regulations will be 'tested by exposure to diverse public comment.'" There is general consensus in the record on the need for the Commission to provide certainty with clear, enforceable rules. There is also general consensus on the need to have such rules. Today the Commission, informed by all of those views, makes a decision grounded in the record. The Commission has considered the arguments, data, and input provided by the commenters, even if not in agreement with the particulars of this Order; that public input has created a robust record, enabling the Commission to adopt new rules that are clear and sustainable.

A. Strong Rules That Protect Consumers from Past and Future Tactics that Threaten the Open Internet

1. Clear, Bright-Line Rules

14. Because the record overwhelmingly supports adopting rules and demonstrates that three specific practices invariably harm the open Internet—Blocking, Throttling, and Paid Prioritization—this Order bans each of them, applying the same rules to both fixed and mobile broadband Internet access service.

15. *No Blocking.* Consumers who subscribe to a retail broadband Internet access service must get what they have paid for—access to all (lawful) destinations on the Internet. This essential and well-accepted principle has long been a tenet of Commission policy, stretching back to its landmark decision in *Carterfone*, which protected a customer's right to connect a telephone to the monopoly telephone network. Thus, this Order adopts a straightforward ban:

> *A person engaged in the provision of broadband Internet access service, insofar as such person is so engaged, shall not block lawful content, applications, services, or non-harmful devices, subject to reasonable network management.*

16. *No Throttling.* The 2010 open Internet rule against blocking contained an ancillary prohibition against the degradation of lawful content, applications, services, and devices, on the ground that such degradation would be tantamount to blocking. This Order creates a separate rule to guard against degradation targeted at specific uses of a customer's broadband connection:

> *A person engaged in the provision of broadband Internet access service, insofar as such person is so engaged, shall not impair or degrade lawful Internet traffic on the basis of Internet content, application, or service, or use of a non-harmful device, subject to reasonable network management.*

17. The ban on throttling is necessary both to fulfill the reasonable expectations of a customer who signs up for a broadband service that promises access to all of the lawful Internet, and to avoid gamesmanship designed to avoid the no-blocking rule by, for example, rendering an application effectively, but not technically, unusable. It prohibits the degrading of Internet traffic based on source, destination, or content. It also specifically prohibits conduct that singles out content competing with a broadband provider's business model.

18. *No Paid Prioritization.* Paid prioritization occurs when a broadband provider accepts payment (monetary or otherwise) to manage its network in a way that benefits particular content, applications, services, or devices. To protect against "fast lanes," this Order adopts a rule that establishes that:

> *A person engaged in the provision of broadband Internet access service, insofar as such person is so engaged, shall not engage in paid prioritization.*
>
> *"Paid prioritization" refers to the management of a broadband provider's network to directly or indirectly favor some traffic over other traffic, including*

through use of techniques such as traffic shaping, prioritization, resource reservation, or other forms of preferential traffic management, either (a) in exchange for consideration (monetary or otherwise) from a third party, or (b) to benefit an affiliated entity.

19. The record demonstrates the need for strong action. The *Verizon* court itself noted that broadband networks have "powerful incentives to accept fees from edge providers, either in return for excluding their competitors or for granting them prioritized access to end users." Mozilla, among many such commenters, explained that "[p]rioritization . . . inherently creates fast and slow lanes." Although there are arguments that some forms of paid prioritization could be beneficial, the practical difficulty is this: the threat of harm is overwhelming, case-by-case enforcement can be cumbersome for individual consumers or edge providers, and there is no practical means to measure the extent to which edge innovation and investment would be chilled. And, given the dangers, there is no room for a blanket exception for instances where consumer permission is buried in a service plan—the threats of consumer deception and confusion are simply too great.

2. No Unreasonable Interference or Unreasonable Disadvantage to Consumers or Edge Providers

20. The key insight of the virtuous cycle is that broadband providers have both the incentive and the ability to act as gatekeepers standing between edge providers and consumers. As gatekeepers, they can block access altogether; they can target competitors, including competitors to their own video services; and they can extract unfair tolls. Such conduct would, as the Commission concluded in 2010, "reduce the rate of innovation at the edge and, in turn, the likely rate of improvements to network infrastructure." In other words, when a broadband provider acts as a gatekeeper, it actually chokes consumer demand for the very broadband product it can supply.

21. The bright-line bans on blocking, throttling, and paid prioritization will go a long way to preserve the virtuous cycle. But not all the way. Gatekeeper power can be exercised through a variety of technical and economic means, and without a catch-all standard, it would be that, as Benjamin Franklin said, "a little neglect may breed great mischief." Thus, the Order adopts the following standard:

Any person engaged in the provision of broadband Internet access service, insofar as such person is so engaged, shall not unreasonably interfere with or unreasonably disadvantage (i) end users' ability to select, access, and use broadband Internet access service or the lawful Internet content, applications, services, or devices of their choice, or (ii) edge providers' ability to make lawful content, applications, services, or devices available to end users. Reasonable network management shall not be considered a violation of this rule.

22. This "no unreasonable interference/disadvantage" standard protects free expression, thus fulfilling the congressional policy that "the Internet offer[s] a forum for a true diversity of political discourse, unique opportunities for cultural development, and myriad avenues for intellectual activity." And the standard will permit considerations of asserted benefits of innovation as well as threatened harm to end users and edge providers.

3. Enhanced Transparency

23. The Commission's 2010 transparency rule, upheld by the *Verizon* court, remains in full effect:

> *A person engaged in the provision of broadband Internet access service shall publicly disclose accurate information regarding the network management practices, performance, and commercial terms of its broadband Internet access services sufficient for consumers to make informed choices regarding use of such services and for content, application, service, and device providers to develop, market, and maintain Internet offerings.*

24. Today's Order reaffirms the importance of ensuring transparency, so that consumers are fully informed about the Internet access they are purchasing and so that edge providers have the information they need to understand whether their services will work as advertised. To do that, the Order builds on the strong foundation established in 2010 and enhances the transparency rule for both end users and edge providers, including by adopting a requirement that broadband providers always must disclose promotional rates, all fees and/or surcharges, and all data caps or data allowances; adding packet loss as a measure of network performance that must be disclosed; and requiring specific notification to consumers that a "network practice" is likely to significantly affect their use of the service. Out of an abundance of caution and in response to a request by the American Cable Association, we also adopt a temporary exemption from these enhancements for small providers (defined for the purposes of the temporary exception as providers with 100,000 or fewer subscribers), and we direct our Consumer & Governmental Affairs Bureau to adopt an Order by December 15, 2015 concerning whether to make the exception permanent and, if so, the appropriate definition of "small." Lastly, we create for all providers a "safe harbor" process for the format and nature of the required disclosure to consumers, which we believe will result in more effective presentation of consumer-focused information by broadband providers.

4. Scope of the Rules

25. The open Internet rules described above apply to both fixed and mobile broadband Internet access service. Consistent with the 2010 Order, today's Order applies its rules to the consumer-facing service that broadband networks provide, which is known as "broadband Internet access service" (BIAS) and is defined to be:

> *A mass-market retail service by wire or radio that provides the capability to transmit data to and receive data from all or substantially all Internet endpoints, including any capabilities that are incidental to and enable the operation of the communications service, but excluding dial-up Internet access service. This term also encompasses any service that the Commission finds to be providing a functional equivalent of the service described in the previous sentence, or that is used to evade the protections set forth in this Part.*

26. As in 2010, BIAS does not include enterprise services, virtual private network services, hosting, or data storage services. Further, we decline to apply the open Internet

rules to premises operators to the extent they may be offering broadband Internet access service as we define it today.

27. In defining this service we make clear that we are responding to the *Verizon* court's conclusion that broadband providers "furnish a service to edge providers" (and that this service was being treated as common carriage *per se*). As discussed further below, we make clear that broadband Internet access service encompasses this service to edge providers. Broadband providers sell retail customers the ability to go anywhere (lawful) on the Internet. Their representation that they will transport and deliver traffic to and from all or substantially all Internet endpoints includes the promise to transmit traffic to and from those Internet endpoints back to the user.

28. *Interconnection.* BIAS involves the exchange of traffic between a broadband Internet access provider and connecting networks. The representation to retail customers that they will be able to reach "all or substantially all Internet endpoints" necessarily includes the promise to make the interconnection arrangements necessary to allow that access.

29. As discussed below, we find that broadband Internet access service is a "telecommunications service" and subject to sections 201, 202, and 208 (along with key enforcement provisions). As a result, commercial arrangements for the exchange of traffic with a broadband Internet access provider are within the scope of Title II, and the Commission will be available to hear disputes raised under sections 201 and 202 on a case-by-case basis: an appropriate vehicle for enforcement where disputes are primarily over commercial terms and that involve some very large corporations, including companies like transit providers and Content Delivery Networks (CDNs), that act on behalf of smaller edge providers.

30. But this Order does not apply the open Internet rules to interconnection. Three factors are critical in informing this approach to interconnection. First, the nature of Internet traffic, driven by massive consumption of video, has challenged traditional arrangements—placing more emphasis on the use of CDNs or even direct connections between content providers (like Netflix or Google) and last-mile broadband providers. Second, it is clear that consumers have been subject to degradation resulting from commercial disagreements, perhaps most notably in a series of disputes between Netflix and large last-mile broadband providers. But, third, the causes of past disruption and—just as importantly—the potential for future degradation through interconnection disputes—are reflected in very different narratives in the record.

31. While we have more than a decade's worth of experience with last-mile practices, we lack a similar depth of background in the Internet traffic exchange context. Thus, we find that the best approach is to watch, learn, and act as required, but not intervene now, especially not with prescriptive rules. This Order—for the first time—provides authority to consider claims involving interconnection, a process that is sure to bring greater understanding to the Commission.

32. *Reasonable Network Management.* As with the 2010 rules, this Order contains an exception for reasonable network management, which applies to all but the paid prioritization rule (which, by definition, is not a means of managing a network):

> *A network management practice is a practice that has a primarily technical network management justification, but does not include other business practices. A network management practice is reasonable if it is primarily used for and tailored to achieving a legitimate network management purpose, taking into account the particular network architecture and technology of the broadband Internet access service.*

33. Recently, significant concern has arisen when mobile providers' have attempted to justify certain practices as reasonable network management practices, such as applying speed reductions to customers using "unlimited data plans" in ways that effectively force them to switch to price plans with less generous data allowances. For example, in the summer of 2014, Verizon announced a change to its "unlimited" data plan for LTE customers, which would have limited the speeds of LTE customers using grandfathered "unlimited" plans once they reached a certain level of usage each month. Verizon briefly described this change as within the scope of "reasonable network management," before changing course and withdrawing the change.

34. With mobile broadband service now subject to the same rules as fixed broadband service, the Order expressly recognizes that evaluation of network management practices will take into account the additional challenges involved in the management of mobile networks, including the dynamic conditions under which they operate. It also recognizes the specific network management needs of other technologies, such as unlicensed Wi-Fi networks.

35. *Non-Broadband Internet Access Service Data Services.* The 2010 rules included an exception for "specialized services." This Order likewise recognizes that some data services—like facilities-based VoIP offerings, heart monitors, or energy consumption sensors—may be offered by a broadband provider but do not provide access to the Internet generally. The term "specialized services" can be confusing because the critical point is not whether the services are "specialized;" it is that they are not broadband Internet access service. IP-services that do not travel over broadband Internet access service, like the facilities-based VoIP services used by many cable customers, are not within the scope of the open Internet rules, which protect access or use of broadband Internet access service. Nonetheless, these other non-broadband Internet access service data services could be provided in a manner that undermines the purpose of the open Internet rules and that will not be permitted. The Commission expressly reserves the authority to take action if a service is, in fact, providing the functional equivalent of broadband Internet access service or is being used to evade the open Internet rules. The Commission will vigilantly watch for such abuse, and its actions will be aided by the existing transparency requirement that non-broadband Internet access service data services be disclosed.

5. Enforcement

36. The Commission may enforce the open Internet rules through investigation and the processing of complaints (both formal and informal). In addition, the Commission may provide guidance through the use of enforcement advisories and advisory opinions, and it will appoint an ombudsperson. In order to provide the Commission with additional understanding, particularly of technical issues, the Order delegates to the Enforcement Bureau the authority to request a written opinion from an outside technical organization or otherwise to obtain objective advice from industry standard-setting bodies or similar organizations.

B. Promoting Investment with a Modern Title II

37. Today, our forbearance approach results in over 700 codified rules being inapplicable, a "light-touch" approach for the use of Title II. This includes no unbundling

of last-mile facilities, no tariffing, no rate regulation, and no cost accounting rules, which results in a carefully tailored application of only those Title II provisions found to directly further the public interest in an open Internet and more, better, and open broadband. Nor will our actions result in the imposition of any new federal taxes or fees; the ability of states to impose fees on broadband is already limited by the congressional Internet tax moratorium.

38. This is Title II tailored for the 21st Century. Unlike the application of Title II to incumbent wireline companies in the 20th Century, a swath of utility-style provisions (including tariffing) will *not* be applied. Indeed, there will be fewer sections of Title II applied than have been applied to Commercial Mobile Radio Service (CMRS), where Congress expressly required the application of Sections 201, 202, and 208, and permitted the Commission to forbear from others. In fact, Title II has never been applied in such a focused way.

39. History demonstrates that this careful approach to the use of Title II will not impede investment. First, mobile voice services have been regulated under a similar light-touch Title II approach since 1994 — and investment and usage boomed. For example, between 1993 and 2009 (while voice was the primary driver of mobile revenues), the mobile industry invested more than $271 billion in building out networks, during a time in which industry revenues increased by 1300 percent and subscribership grew over 1600 percent. Moreover, more recently, Verizon Wireless has invested tens of billions of dollars in deploying mobile wireless services since being subject to the 700 MHz C Block open access rules, which overlap in significant parts with the open Internet rules we adopt today. But that is not all. Today, key provisions of Title II apply to certain enterprise broadband services that AT&T has described as "the epicenter of the broadband investment" the Commission seeks to promote. Title II has been maintained by more than 1000 rural local exchange carriers that have chosen to offer their DSL and fiber broadband services as common carrier offerings. And, of course, wireline DSL was regulated as a common-carrier service until 2005—including a period in the late '90s and the first five years of this century that saw the highest levels of wireline broadband infrastructure investment to date.

40. In any event, recent events have demonstrated that our rules will not disrupt capital markets or investment. Following recent discussions of the potential application of Title II to consumer broadband, investment analysts have issued reports concluding that Title II with appropriate forbearance is unlikely to alter broadband provider conduct or have any negative effect on their value or future profitability. Executives from large broadband providers have also repeatedly represented to investors that the prospect of regulatory action will not influence their investment strategies or long-term profitability; indeed, Sprint has gone so far to say that it "does not believe that a light touch application of Title II, including appropriate forbearance, would harm the continued investment in, and deployment of, mobile broadband services." Finally, the recent AWS auction, conducted under the prospect of Title II regulation, generated bids (net of bidding credits) of more than $41 billion—further demonstrating that robust investment is not inconsistent with a light-touch Title II regime.

C. Sustainable Open Internet Rules

41. We ground our open Internet rules in multiple sources of legal authority—including both section 706 and Title II of the Communications Act. The *Verizon* court upheld the

Commission's use of section 706 as a substantive source of legal authority to adopt open Internet protections. But it held that, "[g]iven the Commission's still-binding decision to classify broadband providers . . . as providers of 'information services,'" open Internet protections that regulated broadband providers as common carriers would violate the Act. Rejecting the Commission's argument that broadband providers only served retail consumers, the *Verizon* court went on to explain that "broadband providers furnish a service to edge providers, thus undoubtedly functioning as edge providers' 'carriers,'" and held that the 2010 no blocking and no unreasonable discrimination rules impermissibly "obligated [broadband providers] to act as common carriers."

42. The *Verizon* decision thus made clear that section 706 affords the Commission substantive authority, and that open Internet protections are within the scope of that authority. And this Order relies on section 706 for the open Internet rules. But, in light of *Verizon*, absent a classification of broadband providers as providing a "telecommunications service," the Commission could only rely on section 706 to put in place open Internet protections that steered clear of regulating broadband providers as common carriers *per se*. Thus, in order to bring a decade of debate to a certain conclusion, we conclude that the best path is to rely on all available sources of legal authority—while applying them with a light touch consistent with further investment and broadband deployment. Taking the *Verizon* decision's implicit invitation, we revisit the Commission's classification of the retail broadband Internet access service as an information service and clarify that this service encompasses the so-called "edge service."

42. Exercising our delegated authority to interpret ambiguous terms in the Communications Act, as confirmed by the Supreme Court in *Brand X*, today's Order concludes that the facts in the market today are very different from the facts that supported the Commission's 2002 decision to treat cable broadband as an information service and its subsequent application to fixed and mobile broadband services. Those prior decisions were based largely on a factual record compiled over a decade ago, during an earlier time when, for example, many consumers would use homepages supplied by their broadband provider. In fact, the *Brand X* Court explicitly acknowledged that the Commission had previously classified the transmission service, which broadband providers offer, as a telecommunications service and that the Commission could return to that classification if it provided an adequate justification. Moreover, a number of parties who, in this proceeding, now oppose our reclassification of broadband Internet access service, previously argued that cable broadband should be deemed a telecommunications service. As the record reflects, times and usage patterns have changed and it is clear that broadband providers are offering both consumers and edge providers straightforward transmission capabilities that the Communications Act defines as a "telecommunications service."

44. The *Brand X* decision made famous the metaphor of pizza delivery. Justice Scalia, in dissent, concluded that the Commission had exceeded its legal authority by classifying cable-modem service as an "information service." To make his point, Justice Scalia described a pizzeria offering delivery services as well as selling pizzas and concluded that, similarly—broadband providers were offering "telecommunications services" even if that service was not offered on a "stand-alone basis."

45. To take Justice Scalia's metaphor a step further, suppose that in 2014, the pizzeria owners discovered that other nearby restaurants did not deliver their food and thus concluded that the pizza-delivery drivers could generate more revenue by delivering from any neighborhood restaurant (including their own pizza some of the time). Consumers would clearly understand that they are being offered a delivery service.

46. Today, broadband providers are offering stand-alone transmission capacity and that conclusion is not changed even if, as Justice Scalia recognized, other products may be offered at the same time. The trajectory of technology in the decade since the *Brand X* decision has been towards greater and greater modularity. For example, consumers have considerable power to combine their mobile broadband connections with the device, operating systems, applications, Internet services, and content of their choice. Today, broadband Internet access service is fundamentally understood by customers as a trans-mission platform through which consumers can access third-party content, applications, and services of their choosing.

47. Based on this updated record, this Order concludes that the retail broadband Internet access service available today is best viewed as separately identifiable offers of (1) a broadband Internet access service that is a telecommunications service (including assorted functions and capabilities used for the management and control of that telecom-munication service) and (2) various "add-on" applications, content, and services that gen-erally are information services. This finding more than reasonably interprets the ambiguous terms in the Communications Act, best reflects the factual record in this pro-ceeding, and will most effectively permit the implementation of sound policy consistent with statutory objectives, including the adoption of effective open Internet protections.

48. This Order also revisits the Commission's prior classification of mobile broadband Internet access service as a private mobile service, which cannot be subject to common car-rier regulation, and finds that it is best viewed as a commercial mobile service or, in the alternative, the functional equivalent of commercial mobile service. Under the statutory definition, commercial mobile services must be "interconnected with the public switched network (as such terms are defined by regulation by the Commission)." Consistent with that delegation of authority to define these terms, and with the Commission's previous recogni-tion that the public switched network will grow and change over time, this Order updates the definition of public switched network to reflect current technology, by including ser-vices that use public IP addresses. Under this revised definition, the Order concludes that mobile broadband Internet access service is interconnected with the public switched net-work. In the alternative, the Order concludes that mobile broadband Internet access service is the functional equivalent of commercial mobile service because, like commercial mobile service, it is a widely available, for profit mobile service that offers mobile subscribers the capability to send and receive communications, including voice, on their mobile device.

49. By classifying broadband Internet access service under Title II of the Act, in our view the Commission addresses any limitations that past classification decisions placed on the ability to adopt strong open Internet rules, as interpreted by the D.C. Circuit in the *Verizon* case.

50. Having classified broadband Internet access service as a telecommunications service, we respond to the *Verizon* court's holding, supporting our open Internet rules under the Commission's Title II authority and removing any common carriage limita-tion on the exercise of our section 706 authority. For mobile broadband services, we also ground the open Internet rules in our Title III authority to protect the public interest through the management of spectrum licensing.

D. Broad Forbearance

51. In finding that broadband Internet access service is subject to Title II, we simulta-neously exercise the Commission's forbearance authority to forbear from 30 statutory

provisions and render over 700 codified rules inapplicable, to establish a light-touch regulatory framework tailored to preserving those provisions that advance our goals of more, better, and open broadband. We thus forbear from the vast majority of rules adopted under Title II. We do not, however, forbear from sections 201, 202, and 208 (or from related enforcement provisions), which are necessary to support adoption of our open Internet rules. We also grant extensive forbearance, minimizing the burdens on broadband providers while still adequately protecting the public.

52. In addition, we do not forbear from a limited number of sections necessary to ensure consumers are protected, promote competition, and advance universal access, all of which will foster network investment, thereby helping to promote broadband deployment.

53. *Section 222: Protecting Consumer Privacy.* Ensuring the privacy of customer information both directly protects consumers from harm and eliminates consumer concerns about using the Internet that could deter broadband deployment. Among other things, section 222 imposes a duty on every telecommunications carrier to take reasonable precautions to protect the confidentiality of its customers' proprietary information. We take this mandate seriously. For example, the Commission recently took enforcement action under section 222 (and section 201(b)) against two telecommunications companies that stored customers' personal information, including social security numbers, on unprotected, unencrypted Internet servers publicly accessible using a basic Internet search. This unacceptably exposed these consumers to the risk of identity theft and other harms.

54. As the Commission has recognized, "[c]onsumers' privacy needs are no less important when consumers communicate over and use broadband Internet access than when they rely on [telephone] services." Thus, this Order finds that consumers concerned about the privacy of their personal information will be more reluctant to use the Internet, stifling Internet service competition and growth. Application of section 222's protections will help spur consumer demand for those Internet access services, in turn "driving demand for broadband connections, and consequently encouraging more broadband investment and deployment," consistent with the goals of the 1996 Act.

55. *Sections 225/255/251(a)(2): Ensuring Disabilities Access.* We do not forbear from those provisions of Title II that ensure access to broadband Internet access service by individuals with disabilities. All Americans, including those with disabilities, must be able to reap the benefits of an open Internet, and ensuring access for these individuals will further the virtuous cycle of consumer demand, innovation, and deployment. This Order thus concludes that application of sections 225, 255, and 251(a)(2) is necessary to protect consumers and furthers the public interest, as explained in greater detail below.

56. *Section 224: Ensuring Infrastructure Access.* For broadband Internet access service, we do not forbear from section 224 and the Commission's associated procedural rules (to the extent they apply to telecommunications carriers and services and are, thus, within the Commission's forbearance authority). Section 224 of the Act governs the Commission's regulation of pole attachments. In particular, section 224(f)(1) requires utilities to provide cable system operators and telecommunications carriers the right of "nondiscriminatory access to any pole, duct, conduit, or right-of-way owned or controlled" by a utility. Access to poles and other infrastructure is crucial to the efficient deployment of communications networks including, and perhaps especially, new entrants.

57. *Section 254: Promoting Universal Broadband.* Section 254 promotes the deployment and availability of communications networks to all Americans, including rural

and low-income Americans—furthering our goals of more and better broadband. With the exception of 254(d), (g), and (k) as discussed below, we therefore do not find the statutory test for forbearance from section 254 (and the related provision in section 214(e)) is met. We recognize that supporting broadband-capable networks is already a key component of Commission's current universal service policies. The Order concludes, however, that directly applying section 254 provides both more legal certainty for the Commission's prior decisions to offer universal service subsidies for deployment of broadband networks and adoption of broadband services and more flexibility going forward.

58. We partially forbear from section 254(d) and associated rules insofar as they would immediately require mandatory universal service contributions associated with broadband Internet access service.

59. Below, we first adopt three bright-line rules banning blocking, throttling, and paid prioritization, and make clear the no-unreasonable interference/disadvantage standard by which the Commission will evaluate other practices, according to their facts. These rules are grounded in multiple sources of statutory authority, including section 706 and Titles II and III of the Communications Act. Second, based on a current factual record, we reclassify broadband Internet access service as a telecommunications service under Title II. And, third, guided by our goals of more, better, and open broadband, we exercise our forbearance authority to put in place a "light touch" Title II regulatory framework that protects consumers and innovators, without deterring investment.

[The remainder of the Order has been omitted.]

Source: Federal Communications Commission. "Report and Order on Remand, Declaratory Ruling, and Order." Adopted February 26, 2015 (released March 12, 2015). www.fcc.gov/document/fcc-releases-open-internet-order.

FCC Issues Press Release Detailing New Internet Rules

February 26, 2015

Ending lingering uncertainty about the future of the Open Internet, the Federal Communications Commission today set sustainable rules of the roads that will protect free expression and innovation on the Internet and promote investment in the nation's broadband network.

The FCC has long been committed to protecting and promoting an Internet that nurtures freedom of speech and expression, supports innovation and commerce, and incentivizes expansion and investment by America's broadband providers. But the agency's attempts to implement enforceable, sustainable rules to protect the Open Internet have been twice struck down by the courts.

Today, the Commission—once and for all—enacts strong, sustainable rules, grounded in multiple sources of legal authority, to ensure that Americans reap the economic, social, and civic benefits of an Open Internet today and into the future.

These new rules are guided by three principles: America's broadband networks must be fast, fair and open—principles shared by the overwhelming majority of the nearly 4 million commenters who participated in the FCC's Open Internet proceeding.

Absent action by the FCC, Internet openness is at risk, as recognized by the very court that struck down the FCC's 2010 Open Internet rules last year in *Verizon v. FCC.*

Broadband providers have economic incentives that "represent a threat to Internet openness and could act in ways that would ultimately inhibit the speed and extent of future broadband deployment," as affirmed by the U.S. Court of Appeals for the District of Columbia. The court upheld the Commission's finding that Internet openness drives a "virtuous cycle" in which innovations at the edges of the network enhance consumer demand, leading to expanded investments in broadband infrastructure that, in turn, spark new innovations at the edge.

However, the court observed that nearly 15 years ago, the Commission constrained its ability to protect against threats to the open Internet by a regulatory classification of broadband that precluded use of statutory protections that historically ensured the openness of telephone networks. The Order finds that the nature of broadband Internet access service has not only changed since that initial classification decision, but that broadband providers have even more incentives to interfere with Internet openness today. To respond to this changed landscape, the new Open Internet Order restores the FCC's legal authority to fully address threats to openness on today's networks by following a template for sustainability laid out in the D.C. Circuit Opinion itself, including reclassification of broadband Internet access as a telecommunications service under Title II of the Communications Act.

With a firm legal foundation established, the Order sets three "bright-line" rules of the road for behavior known to harm the Open Internet, adopts an additional, flexible standard to future-proof Internet openness rules, and protects mobile broadband users with the full array of Open Internet rules. It does so while preserving incentives for investment and innovation by broadband providers by affording them an even more tailored version of the light-touch regulatory treatment that fostered tremendous growth in the mobile wireless industry.

Following are the key provisions and rules of the FCC's Open Internet Order:

New Rules to Protect an Open Internet

While the FCC's 2010 Open Internet rules had limited applicability to mobile broadband, the new rules—in their entirety—would apply to fixed and mobile broadband alike, recognizing advances in technology and the growing significance of wireless broadband access in recent years (while recognizing the importance of reasonable network management and its specific application to mobile and unlicensed Wi-Fi networks). The Order protects consumers no matter how they access the Internet, whether on a desktop computer or a mobile device.

Bright Line Rules: The first three rules ban practices that are known to harm the Open Internet:

- **No Blocking:** broadband providers may not block access to legal content, applications, services, or non-harmful devices.

- **No Throttling:** broadband providers may not impair or degrade lawful Internet traffic on the basis of content, applications, services, or non-harmful devices.

- **No Paid Prioritization:** broadband providers may not favor some lawful Internet traffic over other lawful traffic in exchange for consideration of any kind—in other words, no "fast lanes." This rule also bans ISPs from prioritizing content and services of their affiliates.

The bright-line rules against blocking and throttling will prohibit harmful practices that target specific applications or classes of applications. And the ban on paid prioritization ensures that there will be no fast lanes.

A Standard for Future Conduct: Because the Internet is always growing and changing, there must be a known standard by which to address any concerns that arise with new practices. The Order establishes that ISPs cannot "unreasonably interfere with or unreasonably disadvantage" the ability of consumers to select, access, and use the lawful content, applications, services, or devices of their choosing; or of edge providers to make lawful content, applications, services, or devices available to consumers. Today's Order ensures that the Commission will have authority to address questionable practices on a case-by-case basis, and provides guidance in the form of factors on how the Commission will apply the standard in practice.

Greater Transparency: The rules described above will restore the tools necessary to address specific conduct by broadband providers that might harm the Open Internet. But the Order recognizes the critical role of transparency in a well-functioning broadband ecosystem. In addition to the existing transparency rule, which was not struck down by the court, the Order requires that broadband providers disclose, in a consistent format, promotional rates, fees and surcharges and data caps. Disclosures must also include packet loss as a measure of network performance, and provide notice of network management practices that can affect service. To further consider the concerns of small ISPs, the Order adopts a temporary exemption from the transparency enhancements for fixed and mobile providers with 100,000 or fewer subscribers, and delegates authority to our Consumer and Governmental Affairs Bureau to determine whether to retain the exception and, if so, at what level.

The Order also creates for all providers a "safe harbor" process for the format and nature of the required disclosure to consumers, which the Commission believes will lead to more effective presentation of consumer-focused information by broadband providers.

Reasonable Network Management: For the purposes of the rules, other than paid prioritization, an ISP may engage in reasonable network management. This recognizes the need of broadband providers to manage the technical and engineering aspects of their networks.

- In assessing reasonable network management, the Commission's standard takes account of the particular engineering attributes of the technology involved—whether it be fiber, DSL, cable, unlicensed Wi-Fi, mobile, or another network medium.

- However, the network practice must be primarily used for and tailored to achieving a legitimate network management—and not business—purpose. For example, a provider can't cite reasonable network management to justify reneging on its promise to supply a customer with "unlimited" data.

Broad Protection

Some data services do not go over the public Internet, and therefore are not "broadband Internet access" services (VoIP from a cable system is an example, as is a dedicated heart-monitoring service). The Order ensures that these services do not undermine the effectiveness of the Open Internet rules. Moreover, all broadband providers' transparency disclosures will continue to cover any offering of such non-Internet access data services—ensuring that the public and the Commission can keep a close eye on any tactics that could undermine the Open Internet rules.

Interconnection: New Authority to Address Concerns

For the first time the Commission can address issues that may arise in the exchange of traffic between mass-market broadband providers and other networks and services. Under the authority provided by the Order, the Commission can hear complaints and take appropriate enforcement action if it determines the interconnection activities of ISPs are not just and reasonable.

Legal Authority: Reclassifying Broadband Internet Access under Title II

The Order provides the strongest possible legal foundation for the Open Internet rules by relying on multiple sources of authority including both Title II of the Communications Act and Section 706 of the Telecommunications Act of 1996. At the same time, the Order refrains—or forbears—from enforcing 27 provisions of Title II and over 700 associated regulations that are not relevant to modern broadband service. Together Title II and Section 706 support clear rules of the road, providing the certainty needed for innovators and investors, and the competitive choices and freedom demanded by consumers, while not burdening broadband providers with anachronistic utility-style regulations such as rate regulation, tariffs or network sharing requirements.

- First, the Order reclassifies "broadband Internet access service"—that's the retail broadband service Americans buy from cable, phone, and wireless providers—as a telecommunications service under Title II. This decision is fundamentally a factual one. It recognizes that today broadband Internet access service is understood by the public as a transmission platform through which consumers can access third-party content, applications, and services of their choosing. Reclassification of broadband Internet access service also addresses any limitations that past classification decisions placed on the ability to adopt strong open Internet rules, as interpreted by the D.C. Circuit in the *Verizon* case. And it supports the Commission's authority to address interconnection disputes on a case-by-case basis, because the promise to consumers that they will be able to travel the Internet encompasses the duty to make the necessary arrangements that allow consumers to use the Internet as they wish.

- Second, the proposal finds further grounding in Section 706 of the Telecommunications Act of 1996. Notably, the *Verizon* court held that Section 706 is an independent grant of authority to the Commission that supports adoption of Open Internet rules. Using it here—without the limitations of the common carriage prohibition that flowed from the earlier "information service" classification—bolsters the Commission's authority.

- Third, the Order's provisions on mobile broadband also are based on Title III of the Communications Act. The Order finds that mobile broadband access service is best viewed as a commercial mobile service or its functional equivalent.

Forbearance: A modernized, light-touch approach

Congress requires the FCC to refrain from enforcing—forbear from—provisions of the Communications Act that are not in the public interest. The Order applies some key provisions of Title II, and forbears from most others. Indeed, the Order ensures that some 27 provisions of Title II and over 700 regulations adopted under Title II will not apply to broadband. There is no need for any further proceedings before the forbearance is adopted. *The proposed Order would apply fewer sections of Title II than have applied to mobile voice networks for over twenty years.*

- *Major Provisions of Title II that the Order WILL APPLY:*
   - The proposed Order applies "core" provisions of Title II: Sections 201 and 202 (e.g., no unjust or unreasonable practices or discrimination)
   - Allows investigation of consumer complaints under section 208 and related enforcement provisions, specifically sections 206, 207, 209, 216 and 217
   - Protects consumer privacy under Section 222
   - Ensures fair access to poles and conduits under Section 224, which would boost the deployment of new broadband networks
   - Protects people with disabilities under Sections 225 and 255
   - Bolsters universal service fund support for broadband service in the future through partial application of Section 254.

- *Major Provisions Subject to Forbearance:*
   - Rate regulation: the Order makes clear that broadband providers **shall not** be subject to utility-style rate regulation, including rate regulation, tariffs, and last-mile unbundling.
   - Universal Service Contributions: the Order **DOES NOT** require broadband providers to contribute to the Universal Service Fund under Section 254. The question of how best to fund the nation's universal service programs is being considered in a separate, unrelated proceeding that was already underway.
   - Broadband service will remain exempt from state and local taxation under the Internet Tax Freedom Act. This law, recently renewed by Congress and signed by the President, bans state and local taxation on Internet access regardless of its FCC regulatory classification.

Effective Enforcement

- The FCC will enforce the Open Internet rules through investigation and processing of formal and informal complaints.

- Enforcement advisories, advisory opinions and a newly-created ombudsman will provide guidance.

- The Enforcement Bureau can request objective written opinions on technical matters from outside technical organizations, industry standards-setting bodies and other organizations.

Fostering Investment and Competition

All of this can be accomplished while encouraging investment in broadband networks. To preserve incentives for broadband operators to invest in their networks, the Order will modernize Title II using the forbearance authority granted to the Commission by Congress—tailoring the application of Title II for the 21st century, encouraging Internet Service Providers to invest in the networks on which Americans increasingly rely.

- The Order forbears from applying utility-style rate regulation, including rate regulation or tariffs, last-mile unbundling, and burdensome administrative filing requirements or accounting standards.

- Mobile voice services have been regulated under a similar light-touch Title II approach, and investment and usage boomed.

- Investment analysts have concluded that Title II with appropriate forbearance is unlikely to have any negative on the value or future profitability of broadband providers. Providers such as Sprint, Frontier, as well as representatives of hundreds of smaller carriers that have voluntarily adopted Title II regulation, have likewise said that a light-touch, Title II classification of broadband will not depress investment.

Action by the Commission February 26, 2015, by Report and Order on Remand, Declaratory Ruling, and Order (FCC 15-24). Chairman Wheeler, Commissioners Clyburn and Rosenworcel with Commissioners Pai and O'Rielly dissenting. Chairman Wheeler, Commissioners Clyburn, Rosenworcel, Pai and O'Rielly issuing statements.
Docket No.: 14-28

SOURCE: Federal Communications Commission. "FCC Adopts Strong, Sustainable Rules to Protect the Open Internet." February 26, 2015. www.fcc.gov/document/fcc-adopts-strong-sustainable-rules-protect-open-internet.

FCC Chairman Tom Wheeler Issues Statement on New ISP Rules

February 26, 2015

Re: *Protecting and Promoting the Open Internet, GN Docket No. 14-28.*

For over a decade, the Commission has endeavored to protect and promote the open Internet. FCC Chairs and Commissioners, Republican and Democrat alike, have embraced the importance of the open Internet, and the need to protect and promote that openness. Today is the culmination of that effort, as we adopt the strongest possible open Internet protections. . . .

We heard from startups and world-leading tech companies. We heard from ISPs, large and small. We heard from public-interest groups and public-policy think tanks. We heard from Members of Congress, and, yes, the President. Most important, we heard from nearly 4 million Americans who overwhelmingly spoke up in favor of preserving a free and open Internet.

We listened. We learned. And we adjusted our approach based on the public record. In the process we saw a graphic example of why open and unfettered communications are essential to freedom of expression in the 21st century.

I am incredibly proud of the process the Commission has run in developing today's historic open Internet protections. I say that not just as the head of this agency, but as a U.S. citizen. Today's Open Internet Order is a shining example of American democracy at work. . . .

Broadband networks are the most powerful and pervasive connectivity in history. Broadband is reshaping our economy and recasting the patterns of our lives. Every day, we rely on high-speed connectivity to do our jobs, access entertainment, keep up with the news, express our views, and stay in touch with friends and family.

There are three simple keys to our broadband future. Broadband networks must be fast. Broadband networks must be fair. Broadband networks must be open. . . .

Our challenge is to achieve two equally important goals: ensure incentives for private investment in broadband infrastructure so the U.S. has world-leading networks and ensure that those networks are fast, fair, and open for all Americans.

The Open Internet Order achieves those goals, giving consumers, innovators, and entrepreneurs the protections they deserve, while providing certainty for broadband providers and the online marketplace.

[A page detailing the order's key provisions has been omitted.]

The American people reasonably expect and deserve an Internet that is fast, fair, and open. Today they get what they deserve: strong, enforceable rules that will ensure the Internet remains open, now and in the future.

SOURCE: Federal Communications Commission. "Statement of Chairman Tom Wheeler." GN Docket No. 14-28. February 26, 2015. https://apps.fcc.gov/edocs_public/attachmatch/DOC-332260A2.pdf.

FCC Commissioner Clyburn on New ISP Rules

February 26, 2015

Re: *Protecting and Promoting the Open Internet*, GN Docket No. 14-28.

Following years of vigorous debate, the United States adopted the Bill of Rights in 1791. The Framers recognized that basic freedoms, as enshrined in the first ten amendments to the Constitution, were fundamental to a free and open democratic society. . . .

So here we are, 224 years later, at a pivotal fork in the road, poised to preserve those very same virtues of a democratic society—free speech, freedom of religion, a free press, freedom of assembly and a functioning free market.

As we look around the world we see foreign governments blocking access to websites including social media—in sum, curtailing free speech. There are countries where it is routine for governments, not the consumer, to determine the type of websites and content that can be accessed by its citizens. I am proud to be able to say that we are not among them.

Absent the rules we adopt today, however, any Internet Service Provider (ISP) has the liberty to do just that. They would be free to block, throttle, favor or discriminate against traffic or extract tolls from any user for any reason or for no reason at all.

This is more than a theoretical exercise. Providers here in the United States have, in fact, blocked applications on mobile devices, which not only hampers free expression but also restricts competition and innovation by allowing companies, not the consumer, to pick winners and losers.

As many of you know, this is not my first Open Internet rodeo. While I did vote to approve the 2010 rules, it was no secret that I preferred a different path than the one the Commission ultimately adopted. Specifically, I preferred: (1) Title II with forbearance, (2) mobile parity, (3) a ban on paid prioritization, and (4) preventing the specialized services exemption from becoming a loophole.

So, I am sincerely grateful to the Chairman for his willingness to work with my office to better ensure that this Order strikes the right balance and is positioned to provide us with strong, legally sustainable rules. This is our third bite at the apple and we must get it right. . . .

In the seemingly endless meetings with stakeholders, my office has heard concerns from many sides. To some, the item does not go far enough, others want a ban on "access fees," and there are those who advocate a ban on zero rating, and others, who feel that it goes too far, whether on the scope of forbearance or the focus on interconnection.

We worked closely with the Chairman's office to strike an appropriate balance and yes, it is true, that significant changes were made at the request of my office, including the elimination of the sender-side classification. I firmly believe these edits have strengthened this item. Reports that this weakens our legal authority over interconnection are completely inaccurate.

But it should come as no surprise that, with any item in excess of 300 pages, there are a few issues I would have decided differently.

First, I would have preferred to readopt the unreasonable discrimination and reasonable network management rules from 2010. . . .

And I repeat this challenge to anyone willing to accept it: Highlight examples, where the FCC has ruled that a rate is unreasonable in a context other than inmate calling or a tariff investigation over the last decade. To date, no one has come forth with any examples, and that in and of itself is telling.

And, lest we forget, over 700 small broadband providers in rural America offer broadband Internet access pursuant to the full panoply of Title II regulation. They contribute to universal service and, amazingly, the sky has not fallen and things are okay. . . .

Mr. Chairman, today I support this item because I believe it provides the strong protections we need and balances the concerns raised by stakeholders, large and small. . . .

Source: Federal Communications Commission. "Statement of Commissioner Mignon L. Clyburn." GN Docket No. 14-28. February 26, 2015. https://apps.fcc.gov/edocs_public/attachmatch/DOC-332260A3.pdf.

Commissioner Rosenworcel Releases Statement in Support of ISP Rules

February 26, 2015

Re: *Protecting and Promoting the Open Internet, GN Docket No. 14-28.*

Our Internet economy is the envy of the world. We invented it. The applications economy began here—on our shores. The broadband below us and the airwaves all around us deliver its collective might to our homes and businesses in communities across the country. What produced this dynamic engine of entrepreneurship and experimentation is a foundation of openness. Sustaining what has made us innovative, fierce, and creative should not be a choice—it should be an obligation.

We also have a duty—a duty to protect what has made the Internet the most dynamic platform for free speech ever invented. It is our printing press. It is our town square. It is our individual soapbox—and our shared platform for opportunity.

That is why open Internet policies matter. That is why I support network neutrality.

We cannot have a two-tiered Internet with fast lanes that speed the traffic of the privileged and leave the rest of us lagging behind. We cannot have gatekeepers who tell us what we can and cannot do and where we can and cannot go online. And we do not need blocking, throttling, and paid prioritization schemes that undermine the Internet as we know it.

For these reasons, I support Chairman Wheeler's efforts and rules today. They use our existing statutory tools, including Title II authority, to put back in place basic open Internet policies that we all rely on but last year our courts took away. The result honors the creative, collaborative, and open Internet envisioned by those who were there at the start, including the legendary Sir Tim Berners-Lee, the creator of the World Wide Web—whom we have had the privilege of hearing from today.

This is a big deal. What is also a big deal is 4 million voices. Four million Americans wrote this agency to make known their ideas, thoughts, and deeply-held opinions about Internet openness. They lit up our phone lines, clogged our e-mail in-boxes, and jammed our online comment system. That might be messy, but whatever our disagreements on network neutrality are, I hope we can agree that's democracy in action and something we can all support.

SOURCE: Federal Communications Commission. "Statement of Commissioner Jessica Rosenworcel." GN Docket No. 14-28. February 26, 2015. www.fcc.gov/article/doc-332260a4.

Oral Dissenting Statement of Commissioner Pai

February 26, 2015

Re: *Protecting and Promoting the Open Internet, GN Docket No. 14-28.*

Americans love the free and open Internet. We relish our freedom to speak, to post, to rally, to learn, to listen, to watch, and to connect online. The Internet has become a powerful force for freedom, both at home and abroad. So it is sad this morning to witness the FCC's unprecedented attempt to replace that freedom with government control.

It shouldn't be this way. For twenty years, there's been a bipartisan consensus in favor of a free and open Internet. A Republican Congress and a Democratic President enshrined in the Telecommunications Act of 1996 the principle that the Internet should be a "vibrant and competitive free market . . . unfettered by Federal or State regulation." And dating back to the Clinton Administration, every FCC Chairman—Republican and Democrat—has let the Internet grow free from utility-style regulation. The results speak for themselves.

But today, the FCC abandons those policies. It reclassifies broadband Internet access service as a Title II telecommunications service. It seizes unilateral authority to regulate Internet conduct, to direct where Internet service providers (ISPs) make their investments, and to determine what service plans will be available to the American public. This is not only a radical departure from the bipartisan, market-oriented policies that have served us so well for the last two decades. It is also an about-face from the proposals the FCC made just last May.

So why is the FCC turning its back on Internet freedom? Is it because we now have evidence that the Internet is broken? No. We are flip-flopping for one reason and one reason alone. President Obama told us to do so. . . .

The courts will ultimately decide this *Order*'s fate. Litigants are already lawyering up to seek judicial review of these new rules. Given the *Order*'s many glaring legal flaws, they will have plenty of fodder.

But if this *Order* manages to survive judicial review, these will be the consequences: higher broadband prices, slower speeds, less broadband deployment, less innovation, and fewer options for American consumers. To paraphrase Ronald Reagan, President Obama's plan to regulate the Internet isn't the solution to a problem. His plan is the problem.

In short, because this *Order* imposes intrusive government regulations that won't work to solve a problem that doesn't exist using legal authority the FCC doesn't have, I dissent.

SOURCE: Federal Communications Commission. "Oral Dissenting Statement of Commissioner Ajit Pai." GN Docket No. 14-28. February 26, 2015. www.fcc.gov/article/doc-332260a5.

Dissenting Statement of Commissioner O'Rielly

DOCUMENT

February 26, 2015

[Footnotes have been omitted.]

Re: *Protecting and Promoting the Open Internet*, GN Docket No. 14-28.

Today a majority of the Commission attempts to usurp the authority of Congress by re-writing the Communications Act to suit its own "values" and political ends. The item claims to forbear from certain monopoly-era Title II regulations while reserving the right to impose them using other provisions or at some point in the future. The Commission abdicates its role as an expert agency by defining and classifying services based on unsupported and unreasonable findings. It fails to account for substantial differences between fixed and mobile technologies. It opens the door to apply these rules to edge providers. It delegates substantial authority to the Bureaus, including how the rules will be interpreted and enforced on a case-by-case basis. And, lest we forget how this proceeding started, it also reinstates net neutrality rules. Indeed, it seems that every bad idea ever floated in the name of net neutrality has come home to roost in this item.

To read public statements over the last few weeks, one might think that this item uses Title II in some limited way solely to provide support for net neutrality rules and to protect consumers. And a casual observer might be misled to believe that the ends justify the means.

Along the way, however, the means became the end. Net neutrality is now the pretext for deploying Title II to a far greater extent than anyone could have imagined just months ago. And that is the reality that the Commission tried to hide by keeping the draft from the public and releasing a carefully worded "fact" sheet in its place.

While I see no need for net neutrality rules, I am far more troubled by the dangerous course that the Commission is now charting on Title II and the consequences it will have for broadband investment, edge providers, and consumers. The Commission attempts to downplay the significance of Title II, but make no mistake: this is not some make believe modernized Title II light that is somehow tailored to preserve investment while protecting consumers from blocking or throttling. It is fauxbearance: all of Title II applied through the backdoor of sections 201 and 202 of the Act, and section 706 of the 1996 Act. Moreover, all of it is premised on a mythical "virtuous cycle"—not actual harms to edge providers or consumers.

In some ways, this evolution is not surprising. I have consistently expressed concerns, across a number of proceedings—tech transitions, text-to-911, over-the-top video, VoIP symmetry, etc.—that this Commission has been slowly but steadily attempting to bring over-the-top and other IP services within its reach. Now the Commission goes all in and subjects broadband networks—the foundation of the Internet—to Title II itself. Furthermore, because there is no limiting principle, other providers will eventually be drawn in as well. I cannot support this monumental and unlawful power grab.

[The remainder of the dissent has been omitted, and contains further detail on those concerns outlined in the above paragraphs.]

SOURCE: Federal Communications Commission. "Dissenting Statement of Commissioner Michael O'Rielly." GN Docket No. 14-28. February 26, 2015. www.fcc.gov/article/doc-332260a6.

OTHER HISTORIC DOCUMENTS OF INTEREST

FROM PREVIOUS *HISTORIC DOCUMENTS*

■ Federal Communications Commission Proposes Net Neutrality Rules, *2014*, p. 184

■ Federal Court Rules in Net Neutrality Case, *2010*, p. 119

March

Israeli Prime Minister
Addresses Congress

MARCH 3, 2015

In the midst of U.S. negotiations with Iran over its nuclear program, Israeli prime minister Benjamin Netanyahu was invited by Congressional Republicans to address a joint session of Congress. This marked a break from tradition in that the Speaker of the House invited the prime minister without consultation with the White House. The speech, which focused primarily on Iranian nuclear weapons and threats made against Israel, was well received by both Democrats and Republicans in Congress, while the White House criticized the engagement as a political ploy for Netanyahu's upcoming election that could have dire effects on the ongoing negotiations.

SPEAKER EXTENDS AN INVITATION

Speaker of the House John Boehner, R-Ohio, sent an official invitation to Netanyahu on January 21, 2015. It read simply, "It is my honor, on behalf of the bipartisan leadership of the U.S. House of Representatives and the U.S. Senate, to extend to you an invitation to appear before and address a joint meeting of Congress on Wednesday, February 11, 2015." In sending the letter, Boehner said he was "asking the Prime Minister to address Congress on the grave threats radical Islam and Iran pose to our security and way of life."

Boehner extended the invitation without consulting with the White House or State Department, instead choosing to coordinate with the Israeli ambassador to the United States, Ron Dermer, and told the press that he did not find fault with his actions. "Congress can make this decision on its own," Boehner stated. "The fact is that there needs to be a more serious conversation in America about how serious the threat is from radical Islamic jihadists and the threat posed by Iran." The White House called the move "a departure" from protocol, saying that traditionally the leader of one nation contacts the other to extend an invitation. There is no precedent for Boehner's actions in American history, largely because the Constitution states that it is the sole responsibility of the president to "receive ambassadors and other public ministers." The White House, however, did not go so far as to accuse the Speaker of a Constitutional violation.

The invitation came just one day after President Barack Obama's State of the Union address in which he stated that he would veto any bill passed by Congress that called for new sanctions against Iran, believing that it would deal a serious blow to the ongoing nuclear negotiations. "New sanctions passed by this Congress, at this moment in time, will all but guarantee that diplomacy fails—alienating America from its allies; and ensuring that Iran starts up its nuclear program again," the president said.

Netanyahu Speaks to Congress

Although initially planned with the Israel embassy to take place the week of February 9, it was eventually determined that Netanyahu would speak before a joint session of Congress on March 3 at 10:45 a.m. Eastern time, just two weeks before his Likud Party would face a tough election in Israel. President Obama, Vice President Joe Biden, and Secretary of State John Kerry all had prior engagements and did not attend. President Obama also declined to meet with Netanyahu separately at the White House, fearing that it would appear that he was meddling in a foreign election. Nearly sixty congressional Democrats boycotted the speech, most notably Sen. Elizabeth Warren, D-Mass., who said that while she supports Israel, she found it "unfortunate that Speaker Boehner's actions on the eve of a national election in Israel have made Tuesday's event more political and less helpful for addressing the critical issue of nuclear nonproliferation and the safety of our most important ally in the Middle East." The speech marked Netanyahu's third before a joint session of Congress, the first two occurring in 1996 and 2011.

Netanyahu entered the House Chamber to raucous applause and began his speech by thanking President Obama for his support of Israel and noting that he regretted that some believed his Congressional appearance was solely for his own political purposes. On the contrary, Netanyahu said, "[A]s Prime Minister of Israel, I feel a profound obligation to speak to you about an issue that could well threaten the survival of my country and the future of my people, Iran's quest for nuclear weapons." The prime minister had been warned by U.S. officials ahead of his speech not to reveal secret details of the ongoing nuclear negotiations with Iran, fearful that it could disrupt the effort to reach an agreement. He largely abided by that request.

Netanyahu's primary argument during his speech was that the agreement currently being worked out in the P5+1 negotiations would not entirely prohibit Iran from continuing its nuclear programs and was therefore dangerous. "That deal would not prevent Iran developing nuclear weapons. It would all but guarantee that Iran gets those weapons, lots of them," he said. Officials in the Obama administration have vehemently denied such claims, noting that expecting Iran to agree to cease all nuclear activities is unrealistic. Netanyahu noted that "the alternative to this bad deal is a much better deal." However, he offered no alternatives.

According to Netanyahu, the reported 6,000 centrifuges Iran would be allowed to keep under the deal, coupled with its ability to continue researching and developing its nuclear program, would allow it to build a nuclear weapon in less than a year. This weapon, Netanyahu argued, would be used against the Israeli people. "Iran's supreme leader, Ayatollah Khamenei, spews the oldest hatred . . . of anti-Semitism with the newest technology," he said. "He tweets that Israel must be annihilated. . . . In Iran there isn't exactly free Internet, but he tweets in English that Israel must be destroyed."

Netanyahu encouraged the United States to leave sanctions against Iran in place until Iran "changes its behavior." That spoke to a key talking point of Republicans in Congress, who have sought to impose additional sanctions against the nation, despite promises from the White House that the president would veto any such measure. Netanyahu did concede somewhat on this point, stating, "If the world powers are not prepared to insist that Iran change its behavior before a deal is signed, they should at the very least be prepared to insist that Iran changes its behavior before the deal expires." He added, "Before lifting those restrictions, the world should demand that Iran do three things: first, stop its aggression against its neighbors in the Middle East; second, stop supporting terrorism around the world; and, third, stop threatening to annihilate my country, Israel, the one and only Jewish state."

WHITE HOUSE, DEMOCRATS RESPOND TO NETANYAHU SPEECH

The Obama administration has often been at odds with Netanyahu, particularly with regard to the multi-nation negotiations with Iran over its nuclear program. Shortly after the prime minister's speech, Obama said that "the prime minister didn't offer any viable alternatives" to the agreement with Iran currently being negotiated in the P5+1 talks. "The alternative that the Prime Minister offers is no deal, in which case Iran will immediately begin once again pursuing its nuclear program, accelerate its nuclear program, without us having any insight into what they're doing and without constraint. And his essential argument is that if we just double down on sanctions, Iran won't want to do that," the president said, before asking the nation to wait until the final deal is presented rather than speculating on what might be included.

Susan Rice, the national security advisor, sought to allay Netanyahu's fears by noting prior to his speech that the United States would not sign any agreement that would jeopardize the security of Israel. "A bad deal is worse than no deal. If that is the choice, there will be no deal," she said at the annual meeting of the America Israel Public Affairs Committee (AIPAC). Similarly, the day before Netanyahu's speech, Obama spoke with Reuters and argued that the agreement currently being negotiated would essentially freeze Iran's nuclear capabilities for the next decade, and would leave the world enough time to respond should it be discovered that Iran was again working to develop a nuclear weapon. Speaking to the prime minister's concerns, Obama noted that when the P5+1 signed an interim agreement with Iran in 2013, "Prime Minister Netanyahu made all sorts of claims: This is going to be a terrible deal. This was going to result in Iran getting $50 billion worth of relief. Iran would not abide by the agreement. None of that has come true."

Although Netanyahu has enjoyed support in the United States from both Democrats and Republicans, his speech before Congress put those Democrats who backed U.S. negotiations with Iran in a difficult position. Rep. Nancy Pelosi, D-Calif., the highest-ranking Democrat in the House, said she was "saddened by the insult to the intelligence of the United States as part of the P5+1 nations and saddened by the condescension toward our knowledge of the threat posed by Iran and our broader commitment to preventing nuclear proliferation." Sen. Dianne Feinstein, D-Calif., echoed the president's remarks, noting that Netanyahu proposed no solution that would be "agreeable" for Israel, although she also shared her own concerns with the deal currently being negotiated.

ISRAELI ELECTION LEAVES NETANYAHU IN POWER

A major criticism of Netanyahu's appearance before Congress was that it seemed to be simply meant to give him a platform to move further to the right and secure an election victory for his Likud Party in Israel's March 17 election. Analysts said that such a claim had merit; during Israel's 2011 election Netanyahu used in his campaign advertisements portions of that year's Congressional speech to support his platform, affirming that "when Netanyahu speaks, the world listens."

In the weeks leading up to the election, the Likud Party appeared poised to lose roughly four seats—and its grip on power—as the center-left Zionist Union gained support across the country. Sensing a defeat, Netanyahu dropped earlier rhetoric about continuing to negotiate on a Palestinian state and instead moved further right, noting that he would continue building settlements on occupied land in the West Bank. That appeared to be enough to push Likud to a thirty-seat victory, picking up six more seats than the Zionist Union. Celebrating his election win, Netanyahu said he was "moved by the responsibility Israel has given me" and appreciative of "the decision by Israel's citizens to elect me and my friends, against all odds and in the face of powerful forces."

The Likud Party did not win an overwhelming majority, but it was given the first opportunity by Israel's president to form a coalition government. Minutes before the legal deadline for forming a government, on May 6, the Likud party announced that it had managed to form a coalition with sixty-one of parliament's 120 seats. The Likud coalition included United Torah Judaism and Shas, two ultra-Orthodox parties; Jewish Home, a group that was pulled into Netanyahu's coalition with promises of new settlements in the West Bank; and a new center-right party known as Kulanu. The prime minister's slim majority was the smallest in Israel in two decades, and analysts said the parties had many disparate opinions about how to lead the nation. As such, Netanyahu will likely face difficulty in winning approval for many of his policies.

—Heather Kerrigan

Following is the text of the speech delivered by Prime Minister Benjamin Netanyahu before a joint session of Congress on March 3, 2015; and the text of a response to the speech by President Barack Obama, also on March 3, 2015.

DOCUMENT

Netanyahu Speaks Before Joint Session of Congress

March 3, 2015

. . . My friends, I am deeply humbled by the opportunity to speak for a third time before the most important legislative body in the world, the U.S. Congress. I want to thank you all for being here today.

I know that my speech has been the subject of much controversy. I deeply regret that some perceive my being here as political. That was never my intention.

I want to thank you, Democrats and Republicans, for your common support for Israel year after year, decade after decade. I know that no matter on which side of the aisle you sit, you stand with Israel.

The remarkable alliance between Israel and the United States has always been above politics. It must always remain above politics because America and Israel, we share a common destiny, the destiny of promised lands that cherish freedom and offer hope.

Israel is grateful for the support of America's people and of America's Presidents, from Harry Truman to Barack Obama.

We appreciate all that President Obama has done for Israel. Now, some of that is widely known, like strengthening security cooperation and intelligence sharing, opposing anti-Israel resolutions at the U.N.

Some of what the President has done for Israel is less well known. . . .

And Israel is grateful to you, the American Congress, for your support, for supporting us in so many ways. . . .

My friends, I have come here today because, as Prime Minister of Israel, I feel a profound obligation to speak to you about an issue that could well threaten the survival of my country and the future of my people, Iran's quest for nuclear weapons.

We are an ancient people. In our nearly 4,000 years of history, many have tried repeatedly to destroy the Jewish people. . . .

Today, the Jewish people face another attempt by yet another Persian potentate to destroy us. Iran's Supreme Leader, Ayatollah Khamenei, spews the oldest hatred, the oldest hatred of anti-Semitism with the newest technology.

He tweets that Israel must be annihilated. He tweets. In Iran there isn't exactly free Internet, but he tweets in English that Israel must be destroyed.

For those who believe that Iran threatens the Jewish state but not the Jewish people, listen to Hassan Nasrallah, the leader of Hezbollah, Iran's chief terrorist proxy. He said: If all the Jews gather in Israel, it will save us the trouble of chasing them down around the world. . . .

[A brief history of Iran's targeting of Israelis, Americans, and others in the Middle East has been omitted.]

We must all stand together to stop Iran's march of conquest, subjugation, and terror. . . .

Iran's regime is as radical as ever, its cries of "Death to America," that same America that it calls the great Satan, as loud as ever. Now this shouldn't be surprising because the ideology of Iran's revolutionary regime is deeply rooted in militant Islam, and that is why this regime will always be an enemy of America.

And don't be fooled. The battle between Iran and ISIS doesn't turn Iran into a friend of America. Iran and ISIS are competing for the crown of militant Islam. One calls itself the Islamic Republic; the other calls itself the Islamic State. Both want to impose a militant Islamic empire, first on the region, and then on the entire world. They just disagree among themselves who will be the ruler of that empire.

In this deadly game of thrones, there is no place for America or for Israel; no peace for Christians, Jews, or Muslims who don't share the Islamist medieval creed; no rights for women; no freedom for anyone.

So when it comes to Iran and ISIS, the enemy of your enemy is your enemy. The difference is that ISIS is armed with butcher knives, captured weapons, and YouTube; whereas, Iran could soon be armed with intercontinental ballistic missiles and nuclear bombs.

We must always remember—I will say it one more time—the greatest danger facing our world is the marriage of militant Islam with nuclear weapons. To defeat ISIS and let Iran get nuclear weapons would be to win the battle but lose the war. We can't let that happen. But that, my friends, is exactly what could happen if the deal now being negotiated is accepted by Iran. That deal will not prevent Iran from developing nuclear weapons. It would all but guarantee that Iran gets those weapons, lots of them.

Let me explain why.

While the final deal has not yet been signed, certain elements of any potential deal are now a matter of public record. You don't need intelligence agencies and secret information to know this. You can Google it.

Absent a dramatic change, we know for sure that any deal with Iran will include two major concessions to Iran. The first major concession would leave Iran with a vast nuclear infrastructure, providing it with a short breakout time to the bomb. "Breakout time" is the time it takes to amass enough weapons-grade uranium or plutonium for a nuclear bomb.

According to the deal, not a single nuclear facility would be demolished. Thousands of centrifuges used to enrich uranium would be left spinning. Thousands more would be temporarily disconnected but not destroyed. Because Iran's nuclear program would be left largely in tact [sic], Iran's breakout time would be very short—about a year by U.S. assessment, even shorter by Israel's. And if Iran's work on advanced centrifuges—faster and faster centrifuges—is not stopped, that breakout time could still be shorter—a lot shorter.

True, certain restrictions would be imposed on Iran's nuclear program, and Iran's adherence to those restrictions would be supervised by international inspectors. But here is the problem, you see: inspectors document violations; they don't stop them.

Now, I know this is not going to come as a shock to any of you, but Iran not only defies inspectors, it also plays a pretty good game of hide-and-cheat with them.

The U.N.'s nuclear watchdog agency, the IAEA, said again yesterday that Iran still refuses to come clean about its military nuclear program. Iran was also caught—caught twice, not once—twice operating secret nuclear facilities in Natanz and Qom, facilities that inspectors didn't even know existed. Right now, Iran could be hiding nuclear facilities that we—the U.S. and Israel—don't know about.

As the former head of inspections for the IAEA said in 2013: "If there is no undeclared installation today in Iran, it will be the first time in 20 years that it doesn't have one." Iran has proven time and again that it cannot be trusted, and that is why the first major concession is a source of grave concern.

It leaves Iran with a vast nuclear infrastructure and relies on inspectors to prevent a breakout. That concession creates a real danger that Iran could get to the bomb by violating the deal.

But the second major concession creates an even greater danger that Iran could get to the bomb by keeping the deal because virtually all the restrictions on Iran's nuclear program will automatically expire in about a decade.

Now, a decade may seem like a long time in political life, but it is the blink of an eye in the life of a nation. It is the blink of an eye in the life of our children. We all have a responsibility to consider what will happen when Iran's nuclear capabilities are virtually unrestricted and all the sanctions will have been lifted. Iran would then be free to build a huge nuclear capacity that could produce many, many nuclear bombs.

Iran's Supreme Leader says that openly. He says that Iran plans to have 190,000 centrifuges—not 6,000 or even the 19,000 that Iran has today, but ten times that amount—190,000 centrifuges enriching uranium. With this massive capacity, Iran could make the fuel for an entire nuclear arsenal and this in a matter of weeks once it makes that decision.

My longtime friend John Kerry, Secretary of State, confirmed last week that Iran could legitimately possess that massive centrifuge capacity when the deal expires. Now, I want you to think about that. The foremost sponsor of global terrorism could be weeks away from having enough enriched uranium for an entire arsenal of nuclear weapons—and this with full international legitimacy.

By the way, if Iran's intercontinental ballistic missile program is not part of the deal—and, so far, Iran refuses to even put it on the negotiating table—well, Iran could have the means to deliver that nuclear arsenal to the far-reaching corners of the Earth, including to every part of the United States.

You see, my friends, this deal has two major concessions: one, leaving Iran with a vast nuclear program; and, two, lifting the restrictions on that program in about a decade.

That is why this deal is so bad. It doesn't block Iran's path to the bomb; it paves Iran's path to the bomb.

Why would anyone make this deal? Because they hope that Iran will change for the better in the coming years or they believe that the alternative to this deal is worse.

Well, I disagree. I don't believe that Iran's radical regime will change for the better after this deal. This regime has been in power for 36 years, and its voracious appetite for aggression grows with each passing year. This deal would only whet Iran's appetite for more.

Would Iran be less aggressive when sanctions are removed and its economy is stronger? If Iran is gobbling up four countries right now while it is under sanctions, how many more countries will Iran devour when sanctions are lifted?

Would Iran fund less terrorism when it has mountains of cash with which to fund more terrorism? Why should Iran's radical regime change for the better when it can enjoy the best of both worlds: aggression abroad and prosperity at home?

This is a question that everyone asks in our region. Israel's neighbors—Iran's neighbors—know that Iran will become even more aggressive and sponsor even more terrorism when its economy is unshackled and it has been given a clear path to the bomb. Many of these neighbors say that they will respond by racing to get nuclear weapons of their own.

This deal won't change Iran for the better; it will only change the Middle East for the worse. A deal that is supposed to prevent nuclear proliferation would instead spark a nuclear arms race in the most dangerous part of the planet.

This deal won't be a farewell to arms. It would be a farewell to arms control, and the Middle East would soon be crisscrossed by nuclear tripwires. A region where small skirmishes can trigger big wars would turn into a nuclear tinderbox.

If anyone thinks this deal kicks the can down the road, think again. When we get down that road, we will face a much more dangerous Iran, a Middle East littered with nuclear bombs, and a countdown to a potential nuclear nightmare.

Ladies and gentlemen, I have come here today to tell you we don't have to bet the security of the world on the hope that Iran will change for the better. We don't have to gamble with our future and with our children's future. We can insist that restrictions on Iran's nuclear program not be lifted for as long as Iran continues its aggression in the region and in the world.

Before lifting those restrictions, the world should demand that Iran do three things: first, stop its aggression against its neighbors in the Middle East; second, stop supporting terrorism around the world; and, third, stop threatening to annihilate my country, Israel, the one and only Jewish state.

If the world powers are not prepared to insist that Iran change its behavior before a deal is signed, at the very least, they should insist that Iran change its behavior before a deal expires. . . .

Iran's nuclear program can be rolled back well beyond the current proposal by insisting on a better deal and keeping up the pressure on a very vulnerable regime, especially given the recent collapse in the price of oil.

Now, if Iran threatens to walk away from the table—and this often happens in a Persian bazaar—call their bluff. They will be back because they need the deal a lot more than you do. And by maintaining the pressure on Iran, and on those who do business with Iran, you have the power to make them need it even more.

My friends, for over a year, we have been told that no deal is better than a bad deal. Well, this is a bad deal, it is a very bad deal. We are better off without it.

Now we are being told that the only alternative to this bad deal is war. That is just not true. The alternative to this bad deal is a much better deal, a better deal that doesn't leave Iran with a vast nuclear infrastructure in such a short breakout time, a better deal that keeps the restrictions on Iran's nuclear program in place until Iran's aggression ends, a better deal that won't give Iran an easy path to the bomb, a better deal that Israel and its neighbors may not like but with which we could live, literally. And no country, no country has a greater stake, no country has a greater stake than Israel in a good deal that peacefully removes this threat.

Ladies and gentlemen, history has placed us at a fateful crossroads. We must now choose between two paths.

One path leads to a bad deal that will, at best, curtail Iran's nuclear ambitions for a while, but it will inexorably lead to a nuclear-armed Iran whose unbridled aggression will inevitably lead to war.

The second path, however difficult, could lead to a much better deal that would prevent a nuclear-armed Iran, a nuclearized Middle East, and the horrific consequences of both to all of humanity. . . . My friends, standing up to Iran is not easy; standing up to dark and murderous regimes never is. . . .

But I can guarantee you this: the days when the Jewish people remain passive in the face of genocidal enemies, those days are over. We are no longer scattered among the nations, powerless to defend ourselves. We have restored our sovereignty in our ancient home, and the soldiers who defend our home have boundless courage.

For the first time in 100 generations, we, the Jewish people, can defend ourselves. This is why, as Prime Minister of Israel, I can promise you one more thing. Even if Israel has to stand alone, Israel will stand. But I know that Israel does not stand alone. I know that America stands with Israel, I know that you stand with Israel. . . .

I leave you with his message today:

Be strong and resolute. Neither fear nor dread them.

My friends, may Israel and America always stand together, strong and resolute. May we neither fear nor dread the challenges ahead. May we face the future with confidence, strength, and hope.

May God bless the State of Israel, and may God bless the United States of America. . . .

SOURCE: House of Representatives. "Joint Meeting to Hear an Address by His Excellency Binyamin Netanyahu, Prime Minister of Israel." *Congressional Record* 2015, pt. 161, H1528-H1531. www.gpo.gov/fdsys/pkg/CREC-2015-03-03/pdf/CREC-2015-03-03-pt1-PgH1528.pdf.

President Obama Speaks with Reporters about Netanyahu Speech

March 3, 2015

[The president's opening remarks have been omitted.]

Prime Minister Benjamin Netanyahu of Israel's Address to the U.S. Congress/Iran

One issue that we will be discussing is Iran. And obviously, that's been a topic of great interest today, so let me just make a couple comments on that. I did not have a chance to watch Prime Minister Netanyahu's speech. I was on a video conference with our European partners with respect to Ukraine. I did have a chance to take a look at the transcript, and as far as I can tell, there was nothing new.

The Prime Minister, I think, appropriately pointed out that the bond between the United States of America is unbreakable, and on that point, I thoroughly agree. He also pointed out that Iran has been a dangerous regime and continues to engage in activities that are contrary to the interests of the United States, to Israel, and to the region. And on that, we agree. He also pointed out the fact that Iran has repeatedly threatened Israel and engaged in the most venomous of anti-Semitic statements. And no one can dispute that.

But on the core issue, which is how do we prevent Iran from obtaining a nuclear weapon, which would make it far more dangerous and would give it scope for even greater action in the region, the Prime Minister didn't offer any viable alternatives. So let's be clear about what exactly the central concern should be, both for the United States and for Israel.

I've said since before I became President that one of my primary goals in foreign policy would be preventing Iran from getting nuclear weapons. And with the help of Congress and our international partners, we constructed an extraordinarily effective sanctions regime that pressured Iran to come to the table to negotiate in a serious fashion. They have now been negotiating over the last year, and during that period, Iran has, in fact, frozen its program, rolled back some of its most dangerous highly enriched uranium, and subjected itself to the kinds of verifications and inspections that we had not previously seen. Keep in mind that when we shaped that interim deal, Prime Minister Netanyahu made almost the precise same speech about how dangerous that deal was going to be. And yet, over a year later, even Israeli intelligence officers and, in some cases, members of the Israeli Government, have to acknowledge that, in fact, it has kept Iran from further pursuing its nuclear program.

Now, the deal that we are trying to negotiate, that is not yet completed, would cut off the different pathways for Iran to advance its nuclear capabilities. It would roll back some elements of its program. It would ensure that it did not have what we call a breakout capacity that was shorter than a year's time. And it would subject Iran to the most vigorous inspections and verifications regimes that have ever been put in place.

And the alternative that the Prime Minister offers is no deal, in which case Iran will immediately begin once again pursuing its nuclear program, accelerate its nuclear program, without us having any insight into what they're doing and without constraint. And his essential argument is that if we just double down on sanctions, Iran won't want to do that.

Well, we have evidence from the past decade that sanctions alone are not sufficient to prevent Iran from pursuing its nuclear ambitions. And if it, in fact, does not have some sense that sanctions will be removed, it will not have an interest in avoiding the path that it's currently on.

So the bottom line is this: We don't yet have a deal. It may be that Iran cannot say yes to a good deal. I have repeatedly said that I would rather have no deal than a bad deal. But if we're successful in negotiating, then in fact, this will be the best deal possible to prevent Iran from obtaining a nuclear weapon. Nothing else comes close. Sanctions won't do it. Even military action would not be as successful as the deal that we have put forward.

And I think it is very important not to be distracted by the nature of the Iranian regime's ambitions when it comes to territory or terrorism, all issues which we share a concern with Israel about and are working consistently with Israel on. Because we know that if in fact they obtained a nuclear weapon, all those problems would be worse.

So we're staying focused on the central issue here: How do we prevent Iran from getting a nuclear weapon? The path that we've proposed, if successful, by far is the best way to do that. That's demonstrable. And Prime Minister Netanyahu has not offered any kind of viable alternative that would achieve the same verifiable mechanism to prevent Iran from getting a nuclear weapon.

So I would urge the Members of Congress who were there to continue to express their strong support for Israel's security, to continue to express their strong interest in providing the assistance Israel needs to repel attacks. I think it's important for Members of Congress, on a bipartisan basis, to be unified in pushing back against terrorism in the region and the destabilizing efforts that Iran may have engaged in with our partners. Those are all things in which this administration and Israel agree.

But when it comes to this nuclear deal, let's wait until there's actually a deal on the table that Iran has agreed to, at which point everybody can evaluate it; we don't have to speculate. And what I can guarantee is that if it's a deal I've signed off on, I will be able to prove that it is the best way for us to prevent Iran from getting a nuclear weapon.

And for us to pass up on that potential opportunity would be a grave mistake. It's not one that I intend to make, and I will take that case to every Member of Congress once we actually have a deal. All right? . . .

Prime Minister Benjamin Netanyahu of Israel's Address to the U.S. Congress/Speaker of the House of Representatives John A. Boehner/Israel-U.S. Relations/Iran

Q. Thank you. Now that you've had a chance to read the Prime Minister's remarks at least, do you feel like the speech he gave was appropriate, considering his upcoming elections and the upcoming deadline? And you also talked to other foreign leaders today in the call on Ukraine. Did Iran come up at all, and are you expecting any signs of support from them vis-a-vis your position versus the Prime Minister?

The President. No. The—well, all the folks on the call today share my position that we should see if we can get this deal done. It was not a topic of conversation.

With respect to the decision of the Speaker to offer up the House Chamber 2 weeks before Mr. Netanyahu's election to make this case, I think that question should be directed to Mr. Boehner.

As I said, it is very important for us not to politicize the relationship between Israel and the United States. It's very important for all of us Americans to realize that we have a system of government in which foreign policy runs through the executive branch and the President, not through other channels.

And I think it's important for us to stay focused on the problem at hand. And the specific problem that is being debated right now is not whether we trust the Iranian regime or not, it—we don't trust them. It's not whether Iran engages in destabilizing activities— everybody agrees with that. The central question is, how can we stop them from getting a nuclear weapon?

And what we know is that if we're able to get a deal, not only do we cut off all the various pathways for Iran getting a nuclear weapon, but we also know that we'll have a verification mechanism and an inspection mechanism where, if they cheat and if they engage in a covert program, we are far more likely to see it in time to do something about it.

What I also know is, if we don't have a deal, as Prime Minster Netanyahu suggested—if in fact he's right that they're not trustworthy, they intend to pursue a covert program, and they cheat—we'll be far less aware of it until it is potentially too late.

What I also know is, is that he made the same argument before this current interim deal, and even his officials in his own government had had to acknowledge that Iran has in fact maintained their end of the bargain.

So what I'm focused on right now is solving this problem. I'm not focused on the politics of it, I'm not focused on the theater of it. And my strong suggestion would be that Members of Congress, as they evaluate it, stay similarly focused.

SOURCE: Executive Office of the President. "Remarks Prior to a Meeting With Secretary of Defense Ashton B. Carter and an Exchange With Reporters." March 3, 2015. *Compilation of Presidential Documents* 2015, no. 00145 (March 3, 2015). www.gpo.gov/fdsys/pkg/DCPD-201500145/pdf/DCPD-201500145.pdf.

OTHER HISTORIC DOCUMENTS OF INTEREST

FROM THIS VOLUME

FROM PREVIOUS *HISTORIC DOCUMENTS*

Justice Department and Missouri Governor Respond to Ferguson Police Violations

MARCH 4, 2015

In August 2014, a white police officer in a town outside St. Louis, Missouri, shot and killed an unarmed African American teenager named Michael Brown. The shooting set off weeks of widespread, sometimes violent, demonstrations and protests, and focused national attention on the small town of Ferguson. The Civil Rights Division of the United States Department of Justice opened an investigation into the shooting and into the practices of the Ferguson Police Department. Seven months later, on March 4, 2015, it released two reports. The first explained at length the Justice Department findings that the shooting of Michael Brown, while tragic, did not support the filing of federal charges against the officer involved, Darren Wilson. The second report, however, provided a searing indictment of police and court practices in Ferguson, revealing a long-standing pattern of unlawful conduct in violation of the United States Constitution and federal statutory law. This report exhaustively detailed the routine police practices of stopping and handcuffing residents without probable cause, arrests for questioning police tactics, and excessive and dangerous use of force, all brought to bear disproportionally on the African American population of the town. The report gave context to the outrage witnessed in Ferguson, making it clear that it was not a response to a single isolated confrontation. Attorney General Eric Holder said, "[A]mid a highly toxic environment, defined by mistrust and resentment, stoked by years of bad feelings, and spurred by illegal and misguided practices—it is not difficult to imagine how a single tragic incident set off the city of Ferguson like a powder keg." Attorney General Holder also emphasized that, while the concerns of this report were focused on Ferguson, they "implicate questions about fairness and trust that are national in scope."

THE FERGUSON REPORT: POLICING AS REVENUE GENERATION

The Department of Justice report characterized Ferguson's approach to law enforcement not as a way to protect public safety, but rather as a means to generate revenue. From 2010 to 2015, money collected from fines and fees more than doubled, despite the fact that there was no corresponding rise in crime. The report documented intense pressure from city officials on the police department to aggressively write citations, explicitly stating that the city relied on citation productivity to fund the budget, almost a quarter of which came from these fines. Ferguson, according to Attorney General Holder, relied on the police to serve as a "collection agency" rather than a law enforcement entity focused on promoting public safety. Officer promotions and evaluations were tied to "productivity" with tickets, and officers were encouraged to charge multiple violations for the same conduct. Three or four charges stemming from a single stop was considered routine and officers had informal competitions to see who could issue the largest number of citations during a single stop.

Equally harsh was the report's criticism of Ferguson's court system, which did not operate as an independent, neutral arbitrator of justice, but instead was controlled by the city council and operated to maximize revenue. Almost every ticket written had to be paid in person at a specific court date, even if it was uncontested. The courts, however, faced bureaucratic challenges with wrong court dates and improvised procedures, making it difficult to determine when a hearing was or how much was owed. If someone missed a court date for any reason, the court regularly imposed a separate Failure to Appear charge. Since 2010, the court collected more revenue from Failure to Appear charges than for any other charge. Most damaging, according to the report, was the Court's routine and "staggering" use of arrest warrants to secure collection and compliance whenever someone missed a court appearance or even a single payment, with no opportunity to explain why the payment was missed. These frequently led to arrest, jail time, and additional fees, even though the underlying offense, usually noncriminal traffic cases, reasonably should not result in imprisonment. As the report concluded, this practice of "automatically treating a missed payment as a failure to appear—thus triggering an arrest warrant and possible incarceration—is directly at odds with well-established law that prohibits 'punishing a person for his poverty.'"

Unconstitutional Police Practices in Ferguson

Not only did the police department communicate to officers that they must focus on bringing in revenue, and then penalize officers who did not write enough tickets, but the report also found that "the department has little concern with how officers do this." This pressure to raise revenue, together with lack of supervision and training, resulted in a pattern and practice of constitutional violations.

Despite Fourth Amendment rights, in Ferguson it was commonplace for officers to stop pedestrians and ask for identification for no reason at all. These unjustified stops routinely escalated into arrests often unsupported by probable cause. One officer admitted that when he conducts traffic stops, he asks for identification from all passengers as a matter of course. Any who refuse, as is their right, he regards as suspicious and typically arrests them on a charge termed "Failure to Comply." According to the report, the Failure to Comply statute was routinely abused by officers who used it to charge people who did not do as police asked, even though refusal is not a crime.

The Justice Department also documented a pattern of excessive force in violation of the Fourth Amendment. Reliance on Electronic Control Weapons (ECW) such as Tasers was routine even when "less force—or no force at all—would do." In the report, many examples of Taser use demonstrate that it was punitive, and often used against people already in custody or against vulnerable groups, such as people with mental health problems or cognitive disabilities. "FPD officers' swift, at times automatic, resort to using ECWs against individuals who typically have committed low-level crimes and who pose no immediate threat," the report concludes, "violates the Constitution." The report also documented multiple instances of police releasing canines on unarmed suspects, many of them children and nonviolent offenders, before attempting to use force less likely to cause injuries, often leaving the suspects with serious puncture wounds.

The report also charged the Ferguson Police Department with a pattern of First Amendment violations. In Ferguson, people were punished routinely for talking back to officers, recording public police activities, and lawfully protesting perceived injustices, which are all protected activities. In reviewing arrest reports, it was clear from the officers' own descriptions that they believed criticism and insolence to be grounds for arrest, and they had no tools for deescalating emotionally charged scenes. As recently as February 9, 2015, video footage showed police officers speeding out of the police parking lot toward peaceful protesters announcing that "everybody here's going to jail." One man video recording the arrests, an activity protected by the First Amendment, was pushed to the ground, threated with a Taser, and arrested for "interfering with police action."

RACIAL BIAS IN FERGUSON LAW ENFORCEMENT

Extensive statistics show that the harm stemming from these unconstitutional policing practices disproportionally impacted Ferguson's African American residents. To cite a few of the report's statistics, from 2012 to 2014, African Americans comprised 67 percent of the population, and accounted for 85 percent of the traffic stops, 90 percent of the citations, and 93 percent of the arrests. African Americans were twice as likely as white residents to be searched during a routine traffic stop, even though they were 26 percent less likely to carry contraband. The more discretionary the offense, the more racial disparity seemingly existed in the charges. For example, African Americans made up 95 percent of those charged with the highly discretionary offense described as Manner of Walking Along Roadway, 94 percent of all Resisting Arrest charges, 92 percent of all Peace Disturbance charges, and 89 percent of all Failure to Obey charges. According to the report, "Ferguson's pattern of using excessive force disproportionately harms African-American members of the community. The overwhelming majority of force—almost 90%—is directed against African Americans." In every documented instance in which a police dog bit someone, that person was African American.

Disparate results continued at the courthouse where African Americans were 68 percent less likely than others to have their cases dismissed by the municipal judge, and in 2013, African Americans accounted for 92 percent of cases in which an arrest warrant was issued and 96 percent of those arrested for an outstanding municipal warrant. In this way, the unequal impact of Ferguson's enforcement actions compounded such that, as the consequences grew more severe, those consequences were imposed more and more disproportionally against African Americans.

None of these disparities can be explained by any legitimate public safety effort; in fact, Attorney General Holder stated that the Justice Department's "review of the evidence found *no* alternative explanation for the disproportionate impact on African American residents other than implicit and explicit racial bias." Beyond disparate impact, alone enough to violate federal law, investigators found evidence of explicit racial bias in the examined e-mail communications between police and court supervisors, rife with racist comments and grotesque characterizations.

FERGUSON'S LAW ENFORCEMENT
PRACTICES ERODE COMMUNITY TRUST

The report concluded by describing the impact these unlawful and unfair police practices have had on the community over the years, long before Brown's shooting death. African American residents described "being belittled, disbelieved, and treated with little regard for their legal rights by the Ferguson Police Department." During routine interactions, verbal abuse and intimidation by police officers were common, including threats to fire weapons, often for little or no cause. Residents say these behaviors have generated a great distrust of Ferguson police, especially among African Americans. This erosion of community trust makes policing less effective, more difficult, and less safe.

The end of the report included recommendations for changes that Ferguson should make to correct the constitutional violations. In his public remarks about the findings, Attorney General Holder stated that "it is time for Ferguson's leaders to take immediate, wholesale and structural corrective action. Let me be clear: the United States Department of Justice reserves all its rights and abilities to force compliance and implement basic change."

ONGOING IMPACT OF THE JUSTICE DEPARTMENT REPORT

In the year that followed Brown's shooting in Ferguson, media attention focused on the deaths of more unarmed black men by police in towns across the nation. In Cleveland, Ohio, twelve-year old Tamir Rice was shot by police who saw him playing with a toy gun; in North Charleston, South Carolina, Walter Scott was shot following a daytime traffic stop; and in Baltimore, Maryland, violent protests erupted following the death of Freddie Gray in police custody. These incidents exposed a more widespread breakdown of trust between police departments and African American communities, sparking continued national conversations and additional involvement of the Department of Justice.

In Ferguson, the city has been in negotiations with the Justice Department to create formal guidelines for reforming its police and court systems, and there have been some significant changes in personnel. Almost immediately after the release of the scathing report, the Ferguson police chief resigned and was replaced by an African American interim chief. The police officers and county clerks who sent racist e-mail had already stepped down. The municipal judge resigned and was replaced by a new judge empowered to overhaul the court policies and restore integrity to the system.

The town also adopted new policing strategies, including police officer body cameras, and it is enforcing a series of tough new court reforms. The new municipal court judge, Donald McCullin, promising a "fresh start" for residents, ordered all arrest warrants issued for traffic offenses to be withdrawn and specifically barred jail time for minor offenders. More than 6,000 suspended and revoked drivers' licenses were ordered restored within the first hours of the reforms' enforcement. Missouri governor Jay Nixon backed these new reforms and promised that "cops will stop being revenue agents and go back to being cops." Further, while thanking the Justice Department for its diligence in its investigation, Nixon stated, "Discrimination has no place in our justice system and no place in a democratic society. All Missourians deserve to be treated with fairness, dignity and respect. . . . I will continue to work to enact policies and legislation that promote greater fairness, equality and inclusion in all our communities."

—Melissa Feinberg

Following is the edited text of the summary of the report issued by the Department of Justice on March 4, 2015, in relation to its investigation into the policing practices in Ferguson, Missouri; and the text of a statement by Missouri governor Jay Nixon also on March 4, 2015, in response to the report.

Department of Justice Ferguson Police Investigation Report

March 4, 2015

[The table of contents and title page have been omitted.]

I. REPORT SUMMARY

The Civil Rights Division of the United States Department of Justice opened its investigation of the Ferguson Police Department ("FPD") on September 4, 2014. This investigation was initiated under the pattern-or-practice provision of the Violent Crime Control and Law Enforcement Act of 1994, 42 U.S.C. § 14141, the Omnibus Crime Control and Safe Streets Act of 1968, 42 U.S.C. § 3789d ("Safe Streets Act"), and Title VI of the Civil Rights Act of 1964, 42 U.S.C. § 2000d ("Title VI"). This investigation has revealed a pattern or practice of unlawful conduct within the Ferguson Police Department that violates the First, Fourth, and Fourteenth Amendments to the United States Constitution, and federal statutory law.

Over the course of the investigation, we interviewed City officials, including City Manager John Shaw, Mayor James Knowles, Chief of Police Thomas Jackson, Municipal Judge Ronald Brockmeyer, the Municipal Court Clerk, Ferguson's Finance Director, half of FPD's sworn officers, and others. We spent, collectively, approximately 100 person-days onsite in Ferguson. We participated in ride-alongs with on-duty officers, reviewed over 35,000 pages of police records as well as thousands of emails and other electronic materials provided by the police department. Enlisting the assistance of statistical experts, we analyzed FPD's data on stops, searches, citations, and arrests, as well as data collected by the municipal court. We observed four separate sessions of Ferguson Municipal Court, interviewing dozens of people charged with local offenses, and we reviewed third-party studies regarding municipal court practices in Ferguson and St. Louis County more broadly. As in all of our investigations, we sought to engage the local community, conducting hundreds of in-person and telephone interviews of individuals who reside in Ferguson or who have had interactions with the police department. We contacted ten neighborhood associations and met with each group that responded to us, as well as several other community groups and advocacy organizations. Throughout the investigation, we relied on two police chiefs who accompanied us to Ferguson and who themselves interviewed City and police officials, spoke with community members, and reviewed FPD policies and incident reports.

We thank the City officials and the rank-and-file officers who have cooperated with this investigation and provided us with insights into the operation of the police department, including the municipal court. Notwithstanding our findings about Ferguson's approach to law enforcement and the policing culture it creates, we found many Ferguson police officers and other City employees to be dedicated public servants striving each day to perform their duties lawfully and with respect for all members of the Ferguson community. The importance of their often-selfless work cannot be overstated.

We are also grateful to the many members of the Ferguson community who have met with us to share their experiences. It became clear during our many conversations with

Ferguson residents from throughout the City that many residents, black and white, genuinely embrace Ferguson's diversity and want to reemerge from the events of recent months a truly inclusive, united community. This Report is intended to strengthen those efforts by recognizing the harms caused by Ferguson's law enforcement practices so that those harms can be better understood and overcome.

Ferguson's law enforcement practices are shaped by the City's focus on revenue rather than by public safety needs. This emphasis on revenue has compromised the institutional character of Ferguson's police department, contributing to a pattern of unconstitutional policing, and has also shaped its municipal court, leading to procedures that raise due process concerns and inflict unnecessary harm on members of the Ferguson community. Further, Ferguson's police and municipal court practices both reflect and exacerbate existing racial bias, including racial stereotypes. Ferguson's own data establish clear racial disparities that adversely impact African Americans. The evidence shows that discriminatory intent is part of the reason for these disparities. Over time, Ferguson's police and municipal court practices have sown deep mistrust between parts of the community and the police department, undermining law enforcement legitimacy among African Americans in particular.

Focus on Generating Revenue

The City budgets for sizeable increases in municipal fines and fees each year, exhorts police and court staff to deliver those revenue increases, and closely monitors whether those increases are achieved. City officials routinely urge Chief Jackson to generate more revenue through enforcement. In March 2010, for instance, the City Finance Director wrote to Chief Jackson that "unless ticket writing ramps up significantly before the end of the year, it will be hard to significantly raise collections next year. . . . Given that we are looking at a substantial sales tax shortfall, it's not an insignificant issue." Similarly, in March 2013, the Finance Director wrote to the City Manager: "Court fees are anticipated to rise about 7.5%. I did ask the Chief if he thought the PD could deliver 10% increase. He indicated they could try." The importance of focusing on revenue generation is communicated to FPD officers. Ferguson police officers from all ranks told us that revenue generation is stressed heavily within the police department, and that the message comes from City leadership. The evidence we reviewed supports this perception.

Police Practices

The City's emphasis on revenue generation has a profound effect on FPD's approach to law enforcement. Patrol assignments and schedules are geared toward aggressive enforcement of Ferguson's municipal code, with insufficient thought given to whether enforcement strategies promote public safety or unnecessarily undermine community trust and cooperation. Officer evaluations and promotions depend to an inordinate degree on "productivity," meaning the number of citations issued. Partly as a consequence of City and FPD priorities, many officers appear to see some residents, especially those who live in Ferguson's predominantly African American neighborhoods, less as constituents to be protected than as potential offenders and sources of revenue.

This culture within FPD influences officer activities in all areas of policing, beyond just ticketing. Officers expect and demand compliance even when they lack legal authority. They are inclined to interpret the exercise of free-speech rights as unlawful disobedience, innocent movements as physical threats, indications of mental or physical illness as belligerence. Police supervisors and leadership do too little to ensure that officers act in accordance with law and policy, and rarely respond meaningfully to civilian complaints of officer misconduct. The result is a pattern of stops without reasonable suspicion and arrests without probable cause in violation of the Fourth Amendment; infringement on free expression, as well as retaliation for protected expression, in violation of the First Amendment; and excessive force in violation of the Fourth Amendment.

Even relatively routine misconduct by Ferguson police officers can have significant consequences for the people whose rights are violated. For example, in the summer of 2012, a 32-year-old African-American man sat in his car cooling off after playing basketball in a Ferguson public park. An officer pulled up behind the man's car, blocking him in, and demanded the man's Social Security number and identification. Without any cause, the officer accused the man of being a pedophile, referring to the presence of children in the park, and ordered the man out of his car for a pat-down, although the officer had no reason to believe the man was armed. The officer also asked to search the man's car. The man objected, citing his constitutional rights. In response, the officer arrested the man, reportedly at gunpoint, charging him with eight violations of Ferguson's municipal code. One charge, Making a False Declaration, was for initially providing the short form of his first name (e.g., "Mike" instead of "Michael"), and an address which, although legitimate, was different from the one on his driver's license. Another charge was for not wearing a seat belt, even though he was seated in a parked car. The officer also charged the man both with having an expired operator's license, and with having no operator's license in his possession. The man told us that, because of these charges, he lost his job as a contractor with the federal government that he had held for years.

Municipal Court Practices

Ferguson has allowed its focus on revenue generation to fundamentally compromise the role of Ferguson's municipal court. The municipal court does not act as a neutral arbiter of the law or a check on unlawful police conduct. Instead, the court primarily uses its judicial authority as the means to compel the payment of fines and fees that advance the City's financial interests. This has led to court practices that violate the Fourteenth Amendment's due process and equal protection requirements. The court's practices also impose unnecessary harm, overwhelmingly on African-American individuals, and run counter to public safety.

Most strikingly, the court issues municipal arrest warrants not on the basis of public safety needs, but rather as a routine response to missed court appearances and required fine payments. In 2013 alone, the court issued over 9,000 warrants on cases stemming in large part from minor violations such as parking infractions, traffic tickets, or housing code violations. Jail time would be considered far too harsh a penalty for the great majority of these code violations, yet Ferguson's municipal court routinely issues warrants for people to be arrested and incarcerated for failing to timely pay related fines and fees. Under state law, a failure to appear in municipal court on a traffic charge involving a moving violation also results in a license suspension. Ferguson has made this penalty even more onerous by only allowing the suspension to be lifted after payment of an owed fine is made in full. Further, until recently, Ferguson also added charges, fines, and fees for each missed appearance and payment. Many pending cases still include such charges that were imposed before the court recently eliminated them, making it as difficult as before for people to resolve these cases.

The court imposes these severe penalties for missed appearances and payments even as several of the court's practices create unnecessary barriers to resolving a municipal violation. The court often fails to provide clear and accurate information regarding a person's charges or court obligations. And the court's fine assessment procedures do not adequately provide for a defendant to seek a fine reduction on account of financial incapacity or to seek alternatives to payment such as community service. City and court officials have adhered to these court practices despite acknowledging their needlessly harmful consequences. In August 2013, for example, one City Councilmember wrote to the City Manager, the Mayor, and other City officials lamenting the lack of a community service option and noted the benefits of such a program, including that it would "keep those people that simply don't have the money to pay their fines from constantly being arrested and going to jail, only to be released and do it all over again."

Together, these court practices exacerbate the harm of Ferguson's unconstitutional police practices. They impose a particular hardship upon Ferguson's most vulnerable residents, especially upon those living in or near poverty. Minor offenses can generate crippling debts, result in jail time because of an inability to pay, and result in the loss of a driver's license, employment, or housing.

We spoke, for example, with an African-American woman who has a still-pending case stemming from 2007, when, on a single occasion, she parked her car illegally. She received two citations and a $151 fine, plus fees. The woman, who experienced financial difficulties and periods of homelessness over several years, was charged with seven Failure to Appear offenses for missing court dates or fine payments on her parking tickets between 2007 and 2010. For each Failure to Appear, the court issued an arrest warrant and imposed new fines and fees. From 2007 to 2014, the woman was arrested twice, spent six days in jail, and paid $550 to the court for the events stemming from this single instance of illegal parking. Court records show that she twice attempted to make partial payments of $25 and $50, but the court returned those payments, refusing to accept anything less than payment in full. One of those payments was later accepted, but only after the court's letter rejecting payment by money order was returned as undeliverable. This woman is now making regular payments on the fine. As of December 2014, over seven years later, despite initially owing a $151 fine and having already paid $550, she still owed $541.

Racial Bias

Ferguson's approach to law enforcement both reflects and reinforces racial bias, including stereotyping. The harms of Ferguson's police and court practices are borne disproportionately by African Americans, and there is evidence that this is due in part to intentional discrimination on the basis of race.

Ferguson's law enforcement practices overwhelmingly impact African Americans. Data collected by the Ferguson Police Department from 2012 to 2014 shows that African Americans account for 85% of vehicle stops, 90% of citations, and 93% of arrests made by FPD officers, despite comprising only 67% of Ferguson's population. African Americans are more than twice as likely as white drivers to be searched during vehicle stops even after controlling for non-race based variables such as the reason the vehicle stop was initiated, but are found in possession of contraband 26% less often than white drivers, suggesting officers are impermissibly considering race as a factor when determining whether to search. African

Americans are more likely to be cited and arrested following a stop regardless of why the stop was initiated and are more likely to receive multiple citations during a single incident. From 2012 to 2014, FPD issued four or more citations to African Americans on 73 occasions, but issued four or more citations to non-African Americans only twice. FPD appears to bring certain offenses almost exclusively against African Americans. For example, from 2011 to 2013, African Americans accounted for 95% of Manner of Walking in Roadway charges, and 94% of all Failure to Comply charges. Notably, with respect to speeding charges brought by FPD, the evidence shows not only that African Americans are represented at disproportionately high rates overall, but also that the disparate impact of FPD's enforcement practices on African Americans is 48% larger when citations are issued not on the basis of radar or laser, but by some other method, such as the officer's own visual assessment.

These disparities are also present in FPD's use of force. Nearly 90% of documented force used by FPD officers was used against African Americans. In every canine bite incident for which racial information is available, the person bitten was African American.

Municipal court practices likewise cause disproportionate harm to African Americans. African Americans are 68% less likely than others to have their cases dismissed by the court, and are more likely to have their cases last longer and result in more required court encounters. African Americans are at least 50% more likely to have their cases lead to an arrest warrant, and accounted for 92% of cases in which an arrest warrant was issued by the Ferguson Municipal Court in 2013. Available data show that, of those actually arrested by FPD only because of an outstanding municipal warrant, 96% are African American.

Our investigation indicates that this disproportionate burden on African Americans cannot be explained by any difference in the rate at which people of different races violate the law. Rather, our investigation has revealed that these disparities occur, at least in part, because of unlawful bias against and stereotypes about African Americans. We have found substantial evidence of racial bias among police and court staff in Ferguson. For example, we discovered emails circulated by police supervisors and court staff that stereotype racial minorities as criminals, including one email that joked about an abortion by an African-American woman being a means of crime control.

City officials have frequently asserted that the harsh and disparate results of Ferguson's law enforcement system do not indicate problems with police or court practices, but instead reflect a pervasive lack of "personal responsibility" among "certain segments" of the community. Our investigation has found that the practices about which area residents have complained are in fact unconstitutional and unduly harsh. But the City's personal-responsibility refrain is telling: it reflects many of the same racial stereotypes found in the emails between police and court supervisors. This evidence of bias and stereotyping, together with evidence that Ferguson has long recognized but failed to correct the consistent racial disparities caused by its police and court practices, demonstrates that the discriminatory effects of Ferguson's conduct are driven at least in part by discriminatory intent in violation of the Fourteenth Amendment.

Community Distrust

Since the August 2014 shooting death of Michael Brown, the lack of trust between the Ferguson Police Department and a significant portion of Ferguson's residents, especially African Americans, has become undeniable. The causes of this distrust and division, however, have been the subject of debate. Police and other City officials, as well as some Ferguson residents, have insisted to us that the public outcry is attributable to "outside agitators" who do not reflect the opinions of "real Ferguson residents." That view is at odds with the facts we have gathered during our investigation. Our investigation has shown that distrust of the Ferguson Police Department is longstanding and largely attributable to Ferguson's approach to law enforcement. This approach results in patterns of unnecessarily aggressive and at times unlawful policing; reinforces the harm of discriminatory stereotypes; discourages a culture of accountability; and neglects community engagement. In recent years, FPD has moved away from the modest community policing efforts it previously had implemented, reducing opportunities for positive police-community interactions, and losing the little familiarity it had with some African American neighborhoods. The confluence of policing to raise revenue and racial bias thus has resulted in practices that not only violate the Constitution and cause direct harm to the individuals whose rights are violated, but also undermine community trust, especially among many African Americans. As a consequence of these practices, law enforcement is seen as illegitimate, and the partnerships necessary for public safety are, in some areas, entirely absent.

Restoring trust in law enforcement will require recognition of the harms caused by Ferguson's law enforcement practices, and diligent, committed collaboration with the entire Ferguson community. At the conclusion of this report, we have broadly identified the changes that are necessary for meaningful and sustainable reform. These measures build upon a number of other recommended changes we communicated verbally to the Mayor, Police Chief, and City Manager in September so that Ferguson could begin immediately to address problems as we identified them. As a result of those recommendations, the City and police department have already begun to make some changes to municipal court and police practices. We commend City officials for beginning to take steps to address some of the concerns we have already raised. Nonetheless, these changes are only a small part of the reform necessary. Addressing the deeply embedded constitutional deficiencies we found demands an entire reorientation of law enforcement in Ferguson. The City must replace revenue-driven policing with a system grounded in the principles of community policing and police legitimacy, in which people are equally protected and treated with compassion, regardless of race.

[The remainder of the report, which describes in detail the background and findings of the Department of Justice investigation into the Ferguson, Missouri, Police Department has been omitted.]

Source: U.S. Department of Justice. "Investigation of the Ferguson Police Department." March 4, 2015. www .justice.gov/sites/default/files/opa/press-releases/attachments/2015/03/04/ferguson_police_ department_report.pdf.

Governor Nixon Responds to Justice Department Report

March 4, 2015

Gov. Jay Nixon released the following statement regarding today's announcement by the U.S. Department of Justice:

"On Aug. 11, I asked the Department of Justice to conduct an independent investigation following the shooting of Michael Brown. I appreciate their diligent efforts as well as their specific recommendations for how to restore confidence, build trust, and promote greater fairness in the City of Ferguson's courts and police department.

"Facts exposed in the Department of Justice's report on the Ferguson Police Department are deeply disturbing, and demonstrate the urgent need for the reforms I have called for, some of which the General Assembly is now considering, including reforms to municipal courts.

"Discrimination has no place in our justice system and no place in a democratic society. All Missourians deserve to be treated with fairness, dignity and respect. That is why I will continue to work to enact policies and legislation that promote greater fairness, equality and inclusion in all our communities."

SOURCE: Office of Missouri Governor Jay Nixon. "Gov. Nixon issues statement regarding today's announcement by Department of Justice." March 4, 2015. https://governor.mo.gov/news/archive/gov-nixon-issues-statement-regarding-today's-announcement-department-justice.

OTHER HISTORIC DOCUMENTS OF INTEREST

FROM PREVIOUS *HISTORIC DOCUMENTS*

- Federal Response to Racial Profiling, *2014*, p. 579
- Local Officials Respond to Officer-Involved Shootings, *2014*, p. 346

Solar-Powered Plane Attempts
Around-the-World Flight

MARCH 9, AND JULY 3 AND 15, 2015

An attempt at completing the first-ever solar flight around the world ended in July 2015, when the batteries in an aircraft known as Solar Impulse overheated and required repairs. The flight was part of an initiative to prove that solar power is a viable alternative to fossil fuels, even for high-risk efforts such as flight. During the four-month journey, the Swiss pilots, André Borschberg and Bertrand Piccard, said they broke the world records for distance and duration for a flight powered only by energy from the sun as well as the record for the longest-ever solo flight. The longest nonstop leg of the trip lasted 117 hours and 52 minutes. The pilots said they would continue the flight in the spring of 2016 after the necessary repairs were made.

EARLIER EFFORTS AT SOLAR FLIGHT

The high-profile solar flight experiment built on more than a decade of efforts by Borschberg, an engineer who studied at the Massachusetts Institute of Technology, and Piccard, a psychiatrist and descendant of explorers. Piccard, an aeronaut who made the first ever nonstop around-the-world balloon flight, is the Solar Impulse project's chairman and founder. Borschberg, a trained fighter pilot who is also a professional plane and helicopter pilot, is the initiative's chief executive officer.

An earlier version of the aircraft, commonly referred to as Solar Impulse 1, began operating in late 2009. The plane was constructed with 11,628 photovoltaic cells used to create energy during daylight hours to operate the plane's electric motors. The cells also charge the plane's lithium polymer batteries to continue to power the plane after dark.

The model plane set a number of world records. In 2010, Solar Impulse 1 was used for the first manned solar-powered flight. In July of that year, Borschberg achieved the first twenty-six-hour overnight trip using solar energy. Two years later, the plane finished the first intercontinental solar-energy flight during a trip from Spain to Morocco. In 2013, the aircraft was flown on a two-month tour of the United States, drawing attention to the project's goal of encouraging the use of alternative energy considered to be less damaging to the environment.

Other unmanned solar-fueled aircraft flights had been attempted before the Solar Impulse project began. The U.S. company, AstroFlight, is credited with building the first aircraft to use solar energy. Its plane, AstroFlight Sunrise, took off from California in 1974 and was destroyed by turbulence during its twenty-eighth flight.

DEVELOPMENT OF SOLAR IMPULSE 2

Solar Impulse 2, funded by private companies and the Swiss government, was a refined and more powerful version of the prototype. The design team began work in 2011, with plans to add more solar cells and improve the vehicle's energy efficiency. The initial goal was to finish construction in 2013, but that timeline was ultimately delayed until 2014. By 2015, the Solar Impulse team comprised about ninety people, including engineers, technicians, and mission controllers.

The project's early partners included corporations such as Semper, Altran, and Solvay. In April 2014, energy and automation company ABB became a main sponsor of the project. Other significant partners include watch manufacturer Omega and elevator and escalator provider Schindler. Google and telecommunications company Swisscom also contributed to the project, while Swiss Re Corporate Solutions provided insurance. The governments of Monaco and the United Arab Emirates also lent their support.

The second version of the aircraft was built in Switzerland with 17,248 solar cells mounted on the wings, fuselage, and horizontal part of the plane's tail. As the aircraft took in sunlight during the day, it collected up to 340 kilowatt hours of solar energy per day and recharged the four lithium polymer batteries. The batteries permitted the plane to fly at night and comprised about one-fourth of the plane's weight. The craft's seventy-two meter wingspan was larger than that of a Boeing 747 jet, and weighed about as much as a large car. The single-seat aircraft was fitted with an unpressurized cockpit and was made of carbon fiber.

ATTEMPT TO CIRCUMNAVIGATE THE GLOBE

The historic around-the-world flight attempt began March 9, 2015, and the pilots hoped to complete their journey by August 2015. Borschberg was at the controls, with Piccard as his copilot, when the plane left Abu Dhabi in the United Arab Emirates. Piccard called the departure point symbolic because Abu Dhabi, a major oil producer, is working toward diversifying to more clean energy technologies.

Borschberg and Piccard planned a series of twelve stops, with each pilot taking a turn in the cockpit. During the legs, which lasted several days without a stop, the pilots took brief naps and did exercises such as yoga to stay alert and avoid the effects of immobility while the plane operated on autopilot.

The plane made it through Oman, India, and Myanmar in March. The trip then continued through China, but unexpected problems arose when poor weather conditions forced an unscheduled stop in Japan. When the flight resumed in late June for the leg from Japan to Hawaii, the plane's batteries were damaged. Although the craft was able to fly across the Pacific Ocean to land in Hawaii on July 3, the damage to the batteries grounded the aircraft until 2016.

In a press release, Solar Impulse stated that the batteries became hot during the ascent on the first day of the flight from Japan to Hawaii because the plane was climbing quickly and the equipment was overinsulated. "While the Mission Team was monitoring this very closely during the flight, there was no way to decrease the temperature for the remaining duration as each daily cycle requires an ascent to 28,000 feet and descent for optimal energy management," according to the statement. The group said that "the damage to the batteries is not a technical failure or a weakness in the technology but rather an evaluation error in terms of the profile of the mission and the cooling design specifications of the batteries. The temperature of the batteries in a quick ascent/descent in tropical climates was not properly anticipated."

The irreversible damage to parts of the batteries meant several months of delay because of the time required for repair and the subsequent difficulty of operating long flights during that time of year for a variety of reasons, including limited daylight hours.

The team said that it would also investigate methods of improving the cooling and heating processes for very long flights.

During the flight from Japan to Hawaii, Borschberg set records for the longest solar-powered flight for both duration and distance. The journey also set the record for the longest solo flight for any kind of plane. According to Piccard, "Andre's flight was longer than all the other single-seater flights that had fuel. That's an incredible message. Now you can fly longer with no fuel than you can with fuel. So, what Andre has done is not only a historic first for aviation, it's a historic first for renewable energies."

AFTERMATH OF ABORTED TRIP AND FUTURE PLANS

Piccard sought to raise €20 million ($23 million) to update the aircraft and finish the around-the-world flight. The total cost of the work, from its earliest stages in 2003 to the time the aircraft was grounded in Hawaii, was about €150 million, he said.

While the team is conducting repairs and waiting to re-embark when daylight hours are longer, the airplane is being stored in a hangar at Kalaeloa airport maintained by the University of Hawaii and the Department of Transportation. The new battery heating and cooling systems will be tested before the around-the-world mission is expected to resume in early April 2016. It is anticipated that the first leg of the resumption of flight will be from Hawaii to the West Coast of the United States. The plane will then travel across the United States before landing in New York, after which it will fly across the Atlantic Ocean to Europe, and ultimately back to Abu Dhabi.

Although the project was built around the premise of proving the reliability of solar energy, heavy commercial aircraft are not expected to be sun-powered anytime soon. Part of the reason why the plane is able to fly without any fuel is that it was engineered to be extremely lightweight in comparison to typical jets. Piccard and Borschberg are also part of an advocacy campaign known as the Future Is Clean movement, which draws attention to the underlying goals of the Solar Impulse initiative. The campaign intends to encourage greater use of renewable energy worldwide, not only in aviation but also in many other fields. The Solar Impulse project's leadership attended the United Nations Climate Change Conference in November and December 2015 in Paris, France, to gain further traction for their efforts.

—Rebecca Adams

Following are three press releases issued by Solar Impulse on March 9, and July 3 and 15, 2015, documenting the first around-the-world solar-powered plane flight attempt.

Solar Plane Embarks on Around-the-World Flight Attempt

DOCUMENT

March 9, 2015

Under intense and watchful eyes, the Solar Impulse team in Abu Dhabi along with the Mission Control Center (MCC) in Monaco, witnessed Solar Impulse take-off this morning to reach Muscat (Oman), before crossing the Arabian Sea to Ahmedabad (India).

André Borschberg flew Si2 at 7:12 (GMT +4) on Monday, performing the first stage of the Round-The-World Flight using zero fuel. Piccard will take the reins in Oman and continue onward to Ahmedabad (India). Co-pilots Piccard and Borschberg will take turns flying the single-seater experimental solar aircraft which is able to fly with perpetual endurance.

It has taken twelve years for Bertrand Piccard (initiator and chairman) and André Borschberg (founder and CEO), to be able to finally attempt to make their dream a reality—demonstrating the importance of renewable energy conceived through a pioneering spirit and innovation.

Capable of flying over oceans for several days and nights in a row, Solar Impulse will travel 35,000 kilometers around the world in 25 days over the course of roughly 5 months. Si2 will pass over the Arabian Sea, India, Myanmar, China and the Pacific Ocean. After crossing the Atlantic Ocean, the final legs include a stop-over in Southern Europe or North Africa before completing the Round-The-World flight at its final destination in Abu Dhabi, Solar Impulse's official host city. During the 12 scheduled stops, the Solar Impulse team and its partners will organize public events for governments, schools and universities.

Solar Impulse is an ambitious scientific project, but for those passionate about exploration, this visionary journey is also a strong message for clean technologies. Supported by Prince Albert of Monaco, UAE Minister of State and Chairman of Masdar H.E. Dr. Sultan Al Jaber, Richard Branson and Al Gore, the #FutureIsClean initiative has been launched on www.solarimpulse.com to recruit the severely needed support for the adoption of clean technologies worldwide.

"We are very ambitious in our goal, but modest given the magnitude of the challenge. This is an attempt, and only time will tell if we can overcome the numerous weather, technical, human and administrative issues", said Bertrand Piccard and André Borschberg.

On the tarmac ahead of the take-off, His Excellency Dr. Sultan Al Jaber, UAE Minister of State and Chairman of Masdar, wished pilots Piccard and Borschberg a safe and successful journey.

"The historic day has finally arrived. After months of intense preparation and collaboration with Masdar, Solar Impulse 2 is ready to embark on its attempt to circumnavigate the world using only the sun's energy, demonstrating the power of clean technology. This journey is a moment of national pride for the United Arab Emirates, as Abu Dhabi helped the mission team prepare for success. Together, we inspired thousands of students and professionals across the country, and I'm confident that such community engagement initiatives will be replicated across the globe, capturing the hearts and imaginations of the world and reaching our collective goal of a cleaner future," said H.E. Dr. Sultan Al Jaber.

At approximately 10:00 am local time (GMT +4), Solar Impulse 2 will enter Omanian aerial space in the region of Al Ain at an altitude of approximately, 3,600 meters (12,000 ft.). Solar Impulse 2 will continue its ascension in the direction of Muscat reaching an altitude of approximately 5,800 meters (19,000 ft.). Once the aircraft reaches northern Muscat, André Borschberg will position the plane above the sea and loiter on a waiting pattern until traffic and weather conditions are suitable for landing. Solar Impulse 2's estimated arrival at Muscat International Airport is 7:00 pm local time (GMT +4).

Solar Impulse is an airborne laboratory, genuinely made from technological solutions developed by a multidisciplinary team of 80 specialists and more than a hundred partners and consultants. Si2 is the largest aircraft ever built with such a low weight, equivalent to that of a small car. With a wing covered by more than 17,000 solar cells greater than a Boeing 747, the plane can fly up to an altitude of 8,500 meters at speeds ranging from 50 to 100 km/h.

The two pioneers will be required to demonstrate extraordinary endurance under extreme conditions, living in a 3.8m3 non-pressurized cockpit, unheated, with external temperatures ranging from -40 to +40 degrees Celsius. Crossing the Pacific and Atlantic Oceans in 5 days and 5 nights will certainly represent the highlights of this adventure.

SOURCE: Solar Impulse. "Swiss explorers Bertrand Piccard and Andre Borschberg launch their attempt at flying Round-The-World in a solar-powered airplane. Their experimental aircraft, Solar Impulse 2 took-off this morning from Abu Dhabi." March 9, 2015. www.solarimpulse.com. Used with permission of Solar Impulse.

Solar Flight Reaches Hawaii after Five Days

DOCUMENT

July 3, 2015

The longest and most difficult leg of the Round the World Solar Flight attempted since last March by Swiss explorers Bertrand Piccard and André Borschberg ended successfully in Hawaii. At the controls of Solar Impulse 2, pilot André Borschberg landed safely in Hawaii after flying 117 hours and 52 minutes over the Pacific Ocean from Japan powered only by the sun.

A historic landing took place in Hawaii after a perilous nonstop flight for 5 days and 5 nights. With the sun rising this morning at 5:55 am local time Hawaii (15:55 GMT), Solar Impulse 2 touched down at the Kalaeloa Airport after traveling a distance of roughly 4480 miles (7'200 km). Pilot André Borschberg, also co-founder of Solar Impulse with Bertrand Piccard, broke the world records of distance and duration for solar aviation, as well as the world record for the longest solo flight ever (117: 52 hours and around 7'200 km). These world records will be ratified upon landing by the International Aeronautical Federation.

André endured many challenges requiring him to carefully maintain a balance between wearing an oxygen mask for long stretches of time during high altitude, getting enough rest and maximizing the energy levels of the plane, particularly during turbulent weather conditions. Successfully accomplishing this 8th leg by remaining airborne for 5 consecutive days and nights has now proven that the airplane's critical components perform exceptionally and that Solar Impulse's vision of reaching unlimited endurance without fuel, using solely the power of the sun, was not only a dream: perpetual flight is a reality.

"I feel exhilarated by this extraordinary journey. I have climbed the equivalent altitude of Mount Everest five times without much rest. The team at the Mission Control Center in Monaco (MCC) was my eyes and my ears. . . . The MCC was battling to give me the possibility to rest and recover, but also maximizing the aircraft's energy levels and sending me trajectories and flight strategies simulated by computer", said André Borschberg, "This success fully validates the vision that my partner Bertrand Piccard had after his round-the-world balloon flight to reach unlimited endurance in an airplane without fuel", he adds.

"What André has achieved is extraordinary from the perspective of a pilot. But furthermore, he has also led the technical team during the construction of this revolutionary prototype. It is not only a historic first in aviation it is also a historic first for renewable energies," said Bertrand Piccard, initiator of Solar Impulse, chairman and pilot.

Solar Impulse's bold mission of building a solar plane was created to demonstrate how pioneering spirit, innovation and clean technologies can change the world and to encourage people to save energy and promote the use of clean technologies globally. Departing from Abu Dhabi in March, the explorers are not on this endeavor for the sake of it, as mankind is facing a much bigger problem with pollution, depletion of natural resources and climate change. For Bertrand Piccard, the unprecedented accomplishment is to demonstrate that if technological solutions exist to fly a plane day and night without fuel—which has been successfully proven—then there is potential for these same efficient technologies to be used in our daily lives, and to achieve energy savings to reduce CO_2 emissions. To catapult this idea to the next level, Solar Impulse initiated the Future Is Clean campaign, calling on supporters to add their voice to the message on www.future isclean.org: a website serving as a petition to convince governments around the globe to implement the necessary clean technology solutions and help ensure that the United Nations' upcoming Conference on Climate Change (COP21) is successful in renewing the Kyoto protocol this December in Paris.

During a typical 24-hour flight cycle, the pilot rests eight times averaging between 5 and 20 minutes per day. This is possible only at lower altitudes when the oxygen mask is required to be worn. The pilot's daily intake is 2.4 kg (5.2 lbs) of food, 2.5 L (84.5 oz) of water, and 1 L (33.8 oz) of sports drink per day. His meals include a breakfast, a lunch prepared to be as similar as possible to home-made meals, and snacks including dried fruits and chocolate. The nutritional composition of the food will fluctuate with respect to altitudes and temperatures because the pilots require more energy when flying at higher altitudes—in spite of decreased appetites due to increased elevation. Borschberg performed yoga 30 to 45 minutes a day to stay fit and prevent any potential negative effects of immobility. Bertrand Piccard will fly to Phoenix for the next leg of the Round-The-World attempt before the mission continues onward to New York, Europe and Abu Dhabi where it all started.

SOURCE: Solar Impulse. "Record-breaking solar flight reaches Hawaii after 5 nights and days airborne without fuel. Unlimited endurance is now proven thanks to clean technology." July 3, 2015. www.solar impulse.com. Used with permission of Solar Impulse.

Damage to Solar Aircraft Delays Second Half of Flight to 2016

July 15, 2015

Despite the hard work of the Solar Impulse team to repair the batteries which overheated in the record breaking oceanic flight from Nagoya to Hawaii, the solar powered airplane of Bertrand Piccard and André Borschberg will stay in Hawaii until early spring 2016.

Following the longest and most difficult leg of the round-the-world journey which lasted 5 days and 5 nights (117 hours and 52 minutes), Solar Impulse will undergo maintenance repairs on the batteries due to damage brought about by overheating.

During the first ascent on day one of the flight from Nagoya to Hawaii, the battery temperature increased due to a high climb rate and an over-insulation of the gondolas. And while the Mission Team was monitoring this very closely during the flight, there was no way to decrease the temperature for the remaining duration as each daily cycle requires an ascent to 28'000 feet and descent for optimal energy management.

Overall the airplane performed very well during the flight. The damage to the batteries is not a technical failure or a weakness in the technology but rather an evaluation error in terms of the profile of the mission and the cooling design specifications of the batteries. The temperature of the batteries in a quick ascent / descent in tropical climates was not properly anticipated.

Irreversible damage to certain parts of the batteries will require repairs which will take several months. In parallel, the Solar Impulse engineering team will be studying various options for better cooling and heating processes for very long flights.

The University of Hawaii with the support of the Department of Transportation will host the airplane in its hangar at Kalaeloa airport. Post-maintenance check flights will start in 2016 to test the new battery heating and cooling systems. The round-the-world mission will resume early April from Hawaii to the USA West Coast. From there Solar Impulse will cross the USA to JFK in New York before making the Atlantic crossing to Europe and then returning the point of departure in Abu Dhabi.

Solar Impulse is attempting a historic first of flying around the world only on solar energy.

And while Solar Impulse has completed 8 legs, covering nearly half of the journey, setbacks are part of the challenges of a project which is pushing technological boundaries to the limits.

Solar Impulse will try to complete the first ever round-the-world solar flight in 2016 and this delay will in no way influence the overall objectives of this pioneering endeavour.

SOURCE: Solar Impulse. "Irreversible damage to overheated batteries in the Solar Impulse airplane pushes the second half of Round-the-World solar flight to April 2016." July 15, 2015. www.solarimpulse.com. Used with permission of Solar Impulse.

NASA Announces Successful Orbiting of Dwarf Planet

MARCH 6, JUNE 22, AND OCTOBER 26, 2015

In March 2015, National Aeronautics and Space Administration (NASA) scientists celebrated a new milestone in space exploration as the *Dawn* spacecraft became the first to orbit a dwarf planet. The mission had already achieved two other firsts—orbiting two extraterrestrial targets in one trip and orbiting a main-belt asteroid—before the spacecraft arrived at the dwarf planet Ceres, located in the main asteroid belt between Mars and Jupiter. The spacecraft has been collecting data about its targets since 2011, with the goal of advancing scientific understanding of how planets evolve and the conditions that shaped our early solar system. It will continue its mission through June 2016.

THE *DAWN* MISSION BEGINS

The *Dawn* mission is managed by NASA's Jet Propulsion Laboratory for the agency's Science Mission Directorate in Washington. It is part of the directorate's Discovery Program, which encompasses a series of lower-cost missions that require shorter development times and seek to enhance our understanding of the solar system by exploring planets, comets, and asteroids. *Dawn's* primary objective was to visit and extensively observe two protoplanets, which are large bodies of matter, orbiting the sun or a star, that are thought to be developing into new planets. By studying these bodies, scientists hoped to learn more about the characteristics, conditions, and processes that defined the first several million years of our solar system's existence and influenced the formation and evolution of planets. In particular, the mission focused on exploring the roles that size and water play in planetary evolution.

The team selected as its mission targets Vesta and Ceres—two of the largest protoplanets remaining intact since their formation and the two most massive bodies in the solar system's main asteroid belt. Ceres is also classified as a dwarf planet, which resembles small planets, but is unable to clear its orbital path to the extent that there are no other similarly-sized bodies in its space at roughly the same distance from the sun. Both were thought to have formed within the first fifteen million years of our solar system, before Jupiter's formation interrupted their growth, and to have evolved very differently over time. Vesta was thought to be more evolved and a drier protoplanet, while Ceres was thought to be primitive and wet. Scientists believed that by comparing the two, NASA would gain insights into the key factors controlling planetary evolution. Scientists hypothesized that Ceres may have a thin, permanent atmosphere—a distinguishing feature among minor planets— as well as active hydrological processes that create seasonal polar caps of water frost. If true, the latter would change scientists' previous understanding of Ceres's composition. Some also thought *Dawn* would find that Vesta had more strongly magnetized rocks than those found on Mars, which would alter existing theories about how and when dynamos—the molten metal cores that create planets' magnetic fields—arise, and have important implications for ongoing studies of Mercury, Earth, and Mars. Upon arriving at each protoplanet, *Dawn* would complete a series of near-circular, near-polar orbits at different altitudes to provide scientists with a variety of angles and vantage points for examining Vesta and Ceres' surfaces.

The *Dawn* spacecraft was designed as an orbiter about five feet long, four feet wide, and six feet high. It had solar arrays on either side that, when extended, gave the spacecraft a wingspan of about sixty-five feet. The solar panels provided power to *Dawn's* ion thruster, a newer, highly efficient propulsion system that was critical to fueling *Dawn's* long mission and ability to ultimately orbit two different bodies. The spacecraft weighed nearly 2,700 pounds, of which approximately 1,000 pounds were fuel. It launched on September 27, 2007, from Cape Canaveral Air Force Station in Florida, beginning its long journey to the asteroid belt.

First Stop: Vesta

Vesta was discovered by astronomer Heinrich Wilhelm Olbers in 1807 and was named for the Roman virgin goddess of home and hearth. At 326 miles in diameter, the protoplanet is approximately the length of Arizona and is the second most massive object in our solar system's asteroid belt. Prior to the *Dawn* mission, Vesta, which had yet to be explored, was mostly known only from a series of images taken by the Hubble Space Telescope. Geochemists carefully dissected and analyzed a series of meteorites, known as HED meteorites, which had fallen to Earth's crust and were believed to have originated from Vesta's crust. Scientists used their findings to develop a model of Vesta's composition and our solar system's evolution, and hoped *Dawn's* exploration would confirm their theories.

Dawn arrived at Vesta on July 16, 2011, and began orbiting the surface and capturing images at various distances. The images confirmed that Vesta was a dynamic terrestrial world, similar to other planets in the inner solar system. *Dawn* found a variety of surface mineral and rock patterns that enabled scientists to identify material that was once molten below Vesta's surface, and also discovered rocks that had been fused together when space debris crashed into the protoplanet. Many of the materials of which Vesta is comprised were found to be iron-rich and magnesium-rich minerals that are also found in Earth's volcanic rocks. *Dawn* also identified two giant craters from which scientists believe five percent of all meteorites found on Earth originated. At one of the craters, *Dawn* captured images of different bands of materials, which scientists will study to gain further insights into Vesta's earliest geological history. Additionally, *Dawn's* measurements showed that Vesta's temperature could be as high as 10 degrees Fahrenheit where the sun touched the surface and as low as −150 degrees Fahrenheit in shadowy parts, demonstrating how quickly the surface responded to temperature changes without any atmosphere to trap in heat. Chris Russell, a professor of geophysics and space physics at the University of California, Los Angeles, and the mission's principal investigator, noted that *Dawn* also confirmed the accuracy of the models developed from the HED meteorites. "We went to Vesta, and the first thing we did was show that the body the geochemists had predicted from the meteoritic evidence was the body that we found. That in turn validated the solar system model," he told Space.com. "I consider that an important legacy."

Dawn left its orbit around Vesta on September 5, 2012, continuing on its journey to Ceres. Carol Raymond, *Dawn* deputy principal investigator at the Jet Propulsion Lab, said that the spacecraft's nine months at Vesta has "enabled us to peel back the layers of mystery that have surrounded this giant asteroid since humankind first saw it as just a bright spot in the night sky," adding, "We are closing in on [its] secrets."

Onward to Ceres

Discovered by astronomer Father Giuseppe Piazzi in 1801, Ceres was the first object to be found in the solar system's asteroid belt. First classified as a planet and later as an asteroid, Ceres was officially designated as a dwarf planet in 2006 along with Pluto and Eris. It is named for the Roman goddess of agriculture and harvests and has an average diameter of 590 miles. Prior to the *Dawn* mission, scientists suspected that Ceres had more in common with the planets in the outer solar system. Previous observations suggested that Ceres contained large amounts of water ice beneath its surface—perhaps even more water than all the fresh water on Earth combined—and some scientists believe there may be, or may have been, a subsurface ocean on Ceres. Using the Herschel Space Observatory, in 2014, scientists found evidence of water vapor emitting from the planet's surface, which they hypothesized could either be coming from icy volcanoes or be the result of meteor strikes that exposed subsurface ice to space. These were just a few of the theories that NASA hoped to explore further with *Dawn*.

"At Ceres, we're basically finding the water," Russell told Space.com. "There's certainly a lot of water at Ceres; that suggests there were other bodies similar to Ceres that are not with us anymore but delivered their water to other places in the solar system. So we're learning more about the delivery of water, how water was gathered and maintained for 4.6 billion years out in the middle of the asteroid belt."

On March 6, 2015, at 7:39 a.m. EST, *Dawn* officially became the first spacecraft to orbit a dwarf planet, after traveling 3.1 billion miles over seven and a half years to reach Ceres. At 8:36 a.m., the Jet Propulsion Lab received a signal from the spacecraft indicating that it was "healthy and thrusting with its ion engine" and that it had entered Ceres's orbit as planned. "We feel exhilarated," said Russell. "We have much to do over the next year and a half, but we are now on station with ample reserves, and a robust plan to obtain our science objectives."

With orbit achieved, the mission began a series of phases which will guide *Dawn's* exploration of Ceres. The first phase was completed in April and May when the spacecraft took its first full look at Ceres from a distance of roughly 8,400 miles. The second phase occurred in June when Dawn surveyed Ceres for a second time at a lower altitude of approximately 2,700 miles. The third phase, known as the high-altitude mapping orbit, or HAMO, took place from August through mid-October, and involved capturing higher resolution and 3-D images of the surface from a distance of about 910 miles. The final phase is set to begin in mid-December, during which time *Dawn* will complete a low-altitude mapping orbit at a distance of 230 miles by gathering surface element data with gamma ray and neutron detectors and experimenting with the planet's gravity.

To date, *Dawn* has uncovered a number of interesting details about Ceres's composition and surface. Even before it reached the planet, *Dawn* took a series of photos early in 2015 that showed two bright spots inside a crater on Ceres's surface. These spots appeared to be unique from any other body in the solar system and suggested the presence of a highly reflective material, such as water ice or salt. Then in July, Dawn found evidence that the spots are emitting gaseous material into space, creating a localized atmosphere within the walls of the crater. The spots continue to be a subject of study for the mission.

Dawn also confirmed the presence of water vapor in Ceres's thin atmosphere. It captured images of numerous long, linear features on the surface whose cause is unknown, as well as a large mountain named "The Pyramid" that had a flat top and "strangely streaked flanks." Thus far, Dawn's observations have shown Ceres to be a relatively active world rather than an inert planet of rock and ice: Some areas are less densely cratered than others, suggesting certain geological processes may have erased some craters; others show signs that mud or slush may have once flowed over the surface.

Dawn will continue collecting images and other observations of Ceres through June 2016. The spacecraft is expected to remain in orbit once its fuel has run out, though its instruments will stop working.

—Linda Fecteau Grimm

Following is the statement released by NASA on March 6, 2015, announcing Dawn's *successful orbiting of a dwarf planet; and two press releases dated June 22 and October 26, 2015 on* Dawn's *continuing journey.*

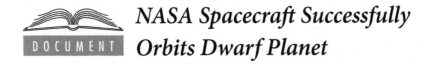

NASA Spacecraft Successfully Orbits Dwarf Planet

DOCUMENT

March 6, 2015

NASA's Dawn spacecraft has become the first mission to achieve orbit around a dwarf planet. The spacecraft was approximately 38,000 miles (61,000) kilometers from Ceres when it was captured by the dwarf planet's gravity at about 4:39 a.m. PST (7:39 a.m. EST) Friday.

Mission controllers at NASA's Jet Propulsion Laboratory (JPL) in Pasadena, California received a signal from the spacecraft at 5:36 a.m. PST (8:36 a.m. EST) that Dawn was healthy and thrusting with its ion engine, the indicator Dawn had entered orbit as planned.

"Since its discovery in 1801, Ceres was known as a planet, then an asteroid and later a dwarf planet," said Marc Rayman, Dawn chief engineer and mission director at JPL. "Now, after a journey of 3.1 billion miles (4.9 billion kilometers) and 7.5 years, Dawn calls Ceres, home."

In addition to being the first spacecraft to visit a dwarf planet, Dawn also has the distinction of being the first mission to orbit two extraterrestrial targets. From 2011 to 2012, the spacecraft explored the giant asteroid Vesta, delivering new insights and thousands of images from that distant world. Ceres and Vesta are the two most massive residents of our solar system's main asteroid belt between Mars and Jupiter.

The most recent images received from the spacecraft, taken on March 1 show Ceres as a crescent, mostly in shadow because the spacecraft's trajectory put it on a side of Ceres that faces away from the sun until mid-April. When Dawn emerges from Ceres' dark side, it will deliver ever-sharper images as it spirals to lower orbits around the planet.

"We feel exhilarated," said Chris Russell, principal investigator of the Dawn mission at the University of California, Los Angeles (UCLA). "We have much to do over the next year and a half, but we are now on station with ample reserves, and a robust plan to obtain our science objectives."

Dawn's mission is managed by JPL for NASA's Science Mission Directorate in Washington. Dawn is a project of the directorate's Discovery Program, managed by NASA's Marshall Space Flight Center in Huntsville, Alabama. UCLA is responsible for overall Dawn mission science. Orbital ATK Inc., in Dulles, Virginia, designed and built the spacecraft. The German Aerospace Center, Max Planck Institute for Solar System Research, Italian Space Agency and Italian National Astrophysical Institute are international partners on the mission team.

SOURCE: National Aeronautics and Space Administration. "NASA Spacecraft Becomes First to Orbit a Dwarf Planet." March 6, 2015. www.nasa.gov/press/2015/march/nasa-spacecraft-becomes-first-to-orbit-a-dwarf-planet.

Dawn Spacecraft Returns Bright Spot Images

June 22, 2015

The closer we get to Ceres, the more intriguing the distant dwarf planet becomes. New images of Ceres from NASA's Dawn spacecraft provide more clues about its mysterious bright spots, and also reveal a pyramid-shaped peak towering over a relatively flat landscape.

"The surface of Ceres has revealed many interesting and unique features. For example, icy moons in the outer solar system have craters with central pits, but on Ceres central pits in large craters are much more common. These and other features will allow us to understand the inner structure of Ceres that we cannot sense directly," said Carol Raymond, deputy principal investigator for the Dawn mission, based at NASA's Jet Propulsion Laboratory in Pasadena, California.

Dawn has been studying the dwarf planet in detail from its second mapping orbit, which is 2,700 miles (4,400 kilometers) above Ceres. A new view of its intriguing bright spots, located in a crater about 55 miles (90 kilometers) across, shows even more small spots in the crater than were previously visible.

At least eight spots can be seen next to the largest bright area, which scientists think is approximately 6 miles (9 kilometers) wide. A highly reflective material is responsible for these spots—ice and salt are leading possibilities, but scientists are considering other options, too.

Dawn's visible and infrared mapping spectrometer allows scientists to identify specific minerals present on Ceres by looking at how light is reflected. Each mineral reflects the range of visible and infrared-light wavelengths in a unique way, and this signature helps scientists determine the components of Ceres. So, as the spacecraft continues to send back more images and data, scientists will learn more about the mystery bright spots.

In addition to the bright spots, the latest images also show a mountain with steep slopes protruding from a relatively smooth area of the dwarf planet's surface. The structure rises about 3 miles (5 kilometers) above the surface.

Ceres also has numerous craters of varying sizes, many of which have central peaks. There is ample evidence of past activity on the surface, including flows, landslides and collapsed structures. It seems that Ceres shows more remnants of activity than the proto-planet Vesta, which Dawn studied intensively for 14 months in 2011 and 2012.

Dawn is the first mission to visit a dwarf planet, and the first to orbit two distinct targets in our solar system. It arrived at Ceres, the largest object in the main asteroid belt between Mars and Jupiter, on March 6, 2015.

Dawn will remain in its current altitude until June 30, continuing to take images and spectra of Ceres in orbits of about three days each. It then will move into its next orbit at an altitude of 900 miles (1,450 kilometers), arriving in early August.

Dawn's mission is managed by JPL for NASA's Science Mission Directorate in Washington. Dawn is a project of the directorate's Discovery Program, managed by NASA's Marshall Space Flight Center in Huntsville, Alabama. UCLA is responsible for overall Dawn mission science. Orbital ATK Inc., in Dulles, Virginia, designed and built the spacecraft. The German Aerospace Center, Max Planck Institute for Solar System Research, Italian Space Agency and Italian National Astrophysical Institute are international partners on the mission team.

SOURCE: National Aeronautics and Space Administration. "Ceres Spots Continue to Mystify in Latest Dawn Images." June 22, 2015. www.nasa.gov/jpl/dawn/ceres-spots-continue-to-mystify-in-latest-dawn-images.

DOCUMENT

Dawn Spacecraft Prepares for Final Orbit

October 26, 2015

NASA's Dawn spacecraft fired up its ion engine on Friday, Oct. 23, to begin its journey toward its fourth and final science orbit at dwarf planet Ceres. The spacecraft completed two months of observations from an altitude of 915 miles (1,470 kilometers) and transmitted extensive imagery and other data to Earth.

The spacecraft is now on its way to the final orbit of the mission, called the low-altitude mapping orbit. Dawn will spend more than seven weeks descending to this vantage point, which will be less than 235 miles (380 kilometers) from the surface of Ceres. In mid-December, Dawn will begin taking observations from this orbit, including images at a resolution of 120 feet (35 meters) per pixel.

Of particular interest to the Dawn team is Occator crater, home to Ceres' bright spots. A new mosaic of images from Dawn's third science orbit highlights the crater and surrounding terrain.

SOURCE: National Aeronautics and Space Administration. "Dawn Heads Toward Final Orbit." October 26, 2015. www.nasa.gov/feature/jpl/dawn-heads-toward-final-orbit.

OTHER HISTORIC DOCUMENTS OF INTEREST

FROM THIS VOLUME

- New Horizons Spacecraft Reaches Pluto, p. 384

FROM PREVIOUS *HISTORIC DOCUMENTS*

- NASA's Voyager 1 Reaches Interstellar Space, *2013*, p. 423
- NASA Rover Lands on Mars, *2012*, p. 373
- NASA on End of Space Shuttle Program, Future of U.S. Space Exploration, *2011*, p. 352

Indiana Governor Signs Religious Freedom Bill into Law and Approves Revisions

MARCH 26 AND APRIL 2, 2015

On March 26, 2015, Republican governor Mike Pence of Indiana signed into law the Religious Freedom Restoration Act (RFRA), an act that supporters said would protect those of any faith from being compelled by the state to provide services for same-sex weddings or similar events. Detractors said it had the potential to provide legal cover to businesses that choose to discriminate against the lesbian, gay, bisexual, and transgender (LGBT) community. Immediately after the RFRA was signed, criticism poured in and national organizations threatened to pull their business out of the state. Under intense pressure from groups around the country, the Indiana legislature passed a second bill in April aimed at clarifying the language in the RFRA, although it stopped short of specifically providing antidiscrimination protections for the LGBT community. Governor Pence quickly signed the clarifying bill.

CONGRESSIONAL DEBATE ON RELIGIOUS FREEDOM

In 1993, then-President Bill Clinton signed a federal RFRA into law to ensure "that interests in religious freedom are protected." In 1997, the U.S. Supreme Court ruled that the law did not apply to the states. Following the U.S. Supreme Court decision in 2014's *Burwell v. Hobby Lobby Stores, Inc.*, which offered for-profit corporations legal protections for their religious beliefs, a number of conservative governors sought to expand their existing RFRA laws to offer citizens protections similar to those under the federal RFRA, and some even sought to include for-profit entities.

In January 2015, Indiana Senate Republicans introduced Senate Bill 101, which they said had the primary intent of ensuring the state could not compel anyone to provide services in violation of their religious beliefs, and closely tracked similar laws in other states. Democrats, however, argued that such a bill could essentially provide legal coverage to those who discriminate against the LGBT community.

There are key differences between Indiana's law and both the federal language and the nineteen other state laws, which raised suspicion among detractors about the bill's ultimate intent. Specifically, Indiana's law gives for-profit businesses the ability to assert a right to "the free exercise of religion." South Carolina is the only other state to include such a statement in its RFRA, while Louisiana and Pennsylvania actually exclude for-profit businesses from RFRA protections. Additionally, the Indiana law says any that "person whose exercise of religion has been substantially burdened, or is likely to be substantially burdened, by a violation of this chapter may assert the violation or impending violation as a claim or defense in a judicial or administrative proceeding, regardless of whether the state or any other governmental entity is a party to the proceeding." This portion of the law equates for-profit corporations with individuals and churches, and allows businesses to use the statute for legal protection in a lawsuit brought by another person instead of one brought solely by the government. Only Texas has similar language in its legislation.

The final version of Senate Bill 101 passed the House on March 23 by a mainly party-line vote of 63–31, with only five Republicans joining the Democrats in opposition. Rep. Tom Washburne said that the RFRA was important to "allow our citizens to hold religious beliefs, maybe even those we might be appalled by, and to be able to express those." The RFRA passed the Senate on March 24 by a vote of 40–10, with Senate Minority Leader Tim Lanane calling the legislation "unnecessary" and said that it "portrayed our state as intolerant, unfriendly, and backwards." Governor Pence had already said that he would sign the bill once it reached his desk, saying that although Indiana's citizens already enjoyed similar protections under federal law, "many people of faith feel their religious liberty is under attack by government action."

Pence's signing event for Senate Bill 101 was closed to the public and press. With him were approximately seventy guests, including representatives of various religions supporting the bill and conservative lobbyists who had been behind the 2014 attempt to ban gay marriage in Indiana. With the governor's signature, the new law was set to take effect on July 1, and the state became the twentieth to adopt a bill modeled after the federal RFRA.

INDIANA BUSINESSES, POLITICIANS REACT

The outcry against the bill was swift, and the hashtag BoycottIndiana quickly began trending on social media. The weekend after the bill was signed, hundreds gathered at the statehouse in protest of the new law, some holding signs reading "No Hate in Our State" and "Pence Must Go." The signing of the religious freedom bill came just a week ahead of the NCAA men's basketball Final Four, which was slated to be held in Indianapolis. While noting that it would "work diligently" to ensure the athletes, staff, and spectators coming to the event would not be negatively impacted by the bill, NCAA president Mark Emmert said that the group was "especially concerned about how this legislation could affect our student-athletes and employees." Major organizations threatened to pull their annual conventions out of the state, including Gen Con LLC, one of the largest gamer conventions, and the Christian Church (Disciples of Christ). Salesforce, which was considering an expansion in the state, said it would now stop corporate travel into Indiana and would help move current employees out of Indiana.

Pence said that he "can't account for the hostility that's been directed at our state" by outside groups but said that there was a "tremendous amount of misinformation and misunderstanding" about what was included in the bill. He told ABC News's George Stephanopoulos, "Indiana steps forward to protect the constitutional rights and privileges of freedom of religion for people of faith and families of faith for people in our state and this avalanche of intolerance has been poured upon the people of our state."

REVISIONS MADE TO RELIGIOUS FREEDOM LAW

As the debate raged on, Pence said that he would not support the Democrats' attempt to write a new state law or amend the RFRA to include antidiscrimination protections for the LGBT community. Citing Democrats who had argued that the law gave too much power to for-profit corporations in private lawsuits, the governor noted, "This isn't about disputes between individuals, it's about government overreach." However, he did indicate a willingness to back the Republican-controlled legislature's attempt to clarify the law.

The Senate drafted its version of a revision bill days after Senate Bill 101 was signed. According to Senate President Pro Tem David Long, the revisions would "unequivocally state that Indiana's law does not and will not be able to discriminate against anyone, anywhere at any time." Congressional leaders drafted the bill behind closed doors with the governor's chief of staff and a group of business leaders. Many conservatives in the legislature did not find the fix necessary from a legal standpoint, but understood how perception could impact Indiana's economic climate.

At the same time, the House drafted its own fix to the bill, which quickly went to committee. The Democrats on the committee met privately to determine whether they would support the fix, which they had publicly noted did not go far enough to offer appropriate protections to the LGBT community. Republicans on the committee removed the Democrats and held a vote to send the measure to the floor without Democratic support. The bill passed the House 66–30 on April 2, and passed the Senate shortly after 34–16.

The governor immediately signed the Religious Freedom Restoration Act Clarification Bill into law. In a signing statement, Governor Pence said, "Over the past week this law has become a subject of great misunderstanding and controversy across our state and nation," and as such, the governor "called upon the Indiana General Assembly to clarify that this new judicial standard would not create a license to discriminate or to deny services to any individual as its critics have alleged." Now, he said, Hoosiers could rest assured that "the Religious Freedom Restoration Act enhances protections for every church, non-profit religious organization or society, religious school, rabbi, priest, preacher, minister or pastor in the review of government action where their religious liberty is infringed. The law also enhances protection in religious liberty cases for groups of individuals and businesses in conscience decisions that do not involve provision of goods and services, employment and housing." LGBT groups saw the revision as a necessary first step toward one day passing an antidiscrimination bill.

ARKANSAS LEARNS LESSONS FROM INDIANA

In Arkansas, the legislature passed a measure similar to Indiana's RFRA in late March. A variety of organizations and for-profit businesses, including the state's biggest corporation, Walmart, encouraged Governor Asa Hutchinson to veto the legislation. After seeing the ongoing outrage in Indiana, before signing any such bill Gov. Hutchinson asked the legislature to submit to him a version that would be more palatable to citizens, businesses, and civic groups. With bipartisan support, the Arkansas legislature was able to pass a revision on April 1, which the governor immediately signed. "The fact that it might not solve every problem for everyone probably means it's a good bill," Hutchinson said of the revision. "It does the three things that I outlined: It protects religious freedom. It establishes a balancing act that the courts must determine in these types of cases. And thirdly, I think it does recognize the diversity of our culture and our work force."

—Heather Kerrigan

Following is a statement from Indiana governor Mike Pence dated March 26, 2015, upon signing the Religious Freedom Restoration Act (RFRA); the text of the RFRA passed on March 26, 2015; and a statement from Gov. Pence, given April 2, 2015, clarifying the RFRA bill.

DOCUMENT

Governor Pence Statement Upon Signing Religious Freedom Law

March 26, 2015

Governor Mike Pence today issued the following statement after signing the Religious Freedom Restoration Act (SEA 101) in a private ceremony.

"Today I signed the Religious Freedom Restoration Act, because I support the freedom of religion for every Hoosier of every faith.

"The Constitution of the United States and the Indiana Constitution both provide strong recognition of the freedom of religion but today, many people of faith feel their religious liberty is under attack by government action.

"One need look no further than the recent litigation concerning the Affordable Care Act. A private business and our own University of Notre Dame had to file lawsuits challenging provisions that required them to offer insurance coverage in violation of their religious views.

"Fortunately, in the 1990s Congress passed, and President Clinton signed, the Religious Freedom Restoration Act—limiting government action that would infringe upon religion to only those that did not substantially burden free exercise of religion absent a compelling state interest and in the least restrictive means.

"Last year the Supreme Court of the United States upheld religious liberty in the Hobby Lobby case based on the federal Religious Freedom Restoration Act, but that act does not apply to individual states or local government action. At present, nineteen states—including our neighbors in Illinois and Kentucky—have adopted Religious Freedom Restoration statutes. And in eleven additional states, the courts have interpreted their constitutions to provide a heightened standard for reviewing government action.

"In order to ensure that religious liberty is fully protected under Indiana law, this year our General Assembly joined those 30 states and the federal government to enshrine these principles in Indiana law, and I fully support that action.

"This bill is not about discrimination, and if I thought it legalized discrimination in any way in Indiana, I would have vetoed it. In fact, it does not even apply to disputes between private parties unless government action is involved. For more than twenty years, the federal Religious Freedom Restoration Act has never undermined our nation's anti-discrimination laws, and it will not in Indiana.

"Indiana is rightly celebrated for the hospitality, generosity, tolerance, and values of our people, and that will never change. Faith and religion are important values to millions of Hoosiers and with the passage of this legislation, we ensure that Indiana will continue to be a place where we respect freedom of religion and make certain that government action will always be subject to the highest level of scrutiny that respects the religious beliefs of every Hoosier of every faith."

SOURCE: Office of the Governor of Indiana. "Governor Pence Issues Statement Regarding the Religious Freedom Restoration Act." March 26, 2015. www.in.gov/activecalendar/EventList.aspx?fromdate=3/26/2015&todate=3/26/2015&display=Day&type=public&eventid=214653&view=EventDetails&information_id=212489.

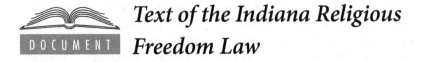

Text of the Indiana Religious Freedom Law

March 26, 2015

SENATE ENROLLED ACT No. 101

AN ACT to amend the Indiana Code concerning civil procedure.

Be it enacted by the General Assembly of the State of Indiana:

SECTION1.IC34-13-9 IS ADDED TO THE INDIANA CODE AS A NEW CHAPTER TO READ AS FOLLOWS [EFFECTIVE JULY 1, 2015]:

Chapter 9. Religious Freedom Restoration

Sec. 1. This chapter applies to all governmental entity statutes, ordinances, resolutions, executive or administrative orders, regulations, customs, and usages, including the implementation or application thereof, regardless of whether they were enacted, adopted, or initiated before, on, or after July 1, 2015.

Sec. 2. A governmental entity statute, ordinance, resolution, executive or administrative order, regulation, custom, or usage may not be construed to be exempt from the application of this chapter unless a state statute expressly exempts the statute, ordinance, resolution, executive or administrative order, regulation, custom, or usage from the application of this chapter by citation to this chapter.

Sec. 3. (a) The following definitions apply throughout this section: (1) "Establishment Clause" refers to the part of the First Amendment of the Constitution of the United States or the Constitution of the State of Indiana prohibiting laws respecting the establishment of religion. (2) "Granting", used with respect to government funding, benefits, or exemptions, does not include the denial of government funding, benefits, or exemptions. (b) This chapter may not be construed to affect, interpret, or in any way address the Establishment Clause. (c) Granting government funding, benefits, or exemptions, to the extent permissible under the Establishment Clause, does not constitute a violation of this chapter.

Sec. 4. As used in this chapter, "demonstrates" means meets the burdens of going forward with the evidence and of persuasion.

Sec. 5. As used in this chapter, "exercise of religion" includes any exercise of religion, whether or not compelled by, or central to, a system of religious belief.

Sec. 6. As used in this chapter, "governmental entity" includes the whole or any part of a branch, department, agency, instrumentality, official, or other individual or entity acting under color of law of any of the following: (1) State government. (2) A political subdivision (as defined in IC 36-1-2-13). (3) An instrumentality of a governmental entity described in subdivision (1) or (2), including a state educational institution, a body politic, a body corporate and politic, or any other similar entity established by law.

Sec. 7. As used in this chapter, "person" includes the following: (1) An individual. (2) An organization, a religious society, a church, a body of communicants, or a group organized and operated primarily for religious purposes. (3) A partnership, a limited liability company, a corporation, a company, a firm, a society, a joint-stock company, an unincorporated association, or another entity that: (A) may sue and be sued; and (B) exercises practices that are compelled or limited by a system of religious belief held by: (i) an individual; or (ii) the individuals; who have control and substantial ownership of the entity, regardless of whether the entity is organized and operated for profit or nonprofit purposes.

Sec. 8. (a) Except as provided in subsection (b), a governmental entity may not substantially burden a person's exercise of religion, even if the burden results from a rule of general applicability. (b) A governmental entity may substantially burden a person's exercise of religion only if the governmental entity demonstrates that application of the burden to the person: (1) is in furtherance of a compelling governmental interest; and (2) is the least restrictive means of furthering that compelling governmental interest.

Sec. 9. A person whose exercise of religion has been substantially burdened, or is likely to be substantially burdened, by a violation of this chapter may assert the violation or impending violation as a claim or defense in a judicial or administrative proceeding, regardless of whether the state or any other governmental entity is a party to the proceeding. If the relevant governmental entity is not a party to the proceeding, the governmental entity has an unconditional right to intervene in order to respond to the person's invocation of this chapter.

Sec. 10. (a) If a court or other tribunal in which a violation of this chapter is asserted in conformity with section 9 of this chapter determines that: (1) the person's exercise of religion has been substantially burdened, or is likely to be substantially burdened; and (2) the governmental entity imposing the burden has not demonstrated that application of the burden to the person: (A) is in furtherance of a compelling governmental interest; and (B) is the least restrictive means of furthering that compelling governmental interest; the court or other tribunal shall allow a defense against any party and shall grant appropriate relief against the governmental entity. (b) Relief against the governmental entity may include any of the following: (1) Declaratory relief or an injunction or mandate that prevents, restrains, corrects, or abates the violation of this chapter. (2) Compensatory damages. (c) In the appropriate case, the court or other tribunal also may award all or part of the costs of litigation, including reasonable attorney's fees, to a person that prevails against the governmental entity under this chapter.

Sec. 11. This chapter is not intended to, and shall not be construed or interpreted to, create a claim or private cause of action against any private employer by any applicant, employee, or former employee.

SOURCE: Indiana Senate. "Senate Enrolled Act No. 101." March 26, 2015. https://iga.in.gov/static-documents/9/2/b/a/92bab197/SB0101.05.ENRS.pdf.

Governor Pence Signs RFRA Clarification Bill

April 2, 2015

"The freedom of religion for every Hoosier is enshrined in the Constitution of the United States and in the Indiana Constitution, which reads, 'No law shall, in any case whatever, control the free exercise and enjoyment of religious opinions, or interfere with the rights of conscience.' For generations, these protections have served as a bulwark of religious liberty for Hoosiers and remain a foundation of religious liberty in the State of Indiana, and that will not change.

"Last week the Indiana General Assembly passed the Religious Freedom Restoration Act raising the judicial standard that would be used when government action intrudes upon the religious liberty of Hoosiers, and I was pleased to sign it.

"Over the past week this law has become a subject of great misunderstanding and controversy across our state and nation. However we got here, we are where we are, and it is important that our state take action to address the concerns that have been raised and move forward.

"Last weekend I called upon the Indiana General Assembly to clarify that this new judicial standard would not create a license to discriminate or to deny services to any individual as its critics have alleged. I am grateful for the efforts of legislators, business and other community leaders who came together to forge this clarifying language in the law.

"Hoosiers deserve to know, that even with this legislation, the Religious Freedom Restoration Act enhances protections for every church, non-profit religious organization or society, religious school, rabbi, priest, preacher, minister or pastor in the review of government action where their religious liberty is infringed. The law also enhances protection in religious liberty cases for groups of individuals and businesses in conscience decisions that do not involve provision of goods and services, employment and housing.

"In the midst of this furious debate, I have prayed earnestly for wisdom and compassion, and I have felt the prayers of people across this state and across this nation. For that I will be forever grateful.

"There will be some who think this legislation goes too far and some who think it does not go far enough, but as governor I must always put the interest of our state first and ask myself every day, 'What is best for Indiana?' I believe resolving this controversy and making clear that every person feels welcome and respected in our state is best for Indiana.

"Our state is rightly celebrated for our pro-business environment, and we enjoy an international reputation for the hospitality, generosity, tolerance and kindness of our people. Hoosier hospitality is not a slogan; it is our way of life. Now that this is behind us, let's move forward together with a renewed commitment to the civility and respect that make this state great."

SOURCE: Office of the Governor of Indiana. "Governor Pence Signs Religious Freedom Restoration Act Clarification Bill; Pence: 'Resolving this controversy, making clear that every person feels welcome and respected in our state is best for IN.'" April 2, 2015. www.in.gov/activecalendar/EventList.aspx?fromdate=7/1/2015&todate=7/31/2015&display=Month&type=public&eventidn=215938&view=EventDetails&information_id=212917&print=print.

OTHER HISTORIC DOCUMENTS OF INTEREST

April

California Governor Declares State of Emergency and Encourages Water Conservation

APRIL 1 AND JULY 31, 2015

Throughout 2015, California continued exploring new solutions to overcoming its greatest environmental challenge: a worsening drought. In April, Governor Jerry Brown issued an executive order that mandated water savings of 25 percent at the residential and urban levels, forcing California citizens to undertake a number of measures—from replacing lawns with drought-tolerant landscapes and reducing shower times—to avoid warnings and fines. The state was able to meet its overall conservation goal throughout the summer months; however, the widespread dry conditions created a secondary problem, the threat of wildfires.

Governor Brown Declares State of Emergency

In January 2014, Governor Brown declared a state of emergency and called on all officials to take any means necessary to make emergency water supplies available and conserve where necessary. The 2014 declaration called on the State Water Resources Control Board to work with suppliers to make water transfer more efficient, encouraged the Department of Water Resources to accelerate funding for projects that would increase water supplies, gave notice to water rights holders that they might be asked to reduce or end water diversions, and required the consideration of modifications made to requirements for releasing water from reservoirs to ensure enough cold water is left for salmon while subsequently improving water quality and conserving supply. By July, the state Water Board voted to approve fines for wasteful water usage. Felicia Marcus, chair of the Water Board, defended the move, saying that the state was in an unprecedented time of drought and that "we don't know when it's going to rain again, . . . this is a dramatic action, but these are dramatic times." By summer 2014, 70,000 warnings and 20,000 penalties had been issued by state water resource agencies for overuse. Fines varied, but most amounted to a few hundred dollars or less. A majority of warnings and penalties were handed out after a neighbor or passerby called to report excessive water use.

Additional drought-related executive orders were issued in April and December 2014, both of which called on the state to increase its efforts to reduce the impact of the drought and to extend the drought declaration into mid-2016. Executive Order B-29-15, issued on April 1, 2015, added new efforts to drought reduction policies. Specifically, the state Water Board was called on to develop restrictions on potable urban water usage that would reduce use by 25 percent. It also called on the Department of Water Resources to work with local agencies to replace 50 million square feet of lawns and ornamental turf with more drought tolerant landscapes. The California Energy Commission was also given approval for a statewide rebate program for residents who agreed to replace old, energy-inefficient appliances.

CRACKDOWN ON PERSONAL WATER USE CONTINUES

As California entered its fourth year of severe drought that continued to worsen, and also faced a snowpack that usually supplies one third of the state's water at its lowest levels, on April 1, 2015, Governor Brown's executive order implemented mandatory water usage cutbacks of 25 percent for residents and businesses, marking the first compulsory reduction in state history. The 411 California water districts were permitted to develop their own enforcement and conservation techniques to ensure an average 25 percent savings in their communities. In some areas, this meant drought surcharges assessed to homeowners who exceeded a monthly allotment of water. Such enforcement policies affected Californians differently. For example, the top ten residential water users in Los Angeles collectively consumed 80 million gallons of water in a year—the equivalent of ninety families-worth of use—but were not fined, primarily because less affluent families cut back enough to help the city meet its water conservation goal.

The strict crackdown on personal water use was the strongest response to drought the state had ever undertaken. Even during widespread severe drought in the 1970s and 1980s, residents were simply encouraged to conserve water, but no enforcement mechanism was put in place. The governor's policies, however, appeared to be in line with public opinion on the severity of the situation. A poll conducted by the Public Policy Institute of California in March 2015 showed that of those surveyed, concern about the ongoing drought matched concern about the economy.

For the first time, in October 2015, the state began fining California water suppliers who were not hitting their 25 percent conservation goal. Fines were distributed despite the fact that the state as a whole hit and exceeded its 25 percent goal in June to December. "Millions of Californians have saved water during the summer months, which are the four most critical months to save water," Marcus said, adding that individuals and water agencies alike needed to keep up the hard work throughout the fall and winter. The first water suppliers to receive $61,000 fines included Beverly Hills, Indio, Redlands, and Coachella Valley.

A number of groups questioned the state's reliance on cutbacks in personal water use as a primary component of its drought policy. Residential and urban water districts make up 20 percent of water usage in the state, while agriculture, which accounts for 80 percent, was not included in the governor's renewed push for water conservation. The governor argued that he was not including farmers in the 25 percent reduction because they had already been impacted deeply by the reduction of water released from state reservoirs during the years of drought, forcing them to plant fewer fields each year.

Encouraging residents to save so much water has a hidden downside. When residents and businesses consume less, water agencies sell less, and thus generate lower revenue. What this means is that to make up budget shortfalls, agencies turn to funds that would have been used to upgrade or replace aging and failing infrastructure. Instead, they need that money now to keep running water processing facilities and pay staff. In response, some districts began implementing surcharges on each gallon of water to help cover the shortfall.

In addition to asking residents to conserve personal water usage in any way possible, the state of California encouraged creativity in response to the drought. One method that gained nationwide attention was the use of millions of black rubber balls to prevent water evaporation. A total of nearly 96 million balls were placed on top of the Los Angeles reservoir in August. The balls were part of a $34.5 million water quality project launched by the city in response to Environmental Protection Agency (EPA) mandates that reservoirs be covered in some fashion. This was not the first time the city deployed the black rubber balls, and the current batch was expected to save 300 million gallons of water per year.

DROUGHT BREEDS WILDFIRES; WEATHER PATTERN BRINGS POSSIBLE RELIEF

The dry conditions around the state were the catalyst for wildfires that spread primarily across Northern California. As of the end of November, more than 6,000 wildfires had been recorded and more than 300,000 acres had been burned. Massive mandatory evacuations were enacted, with an estimated 23,000 residents forced to flee their homes. Governor Brown declared a state of emergency in September in Amador, Lake, Napa, and Calaveras counties in the northern half of the state. On September 21, Governor Brown requested a presidential major disaster declaration for California following the Valley and Butte fires, which would allow for the release of federal funds to help with disaster recovery efforts. The day after the request was submitted, it was approved and the Federal Emergency Management Agency (FEMA) began disbursement of funds and assistance.

The Valley and Butte fires were among the worst and costliest in state history, with an economic impact totaling more than $2 billion. The two fires claimed five lives and destroyed more than 1,400 homes. Most of the fires had been extinguished or contained by early October by the 10,000 firefighters who were spread out across the fires. California was not alone in its severe fire season. A large portion of the Western United States was impacted, with nearly nine million acres destroyed by the end of September, compared with three million acres the year before. Governor Brown called the wildfires a "wake-up call" and "a new normal." He added, "We're going to get ready. We have resources, we'll need more, but you can be sure that the California firefighting personnel and all their different departments are ready and we're going to do everything we possibly can."

In November, the California Department of Water Resources announced the likelihood that the state would be hit by a strong El Niño event during the winter. This came on the heels of an announcement by the U.S. drought monitor that the Sierra Nevada snowpack, which supplies a significant portion of California's water supply, was above normal. Even so, caution was urged, and the Department of Water Resources stated that it would be unlikely that the snowpack, increased rainfall, and lower temperatures would erase the four-year drought. According to the department, "Based on past drought-busting years, precipitation would need to be about 120% of average—about 60 inches—in key Northern California watersheds." Above-average rainfall might have downsides for California, because it can cause flooding and mudslides.

—Heather Kerrigan

Following is an executive order given on April 1, 2015, calling for mandatory cutbacks in personal water use; and a statement from the office of California governor Jerry Brown, issued on July 31, 2015, declaring a state of emergency in response to widespread wildfires in Northern California.

Governor Brown Issues Executive Order on Water Conservation

April 1, 2015

Executive Order B-29-15

WHEREAS on January 17, 2014, proclaimed a State of Emergency to exist throughout the State of California due to severe drought conditions; and

WHEREAS on April 25, 2014, proclaimed a Continued State of Emergency to exist throughout the State of California due to the ongoing drought; and

WHEREAS California's water supplies continue to be severely depleted despite a limited amount of rain and snowfall this winter, with record low snowpack in the Sierra Nevada mountains, decreased water levels in most of California's reservoirs, reduced flows in the state's rivers and shrinking supplies in underground water basins; and

WHEREAS the severe drought conditions continue to present urgent challenges including: drinking water shortages in communities across the state, diminished water for agricultural production, degraded habitat for many fish and wildlife species, increased wildfire risk, and the threat of saltwater contamination to fresh water supplies in the Sacramento–San Joaquin Bay Delta; and

WHEREAS a distinct possibility exists that the current drought will stretch into a fifth straight year in 2016 and beyond; and

WHEREAS new expedited actions are needed to reduce the harmful impacts from water shortages and other impacts of the drought; and

WHEREAS the magnitude of the severe drought conditions continues to present threats beyond the control of the services, personnel, equipment, and facilities of any single local government and require the combined forces of a mutual aid region or regions to combat; and

WHEREAS under the provisions of section 8558(b) of the Government Code, find that conditions of extreme peril to the safety of persons and property continue to exist in California due to water shortage and drought conditions with which local authority is unable to cope; and

WHEREAS under the provisions of section 8571 of the California Government Code, I find that strict compliance with various statutes and regulations specified in this order would prevent, hinder, or delay the mitigation of the effects of the drought.

NOW, THEREFORE, I, EDMUND G. BROWN JR., Governor of the State of California, in accordance with the authority vested in me by the Constitution and statutes of the State of California, in particular Government Code sections 8567 and 8571 of the California Government Code, do hereby issue this Executive Order, effective immediately.

IT IS HEREBY ORDERED THAT:

1. The orders and provisions contained in my January 17, 2014 Proclamation, my April 25, 2014 Proclamation, and Executive Orders and remain in full force and effect except as modified herein.

SAVE WATER

2. The State Water Resources Control Board (Water Board) shall impose restrictions to achieve a statewide 25% reduction in potable urban water usage through February 28, 2016. These restrictions will require water suppliers to California's cities and towns to reduce usage as compared to the amount used in 2013. These restrictions should consider the relative per capita water usage of each water suppliers' service area, and require that those areas with high per capita use achieve proportionally greater reductions than those with low use. The California Public Utilities Commission is requested to take similar action with respect to investor-owned utilities providing water services.

3. The Department of Water Resources (the Department) shall lead a statewide initiative, in partnership with local agencies, to collectively replace 50 million square feet of lawns and ornamental turf with drought tolerant landscapes. The Department shall provide funding to allow for lawn replacement programs in underserved communities, which will complement local programs already underway across the state.

4. The California Energy Commission, jointly with the Department and the Water Board, shall implement a time-limited statewide appliance rebate program to provide monetary incentives for the replacement of inefficient household devices.

5. The Water Board shall impose restrictions to require that commercial, industrial, and institutional properties, such as campuses, golf courses, and cemeteries, immediately implement water efficiency measures to reduce potable water usage in an amount consistent with the reduction targets mandated by Directive 2 of this Executive Order.

6. The Water Board shall prohibit irrigation with potable water of ornamental turf on public street medians.

7. The Water Board shall prohibit irrigation with potable water outside of newly constructed homes and buildings that is not delivered by drip or microspray systems.

8. The Water Board shall direct urban water suppliers to develop rate structures and other pricing mechanisms, including but not limited to surcharges, fees, and penalties, to maximize water conservation consistent with statewide water restrictions. The Water Board is directed to adopt emergency regulations, as it deems necessary, pursuant to Water Code section 1058.5 to implement this directive. The Water Board is further directed to work with state agencies and water suppliers to identify mechanisms that would encourage and facilitate the adoption of rate structures and other pricing mechanisms that promote water conservation. The California Public Utilities Commission is requested to take similar action with respect to investor-owned utilities providing water services.

INCREASE ENFORCEMENT AGAINST WATER WASTE

9. The Water Board shall require urban water suppliers to provide information on water usage, conservation, and enforcement on a permanent basis.

10. The Water Board shall require frequent reporting of water diversion and use by water right holders, conduct inspections to determine whether illegal diversions or wasteful and unreasonable use of water are occurring, and bring enforcement actions against illegal diverters and those engaging in the wasteful and unreasonable use of water. Pursuant to Government Code sections 8570 and 8627, the Water Board is granted authority to inspect property or diversion facilities to ascertain compliance with water rights laws and regulations where there is cause to believe such laws and regulations have been violated. When access is not granted by a property owner, the Water Board may obtain an inspection warrant pursuant to the procedures set forth in Title 13 (commencing with section 1822.50) of Part 3 of the Code of Civil Procedure for the purposes of conducting an inspection pursuant to this directive.

11. The Department shall update the State Model Water Efficient Landscape Ordinance through expedited regulation. This updated Ordinance shall increase water efficiency standards for new and existing landscapes through more efficient irrigation systems, greywater usage, onsite storm water capture, and by limiting the portion of landscapes that can be covered in turf. It will also require reporting on the implementation and enforcement of local ordinances, with required reports due by December 31, 2015. The Department shall provide information on local compliance to the Water Board, which shall consider adopting regulations or taking appropriate enforcement actions to promote compliance. The Department shall provide technical assistance and give priority in grant funding to public agencies for actions necessary to comply with local ordinances.

12. Agricultural water suppliers that supply water to more than 25,000 acres shall include in their required 2015 Agricultural Water Management Plans a detailed drought management plan that describes the actions and measures the supplier will take to manage water demand during drought. The Department shall require those plans to include quantification of water supplies and demands for 2013, 2014, and 2015 to the extent data is available. The Department will provide technical assistance to water suppliers in preparing the plans.

13. Agricultural water suppliers that supply water to 10,000 to 25,000 acres of irrigated lands shall develop Agricultural Water Management Plans and submit the plans to the Department by July 1, 2016. These plans shall include a detailed drought management plan and quantification of water supplies and demands in 2013, 2014, and 2015, to the extent that data is available. The Department shall give priority in grant funding to agricultural water suppliers that supply water to 10,000 to 25,000 acres of land for development and implementation of Agricultural Water Management Plans.

14. The Department shall report to Water Board on the status of the Agricultural Water Management Plan submittals within one month of receipt of those reports.

15. Local water agencies in high and medium priority groundwater basins shall immediately implement all requirements of the California Statewide Groundwater Elevation Monitoring Program pursuant to Water Code section 10933. The Department shall refer noncompliant local water agencies within high and medium priority groundwater basins to the Water Board by December 31, 2015,

which shall consider adopting regulations or taking appropriate enforcement to promote compliance.

16. The California Energy Commission shall adopt emergency regulations establishing standards that improve the efficiency of water appliances, including toilets, urinals, and faucets available for sale and installation in new and existing buildings.

INVEST IN NEW TECHNOLOGIES

17. The California Energy Commission, jointly with the Department and the Water Board, shall implement a Water Energy Technology (WET) program to deploy innovative water management technologies for businesses, residents, industries, and agriculture. This program will achieve water and energy savings and greenhouse gas reductions by accelerating use of cutting-edge technologies such as renewable energy-powered desalination, integrated on-site reuse systems, water-use monitoring software, irrigation system timing and precision technology, and on-farm precision technology.

STREAMLINE GOVERNMENT RESPONSE

18. The Office of Emergency Services and the Department of Housing and Community Development shall work jointly with counties to provide temporary assistance for persons moving from housing units due to a lack of potable water who are served by a private well or water utility with less than 15 connections, and where all reasonable attempts to find a potable water source have been exhausted.

19. State permitting agencies shall prioritize review and approval of water infrastructure projects and programs that increase local water supplies, including water recycling facilities, reservoir improvement projects, surface water treatment plants, desalination plants, storm water capture, and grey water systems. Agencies shall report to the Governor's Office on applications that have been pending for longer than 90 days.

20. The Department shall take actions required to plan and, if necessary, implement Emergency Drought Salinity Barriers in coordination and consultation with the Water Board and the Department of Fish and Wildlife at locations within the Sacramento–San Joaquin delta estuary. These barriers will be designed to conserve water for use later in the year to meet state and federal Endangered Species Act requirements, preserve to the extent possible water quality in the Delta, and retain water supply for essential human health and safety uses in 2015 and in the future.

21. The Water Board and the Department of Fish and Wildlife shall immediately consider any necessary regulatory approvals for the purpose of installation of the Emergency Drought Salinity Barriers.

22. The Department shall immediately consider voluntary crop idling water transfer and water exchange proposals of one year or less in duration that are initiated by local public agencies and approved in 2015 by the Department subject to the criteria set forth in Water Code section 1810.

23. The Water Board will prioritize new and amended safe drinking water permits that enhance water supply and reliability for community water systems facing water shortages or that expand service connections to include existing residences facing water shortages. As the Department of Public Health's drinking water program was transferred to the Water Board, any reference to the Department of Public Health in any prior Proclamation or Executive Order listed in Paragraph 1 is deemed to refer to the Water Board.

24. The California Department of Forestry and Fire Protection shall launch a public information campaign to educate the public on actions they can take to help to prevent wildfires including the proper treatment of dead and dying trees. Pursuant to Government Code section 8645, $1.2 million from the State Responsibility Area Fire Prevention Fund (Fund 3063) shall be allocated to the California Department of Forestry and Fire Protection to carry out this directive.

25. The Energy Commission shall expedite the processing of all applications or petitions for amendments to power plant certifications issued by the Energy Commission for the purpose of securing alternate water supply necessary for continued power plant operation. Title 20, section 1769 of the California Code of Regulations is hereby waived for any such petition, and the Energy Commission is authorized to create and implement an alternative process to consider such petitions. This process may delegate amendment approval authority, as appropriate, to the Energy Commission Executive Director. The Energy Commission shall give timely notice to all relevant local, regional, and state agencies of any petition subject to this directive, and shall post on its website any such petition.

26. For purposes of carrying out directives 2-9, 11, 16-17, 20-23, and 25, Division 13 (commencing with section 21000) of the Public Resources Code and regulations adopted pursuant to that Division are hereby suspended. This suspension applies to any actions taken by state agencies, and for actions taken by local agencies where the state agency with primary responsibility for implementing the directive concurs that local action is required, as well as for any necessary permits or approvals required to complete these actions. This suspension, and those specified in paragraph 9 of the January 17, 2014 Proclamation, paragraph 19 of the April 25, 2014 proclamation, and paragraph 4 of Executive Order B-28-14, shall remain in effect until May 31, 2016. Drought relief actions taken pursuant to these paragraphs that are started prior to May 31, 2016, but not completed, shall not be subject to Division 13 (commencing with section 21000) of the Public Resources Code for the time required to complete them.

27. For purposes of carrying out directives 20 and 21, section 13247 and Chapter 3 of Part 3 (commencing with section 85225) of the Water Code are suspended.

28. For actions called for in this proclamation in directive 20, the Department shall exercise any authority vested in the Central Valley Flood Protection Board, as codified in Water Code section 8521, et seq., that is necessary to enable these urgent actions to be taken more quickly than otherwise possible. The Director of the Department of Water Resources is specifically authorized, on behalf of the State of California, to request that the Secretary of the Army, on the recommendation of the Chief of Engineers of the Army Corps of Engineers, grant any permission

required pursuant to section 14 of the Rivers and Harbors Act of 1899 and codified in section 48 of title 33 of the United States Code.

29. The Department is directed to enter into agreements with landowners for the purposes of planning and installation of the Emergency Drought Barriers in 2015 to the extent necessary to accommodate access to barrier locations, land-side and water-side construction, and materials staging in proximity to barrier locations. Where the Department is unable to reach an agreement with landowners, the Department may exercise the full authority of Government Code section 8572.

30. For purposes of this Executive Order, chapter 3.5 (commencing with section 11340) of part 1 of division 3 of the Government Code and chapter 5 (commencing with section 25400) of division 15 of the Public Resources Code are suspended for the development and adoption of regulations or guidelines needed to carry out the provisions in this Order. Any entity issuing regulations or guidelines pursuant to this directive shall conduct a public meeting on the regulations and guidelines prior to adopting them.

31. In order to ensure that equipment and services necessary for drought response can be procured quickly, the provisions of the Government Code and the Public Contract Code applicable to state contracts, including, but not limited to, advertising and competitive bidding requirements, are hereby suspended for directives 17, 20, and 24. Approval by the Department of Finance is required prior to the execution of any contract entered into pursuant to these directives.

This Executive Order is not intended to, and does not, create any rights or benefits, substantive or procedural, enforceable at law or in equity, against the State of California, its agencies, departments, entities, officers, employees, or any other person.

I FURTHER DIRECT that as soon as hereafter possible, this Order be filed in the Office of the Secretary of State and that widespread publicity and notice be given to this Order.

IN WITNESS WHEREOF

I have hereunto set my hand and caused the Great Seal of the State of California to be affixed this 1st day of April 2015.

EDMUND G. BROWN JR.
Governor of California

ATTEST:
ALEX PADILLA
Secretary of State

Source: Office of the Governor of California. "Executive Order B-29-15." April 1, 2015. http://www .gov.ca.gov/docs/4.1.15_Executive_Order.pdf.

Governor Brown Declares State of Emergency

July 31, 2015

With wildfires burning across the state—exacerbated by severe drought conditions and extreme weather—Governor Edmund G. Brown Jr. today declared a state of emergency in California to help mobilize additional firefighting and disaster response resources.

"California's severe drought and extreme weather have turned much of the state into a tinderbox," said Governor Brown. "Our courageous firefighters are on the front lines and we'll do everything we can to help them."

The full text of the proclamation is below:

PROCLAMATION OF A STATE OF EMERGENCY

WHEREAS since June 17, 2015, a series of wildfires has started in the Counties of Butte, El Dorado, Humboldt, Lake, Madera, Napa, Nevada, Sacramento, San Bernardino, San Diego, Shasta, Solano, Tulare, Tuolumne, and Yolo. These fires have burned thousands of acres of land and continue to burn; and

WHEREAS these fires have destroyed structures and continue to threaten hundreds of homes, necessitating the evacuation of residents; and

WHEREAS the fires have damaged and continue to threaten critical infrastructure and have forced the closure of major highways and local roads; and

WHEREAS on January 17, 2014, I declared a State of Emergency based on the extreme drought that has now persisted in the State for four years; and

WHEREAS the drought conditions have increased the State's risk of wildfires, caused millions of trees to die, and increased the severity and spread of the fires throughout the State; and

WHEREAS extreme weather conditions, lightning storms, and high temperatures have increased the risk and severity of fires throughout the State; and

WHEREAS as a result of the numerous fires burning throughout the State, combined with the drought conditions, California's air quality has significantly deteriorated and impacted public health; and

WHEREAS Federal Fire Management Assistance Grants have been requested and approved for the Wragg Fire burning in the Counties of Napa, Solano, and Yolo and for the North Fire burning in the County of San Bernardino; and

WHEREAS by virtue of the number of fires burning simultaneously, the State's resources have been significantly committed such that the State will seek the assistance and resources of other states, as necessary, pursuant to the Emergency Management Assistance Compact, Public Law 104-321, and sections 179 through 179.9 of the California Government Code; and

WHEREAS the circumstances of these wildfires, by reason of their magnitude, are or are likely to be beyond the control of the services, personnel, equipment, and facilities of any single local government and require the combined forces of a mutual aid region or regions to combat; and

WHEREAS under the provisions of section 8558(b) of the California Government Code, I find that conditions of extreme peril to the safety of persons and property exists in California due to these wildfires.

NOW, THEREFORE, I, EDMUND G. BROWN JR., Governor of the State of California, in accordance with the authority vested in me by the State Constitution and statutes, including the California Emergency Services Act, and in particular, section 8625 of the California Government Code, HEREBY PROCLAIM A STATE OF EMERGENCY to exist in the State of California due to the wildfires burning throughout the State.

IT IS HEREBY ORDERED THAT:

1. All agencies of the state government shall utilize and employ state personnel, equipment, and facilities for the performance of any and all activities consistent with the direction of the Governor's Office of Emergency Services and the State Emergency Plan. Also, all citizens are to heed the advice of emergency officials with regard to this emergency in order to protect their safety.

2. The California National Guard shall mobilize under California Military and Veterans Code section 146 (mobilization in case of catastrophic fires) to support disaster response and relief efforts and coordinate with all relevant state agencies, including the Governor's Office of Emergency Services, and all relevant state and local emergency responders and law enforcement within the impacted areas.

I FURTHER DIRECT that as soon as hereafter possible, this proclamation be filed in the Office of the Secretary of State and that widespread publicity and notice be given of this proclamation.

IN WITNESS WHEREOF I have hereunto set my hand and caused the Great Seal of the State of California to be affixed this 31st day of July 2015.

EDMUND G. BROWN JR.
Governor of California

ATTEST:
ALEX PADILLA
Secretary of State

SOURCE: Office of the Governor of California. "Governor Brown Declares State of Emergency in California to Bolster Wildfire Response." July 31, 2015. http://www.gov.ca.gov/news.php?id=19053.

OTHER HISTORIC DOCUMENTS OF INTEREST

FROM PREVIOUS *HISTORIC DOCUMENTS*

- ■ NOAA on 2011 Extreme Weather, *2011*, p. 273

Iranian Nuclear Deal Reached

APRIL 2, MAY 22, AND JULY 14, 2015

Led by the United States, European Union (EU), and United Nations (UN), international efforts to restrict Iran's nuclear program, primarily through economic sanctions, have been ongoing for approximately twenty years. Western countries suspect that Iran has long been attempting to build nuclear weapons in violation of the Nuclear Non-Proliferation Treaty—fueled in part by the country's history of attempting to conceal these activities— despite Iranian officials' insistence that their nuclear program has only peaceful goals, such as electricity generation. The hardline conservatism of many in Iran's government contributed to these concerns and made a diplomatic solution to the issue seemingly impossible. The June 2013 election of Hassan Rouhani as Iran's new president, however, raised hopes of greater cooperation and an easing of tensions, particularly given Rouhani's call for a nuclear deal with the international community, highlighted during a speech before the UN General Assembly.

In November 2013, negotiators from China, France, Germany, Russia, the United Kingdom, the United States, and Iran reached a six-month agreement known as the Joint Plan of Action (JPA). The plan required Iran to take several immediate steps to reduce its nuclear activities in return for approximately $7 billion in international sanctions relief, with the goal of providing additional time for the parties to negotiate a longer-term arrangement. The JPA took effect on January 20, 2014, and set a deadline of July 20, 2014 for a final agreement to be reached.

Negotiators met several times throughout the first half of 2014, but progress was slow, and those involved reported "significant gaps" between the two sides, caused namely by disagreement over the number and type of uranium-enriching centrifuges that Iran should be permitted to have. On July 19, 2014, high representative of the EU for foreign affairs and security policy Catherine Ashton and Iranian foreign minister Javad Zarif issued a statement announcing an extension of the JPA to November 24, 2014. All parties would continue meeting the terms of the initial JPA, and Iran committed to taking several additional steps, such as converting diluted enriched uranium into fuel for the Tehran Research Reactor, rendering the material nearly impossible to use for weapons.

Talks resumed in September 2014 and continued with periodic meetings through November. On November 24, negotiators announced another, seven-month extension for the talks, with a new deadline of June 30, 2015. The continued delays led many observers to question whether negotiators would ever reach a final agreement.

2015 NEGOTIATIONS RESULT IN AGREEMENT

On March 26, 2015, negotiators reconvened in Lausanne, Switzerland, to continue their discussions. After a week of meetings, the parties announced a framework agreement with Iran that outlined parameters for a final Joint Comprehensive Plan of Action (JCPOA). Under this framework, Iran tentatively agreed to a number of limits on its nuclear program for at least ten years and to allow international inspections to verify its compliance with the agreement, in exchange for the lifting of certain sanctions. Details of the JCPOA were to be negotiated and finalized by the end of June.

Zarif and high representative of the EU Federica Mogherini issued a joint statement celebrating the group's accomplishment. "The political determination, the good will and the hard work of all parties made it possible," they said. "This is a crucial decision laying the agreed basis for the final text of the JCPOA."

UN secretary general Ban Ki-moon also applauded the arrangement, saying it would "contribute to peace and stability in the region and enable all countries to cooperate urgently to deal with the many serious security challenges they face." U.S. president Barack Obama described the framework as "a good deal, a deal that meets our core objectives," claiming it "would cut off every pathway that Iran could take to develop a nuclear weapon." He added that the deal was "not based on trust, it's based on unprecedented verification."

KEY TERMS OF THE AGREEMENT

On July 15, negotiators signed and released the final JCPOA in Vienna. Under the agreement, Iran reaffirmed that it would not seek, develop, or acquire any nuclear weapons. It retained the ability to enrich uranium, but for the next fifteen years, it can only maintain a 300kg stockpile of low-enriched uranium, as opposed to the 10,000kg it had at the time the agreement was signed. The JCPOA also limits the number of Iran's centrifuges. For the next fifteen years Iran's Fordow facility can only have 1,044 centrifuges, which cannot be used for uranium enrichment, and for the next ten years Iran can have no more than about 5,000 first-generation centrifuges at its Natanz facility, which can be used for low-enriched uranium production. Iran's remaining centrifuges, about 13,500, would be placed in storage until these time limits expired.

In addition, the agreement limits Iran's research and development activities related to its nuclear program over the next eight years, after which time the country will be allowed to resume some activities, such as testing more advanced centrifuges. Iran also agreed to convert its Fordow facility into a nuclear, physics, and technology center and to redesign the heavy water research reactor at its Arak facility to support only "peaceful nuclear research." Other key provisions included Iran's commitment to allow the International Atomic Energy Agency (IAEA) to have a long-term presence in Iran and monitor its implementation of these measures.

In return, once the UN Security Council had passed a resolution endorsing the JCPOA and the IAEA verified Iran's implementation of all nuclear-related measures, all previous Security Council resolutions relating to Iran's nuclear program would be terminated. At that time, the EU would also lift its sanctions, and the United States would lift its secondary sanctions, which apply to other countries doing business with Iran. Eight years after the agreement's adoption, or once it has been concluded that all nuclear material in Iran is only being used peacefully, the United States would then seek congressional action to terminate its remaining sanctions, with the exception of sanctions relating to human rights, missiles, and support for terrorism. Iran will also receive between $100 billion and $150 billion of oil revenue that had been frozen in offshore accounts, and the United Nations committed to lifting its arms embargo on Iran after five years and its ballistic missile restrictions after eight years.

The JCPOA established a Joint Commission to help monitor the agreement's implementation and manage dispute resolutions. Under the dispute resolution process, any party that believed another party was not meeting its commitments under the JCPOA could refer the issue to the Joint Commission, which would have fifteen days to reach a resolution. If the complainant did not believe the Joint Commission's action had resolved the problem, it could refer the issue to the UN Security Council, which would also have fifteen days to achieve resolution. At that time, the Security Council would have an opportunity to vote on whether to continue lifting sanctions on Iran. If such a resolution did not pass within thirty days, sanctions would then snap back into place and the JCPOA would be terminated.

DEBATE ABOUT AGREEMENT RAGES ON

Supporters of the negotiations continued to celebrate the agreement as an international diplomatic success following the announcement of the JCPOA. President Rouhani even offered his own supportive comments, stating, "Today is the end to acts of tyranny against our nation and the start of cooperation with the world." Several reports indicated that Iranians celebrated the announcement in the streets of Tehran.

While many openly welcomed the deal, others urged caution. Saudi officials, for example, did not publicly criticize the deal, but one anonymous official told Reuters, "We have learned as Iran's neighbors in the last 40 years that goodwill only led us to harvest sour grapes." Still others expressed complete opposition, including Iran Revolutionary Guard commander Mohammed Ali Jafari, who said, "We will never accept it." Israeli prime minister Benjamin Netanyahu was perhaps the agreement's most vocal opponent, claiming that it "would threaten the survival of Israel." He added, "This deal would legitimize Iran's nuclear program, bolster Iran's economy and increase Iran's aggression and terror throughout the Middle East and beyond." He also demanded that the final deal include a clear acknowledgment by Iran of Israel's right to exist.

The JCPOA's announcement also fed an intense, ongoing public debate in the United States where the Obama administration faced a number of skeptics and opponents, particularly among the Republic Party. Speaker of the House John Boehner, R-Ohio, called the agreement a "bad deal," and Senate majority leader Mitch McConnell, R-Ky., said that "the Obama Administration approached these talks from a flawed perspective: reaching the best deal acceptable to Iran, rather than actually advancing our national goal of ending Iran's nuclear program."

In February, Sen. Bob Corker, R-Tenn., introduced the Iran Nuclear Agreement Review Act of 2015, which required President Obama to submit the terms of the final agreement to Congress for review. Congress would have sixty days to review and vote to approve or reject the agreement, thus determining whether it would lift congressionally imposed sanctions as called for by the JCPOA. The bill created a potential scenario in which Congress could disapprove of the deal, override an expected Obama veto, and prevent the complete lifting of U.S. sanctions, in which case Iran would likely back out of the agreement. The bill passed the House of Representatives on March 17 and the Senate on May 7, becoming law on May 22. On July 19, the U.S. State Department provided all details and documents related to the deal to Congress, with the congressional review period officially beginning on July 20. However, Congress did not pass a resolution disapproving of the deal by the established deadline of September 17.

The criticisms voiced by congressional Republicans were echoed by the 2016 presidential candidates. This included former Florida governor Jeb Bush's claims that the JCPOA was "a dangerous, deeply flawed, and short sighted deal." Sen. Lindsey Graham, R-S.C., described it as "the most dangerous, irresponsible step I've ever seen in the history of watching the Mideast." By contrast, Democratic candidates praised the deal. Former secretary of state Hillary Clinton said it was an "important step that puts the lid on Iran's nuclear programs," while Sen. Bernie Sanders, D-Vt., said it was "a victory for diplomacy over saber-rattling" that could help prevent another war in the Middle East.

A number of wealthy donors, special interest groups, and nonprofits invested in campaigns aimed at swaying the debate one way or another. The American Israel Public Affairs Committee, for example, founded a new group called Citizens for a Nuclear Free Iran and spent at least $11 million in advertising to help foment opposition to the deal. A host of former government officials and foreign policy experts also weighed in. On July 17, a group of more than 100 former U.S. ambassadors and State Department officials signed an open letter endorsing the agreement. This was followed by the July 20 release of an open letter to Congress, urging them to approve the deal, which had been signed by more than sixty national security leaders, including former Sen. George Mitchell, D-Maine, former secretary of state Madeleine Albright, and former national security advisor Brent Scowcroft.

THE AGREEMENT MOVES FORWARD

On July 20, the UN Security Council unanimously adopted a resolution endorsing the JCPOA. Some in Congress had called for the Council to delay the vote until the congressional review period had been completed, a request Secretary of State John Kerry called "presumptuous." However, the resolution did delay the JCPOA's implementation for ninety days, a nod to Congress. The EU also approved the deal on July 20, committing to a gradual lifting of sanctions, but noting that it would maintain its ban on supplying ballistic missile technology to Iran as well as its human rights sanctions.

Iran's *Majilis*, or parliament, formed a committee to study the agreement and announced it would wait at least eighty days before voting on it. Lawmakers approved the deal on October 18, also known as "Adoption Day," or the day the agreement became effective and signatories were to begin preparing to implement their portions of the plan. The next step in implementation will be "Implementation Day," when the IAEA verifies that Iran has implemented key nuclear-related measures, and the EU and United States lift sanctions.

—Linda Fecteau Grimm

Following is the edited text of a statement delivered by President Barack Obama on April 2, 2015, announcing the agreement reached with Iran and international partners regarding Iran's nuclear program; an April 2, 2015, joint statement by the European Union high representative Federica Mogherini and Iranian foreign minister Javad Zarif regarding the nuclear agreement; the edited text of Public Law No. 114-17, signed by the president on May 22, 2015, which gave Congress the ability to review any such agreement with Iran before it is formally signed; the text of the Iranian nuclear agreement, formally signed on July 14, 2015; and the text of a televised speech delivered by Iranian president Hassan Rouhani on July 14, 2015, regarding the nuclear agreement.

President Obama Announces Iranian Nuclear Agreement

April 2, 2015

Good afternoon, everybody. Today the United States, together with our allies and partners, has reached a historic understanding with Iran, which, if fully implemented, will prevent it from obtaining a nuclear weapon.

As President and Commander in Chief, I have no greater responsibility than the security of the American people. And I am convinced that if this framework leads to a final, comprehensive deal, it will make our country, our allies, and our world safer.

This has been a long time coming. The Islamic Republic of Iran has been advancing its nuclear program for decades . . . I made clear that we were prepared to resolve this issue diplomatically, but only if Iran came to the table in a serious way. When that did not happen, we rallied the world to impose the toughest sanctions in history, sanctions which had a profound impact on the Iranian economy.

Now, sanctions alone could not stop Iran's nuclear program, but they did help bring Iran to the negotiating table. Because of our diplomatic efforts, the world stood with us, and we were joined at the negotiating table by the world's major powers: the United Kingdom, France, Germany, Russia, and China, as well as the European Union.

Over a year ago, we took the first step towards today's framework with a deal to stop the progress of Iran's nuclear program and roll it back in key areas. And recall that at the time, skeptics argued that Iran would cheat and that we could not verify their compliance and the interim agreement would fail. Instead, it has succeeded exactly as intended. Iran has met all of its obligations. It eliminated its stockpile of dangerous nuclear material. Inspections of Iran's program increased. And we continued negotiations to see if we could achieve a more comprehensive deal.

Today, after many months of tough, principled diplomacy, we have achieved the framework for that deal. And it is a good deal, a deal that meets our core objectives. This framework would cut off every pathway that Iran could take to develop a nuclear weapon. Iran will face strict limitations on its program, and Iran has also agreed to the most robust and intrusive inspections and transparency regime ever negotiated for any nuclear program in history. So this deal is not based on trust, it's based on unprecedented verification.

[The following page has been omitted and includes discussion of the deal's key provisions.]

. . . If there is backsliding on the part of the Iranians, if the verification and inspection mechanisms don't meet the specifications of our nuclear and security experts, there will be no deal. But if we can get this done and Iran follows through on the framework that our negotiators agreed to, we will be able to resolve one of the greatest threats to our security and to do so peacefully.

Given the importance of this issue, I have instructed my negotiators to fully brief Congress and the American people on the substance of the deal, and I welcome a robust debate in the weeks and months to come. I am confident that we can show that this deal is good for the security of the United States, for our allies, and for the world. . . .

Iran is not going to simply dismantle its program because we demand it to do so. That's not how the world works, and that's not what history shows us . . . Should negotiations collapse because we, the United States, rejected what the majority of the world considers a fair deal, what our scientists and nuclear experts suggest would give us confidence that they are not developing a nuclear weapon, it's doubtful that we can even keep our current international sanctions in place. . . .

To the Iranian people, I want to reaffirm what I've said since the beginning of my Presidency: We are willing to engage you on the basis of mutual interests and mutual respect. This deal offers the prospect of relief from sanctions that were imposed because of Iran's violation of international law. . . . It demonstrates that if Iran complies with its international obligations, then it can fully rejoin the community of nations, thereby fulfilling the extraordinary talent and aspirations of the Iranian people. That would be good for Iran, and it would be good for the world.

Of course, this deal alone, even if fully implemented, will not end the deep divisions and mistrust between our two countries. We have a difficult history between us, and our concerns will remain with respect to Iranian behavior so long as Iran continues its sponsorship of terrorism, its support for proxies who destabilize the Middle East, its threats against America's friends and allies, like Israel. So make no mistake: We will remain vigilant in countering those actions and standing with our allies.

It's no secret that the Israeli Prime Minister and I don't agree about whether the United States should move forward with a peaceful resolution to the Iranian issue. If in fact Prime Minister Netanyahu is looking for the most effective way to ensure Iran doesn't get a nuclear weapon, this is the best option. And I believe our nuclear experts can confirm that.

More importantly, I will be speaking with the Prime Minister today to make clear that there will be no daylight—there is no daylight, when it comes to our support for Israel's security and our concerns about Iran's destabilizing policies and threats toward Israel. . . .

Today I also spoke with the King of Saudi Arabia to reaffirm our commitment to the security of our partners in the Gulf. And I'm inviting the leaders of the six countries who make up the Gulf Cooperation Council—Saudi Arabia, the United Arab Emirates, Kuwait, Oman, Qatar, and Bahrain—to meet me at Camp David this spring to discuss how we can further strengthen our security cooperation, while resolving the multiple conflicts that have caused so much hardship and instability throughout the Middle East.

Finally, it's worth remembering that Congress has, on a bipartisan basis, played a critical role in our current Iran policy, helping to shape the sanctions regime that applied so much pressure on Iran and ultimately forced them to the table. In the coming days and weeks, my administration will engage Congress once again about how we can play a—how it can play a constructive oversight role. I'll begin that effort by speaking to the leaders of the House and Senate today.

In those conversations, I will underscore that the issues at stake here are bigger than politics. These are matters of war and peace, and they should be evaluated based on the facts and what is ultimately best for the American people and for our national security. For this is not simply a deal between my administration and Iran. This is a deal between Iran, the United States of America, and the major powers in the world, including some of our closest allies. If Congress kills this deal, not based on expert analysis and without offering any reasonable alternative, then it's the United States that will be blamed for the failure of diplomacy. International unity will collapse, and the path to conflict will widen. . . .

But we have an historic opportunity to prevent the spread of nuclear weapons in Iran, and to do so peacefully, with the international community firmly behind us. We should seize that chance.

Thank you. God bless you, and God bless the United States of America.

Source: Executive Office of the President. "Remarks on International Diplomatic Efforts to Prevent Iran from Developing Nuclear Weapons." April 2, 2015. *Compilation of Presidential Documents* 2015, no. 00230 (April 2, 2015). http://www.gpo.gov/fdsys/pkg/DCPD-201500230/pdf/DCPD-201500230.pdf.

European Union and Iranian Representatives Remark on Nuclear Agreement

DOCUMENT

April 2, 2015

We, the EU High Representative and the Foreign Minister of the I. R. of Iran, together with the Foreign Ministers of the E3+3 (China, France, Germany, the Russian Federation, the United Kingdom and the United States), met from 26 March to 2nd April 2015 in Switzerland. As agreed in November 2013, we gathered here to find solutions towards reaching a comprehensive resolution that will ensure the exclusively peaceful nature of the Iranian nuclear programme and the comprehensive lifting of all sanctions.

Today, we have taken a decisive step: we have reached solutions on key parameters of a Joint Comprehensive Plan of Action (JCPOA). The political determination, the good will and the hard work of all parties made it possible. Let us thank all delegations for their tireless dedication.

This is a crucial decision laying the agreed basis for the final text of the JCPOA. We can now restart drafting the text and annexes of the JCPOA, guided by the solutions developed in these days.

As Iran pursues a peaceful nuclear programme, Iran's enrichment capacity, enrichment level and stockpile will be limited for specified durations, and there will be no other enrichment facility than Natanz. Iran's research and development on centrifuges will be carried out on a scope and schedule that has been mutually agreed. . . .

A new UN Security Council Resolution will endorse the JCPOA, terminate all previous nuclear-related resolutions and incorporate certain restrictive measures for a mutually agreed period of time.

We will now work to write the text of a Joint Comprehensive Plan of Action including its technical details in the coming weeks and months at the political and experts levels. We are committed to complete our efforts by June 30th. We would like to thank the Swiss government for its generous support in hosting these negotiations.

Source: European Union. "Joint Statement by EU High Representative Federica Mogherini and Iranian Foreign Minister Javad Zarif." April 2, 2015. © European Union, 2015. http://eeas.europa.eu/statements-eeas/2015/150402_03_en.htm.

Public Law on Congressional Review of Iranian Nuclear Agreement

May 22, 2015

[Parenthetical notes have been removed.]

Public Law No: 114-17 (05/22/2015)

An Act

To provide for congressional review and oversight of agreements relating to Iran's nuclear program, and for other purposes.

Be it enacted by the Senate and House of Representatives of the United States of America in Congress assembled,

SECTION 1.   SHORT TITLE.

This Act may be cited as the "Iran Nuclear Agreement Review Act of 2015".

SEC. 2.   CONGRESSIONAL REVIEW AND OVERSIGHT OF AGREEMENTS WITH IRAN RELATING TO THE NUCLEAR PROGRAM OF IRAN.

The Atomic Energy Act of 1954 (42 U.S.C. 2011 et seq.) is amended by inserting after section 134 the following new section:

"SEC. 135.   CONGRESSIONAL REVIEW AND OVERSIGHT OF AGREEMENTS WITH IRAN.

"(a) Transmission To Congress Of Nuclear Agreements With Iran And Verification Assessment With Respect To Such Agreements.—

"(1) TRANSMISSION OF AGREEMENTS.—Not later than 5 calendar days after reaching an agreement with Iran relating to the nuclear program of Iran, the President shall transmit to the appropriate congressional committees and leadership—

"(A) the agreement, as defined in subsection (h)(1), including all related materials and annexes;

"(B) a verification assessment report of the Secretary of State prepared under paragraph (2) with respect to the agreement; and

"(C) a certification that—

"(i) the agreement includes the appropriate terms, conditions, and duration of the agreement's requirements with respect to Iran's nuclear activities and provisions describing any sanctions to be waived, suspended, or otherwise reduced by the United States, and any other nation or entity, including the United Nations; and

"(ii) the President determines the agreement meets United States non-proliferation objectives, does not jeopardize the common defense and security, provides an adequate framework to ensure that Iran's nuclear activities permitted thereunder will not be inimical to or constitute an unreasonable risk to the common defense and security, and ensures that Iran's nuclear activities permitted thereunder will not be used to further any nuclear-related military or nuclear explosive purpose. . . .

"(2) VERIFICATION ASSESSMENT REPORT.—

"(A) IN GENERAL.—The Secretary of State shall prepare, with respect to an agreement described in paragraph (1), a report assessing—

"(i) the extent to which the Secretary will be able to verify that Iran is complying with its obligations and commitments under the agreement;

"(ii) the adequacy of the safeguards and other control mechanisms and other assurances contained in the agreement. . . .

"(b) Period For Review By Congress Of Nuclear Agreements With Iran.—

"(1) IN GENERAL.—During the 30-calendar day period following transmittal by the President . . . the Committee on Foreign Relations of the Senate and the Committee on Foreign Affairs of the House of Representatives shall, as appropriate, hold hearings and briefings and otherwise obtain information in order to fully review such agreement.

"(2) EXCEPTION.—The period for congressional review under paragraph (1) shall be 60 calendar days if an agreement, including all materials required to be transmitted to Congress pursuant to subsection (a)(1), is transmitted pursuant to subsection (a) between July 10, 2015, and September 7, 2015.

[The following paragraphs have been omitted and include language prohibiting the president from changing or lifting sanctions during the congressional review period or his consideration of a vote of disapproval, if passed.]

"(c) Effect Of Congressional Action With Respect To Nuclear Agreements With Iran.—

"(1) SENSE OF CONGRESS.—It is the sense of Congress that—

"(A)   the sanctions regime imposed on Iran by Congress is primarily responsible for bringing Iran to the table to negotiate on its nuclear program;

"(B)   these negotiations are a critically important matter of national security and foreign policy for the United States and its closest allies;

"(C)   this section does not require a vote by Congress for the agreement to commence;

"(D)   this section provides for congressional review, including, as appropriate, for approval, disapproval, or no action on statutory sanctions relief under an agreement; and

"(E)   even though the agreement may commence, because the sanctions regime was imposed by Congress and only Congress can permanently modify or eliminate that regime, it is critically important that Congress have the opportunity, in an orderly and deliberative manner, to consider and, as appropriate, take action affecting the statutory sanctions regime imposed by Congress.

"(2)   IN GENERAL.—Notwithstanding any other provision of law, action involving any measure of statutory sanctions relief by the United States pursuant to an agreement subject to subsection (a) or the Joint Plan of Action—

"(A)   may be taken, consistent with existing statutory requirements for such action, if, during the period for review provided in subsection (b), the Congress adopts, and there is enacted, a joint resolution stating in substance that the Congress does favor the agreement;

"(B)   may not be taken if, during the period for review provided in subsection (b), the Congress adopts, and there is enacted, a joint resolution stating in substance that the Congress does not favor the agreement; or

"(C)   may be taken, consistent with existing statutory requirements for such action, if, following the period for review provided in subsection (b), there is not enacted any such joint resolution. . . .

[The following three pages have been omitted and outline a process for the president and federal agencies to provide regular reports to Congress on the deal's implementation and certifications that Iran is meeting its obligations.]

"(7)   SENSE OF CONGRESS.—It is the sense of Congress that—

"(A)   United States sanctions on Iran for terrorism, human rights abuses, and ballistic missiles will remain in place under an agreement, as defined in subsection (h)(1); . . . .

"(C) the President should determine the agreement in no way compromises the commitment of the United States to Israel's security, nor its support for Israel's right to exist; . . . .

"(e) Expedited Consideration Of Legislation.—

"(1) IN GENERAL.—In the event the President does not submit a certification pursuant to subsection (d)(6) or has determined pursuant to subsection (d)(3) that Iran has materially breached an agreement subject to subsection (a) and the material breach has not been cured, Congress may initiate within 60 calendar days expedited consideration of qualifying legislation pursuant to this subsection.

[The following five pages have been omitted and outline rules for the expedited legislative process, as well as definitions of terms included in this law.]

SOURCE: Library of Congress. "Public Law No: 114-17." Signed into law May 22, 2015. http://www.congress.gov/114/plaws/publ17/PLAW-114publ17.pdf.

Joint Comprehensive Plan of Action on Iranian Nuclear Program

July 14, 2015

PREFACE

The E3/EU+3 (China, France, Germany, the Russian Federation, the United Kingdom and the United States, with the High Representative of the European Union for Foreign Affairs and Security Policy) and the Islamic Republic of Iran welcome this historic Joint Comprehensive Plan of Action (JCPOA), which will ensure that Iran's nuclear programme will be exclusively peaceful, and mark a fundamental shift in their approach to this issue. They anticipate that full implementation of this JCPOA will positively contribute to regional and international peace and security. Iran reaffirms that under no circumstances will Iran ever seek, develop or acquire any nuclear weapons.

Iran envisions that this JCPOA will allow it to move forward with an exclusively peaceful, indigenous nuclear programme, in line with scientific and economic considerations, in accordance with the JCPOA, and with a view to building confidence and encouraging international cooperation. In this context, the initial mutually determined limitations described in this JCPOA will be followed by a gradual evolution, at a reasonable pace, of Iran's peaceful nuclear programme, including its enrichment activities, to a commercial programme for exclusively peaceful purposes, consistent with international nonproliferation norms.

The E3/EU+3 envision that the implementation of this JCPOA will progressively allow them to gain confidence in the exclusively peaceful nature of Iran's programme. The

JCPOA reflects mutually determined parameters, consistent with practical needs, with agreed limits on the scope of Iran's nuclear programme, including enrichment activities and R&D. The JCPOA addresses the E3/EU+3's concerns, including through comprehensive measures providing for transparency and verification.

The JCPOA will produce the comprehensive lifting of all UN Security Council sanctions as well as multilateral and national sanctions related to Iran's nuclear programme, including steps on access in areas of trade, technology, finance, and energy.

PREAMBLE AND GENERAL PROVISIONS

i. The Islamic Republic of Iran and the E3/EU+3 (China, France, Germany, the Russian Federation, the United Kingdom and the United States, with the High Representative of the European Union for Foreign Affairs and Security Policy) have decided upon this long-term Joint Comprehensive Plan of Action (JCPOA). This JCPOA, reflecting a step-by-step approach, includes the reciprocal commitments as laid down in this document and the annexes hereto and is to be endorsed by the United Nations (UN) Security Council.

ii. The full implementation of this JCPOA will ensure the exclusively peaceful nature of Iran's nuclear programme.

iii. Iran reaffirms that under no circumstances will Iran ever seek, develop or acquire any nuclear weapons.

iv. Successful implementation of this JCPOA will enable Iran to fully enjoy its right to nuclear energy for peaceful purposes under the relevant articles of the nuclear Non-Proliferation Treaty (NPT) in line with its obligations therein, and the Iranian nuclear programme will be treated in the same manner as that of any other non-nuclear-weapon state party to the NPT.

v. This JCPOA will produce the comprehensive lifting of all UN Security Council sanctions as well as multilateral and national sanctions related to Iran's nuclear programme, including steps on access in areas of trade, technology, finance and energy. . . .

vi. The E3/EU+3 and Iran commit to implement this JCPOA in good faith and in a constructive atmosphere, based on mutual respect, and to refrain from any action inconsistent with the letter, spirit and intent of this JCPOA that would undermine its successful implementation. . . .

vii. A Joint Commission consisting of the E3/EU+3 and Iran will be established to monitor the implementation of this JCPOA and will carry out the functions provided for in this JCPOA. . . .

viii. The International Atomic Energy Agency (IAEA) will be requested to monitor and verify the voluntary nuclear-related measures as detailed in this JCPOA. The IAEA will be requested to provide regular updates to the Board of Governors, and as provided for in this JCPOA, to the UN Security Council. . . .

ix. All provisions and measures contained in this JCPOA are only for the purpose of its implementation between E3/EU+3 and Iran. . . .

x. The EU and E3+3 countries and Iran, in the framework of the JCPOA, will cooperate, as appropriate, in the field of peaceful uses of nuclear energy and engage in mutually determined civil nuclear cooperation projects. . . .

xi. The E3+3 will submit a draft resolution to the UN Security Council endorsing this JCPOA affirming that conclusion of this JCPOA marks a fundamental shift in its consideration of this issue and expressing its desire to build a new relationship with Iran. This UN Security Council resolution will also provide for the termination on Implementation Day of provisions imposed under previous resolutions; establishment of specific restrictions; and conclusion of consideration of the Iran nuclear issue by the UN Security Council 10 years after the Adoption Day. . . .

xii. The E3/EU+3 and Iran will meet at the ministerial level every 2 years, or earlier if needed, in order to review and assess progress and to adopt appropriate decisions by consensus.

Iran and E3/EU+3 will take the following voluntary measures within the timeframe as detailed in this JCPOA and its Annexes

NUCLEAR

A. ENRICHMENT, ENRICHMENT R&D, STOCKPILES

1. Iran's long term plan includes certain agreed limitations on all uranium enrichment and uranium enrichment-related activities including certain limitations on specific research and development (R&D) activities for the first 8 years, to be followed by gradual evolution, at a reasonable pace, to the next stage of its enrichment activities for exclusively peaceful purposes, as described in Annex I. . . .

2. Iran will begin phasing out its IR-1 centrifuges in 10 years. During this period, Iran will keep its enrichment capacity at Natanz at up to a total installed uranium enrichment capacity of 5060 IR-1 centrifuges. Excess centrifuges and enrichment-related infrastructure at Natanz will be stored under IAEA continuous monitoring, as specified in Annex I.

3. Iran will continue to conduct enrichment R&D in a manner that does not accumulate enriched uranium. Iran's enrichment R&D with uranium for 10 years will only include IR-4, IR-5, IR-6 and IR-8 centrifuges as laid out in Annex I, and Iran will not engage in other isotope separation technologies for enrichment of uranium as specified in Annex I. Iran will continue testing IR-6 and IR-8 centrifuges, and will commence testing of up to 30 IR-6 and IR-8 centrifuges after eight and a half years, as detailed in Annex I.

4. As Iran will be phasing out its IR-1 centrifuges, it will not manufacture or assemble other centrifuges, except as provided for in Annex I, and will replace failed centrifuges with centrifuges of the same type. Iran will manufacture advanced centrifuge machines only for the purposes specified in this JCPOA. From the end of the eighth year, and as described in Annex I, Iran will start to manufacture agreed numbers of IR-6 and IR-8 centrifuge machines without

rotors and will store all of the manufactured machines at Natanz, under IAEA continuous monitoring until they are needed under Iran's long-term enrichment and enrichment R&D plan.

5. Based on its own long-term plan, for 15 years, Iran will carry out its uranium enrichment-related activities, including safeguarded R&D exclusively in the Natanz Enrichment facility, keep its level of uranium enrichment at up to 3.67%, and, at Fordow, refrain from any uranium enrichment and uranium enrichment R&D and from keeping any nuclear material.

6. Iran will convert the Fordow facility into a nuclear, physics and technology centre. International collaboration including in the form of scientific joint partnerships will be established in agreed areas of research. 1044 IR-1 centrifuges in six cascades will remain in one wing at Fordow. Two of these cascades will spin without uranium and will be transitioned, including through appropriate infrastructure modification, for stable isotope production. The other four cascades with all associated infrastructure will remain idle. All other centrifuges and enrichment-related infrastructure will be removed and stored under IAEA continuous monitoring as specified in Annex I.

7. During the 15 year period, and as Iran gradually moves to meet international qualification standards for nuclear fuel produced in Iran, it will keep its uranium stockpile under 300 kg of up to 3.67% enriched uranium hexafluoride (UF6) or the equivalent in other chemical forms. The excess quantities are to be sold based on international prices and delivered to the international buyer in return for natural uranium delivered to Iran, or are to be down-blended to natural uranium level. Enriched uranium in fabricated fuel assemblies from Russia or other sources for use in Iran's nuclear reactors will not be counted against the above stated 300 kg UF6 stockpile, if the criteria set out in Annex I are met with regard to other sources. The Joint Commission will support assistance to Iran, including through IAEA technical cooperation as appropriate, in meeting international qualification standards for nuclear fuel produced in Iran. All remaining uranium oxide enriched to between 5% and 20% will be fabricated into fuel for the Tehran Research Reactor (TRR). Any additional fuel needed for the TRR will be made available to Iran at international market prices.

B. ARAK, HEAVY WATER, REPROCESSING

8. Iran will redesign and rebuild a modernised heavy water research reactor in Arak, based on an agreed conceptual design, using fuel enriched up to 3.67%, in a form of an international partnership which will certify the final design. The reactor will support peaceful nuclear research and radioisotope production for medical and industrial purposes. The redesigned and rebuilt Arak reactor will not produce weapons grade plutonium . . . All spent fuel from Arak will be shipped out of Iran for the lifetime of the reactor. This international partnership will include participating E3/EU+3 parties, Iran and such other countries as may be mutually determined. . . .

9. Iran plans to keep pace with the trend of international technological advancement in relying on light water for its future power and research reactors with enhanced international cooperation, including assurance of supply of necessary fuel.

10. There will be no additional heavy water reactors or accumulation of heavy water in Iran for 15 years. All excess heavy water will be made available for export to the international market.

11. Iran intends to ship out all spent fuel for all future and present power and research nuclear reactors, for further treatment or disposition as provided for in relevant contracts to be duly concluded with the recipient party.

12. For 15 years Iran will not, and does not intend to thereafter, engage in any spent fuel reprocessing or construction of a facility capable of spent fuel reprocessing, or reprocessing R&D activities leading to a spent fuel reprocessing capability, with the sole exception of separation activities aimed exclusively at the production of medical and industrial radio-isotopes from irradiated enriched uranium targets.

C. TRANSPARENCY AND CONFIDENCE BUILDING MEASURES

13. Consistent with the respective roles of the President and Majlis (Parliament), Iran will provisionally apply the Additional Protocol to its Comprehensive Safeguards Agreement in accordance with Article 17(b) of the Additional Protocol, proceed with its ratification within the timeframe as detailed in Annex V and fully implement the modified Code 3.1 of the Subsidiary Arrangements to its Safeguards Agreement.

14. Iran will fully implement the "Roadmap for Clarification of Past and Present Outstanding Issues" agreed with the IAEA, containing arrangements to address past and present issues of concern relating to its nuclear programme as raised in the annex to the IAEA report of 8 November 2011 (GOV/2011/65). . . .

15. Iran will allow the IAEA to monitor the implementation of the voluntary measures for their respective durations, as well as to implement transparency measures, as set out in this JCPOA and its Annexes. These measures include: a long-term IAEA presence in Iran; IAEA monitoring of uranium ore concentrate produced by Iran from all uranium ore concentrate plants for 25 years; containment and surveillance of centrifuge rotors and bellows for 20 years; use of IAEA approved and certified modern technologies including on-line enrichment measurement and electronic seals; and a reliable mechanism to ensure speedy resolution of IAEA access concerns for 15 years, as defined in Annex I.

16. Iran will not engage in activities, including at the R&D level, that could contribute to the development of a nuclear explosive device, including uranium or plutonium metallurgy activities, as specified in Annex I.

17. Iran will cooperate and act in accordance with the procurement channel in this JCPOA, as detailed in Annex IV, endorsed by the UN Security Council resolution.

SANCTIONS

18. The UN Security Council resolution endorsing this JCPOA will terminate all provisions of previous UN Security Council resolutions on the Iranian nuclear

issue—1696 (2006), 1737 (2006), 1747 (2007), 1803 (2008), 1835 (2008), 1929 (2010) and 2224 (2015)—simultaneously with the IAEA-verified implementation of agreed nuclear-related measures by Iran and will establish specific restrictions, as specified in Annex V. *[footnote: The provisions of this Resolution do not constitute provisions of this JCPOA.]*

19. The EU will terminate all provisions of the EU Regulation, as subsequently amended, implementing all nuclear-related economic and financial sanctions, including related designations, simultaneously with the IAEA-verified implementation of agreed nuclear-related measures by Iran as specified in Annex V, which cover all sanctions and restrictive measures in the following areas, as described in Annex II:

    i. Transfers of funds between EU persons and entities . . . ;

    ii. Banking activities . . . ;

    iii. Provision of insurance and reinsurance;

    iv. Supply of specialised financial messaging services . . . ;

    v. Financial support for trade with Iran (export credit, guarantees or insurance);

    vi. Commitments for grants, financial assistance and concessional loans to the Government of Iran;

    vii. Transactions in public or public-guaranteed bonds;

    viii. Import and transport of Iranian oil, petroleum products, gas and petrochemical products;

    ix. Export of key equipment or technology for the oil, gas and petrochemical sectors;

    x. Investment in the oil, gas and petrochemical sectors;

    xi. Export of key naval equipment and technology;

    xii. Design and construction of cargo vessels and oil tankers;

    xiii. Provision of flagging and classification services;

    xiv. Access to EU airports of Iranian cargo flights;

    xv. Export of gold, precious metals and diamonds;

    xvi. Delivery of Iranian banknotes and coinage;

    xvii. Export of graphite, raw or semi-finished metals such as aluminum and steel, and export or software for integrating industrial processes;

    xviii. Designation of persons, entities and bodies (asset freeze and visa ban) set out in Attachment 1 to Annex II; and

    xix. Associated services for each of the categories above.

20. The EU will terminate all provisions of the EU Regulation implementing all EU proliferation-related sanctions, including related designations, 8 years after Adoption Day or when the IAEA has reached the Broader Conclusion that all nuclear material in Iran remains in peaceful activities, whichever is earlier.

21. The United States will cease the application, and will continue to do so, in accordance with this JCPOA of the sanctions specified in Annex II to take effect simultaneously with the IAEA-verified implementation of the agreed nuclear-related measures by Iran as specified in Annex V. Such sanctions cover the following areas as described in Annex II:

    i. Financial and banking transactions with Iranian banks and financial institutions as specified in Annex II . . . ;

    ii. Transactions in Iranian Rial;

    iii. Provision of U.S. banknotes to the Government of Iran;

    iv. Bilateral trade limitations on Iranian revenues abroad . . . ;

    v. Purchase, subscription to, or facilitation of the issuance of Iranian 12 sovereign debt . . . ;

    vi. Financial messaging services to the Central Bank of Iran and Iranian financial institutions set out in Attachment 3 to Annex II;

    vii. Underwriting services, insurance, or reinsurance;

    viii. Efforts to reduce Iran's crude oil sales;

    ix. Investment, including participation in joint ventures, goods, services, information, technology and technical expertise and support for Iran's oil, gas and petrochemical sectors;

    x. Purchase, acquisition, sale, transportation or marketing of petroleum, petrochemical products and natural gas from Iran;

    xi. Export, sale or provision of refined petroleum products and petrochemical products to Iran;

    xii. Transactions with Iran's energy sector;

    xiii. Transactions with Iran's shipping and shipbuilding sectors and port operators;

    xiv. Trade in gold and other precious metals;

    xv. Trade with Iran in graphite, raw or semi-finished metals such as aluminum and steel, coal, and software for integrating industrial processes;

    xvi. Sale, supply or transfer of goods and services used in connection with Iran's automotive sector;

    xvii. Sanctions on associated services for each of the categories above;

    xviii. Remove individuals and entities set out in Attachment 3 to Annex II from the SDN List, the Foreign Sanctions Evaders List, and/or the Non-SDN Iran Sanctions Act List; and

    xix. Terminate Executive Orders 13574, 13590, 13622, and 13645, and Sections 5 – 7 and 15 of Executive Order 13628.

22. The United States will, as specified in Annex II and in accordance with Annex V, allow for the sale of commercial passenger aircraft and related parts and services

to Iran; license non-U.S. persons that are owned or controlled by a U.S. person to engage in activities with Iran consistent with this JCPOA; and license the importation into the United States of Iranian-origin carpets and foodstuffs.

23. Eight years after Adoption Day or when the IAEA has reached the Broader Conclusion that all nuclear material in Iran remains in peaceful activities, whichever is earlier, the United States will seek such legislative action as may be appropriate to terminate, or modify to effectuate the termination of, the sanctions specified in Annex II on the acquisition of nuclear-related commodities and services for nuclear activities contemplated in this JCPOA, to be consistent with the U.S. approach to other non-nuclear-weapon states under the NPT.

24. The E3/EU and the United States specify in Annex II a full and complete list of all nuclear-related sanctions or restrictive measures and will lift them in accordance with Annex V. Annex II also specifies the effects of the lifting of sanctions beginning on "Implementation Day". If at any time following the Implementation Day, Iran believes that any other nuclear-related sanction or restrictive measure of the E3/EU+3 is preventing the full implementation of the sanctions lifting as specified in this JCPOA, the JCPOA participant in question will consult with Iran with a view to resolving the issue and, if they concur that lifting of this sanction or restrictive measure is appropriate, the JCPOA participant in question will take appropriate action. If they are not able to resolve the issue, Iran or any member of the E3/EU+3 may refer the issue to the Joint Commission.

25. If a law at the state or local level in the United States is preventing the implementation of the sanctions lifting as specified in this JCPOA, the United States will take appropriate steps, taking into account all available authorities, with a view to achieving such implementation. . . .

26. The EU will refrain from re-introducing or re-imposing the sanctions that it has terminated implementing under this JCPOA, without prejudice to the dispute resolution process provided for under this JCPOA. There will be no new nuclear related UN Security Council sanctions and no new EU nuclear-related sanctions or restrictive measures. The United States will make best efforts in good faith to sustain this JCPOA and to prevent interference with the realisation of the full benefit by Iran of the sanctions lifting specified in Annex II. . . . The U.S. Administration, acting consistent with the respective roles of the President and the Congress, will refrain from imposing new nuclear-related sanctions. Iran has stated that it will treat such a re-introduction or re-imposition of the sanctions 14 specified in Annex II, or such an imposition of new nuclear-related sanctions, as grounds to cease performing its commitments under this JCPOA in whole or in part. . . .

27. The E3/EU+3 will take adequate administrative and regulatory measures to ensure clarity and effectiveness with respect to the lifting of sanctions under this JCPOA. The EU and its Member States as well as the United States will issue relevant guidelines that make publicly accessible statements on the details of sanctions or restrictive measures which have been lifted under this JCPOA. The EU and its Member States and the United States commit to consult with Iran regarding the content of such guidelines and statements, on a regular basis and whenever appropriate.

28. The E3/EU+3 and Iran commit to implement this JCPOA in good faith and in a constructive atmosphere, based on mutual respect, and to refrain from any action inconsistent with the letter, spirit and intent of this JCPOA that would undermine its successful implementation. Senior Government officials of the E3/EU+3 and Iran will make every effort to support the successful implementation of this JCPOA including in their public statements. *[footnote: 'Government officials' for the U.S. means senior officials of the U.S. Administration.]* The E3/EU+3 will take all measures required to lift sanctions and will refrain from imposing exceptional or discriminatory regulatory and procedural requirements in lieu of the sanctions and restrictive measures covered by the JCPOA.

29. The EU and its Member States and the United States, consistent with their respective laws, will refrain from any policy specifically intended to directly and adversely affect the normalisation of trade and economic relations with Iran inconsistent with their commitments not to undermine the successful implementation of this JCPOA.

30. The E3/EU+3 will not apply sanctions or restrictive measures to persons or entities for engaging in activities covered by the lifting of sanctions provided for in this JCPOA, provided that such activities are otherwise consistent with E3/EU+3 laws and regulations in effect. Following the lifting of sanctions under this JCPOA as specified in Annex II, ongoing investigations on possible infringements of such sanctions may be reviewed in accordance with applicable national laws.

31. Consistent with the timing specified in Annex V, the EU and its Member States will terminate the implementation of the measures applicable to designated entities and individuals, including the Central Bank of Iran and other Iranian banks and financial institutions, as detailed in Annex II and the attachments thereto. Consistent with the timing specified in Annex V, the United States will remove designation of certain entities and individuals on the Specially Designated Nationals and Blocked Persons List, and entities and individuals listed on the Foreign Sanctions Evaders List, as detailed in Annex II and the attachments thereto.

32. EU and E3+3 countries and international participants will engage in joint projects with Iran, including through IAEA technical cooperation projects, in the field of peaceful nuclear technology, including nuclear power plants, research reactors, fuel fabrication, agreed joint advanced R&D such as fusion, establishment of a state-of-the-art regional nuclear medical centre, personnel training, nuclear safety and security, and environmental protection, as detailed in Annex III. They will take necessary measures, as appropriate, for the implementation of these projects.

33. The E3/EU+3 and Iran will agree on steps to ensure Iran's access in areas of trade, technology, finance and energy. The EU will further explore possible areas for cooperation between the EU, its Member States and Iran, and in this context consider the use of available instruments such as export credits to facilitate trade, project financing and investment in Iran.

IMPLEMENTATION PLAN

34. Iran and the E3/EU+3 will implement their JCPOA commitments according to the sequence specified in Annex V. The milestones for implementation are as follows:

   i. Finalisation Day is the date on which negotiations of this JCPOA are concluded among the E3/EU+3 and Iran, to be followed promptly by submission of the resolution endorsing this JCPOA to the UN Security Council for adoption without delay.

   ii. Adoption Day is the date 90 days after the endorsement of this JCPOA by the UN Security Council, or such earlier date as may be determined by mutual consent of the JCPOA participants, at which time this JCPOA and the commitments in this JCPOA come into effect. Beginning on that date, JCPOA participants will make necessary arrangements and preparations for the implementation of their JCPOA commitments.

   iii. Implementation Day is the date on which, simultaneously with the IAEA report verifying implementation by Iran of the nuclear-related measures described in Sections 15.1. to 15.11 of Annex V, the EU and the United States take the actions described in Sections 16 and 17 of Annex V respectively and in accordance with the UN Security Council resolution, the actions described in Section 18 of Annex V occur at the UN level.

   iv. Transition Day is the date 8 years after Adoption Day or the date on which the Director General of the IAEA submits a report stating that the IAEA has reached the Broader Conclusion that all nuclear material in Iran remains in peaceful activities, whichever is earlier. On that date, the EU and the United States will take the actions described in Sections 20 and 21 of Annex V respectively and Iran will seek, consistent with the Constitutional roles of the President and Parliament, ratification of the Additional Protocol.

   v. UN Security Council resolution Termination Day is the date on which the UN Security Council resolution endorsing this JCPOA terminates according to its terms, which is to be 10 years from Adoption Day, provided that the provisions of previous resolutions have not been reinstated. On that date, the EU will take the actions described in Section 25 of Annex V. . . .

35. The sequence and milestones set forth above and in Annex V are without prejudice to the duration of JCPOA commitments stated in this JCPOA.

DISPUTE RESOLUTION MECHANISM

36. If Iran believed that any or all of the E3/EU+3 were not meeting their commitments under this JCPOA, Iran could refer the issue to the Joint Commission for resolution; similarly, if any of the E3/EU+3 believed that Iran was not meeting its commitments under this JCPOA, any of the E3/EU+3 could do the same. The Joint Commission would have 15 days to resolve the issue, unless the time

period was extended by consensus. After Joint Commission consideration, any participant could refer the issue to Ministers of Foreign Affairs, if it believed the compliance issue had not been resolved. Ministers would have 15 days to resolve the issue, unless the time period was extended by consensus. After Joint Commission consideration—in parallel with (or in lieu of) review at the Ministerial level—either the complaining participant or the participant whose performance is in question could request that the issue be considered by an Advisory Board, which would consist of three members (one each appointed by the participants in the dispute and a third independent member). The Advisory Board should provide a non-binding opinion on the compliance issue within 15 days. If, after this 30-day process the issue is not resolved, the Joint Commission would consider the opinion of the Advisory Board for no more than 5 days in order to resolve the issue. If the issue still has not been resolved to the satisfaction of the complaining participant, and if the complaining participant deems the issue to constitute significant non-performance, then that participant could treat the unresolved issue as grounds to cease performing its commitments under this JCPOA in whole or in part and/or notify the UN Security Council that it believes the issue constitutes significant non-performance.

37. Upon receipt of the notification from the complaining participant, as described above, including a description of the good-faith efforts the participant made to exhaust the dispute resolution process specified in this JCPOA, the UN Security Council, in accordance with its procedures, shall vote on a resolution to continue the sanctions lifting. If the resolution described above has not been adopted within 30 days of the notification, then the provisions of the old UN Security Council resolutions would be re-imposed, unless the UN Security Council decides otherwise. . . . Iran has stated that if sanctions are reinstated in whole or in part, Iran will treat that as grounds to cease performing its commitments under this JCPOA in whole or in part.

SOURCE: European Union. "Joint Comprehensive Plan of Action." July 14, 2015. © European Union, 2015. http://eeas.europa.eu/statements-eeas/docs/iran_agreement/iran_joint-comprehensive-plan-of-action_en.pdf.

Iranian President Remarks on Nuclear Agreement

July 14, 2015

President Hassan Rouhani in a live TV speech on Tuesday addresses nation on conclusion of nuclear talks, said Iran was after maintaining its national interests in this negotiations including protecting Iran's capabilities in nuclear energy industry, see an end to the "wrong, cruel and inhumane sanctions", see all "illegal" resolutions imposed by the UN Security Council scrapped, and see its nuclear dossier excluded from the Chapter 7 of the UN charter. . . .

President Rouhani said, 'I announce to the great Iranian nation that a new chapter has opened in an important juncture of country's history. The 12-year dispute emanated from illusions of the western governments and the propaganda to spread such illusions in the international community, are over.'

'I am happy that with the 23-month nuclear talks of Iran with the world six major powers, we have today been able to reach a new point; of course the month of Ramadan has always been source of blessing and destiny making for the 11th Government.'

. . . 'We should take necessary steps in various sections to settle nuclear issue and problem; politically speaking, we should prepare necessary political conditions; as far as public opinion is concerned, they should know that negotiations does not mean reading statements. Negotiation means give and take. Negotiation means money that is given and a house that is purchased. We did not seek charity so that somebody will give us something for free; we were for talks; we wanted fair Give & Take based on national interests.'

He added, 'We have always emphasized that the talks will not win-loss in kind; any talks, being win-loss in nature, will not last long. The talks and agreement will be durable that is win-win for both sides.' . . .

We had to bring order to economy under sanctions; when we started negotiations, the economic growth was well under zero per cent; however, during negotiations, we both controlled the inflation and stabilized economy, which was a clear message to the 5+1; resistance by the Iranian nation was also effective; the national resistance brought the western negotiators back to negotiation table; we sought four objectives in the negotiations; to secure a continuous nuclear activity inside the country; to remove inhumane and cruel sanctions; to have cancelled in the UN all resolutions against Iran; to remove out of the UN arrangements Iran's nuclear program; we reached almost all four objectives; however, to adhere to redlines, considerable efforts have been waged by our experts, politicians, and negotiators in the negotiation. . . .

With implementation of the deal, after 10 years, no dossier will remain in the UN; It would be objected that trust upon the 5+1 makes the basis for the deal; for us, implementation of the deal is a real test: if it is implemented well, it would destroy every brick of the wall of distrust. We will continue to go forward with the deal, without investing trust in countries in the region which are either enemies or rivals. We have once implemented [the deal] unilaterally; now the deal is bilateral if they remain committed to the deal; the Iranian nation has always lived to its promise, and will do this time as well. However, deal has different stages; all seven countries have agreed unanimously on all articles of the deal; with the UN, it should approve of the deal where it relates to removal of resolutions approved by the UN.

Today is the day of joint statement; the day when the UN approves of the deal, it is the day when the US and the EU will clearly announce removal of all sanctions, and after that Iran's commitment will go into effect, which will last for at least two months, which will be the day for deal implementation. . . .

Today, powers might say that they prevented Iran from making a nuclear bomb has been their major achievements; however, all know well that our Leader's fatwa prohibits nuclear weapon; Iran has never been and will never be after achieving nuclear weapons; so I call them to speak of other achievements which would usher a new era in international community. . . .

I would welcome constructive criticism; however, I would not allow criticism through scandal, through gossip, through defamation, to damage the trust of the public, to extinguish their hope for a new start; fresh start to a new hope, a better future for our youth, a more rapid movement toward development; and finally, you all our neighbors, beware of being trapped in Israeli propaganda. . . .

And as to our nation, we will have your help and support, in the path to the future.

SOURCE: Government of Iran. "Dr. Rouhani addresses nation on conclusion of nuclear talks." July 14, 2015. www.president.ir/en/88109.

OTHER HISTORIC DOCUMENTS OF INTEREST

FROM PREVIOUS *HISTORIC DOCUMENTS*

Response to al Qaeda-Affiliated Terrorist Attacks in Kenya and Mali

APRIL 4 AND NOVEMBER 23, 2015

Al Qaeda-affiliated groups carried out a number of attacks on African soil in 2014, two of the most notable taking place in Kenya where 148 were killed at a university and in Mali where nearly 170 hostages were taken, of which two dozen were killed. The attacks were carried out by two separate groups, al-Shabaab and al Mourabitoun, in cooperation with al Qaeda in the Islamic Maghreb, and came as little surprise to many in the international community. Kenya has become a hotbed of terrorist activity since the nation invaded Somalia in 2013, and Mali has been racked by government instability that invited the strengthening of Islamic extremists operating in the region.

University Students Gunned Down in Kenya

In the early morning of April 2, 2015, militants entered Garissa University in southeastern Kenya and opened fire on students in their dorms. In total, 142 students, three soldiers, and three police officers were killed, and seventy-nine were injured. According to witnesses, the gunmen targeted Christian students and allowed Muslims to leave the campus unharmed. Kenyan Defense Forces and other local security groups were quickly deployed to the university. They cordoned off the area, and a fifteen-hour siege to locate and capture the attackers ensued. Four of the attackers were killed in the siege. The attack was the most deadly in Kenya since 1998 when al Qaeda bombed the United States embassy and killed more than 200.

Al-Shabaab, the al Qaeda-affiliated terrorist organization functioning primarily out of Somalia, claimed responsibility for the attack, and the Kenyan government said that former Kenyan Islamic school headmaster Mohamed Kuno was the likely mastermind. In a statement on April 2, al-Shabaab said that the attack was an "operation against the infidels." Al-Shabaab spokesperson Ali Mohamoud Raghe said the group was fighting against "the Christian government of Kenya" that "invaded our country." In particular, Garissa University was targeted because of its large population of Christians. Al-Shabaab said it would continue its attacks in Kenya until the cities ran "red with blood," adding, "This will be a long, gruesome war of which you, the Kenyan public, are its first casualities."

Kenyan president Uhuru Kenyatta declared the event "an attack on our humanity," adding that those responsible were "not expressing a legitimate political aspiration" or "reflecting the tenets of faith and Godliness. They are motivated to worship suicide and the murder of children by a tyrannical ideology." During an address to the nation, the president urged Kenyans to be an example of the resiliency of the human spirit and not to victimize any member of Kenyan society despite their faith. "It is unfortunate that a false narrative is being propagated that Kenyan Somalis and Muslims are victims of marginalisation and oppression by the rest of Kenya. Nothing could be further from the truth. They enjoy the full rights, privileges and duties of every Kenyan. In those areas that have received less recognition and support from past governments, our Constitution has made provisions." He further encouraged the nation to come together in the wake of the university attack to root out terrorism wherever it lives in Kenya to prevent the nation from becoming a bastion of terrorist activity. "I urge all my brothers and sisters in the affected regions, and across the country, to not allow those who hide and abet the terrorists to compromise and even destroy the development that is fast growing in your area," he said.

On April 4, five men were arrested for suspected involvement in the attack. Three were Kenyan citizens of Somali descent, and the fourth was Tanzanian. Following the arrests, the government speculated that university guards may have permitted entrance to the university, though two guards were killed first by the al-Shabaab attackers. Curfews were established from the day of the attack through April 16 in the counties of Garissa, Wajir, Mandera, and Tana River. Critics of Kenyatta's government saw the curfew as permission for security forces to detain and harass Muslim Kenyans.

Immediately following the attacks, the Kenyan government and its primary allies, including the United States, vowed to continue to root out terrorists in the region. While offering his condolences to the friends and families of the victims during a speech to the nation, Kenyatta blamed the extensive deaths on a lack of military forces. "We have suffered unnecessarily due to shortage of security personnel," he said, adding that his government would take "urgent steps" to ensure that police and military forces were immediately trained to prevent such attacks in the future. This included ordering 10,000 new police recruits to report for duty, despite ongoing allegations that the recruits had been hired illegally.

Al-Shabaab's Ongoing War against Kenya

Kenya, which shares a border with Somalia, sent troops into the neighboring nation in October 2011 to stop Islamic terrorists from kidnapping and attacking Kenyans. This set off an almost immediate conflict between the two nations, in which al-Shabaab has ramped up its attacks year after year within Kenya. In 2013, al-Shabaab carried out an attack on a popular Kenyan mall that attracts many Westerners, resulting in sixty-seven people being killed. The ongoing attacks against citizens and civilians alike has harmed Kenya's reputation as a pillar of stability in the Middle East and stalled its tourism market, a primary component of the Kenyan economy.

Kenyatta's ability to handle al-Shabaab has been questioned since his inauguration in 2013. Since that time, more than 400 people have been killed in Kenya by the group. According to international human rights observers, the president is using the attacks as a means to consolidate his power and oppress civil rights. In December 2014, for example, Kenya's parliament passed a law backed by the president that would allow security forces to arrest and hold someone for as long as a year without charging the person with a crime.

Gunmen Hold Hostages in Mali Hotel

Seven months after the siege in Kenya, on November 20, 170 hostages were taken by another al Qaeda-affiliated group, al Mourabitoun, which stated it was working in cooperation with al Qaeda in the Islamic Maghreb, this time in the Malian capital of Bamako at the Radisson Blu hotel, just blocks away from the U.S. embassy. Al Mourabitoun came to power in 2013 and was led by former al Qaeda member Mokhtar Belmokhtar. Reports have indicated that he was killed in Libya during a U.S. airstrike, but as of the close of 2015 his death had not yet been confirmed. Macina Liberation Front has also claimed responsibility for the attack; however, its claims have not been verified.

Before dawn, cars full of gunmen with fake diplomatic license plates easily moved past security guards as they pulled up to the hotel. Once inside, they moved past hotel security and began firing. According to hotel employee Tamba Couye, when they entered, they were silent and began to shoot at "anything that moved." According to reports from witnesses, the attackers were heard shouting "Allah Akbar," or "God is great." Others indicated that the gunmen were speaking English. Forces responding to the attack said that those hotel guests who were able to recite portions of the Koran were allowed to leave the hotel unharmed. French, U.S., and Malian security forces all participated in the hostage rescue, along with the United Nations. More than two dozen people were killed in the attack, including six Malians, six Russians, three Chinese, two Belgians, one American, one Israeli, and one Senegalese. Three attackers were also killed during the standoff that stretched into the late afternoon. On November 27, Malian Special Forces announced that they had arrested two Malian men in connection with the attack, but that they were likely still seeking three of four accomplices.

The attack was viewed by many in the international community as an attempt to undermine ongoing work toward securing peace between the Malian government and rebel groups operating in the country. A peace accord signed in June had already been broken multiple times, and a number of those staying in the hotel were there to monitor the peace efforts. Mali's president, Ibrahim Boubacar Keita, who was in Chad at the time of the attack, reiterated the point he had made many times earlier that "Mali will have to get used to situations like this," adding, "no one, nowhere, is safe, given the danger of terrorism." In a brief statement following the attack, Mali's Prime Minister Modibo Keita stated that support had poured in from around the world and called it a show of solidarity and condemnation against the terrorists who perpetrated the "barbarous and cowardly act."

LACK OF STABILITY IN MALI

Although local military forces and support from international troops has helped make progress in removing some terrorist cells from countries across Africa, a lot of work remains to be done in Mali, where a variety of organizations—including al Qaeda in the Islamic Maghreb, Islamic Movement for Azawad, Movement for Unity and Jihad in West Africa, Signed in Blood Battalion, the National Movement Liberation of Azawad, and Ansar Dine—continue to operate. Primarily, these groups desire to take control of various portions of the country and institute a strict version of seventh-century Islamic law, which, among other things, calls for the destruction of non-Salafi religious sects and the amputation of limbs as punishment.

Mali has been locked in deep political crisis since it gained independence from France in 1960. The ongoing unrest and lack of a stable government has allowed terrorism to flourish within its borders. In 2012, a coup overthrew the ruling Malian government, which put Islamic extremists in control. These extremists were pushed back, in part through the cooperation of 1,000 French military forces that remain stationed in its former colony. Despite putting a Western-backed government in power, stability has still not been secured, and international analysts predict that the nation will continue to experience attacks similar to the hostage taking at the Radisson Blu. Regardless, President Keita said, "Terrorism will not win."

—Heather Kerrigan

Following is the text of an address delivered by Kenyan president Uhuru Kenyatta on April 4, 2015, following the al-Shabaab terrorist attack at Garissa University; a November 23, 2015, press release from the United Nations special mission in Mali regarding the Bamako hotel attack; and a statement by Malian prime minister Modibo Keita responding to the hotel attack.

DOCUMENT

Kenyan President Responds to Terror Attack

April 4, 2015

My Fellow Kenyans,

1. Our Nation is in a profound state of mourning following the heinous attack and mindless slaughter of 147 Kenyans in Garissa at Garissa University College on Thursday 2nd April 2015. It was the most lethal terrorist attack on Kenya since the 1998 US Embassy bombing. During the day-long ordeal, the terrorists took more than 800 students hostage; thankfully, more than 600 were rescued.

2. Our security forces responded and killed 4 of the terrorists while arresting 5. I commend the three officers who paid the ultimate price in their selfless service to Kenya.

My compatriots,

3. I stand before you, with profound sadness at a time of great sorrow for Kenya.

4. Let us take a moment to remember those who died and pray for the eternal repose of their souls. Let us also pray for those who were injured and for solace to all affected families. Today, villages and towns throughout Kenya are in mourning.

5. As we mourn together, and pray together for the fallen and for this our precious Republic of Kenya, I declare three days of national mourning during which our flag shall fly at half-mast.

I also want to assure the families, that government will support all possible support to the victims.

6. We have received many messages of condolence and strong expressions of support and goodwill from our friends and people of goodwill across the globe.

In this regard, we wish to thank our brothers and sisters from the East African Community and IGAD, the African continent, as well as global leaders including the Secretary General of the United Nations, the President of the United States of America, and His Holiness Pope Francis, amongst others. This solidarity underlines the oneness of humanity and consensus that terrorism is a global threat requiring robust international partnerships.

7. To the families and friends of the survivors, and indeed all Kenyans, I want you to know that our security forces are pursuing leads on the remaining accomplices. We shall employ all means at our disposal to bring the perpetrators to justice. We are also in active pursuit of the mastermind of the attack, and have placed a reward for the information leading to his capture.

8. To the students who survived the attack on Garissa University College, I want you to understand our nation's deep regret that such a calamity should befall you in your formative years. However difficult, you must remain resolved to finish your studies and graduate. Because in doing so, you will demonstrate to yourselves, and to the world, that terror and evil can never prevail over the hard work and resilience that characterises the Kenyan spirit.

9. In the next few days, as funerals are held across the length and breadth of Kenya, we will be filled with anguish and great anger. During this holy period of Easter, the families and communities of the fallen should take solace in recalling that after the evil of the cross on Friday, and when the Devil thought he had triumphed, Sunday's hope arrived. As we remember those that fell at Garissa, we recognise that the resurrection of Jesus demonstrates that the power of hatred and violence will never prevail. We shall prevail.

10. I urge every Kenyan, every church and every local leader to speak up for our unity and ensure that our justified anger does not spill over and lead to the victimisation of anyone. This would only play into the hands of the terrorists. Let us remain in unity as we safeguard our peace and stability.

Fellow Kenyans,

11. On Thursday, the Garissa University College was turned from a place of learning and hope into an arena of pain, despair and death. As a nation, we are betrayed by those who attempt to turn our diversity, our openness, and our freedom against us.

12. Humanity's existence is defined by the sanctity of life. By separating our children in the name of religion, before slaughtering them, the terrorists aimed to shatter this sanctity, which defines all communities and peoples globally.

I stand here today, to declare that what we have witnessed in Garissa and other parts of the world is an attack on our humanity.

13. These terrorists are not expressing a legitimate political aspiration; they are not killing in response to oppression or marginalisation; and they are not reflecting the tenets of faith and Godliness.

They are motivated to worship suicide and the murder of children by a tyrannical ideology that seeks to establish a Caliphate in Somalia, and the north-eastern and coastal counties of our country, and across large parts of the world.

14. Such an entity would then embark on the evil brutality that we see being daily perpetrated by ISIS in Iraq and Syria, and Boko Haram in West Africa.

It would offer no future except for more death and destruction, and, in this sense, the Garissa attack is aimed at humanity, at the deep common bonds of openness, respect for difference and empathy that form the global community.

My Fellow Kenyans,

15. We tell those who believe that a Caliphate is possible in Kenya that we are one indivisible, sovereign, and democratic state. That fact will never change.

Our forefathers bled and died for this nation and we will do everything to defend our way of life.

16. When I addressed Parliament on the 26th of March about the State of the Nation, I emphasised the need for a national reconciliation to allow us to move forward together as one nation. By drawing a line under a shared painful past, Kenyans should embrace a future of shared prosperity and security.

Today, however, I am saddened to stand before you after the massacre in Garissa.

17. It is unfortunate that a false narrative is being propagated that Kenyan Somalis and Muslims are victims of marginalisation and oppression by the rest of Kenya. Nothing could be further from the truth. They enjoy the full rights, privileges and duties of every Kenyan. In those areas that have received less recognition and support from past governments, our Constitution has made provisions.

A large amount of extra financial resources and services are being provided, and Kenyan Somalis and Muslims form a vital part of our national economic and political life. We are one.

18. I urge all my brothers and sisters in the affected regions, and across the country, to not allow those who hide and abet the terrorists to compromise and even destroy the development that is fast growing in your area.

There is more infrastructure being built than ever before; more of your children are being enrolled in schools and colleges; more services are being delivered; and the economic transformation of the country will benefit you and your descendants, as they will all Kenyans.

19. The terrorists promise only death, poverty and terror; I am certain that your choice, as expressed in your determination to work with the government to defeat them, will be for development and progress.

20. Through the pain and anger that we are all feeling, we must come to the painful realisation that evil with its persistent desire to destroy and undermine need succeed only once for every hundred attempts that we foil. One chance is all they need to unleash their barbaric medieval slaughter upon our people and children.

21. Our security demands that we continue the difficult and daunting task of identifying, separating, tracking and deterring the enemy not only in Kenya but in Somalia, alongside our African and international allies. This is why I am calling on all leaders, at all levels of government, in civil society and in the political opposition to speak in a united voice that reflects the importance of sustaining this initiative. All leaders should treat national security as a subject that demands the weightiest consideration.

Fellow Kenyans,

22. Since independence, Kenya has embraced its diversity.

Our multi-ethnic, multi-cultural, and multi-religious character has been embraced in law and by deep tolerance among our people. It is a point of pride for our nation and a source of great strength against adversity.

23. I personally believe that Islam is a religion of peace and tolerance, tenets which the vast majority of Muslims uphold. However, the time has come for us to be honest with ourselves and each other.

24. The radicalisation that breeds terrorism is not conducted in the bush at night. It occurs in the full glare of day, in madrassas, in homes and in Mosques with rogue Imams. We must ask where are the religious leaders, the community leadership, and the parents and families of those who are radicalising our young people? The government must get the information and cooperation of all these parties if we are to effectively combat the terrorists.

25. It is a fact that our task of countering terrorism work has been made all the more difficult by the fact that the planners and financiers of this brutality are deeply embedded in our communities and were seen as ordinary, harmless people.

26. We will not allow them to continue their lives as normal. The full force of the law will be brought to bear with even greater intensity than has been the case in previous years.

27. During the State of the Nation address, and on many occasions before then, I spoke of the pervasive threat of corruption to our aspirations as a people. What else but corruption of the worst and most criminal kind is it for Kenyans to finance, hide and recruit on behalf of Al Shabaab? There is no form of legal penalty, social shaming and Godly condemnation that they do not deserve to the fullest extent.

Fellow Kenyans,

28. The leadership of this nation, under my stewardship, has been in continuous deliberation to elaborate a robust framework to deal with that [which] has become an existential threat to our Republic. I guarantee Kenyans that my administration shall respond in the severest ways possible to the Garissa attack, and any other threat to us.

29. Thursday wounded Kenya, Thursday wounded families, friends and the communities of the victims of the attack. Despite adversity, we have been, and will always be, unbowed and shall continue to build a strong, prosperous and secure nation. That is the greatest testimony we can offer to those precious departed we have lost.

God bless you, and God Bless Kenya.

UHURU KENYATTA, CGH
PRESIDENT AND COMMANDER IN CHIEF OF THE KENYA DEFENCE FORCES.

Source: Official Website of the President of Kenya. "Statement by H. E. Uhuru Kenyatta on the Terrorist Attack at Garissa University College, Garissa County, Delivered During a Live Address to the Nation." April 4, 2015. www.president.go.ke/2015/04/04/statement-by-h-e-uhuru-kenyatta-on-the-terrorist-attack-at-garissa-university-college-garissa-county-delivered-during-a-live-address-to-the-nation.

United Nations Special Mission in Mali on Hotel Hostage Taking

November 23, 2015

The Special Representative of the Secretary-General for Mali (SRSG) and Head of MINUSMA, Mr. Mongi Hamdi, commends the professionalism of the Malian Defense and Security Forces (MDSF), in the aftermath of the terrorist attack against a Bamako hotel on 20 November 2015, and expresses his gratitude to countries having provided support during the crisis.

"I also extend my great appreciation to the various divisions of MINUSMA who mobilized alongside their Malian and international partners," he said.

"On the morning of 20 November, shortly after having been informed of this despicable terrorist attack, I ordered the establishment and immediate deployment to the site of a security force composed of elements from our UN security and safety section, our Quick Reaction Force and police specialists*. Supporting this team was a first-aid cell providing medical care to the injured and psychological support to evacuees," Mr. Mongi Hamdi said.

MINUSMA also deployed onsite ambulances and firetrucks.

"I am impressed by the good coordination with the Malian Defense and Security Forces. I want to renew my appreciation to our police officers from UNPOL, to the UN Security personnel, and to all firefighters and rescuers who have joined forces with our Malian and international partners with a great deal of passion and professionalism. I finally salute the composure and courage of hotel guests and staff who had [to] overcome this ordeal," the Special Representative to the Secretary-General added.

The Secretary General of the United Nations, the Security Council and SRSG Hamdi had all previously condemned the heinous terrorist attack in which at least

22 people have been killed—including two attackers—and dozens injured, including 6 seriously wounded.

The United Nations Police (UNPOL) is now providing support and technical expertise to the ongoing investigation.

MINUSMA extends its sincere condolences to the bereaved families, to the peoples and Governments of the countries affected by this tragedy, and wish a speedy recovery to the injured.

MINUSMA strongly condemns any action aiming to jeopardize the Peace Process and remains committed to support the people and Government of Mali in their efforts to bring back lasting peace to the country.

* United Nations personnel involved on site during the crisis:

45 Police Officers from UNPOL (UN Police)
14 UN Security Officers

SOURCE: United Nations Multidimensional Integrated Stabilization Mission in Mali. "Bamako Attack: MINUSMA Working Alongside Malian Defense and Security Forces." November 23, 2015. http://minusma.unmissions.org/en/bamako-attack-minusma-working-alongside-malian-defense-and-security-forces.

Malian Prime Minister Remarks on International Response to Hotel Attack

DOCUMENT

November 23, 2015

Primature: Prime Minister Modibo KEITA welcomes his counterpart from Burkina Faso on Monday.

Following the vile terrorist attack on the Radisson BLU perpetrated last Friday and for which two terrorist organizations, Al mourabitoune and the Mouvement de libération du Macina (*Macina Liberation Movement*), have claimed responsibility, our country continues to receive signs of solidarity and compassion from the entire international community, who condemns in the strongest terms this barbarous and cowardly act committed by men who fear neither God nor man. In addition to messages of support from heads of state and of government throughout the world, the ECOWAS sent President Macky SALL on a visit to President Ibrahim Boubakar KEITA on Sunday, and Burkina Faso is sending the president of its transition parliament as well as its prime minister on Monday 23 November. They all bring messages of condolence and support from the President and the people of Burkina Faso to the highest authorities of our country. Other public figures are also expected in the coming hours and days!

SOURCE: Malinet. "PRIME MINISTER: Prime Minister Modibo Keita hosts Monday his counterpart from Burkina Faso." November 23, 2015. Translated from French by SAGE Publishing. www.malinet .net/flash-info/primature-le-premier-ministre-modibo-keita-accueille-ce-lundi-son-homologue-du-burkina-faso.

OTHER HISTORIC DOCUMENTS OF INTEREST

United States and Cuban Officials Remark on Renewed Relations

APRIL 11 AND 14, MAY 29, JULY 1, AUGUST 14, AND
SEPTEMBER 28, 2015

In December 2014, President Barack Obama surprised many when he announced the intent of the United States and its long-time enemy, Cuba, to begin working toward normalization of relations. Since Fidel Castro came to power in 1959, the two nations have had a nearly nonexistent relationship that stopped most trade and prevented Americans from traveling to the island nation. Throughout 2015, Secretary of State John Kerry and a team of diplomats negotiated with Cuban leaders to lift economic sanctions and restore diplomatic ties, including the reopening of the U.S. embassy in Havana and the Cuban embassy in Washington, D.C.

HISTORY OF U.S.–CUBA RELATIONS

Castro came to power in 1959 as the result of a coup that toppled the U.S.-backed government of General Fulgencio Batista. Although the United States recognized Castro as the rightful ruler of the nation, Castro began looking for other international partners, and specifically turned to the Soviet Union, then a fierce enemy of the United States. As Cuba increased trade with the Soviet government, it also raised taxes on American imports, which led to economic sanctions from the United States, including a complete embargo on all trade. Any remaining diplomatic ties officially ended in 1961, and the United States quickly acted with multiple attempts to overthrow the Castro regime, including the infamous 1961 Bay of Pigs invasion. Cuba responded to the invasion by further strengthening its relationship with the Soviet Union, even allowing the Soviets to build a secret missile base in Cuba. This missile base led to the fourteen-day Cuban Missile Crisis standoff, during which then-President John Kennedy ordered a naval blockade around the island and demanded the removal of the base. In the end, the United States agreed not to invade and to remove its own missiles from Turkey, as long as Cuba agreed to dismantle the Soviet Union's base.

Even after the fall of the Soviet Union, the United States still failed to lift its embargo against Cuba, and in fact strengthened it through Congressional action in 1992 and 1996. In 1982, Cuba was added to the State Department's list of state sponsors of terrorism. When Fidel Castro stepped down from his position in 2008 due to ill health and was replaced by his brother, Raúl, there was hope that the United States would use the opportunity to begin restoring its relationship with the island nation.

THE LONG ROAD TO RESTORATION

President Obama began working to soften the United States' relationship with Cuba when he took office in early 2009. At that time he reversed many of the restrictions put in place by his predecessor, President George W. Bush, including allowing Americans with Cuban relatives to make unlimited visits to Cuba and send financial aid. The president also eased restrictions on wireless providers and allowed them to establish cellphone and television services in Cuba. According to the White House, these moves were undertaken to encourage Cuban citizens to become less dependent on the Castro regime. Obama even continued his push to restore diplomatic ties late in 2009 when U.S. Agency for International Development (USAID) subcontractor Alan Gross was arrested, charged with attempting to overthrow the Castro regime, and sentenced to fifteen years in prison.

Throughout 2013 and 2014, U.S. and Cuban officials met secretly to examine the potential of normalization of the relationship. The eighteen-month talks resulted in a framework for restoring full diplomatic ties, as long as certain concessions were met, including the release of three of the remaining Cuban Five, Gross, Rolando Sarraff Trujillo, a Cuban intelligence officer who spied for the CIA, and fifty-three individuals being held in Cuban jails who were considered political prisoners by U.S. officials. The new approach to Cuban relations included fourteen key provisions: establishment of diplomatic relations; adjustment of relations to empower Cubans; expanded travel to Cuba; increased remittance levels; expanded commercial sales and exports to Cuba; allowance of additional imports from Cuba; facilitation of authorized transactions between the two countries; new efforts to help Cubans access communications technologies; updated Cuban sanctions in third countries; discussion of the maritime boundary in the Gulf of Mexico; review of the State Department designation of Cuba as a state sponsor of terrorism; possible allowance of Cuban civil society groups to participate in the 2015 Summit of the Americans in Panama; and continuing commitment to human rights and democracy.

The first change made under the agreement came in January 2015, when the United States began scaling back its trade and travel restrictions. For the first time since 1961, Americans would be able to travel to Cuba without first obtaining a government license. However, some travel restrictions were maintained. Travelers to Cuba were required to be visiting for one of twelve reasons, including conducting research, participating in an educational activity, participating in a sporting event, or performing a concert. As of 2015, tourism did not meet the requirements for travel. And to that end, although American air carriers such as Jet Blue and American Airlines opened up routes from cities in Florida and New York to Havana, U.S. citizens could not directly purchase tickets. Instead, they were required to go through a third party with a license to provide such tickets. As such, a number of tour companies began offering what they called educational experiences to Cuba.

The economic sanctions lifted in January included allowed shipment of building materials to private Cuban companies, U.S. corporate investment in some small Cuban businesses, the ability of banks to authorize transactions, the ability of U.S. travelers to Cuba to use American credit and debit cards, and permission for U.S. insurance companies to provide coverage for those visiting or living in Cuba.

On April 11, 2015, Obama and Castro met on the sidelines of the Summit of the Americas, marking the first time a U.S. and Cuban head of state had met since 1961. In a brief press conference, the leaders agreed that they were both willing to put all of their issues on the table for debate as they continued the dialogue to normalize relations. "I think what we have both concluded is that we can disagree with a spirit of respect and civility and that, over time, it is possible for us to turn the page and develop a new relationship between our two countries," Obama said. Castro echoed those remarks, noting,

"We shall continue advancing in the meetings which are taking place in order to reestablish relations between our countries."

In December 2014, President Obama recommended that, as part of the work to normalize relations with Cuba, the Secretary of State review Cuba's designation as a state sponsor of terrorism. Secretary of State John Kerry completed his review on April 8, and on April 14, President Obama delivered the requisite information to Congress to note that it would remove Cuba from the list based on Kerry's review. Congress was given forty-five days to review the information, which stated that Cuba had not supported international terrorism during the previous six months and had provided the United States assurances that it would no longer do so. On May 29, Secretary Kerry made the final decision to have Cuba removed from the State Sponsors of Terrorism List.

EMBASSIES REOPEN, MANY ECONOMIC SANCTIONS REMAIN

On July 20, 2015, Cuba and the United States reopened their embassies in each other's capitals. No official celebration took place on that date in Havana, and business as usual continued in the newly established embassy, previously the U.S. Interests Section of the Embassy of Switzerland. In Washington, D.C., Cuba's Foreign Minister Bruno Rodriguez called for continuing "a dialogue based on mutual respect and sovereign equality" between the two countries. Opponents of the Cuban government stood outside the D.C. embassy, pressing for improvements in Cuban human rights and an end to the Castro regime. Secretary Kerry noted that the opening of the embassies "does not signify the end to differences that still separate our governments," adding that "it does reflect the reality that the Cold War ended long ago, and that the interests of both countries are better served by engagement than by estrangement." When he presided over the official reopening on August 15, Kerry said the renewed relationship would mean recognition "that U.S. policy is not the anvil on which Cuba's future will be forged." Instead, he said it would be "for the Cubans to shape."

However, even while this historic step was taken, both Cuban and U.S. officials continued their rhetoric about the remaining problems in restoring relations. Rodriguez spoke about the "nefarious consequences" of the Cuban Constitution's Platt Amendment, which allows the United States to establish bases like Guantánamo on Cuban soil and exercise some control over Cuban affairs, and added that Cuba has its "own concerns in the area of human rights in the United States." Bruno said that of those issues still outstanding between the two countries, Cuba would be willing to continue negotiations, but that there were some solutions on which it "would be very difficult to reach an agreement."

Although President Obama had the ability to use his executive authority to control some areas related to the normalization of relations, Congress was in charge of nearly all economic sanctions. Fully normalizing relations with Cuba would require the repeal of the Helms-Burton Act, the 1996 law that prohibited the lifting of economic sanctions until Cuba allowed for full democratic rights for its people. Kerry admitted during the embassy opening in August that there would be "no way Congress is going to vote to lift the embargo if [the Cuban government is] not moving with respect to issues of conscience." But Kerry said that he continued to believe that Cubans "would be best served by a genuine democracy where people are free to choose their leaders, express their ideas and practice their faith."

Reaction to Normalization Efforts

When Obama first announced his plans in December 2014, he was met with criticism from Republican lawmakers who disagreed with the push to restore economic and diplomatic ties with a nation that still had not granted full democratic freedoms to its citizens. Sen. Marco Rubio, R-Fla., a Cuban American and 2016 presidential contender, called the plans "a concession to tyranny." Republican-controlled House and Senate leadership promised to attempt to block some of the president's normalization plans, specifically the lifting of economic sanctions and funds for a new U.S. embassy in Cuba. Likely, Congress will have to use its power of the purse to undo the president's plans. There are Democrats and Republicans on both sides of the debate, which will likely carry into 2016 and beyond.

U.S. public opinion on restoration of the U.S.–Cuban relationship has remained high since late 2014. According to a Pew Research poll conducted shortly after the president's announcement on December 17, 2014, 63 percent of those surveyed supported the resumption of diplomatic relations. In Cuba, 97 percent of those surveyed favored the normalization of the U.S.–Cuban relationship, according to a 2015 poll conducted by Bendixen and Amandi.

—Heather Kerrigan

Following are the remarks from a press conference between U.S. president Barack Obama and Cuban president Raúl Castro on April 11, 2015, regarding the ongoing negotiations to restore diplomatic ties; a press statement from Secretary of State John Kerry on April 14, 2015, recommending that Cuba be removed from the Department's list of state sponsors of terrorism; a press statement from the Department of State on May 29, 2015, announcing the removal of Cuba from the list of state sponsors of terrorism; remarks from Secretary Kerry on July 1, 2015, on the formal agreement between Cuba and the United States; the remarks by Secretary Kerry on August 14, 2015, at the flag-raising ceremony at the U.S. embassy in Cuba; and a portion of the statement by President Castro before the United Nations on September 28, 2015, regarding renewed relations with the United States.

DOCUMENT

U.S. and Cuban Presidents on Renewed Relationship

April 11, 2015

President Obama. This is obviously a historic meeting. The history between the United States and Cuba is obviously complicated, and over the years, a lot of mistrust has developed. But during the course of the last several months, there have been contacts between the U.S. and the Cuban Government. And in December, as a consequence of some of the groundwork that had been laid, both myself and President Castro announced a significant change in policy and the relationship between our two governments.

I think that after 50 years of a policy that had not changed on the part of the United States, it was my belief that it was time to try something new: that it was important for us to engage more directly with the Cuban Government and the Cuban people. And as a consequence, I think we are now in a position to move on a path towards the future and leave behind some of the circumstances of the past that have made it so difficult, I think, for our countries to communicate.

Already, we've seen majorities of the American people and the Cuban people respond positively to this change. And I truly believe that as more exchanges take place, more commerce and interactions resume between the United States and Cuba, that the deep connections between the Cuban people and the American people will reflect itself in a more positive and constructive relationship between our governments.

Now, obviously, there are still going to be deep and significant differences between our two governments. We will continue to try to lift up concerns around democracy and human rights. And as we heard from President Castro's passionate speech this morning, they will lift up concerns about U.S. policy as well. But I think what we have both concluded is that we can disagree with a spirit of respect and civility and that, over time, it is possible for us to turn the page and develop a new relationship between our two countries.

And some of our immediate tasks include normalizing diplomatic relations and ultimately opening an Embassy in Havana and Cuba being able to open an Embassy in Washington, DC, so that our diplomats are able to interact on a more regular basis.

So I want to thank President Castro for the spirit of openness and courtesy that he has shown during our interactions. And I think that if we can build on this spirit of mutual respect and candidness, that over time, we will see not just a transformation in the relationship between our two countries, but a positive impact throughout the hemisphere and the world.

And President Castro earlier today spoke about the significant hardships that the people of Cuba have undergone over many decades. I can say with all sincerity that the essence of my policy is to do whatever I can to make sure that the people of Cuba are able to prosper and live in freedom and security and enjoy a connection with the world where their incredible talents and ingenuity and hard work can thrive.

President Castro. Muchas gracias.

President Obama. Thank you. . . .

President Castro. Well, Mr. President, friends from the press, we have been making long speeches and listening to many long speeches too . . . so I do not want to abuse the time of President Obama or your time.

I think that what President Obama has just said, it's practically the same as we feel about these topics, including human rights, freedom of the press. We have said on previous occasions to some American friends that we are willing to discuss every issue between the United States and Cuba. We are willing to discuss about those issues that I have mentioned and about many others, as these reforms, both in Cuba, but also in the United States.

I think that everything can be on the table. I think that we can do it, as President Obama has just said, with respect for the ideas of the other. We could be persuaded of some things; of others, we might not be persuaded. But when I say that I agree with everything that the President has just said, I include that we have agreed to disagree. No one should entertain illusions. It is true that we have many differences. Our countries have a long and complicated history behind them, but we are willing to make progress in the way the President has described.

We can develop a friendship between our two peoples. We shall continue advancing in the meetings which are taking place in order to reestablish relations between our countries. We shall open our Embassies. We shall visit each other, have exchanges, people to people. And now all that matters is what close neighbors can do; we are close neighbors, and there are many things that we can have.

So we are willing to discuss everything, but we need to be patient, very patient. Some things we will agree on; others we will disagree. The pace of life at the present moment in the world, it's very fast. We might disagree on something today on which we could agree tomorrow. And we hope that our closest assistants—part of them are here with us today—we hope that they will follow the instructions of both Presidents.

Thank you so much. *Muchas gracias*. Thank you, everybody.

SOURCE: Executive Office of the President. "Remarks Prior to a Meeting With President Raúl Castro Ruz of Cuba in Panama City, Panama." April 11, 2015. *Compilation of Presidential Documents* 2015, no. 00260 (April 11, 2015). www.gpo.gov/fdsys/pkg/DCPD-201500260/pdf/DCPD-201500260.pdf.

Secretary Kerry Recommends Removal of Cuba from List of State Sponsors of Terrorism

DOCUMENT

April 14, 2015

In December 2014, as a critical component of establishing a new direction for U.S.–Cuba relations, the President directed the State Department to launch a review of Cuba's designation as a State Sponsor of Terrorism and provide a report to him within six months. Last week, the State Department submitted a report to the White House recommending, based on the facts and the statutory standard, that President Obama rescind Cuba's designation as a State Sponsor of Terrorism.

This recommendation reflects the Department's assessment that Cuba meets the criteria established by Congress for rescission. While the United States has had, and continues to have, significant concerns and disagreements with a wide range of Cuba's policies and actions, these concerns and disagreements fall outside of the criteria for designation as a State Sponsor of Terrorism. This review focused on the narrow questions of whether Cuba provided any support for international terrorism during the previous six months, and whether Cuba has provided assurances that it will not support acts of international terrorism in the future, consistent with the statutory standard for rescission.

Circumstances have changed since 1982, when Cuba was originally designated as a State Sponsor of Terrorism because of its efforts to promote armed revolution by forces in Latin America. Our Hemisphere, and the world, look very different today than they did 33 years ago. Our determination, pursuant to the facts, including corroborative assurances received from the Government of Cuba and the statutory standard, is that the time has come to rescind Cuba's designation as a State Sponsor of Terrorism.

SOURCE: U.S. Department of State. "Recommendation to Rescind Cuba's Designation as a State Sponsor of Terrorism." April 14, 2015. www.state.gov/secretary/remarks/2015/04/240687.htm.

State Department Announces Removal of Cuban Designation as Terrorism Sponsor

May 29, 2015

In December 2014, the President instructed the Secretary of State to immediately launch a review of Cuba's designation as a State Sponsor of Terrorism, and provide a report to him within six months regarding Cuba's support for international terrorism. On April 8, 2015, the Secretary of State completed that review and recommended to the President that Cuba no longer be designated as a State Sponsor of Terrorism.

Accordingly, on April 14, the President submitted to Congress the statutorily required report indicating the Administration's intent to rescind Cuba's State Sponsor of Terrorism designation, including the certification that Cuba has not provided any support for international terrorism during the previous six-months; and that Cuba has provided assurances that it will not support acts of international terrorism in the future. The 45-day Congressional pre-notification period has expired, and the Secretary of State has made the final decision to rescind Cuba's designation as a State Sponsor of Terrorism, effective today, May 29, 2015.

The rescission of Cuba's designation as a State Sponsor of Terrorism reflects our assessment that Cuba meets the statutory criteria for rescission. While the United States has significant concerns and disagreements with a wide range of Cuba's policies and actions, these fall outside the criteria relevant to the rescission of a State Sponsor of Terrorism designation.

SOURCE: U.S. Department of State. "Rescission of Cuba as a State Sponsor of Terrorism." May 29, 2015. www.state.gov/r/pa/prs/ps/2015/05/242986.htm.

Secretary Kerry Announces Formal Agreement to Reestablish Diplomatic Ties

July 1, 2015

SECRETARY KERRY: Good afternoon, everybody. Thank you for your patience. In Washington a few moments ago, President Obama announced that we had reached an agreement to formally re-establish diplomatic relations with the Republic of Cuba and that we will reopen embassies in our respective countries.

Later this summer, as the President announced, I will travel to Cuba to personally take part in the formal reopening of our United States Embassy in Havana. This will mark the resumption of embassy operations after a period of 54 years. It will also be the first visit by a Secretary of State to Cuba since 1945. The reopening of our embassy, I will tell you, is an important step on the road to restoring fully normal relations between the United States and Cuba. Coming a quarter of a century after the end of the Cold War, it recognizes the reality of the changed circumstances, and it will serve to meet a number of practical needs.

The United States and Cuba continue to have sharp differences over democracy, human rights, and related issues, but we also have identified areas for cooperation that include law enforcement, safe transportation, emergency response, environmental protection, telecommunications, and migration. The resumption of full embassy activities will help us engage the Cuban Government more often and at a higher level, and it will also allow our diplomats to interact more frequently, and frankly more broadly and effectively, with the Cuban people. In addition, we will better be able to assist Americans who travel to the island nation in order to visit family members or for other purposes.

This transition, this moment in history, is taking place because President Obama made a personal, fundamental decision to change a policy that didn't work and that had been in place not working for far too long. I believe that's leadership, and I appreciate that leadership. And President Castro felt similarly that it was time for a change. Both leaders agree that concentrating on the issues and possibilities of the future is far more productive than remaining mired in the past. And I would say as we look at the world today with conflicts that we see and even these negotiations taking place here in Vienna, it is important for people to understand that things can change, that leadership can be effective and can make a difference.

This step has been long overdue, and the response of the international community has reflected the relief and the welcoming that people all over the world feel for this step. This step will advance the President's vision—President Obama's vision—of an Americas where responsibilities are widely shared and where countries combine their strengths to advance common interests and values. And we, frankly, also believe that this opening will help to change relationships in the region as a whole.

I want to thank Assistant Secretary of State Roberta Jacobson and her team, our team at the State Department, together with those at the White House who have worked to lead these discussions with their Cuban counterparts in order to enable the normalization of our diplomatic relations and the reopening of our embassies. I also want to thank the Government of Switzerland for the essential role that they have played in serving as the United States protecting power in Cuba for more than 50 years.

And finally, I want to acknowledge the efforts of many in the United States Congress, the Cuban American community, civil society, faith-based organizations, the private sector, and others throughout our country and beyond who have supported the start of a new chapter of relations between the United States and Cuba. I look forward to meeting again with my Cuban counterpart, Bruno Rodriguez, who I saw most recently in Panama, and I also look forward to greeting our embassy personnel and the Cuban people in Havana later this summer. I look forward to taking part in the reopening of our United States embassy and in the raising of the Stars and Stripes over that embassy, and the beginning of a new era of a new relationship with the people of Cuba. Thank you all very much.

[The brief question and answer section has been omitted.]

Source: U.S. Department of State. "Statement on Cuba." July 1, 2015. www.state.gov/secretary/remarks/2015/07/244542.htm.

Secretary Kerry Remarks on Flag-Raising Ceremony at U.S. Embassy in Havana

DOCUMENT

August 14, 2015

SECRETARY KERRY: Please be seated, everybody. Thank you very, very much. *Muchas gracias. Buenos dias.* I'm so sorry that we are a little bit late today, but what a beautiful ride in and how wonderful to be here. And I thank you for leaving my future transportation out here in back of me. I love it. (Laughter.)

Distinguished members of the Cuban delegation—Josefina, thank you for your leadership and for all your work of your delegation; excellencies from the diplomatic corps; my colleagues from Washington, past and present; Ambassador DeLaurentis and all of the embassy staff; and friends watching around the world, thank you for joining us at this truly historic moment as we prepare to raise the United States flag here at our embassy in Havana, symbolizing the re-establishment of diplomatic relations after 54 years. This is also the first time that a United States Secretary of State has been to Cuba since 1945. (Applause.)

This morning I feel very much at home here, and I'm grateful to those who have come to share in this ceremony who are standing around outside of our facilities, and I feel at home here because this is truly a memorable occasion—a day for pushing aside old barriers and exploring new possibilities.

And it is in that spirit that I say on behalf of my country, *Los Estados Unidos acogen con beneplacito este nuevo comienzo de su relacion con el pueblo y el Gobierno de Cuba. Sabemos que el camino hacia unas relaciones plenamente normales es largo, pero es precisamente por ello que tenemos que empezar en este mismo instante. No hay nada que temer, ya que seran muchos los beneficios de los que gozaremos cuando permitamos a nuestros ciudadanos conocerse mejor, visitarse con mas frecuencia, realizar negocios de forma habitual, intercambiar ideas y aprender los unos de los otros.*

[Translation by SAGE: The United States welcomes this new beginning of our relationship with the people and the government of Cuba. We know that the road to a fully normal relationship is long, but it is precisely why we have to start right now. There is nothing to fear, there are many benefits to celebrate as we let our citizens know each other better, visit more often, conduct business as usual, exchange ideas, and learn from each other.]

My friends, we are gathered here today because our leaders—President Obama and President Castro—made a courageous decision to stop being the prisoners of history and to focus on the opportunities of today and tomorrow. This doesn't mean that we should or will forget the past; how could we, after all? At least for my generation, the images are indelible.

In 1959, Fidel Castro came to the United States and was greeted by enthusiastic crowds. Returning the next year for the UN General Assembly, he was embraced by then-Soviet Premier Nikita Khrushchev. In 1961, the Bay of Pigs tragedy unfolded with President Kennedy accepting responsibility. And in October 1962, the missile crisis arose—13 days that pushed us to the very threshold of nuclear war. I was a student then, and I can still remember the taut faces of our leaders, the grim map showing the movement of opposing ships, the approaching deadline, and that peculiar word—quarantine. We were unsettled and uncertain about the future because we didn't know when closing our eyes at night what we would find when we woke up.

In that frozen environment, diplomatic ties between Washington and this capital city were strained, then stretched thin, then severed. In late 1960, the U.S. ambassador left Havana. Early the following January, Cuba demanded a big cut in the size of our diplomatic mission, and President Eisenhower then decided he had no choice but to shut the embassy down.

Most of the U.S. staff departed quickly, but a few stayed behind to hand the keys over to our Swiss colleagues, who would serve diligently and honorably as our protecting power for more than 50 years. I just met with the Foreign Minister Didier Burkhalter, and we're grateful to Switzerland always for their service and their help. (Applause.)

Among those remaining at the embassy were three Marine guards: Larry Morris, Mike East, and Jim Tracy. As they stepped outside, they were confronted by a large crowd standing between them and the flagpole. Tensions were high. No one felt safe. But the Marines had a mission to accomplish. And slowly, the crowd just parted in front of them as they made their way to the flagpole, lowered Old Glory, folded it, and returned to the building.

Larry, Mike, and Jim had done their jobs, but they also made a bold promise that one day they would return to Havana and raise the flag again. (Applause.)

At the time, no one could have imagined how distant that day would be.

For more than half a century, U.S.–Cuban relations have been suspended in the amber of Cold War politics. In the interim, a whole generation of Americans and Cubans have grown up and grown old. The United States has had ten new presidents. In a united Germany, the Berlin Wall is a fading memory. Freed from Soviet shackles, Central Europe is again home to thriving democracies.

And last week, I was in Hanoi to mark the 20th anniversary of normalization of relations between the United States and Vietnam. Think about that. A long and terrible war that inflicted indelible scars on body and mind, followed by two decades of mutual healing, followed by another two decades of diplomatic and commercial engagement. In this period, Vietnam evolved from a country torn apart by violence into a dynamic society with one of the world's fastest growing economies. And all that time, through reconciliation, through normalization, Cuban-American relations remained locked in the past.

Meanwhile, new technologies enabled people everywhere to benefit from shared projects across vast stretches of ocean and land. My friends, it doesn't take a GPS to realize that the road of mutual isolation and estrangement that the United States and Cuba were traveling was not the right one and that the time has come for us to move in a more promising direction.

In the United States, that means recognizing that U.S. policy is not the anvil on which Cuba's future will be forged. Decades of good intentions aside, the policies of the past have not led to a democratic transition in Cuba. It would be equally unrealistic to expect normalizing relations to have, in a short term, a transformational impact. After all, Cuba's future is for Cubans to shape. Responsibility for the nature and quality of governance and accountability rests, as it should, not with any outside entity; but solely within the citizens of this country.

But the leaders in Havana—and the Cuban people—should also know that the United States will always remain a champion of democratic principles and reforms. Like many other governments in and outside this hemisphere, we will continue to urge the Cuban Government to fulfill its obligations under the UN and inter-American human rights covenants—obligations shared by the United States and every other country in the Americas.

And indeed, we remain convinced the people of Cuba would be best served by genuine democracy, where people are free to choose their leaders, express their ideas, practice their faith; where the commitment to economic and social justice is realized more fully; where institutions are answerable to those they serve; and where civil society is independent and allowed to flourish.

Let me be clear: The establishment of normal diplomatic relations is not something that one government does as a favor to another; it is something that two countries do together when the citizens of both will benefit. And in this case, the reopening of our embassies is important on two levels: People-to-people and government-to-government.

First, we believe it's helpful for the people of our nations to learn more about each other, to meet each other. That is why we are encouraged that travel from the United States to Cuba has already increased by 35 percent since January and is continuing to go up. We are encouraged that more and more U.S. companies are exploring commercial ventures here that would create opportunities for Cuba's own rising number of entrepreneurs, and we are encouraged that U.S. firms are interested in helping Cuba expand its telecommunications and internet links, and that the government here recently pledged to create dozens of new and more affordable Wi-Fi hotspots.

We also want to acknowledge the special role that the Cuban American community is playing in establishing a new relationship between our countries. And in fact, we have with us this morning representatives from that community, some of whom were born here and others who were born in the United States. With their strong ties of culture and family, they can contribute much to the spirit of bilateral cooperation and progress that we are seeking to create, just as they have contributed much to their communities in their adopted land.

The restoration of diplomatic ties will also make it easier for our governments to engage. After all, we are neighbors, and neighbors will always have much to discuss in such areas as civil aviation, migration policy, disaster preparedness, protecting marine environment, global climate change, and other tougher and more complicated issues. Having normal relations makes it easier for us to talk, and talk can deepen understanding even when we know full well we will not see eye to eye on everything.

We are all aware that notwithstanding President Obama's new policy, the overall U.S. embargo on trade with Cuba remains in place and can only be lifted by congressional action—a step that we strongly favor. For now—(applause). For now, the President has taken steps to ease restrictions on remittances, on exports and imports to help Cuban private entrepreneurs, on telecommunications, on family travel, but we want to go further. The goal of all of these changes is to help Cubans connect to the world and to improve their lives. And just as we are doing our part, we urge the Cuban Government to make it less difficult for their citizens to start businesses, to engage in trade, access information online. The embargo has always been something of a two-way street—both sides need to remove restrictions that have been holding Cubans back.

Before closing, I want to sincerely thank leaders throughout the Americas who have long urged the United States and Cuba to restore normal ties. I thank the Holy Father Pope

Francis and the Vatican for supporting the start of a new chapter in relations between our countries. And I think it is not accidental that the Holy Father will come here and then to Washington, the United States at this moment. I applaud President Obama and President Castro both for having the courage to bring us together in the face of considerable opposition. I am grateful to Assistant Secretary of State Roberta Jacobson and her team, to our counterparts in the Cuban Foreign Ministry, to our chief of mission, Ambassador Jeff DeLaurentis and his extraordinary staff, for all of the hard work that has led up to this day. And I just say to our wonderful embassy staff, if you think you've been busy these past months, hold on to your seatbelts. (Laughter.)

But above all, above all, I want to pay tribute to the people of Cuba and to the Cuban American community in the United States. Jose Marti once said that "everything that divides men . . . is a sin against humanity." Clearly, the events of the past—the harsh words, the provocative and retaliatory actions, the human tragedies—all have been a source of deep division that has diminished our common humanity. There have been too many days of sacrifice and sorrow; too many decades of suspicion and fear. That is why I am heartened by the many on both sides of the Straits who—whether because of family ties or a simple desire to replace anger with something more productive—have endorsed this search for a better path.

We have begun to move down that path without any illusions about how difficult it may be. But we are each confident in our intentions, confident in the contacts that we have made, and pleased with the friendships that we have begun to forge.

And we are certain that the time is now to reach out to one another, as two peoples who are no longer enemies or rivals, but neighbors—time to unfurl our flags, raise them up, and let the world know that we wish each other well.

Estamos seguros de que este es el momento de acercarnos: dos pueblos ya no enemigos ni rivales, sino vecinos. Es el momento de desplegar nuestras banderas, enarbolarlas y hacerle saber al resto del mundo que nos deseamos lo mejor los unos a los otros.

[Translation by SAGE: We are sure this is the right time: two people who are not enemies or rivals, but neighbors. This is the moment to unfurl our flags, raise them, and let the rest of the world know that we wish the best to each other.]

It is with that healing mission in mind that I turn now to Larry Morris, Jim Tracy, and Mike East. Fifty-four years ago, you gentlemen promised to return to Havana and hoist the flag over the United States Embassy that you lowered on that January day long ago. Today, I invite you on behalf of President Obama and the American people to fulfill that pledge by presenting the Stars and Stripes to be raised by members of our current military detachment.

Larry, Jim, and Mike, this is your cue to deliver on words that would make any diplomat proud, just as they would any member of the United States Marine Corps: Promise made, promise kept. Thank you.

SOURCE: U.S. Department of State. "Remarks at Flag Raising Ceremony." August 14, 2015. www.state.gov/secretary/remarks/2015/08/246121.htm.

President Castro Speaks
Before the United Nations

September 28, 2015

[All portions of Castro's statement not pertaining to the United States have been omitted.]

Mr. President,

After 56 years in which the Cuban people put up a heroic and selfless resistance, diplomatic relations have been reestablished between Cuba and the United States of America.

Now, a long and complex process begins toward the normalization of relations that will only be achieved with the end of the economic, commercial and financial blockade against Cuba; the return to our country of the territory illegally occupied by Guantanamo Naval Base; the cessation of radio and TV broadcasts, and of subversion and destabilization programs against the Island; and, when our people are compensated for the human and economic damages they still endure.

While the blockade remains in force, we shall continue introducing the Draft Resolution entitled "Necessity of Ending the Economic, Commercial and Financial Embargo imposed by the United States of America against Cuba."

SOURCE: United Nations. "Remarks by Raúl Castro Ruz, President of the Councils of State and Ministers of the Republic of Cuba, in his address to the General Debate of the 70th Session of the UNGA, New York, September 28, 2015." September 28, 2015. http://gadebate.un.org/sites/default/files/gastatements/70/70_CU_en.pdf.

OTHER HISTORIC DOCUMENTS OF INTEREST

FROM PREVIOUS *HISTORIC DOCUMENTS*

Congress Approves Fast-Track Authority; President Obama Signs Assistance Bill for Workers Affected by Trade Acts

APRIL 16, MAY 22, AND JUNE 29, 2015

Throughout his second term, President Barack Obama requested that Congress act to renew the authority that allows a president to negotiate trade agreements without threat of Congressional filibuster or amendments. This "fast-track" authority, as it is known, had been available to every president from 1974 through 2007, when Congress allowed it to lapse. According to the president, such authority was necessary to ensure passage of the Trans-Pacific Partnership (TPP), a major trade agreement with eleven countries, most of which were located in the Pacific Rim. Ultimately, the president worked with Republican leaders in Congress to pass a bill that would reinstate fast-track authority, but he faced criticism from many Democrats who said that the free trade agreements negotiated with fast-track authority harm the American workforce by moving jobs overseas and reducing wages.

FAST-TRACK AUTHORITY AND FREE TRADE AGREEMENTS

Fast-track authority, the ability of a president to negotiate trade deals which can be approved or rejected by Congress but which cannot be filibustered or amended, was first granted under the Trade Act of 1974. The authority has been continually approved since its inception each time it was due to expire and has been responsible for the negotiation of trade agreements with the nations of Australia, Bahrain, Canada, Chile, Colombia, Costa Rica, Dominican Republic, El Salvador, Guatemala, Honduras, Israel, Jordan, Mexico, Morocco, Nicaragua, Oman, Panama, Peru, Singapore, and South Korea.

Fast-track authority most recently expired on July 1, 2007, and although free trade agreements have been enacted since that time, it is only because they were originally agreed to and signed prior to expiration. This left President Obama as the only sitting president since 1974 to not have access to fast-track authority. In 2012, the president argued that such authority was necessary to ensure that the Trans-Pacific Partnership (TPP) with the Asia-Pacific region and the Transatlantic Trade and Investment Partnership (T-TIP) with the European Union could be finalized.

PRESIDENT OBAMA SEEKS FAST-TRACK RENEWAL

Members of the Democratic Party, which draws a significant amount of support from labor unions, have long argued that free trade agreements are harmful to labor in the United States, particularly to the manufacturing sector if jobs are outsourced as a result of the agreement. Unions also argue that free trade agreements result in overall lower wages for the blue-color American workforce. In a statement opposing fast-track authority, AFL-CIO president Richard Trumka said, "For decades, we've seen how fast-tracked trade deals devastated our communities through lost jobs and eroded public services. We can't afford another bad deal that lowers wages and outsources jobs." In 1993, labor unions came out strongly against the North Atlantic Free Trade Agreement (NAFTA), which they believed would send a significant portion of manufacturing jobs to Mexico. Rallies were held around the United States, specifically in Washington, D.C., and manufacturing hubs in the Midwest. Labor leaders squared off with then-President Bill Clinton, a Democrat, who argued that, even if NAFTA was not passed, factory jobs could still be moved to Mexico where labor is cheaper. However, he said, if passed, the agreement would mean "dramatically increased sales of American products made right here in America." Ultimately, NAFTA passed, and labor unions continue to argue that they are hurt at the bargaining table by companies that are willing to lay off American workers to find cheaper labor elsewhere.

Given the fraught history surrounding free trade agreements, President Obama found few Democrats in Congress willing to support his drive for new fast-track approval. Republicans, however, came to the table. On January 9, 2014, the Bipartisan Congressional Trade Priorities Act of 2014 was introduced in the Senate by Sen. Max Baucus, D-Mont., and Sen. Dave Camp, R-Mich. The legislation would permit the president to enter into trade agreements that would reduce or eliminate export tariffs and other barriers to trade. If passed and signed into law, the legislation would remain intact until at least July 1, 2018, at which point Congress would be forced to pass an extension or allow the law to lapse. The legislation failed to pass out of committee to the full Senate. Following the November 2014 midterm elections, in which Republicans took control of both the House and Senate, the president again pushed Congress to approve a bill to give him the negotiating power that would allow the TPP to be finalized. A trade authority bill, sponsored by Sen. Orrin Hatch, R-Utah, Sen. Ron Wyden, D-Ore., and Rep. Paul Ryan, R-Wis., was introduced in the Senate on April 16, 2015. On the same day, the bill was also introduced on the House floor. The bill would allow the president fast-track authority, but would also require that Congress, and the public, receive detailed updates regarding any trade agreement and be given ample time to review such information before an up-down vote is held.

HOUSE AND SENATE APPROVE FAST-TRACK AUTHORITY

In the months preceding the House and Senate votes on the Trade Promotion Authority (TPA) bill, Republicans and Democrats in Congress squabbled with the White House over the necessity of such legislation and its ultimate impact on American workers. In a debate that Speaker of the House John Boehner, R-Ohio, labeled as "close to bizarre," Democrats were pitted against the president while Republicans worked with the White House toward passage. There was, however, a small group of fourteen pro-trade Democrats who faced backlash from labor groups for their support of the TPA.

The TPA came to a vote on the House floor on June 18. Raucous debate ensued, during which Sen. Elizabeth Warren, D-Mass., accused those behind the bill of potentially allowing companies to evade U.S. laws. President Obama responded, noting that Warren's arguments did not "stand the test of fact and scrutiny," a comment Sen. Sherrod Brown, D-Ohio, called "disrespectful." Ultimately, the bill passed by only ten votes. All but fifty

Republicans approved the measure, while only twenty-eight Democrats voted in favor. In the Senate, there was stronger support for the TPA. During the July 6 vote, the measure passed 60–38, with thirteen Democrats joining all but five Republicans. "We had plenty of bumps along the road. Frankly, a few big potholes too," said Senate majority leader Mitch McConnell, R-Ky., following passage. "But we worked across the aisle to get through all of them. That's an example of a new Congress that's back to work for the American people," he added. The TPA would give President Obama and his successor fast-track authority until 2018, with an extension until 2021 possible.

Shortly after passage of the TPA, the House and Senate voted on a similar bill, a Trade Adjustment Assistance (TAA) extension, which was intended to help American workers whose jobs were sent overseas by extending worker assistance through 2022. A total of $2.7 billion was set aside to provide worker education and retraining for all those in service industries if their job is sent overseas. Such assistance had been in place for workers since the 1960s. Rep. Steve Israel, D-NY., who voted against the TPA, said that he would support the TAA because failure to pass such protection "is the quintessential cutting of our noses to spite our face. And it's not cutting off our noses—it's cutting off the noses of working people," he said. The Senate voted on the bill on July 6, which it passed 76–22. The House voted to pass the TAA on June 25, after previously rejecting the bill just weeks earlier. On June 29, President Obama signed both the TAA and the TPA into law. During the signing ceremony, the president shared his belief that the "legislation will help turn global trade, which can often be a race to the bottom, into a race to the top. It will reinforce America's leadership role in the world: in Asia and in Europe and beyond. If I didn't believe it, I wouldn't have fought so hard to get these things done."

Trans-Pacific Partnership Finalized

According to President Obama, the nations party to the TPP—Australia, Brunei, Canada, Chile, Japan, Malaysia, Mexico, New Zealand, Peru, Singapore, and Vietnam—viewed fast-track authority as vital to ensuring successful passage of the massive free trade agreement, which would encompass 40 percent of the world's population and 60 percent of its gross domestic product (GDP). Negotiations on the TPP had been taking place for five years, largely behind closed doors. The secrecy surrounding the agreement drew sharp criticism from Democrats and Republicans alike and was a primary reason why Congress wrote the TPA to force the president to share specific information on any free trade agreement being negotiated.

A final version of the TPP was agreed to by the twelve nations party to the deal and released on October 5, 2015. As written, the TPP would remove more than 18,000 tariffs that are currently placed on exports from the United States to participating nations, including those on automobiles, information technology, consumer goods, agricultural products, pork and beef, and machinery. If approved by Congress, the agreement would increase economic ties between the twelve nations and open up additional trade opportunities. Opponents, primarily labor unions, argued that the TPP presents a significant threat to the American workforce, while supporters said that it would create additional higher-paying jobs in America by increasing the market for American exports. At the announcement that a final agreement had been reached, the president said in a statement, "When more than 95 percent of our potential customers live outside our borders, we can't let countries like China write the rules of the global economy. We should write those rules, opening new markets to American products while setting high standards for protecting workers and preserving our environment."

As signed into law, a portion of the TPA would allow the U.S. public and Congress the first chance to view and consider the free trade agreement. The president would not be able to sign any final agreement until two months after its release to the public, and Congress would not be able to hold a yes/no majority vote until two months after that. This, some argued, would put the TPP at risk because debate would be playing out during the 2016 presidential campaign. The White House said it would begin working to gather support in Congress for approval of the TPP, which will likely require encouraging more Democrats to vote for passage, a difficult task during an election year.

—Heather Kerrigan

Following is a statement from the AFL-CIO released on April 16, 2015, opposing passage of fast-track trade approval; a statement from the United Steelworkers, also on April 16, 2015, in opposition to fast-track approval; a statement delivered by President Barack Obama on May 22, 2015, in response to Senate passage of Trade Promotion Authority and Trade Adjustment Assistance legislation; the president's June 29, 2015, statement upon signing the trade adjustment assistance extension and trade promotion authority bills; the text of the trade adjustment assistance bill; and a summary of the trade promotion authority bill.

DOCUMENT

AFL-CIO Calls on Congress Not to Pass TPA

April 16, 2015

"At a time when workers all over the country are standing up for higher wages, Congress is considering legislation that will speed through corporate-driven trade deals. For decades, we've seen how fast-tracked trade deals devastated our communities through lost jobs and eroded public services. We can't afford another bad deal that lowers wages and outsources jobs. That's why Congress must reject Fast Track (TPA-2015) and maintain its constitutional authority and leverage to improve the TPP and other trade deals.

"Trade deals have wide-ranging impacts and shouldn't be negotiated behind closed doors and then rubber-stamped. The current Trans-Pacific Partnership deal under discussion would cover 40 percent of the world's GDP. A deal this big should be debated in a full and open manner like every other piece of legislation. Working people are showing tremendous courage standing up to the low-wage, corporate agenda. It's time for politicians to do the same."

SOURCE: AFL-CIO. "Statement by AFL-CIO President Richard Trumka: Stop the Fast Track to Lower Wages." April 16, 2015. www.aflcio.org/Press-Room/Press-Releases/Statement-by-AFL-CIO-President-Richard-Trumka-Stop-the-Fast-Track-to-Lower-Wages.

United Steelworkers Speak Out Against TPA

April 16, 2015

(Pittsburgh) – United Steelworkers (USW) International President Leo W. Gerard issued the following statement today following the release of legislation today by Senators Orrin Hatch and Ron Wyden and Congressman Paul Ryan to provide the President fast track trade negotiating authority.

"Today's fast track bill will only continue outmoded trade policies that have decimated American manufacturing with more than 60,000 shuttered factories and millions of lost jobs. It's time for a new trade policy, not more of the same.

"The USW is not against trade, but unfortunately the history of trade agreements is clear: I don't know anyone who can name an agreement passed under fast track that has resulted in a net gain of jobs for working Americans. The fast track bill introduced today fails to ensure that future trade agreements will produce the results that will enhance wages and job security, and address income inequality.

"Congress has included negotiating objectives in past fast track authority legislation requiring trade deficit reduction, adequate attention to workers' rights, provisions to address unfair tax rebate policies and other provisions that were not achieved in final trade agreements. New negotiating objectives, such as addressing currency manipulation, are unlikely to be fulfilled even though it is included as an objective in a bill.

"Fast track will only perpetuate existing trade policies which are in dramatic need of change. Providing expedited procedures and preferential treatment for trade agreements that don't provide the results America needs is unacceptable. A good trade agreement doesn't need the protection of fast track—it would have the strong support of the American people.

"For Steelworkers, trade isn't an academic or political issue; it's about kitchen table economics: Will our members be able to keep their jobs and put food on their tables, pay their bills, put their kids through college and have a safe and secure retirement? We have had to spend far too much time, energy and resources fighting to have existing trade agreements enforced. Fast track will only keep the current system in place and that's unacceptable."

SOURCE: United Steelworkers. "USW Opposes Fast Track Bill: It's Time for a New Trade Policy, Not More of the Same." April 16, 2015. www.usw.org/news/media-center/releases/2015/usw-opposes-fast-track-bill-its-time-for-a-new-trade-policy-not-more-of-the-same.

President Applauds Senate Action on TPA and TAA

May 22, 2015

Today's bipartisan Senate vote is an important step toward ensuring the United States can negotiate and enforce strong, high-standards trade agreements. If done right, these agreements are vital to expanding opportunities for the middle class, leveling the playing field for American workers, and establishing rules for the global economy that help our businesses grow and hire by selling goods made in America to the rest of the world. This trade promotion authority (TPA) legislation includes strong standards that will advance workers' rights, protect the environment, promote a free and open Internet, and it supports new robust measures to address unfair currency practices. The legislation also includes an important extension of trade adjustment assistance (TAA) to help all American workers participate in the global economy.

I want to thank Senators of both parties for sticking up for American workers by supporting smart trade and strong enforcement, and I encourage the House of Representatives to follow suit by passing TPA and TAA as soon as possible.

SOURCE: Executive Office of the President. "Statement on Senate Passage of Trade Promotion Authority and Trade Adjustment Assistance Legislation." May 22, 2015. *Compilation of Presidential Documents 2015*, no. 00389 (May 22, 2015). www.gpo.gov/fdsys/pkg/DCPD-201500389/pdf/DCPD-201500389.pdf.

DOCUMENT *President Obama Signs TPA and TAA*

June 29, 2015

Thank you. Well, welcome to the White House. I thought we'd start off the week with something we should do more often: a truly bipartisan bill signing.

For 6½ years, we've worked to rescue the economy from the worst financial crisis since the Great Depression, to get it growing again and to rebuild it on a new foundation for prosperity. Today, our businesses have created more than 12 million new jobs in the past 5 years; that's the longest streak of job growth on record, 401(k)s have been replenished, the housing market is stronger, and more than 16 million Americans have gained the financial security of health insurance.

But a constantly changing economy demands our constant effort to protect hardworking Americans and protect their success. And one of the things we ought to be doing is rewriting the rules of global trade to make sure that they benefit American workers and American businesses and that they reflect American values, especially now, while our economy is in a position of global strength. The two bills that I'll sign today will help America do just that.

The first will help us pass new, 21st-century trade agreements with higher standards and tougher protections than those that we've signed before. The Trans-Pacific Partnership, for example, includes strong protections for workers and the environment. Unlike previous agreements, those provisions will actually be enforceable. And that's good for American businesses and America[n] workers because we already meet high standards than—higher standards than most of the rest of the world. So we want to make sure that everybody else catches up. This agreement will help us level the playing field.

The second bill offers even more support for American workers. It renews and expands the trade adjustment assistance program, which provides job training and other assistance to tens of thousands of American workers every year. It gives us new tools to help American steelworkers and folks in other critical industries fight against unfair practices by other countries. It also reauthorizes AGOA, the African Growth and Opportunity Act, which has had strong bipartisan support for many years now, and which helps open up markets in Africa to American businesses while making it easier for African businesses to sell their products in America. And we're extending a similar program to Haiti and renewing support for other development—developing economies through what's known as the Generalized System of Preferences.

Now, I think it's fair to say that getting these bills through Congress has not been easy. *[Laughter]* They've been declared dead more than once. They have inspired long and passionate debates, and that's entirely appropriate for our democracy. That's how this country is supposed to work. We're supposed to make sure that we air our differences, and then, ultimately, Congress works its will, especially on issues that inspire strongly held feelings on all sides.

But I would not be doing this, I would not be signing these bills if I was not absolutely convinced that these two pieces of legislation are ultimately good for American workers. I would not be signing them if I wasn't convinced they'd be good for American businesses. I would not be signing them if I did not know that they will give us a competitive edge in this new economy and that that new economy cannot be reversed. We have to embrace it.

This legislation will help turn global trade, which can often be a race to the bottom, into a race to the top. It will reinforce America's leadership role in the world: in Asia and in Europe and beyond. If I didn't believe it, I wouldn't have fought so hard to get these things done.

So this is a good day. And I want to thank everybody who has helped us get it—get to this day. We've got small-business owners here, environmental and global development groups, other advocates who were a big part of this campaign. We've got some outstanding Members of Congress, both Republican and Democrat, who came together to make this happen. I want to name just a few. Although Congress is on recess, I think it's important to acknowledge Speaker John Boehner and Leader Mitch McConnell; Senators Orrin Hatch, Ron Wyden, and Patty Murray; Congressmen Paul Ryan, Ron Kind, and Pat Tiberi. And thanks to all the Senators and Representatives who took tough votes and encouraged their colleagues to do the same.

This was a true bipartisan effort. And it's a reminder of what we can get done—even on the toughest issues—when we work together in a spirit of compromise. I hope we're going to be able to summon that same spirit on future challenges, like starting to rebuild some of our roads and bridges and infrastructure—*[laughter]*—around the country, because the American people deserve nothing less from us.

Let me just make one more comment. The trade authorization that's provided here is not the actual trade agreements. So we still have some tough negotiations that are going to be taking place. There has always been concern that people want transparency in those agreements. Under this authorization, these agreements will be posted on a website for a long period of time for people to scrutinize and take a look at and pick apart.

And so the debate on the particular provisions of trade will not end with this bill signing. But I'm very confident that we're going to be able to say at the end of the day that the trade agreements that come under this authorization are going to improve the system of trade that we have right now. And that's a good thing.

I think it's also important to note that trade is just one part of a broader agenda of middle class economics. And so we've still got more work to do on infrastructure. We've still got more work to do on job training. We've still got more work to do on research and development. And we've still got more work to do to make sure that folks are getting good wages for hard work. We've still got too many communities that are left behind around the country. We've still got more work to do to help support our small businesses, who are extraordinary job creators.

So this is not the end of the road; this is just one step in a long path to making sure that the next generation enjoys the extraordinary prosperity that our parents and grandparents passed down to us. And although there are going to be disagreements between the parties on particular elements, I think what we can agree on is that in this country, if you work hard, you should be able to get ahead no matter where you come from, what you look like, or who you love.

With that, let me sign this piece of legislation.

[At this point, the President signed the bills.]

All right. For those of you who work for me, get back to work. *[Laughter]*
Thank you very much, everybody.

Source: Executive Office of the President. "Remarks on Signing the Defending Public Safety Employees' Retirement Act and the Trade Preferences Extension Act of 2015." June 29, 2015. *Compilation of Presidential Documents* 2015, no. 00468. www.gpo.gov/fdsys/pkg/DCPD-201500468/pdf/DCPD-201500468.pdf.

DOCUMENT   *Trade Adjustment Assistance Bill*

June 29, 2015

[Portions of Public Law 114-27 not related to trade adjustment assistance have been omitted.]

SEC. 403. <<Note: 10 USC 2271 note prec.>> EXTENSION OF TRADE ADJUSTMENT ASSISTANCE PROGRAM.

(a) Extension of Termination Provisions. –Section 285 of the Trade Act of 1974 (19 U.S.C. 2271 note) is amended by striking "December 31, 2013" each place it appears and inserting "June 30, 2021".

(b) Training Funds. –Section 236(a)(2)(A) of the Trade Act of 1974 (19 U.S.C. 2296(a)(2)(A)) is amended by striking "shall not exceed" and all that follows and inserting "shall not exceed $450,000,000 for each of fiscal years 2015 through 2021".

(c) Reemployment Trade Adjustment Assistance. –Section 246(b)(1) of the Trade Act of 1974 (19 U.S.C. 2318(b)(1)) is amended by striking "December 31, 2013" and inserting "June 30, 2021".

(d) Authorizations of Appropriations.—

(1) Trade adjustment assistance for workers. –Section 245(a) of the Trade Act of 1974 (19 U.S.C. 2317(a)) is amended by striking December 31, 2013" and inserting "June 30, 2021".

(2) Trade adjustment assistance for firms. –Section 255(a) of the Trade Act of 1974 (19 U.S.C. 2345(a)) is amended by striking "fiscal years 2012 and 2013" and all that follows through "December 31, 2013" and inserting "fiscal years 2015 through 2021".

(3) Trade adjustment assistance for farmers. –Section 298(a) of the Trade Act of 1974 (19 U.S.C. 2401g(a)) is amended by striking "fiscal years 2012 and 2013" and all that follows through "December 31, 2013" and inserting "fiscal years 2015 through 2021".

SOURCE: Library of Congress. "H.R. 1295—Trade Preferences Extension Act of 2015." Text as signed into law. June 29, 2015. www.congress.gov/bill/114th-congress/house-bill/1295/text/pl.

Summary of Trade Promotion Authority Bill as Signed into Law

June 29, 2015

[The sections of the Congressional summary of Public Law 114-26 not pertaining to trade promotion authority have been omitted.]

TITLE I—TRADE PROMOTION AUTHORITY

Bipartisan Congressional Trade Priorities and Accountability Act of 2015

(Sec. 102) Declares the overall trade negotiating objectives of the United States with respect to any agreement with a foreign country to reduce or eliminate existing tariffs or nontariff barriers of that country or the United States that are unduly burdening and restricting U.S. trade. Includes among such objectives:

- more open, equitable, and reciprocal market access;

- the reduction or elimination of trade barriers and distortions that are directly related to trade and investment and that decrease market opportunities for U.S. exports or otherwise distort U.S. trade;

- stronger international trade and investment disciplines and procedures, including dispute settlement;

- enhanced U.S. competitiveness;

- protection of the environment;

- respect for worker and children rights consistent with International Labor Organization core labor standards;

- equal access of small businesses to international markets; and

- religious freedom.

Declares the principal trade negotiating objectives of the United States with respect to:

- goods and services;

- agriculture;

- foreign investment;

- intellectual property;

- digital goods and services, as well as cross-border data flows;

- regulatory practices;

- state-owned and state-controlled enterprises;

- localization barriers to trade;

- labor and the environment;

- currency and foreign currency manipulation;

- the World Trade Organization (WTO) and multilateral trade agreements;

- trade institution transparency;

- anti-corruption;

- dispute settlement and enforcement;

- trade remedy laws;

- border taxes;

- textile negotiations;

- commercial partnerships, especially with Israel; and

- good governance, transparency, operation of legal regimes, and the rule of law of U.S. trading partners.

Directs the President, in order to maintain U.S. competitiveness in the global economy, to engage in specified capacity building activities with respect to foreign countries that seek to enter into trade agreements with the United States.

(Sec. 103) Authorizes the President to enter into trade agreements with foreign countries for the reduction or elimination of tariff or nontariff barriers before July 1, 2018, or before July 1, 2021, if trade authorities procedures are extended to implementing bills (congressional approval) with respect to such agreements.

Authorizes the President to proclaim necessary or appropriate modifications or continuation of any existing duty, continuation of existing duty-free or excise treatment, or additional duties to carry out any such agreement.

(Sec. 104) Subjects trade agreements to congressional oversight and approval, consultations, and access to information requirements.

Requires the convening each Congress of the House and the Senate Advisory Groups on Negotiations to consult with and advise the United States Trade Representative (USTR) regarding the formulation of specific objectives, negotiating strategies and positions, the development of the applicable trade agreement, and compliance and enforcement of the negotiated commitments under the trade agreement.

Amends the Trade Act of 1974 to establish within the Office of the USTR the position of Chief Transparency Officer to consult with Congress on transparency policy, coordinate transparency in trade negotiations, engage and assist the public, and advise the USTR on transparency policy.

(Sec. 105) Specifies presidential notifications, consultations, reports, and other actions and their deadlines that must take place for any trade agreement to enter into force.

Specifies requirements for negotiations regarding agriculture, the fishing industry, and textiles.

(Sec. 106) Prescribes procedures for resolutions of disapproval in the House and the Senate before the President enters into any trade agreement.

Declares that trade authorities procedures shall not apply to any implementing bill submitted with respect to a trade agreement:

- if both chambers of Congress agree by a certain deadline to a procedural disapproval resolution for lack of notice or consultations, and

- with a country which does not fully comply and is not making significant efforts to comply with minimum standards for the elimination of human trafficking ("tier 3" country).

(Sec. 107) Prescribes requirements for the treatment of trade agreements entered into under the auspices of the WTO or with the Trans-Pacific Partnership countries or the European Union which result from negotiations commenced before enactment of this Act.

(Sec. 108) Declares that any provision of a trade agreement that is inconsistent with any U.S. laws shall be null and void.

(Sec. 109) Expresses the sense of Congress that the USTR should facilitate participation of small businesses in the trade negotiation process.

SOURCE: Library of Congress. "H.R. 2146—Defending Public Safety Employees' Retirement Act." Summary of Public Law. June 29, 2015. www.congress.gov/bill/114th-congress/house-bill/2146?q=%7B %22search%22%3A%5B%22%5C%22pl114-26%5C%22%22%5D%7D&resultIndex=1.

OTHER HISTORIC DOCUMENTS OF INTEREST

FROM PREVIOUS *HISTORIC DOCUMENTS*

European Council Holds Special Meeting on Migrant Crisis

APRIL 23, MAY 18, JUNE 22, AND SEPTEMBER 14 AND 28, 2015

A dramatic increase in the number of migrants crossing the Mediterranean Sea to reach Europe's shores left political leaders struggling to formulate an effective response. One especially tragic incident—approximately 800 migrants drowned in April 2015 when an overcrowded boat traveling from Libya to Italy capsized—propelled the issue to the top of the agenda of the European Union (EU). At an emergency summit convened several days later, EU leaders agreed to reinforce border patrols along the Central Mediterranean, which was the route most of the migrants were taking. They also gave the initial green light to deploy a multinational naval mission tasked with pursuing and intercepting boats used by smugglers to illegally transport migrants.

These actions succeeded in reducing the flow of migrants through that particular part of the Mediterranean, the Libya-to-Italy route, in subsequent months. But these actions also had an unintended consequence: migrant flows were redirected from the Central to the Eastern Mediterranean. Over the summer, hundreds of thousands of migrants embarked on a treacherous journey taking the Turkey-to-Greece route. Some migrants were fleeing the worsening four-year civil war in Syria, while others were escaping repression, persecution, and economic hardship in various parts of Africa and the Middle East.

DROWNINGS REACH CRISIS PROPORTIONS

Since 2000, some 22,400 people have died trying to cross the Mediterranean Sea, most of them on a northward-bound quest to reach Europe. The flow occurred despite Europe's continuing to experiencing economic struggles, with many EU countries seeing little or no growth since 2008, and some suffering periodic recessions, high levels of unemployment, and soaring public debt. Among such economically stressed EU nations were Greece and Italy, two countries that, because of their geographical proximity to the Middle East and North Africa, tended to be where these migrants first arrived. The draw to the EU can be explained partly by its relative peacefulness and prosperity compared to the regions of Africa and the Middle East from where the migrants were leaving.

When the series of prodemocracy political uprisings known as the Arab Spring started in 2011, many hoped it would have a positive impact on the region's political and economic development. However, these hopes had largely faded by 2014 as many countries— namely, Iraq, Libya, and Syria—descended into political chaos, sectarian conflict, and Islamist terrorism. Meanwhile, the large gap in living standards between sub-Saharan African nations and Europe was a draw for migrants from countries in West Africa, including Gambia and Nigeria. In some countries, such as Eritrea, a highly repressive political regime was an additional trigger, while in places such as Somalia endless conflict between Islamist militant groups and weak civil governments were factors. Many migrants trekked hundreds of miles across the Saharan desert just to reach the Mediterranean.

By early 2015, Libya emerged as a primary location for Europe-bound migrants because of its proximity to Italy and because many migrant-smuggling gangs had gained a foothold. Longtime Libyan authoritarian leader Muammar Gaddafi was deposed in 2011, after which some progress was made in building a democratic system of government. However, these efforts suffered a major setback following the June 2014 elections when two rival governments formed, with both claiming legitimacy. The government that gained international recognition based itself in the city of Tobruk in eastern Libya, while a rival, more Islamist-oriented government based itself in the nation's capital of Tripoli in western Libya. The schism helped Islamist terrorist groups entrench themselves along certain Libyan coastal towns. Many of these groups were affiliated with the Islamic State of Iraq and the Levant (ISIL), which succeeded in creating a caliphate in Iraq and Syria in the summer of 2014.

Italy Becomes Prime Migrant Destination

Until 2015, Libya served both as a transit point and as a destination country for migrants. But faced with a rapidly deteriorating security situation, tens of thousands of migrants who were living there fled the growing chaos on a desperate quest to reach Europe. The surge in migration generated huge profits for gangs of smugglers who typically charged several thousand dollars per migrant for passage to Europe. The migrants in their charge often suffered abuse, imprisonment, and maltreatment. They were shuttled over land in overheated vehicles, kept in prison-like conditions before their sea voyage, and then packed tightly into flimsy boats.

Because the smugglers typically had poor navigation skills, many boats crashed against rocks or capsized before they reached shore. In addition, sometimes smugglers abandoned vessels when they saw maritime border control authorities approaching. In 2014, an estimated 3,500 migrants died or went missing making the crossing, marking the deadliest year on record. Italy, a first destination for the migrants, responded by launching an operation called Mare Nostrum, which rescued tens of thousands of migrants at risk of drowning.

However, Italy grew increasingly frustrated with other EU countries for not doing more to help rescue and process migrants. For many of the migrants, Italy was in fact only a midpoint on their intended journey, which they hoped would culminate in other EU countries where their economic prospects were better or where they stood a strong chance of being granted refugee status. Germany and Sweden were particularly popular destinations, and both experienced a large increase in asylum applications.

Matters came to a head on April 19, 2015, when an estimated 800 migrants drowned after their boat capsized while approaching a merchant ship seventy miles from the Libyan coast, south of the Italian island of Lampedusa. This was the single deadliest drowning instance to occur in the Mediterranean in recorded history. In response, EU leaders convened an emergency summit and adopted a joint declaration on April 23 that served as an action plan.

Mixed Results from EU Response

"Our immediate priority is to prevent more people from dying at sea," EU leaders said at the conclusion of their April 23 special meeting to address the migrant crisis. "Instability in Libya creates an ideal environment for the criminal activities of traffickers," they noted. The EU already had some joint border control operations in the Mediterranean—Triton and Poseidon. These operations were reinforced, with more member states contributing to them. The leaders also gave the political green light to establishing a military mission called EUNAVFOR MED Operation SOPHIA whose mandate was to "identify, capture and destroy vessels before they are used by traffickers."

The leaders called for more so-called readmission agreements with non-EU governments to facilitate the deportation of unauthorized economic migrants in the EU and return them to the countries they originally came from or transited through. The EU leaders stressed the need to work closely with countries in the surrounding region, in particular Turkey, where two million Syrian refugees were living, some of whom had started to head toward the European Union. They asked for a plan to be drawn up by the European Commission, the EU's executive arm, to redistribute asylum-seekers more evenly among EU member states. And they agreed to "consider options for organizing emergency relocation between all EU member states on a voluntary basis."

The EUNAVFOR MED operation was one of the more innovative measures developed because it differed from previous operations that focused mainly on rescuing migrants from drowning. The core mission of EUNAVFOR MED, by contrast, was to use military assets to seize and dispose of smugglers' boats and other assets. Formally approved on May 18, the mission was launched on June 22. It was headquartered in Rome and led by Italian rear admiral Enrico Credendino. Phase 1 brought together naval vessels from France, Germany, Italy, Spain, and the United Kingdom to gather intelligence on smuggler operations. Phase 2, launched on October 7, empowered naval authorities to board, search, seize, and divert vessels they spotted in international waters.

Phase 3, the ability to seize and dispose of vessels in Libyan (not international) waters, was the most contested aspect. By December 2015, this phase had yet to begin because it had not received approval from either the United Nations Security Council or the Libyan government. At the United Nations, Russia was withholding consent because it was keen to avoid a repeat of what happened in 2011, when the UN Security Council granted the North Atlantic Treaty Organization (NATO) a legal basis to launch a military operation that ultimately led to the toppling of Gaddafi, much to Moscow's chagrin. The internationally recognized Libyan government in Tobruk withheld consent because it was wary of letting foreign military forces conduct operations in Libyan waters.

As the summer progressed, migrants increasingly started to take a different route to Europe, eschewing the Libya-to-Italy crossing in favor of the Turkey-to-Greece passage further east. As with the Central Mediterranean crossings, there were frequent drownings from capsized dinghies and other flimsy vessels. Those who reached Greece tended to continue their journey over land by bus, train, and foot via the Western Balkans, often entering the European Union through Hungary. In response, Hungarian authorities erected a barbed wire fence at their border to prevent entrance.

The Mediterranean migration crisis laid bare flaws in the EU's border control, asylum, and migration systems. Particularly problematic were the EU rules for determining who is responsible for processing an asylum-seeker because they put an inordinately heavy burden on the relatively few countries in which migrants first arrive, especially Greece and Italy. In response, the European Commission proposed that some asylum-seekers be relocated to other EU countries that had received relatively few migrants. The Commission proposed a relocation total of 60,000 migrants in June and increased this to 160,000 in September as the numbers of migrants continued to increase. The proposals met with stiff resistance from non-Mediterranean countries such as Poland and Slovakia who insisted that the migrants were not, according to EU law, their responsibility. Meanwhile, events on the ground overtook the plan, with an estimated one million economic migrants and refugees having arrived in the EU by the end of 2015.

—Brian Beary

Following is a statement from the European Council following a special meeting on April 23, 2015, on the Mediterranean migrant crisis; and the text of a statement made by European Council president Donald Tusk on April 23, 2015, regarding the outcome of the special meeting; the text of two European Council decisions on May 18 and June 22, 2015, regarding EU military operations in the Southern Central Mediterranean; a September 14, 2015, press release from the European Council announcing the decision to transition into Phase 2 of operations against human traffickers in the Mediterranean; and a September 28, 2015, press release from the European Council announcing the start of Operation Sophia.

European Council Holds Special Meeting on Migrant Crisis

April 23, 2015

1. The situation in the Mediterranean is a tragedy. The European Union will mobilise all efforts at its disposal to prevent further loss of life at sea and to tackle the root causes of the human emergency that we face, in cooperation with the countries of origin and transit. Our immediate priority is to prevent more people from dying at sea.

2. We have therefore decided to strengthen our presence at sea, to fight the traffickers, to prevent illegal migration flows and to reinforce internal solidarity and responsibility. Given that instability in Libya creates an ideal environment for the criminal activities of traffickers, we will actively support all UN-led efforts towards re-establishing government authority in Libya. We will also step up efforts to address conflict and instability as key push factors of migration, including in Syria.

3. We today commit to:

Strengthening our presence at sea

a) rapidly reinforce EU Operations Triton and Poseidon by at least tripling the financial resources for this purpose in 2015 and 2016 and reinforcing the number of assets, thus allowing to increase the search and rescue possibilities within the mandate of FRONTEX. We welcome the commitments already made by Member States which will allow to reach this objective in the coming weeks;

Fighting traffickers in accordance with international law

b) disrupt trafficking networks, bring the perpetrators to justice and seize their assets, through swift action by Member State authorities in co-operation with EUROPOL, FRONTEX, the European Asylum Support Office (EASO) and EUROJUST, as well as through increased intelligence and police-cooperation with third countries;

c) undertake systematic efforts to identify, capture and destroy vessels before they are used by traffickers;

d) at the same time, the High Representative is invited to immediately begin preparations for a possible CSDP operation to this effect;

e) use EUROPOL to detect and request removal of internet content used by traffickers to attract migrants and refugees, in accordance with national constitutions;

Preventing illegal migration flows

f) increase support to Tunisia, Egypt, Sudan, Mali and Niger among others, to monitor and control the land borders and routes, building on current CSDP operations in the region, as well as on regional cooperation frameworks (Rabat and Khartoum processes); step up dialogue with the African Union at all levels on all these issues;

g) reinforce our political cooperation with African partners at all levels in order to tackle the cause of illegal migration and combat the smuggling and trafficking of human beings. The EU will raise these issues with the African Union and the key countries concerned, with whom it will propose the holding of a summit in Malta in the coming months;

h) step up cooperation with Turkey in view of the situation in Syria and Iraq;

i) deploy European migration liaison officers in key countries to gather information on migratory flows, co-ordinate with national liaison officers, and co-operate directly with the local authorities;

j) work with regional partners in building capacity for maritime border management and search and rescue operations;

k) launch Regional Development and Protection programmes for North Africa and the Horn of Africa;

l) invite the Commission and the High Representative to mobilise all tools, including through development cooperation and the implementation of EU and national readmission agreements with third countries, to promote readmission of unauthorised economic migrants to countries of origin and transit, working closely with the International Organisation for Migration;

m) while respecting the right to seek asylum, set up a new return programme for the rapid return of illegal migrants from frontline Member States, coordinated by FRONTEX;

Reinforcing internal solidarity and responsibility

n) rapid and full transposition and effective implementation of the Common European Asylum System by all participating Member States, thereby ensuring common European standards under existing legislation;

o) increase emergency aid to frontline Member States and consider options for organising emergency relocation between all Member States on a voluntary basis;

p) deploy EASO teams in frontline Member States for joint processing of asylum applications, including registration and finger-printing;

q) set up a first voluntary pilot project on resettlement across the EU, offering places to persons qualifying for protection.

4. The EU institutions and the Member States will work immediately on the full implementation of these orientations. The Presidency and the Commission will present next week a roadmap setting out work up to June.

5. The European Council looks forward to the Commission Communication on a European Agenda for Migration, in order to develop a more systemic and geographically comprehensive approach to migration. The European Council will remain seized of the situation and will closely monitor the implementation of these orientations. The Council and the Commission will report to the European Council in June.

SOURCE: Council of the European Union. "Special meeting of the European Council, 23 April 2015 — statement." April 23, 2015. © European Union, 2015. www.consilium.europa.eu/en/press/press-releases/2015/04/23-special-euco-statement.

European Council President Remarks on Outcome of Special Meeting

April 23, 2015

Good evening. Today, we discussed the dramatic situation in the Mediterranean at the highest political level. Saving the lives of innocent people is the number one priority. But saving lives is not just about rescuing people at sea. It is also about stopping the smugglers and addressing irregular migration.

Let me be clear. Europe did not cause this tragedy. But that does not mean we can be indifferent. We are facing a difficult summer and we need to be ready to act. Therefore, leaders have agreed [on] four priority areas for action.

First, leaders have asked the High Representative to propose actions in order to capture and destroy the smugglers' vessels before they can be used. Naturally, this will be in line with international law and respect for human rights. We will step up co-operation against smuggling networks by working through Europol, and by deploying immigration officers to third countries.

Second, we have agreed to triple the resources available to Triton, our border mission in the Central Mediterranean, and to enhance its operational capability. The mission will continue to carry out its mandate and respond to distress calls where necessary. I am happy to announce that leaders have already pledged significantly greater support, including many more vessels, aircraft and experts, and money.

Third, we need to limit irregular migration flows and to discourage people from putting their lives at risk. This means better co-operation with the countries of origin and transit, especially the countries around Libya.

Finally, we will do more on refugee protection. The European Union will help front-line Member States under pressure and co-ordinate the resettlement of more people to Europe on a voluntary basis, and with an option for emergency relocation. For those who do not qualify as refugees, we will operate an effective returns policy.

Leaders had no illusions that we would solve this international human emergency today. Therefore, we have tasked the Commission, the Council and the High Representative to step up their work based on what we have now agreed. This issue remains our priority and the European Council will come back to it in June.

As a final remark, let me repeat that the European Union is completely opposed to the death penalty. It cannot be the answer to drug trafficking. I am referring here to Mr Atlaoui, the French citizen who has been condemned by the Indonesian authorities. Thank you.

SOURCE: Council of the European Union. "Remarks by President Donald Tusk following the special European Council meeting on migratory pressures in the Mediterranean." April 23, 2015. © European Union, 2015. www.consilium.europa.eu/en/press/press-releases/2015/04/23-final-remarks-tusk-european-council-migration.

European Council Adopts Decision on Mediterranean Military Operations

May 18, 2015

[Footnotes have been omitted.]

COUNCIL DECISION (CFSP) 2015/778

of 18 May 2015

on a European Union military operation in the Southern Central Mediterranean (EUNAVFOR MED)

THE COUNCIL OF THE EUROPEAN UNION,

Having regard to the Treaty on European Union, and in particular Articles 42(4) and 43(2) thereof,

Having regard to the proposal from the High Representative of the Union for Foreign Affairs and Security Policy,

Whereas:

(1) On 20 April 2015, the Council confirmed a strong commitment to act in order to prevent human tragedies resulting from the smuggling of people across the Mediterranean.

(2) On 23 April 2015, the European Council expressed its indignation about the situation in the Mediterranean and underlined that the Union will mobilise all efforts at its disposal to prevent further loss of life at sea and to tackle the root causes of this human emergency, in cooperation with the countries of origin and transit, and that the immediate priority is to prevent more people from dying at sea. The European Council committed to strengthening the Union's presence at sea, to preventing illegal migration flows and to reinforcing internal solidarity and responsibility.

(3) The European Council of 23 April 2015 also committed to fighting the traffickers in accordance with international law, by undertaking systematic efforts to identify, capture and destroy vessels before they are used by traffickers, and invited the High Representative of the Union for Foreign Affairs and Security Policy (HR) to start preparations for a possible Common Security and Defence Policy (CSDP) operation to this effect.

(4) On 11 May 2015, the HR informed the UN Security Council about the crisis of migrants in the Mediterranean and the ongoing preparation for a possible Union naval operation, in the framework of the Union's Common Security and Defence Policy. In this regard, she expressed the need for the Union to work with the support of the UN Security Council.

(5) On 18 May 2015, the Council approved the crisis management concept for a CSDP operation to disrupt the business model of smugglers in the Southern Central Mediterranean.

(6) The Union CSDP operation will be conducted in accordance with international law, in particular with the relevant provisions of the 1982 United Nations Convention on the Law of the Sea (UNCLOS), the 2000 Protocols against the Smuggling of Migrants by Land, Sea and Air (the Protocol against the Smuggling of Migrants) and to Prevent, Suppress and Punish Trafficking in Persons, especially Women and Children, supplementing the United Nations Convention against Transnational Organized Crime, the 1974 International Convention for the Safety of Life at Sea (SOLAS), the 1979 International Convention on Maritime Search and Rescue (SAR), the 1976 Convention for the Protection of the Marine Environment and the Coastal Region of the Mediterranean (Barcelona Convention), the 1951 Geneva Convention relating to the Status of Refugees and the principle of non-refoulement and international human rights law.

The UNCLOS, SOLAS and SAR Conventions include the obligation to assist persons in distress at sea and to deliver survivors to a place of safety, and to that end the vessels assigned to EUNAVFOR MED will be ready and equipped to perform the related duties under the coordination of the competent Rescue Coordination Centre.

(7) On the high seas, in accordance with relevant domestic and international law, States may interdict vessels suspected of smuggling migrants, where there is flag State authorisation to board and search the vessel or where the vessel is without nationality, and may take appropriate measures against the vessels, persons and cargo.

(8) Measures may also be taken in the territorial or internal waters, territory or airspace of a State against vessels suspected of involvement in human smuggling or trafficking, with the consent of that State or pursuant to a UN Security Council Resolution, or both.

(9) A State may take appropriate measures against persons present on its territory whom it suspects of smuggling or trafficking humans with a view to their possible arrest and prosecution, in accordance with international law and its domestic law.

(10) The Political and Security Committee (PSC) should exercise, under the responsibility of the Council and of the HR, political control over the Union crisis management operation, provide it with strategic direction and take the relevant decisions in accordance with the third paragraph of Article 38 of the Treaty on European Union (TEU).

(11) Pursuant to Article 41(2) TEU, and in accordance with Council Decision (CFSP) 2015/528 (1), the operational expenditure arising from this Decision, which has military or defence implications, is to be borne by the Member States.

(12) In accordance with Article 5 of Protocol No 22 on the position of Denmark annexed to the Treaty on European Union and to the Treaty on the Functioning of the European Union, Denmark does not participate in the elaboration and implementation of decisions and actions of the Union which have defence implications. Consequently, Denmark is not participating in the adoption of this Decision, is neither bound by it nor subject to its application, and does not participate in the financing of this operation,

HAS ADOPTED THIS DECISION:

Article 1

Mission

1. The Union shall conduct a military crisis management operation contributing to the disruption of the business model of human smuggling and trafficking networks in the Southern Central Mediterranean (EUNAVFOR MED), achieved by undertaking systematic efforts to identify, capture and dispose of vessels and assets used or suspected of being used by smugglers or traffickers, in accordance with applicable international law, including UNCLOS and any UN Security Council Resolution.

2. The area of operation shall be defined, before the launching of EUNAVFOR MED, in the relevant planning documents to be approved by the Council.

Article 2
Mandate

1. EUNAVFOR MED shall operate in accordance with the political, strategic and politico-military objectives set out in the Crisis Management Concept approved by the Council on 18 May 2015.

2. EUNAVFOR MED shall be conducted in sequential phases, and in accordance with the requirements of international law. EUNAVFOR MED shall:

   (a) in a first phase, support the detection and monitoring of migration networks through information gathering and patrolling on the high seas in accordance with international law;

   (b) in a second phase,

      (i) conduct boarding, search, seizure and diversion on the high seas of vessels suspected of being used for human smuggling or trafficking, under the conditions provided for by applicable international law, including UNCLOS and the Protocol against the Smuggling of Migrants;

      (ii) in accordance with any applicable UN Security Council Resolution or consent by the coastal State concerned, conduct boarding, search, seizure and diversion, on the high seas or in the territorial and internal waters of that State, of vessels suspected of being used for human smuggling or trafficking, under the conditions set out in that Resolution or consent;

   (c) in a third phase, in accordance with any applicable UN Security Council Resolution or consent by the coastal State concerned, take all necessary measures against a vessel and related assets, including through disposing of them or rendering them inoperable, which are suspected of being used for human smuggling or trafficking, in the territory of that State, under the conditions set out in that Resolution or consent.

3. The Council shall assess whether the conditions for transition beyond the first phase have been met, taking into account any applicable UN Security Council Resolution and consent by the coastal States concerned.

4. EUNAVFOR MED may collect, in accordance with applicable law, personal data concerning persons taken on board ships participating in EUNAVFOR MED related to characteristics likely to assist in their identification, including fingerprints, as well as the following particulars, with the exclusion of other personal data: surname, maiden name, given names and any alias or assumed name; date and place of birth, nationality, sex; place of residence, profession and whereabouts; driving licenses, identification documents and passport data. It may transmit such data and data related to the vessels and equipment used by such persons to the relevant law enforcement authorities of Member States and/or to competent Union bodies.

Article 3
Appointment of the EU Operation Commander

Rear Admiral Enrico Credendino is hereby appointed EU Operation Commander of EUNAVFOR MED.

Article 4
Designation of the EU Operation Headquarters

The Operation Headquarters of EUNAVFOR MED shall be located in Rome, Italy.

Article 5
Planning and launch of the operation

The Decision to launch EUNAVFOR MED shall be adopted by the Council, upon the recommendation of the Operation Commander of EUNAVFOR MED following approval of the Operation Plan and of the Rules of Engagement necessary for the execution of the mandate.

Article 6
Political control and strategic direction

1. Under the responsibility of the Council and of the HR, the PSC shall exercise the political control and strategic direction of EUNAVFOR MED. The Council hereby authorises the PSC to take the relevant decisions in accordance with Article 38 TEU. This authorisation shall include the powers to amend the planning documents, including the Operations Plan, the Chain of Command and the Rules of Engagement. It shall also include the powers to take decisions on the appointment of the EU Operation Commander and the EU Force Commander. The powers of decision with respect to the objectives and termination of the EU military operation shall remain vested in the Council. Subject to Article 2(3) of this Decision, the PSC shall have the power to decide when to make the transition between the different phases of the operation.

2. The PSC shall report to the Council at regular intervals.

3. The Chairman of the EU Military Committee (EUMC) shall, at regular intervals, report to the PSC on the conduct of EUNAVFOR MED. The PSC may invite the EU Operation Commander or the EU Force Commander to its meetings, as appropriate.

Article 7
Military direction

1. The EUMC shall monitor the proper execution of EUNAVFOR MED conducted under the responsibility of the EU Operation Commander.

2. The EU Operation Commander shall, at regular intervals, report to the EUMC. The EUMC may invite the EU Operation Commander or the EU Force Commander to its meetings, as appropriate.

3. The Chairman of the EUMC shall act as the primary point of contact with the EU Operation Commander.

Article 8
Consistency of the Union's response and coordination

1. The HR shall ensure the implementation of this Decision and its consistency with the Union's external action as a whole, including the Union's development programmes and its humanitarian assistance.

2. The HR, assisted by the European External Action Service (EEAS), shall act as the primary point of contact with the United Nations, the authorities of the countries in the region, and other international and bilateral actors, including NATO, the African Union and the League of Arab States.

3. EUNAVFOR MED shall cooperate with the relevant Member State authorities and shall establish a coordination mechanism, and as appropriate, conclude arrangements with other Union agencies and bodies, in particular FRONTEX, EUROPOL, EUROJUST, European Asylum Support Office and relevant CSDP missions.

Article 9
Participation by third States

1. Without prejudice to the Union's decision-making autonomy or to the single institutional framework, and in accordance with the relevant guidelines of the European Council, third States may be invited to participate in the operation.

2. The Council hereby authorises the PSC to invite third States to offer contributions and to take the relevant decisions on acceptance of the proposed contributions, upon the recommendation of the EU Operations Commander and the EUMC.

3. Detailed arrangements for the participation by third States shall be the subject of agreements concluded pursuant to Article 37 TEU and in accordance with the procedure laid down in Article 218 of the Treaty on the Functioning of the European Union (TFEU). Where the Union and a third State have concluded an agreement establishing a framework for the latter's participation in crisis management missions of the Union, the provisions of such an agreement shall apply in the context of EUNAVFOR MED.

4. Third States making significant military contributions to EUNAVFOR MED shall have the same rights and obligations in terms of day-to-day management of the operation as Member States taking part in the operation.

5. The Council hereby authorises the PSC to take relevant decisions on the setting-up of a Committee of Contributors, should third States provide significant military contributions.

Article 10
Status of Union-led personnel

The status of Union-led units and personnel shall be defined where necessary in accordance with international law.

Article 11
Financial arrangements

1. The common costs of the EU military operation shall be administered in accordance with Decision (CFSP) 2015/528.

2. The financial reference amount for the common costs of EUNAVFOR MED shall be EUR 11,82 million. The percentage of the reference amount referred to in

Article 25(1) of Decision (CFSP) 2015/528 shall be 70% in commitments and 40% for payments.

Article 12
Release of information

1. The HR shall be authorised to release to the third States associated with this Decision, as appropriate and in accordance with the needs of EUNAVFOR MED, EU classified information generated for the purposes of the operation, in accordance with Council Decision 2013/488/EU (1), as follows:

   (a) up to the level provided in the applicable Security of Information Agreements concluded between the Union and the third State concerned; or

   (b) up to the 'CONFIDENTIEL UE/EU CONFIDENTIAL' level in other cases.

2. The HR shall also be authorised to release to the UN, in accordance with the operational needs of EUNAVFOR MED, EU classified information up to 'RESTREINT UE/EU RESTRICTED' level which are generated for the purposes of EUNAVFOR MED, in accordance with Decision 2013/488/EU. Arrangements between the HR and the competent authorities of the United Nations shall be drawn up for this purpose.

3. The HR shall be authorised to release to the third States associated with this Decision any EU non-classified documents connected with the deliberations of the Council relating to the operation and covered by the obligation of professional secrecy pursuant to Article 6(1) of the Council's Rules of Procedure (2).

4. The HR may delegate such authorisations, as well as the ability to conclude the arrangements referred to in this Article, to EEAS officials, to the EU Operation Commander or to the EU Force Commander in accordance with section VII of Annex VI to Decision 2013/488/EU.

Article 13
Entry into force and termination

This Decision shall enter into force on the date of its adoption.

EUNAVFOR MED shall end no later than 12 months after having reached Full Operational Capability (FOC).

This Decision shall be repealed as from the date of closure of the EU Operation Headquarters in accordance with the plans approved for the termination of EUNAVFOR MED, and without prejudice to the procedures regarding the audit and presentation of the accounts of EUNAVFOR MED laid down in Decision (CFSP) 2015/528.

Done at Brussels, 18 May 2015.

For the Council
The President
F. MOGHERINI

SOURCE: Council of the European Union. "Council Decision (CFSP) 2015/778 of 18 May 2015 on a European Union military operation in the Southern Central Mediterranean (EUNAVFOR MED)." May 19, 2015. © European Union, 2015. http://eur-lex.europa.eu/legal-content/EN/TXT/PDF/?uri=CELEX:3 2015D0778&qid=1435825940768&from=EN.

European Council Decision on the Launch of the EUNAVFOR MED Operation

June 22, 2015

COUNCIL DECISION (CFSP) 2015/972

of 22 June 2015

launching the European Union military operation in the southern Central Mediterranean (EUNAVFOR MED)

THE COUNCIL OF THE EUROPEAN UNION,

Having regard to the Treaty on European Union, and in particular Articles 42(4) and 43(2) thereof,

Having regard to Council Decision (CFSP) 2015/778 of 18 May 2015 on a European Union military operation in the southern Central Mediterranean (EUNAVFOR MED) (1), and in particular Article 5 thereof,

Having regard to the proposal from the High Representative of the Union for Foreign Affairs and Security Policy,

Whereas:

(1) On 18 May 2015, the Council adopted Decision (CFSP) 2015/778.

(2) Following the recommendation of the Operation Commander, EUNAVFOR MED should be launched on 22 June 2015.

(3) In accordance with Article 5 of Protocol No 22 on the position of Denmark annexed to the Treaty on European Union and to the Treaty on the Functioning of the European Union, Denmark does not participate in the elaboration and implementation of decisions and actions of the Union which have defence implications. Consequently, Denmark is not participating in the adoption of this Decision, is neither bound by it nor subject to its application, and does not participate in the financing of this operation,

HAS ADOPTED THIS DECISION:

Article 1

The Operation Plan and the Rules of Engagement concerning the European Union military operation in the southern Central Mediterranean (EUNAVFOR MED) are hereby approved.

Article 2

1. EUNAVFOR MED shall be launched on 22 June 2015.

2. In accordance with Article 2(3) of Decision (CFSP) 2015/778, the Council shall assess whether the conditions for transition beyond the first phase of the operation

have been met, taking into account any applicable UN Security Council Resolution and consent by the coastal states concerned. Subject to such assessment by the Council, and in accordance with Article 6(1) of Decision (CFSP) 2015/778, the Political and Security Committee shall have the power to decide when to make the transition between the different phases of the operation.

Article 3

This Decision shall enter into force on the date of its adoption. Done at Luxembourg, 22 June 2015.

For the Council
The President
F. MOGHERINI

European Council Announces Positive Assessment of Mediterranean Operations

September 14, 2015

The Council adopted a positive assessment that the conditions to move to the first step of phase two on the high seas of EUNAVFOR MED have been met, the naval operation having fulfilled all military objectives related to phase 1 focusing upon the collection and analysis of information and intelligence.

This assessment is part of the formal steps required in the process of transitioning the operation to phase 2 on the high seas and will be followed soon by a force generation conference and approval of rules of engagement for phase 2 on the high seas. Once these rules are agreed and the Operation Commander indicates that he has the required assets, the EU Ambassadors within the Political and Security Committee will decide when to launch the first step of phase 2.

This important transition will enable the EU naval operation against human smugglers and traffickers in the Mediterranean to conduct boarding, search, seizure and diversion on the high seas of vessels suspected of being used for human smuggling or trafficking, within international law.

European Council Announces
Start of Operation Sophia

September 28, 2015

Following the political guidance provided by the defence and foreign affairs ministers at their informal meetings on 3 and 5 September, EU Ambassadors within the Political and Security Committee agreed to start the first step of the second phase of the operation as of 7 October 2015 and approved the corresponding rules of engagement.

The EU naval operation against human smugglers in the Mediterranean will be able to board, search, seize and divert vessels suspected of being used for human smuggling or trafficking on the high seas, in line with international law.

The Political and Security Committee also agreed that EUNAVFOR Med should be renamed "Sophia" after the name given to the baby born on the ship of the operation which rescued her mother on 22 August 2015 off the coast of Libya.

"Today's decision takes the EU naval operation from its intelligence-gathering phase to its operational and active phase against human smugglers on the high seas. The European Union has proven its capacity to act in a swift and united manner. We are also united in our diplomatic efforts to find both a political solution to the crises in Syria and Libya, and, in partnership with the countries of origin and transit of the migration flows, to support the economic and social development of these countries." —Federica Mogherini, High Representative for Foreign Affairs and Security Policy

The new name of the operation will be formally adopted by the Council at the earliest opportunity.

The decision by the Political and Security Committee to launch the first step of phase 2 of the operation follows an assessment by the Council on 14 September that the conditions to move to this stage have been met.

The Operation Commander Rear Admiral Credendino has judged the transition possible as member states provided the assets needed for this more active phase in the force generation conference of 16 September 2015.

The operation is aimed at disrupting the business model of human smuggling and trafficking networks in the Mediterranean and to prevent the further loss of life at sea. It is part of a wider EU comprehensive approach to migration, tackling both the symptoms and root causes such as conflict, poverty, climate change and persecution.

SOURCE: Council of the European Union. "EUNAVFOR Med: EU agrees to start the active phase of the operation against human smugglers and to rename it "Operation Sophia"." September 28, 2015. © European Union, 2015. www.consilium.europa.eu/en/press/press-releases/2015/09/28-eunavfor.

OTHER HISTORIC DOCUMENTS OF INTEREST

FROM THIS VOLUME

FROM PREVIOUS *HISTORIC DOCUMENTS*

United Nations and Nepalese Officials Remark on Earthquake and Recovery

APRIL 25, JUNE 25, AND OCTOBER 23, 2015

One of the worst natural disasters in Nepal's history struck the country in April 2015. A major earthquake occurred outside of the capital, killing thousands, displacing millions more, and destroying dozens of historical sites. Weak infrastructure and internal political issues exacerbated the earthquake's impact and hampered international relief efforts, as did continued aftershocks that caused more damage to roads and villages and killed dozens more. Nepal's government later hosted a global conference to discuss the country's reconstruction plans, with the goal of gathering best practices on relief and reconstruction efforts and collecting additional pledges for support from the international community.

DISASTER STRIKES

An earthquake measuring a 7.8 magnitude—the second highest class on the Richter scale—hit Nepal on the morning of April 25, 2015. Its epicenter was located twenty-two miles west of Khudi, the nearest city, and fifty-one miles northwest of Nepal's capital, Kathmandu, but its effects were felt across the country. According to the UN Office for the Coordination of Humanitarian Affairs, the earthquake killed 8,617 people and injured more than 16,000. An estimated 5.6 million people were affected by the earthquake, including nearly 3 million people who were displaced after their homes, or in some cases entire villages, were destroyed. The earthquake also triggered an avalanche on Mount Everest that swept through a base camp, killing twenty people and injuring 120. It also destroyed a key segment of the climbing route between base camp and camps located higher up the mountain, stranding approximately 200 people for several days.

The physical damage caused by the earthquake was extensive. More than 473,000 houses were destroyed and twenty-six hospitals damaged. The United Nations Educational, Scientific and Cultural Organization (UNESCO) reported that more than thirty monuments in the Kathmandu region collapsed during the earthquake and another 120 were partially damaged. Many of these were world-famous historical and cultural sites that draw hundreds of thousands of tourists each year. This included Kathmandu's Durbar Square, a UNESCO World Heritage Site. An estimated 80 percent of the temples in Durbar Square were destroyed by the earthquake, including Kasthamandap, an early 16th-century wooden temple that inspired the city's name. Kathmandu's iconic Dharahara Tower was also destroyed, and at least twenty-four people who had been climbing the tower died when it collapsed. Another historic temple built in 1690, the Maju Deval Temple, was leveled, and Patan Durbar Square, a UNESCO World Heritage Site located south of Kathmandu, was also destroyed.

Hundreds of aftershocks occurred following the initial quake, including another earthquake measuring a magnitude of 7.3 on May 12 that hit forty-seven miles east of Kathmandu near the town of Namche Bazaar. Although nearly the same magnitude of the April 25 earthquake, scientists classified it as an aftershock, due largely to the fact that the quakes occurred along the same fault line. The tremors were also felt in India, Tibet, and Bangladesh. More than 100 people were killed and 2,500 injured. Fearful of the continued aftershocks and the possibility of another major quake, thousands of Nepalese moved outdoors, setting up makeshift tents in open spaces—including a military parade ground—and used tarps to protect themselves from the rain and weather.

The number of casualties and significant damage made the earthquake the worst disaster in Nepal since 1934, when an earthquake killed more than 10,000 people. "On behalf of the United Nations, I send my deepest condolences to the Government of Nepal and to everyone affected, particularly to the families and friends of those killed and injured," said UN secretary general Ban Ki-moon in a statement. "The United Nations is supporting the Government of Nepal in coordinating international search and rescue operations and is preparing to mount a major relief effort."

RELIEF EFFORTS BEGIN

The U.S. Geological Survey initially estimated that economic losses caused by the quake would equal anywhere between 9 percent and 50 percent of Nepal's roughly $20 billion gross domestic product (GDP). Nepal's tourism industry, which accounts for approximately eight percent of the country's economy and employs more than 1 million people, was expected to be particularly hard hit. "Kathmandu is central to the nation's economy, and it's crippled," former finance minister Madhukar S. J. B. Rana told Bloomberg News. "The extent of the impact depends both on the magnitude of the disaster but also on the resources and capacity to cope. We don't have that."

As an initial response to the disaster, the Nepal Army launched Operation Sankat Mochan, an operation focused on search and rescue and on coordinating disaster relief. It involved 90 percent of the Army's forces as well as military personnel from a number of different countries. Pledges of support poured in from the international community. The United Nations requested $432 million in emergency funds to support Nepal's relief efforts and released $15 million from its own central emergency response fund. The Asian Development Bank provided a $3 million grant to Nepal for immediate relief efforts and promised up to $200 million for the first phase of reconstruction. By mid-May, Nepal had received approximately $88 million in aid, including donations of $31 million from the United Kingdom, $22 million from China, $19 million from Norway, and $15 million from the United States. A number of countries also provided technical expertise or sent disaster response teams to support relief efforts on the ground in Nepal. China, for example, sent a sixty-two-member search and rescue team, Israel sent 260 rescue experts and a 200-person medical team, and Japan sent another seventy personnel to support disaster relief.

The United Nations served as coordinator for international efforts to maximize effectiveness, and Nepalese officials reassured the public that the government was taking appropriate action to distribute aid. "The government is doing all it can for rescue and relief on a war footing," said Prime Minister Sushil Koirala. "It is a challenge and a very difficult hour for Nepal."

LACK OF RESOURCES, POLITICAL STRUGGLES HAMPER RELIEF

Prior to the earthquake, it was widely known that Nepal lacked the resources and leadership necessary to ensure its preparedness for a major disaster. Nepal is classified as a "least developed country" by the United Nations—meaning it is among the countries with the lowest indicators of socioeconomic development—and it is one of the poorest countries in Asia. The country has also been racked by internal political issues, including a ten-year civil war that killed roughly 12,000 by the time it ended in 2006. Local elections had not been held in twenty years, and the committees charged with maintaining local governing councils were disorganized. Nepal had nine prime ministers over the course of eight years, creating instability and uncertainty at the national level. A major factor, caused by ineffective governance, contributing to the earthquake's devastating impact was the common practice of many Nepalese building their own houses without professional oversight. The government passed a National Building Code in 1994 following an earthquake that killed 700 people, but failed to enforce it, leading to widespread noncompliance. In addition, Nepal has weak communication and transportation infrastructures due in part to its mountainous terrain. The World Bank reports that more than a third of Nepalese living in hilly regions are more than four hours away from a paved road, and the headquarters of fifteen of the country's seventy-five districts are not connected to any roads.

These factors posed major challenges for Nepal's relief efforts. Nepal has only one international airport, creating congestion at the terminals and stranding many planes carrying supplies on tarmacs. The lack of paved roads made it difficult to transport supplies to the remote areas where they were most needed, and many roads had been blocked by landslides triggered by the earthquake. There was also a shortage of trucks, and many drivers had returned to their villages to help their own families. "Our granaries are full and we have ample food stock, but we are not able to transport supplies at a faster pace," said Shrimani Raj Khanal, a manager at the Nepal Food Corporation.

The UN's resident coordinator in Nepal, Jamie McGoldrick, said that Nepal's customs restrictions were also slowing relief efforts and causing a backup of supplies at the Kathmandu airport, and local media reported that shipments of supplies had been stopped at the Indian border. Nepal's government had exempted some supplies such as tarps and tents from import taxes after the earthquake, but McGoldrick said the rules needed to be relaxed even further to allow faster processing of other supplies. However, Nepal finance secretary Prasad Sharma disputed his claims. "We haven't sent back anything, and there's no duty to pay on anything. These charges are completely irresponsible and I refute them," Sharma said.

International Conference on Nepal's Reconstruction

On June 25, two months after the earthquake hit, the Nepalese government organized a one-day International Conference in Kathmandu to address Nepal's reconstruction. Government leaders from neighboring and supportive countries, officials from the UN, European Commission, World Bank, and Asian Development Bank, and representatives from development partners and other multilateral and regional institutions were invited to attend. The stated goals of the conference were to inform attendees of the current situation in Nepal, distribute the findings from the Nepal National Planning Commission's Post Disaster Needs Assessment (PDNA), share best practices and experiences from effective reconstruction programs, and secure additional pledges of technical and financial support for Nepal's reconstruction.

Foreign Affairs Minister Mahendra Bahadur Pandey gave welcome remarks at the conference in which he acknowledged Nepal's lack of preparation for such a disaster, but defended the government's "prompt" response. Noting that the PDNA estimated Nepal would need approximately $6.7 billion for reconstruction, "a huge amount for a least developed country like Nepal," he called for the international community's increased support. "We are committed to making this tragedy a shifting ground for the settled and safer future by utilizing our national resources and expertise to the extent possible," he said. "For this, an enhanced level of support and cooperation from our neighboring and friendly countries and the international community is extremely critical."

Takehiki Nakao, the president of the Asian Development Bank, also spoke at the event and called on Nepal to follow key principles as it recovers, including building earthquake-resistant facilities, ensuring that the most vulnerable of Nepal's citizens receive the appropriate assistance, and proper oversight of the distribution of donations.

More than 300 delegates from sixty nations attended the conference and pledged $4.4 billion in aid for Nepal's recovery, including half a billion dollars from the World Bank. Half of this amount is to be provided in grants, and the other half will consist of loans.

—Linda Fecteau Grimm

Following is the text of a statement by UN secretary general Ban Ki-moon on April 25, 2015, expressing support following an earthquake in Nepal; the edited text of remarks by Nepal's minister for foreign affairs, Mahendra Bahadur Pandey, on June 25, 2015, regarding earthquake recovery; the text of a speech delivered by Takehiko Nakao, president of the Asian Development Bank, also on June 25, 2015, on the principles of reconstruction for Nepal; the text of a June 25, 2015, World Bank group pledge of support toward Nepal's reconstruction; and the text of a October 23, 2015, press release from the United Nations News Centre regarding ongoing humanitarian aid in Nepal.

DOCUMENT

United Nations Secretary General on Nepal Earthquake

April 25, 2015

Our thoughts are with the people of Nepal and neighbouring countries today in the aftermath of the earthquake that has struck the Kathmandu Valley.

The reports of the devastation are still coming in and the numbers of people killed, injured and affected by this earthquake continue to rise. It is clear that very many lives have been lost. There has also been significant damage to Nepal's irreplaceable cultural heritage.

On behalf of the United Nations, I send my deepest condolences to the Government of Nepal and to everyone affected, particularly to the families and friends of those killed and injured. I thank the first responders in all the affected countries who are working around the clock to save lives.

The United Nations is supporting the Government of Nepal in coordinating international search and rescue operations and is preparing to mount a major relief effort.

SOURCE: United Nations. News Centre. "Statement on Nepal earthquake." April 25, 2015. www.un.org/apps/news/infocus/sgspeeches/statments_full.asp?statID=2587#.Vm7fKLyiox9.

Statement from Nepal's Minister of Foreign Affairs on Earthquake Reconstruction

June 25, 2015

The Right Honourable Prime Minister and Chair of this Session

Hon. Ministers
UN Under-Secretary General
President of ADB
Vice President of the World Bank
Heads of Delegations
Excellencies
Distinguished Delegates
Ladies and Gentlemen

It is my honour and privilege to warmly welcome you all to the International Conference on Nepal's Reconstruction 2015 hosted by the Government of Nepal....

It has exactly been two months since Nepal was struck by the devastating earthquake. The damage caused by the earthquake and its subsequent aftershocks especially with respect to lives and property is incalculable. Our historical and cultural monuments of archaeological significance have been badly damaged. Equally alarming are the adverse impacts on the country's economy and pursuit of internationally agreed development goals including the MDGs. The disaster is certain to unsettle the country's achievements in human and social sectors and upset the national aspirations for swifter progress....

Mr. Chairman,

We should concede that we may have fallen short of the required preparedness for the disaster of this magnitude. However, the Government of Nepal acted promptly during rescue and relief operations in mobilizing its own resources and coordinating outside support. The existing regional and international frameworks have also been of tremendous help. And, the past two months, testing and difficult though they have been, have motivated us to get organized to ensure that we learn from the disaster. The earthquake-induced loss is tragic and irreparable; but it also has brought forth opportunities to rebuild the country better. The necessity now is to 'walk the talk' of 'post disaster period as an opportunity' discourse to ensure that it does not become a mere statement of intent but an expression of reality.

It is against such context that we are hosting this Conference. The preliminary Post Disaster Needs Assessment (PDNA) is now before you. It shows that the pathways to recovery would need about $6.7 billion. This is a huge amount for a least developed country like Nepal....

Translating the vision of 'Resilient Nepal' into reality is not possible without the enhanced level of support from our friendly countries and the international community. For this, our concerted actions and sustained engagement at both national and international levels should be guided by the local conditions and the priorities of the communities. The international community needs to respond in a robust and yet highly coordinated manner. Such response may include, in addition to the financial support to Nepal's recon-struction works, the substantial measures including through market access, technology transfer, announcement of special economic packages, encouragement to foreign direct investment (FDI), and tourism.

Mr. Chairman,

Our land may have been shaken and our physical structures left damaged by the geo-logical movement. The Nepalese people's vigor and will-power to fight such hardships, however, has not diminished a bit. We are committed to making this tragedy a shifting ground for the settled and safer future by utilizing our national resources and expertise to the extent possible. For this, an enhanced level of support and cooperation from our neigh-boring and friendly countries and the international community is extremely critical....

I thank you very much for your attention.

SOURCE: Government of Nepal. Ministry of Foreign Affairs. "Welcome Remarks by Hon. Mahendra Bahadur Pandey, Minister for Foreign Affairs at the International Conference on Nepal's Reconstruction, on 25th June 2015 in Kathmandu." June 25, 2015. www.mofa.gov.np/speech/welcome-remarks-by-hon-mahendra-bahadur-pandey-minister-for-foreign-affairs-at-the-international-conference-on-nepal-s-reconstruction-on-25th-june-2015-in-kathmandu.

Asian Development Bank Outlines Principles for Recovery in Nepal

June 25, 2015

Right Honorable Prime Minister Sushil Koirala,
Your Excellencies,
Ladies and Gentlemen,

I would like to express ADB's deepest sympathy to the people of Nepal. The earthquake last April was by far the worst natural disaster in Nepal's recent history.

The Nepali people, the government, and the international community immediately stepped in to help. On the occasion of ADB's Annual Meeting in Baku, Azerbaijan around one week after the earthquake, ADB hosted the Nepal Partnership Forum co-chaired by Finance Minister Mahat which affirmed international support.

Affected families showed tremendous resilience by initiating rebuilding efforts on their own despite their heavy suffering. Many people also volunteered to deliver relief goods to remote villages, crossing difficult terrain. It is heartening to see the Nepali people's self-help spirit and solidarity. I am sure that the nation will be rebuilt, and will be stronger as a result.

But the remaining challenges are immense. We must consider the sheer magnitude of the damages and suffering, the remoteness of the affected areas, and the monsoon already setting in. Today's conference is very timely.

The government has shown strong leadership in planning the reconstruction efforts. It led the post-disaster needs assessments along with donors, is drafting a rehabilitation and reconstruction policy, and is establishing a special agency for reconstruction.

For our part, just yesterday, ADB's Board approved $200 million in Earthquake Emergency Assistance, to rebuild and restore schools, roads, and public buildings. We are partnering with the Japan International Cooperation Agency and other donors to augment our support. In addition, ADB is providing $50 million in budget support and grant assistance.

For the subsequent phase of reconstruction, we are also ready to allocate up to $350 million from the existing ADB loan portfolio to high-priority rehabilitation activities. This will not affect our ongoing and planned development programs.

All in all, the total assistance from ADB for rebuilding Nepal after the earthquake will reach $600 million. ADB will make best use of its long-term experiences of rehabilitation and reconstruction work after serious disasters such as Typhoon Yolanda in the Philippines and after the tsunami in Sumatra, Indonesia.

I would like to take this opportunity to highlight 5 principles for reconstruction.

The first is "Building Back Better". Buildings should be rebuilt to earthquake-resistant standards. Our assistance will include more resilient school buildings and education for disaster preparedness to provide a better and more secure future for children.

The second principle is inclusiveness. In our reconstruction efforts, we will pay special attention to the needs of the poor, rural residents, and other vulnerable social groups, who have suffered more from the earthquakes.

The third principle is the importance of a robust institutional setup for reconstruction. As I have mentioned, the government is establishing a special purpose agency for reconstruction. This will facilitate swift decision-making in the budget process, implementation, and coordination. It goes without saying that strong leadership is important for the success of the new agency.

The fourth principle is about capacity and governance. ADB will work closely with the government to help build strong institutional capacity, and to ensure sound governance and fiduciary risk management systems for the reconstruction process.

The fifth principle is donor coordination and government ownership. This conference is a testament to the resolve of the government and the international community to work in a coordinated and harmonized manner to plan and implement reconstruction of the affected areas.

Mr. Chair, I visited Nepal just last February and was impressed by the people's hospitality, the country's rich and diverse culture and heritage, and its tremendous development potential in areas such as agribusiness, tourism, and small and medium enterprises. I was also encouraged by the government's commitment to its long-term vision for prosperity.

Moving forward, I truly believe that Nepal will emerge stronger from this catastrophe and continue along the path of inclusive and sustainable growth. Hard-won gains made before the earthquake in poverty reduction, private sector-based growth, and political stability should not be compromised by this tragedy. Reconstruction should go hand-in-hand with development programs already planned.

The international community stands together with the people and government of Nepal at this challenging time.

Thank you very much.

SOURCE: Asian Development Bank. "Speech at the International Conference on Nepal's Reconstruction 2015—Takehiko Nakao." June 25, 2015. This article was first published by the Asian Development Bank (www.adb.org). www.adb.org/news/speeches/speech-international-conference-nepal-s-reconstruction-2015-takehiko-nakao.

World Bank Pledges Monetary Support for Nepal

June 25, 2015

With the Post-Disaster Needs Assessment complete and the Government's new budget cycle beginning in mid-July the World Bank Group is mobilizing resources to align budget support and investments with the recovery and reconstruction needs.

The World Bank Group plans to provide up to half-a-billion dollars to finance the reconstruction of Nepal, of which $300 million is new funding from the International Development Association's Crisis Response Window. The World Bank Group support will consist of:

- **$100 million for budget support:** to be considered by the World Bank Board on June 29. This IDA credit will provide the Government of Nepal with short-term financial support to accelerate and expand relief and recovery efforts. It will also support policy measures to strengthen the country's financial sector as a vehicle that channels resources for reconstruction to the private sector and households.

- **$200 million for housing reconstruction:** submitted to the World Bank Board of Executive Directors for consideration on June 29. This credit will provide grants to home-owners to rebuild about 55,000 houses for the poor in rural areas. The grants will be disbursed in tranches after verification that houses have been constructed to standards resistant to natural disasters. The credit will also finance technical assistance to improve disaster risk management systems.

- **Multi-Donor Trust Fund (MDTF) for housing reconstruction:** we have proposed a facility to enable coordination, increase harmonization and reduce transaction costs for donor financing of housing reconstruction. Additional funding is needed as the World Bank's $200 million credit only covers a small part of the housing reconstruction needs.

- **$100 to $200 million reallocated from the existing portfolio:** we are supporting the Government of Nepal in reallocating resources from existing projects to support the reconstruction effort across multiple sectors (agriculture, health, education, energy, roads and bridges, water and sanitation) without affecting the long-term development agenda. An initial $40 million is proposed for reallocation toward disaster response, of which $12 million has already been redirected to finance nutrition and rural water supply needs in the worst-hit districts.

- **Expected $50 to 70 million liquidity facility and $9.8 million of quick post-earthquake response from IFC:** the liquidity facility from the World Bank Group's private sector arm, will be available to commercial bank clients to support recovery of firms including SMEs in tourism or housing. This USD facility can be used for import of essential capital equipment and for working capital needs of firms, as well as accelerated financing to clients in tourism and agribusiness to ensure business continuity.

- **Joint WBG Hydropower:** Under the joint implementation plan for hydro power, the World Bank Group intends to accelerate existing agreements for development and rehabilitation of approximately 2500MW hydropower generation capacity. This includes required direct IDA and IFC financing and mobilizing necessary financing from partners including the private sector, as well as advisory and technical assistance.

Source: The World Bank. "World Bank Group Pledge Statement at the International Conference on Nepal's Reconstruction 2015." June 25, 2015. www.worldbank.org/en/news/speech/2015/06/25/world-bank-group-pledge-statement-at-the-international-conference-on-nepals-reconstruction-2015.

United Nations Details Ongoing Humanitarian Crisis in Nepal

October 23, 2015

As winter approaches, the top United Nations humanitarian official for Nepal today stressed that shelter and food remain top priorities six months after the devastating earthquakes that shook the country in April.

"While much has been achieved, the humanitarian community remains committed to meet remaining needs," said Jamie McGoldrick, UN Humanitarian Coordinator in Nepal, in a press release.

"With the winter on the way, we must ensure adequate shelter and food security, particularly for more than 80,000 families."

According to the UN Office for the Coordination of Humanitarian Affairs (OCHA), humanitarian partners, with the Government of Nepal, provided emergency shelter to over 700,000 families, but the effect of the coming harsh cold weather is a concern with many people still without permanent durable housing.

The April and May earthquakes left 8,891 people dead, destroyed more than 600,000 houses and damaged 290,000 houses, OCHA estimates. During the height of the emergency, some 188,900 people were temporarily displaced.

Over the last six months, humanitarian partners provided food to over 1.4 million people, established temporary classrooms for 300,000 children and supported health authorities to restore all damaged health facilities by June. Concerted efforts reportedly ensured that there were no disease outbreaks.

Meanwhile, to reach remote and isolated villages, last mile logistics operations employed innovative and traditional methods of delivering assistance with 16,000 porters and hundreds of mules. Over 500,000 people received multi-purpose cash assistance, which helped them bridge the economic gap caused by devastated livelihoods.

"When faced with tough challenges like the monsoon season, landslides and difficult terrain, we are proud of how we have been able to support the Government and people of Nepal and respond to the challenges overall," Mr. McGoldrick said. "But present conditions are a concern."

Since the end of September, fuel in short supply has impeded progress, OCHA reports. The Humanitarian Country Team is urging a quick resolution to the fuel shortage so that winter goods can be quickly delivered to vulnerable households. This massive logistical undertaking can be achieved, Mr. McGoldrick said, but the lack of fuel is significantly affecting distribution of goods. He further noted that there is a brief window of fair weather in which humanitarian actors can respond before the snow.

The Humanitarian Country Team also underlined it is working very closely with the Government and other partners to ensure a smooth transition to recovery and reconstruction.

"The Humanitarian Country Team is looking forward to the establishment of the National Reconstruction Authority," said Mr. McGoldrick. "Once it becomes operational, we anticipate that we will start to see the rapid expansion of reconstruction across the earthquake-affected areas."

SOURCE: United Nations. News Centre. "Six months after earthquake, Nepal 'racing against winter'—UN relief official." October 23, 2015. www.un.org/apps/news/story.asp?NewsID=52348#.VtZiu7w6JVt.

OTHER HISTORIC DOCUMENTS OF INTEREST

FROM PREVIOUS *HISTORIC DOCUMENTS*

- Nepal Election Replaces Monarchy with Constituent Assembly, *2008*, p. 131
- Peace Agreement between Nepalese Government and Maoist Rebels, *2006*, p. 678

May

Federal Court Rules on NSA Domestic Surveillance Program

MAY 7, 2015

In 2013, Edward Snowden, a former National Security Agency (NSA) contractor, leaked information to the press that revealed the previously unknown existence of a top secret government surveillance program that daily collected and stored, in bulk, logs of all the metadata associated with telephone calls made by and to all Americans. The exposure of the secret program led to a public uproar. Unlikely coalitions emerged both in favor of and opposed to the program. Many were outraged at the violation of personal privacy, while some lawmakers argued that it was necessary to prevent terrorism and that revealing details of the program gave the terrorists an advantage. Less than a week after the revelation, the American Civil Liberties Union (ACLU) brought a suit against James Clapper, the director of national intelligence, challenging the legality of the program, arguing that it sweeps up sensitive information in warrantless searches and seizures that violate both the Fourth Amendment rights to privacy and the freedoms of speech and association protected by the First Amendment. The district court dismissed the case and it was appealed to the Court of Appeals for the Second Circuit, which, on May 7, 2015, ruled against the NSA in *ACLU v. Clapper*. Without addressing any of the constitutional issues, the Court ruled that the NSA's collection of bulk telephone metadata "exceeds the scope of what Congress has authorized" in Section 215 of the Patriot Act.

The decision was a large victory for civil libertarians and advocates for privacy rights, but its impact appears short-lived. Just weeks after the Court's ruling, Congress let the challenged provisions of the Patriot Act lapse. It replaced them with the USA Freedom Act, which gives the NSA six months to halt its bulk metadata collection program.

The Patriot Act and the NSA's Metadata Program

Congress originally passed the USA PATRIOT Act by overwhelming bipartisan margins following the September 11, 2001, terrorist attacks. Its official name is an acronym of the first letters of the words: "United and Strengthening America by Providing Appropriate Tools Required to Intercept and Obstruct Terrorism Act of 2001." The Act's passage significantly increased the surveillance and investigative powers of law enforcement agencies.

The government argued that Section 215 of the Act authorized the NSA's telephone metadata collection program. First, it is important to understand exactly what is encompassed by the term "telephone metadata." Metadata includes information detailing the length of the call, the phone numbers of both parties, and the routing of the call, which can convey general, but not precise, location information. It does not directly reveal the content of the calls, although the challengers argue that "the startling amount of detailed information metadata can reveal" still raises privacy concerns. For example, knowing that someone is calling a specialized "hotline" could reveal that the person is a victim of domestic violence or rape, a veteran, an addict, contemplating suicide, or reporting a crime.

Section 215 of the Patriot Act permits the government to apply for "an order requiring the production of any tangible things . . . for an investigation . . . to protect against international terrorism or clandestine intelligence activities." The type of things producible under these orders appears to be "essentially unlimited," but the Act requires that the government make a specific case before it can order communications companies to produce the information. Specifically, to obtain a Section 215 order, the government must provide "a statement of facts showing that there are reasonable grounds to believe that the tangible things sought are relevant to an authorized investigation." Section 215 contained a "sunset" provision, causing it to expire and require renewal. Between 2001 and 2011, it had been amended seven times.

The telephone metadata program became public on June 5, 2013, when a British newspaper published an order to Verizon that had been leaked by Edward Snowden. The order directed Verizon to produce to the NSA "on an ongoing daily basis . . . all call detail records or 'telephony metadata' created by Verizon for communications (i) between the United States and abroad; or (ii) wholly within the United States, including local telephone calls." After the order was made public, the U.S. government acknowledged that it was part of a broader program of bulk collection of telephone metadata from other telecommunications providers. It is undisputed that the government started relying on Section 215 to collect this telephone metadata information in bulk since at least May 2006. The government contests the characterization of the program as collecting "virtually all telephony metadata" but declined to elaborate.

The order contemplates the creation of a "data archive" exclusively operated by the NSA to store and process metadata. This vast data bank is kept in reserve and queried if it becomes relevant to an investigation. The government explained that the data can only be accessed "when NSA has identified a known telephone number for which . . . there are facts giving rise to reasonable, articulable suspicion that the telephone number is associated with . . . terrorist activity or a specific terrorist organization." The government also asserted in its court papers that "it does not conduct any general 'browsing' of the data."

On June 11, 2013, the ACLU sued the government officials responsible for administering the program, challenging it on both statutory and constitutional grounds. It asked the court to permanently enjoin the government from continuing its program and to "purge from their possession all of the call records." The district court dismissed the case, and the ACLU appealed to the 2nd Circuit Court of Appeals.

APPELLATE COURT FINDS GOVERNMENT OVERSTEPPED AUTHORITY

A panel of judges on the Second Circuit Court of Appeals ruled that the NSA's bulk collection of telephone metadata was not authorized by Section 215 of the Patriot Act, the law that the government had cited to justify the program.

The Court reviewed the requirements of Section 215, which required the government to "show reasonable grounds to believe" that what it is seeking is "relevant to an authorized investigation." At its most basic, the law requires that the records be "relevant" and that they be relevant to "an authorized investigation." According to the court, neither of these two requirements was met.

In arguing its case, the government emphasized that "relevance" is an extremely generous standard and compared it to the standard required for grand jury subpoenas. It argued that it is "eminently reasonable to believe that Section 215 bulk telephony metadata is relevant to counterterrorism investigations." The ACLU disputed the idea that "metadata from every phone call with a party in the United States, over a period of years and years, can be considered 'relevant to an authorized investigation,' by any definition of the term."

The Court focused on the sweeping surveillance at issue in the case, creating a "vast repository" of a "staggering volume" of information that is not directly "relevant" but is kept because it "may allow the NSA, at some unknown time in the future, utilizing its ability to sift through the trove of irrelevant data it has collected up to that point, to identify information that *is* relevant." Comparing the type of information ordered under this NSA program to the standard used in grand juries did not, the Court found, help the government's case. Subpoenas typically seek the records of particular people under investigation, and cover particular time periods when the events under investigation occurred. By contrast, the information the NSA ordered through this program concerns "*every* telephone call made or received in the United States" for an "indefinite period of time extending into the future." After finding that such an expansion of the concept of "relevance" would be "unprecedented and unwarranted," the Court concluded that it agrees "with appellants that the government's argument is irreconcilable with the statute's plain text."

Because the Court found that the NSA's program was not authorized by statute, it did not need to reach the ACLU's constitutional arguments, but it did, nevertheless, outline some of the complicated and difficult Fourth Amendment issues implicated by such programs. The ACLU contends that the warrantless seizure of telephone records violates individual's expectations of privacy under the Fourth Amendment. The government has responded to such arguments by focusing on what is known as the "third-party records doctrine," under which individuals have no reasonable expectation of privacy in information voluntarily disclosed to third parties such as phone companies. Courts have been struggling with how and whether this third-party exception to the Fourth Amendment applies in the digital age, where people provide a great deal of information about themselves to technology and communications companies in just the daily course of carrying out mundane tasks. To resolve *ACLU v. Clapper*, the Court did not need to "reach these weighty constitutional issues," and it stressed that this is an area where "a congressional judgment as to what is 'reasonable' under current circumstances would carry weight."

The Second Circuit's opinion sent the case back to the district court to be reheard, but it did not order data collection to be stopped. At the time of the decision, Section 215 was scheduled to expire in just several weeks. "In light of the asserted national security interests at stake," the Court stated, "we deem it prudent to pause to allow an opportunity for debate in Congress that may (or may not) profoundly alter the legal landscape." The opinion also acknowledged that, because it rested its case on statutory issues, the decision could become moot if Congress substantially modifies the statute, or fails to reauthorize it entirely.

Congress Passes Freedom Act

Just a few weeks after the decision, on June 1, 2015, Section 215 expired for the first time since the passage of the Patriot Act in 2001, amid much political maneuvering in Congress. The next day, Congress passed the USA Freedom Act, which amends Section 215 to prohibit the bulk collection of call records that was at issue in *ACLU v. Clapper*. Under the revised law, the NSA has six months to abandon its wholesale collection of phone records and transition to a more narrowly targeted collection of call detail records as needed in intelligence investigations. The new law adds a requirement that the government promptly destroy collected records determined not to have any foreign intelligence information. President Obama had once supported the secret bulk metadata collection but had publically changed his position after the results of two independent review panels found the program not to be necessary to prevent terror attacks. Praising the passage of the Freedom Act, he said, "Enactment of this legislation will strengthen civil liberty safeguards and provide greater public confidence in these programs. I am gratified that Congress has finally moved forward with this sensible reform legislation."

The brief period between when the Patriot Act had expired and the replacement Freedom Act was passed resulted from a stand-off between those who wanted to keep the rules unchanged, including Senate majority leader Mitch McConnell, R-Ky., who argued that it was necessary to America's ability to protect itself, and those critics of the Freedom Act, including such diverse senators as Sen. Rand Paul, R-Ky., and Sen. Bernie Sanders, I-Vt., who say that the new law does not go far enough to curtail surveillance programs.

ACLU deputy legal director Jameel Jaffer commented on the passage of the Freedom Act, calling it "the most important surveillance reform bill since 1978, and its passage is an indication that Americans are no longer willing to give the intelligence agencies a blank check." Although, he added, "The bill leaves many of the government's most intrusive and overbroad surveillance powers untouched, and it makes only very modest adjustments to disclosure and transparency requirements."

—Melissa Feinberg

Following is the edited text of the United States Court of Appeals for the Second Circuit decision in ACLU v. Clapper, *in which the court ruled against the NSA's bulk data collection program.*

DOCUMENT   *ACLU v. Clapper*

May 7, 2015

[All footnotes have been omitted.]

**UNITED STATES COURT OF APPEALS
FOR THE SECOND CIRCUIT**

August Term, 2014 (Argued: September 2, 2014 Decided: May 7, 2015)

Docket No. 14-42-cv

AMERICAN CIVIL LIBERTIES UNION, AMERICAN CIVIL LIBERTIES UNION FOUNDATION, NEW YORK CIVIL LIBERTIES UNION, NEW YORK CIVIL LIBERTIES UNION FOUNDATION,

Plaintiffs-Appellants,

— v. —

JAMES R. CLAPPER, in his official capacity as Director of National Intelligence,
MICHAEL S. ROGERS, in his official capacity as Director of the National Security
Agency and Chief of the Central Security Service, ASHTON B. CARTER, in his
official capacity as Secretary of Defense, LORETTA E. LYNCH, in her official capacity as
Attorney General of the United States, and JAMES B. COMEY, in his official capacity as
Director of the Federal Bureau of Investigation,

Defendants-Appellees.

GERARD E. LYNCH, Circuit Judge:

This appeal concerns the legality of the bulk telephone metadata collection program (the "telephone metadata program"), under which the National Security Agency ("NSA") collects in bulk "on an ongoing daily basis" the metadata associated with telephone calls made by and to Americans, and aggregates those metadata into a repository or data bank that can later be queried. Appellants challenge the program on statutory and constitutional grounds. Because we find that the program exceeds the scope of what Congress has authorized, we vacate the decision below dismissing the complaint without reaching appellants' constitutional arguments. We affirm the district court's denial of appellants' request for a preliminary injunction.

[Background and Sections I and II, summarizing the definition of telephone metadata and Section 215 of the USA PATRIOT ACT, have been omitted.]

III. Statutory Authorization

Although appellants vigorously argue that the telephone metadata program violates their rights under the Fourth Amendment to the Constitution, and therefore cannot be authorized by either the Executive or the Legislative Branch of government, or by both acting together, their initial argument is that the program simply has not been authorized by the legislation on which the government relies for the issuance of the orders to service providers to collect and turn over the metadata at issue. We naturally turn first to that argument.

Section 215 clearly sweeps broadly in an effort to provide the government with essential tools to investigate and forestall acts of terrorism. The statute permits the government to apply for "an order requiring the production of *any tangible things* . . . for an investigation . . . to protect against international terrorism or clandestine intelligence activities." 50 U.S.C. § 1861(a)(1) (emphasis added). A § 215 order may require the production of anything that "can be obtained with a subpoena *duces tecum* issued by a court of the United States in aid of a grand jury investigation" or any other court order. *Id.* § 1861(c)(2)(D).

While the *types* of "tangible things" subject to such an order would appear essentially unlimited, such "things" may only be produced upon a specified factual showing by the government. To obtain a § 215 order, the government must provide the FISC with "a statement of facts showing that there are reasonable grounds to believe that the tangible things sought are relevant to an authorized investigation (other than a threat assessment) conducted [under guidelines approved by the Attorney General]." *Id.* § 1861(b)(2)(A); see *id.* § 1861(a)(2) (requiring that investigations making use of such orders be conducted under guidelines approved by the Attorney General). The basic requirements for metadata collection under § 215, then, are simply that the records be *relevant* to an *authorized* investigation (other than a threat assessment).

For all the complexity of the statutory framework, the parties' respective positions are relatively simple and straightforward. The government emphasizes that "relevance" is an extremely generous standard, particularly in the context of the grand jury investigations to which the statute analogizes orders under § 215. Appellants argue that relevance is not an unlimited concept, and that the government's own use (or non-use) of the records obtained demonstrates that most of the records sought are not relevant to any particular investigation; the government does not seek the records, as is usual in a grand jury investigation, so as to review them in search of evidence bearing on a particular subject, but rather seeks the records to create a vast data bank, to be kept in reserve and queried if and when some particular set of records might be relevant to a particular investigation.

Echoing the district court's statement that "'[r]elevance' has a broad legal meaning," 959 F. Supp. 2d at 746, the government argues that the telephone metadata program comfortably meets the requisite standard. The government likens the relevance standard intended by Congress to the standard of relevance for grand jury and administrative subpoenas, and, to some extent, for civil discovery.

Both the language of the statute and the legislative history support the grand jury analogy. During the 2006 reauthorization debate, Senator Kyl recalled that, in passing the PATRIOT Act shortly after September 11, Congress had realized that "it was time to apply to terrorism many of the same kinds of techniques in law enforcement authorities that we already deemed very useful in investigating other kinds of crimes. Our idea was, if it is good enough to investigate money laundering or drug dealing, for example, we sure ought to use those same kinds of techniques to fight terrorists." 152 Cong. Rec. S1607 (daily ed. Mar. 2, 2006) (statement of Sen. Kyl). He also remarked that "[r]elevance is a simple and well established standard of law. Indeed, it is the standard for obtaining every other kind of subpoena, including administrative subpoenas, grand jury subpoenas, and civil discovery orders." *Id.* at S1606 . . . .

So much, indeed, seems to us unexceptionable. In adopting § 215, Congress intended to give the government, on the approval of the FISC, broad-ranging investigative powers analogous to those traditionally used in connection with grand jury investigations into possible criminal behavior.

The government then points out that, under the accepted standard of relevance in the context of grand jury subpoenas, "courts have authorized discovery of large volumes of information where the requester seeks to identify within that volume smaller amounts of information that could directly bear on the matter." The government asks us to conclude that it is "eminently reasonable to believe that Section 215 bulk telephony metadata is relevant to counterterrorism investigations." Appellees' Br. 31. The government asks us to conclude that it is "eminently reasonable to believe that Section 215 bulk telephony metadata is relevant to counterterrorism investigations." Id. at 32. Appellants, however, dispute that metadata from every phone call with a party in the United States, over a period of years and years, can be considered "relevant to an authorized investigation," by any definition of the term.

The very terms in which this litigation has been conducted by both sides suggest that the matter is not as routine as the government's argument suggests. Normally, the question of whether records demanded by a subpoena or other court order are "relevant" to a proceeding is raised in the context of a motion to quash a subpoena. The grand jury undertakes to investigate a particular subject matter to determine whether there is probable cause to believe crimes have been committed, and seeks by subpoena records that might contain evidence that will help in making that determination. Given the wide investigative scope of a grand jury, the standard is easy to meet, but the determination of relevance is constrained by the subject of the investigation. In resolving a motion to quash, a court compares the records demanded by the particular subpoena with the subject matter of the investigation, however broadly defined.

Here, however, the parties have not undertaken to debate whether the records required by the orders in question are relevant to any particular inquiry. The records demanded are all-encompassing; the government does not even suggest that all of the records sought, or even necessarily any of them, are relevant to any specific defined inquiry. Rather, the parties ask the Court to decide whether § 215 authorizes the "creation of a historical repository of information that bulk aggregation of the metadata allows," Appellees' Br. 32, because bulk collection to create such a repository is "necessary to the application of certain analytic techniques," Appellants' Br. 23. That is not the language in which grand jury subpoenas are traditionally discussed.

Thus, the government takes the position that the metadata collected—a vast amount of which does not contain directly "relevant" information, as the government concedes— are nevertheless "relevant" because they may allow the NSA, at some unknown time in the future, utilizing its ability to sift through the trove of irrelevant data it has collected up to that point, to identify information that is relevant . . . . We agree with appellants that such an expansive concept of "relevance" is unprecedented and unwarranted.

The statutes to which the government points have never been interpreted to authorize anything approaching the breadth of the sweeping surveillance at issue here. The government admitted below that the case law in analogous contexts "d[id] not involve data acquisition on the scale of the telephony metadata collection." *ACLU v. Clapper*, No. 13 Civ. 3994 (S.D.N.Y. Aug. 26, 2013), ECF No. 33 (Mem. of Law of Defs. in Supp. of Mot. to Dismiss) at 24. That concession is well taken. As noted above, if the orders challenged by appellants do not require the collection of metadata regarding every telephone call made or received in the United States (a point asserted by appellants and at least nominally contested by the government), they appear to come very close to doing so. The sheer volume of information sought is staggering; while search warrants and subpoenas for business records may encompass large volumes of paper documents or electronic data, the most expansive of such evidentiary demands are dwarfed by the volume of records obtained pursuant to the orders in question here.

Moreover, the distinction is not merely one of quantity—however vast the quantitative difference—but also of quality. Search warrants and document subpoenas typically seek the records of a particular individual or corporation under investigation, and cover particular time periods when the events under investigation occurred. The orders at issue here contain no such limits. The metadata concerning every telephone call made or received in the United States using the services of the recipient service provider are demanded, for an indefinite period extending into the future. The records demanded are not those of suspects under investigation, or of people or businesses that have contact with such subjects, or of people or businesses that have contact with others who are in contact with the subjects—they extend to every record that exists, and indeed to records that do not yet exist, as they impose a continuing obligation on the recipient of the subpoena to provide such records on an ongoing basis as they are created. The government can point to no grand jury subpoena that is remotely comparable to the real-time data collection undertaken under this program . . . .

[T]he cases cited by the government only highlight the difference between the investigative demands at issue in those cases and the ones at issue here. Both of those examples, and all examples of which we are aware, are bounded either by the facts of the investigation or by a finite time limitation. The telephone metadata program requires that the phone companies turn over records on an "ongoing daily basis"—with no foreseeable end point, no requirement of relevance to any particular set of facts, and no limitations as to subject matter or individuals covered . . .

To the extent that § 215 was intended to give the government, as Senator Kyl proposed, the "same kinds of techniques to fight terrorists" that it has available to fight ordinary crimes such as "money laundering or drug dealing," 152 Cong. Rec. S1607 (daily ed. Mar. 2, 2006) (statement of Sen. Kyl), the analogy is not helpful to the government's position here. The techniques traditionally used to combat such ordinary crimes have not included the collection, via grand jury subpoena, of a vast trove of records of metadata concerning the financial transactions or telephone calls of ordinary Americans to be held in reserve in a data bank, to be searched if and when at some hypothetical future time the records might become relevant to a criminal investigation.

The government's emphasis on the potential breadth of the term "relevant," moreover, ignores other portions of the text of § 215. "Relevance" does not exist in the abstract; something is "relevant" or not in relation to a particular subject. Thus, an item relevant to a grand jury investigation may not be relevant at trial. In keeping with this usage, § 215 does not permit an investigative demand for any information relevant to fighting the war on terror, or anything relevant to whatever the government might want to know. It permits demands for documents "relevant to an authorized *investigation*." The government has not attempted to identify to what particular "authorized investigation" the bulk metadata of virtually all Americans' phone calls are relevant. Throughout its briefing, the government refers to the records collected under the telephone metadata program as relevant to "counterterrorism investigations," without identifying any specific investigations to which such bulk collection is relevant. See, e.g., Appellees' Br. 32, 33, 34.8. . . . Put another way, the government effectively argues that there is only one enormous "anti-terrorism" investigation, and that any records that might ever be of use in developing any aspect of that investigation are relevant to the overall counterterrorism effort . . . .

Such expansive development of government repositories of formerly private records would be an unprecedented contraction of the privacy expectations of all Americans. Perhaps such a contraction is required by national security needs in the face of the dangers of contemporary domestic and international terrorism. But we would expect such a momentous decision to be preceded by substantial debate, and expressed in unmistakable language. There is no evidence of such a debate in the legislative history of § 215, and the language of the statute, on its face, is not naturally read as permitting investigative agencies, on the approval of the FISC, to do any more than obtain the sorts of information routinely acquired in the course of criminal investigations of "money laundering [and] drug dealing."

We conclude that to allow the government to collect phone records only because they may become relevant to a possible authorized investigation in the future fails even the permissive "relevance" test. Just as "the grand jury's subpoena power is not unlimited, *United States v. Calandra*, 414 U.S. 338, 346 (1974), § 215's power cannot be interpreted in a way that defies any meaningful limit. Put another way, we agree with appellants that the government's argument is "irreconcilable with the statute's plain text." Appellants' Br. 26. Such a monumental shift in our approach to combating terrorism requires a clearer signal from Congress than a recycling of oft-used language long held in similar contexts to mean something far narrower. "Congress . . . does not alter the fundamental details of a regulatory scheme in vague terms or ancillary provisions — it does not . . . hide elephants in mouseholes." *Whitman v. Am. Trucking Ass'ns.*, 531 U.S. 457, 468 (2001). The language of § 215 is decidedly too ordinary for what the government would have us believe is such an extraordinary departure from any accepted understanding of the term "relevant to an authorized investigation." . . .

IV. Constitutional Claims

In addition to arguing that the telephone metadata program is not authorized by § 215, appellants argue that, even if the program is authorized by statute, it violates their rights under the Fourth and First Amendments to the Constitution. The Fourth Amendment claim, in particular, presents potentially vexing issues. . . .

Appellants contend that the seizure from their telephone service providers, and eventual search, of records of the metadata relating to their telephone communications violates their expectations of privacy under the Fourth Amendment in the absence of a search warrant based on probable cause to believe that evidence of criminal conduct will be found in the records. The government responds that the warrant and probable cause requirements of the Fourth Amendment are not implicated because appellants have no privacy rights in the records. This dispute touches an issue on which the Supreme Court's jurisprudence is in some turmoil. . . .

Appellants' argument invokes one of the most difficult issues in Fourth Amendment jurisprudence: the extent to which modern technology alters our traditional expectations of privacy. On the one hand, the very notion of an individual's expectation of privacy, considered in *Katz* a key component of the rights protected by the Fourth Amendment, may seem quaint in a world in which technology makes it possible for individuals and businesses (to say nothing of the government) to observe acts of individuals once regarded as protected from public view. On the other hand, rules that permit the government to obtain records and other information that consumers have shared with businesses without a warrant seem much more threatening as the extent of such information grows . . . .

Because we conclude that the challenged program was not authorized by the statute on which the government bases its claim of legal authority, we need not and do not reach these weighty constitutional issues. The seriousness of the constitutional concerns, however, has some bearing on what we hold today, and on the consequences of that holding . . . .

[Additional information on the preliminary injunction has been omitted.]

Conclusion

This case serves as an example of the increasing complexity of balancing the paramount interest in protecting the security of our nation—a job in which, as the President has stated, "actions are second-guessed, success is unreported, and failure can be catastrophic," Remarks [*sic*] by the President on Review of Signals Intelligence—with the privacy interests of its citizens in a world where surveillance capabilities are vast and where it is difficult if not impossible to avoid exposing a wealth of information about oneself to those surveillance mechanisms. Reconciling the clash of these values requires productive contribution from all three branches of government, each of which is uniquely suited to the task in its own way.

For the foregoing reasons, we conclude that the district court erred in ruling that § 215 authorizes the telephone metadata collection program, and instead hold that the telephone metadata program exceeds the scope of what Congress has authorized and therefore violates § 215. Accordingly, we VACATE the district court's judgment dismissing the complaint and REMAND the case to the district court for further proceedings consistent with this opinion.

[A concurring opinion has been omitted.]

SOURCE: U.S. Court of Appeals for the Second Circuit. "*ACLU v. Clapper.*" May 7, 2015. www.ca2.uscourts.gov/decisions/isysquery/5c81be63-c2ed-4c0e-9707-6bff831b4aba/1/doc/14-42_complete_opn.pdf.

OTHER HISTORIC DOCUMENTS OF INTEREST

FROM PREVIOUS *HISTORIC DOCUMENTS*

- President Obama's National Security Agency Reform Proposal Released, *2014*, p. 99
- Federal Review of NSA Surveillance Program Issued, *2013*, p. 633
- U.S. Department of State Responds to WikiLeaks, *2010*, p. 596

African Union and United Nations Respond to Coup Attempt and Violence in Burundi

MAY 18 AND NOVEMBER 12 AND 13, 2015

Burundi, one of the world's poorest nations, was thrown back into a state of ethnic and political violence following an attempted coup in May 2015. The coup quickly failed, and the current president was reelected to another term in office, much to the chagrin of Burundian citizens and international leaders. With his power solidified, the president quickly began to silence critics. Instability in the region quickly increased, and regional organizations worked together to encourage solutions to the violence.

BURUNDI'S HISTORY OF INSTABILITY

Much of Burundi's post-colonial history has been marred by instability and violent conflict. A significant portion of the violence seen in the nation is fueled by racial tensions. A majority of citizens are ethnic Hutus, while Tutsis make up 14 percent, and Twas comprise a mere 1 percent of the population. However, it is the Tutsis who have controlled the government since the end of colonial rule in 1962. From the early 1990s into the early 2000s, the country experienced a widespread civil war that left an estimated 300,000 dead and displaced millions more. That war was brought to an end by the Arusha Accords, signed in 2000, which brought greater stability to the nation. The peace accords encouraged balance of political power between Hutus and Tutsis. Antigovernment forces agreed to lay down their arms and become legitimate political parties, and civil liberties began to expand. In 2005, a new constitution was approved, which required that 60 percent of government posts go to Hutus, while 40 percent would be held by Tutsis. The new constitution was quickly followed by Pierre Nkurunziza, a Hutu, being placed in power by the nation's parliament.

The goodwill ended in 2010 when the government stood for reelection and jailed political opponents, journalists, and leaders of civil society groups. As violence increased, all five opposition candidates announced that they would boycott the election, thus leaving only Nkurunziza on the ballot. Seventy-seven percent of eligible voters turned out, and the president won more than 91 percent of the vote.

In addition to political and ethnic strife, Burundi has faced additional pressures from the spillover of conflict from Rwanda and the Democratic Republic of Congo, two of the landlocked state's neighbors. Border regions have become relatively lawless and are often the site of fierce clashes between local militias and rebel factions from both within and outside Burundi. Burundi also suffers from widespread poverty and resource insecurity—an estimated 60 percent of the 12 million citizens do not have access to enough food—and the government has been unable to provide the funds necessary to overcome the shortfall.

2015 ELECTION RAISES INTERNATIONAL CONCERN

On April 25, Burundi's authoritarian president Nkurunziza announced that he would seek his third term in office during the June 2015 nationwide election. As in the preceding elections, the announcement led to widespread protests, which were quickly quashed by the progovernment security forces. Protesters spoke out about the years under the president's rule, which had all but dismantled the 2000 peace accord that had helped diffuse religious and ethnic tension. The protesters were labeled "terrorists" by the president's government, and to stop the spread of their antigovernment message, Internet and telephone networks were shut down.

Opponents also indicated that the president's bid to seek another term was illegal under Burundi's constitution, which allows only two five-year terms. Nkurunziza, however, has argued that his first election was indirect and therefore the election in 2015 would mark his second term. The nation's high court upheld the president's argument; however, one judge who fled the country after the ruling said that the justices had been coerced into favoring the president's position.

Fearful of the repressive regime, tens of thousands of Burundians began fleeing to neighboring countries. Shortly after Nkurunziza's announcement, the United Nations stated that an estimated 350,000 refugees will require "humanitarian assistance within six months." In May, the United Nations refugee agency reported that a total of 111,000 Burundians had fled to Rwanda, Tanzania, and the Democratic Republic of Congo. By December, the United Nations estimated that 200,000 had fled the country and that refugee camps in the three neighboring nations were struggling to provide the resources necessary to account for the uptick.

MILITARY ATTEMPTS COUP

On May 13, Nkurunziza traveled to Tanzania to attend the Summit of the East African Community that was aimed at ending political violence in Burundi. While he was away from the country, General Godefroid Niyombare, a top commander in Burundi's military, announced that he was deposing Nkurunziza and would commence with the establishment of a transitional government. Senior military and security officials joined Niyombare in his announcement, which came as a surprise to many, because police and military forces had long been viewed as sympathetic to Nkurunziza.

In response to the announcement, Nkurunziza left the summit and attempted to return to Burundi. His flight was sent back to Tanzania after those supporting the coup seized control of the airport. The day following the coup announcement, Prime Niyongabo, the head of the nation's military, announced in a radio address that the coup had been stopped. Soldiers were called out to protect key government installations from the clashes that ensued.

The African Union condemned the coup and called for a "return to constitutional order." Nkurunziza returned to the country on May 14, and the following day coup leader Niyombare announced that he would surrender to government forces. The coup leaders, which included three of the president's cabinet members and twenty-seven security officials, were formally charged in December for their involvement with the coup attempt. They reportedly suffered a number of human rights violations following their surrender.

ELECTION PROCEEDS AS PLANNED

Despite the violence, Nkurunziza decided to hold the presidential election as originally scheduled, although parliamentary elections were delayed for ten days. In the month leading up to the June vote, opposition leaders were attacked and killed and members of the president's own party—and those who opposed him—fled the country in exile. As political tension continued to escalate, approximately 200 student protesters scaled the wall at the U.S. embassy in Burundi to seek refuge. They voluntarily agreed to leave the grounds and in response the U.S. government encouraged the Burundian government to seek a "peaceful resolution" to its ongoing violence.

The leading opposition party, National Liberation Forces (FNL), announced on June 11 that it would boycott what it called a "fake" election that was unlikely to produce credible, fair results. Even so, the vote proceeded on July 21, and Nkurunziza was declared the overwhelming winner, because he was the only candidate on the ballot. Following the vote, the opposition announced that it would seek to form a national unity government in which Nkurunziza would be permitted to hold the position of president for no more than a year. Nkurunziza rejected such a requirement, but did publicly indicate a willingness to form a coalition government that would help end the political violence. During his inauguration on August 20, Nkurunziza called his reelection "a victory for all Burundians, those who elected us, and those who did not." His election drew sharp criticism from Western governments, who noted that his renewal of power would likely end any attempts at negotiations to bring about lasting peace.

VIOLENCE CONTINUES

Following the president's reelection, periodic violence continued around the country. In November, the government called on rebel groups to hand over their arms before a widespread crackdown would take place to root out those who were not loyal to Nkurunziza's rule. December 11 marked the largest attack since April, when eighty-seven were killed in the capital city of Bujumbura. According to news reports, a majority of those killed were in the antigovernment district of Nyakabiga, and residents alleged that some of the dead were killed after being taken from their homes during police raids.

In November, top officials from the United States, European Union, and African Union issued a statement urging Burundi's government leaders to meet with opposition groups in Ethiopia or Uganda for peace talks, to be mediated by the Ugandan president. By the close of 2015, such talks had not yet begun. The African Union and United Nations adopted their own resolutions aimed at encouraging an end to the ongoing violence. In November, the UN Security Council resolution called on Secretary General Ban Ki-moon to determine methods to increase the UN peacekeeping presence in Burundi. "The Security Council must do everything in its power to prevent a countrywide conflagration, with possible regional implications," French ambassador François Delattre said after the measure was approved. The African Union's resolution called for mediated talks to begin among all involved parties that would be based on the notions of the 2000 peace accords and promised to send additional military, security, and human rights personnel to assist in any means necessary to ensure a return to peace.

—Heather Kerrigan

Following is the text of a statement from the African Union on May 18, 2015, condemning the coup attempt in Burundi and calling for the return of the ruling government; the text of a resolution adopted by the United Nations Security Council on November 12, 2015, calling for the end of violence in Burundi; and the text of a November 13, 2015, resolution adopted by the African Union in response to the violence in Burundi.

DOCUMENT

African Union Condemns Coup Attempt

May 18, 2015

The African Union Economic, Social and Cultural Council (ECOSOCC) is deeply concerned about the unfolding political, security and humanitarian situation in the Republic of Burundi.

ECOSOCC deplores the continued acts of violence against civilian people, civil society, media houses and public institutions. Violence against peacefully protesting citizens is unacceptable and must stop. We remain deeply worried about the plight of people fleeing for their safety from Burundi to neighbouring countries.

ECOSOCC strongly condemns the coup attempt in Burundi led by Major General Godefroid Niyombare to oust Pierre Nkurunziza, the president of Burundi. Changing governments through violence and military force is unconstitutional and undemocratic action.

"We urge all political sides in Burundi to show restraint, end violence, embrace national dialogue and take all possible actions to restore constitutional order, rule of law, peace and stability while ensuring that the human rights of all Burundians are respected and protected," said Honourable Joseph Chilengi, Presiding Officer of ECOSOCC.

ECOSOCC particularly calls for full respect and protection for civil society and free media in Burundi who became under attacks from different political forces to advance their political agendas. Burundian civil society must have free space to operate. Closed media houses must be reopened and allowed to resume their operations without fear of violence and intimidations.

While welcoming the efforts of the African Union (AU) and the East Africa Community (EAC), ECOSOCC emphasizes the inevitability for all Burundian political forces to respect the principles of the Arusha Agreements to ensure lasting peace, unity and democratic governance.

"The people of Burundi must be allowed to elect democratic, legitimate and constitutional government through inclusive, credible and transparent elections, held in a conducive environment," declared ECOSOCC Presiding Officer.

SOURCE: African Union. "ECOSOCC Statement on the situation in Burundi." May 18, 2015. http://pages .au.int/sites/default/files/ECOSOCC%20Statement%20on%20the%20situation%20in%20Burundi%20 (3).pdf.

UN Security Council Adopts Resolution on Violence in Burundi

November 12, 2015

The Security Council,

Recalling the statements of its President on Burundi, in particular the statements of 18 February 2015 (2015/6), of 26 June 2015 (2015/13) and of 28 October 2015 (2015/18),

Expressing its deep concern about the ongoing escalation of insecurity and the continued rise in violence in Burundi, as well as the persisting political impasse in the country, marked by a lack of dialogue among Burundian stakeholders,

Stressing that the situation prevailing in Burundi has the potential to seriously undermine the significant gains achieved through the Arusha Agreement, with devastating consequences for Burundi and the region as a whole,

Stressing the primary responsibility of the Government of Burundi for ensuring security in its territory and protecting its population with respect for the rule of law, human rights and international humanitarian law, as applicable,

Reaffirming its strong commitment to the sovereignty, political independence, territorial integrity and unity of Burundi,

Strongly condemning the increased cases of human rights violations and abuses, including those involving extra-judicial killings, acts of torture and other cruel, inhuman and/or degrading treatment, arbitrary arrests, illegal detentions, harassment and intimidation of human rights defenders and journalists, and all violations and abuses of human rights committed in Burundi both by security forces and by militias and other illegal armed groups,

Underscoring its deep concerns on the prevalence of impunity, on the daily assassinations, on the restrictions on enjoyment of the freedom of expression, including for members of the press, and on the continued worsening of the humanitarian situation, marked by the more than 200 000 Burundian citizens seeking refuge in neighbouring countries, and commending the host countries for their efforts,

Strongly condemning all public statements, coming from in or outside of the country, that appear aimed at inciting violence or hatred towards different groups in Burundian society,

Urging the Government of Burundi to bring to justice and hold accountable all those responsible for violations of international humanitarian law or violations and abuses of human rights, as applicable,

Recognizing the role and efforts of the High Commissioner for Human Rights to assess and report on the situation of human rights in Burundi,

Recalling that Burundi is a State Party to the Rome Statute of the International Criminal Court, and has undertaken obligations to fight impunity for crimes falling within the jurisdiction of the Court, and emphasizing that the International Criminal Court is complementary to national criminal jurisdictions,

Stressing the utmost importance of respecting the letter and the spirit of the Arusha Peace and Reconciliation Agreement of 28 August 2000 which has helped to sustain a decade of peace in Burundi,

Reiterating its conviction that only a genuine and inclusive dialogue, based on respect for the Constitution and Arusha Agreement, would best enable the Burundian stakeholders to find a consensual solution to the crisis facing their country, preserve peace and consolidate democracy and the rule of law,

Stressing the urgency of convening an inter-Burundian dialogue in coordination with the Government of Burundi and all concerned and peaceful stakeholders, both who are in Burundi and those outside the country, in order to find a consensual and nationally owned solution to the current crisis, and taking note of the establishment of the National Commission for the inter-Burundian dialogue,

Calling for the reinforcement of the mediation efforts led by President Yoweri Museveni of Uganda on behalf of the East African Community (EAC) and as endorsed by the African Union, welcoming the visit recently undertaken by the representative of the Mediator in Bujumbura for consultations with the Government of Burundi and other stakeholders, and underlining the need to expedite the preparatory process of the dialogue, including the convening of a pre-dialogue consultation involving all relevant international facilitators, under the leadership of the Mediator, to ensure an adequate preparation of the inter-Burundian dialogue and its success,

Urging the Government of Burundi and other concerned stakeholders to extend full cooperation to the Mediator,

Welcoming the continued engagement of all concerned stakeholders, including the Burundi Configuration of the Peacebuilding Commission, and encouraging the continued cooperation between the Government of Burundi and the Peacebuilding Commission,

Welcoming the statement of the African Union Peace and Security Council (PSC) on 17 October 2015, and the proposed next steps adopted on that occasion, and looking forward to their full implementation,

Welcoming the deployment of African Union human rights observers and military experts and urging the Government of Burundi and other stakeholders to provide them full cooperation in order to facilitate the implementation of their mandate,

Noting the decision of the African Union to impose targeted sanctions, including travel ban and asset freeze, against all the Burundian stakeholders whose actions and statements contribute to the perpetuation of violence and impede the search for a solution,

1. *Calls upon* the Government of Burundi and all parties to reject any kind of violence and demands that all sides in Burundi refrain from any action that would threaten peace and stability in the country;

2. *Calls upon* the Government of Burundi to respect, protect and guarantee all human rights and fundamental freedoms for all, in line with the country's international obligations, and to adhere to the rule of law and undertake transparent accountability for acts of violence, and to cooperate fully with the Office of the High Commissioner in the fulfilment of its mandate;

3. *Urges* the Government of Burundi to cooperate with the EAC-led, AU endorsed mediation to enable it to immediately convene an inclusive and genuine inter-Burundian dialogue involving all concerned and peaceful stakeholders, both those who are in Burundi and those outside the country, in order to find a consensual and nationally owned solution to the current crisis;

4. *Expresses* its full support to the mediation efforts led by President Yoweri Museveni of Uganda on behalf of the East African Community (EAC) and as endorsed by the African

Union, and stresses the importance of close coordination between the region and relevant international facilitators;

5. *Welcomes* the decision of the Secretary-General to appoint a Special Advisor on Conflict Prevention, including in Burundi, to work with the government of Burundi and other concerned stakeholders, as well as sub-regional, regional and other international partners, in support of an inclusive inter-Burundian dialogue and peaceful resolution of conflict and in support of national efforts to build and sustain peace;

6. *Expresses* its intention to consider additional measures against all Burundian actors whose actions and statements contribute to the perpetuation of violence and impede the search for a peaceful solution;

7. *Stresses* the importance of the Secretary-General following closely the situation in Burundi and invites him to deploy a team in Burundi to coordinate and work with the Government of Burundi, African Union and other partners to assess the situation and develop options to address political and security concerns;

8. *Requests* the Secretary-General to update the Security Council within 15 days, including by presenting options on the future presence of the United Nations in Burundi, and then regularly on the situation in Burundi, in particular on security and on violations and abuses of human rights, and incitement to violence or hatred against different groups in Burundian society;

9. *Affirms* the importance of United Nations and African Union contingency planning, to enable the international community to respond to any further deterioration of the situation;

10. *Decides* to remain actively seized of the matter.

SOURCE: United Nations Security Council. "Resolution 2248 (2015)." November 12, 2015. http://www .securitycouncilreport.org/atf/cf/%7B65BFCF9B-6D27-4E9C-8CD3-CF6E4FF96FF9%7D/s_res_2248.pdf.

African Union Adopts Resolution on the Situation in Burundi

November 13, 2015

Council,

1. Takes note of the briefing made by the AU Commissioner for Peace and Security on the evolution of the situation in Burundi. Council also takes note of the statements made by the representative of Burundi, as well as by those of the East African Community (EAC), the International Conference on the Great Lakes Region (ICGLR), the European Union (EU), the United Nations (UN) and of the following members of the UN Security Council: China, France, New Zealand, Nigeria, the United Kingdom and the United States of America;

2. Reaffirms its previous pronouncements on the situation in Burundi, including communiqué PSC/PR/COMM.(DLI) adopted at its 551th meeting held on 17 October 2015, as well as the AU's commitment to the scrupulous observance of the letter and spirit

of the August 2000 Arusha Agreement for Peace and Reconciliation in Burundi, which is the cornerstone of peace, security and stability in Burundi;

3. Notes with satisfaction the growing involvement of the international community towards the search for a peaceful solution to the crisis facing Burundi and the support extended to the African-led efforts, including those being undertaken by H.E. President Yoweri Kaguta Museveni of Uganda, the Mediator appointed by the EAC to facilitate dialogue among the Burundian stakeholders. In this regard, Council expresses satisfaction at the adoption by the UN Security Council, on 12 November 2015, of resolution 2248 (2015) in which that organ welcomed communiqué PSC/PR/COMM.(DLI) and the proposed next steps adopted on that occasion, looking forward to their full implementation, and noted the decision of the AU to impose targeted sanctions, including travel bans and asset freezes, against all the Burundian stakeholders whose actions and statements contribute to the perpetuation of violence and impede the search for a solution. Council also welcomes the joint statement issued, on 12 November 2015, by the Chairperson of the Commission, Nkosazana Dlamini-Zuma, the UN Deputy Secretary-General, Jan Eliasson, and the EU High Representative for Foreign Affairs and Security Policy, Federica Mogherini;

4. Reiterates the AU's deep concern at the continuing political impasse in Burundi, as well as at the prevailing insecurity and violence in that country and the resulting humanitarian consequences. Council reaffirms the strong condemnation by the AU of all acts of violence, committed by whomsoever, as well as of human rights abuses, including killings, extra-judicial executions, violations of the physical integrity of persons, acts of torture and other cruel, inhuman and/or degrading treatment, arbitrary arrests and illegal detentions, violations of the freedom of the press and freedom of expression and the prevalence of impunity. Council also strongly condemns the inflammatory statements made by Burundian political leaders, which have the potential of aggravating the current tension and creating conditions conducive to violence of untold consequences for Burundi and the region;

5. Reiterates the AU's determination to ensure that the perpetrators of acts of violence and abuses and all those who aggravate the situation by making inflammatory statements, regardless of their affiliations, are held accountable for their acts;

6. Reaffirms the AU's conviction that only a genuine and truly all-inclusive dialogue, based on the respect of the Arusha Agreement, can enable the Burundian stakeholders to overcome the serious difficulties facing their country, as well as to strengthen social cohesion, democracy and the rule of law, and rejects any recourse to force in pursuit of political objectives. In this regard, Council stresses the centrality of the regional dialogue facilitated by the EAC Mediator, and to be convened outside Burundi, in a location to be determined by the Mediation, in order to enable all Burundian stakeholders, both those within and outside Burundi, to participate in the said dialogue in the required security conditions;

7. Notes with satisfaction the efforts being made by the Mediation, including the recent visits undertaken to Bujumbura, Burundi, by the Minister of Defence of Uganda, Honorable Crispus Kiyonga, in his capacity as emissary of the EAC Mediator, President Yoweri Kaguta Museveni, in order to accelerate the resumption of the dialogue. Council urges the concened [sic] international organizations and other relevant international actors to extend full support to the Mediation, as required. In this regard, Council requests the Chairperson of the Commission to urgently liaise with the Ugandan authorities to determine how best the AU can assist the mediation efforts;

8. Demands that the Government of Burundi and all other concerned stakeholders extend full cooperation to the Mediation and recalls that all those who hinder, in one way

or the other, the holding of the inter-Burundian dialogue and, more generally, the efforts to put an end to the violence and to find a peaceful solution to the crisis will be targeted by the sanctions agreed upon by Council in paragraph 12 of communiqué PSC/PR/COMM. (DLI). In this regard, Council reaffirms its decision, in support of the peace efforts, to impose sanctions against the Burundian stakeholders whose actions and statements contribute to the persistence of violence and impede the search for a solution. Council welcomes the intention expressed by the UN Security Council to consider additional measures against all the Burundian stakeholders whose actions and statements contribute to the perpetuation of violence and impede the search for a solution;

9. Welcomes the steps taken by the Commission as a follow-up to the relevant provisions of communiqué PSC/PR/COMM.(DLI), including:

i. the ongoing compilation by the Commission, for Council's attention, of a list of individuals and entities to be targeted by the sanctions decided by Council. Council requests the Commission to continue this work and to regularly update the list, which should include individuals who are impeding the negotiation process, committing acts of violence and violations of human rights and making inflammatory statements. Council shall, whenever it deems it appropriate, authorize the Chairperson of the Commission to communicate to Member States and international partners, for implementation and cooperation, the names of individuals and entities to be sanctioned;

ii. the generation of additional civilian, military and police personnel to reach the newly authorized strength of 100 human rights observers and military experts to be deployed in Burundi, under the authority of the Special Representative of the Chairperson of the Commission for the Great Lakes Region and Head of the AU Liaison Office in Burundi. Council requests the Commission to do everything possible to ensure that all these personnel are deployed in Burundi by 15 December 2015. Council, recalling the commitment of Member States, as provided for in article 7 (3) of the Protocol Relating to the Establishment of the Peace and Security Council, to accept and implement the decisions of Council, requests the Government of Burundi to promptly extend its full cooperation to the Commission, in order to facilitate the planned deployment. Council also reiterates the need for the urgent finalization of the discussions on the Memorandum of Understanding (MoU) that will govern the activities of the AU human rights observers and military experts in Burundi, on the understanding that the MoU must respect the following principles: conduct, by the human rights observers and the military experts, of their respective mandates in an independent, neutral and impartial fashion; free movement throughout the territory of Burundi; and respect of the privileges and immunities necessary for the effective discharge of their mandates, as provided for in the relevant AU and international instruments. Council requests the Commission to develop a model agreement for the deployment of military and civilian personnel, for Council's expeditious consideration and approval, and should no agreement be reached with Burundi on the draft MoU within 15 days of the adoption of the present communiqué, decides that the model agreement shall apply provisionally; and

iii. the request sent to the African Commission on Human and Peoples' Rights regarding the launching of a thorough investigation on the violations of human rights and other abuses against the civilian populations in Burundi, in order to enable Council to take additional measures. In this regard, Council requests the Commission, on the basis of the AU Constitutive Act and the Protocol Relating to the Establishment of the Peace and Security Council, as well as relevant AU's experience, to identify the additional measures that could be taken on the basis of the report expected to be submitted by the African Commission on Human and Peoples' Rights;

10. Looks forward to the submission by the Commission, on the basis of the reports of human rights observers and the military experts, of the first monthly report on the situation of human rights and acts of violence in Burundi, as requested in paragraph 12 (iii) of communiqué PSC/PR/COMM.(DLI);

11. Takes note of the steps being taken by the Commission to expedite and finalize the contingency planning requested by Council in communiqué PSC/PR/COMM.(DVII), adopted at its 507th meeting held on 14 May 2015, as reiterated in communiqué PSC/PR/COMM.(DLI). Council, noting the affirmation by the UN Security Council, in resolution 2248 (2015), of the importance of contingency planning by the UN and the AU, to enable the international community to respond to any further deterioration of the situation, requests the Commission to coordinate its efforts with those of the UN;

12. Reiterates its call for the mobilization of the necessary assistance in favor of the Burundian refugees in the neighboring countries, and, once again, urges the Chairperson of the Commission to take the necessary initiatives to this effect. Council renews its appreciation to the neighboring countries and other African countries hosting refugees from Burundi, including Tanzania, Rwanda, the Democratic Republic of the Congo and Uganda;

13. Requests the Chairperson of the Commission to forward the present communiqué to all AU Member States, as well as to the UN Secretary-General and, through him, to the UN Security Council, and urges the UN Security Council and its members to fully support the African-led efforts and all the measures provided for in this communiqué. Council also requests the Chairperson of the Commission to forward the present communiqué to the other AU bilateral and multilateral partners and to seek their full support towards the effective implementation of the decisions contained therein;

14. Decides to remain actively seized of the matter.

SOURCE: African Union. "Communiqué." November 13, 2015. www.peaceau.org/uploads/psc-557-comm-burundi-12-11-2015.pdf.

OTHER HISTORIC DOCUMENTS OF INTEREST

FROM PREVIOUS *HISTORIC DOCUMENTS*

■ Peace Agreement Between Government and Rebels in Burundi, *2003*, p. 922

Ireland's Taoiseach Remarks on Same-Sex Marriage Referendum

MAY 23 AND SEPTEMBER 16, 2015

On May 23, 2015, Ireland became the first country in the world to legalize same-sex marriage through popular vote. More than 60 percent of voters supported the referendum, which required a formal bill in the nation's parliament and presidential endorsement to officially take effect. In October, the bill was given formal approval, and same-sex marriage was recognized beginning on November 16, 2015. Given Ireland's historically conservative, Catholic background—85 percent of the population identify as Roman Catholic—the decision to allow same-sex marriage raised the question about whether other European nations such as Germany, Italy, and Northern Ireland, would follow suit.

IRELAND'S EFFORTS TO RECOGNIZE THE LGBT COMMUNITY

Despite its long history of conservative Catholicism, Ireland has been working for more than three decades to afford homosexuals the same rights as their heterosexual counterparts. Today, the nation is considered one of the most liberal regarding its attitude toward the lesbian, gay, bisexual, and transgender (LGBT) community.

In the 1970s, the Campaign for Homosexual Law Reform was founded to work toward the decriminalization of homosexuality. It succeeded in 1988, when the European Court of Human Rights ruled that the nation's law was incompatible with the European Convention on Human Rights. Subsequently, in 1993, same-sex sexual activity was formally decriminalized in Ireland. The Employment Equality Act of 1998 and Equal Status Act of 2000 provided protections for the homosexual community against discrimination.

In 2007, the European High Court ruled that Ireland must allow citizens who define themselves as transgender to obtain new birth certificates with their preferred gender listed. The nation introduced legislation on December 19, 2014, to formalize this process. At that time, those wishing to change their legal gender on an official document, such as a driver's license or birth certificate, were required to obtain statements from endocrinologists and psychiatrists. The new law would seek to change this to simply require a formal declaration by the individual of his or her intent to seek such change. No medical procedures would need to be conducted to approve an individual for legal status as a different gender.

On July 15, 2015, Ireland became one of the small number of countries to have a written law allowing for self-declared gender recognition. The bill was signed into law by President Michael D. Higgins and went into force on September 8, 2015. Sara Phillips, chair of the Transgender Equality Network, said that the "legislation marks an incredible shift in Irish society. Our community is finally stepping out of the shadows."

Some criticism of the new law remained after passage, even from those who supported it overall. As enrolled, the law allowed only those age eighteen or older to make a formal declaration regarding gender identification, which Irish senator Jillian van Turnhout called "slamming the door" on younger citizens. Under the law, sixteen- and seventeen-year-olds would be required to seek a court order to change their official gender identification. Those age fifteen or younger would not be permitted to request a legal change.

REFERENDUM ON SAME-SEX MARRIAGE PASSES

In November 2013, the Irish government announced that it would place a same-sex marriage referendum on the ballot sometime in 2015. At the time of the announcement, same-sex couples were able to enter into civil partnerships and had been doing so since 2009. Critics of the previous law argued that civil partnerships did not afford the same rights as a traditional marriage and thus resulted in discrimination. Those who favored the distinction between civil partnerships and marriage did so primarily on religious grounds, noting that in religious texts marriage is defined as being between one man and one woman and is the basis for procreation.

Ultimately, the decision was made to hold the referendum on May 22, 2015. If passed, the referendum would add language to the constitution that would read, "Marriage may be contracted in accordance with law by two persons without distinction as to their sex." Polls conducted by a variety of media outlets leading up to the referendum showed strong public support for same-sex marriage. On April 25, for example, a poll commissioned by the *Sunday Business Post* found that 72 percent supported the legalization of same-sex marriage, while only 20 percent were opposed. Similarly, on March 27, *The Irish Times* found 74 percent in favor and 26 percent opposed. Unsurprisingly, polls showed the strongest support among Ireland's young voters.

Of the more than 1.9 million votes cast on May 22, approximately 62 percent were in favor of the referendum. Turnout was higher than normal, which some credited to the #hometovote movement that encouraged young Irish expatriates to return to Ireland and cast a vote. Concern had been voiced prior to the vote that there would be a divisive split between those in rural and urban communities; however, of all forty-three constituencies, only one did not vote in favor of the referendum. Following the referendum, thousands of same-sex marriage supporters took to the streets in celebration. Taoiseach Enda Kenny welcomed the outcome and Ireland's new distinction as "the first country in the world to vote for equal marriage." According to Kenny, the vote "disclosed who we are—a generous, compassionate, bold and joyful people," adding that the vote said "Yes to inclusion. Yes to generosity. Yes to love, and Yes to equal marriage." Kenny said the outcome of the same-sex marriage referendum would ultimately strengthen all marriages by ensuring that all Ireland's citizens enjoy the same rights and freedoms.

The decision to legalize same-sex marriage put Ireland at odds with the Catholic Church, which had long held a prominent position in Irish society. Diarmuid Martin, the archbishop of Dublin, said in response to the vote that the "church needs to take a reality check," adding that "it's very clear there's a growing gap between Irish young people and the church, and there's a growing gap between the culture of Ireland that's developing and the church." In the Vatican, Secretary of State Cardinal Pietro Parolin said the vote was a "defeat for humanity." Archbishop Martin attempted to clarify the cardinal's remarks. "I think what he was trying to do was express the loss that has occurred here and we do feel it's a loss. Something very unique and precious has been lost. That's not in any way to say that there are not a lot of people who were very happy with the result." The archbishop went on to affirm the "courageous decision" of individuals to speak up in favor of traditional marriage and said that those who opposed the referendum did not do so "to be offensive or bigoted or homophobic." He added that, although the Church would need to do some internal reflection to determine how to move forward, the vote had not made the Church irrelevant in Irish society.

IRELAND'S GOVERNMENT FORMALIZES RECOGNITION OF SAME-SEX COUPLES

After the public vote, Minister for Justice Frances Fitzgerald announced that legislation permitting same-sex marriage would be brought before Ireland's parliament in the summer of 2015. Despite a brief delay while the nation's High Court reviewed a challenge to the referendum's results (which it ultimately rejected), Ireland's cabinet reviewed the Marriage Bill on September 16, 2015, after which it entered into the parliamentary process.

On October 22, 2015, the bill moved out of parliament and was sent to the Presidential Commission. On October 29, 2015, the president signed the bill into law, thus giving it formal approval and allowing for the recognition of same-sex marriages. This made Ireland the fourteenth nation in Europe to legalize same-sex marriage. Same-sex marriage was formally recognized on November 16, and the first marriage ceremonies took place on November 17, 2015.

The legalization of same-sex marriage in Ireland raised the question of whether other European nations would follow suit. In particular, some questioned whether those in Northern Ireland would gain similar rights. Gavin Boyd, an activist with the Rainbow Project, a gay rights group in Belfast, said the May vote was a "sweet victory . . . tinged with sadness. Northern Ireland is now the only region in western Europe where marriage equality is not a reality." In 2013, the United Kingdom passed a law to afford same-sex couples the right to marry beginning in March 2014. The law did not apply to Scotland or Northern Ireland due to the semiautonomous nature of those nations. A same-sex marriage bill was later approved in Scotland in February 2014.

Two of the continent's largest countries—Germany and Italy—also did not yet allow same-sex marriage. In Germany, civil unions are permitted and carry all the legal rights as marriage with the exception of adoption rights and use of some reproductive technology. Chancellor Angela Merkel has made clear that the issue is not currently on the nation's agenda. In 2012, the leader remarked that she wanted "to preserve the privileged tax position of marriages because our constitution envisions marriage and family as being directly related." She did, however, concede the need for both same-sex and opposite-sex couples to have the same rights in some areas "like in inheritance taxes or in public services law." Calls for same-sex marriage legislation increased after Ireland's referendum, but the chancellor's government continued to refuse action. "You would think what the Irish Catholics can do, we could do, too," said Jens Spahn, an openly gay politician and member of Merkel's center-right Christian Democratic Union.

Italy has come under fire from the European Human Rights Court for its refusal to allow either civil unions or same-sex marriage. There, the strong influence of the Roman Catholic Church has largely kept the issue out of debate. But, as in Germany, public pressure increased after the Irish referendum. Members of the ruling Democratic Union Party revived an attempt to legalize civil unions. Party leader Roberto Speranza remarked that following the "joy" in Ireland, "now it is Italy's turn." Still, the nation has one of the largest

Catholic populations in Europe, which could make it politically dangerous for those who support civil unions or same-sex marriage.

—Heather Kerrigan

Following is the text of a statement delivered by Irish Taoiseach Enda Kenny on May 23, 2015, following the passage of a referendum to legalize same-sex marriage; and an announcement given on September 16, 2015, about the 2015 Marriage Bill.

DOCUMENT

Taoiseach Kenny's Response to Same-Sex Marriage Referendum

May 23, 2015

Today Ireland made history.

The first country in the world to vote for equal marriage. I welcome that and thank all those who voted yesterday. In the privacy of the ballot box they made a public statement.

With today's Yes vote we have disclosed who we are—a generous, compassionate, bold and joyful people.

Yes to inclusion.

Yes to generosity.

Yes to love, and

Yes to equal marriage.

I know that for tens of thousands of couples and their families, the past 24 hours were almost a vigil at the end of a long journey. Would their fragile and deeply personal hopes be realised?

Would a majority of people, in this our Republic, stand with them and stand up for them so that they can live in our shelter and no longer in our shadow?

That having come out to us we could now come out for them—and do it with a single word, a solitary syllable—Yes—marked with an X.

Today they have their answer. The people have answered the call of families and friends, of neighbours and new acquaintances.

Of Jack O'Rourke and Edel Tierney, Finian Curran and Allie Kershaw and Jerry, Leo, Pat and so many others. It was their stories and their voices that inspired the hearts and minds of the Irish people.

Our people have truly answered Ireland's Call.

The referendum was about inclusiveness and equality, about love and commitment being enshrined in the constitution. For a significant proportion who voted against the amendment it was because of genuinely held views which are to be respected.

The decision makes every citizen equal and will strengthen the institution of marriage for all existing and future marriages. All people now have an equal future to look forward to.

So—the people went to the polls.

It passed.

The answer is YES.

Yes to their future.

Yes to their love.

Yes to their equal marriage.

That yes is heard loudly across the living world as a sound of pioneering leadership of our people and hopefully across the generations of gay men and women born as we say, before their time.

The people have spoken.

They have said yes.

Ireland—thank you.

Source: Department of the Taoiseach. "Speech by An Taoiseach, Enda Kenny on the Marriage Equality Referendum, Dublin Castle 23rd May, 2015." May 23, 2015. http://www.taoiseach.gov.ie/eng/News/Taoiseach's_Speeches/Speech_by_An_Taoiseach_Enda_Kenny_on_the_Marriage_Equality_Referendum_Dublin_Castle_23rd_May_2015.html.

DOCUMENT

New Marriage Bill Published

September 16, 2015

Frances Fitzgerald TD, Minister for Justice and Equality, has announced that the Government has today approved the publication of the Marriage Bill 2015 and its presentation to Dáil Éireann.

The Marriage Bill 2015 will update the laws on marriages to enable couples to marry without distinction as to their sex as provided for in Article 41.4 of the Constitution which was approved by the people in the historic Marriage Equality referendum on 22nd May 2015. Article 41.4 provides for two persons to have the right to contract a marriage in accordance with law without distinction as to their sex.

The Minister stated: "I am delighted to be in a position to publish the Marriage Bill 2015 which will, when enacted, enable same-sex couples to marry in Ireland. This Bill implements the strong desire of the Irish people that couples should be able to marry without distinction as to their sex. It will make Marriage Equality a reality in Ireland."

The Minister continued: "In accordance with the priority which the Government is attaching to this matter, the legislative process will begin immediately and I will introduce the Bill into the Dáil next week."

"I hope this legislation can be enacted as soon as possible so that the first same-sex marriages can take place before the end of the year."

The Minister confirmed that the Bill includes a provision allowing a couple to convert a notification of their intention to enter civil partnership into a notification of their intention to marry.

Minister Fitzgerald announced that arrangements are being made separately, in conjunction with the Department of Social Protection, to reduce the fees for civil partners wishing to marry from €200 to €50.

The Minister added: "I am conscious that many couples have married abroad. The Bill includes provisions which will allow such marriages to be recognised without the couple having to go through any additional process.

"Civil partners will also be able to marry one another without having to formally dissolve their civil partnership first though of course the civil partnership will dissolve automatically once the marriage takes place."

The Minister said that the Bill will not change the process of registering marriages.

The Minister added: "The Bill retains the existing protections for religious bodies. They will not be compelled to recognise a particular form of marriage ceremony. Similarly, a religious solemniser will not be compelled to solemnise a marriage that is not in accordance with the form of ceremony recognised by the religious body of which he or she is a member."

The key provisions of the Bill are as follows:

- The statutory impediment in section 2(2)(e) of the Civil Registration Act 2004, preventing parties of the same sex from marrying will be removed. This will enable two persons to marry without distinction as to their sex.

- Each of a couple will be able to accept the other in their marriage vows as a husband, as a wife or as a spouse.

- Those couples who are already in civil partnerships will be able to marry one another without having to dissolve their civil partnership. The civil partnership will be dissolved as of the date of the marriage.

- Couples who have given notice of their intention to enter a civil partnership will be able to opt to convert that notification into notice of their intention to marry.

- Civil partnership will, in general, be closed to new couples. Only couples who have already completed their civil partnership registration forms or whose civil partnership has been delayed by an objection will be able to register in a civil partnership once the relevant sections of Part 7A of the Civil Registration Act 2004, as inserted by the Civil Partnership and Certain Rights and Obligations of Cohabitants Act 2010, have been repealed.

- The Bill specifies that nothing in it can be construed as compelling a religious body to recognise a particular form of marriage ceremony or a religious solemniser to solemnise a marriage with a form of marriage ceremony that is not recognised by the religious body of which he or she is a member.

- Foreign marriages between same sex couples will be recognised under Irish law as marriages.

- Legislative amendments are set out in the Bill providing for situations in which spouses are of the same sex.

The Bill will be published tomorrow on the Houses of the Oireachtas website www.oireachtas.ie.

SOURCE: Ireland Department of Justice and Equality. "Minister Fitzgerald publishes Marriage Bill 2015." September 16, 2015. www.justice.ie/en/JELR/Pages/PR15000470.

OTHER HISTORIC DOCUMENTS OF INTEREST

FROM THIS VOLUME

FROM PREVIOUS *HISTORIC DOCUMENTS*

Nigeria Elects New President amidst Continued Struggle with Boko Haram

MAY 29 AND NOVEMBER 12, 2015

Amid rampant corruption, a flagging economy, and increasing insurgency, General Muhammadu Buhari was elected president of Nigeria, defeating incumbent Goodluck Jonathan. The president campaigned on a platform of growing the economy and rooting out terrorism. One of the president's greatest challenges would be defeating Boko Haram, a terrorist group founded in 2002. Since launching military operations in 2009, Boko Haram has been responsible for thousands of deaths and abductions in Nigeria and seized the northeastern portion of the state where it has declared a caliphate. The Nigerian army undertook missions throughout 2015 to rescue Boko Haram hostages and succeeded in freeing hundreds of women and children and securing former Boko Haram strongholds, but it was unable to fully push the group out of the country.

SECURITY THREATS DELAY ELECTION

In Africa's largest oil-producing state, terrorist organization Boko Haram has gained a strong foothold. The government of President Jonathan, who first took office in 2010, had been unable to make headway in expelling the group from the country. In fact, during Jonathan's tenure, the group ramped up attacks and kidnappings, most notably in 2014 when nearly 300 schoolgirls were kidnapped from Chibok in Nigeria's northeastern Borno State. They remain missing as of the end of 2015. Due to the ongoing threat presented by the terrorist organization, security was the most widely discussed issue of the presidential election of early 2015. Fourteen candidates were pitted against each other, although only two, President Jonathan and Buhari, had a realistic chance at victory. Jonathan's People's Democratic Party (PDP) was expected to face a significant challenge, threatening the power it had held since 1999 when civilian rule was restored in Nigeria. Buhari, who led the country from January 1984 to August 1985 following a military coup, and a member of the All Progressives Congress (APC), had lost his last three elections for president. Both Jonathan and Buhari promised to end the Boko Haram insurgency—which had killed more than 15,000 people—within months following the election.

Voting in Nigeria often takes place in two rounds, unless one candidate secures 25 percent of the vote in the first round in two-thirds of Nigeria's thirty-six states. If there is no clear winner following the first round, a runoff is held within seven days. The victor of the runoff election must only secure a simple majority. For the first time, those displaced by Boko Haram would be permitted to cast ballots at special facilities within displacement camps or their states of origin.

The 2015 presidential elections were initially scheduled to take place in mid-February; however, they were pushed back to late March due to increasing violence led by Boko

Haram. In January, security forces informed the Independent National Electoral Commission that due to the number of militia who had been conscripted to fight against Boko Haram they would not be able to provide effective security for the elections. As the rescheduled March 28 date drew near, concern was raised about whether Buhari supporters, who were located primarily in the northern part of the country where Boko Haram continued to hold power, would be able to vote freely.

NIGERIA ELECTS A NEW LEADER

Since the first round of balloting did not produce a clear victor, a second round was held on March 29. On April 1, the Independent National Electoral Commission certified the election results and announced that Buhari defeated Jonathan by more than 2.5 million votes. The election was historic because a sitting president had never before been defeated. Although there were some allegations of voter fraud, election observers reported little unusual activity and generally agreed that the vote was legitimate. Observers had not been deployed to the northeast part of the country because of the threat of violence from Boko Haram. Jonathan graciously handed power to his successor and called on his supporters not to resort to violence, stating, "I promised the country free and fair elections. I have kept my word." He added, "As I have always affirmed, nobody's ambition is worth the blood of any Nigerian. The unity, stability and progress of our dear country is more important than anything else."

On May 29, Buhari was sworn in as president. During his inaugural address, the new president remarked on the "enormous challenges" facing Nigeria and how important it was to "modernize and uplift" the country. "Insecurity, pervasive corruption, the hitherto unending and seemingly impossible fuel and power shortages are the immediate concerns. We are going to tackle them head on. Nigerians will not regret that they have entrusted national responsibility to us. . . . We can fix our problems," the new president said. Buhari promised that he would take action on all the challenges facing the country through the proper democratic channels, would respect the functions of the legislative and judicial arms of the government, and would operate within the bounds of the nation's constitution.

Buhari spent a bulk of his inaugural address discussing the threat from Boko Haram, which he called one of the nation's most immediate challenges. "Boko Haram is a mindless, godless group who are as far away from Islam as one can think of," he stated. Buhari called on the nation's military forces to root out terrorism and bring the perpetrators to justice while avoiding any human rights violations. The president said that he would not consider the Boko Haram insurgency defeated "without rescuing the Chibok girls and all other innocent persons held hostage by insurgents. This government will do all it can to rescue them alive."

International analysts agreed with the new president, who was previously known as a dictatorial ruler with a record of human rights violations, noting that he would face steep challenges. "The problems are staggering. They are going to require incredible political skill," said John Campbell, former U.S. ambassador to Nigeria. "You don't solve Boko Haram day after tomorrow. You don't solve the economic challenges. You don't resolve corruption when corruption basically impacts on huge areas of national life. You can't solve these things instantaneously."

Nigerian Military Frees Boko Haram Hostages

In March 2015, Boko Haram formally aligned itself with the Islamic State of Iraq and the Levant (ISIL) and ramped up its attacks, killing 800 in the two months after Buhari's inauguration. In response, the Nigerian military accelerated its own action against the terrorist group, including more airstrikes. In September, the Nigerian Army approved promotions for 5,000 soldiers in an attempt to both boost morale and improve its operations.

In late April, the army freed 200 girls and 93 women from Sambisa Forest, a key Boko Haram stronghold. At first, many speculated that those rescued could be the Chibok girls; however, it was later confirmed that they were not. On August 3, the Nigerian military announced that it had attacked Boko Haram strongholds in the northeastern part of the country. During the operation, the military freed 178 hostages, most of whom were women and children, and captured a Boko Haram commander. In late September, the military announced the rescue of another 241 women and children in raids on two camps, along with the capture of many Boko Haram fighters and a key leader. The following month, 338 were rescued near Sambisa Forest. Despite the hundreds of individuals rescued in the actions against Boko Haram, the Chibok schoolgirls had still not been located and freed by the end of 2015.

Nigerian troops have been hampered in their efforts against Boko Haram in a number of ways. The troops are not well equipped or trained, and the lack of resources and rampant corruption among senior officials—even despite a growing military budget—has led to low morale. In its decision to promote 5,000 troops in September, the Nigerian Army also announced that it would give regular awards to those who are assigned to the areas of heaviest fighting in the northeastern part of the nation. Army Chief of Staff Tukur Buratai said he believed the changes would "encourage our troops to fight for our country." In October, the military unveiled a task force that would be assigned to Borno State specifically to combat the insurgency. This fighting force, the army promised, would be better prepared and equipped than Boko Haram militants. Such promises were quickly quashed; in a statement, Buhari explained that the nation's military forces had been denied the weapons to fight Boko Haram because of corruption in the procurement process.

The Nigerian public has also lost confidence in both the government and military to root out Boko Haram fighters. In official statements, the government has downplayed the group's power and has at times failed to issue any response to Boko Haram attacks. In the fall and winter of 2015, the Nigerian military released a number of press releases aimed at bolstering the support of an increasingly skeptical and wary public. In November, for example, Colonel Sani Kukasheka, the acting director of Army Public Relations, explained various activities that had been carried out including the "discovery and destruction of terrorists' camps, weapons and equipment," which caused Boko Haram to flee their bases. In detailing the raids that had been conducted to free Nigerians in Boko Haram captivity and deactivate or confiscate the terrorist organization's weapons, Kukasheka stated that "the public are hereby reassured that the Nigerian Army remains committed to its obligation to Nigerians." He added that Nigerians should go about their lives with patience and understanding for additional security checks and noted that "Nigerian Army troops in all locations are in high spirits and doing their best to ensure expeditious defeat of the Boko Haram terrorists."

—Heather Kerrigan

Following is the text of General Buhari's inaugural address, delivered on May 29, 2015; and a November 12, 2015, statement by the Nigerian military regarding its ongoing mission against Boko Haram.

General Buhari Delivers Inaugural Address

May 29, 2015

I am immensely grateful to God who has preserved us to witness this day and this occasion. Today marks a triumph for Nigeria and an occasion to celebrate her freedom and cherish her democracy. Nigerians have shown their commitment to democracy and are determined to entrench its culture. Our journey has not been easy but thanks to the determination of our people and strong support from friends abroad we have today a truly democratically elected government in place.

I would like to thank President Goodluck Jonathan for his display of statesmanship in setting a precedent for us that has now made our people proud to be Nigerians wherever they are. With the support and cooperation he has given to the transition process, he has made it possible for us to show the world that despite the perceived tension in the land we can be a united people capable of doing what is right for our nation. Together we co-operated to surprise the world that had come to expect only the worst from Nigeria. I hope this act of graciously accepting defeat by the outgoing President will become the standard of political conduct in the country.

I would like to thank the millions of our supporters who believed in us even when the cause seemed hopeless. I salute their resolve in waiting long hours in rain and hot sunshine to register and cast their votes and stay all night if necessary to protect and ensure their votes count and were counted. I thank those who tirelessly carried the campaign on the social media. At the same time, I thank our other countrymen and women who did not vote for us but contributed to make our democratic culture truly competitive, strong and definitive.

I thank all of you.

Having just a few minutes ago sworn on the Holy Book, I intend to keep my oath and serve as President to all Nigerians.

I belong to everybody and I belong to nobody.

A few people have privately voiced fears that on coming back to office I shall go after them.

These fears are groundless. There will be no paying off old scores. The past is prologue.

Our neighbours in the Sub-region and our African brethren should rest assured that Nigeria under our administration will be ready to play any leadership role that Africa expects of it.

Here I would like to thank the governments and people of Cameroon, Chad and Niger for committing their armed forces to fight Boko Haram in Nigeria.

I also wish to assure the wider international community of our readiness to cooperate and help to combat threats of cross-border terrorism, sea piracy, refugees and boat people, financial crime, cyber crime, climate change, the spread of communicable diseases and other challenges of the 21st century.

At home we face enormous challenges. Insecurity, pervasive corruption, the hitherto unending and seemingly impossible fuel and power shortages are the immediate concerns.

We are going to tackle them head on. Nigerians will not regret that they have entrusted national responsibility to us. We must not succumb to hopelessness and defeatism. We can fix our problems.

In recent times Nigerian leaders appear to have misread our mission. Our founding fathers, Mr Herbert Macauley, Dr Nnamdi Azikiwe, Chief Obafemi Awolowo, Alhaji Ahmadu Bello, the Sardauna of Sokoto, Alhaji Abubakar Tafawa Balewa, Malam Aminu Kano, Chief J. S. Tarka, Mr Eyo Ita, Chief Denis Osadeby, Chief Ladoke Akintola and their colleagues worked to establish certain standards of governance. They might have differed in their methods or tactics or details, but they were united in establishing a viable and progressive country.

Some of their successors behaved like spoilt children breaking everything and bringing disorder to the house.

Furthermore, we as Nigerians must remind ourselves that we are heirs to great civilizations: Shehu Othman Dan fodio's caliphate, the Kanem Borno Empire, the Oyo Empire, the Benin Empire and King Jaja's formidable domain. The blood of those great ancestors flow in our veins. What is now required is to build on these legacies, to modernize and uplift Nigeria.

Daunting as the task may be it is by no means insurmountable. There is now a national consensus that our chosen route to national development is democracy. To achieve our objectives we must consciously work the democratic system. The Federal Executive under my watch will not seek to encroach on the duties and functions of the Legislative and Judicial arms of government. The law enforcing authorities will be charged to operate within the Constitution. We shall rebuild and reform the public service to become more effective and more serviceable. We shall charge them to apply themselves with integrity to stabilize the system.

For their part the legislative arm must keep to their brief of making laws, carrying out over-sight functions and doing so expeditiously. The judicial system needs reform to cleanse itself from its immediate past. The country now expects the judiciary to act with dispatch on all cases especially on corruption, serious financial crimes or abuse of office. It is only when the three arms act constitutionally that government will be enabled to serve the country optimally and avoid the confusion all too often bedeviling governance today.

Elsewhere relations between Abuja and the States have to be clarified if we are to serve the country better. Constitutionally there are limits to powers of each of the three tiers of government but that should not mean the Federal Government should fold its arms and close its eyes to what is going on in the states and local governments. Not least the operations of the Local Government Joint Account. While the Federal Government can not interfere in the details of its operations it will ensure that the gross corruption at the local level is checked. As far as the constitution allows me I will try to ensure that there is responsible and accountable governance at all levels of government in the country. For I will not have kept my own trust with the Nigerian people if I allow others abuse theirs under my watch.

However, no matter how well organized the governments of the federation are they cannot succeed without the support, understanding and cooperation of labour unions, organized private sector, the press and civil society organizations. I appeal to employers and workers alike to unite in raising productivity so that everybody will have the opportunity to share in increased prosperity. The Nigerian press is the most vibrant in Africa. My appeal to the media today—and this includes the social media—is to exercise its considerable powers with responsibility and patriotism.

My appeal for unity is predicated on the seriousness of the legacy we are getting into. With depleted foreign reserves, falling oil prices, leakages and debts the Nigerian economy is in deep trouble and will require careful management to bring it round and to tackle the immediate challenges confronting us, namely; Boko Haram, the Niger Delta situation, the power shortages and unemployment especially among young people. For the longer term we have to improve the standards of our education. We have to look at the whole field of medicare. We have to upgrade our dilapidated physical infrastructure.

The most immediate is Boko Haram's insurgency. Progress has been made in recent weeks by our security forces but victory cannot be achieved by basing the Command and Control Centre in Abuja. The command centre will be relocated to Maiduguri and remain until Boko Haram is completely subdued. But we cannot claim to have defeated Boko Haram without rescuing the Chibok girls and all other innocent persons held hostage by insurgents.

This government will do all it can to rescue them alive. Boko Haram is a typical example of small fires causing large fires. An eccentric and unorthodox preacher with a tiny following was given posthumous fame and following by his extra judicial murder at the hands of the police. Since then through official bungling, negligence, complacency or collusion Boko Haram became a terrifying force taking tens of thousands of lives and capturing several towns and villages covering swathes of Nigerian sovereign territory.

Boko Haram is a mindless, godless group who are as far away from Islam as one can think of. At the end of the hostilities when the group is subdued the Government intends to commission a sociological study to determine its origins, remote and immediate causes of the movement, its sponsors, the international connexions to ensure that measures are taken to prevent a recurrence of this evil. For now the Armed Forces will be fully charged with prosecuting the fight against Boko haram. We shall overhaul the rules of engagement to avoid human rights violations in operations. We shall improve operational and legal mechanisms so that disciplinary steps are taken against proven human right violations by the Armed Forces.

Boko Haram is not only the security issue bedeviling our country. The spate of kidnappings, armed robberies, herdsmen/farmers clashes, cattle rustlings all help to add to the general air of insecurity in our land. We are going to erect and maintain an efficient, disciplined people-friendly and well-compensated security forces within an over-all security architecture.

The amnesty programme in the Niger Delta is due to end in December, but the Government intends to invest heavily in the projects, and programmes currently in place. I call on the leadership and people in these areas to cooperate with the State and Federal Government in the rehabilitation programmes which will be streamlined and made more effective. As ever, I am ready to listen to grievances of my fellow Nigerians. I extend my hand of fellowship to them so that we can bring peace and build prosperity for our people.

No single cause can be identified to explain Nigerian's poor economic performance over the years than the power situation. It is a national shame that an economy of 180 million generates only 4,000MW, and distributes even less. Continuous tinkering with the structures of power supply and distribution and close on $20b expanded since 1999 have only brought darkness, frustration, misery, and resignation among Nigerians. We will not allow this to go on. Careful studies are under way during this transition to identify the quickest, safest and most cost-effective way to bring light and relief to Nigerians.

Unemployment, notably youth un-employment features strongly in our Party's Manifesto. We intend to attack the problem frontally through revival of agriculture, solid minerals mining as well as credits to small and medium size businesses to kick-start these enterprises. We shall quickly examine the best way to revive major industries and accelerate the revival and development of our railways, roads and general infrastructure.

Your Excellencies, My fellow Nigerians I cannot recall when Nigeria enjoyed so much goodwill abroad as now. The messages I received from East and West, from powerful and small countries are indicative of international expectations on us. At home the newly elected government is basking in a reservoir of goodwill and high expectations. Nigeria therefore has a window of opportunity to fulfill our long-standing potential of pulling ourselves together and realizing our mission as a great nation.

Our situation somehow reminds one of a passage in Shakespeare's Julius Caesar.

There is a tide in the affairs of men which, taken at the flood, leads on to fortune; Omitted, all the voyage of their life,

Is bound in shallows and miseries.

We have an opportunity. Let us take it. Thank you.

SOURCE: Nigerian National Orientation Agency. "The Full Text of Muhammadu Buhari's Inaugural Speech." May 29, 2015. www.noa.gov.ng/attachments/article/87/MUHAMMADU%20BUHARI'S%20 SPEECH.pdf.

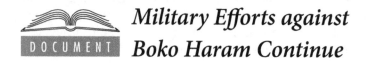

Military Efforts against Boko Haram Continue

November 12, 2015

The fight against Boko Haram terrorists is continuing to maintain its momentum with the discovery and destruction of terrorists camps, weapons and equipment, while the terrorists have been fleeing, and abandoning their bases.

In 25 Task Force Brigades area of responsibility, the troops were able to clear Boko Haram terrorists camps at Nwalemer, Mallemiri and Bale. Similarly in Gwoza axis, troops of 26 Task Force Brigade have also destroyed terrorists camps in Tripkwopta and Gidan Gachi yesterday. The troops however encountered an Improvised Explosive Device (IED) buried along their route of advance near Balazalla Dure that partially affected one of the leading vehicles. The troops also encountered an abandoned truck loaded with IEDs at Uvole village, which was blown up by them.

Also, with close air support by the Nigerian Air Force, troops of 28 Task Force Brigade advancing along Bitta and Damboa axis cleared Boko Haram terrorists camps at Modupe 1, 2 and 3 and in the process rescued 61 persons abducted earlier and held captives by the

Boko Haram terrorists. The rescued persons were mainly women and children and have since been evacuated. The troops also recovered 2 Dane guns in the area after an encounter with the terrorists at Langaran Fulani and also killed 4 terrorists, arrested one.

The public are hereby reassured that the Nigerian Army remains committed to its obligation to Nigerians. This is being demonstrated daily by the personal presence of the army leadership with the forward troops. It is reinforced by the manifest desire and zeal of the rank and file down to the last rifle man to discharge their responsibility for the restoration and maintenance of peace as well as the safeguarding of the safety and security of the citizenry in the North East.

Consequently, Nigerians are hereby advised to go about their legitimate duties and show understanding for security checks and procedures put in place to frustrate the evil intents of the terrorists. Nigerian Army troops in all locations are in high spirits and doing their best to ensure expeditious defeat of the Boko Haram terrorists.

Thank you.

SANI KUKASHEKA USMAN Colonel

Acting Director Army Public Relations

SOURCE: Nigerian Military. "Fight Against Boko Haram Terrorists Continues to Gain Momentum." November 12, 2015. http://army.mil.ng/Press-Release.html.

OTHER HISTORIC DOCUMENTS OF INTEREST

FROM PREVIOUS *HISTORIC DOCUMENTS*

- Nigerian Government and African Union Respond to Kidnapping by Boko Haram, *2014*, p. 161
- Goodluck Jonathan on His Inauguration as President of Nigeria, *2011*, p. 201

June

United Nations Releases Report on Worldwide Refugee Situation

JUNE 18, 2015

On June 18, 2015, the United Nations High Commissioner for Refugees (UNHCR) released the "Global Trends Report: World at War," the 2015 installment of its annual report on displaced persons worldwide. Tabulating the number of refugees, asylum seekers, and those displaced within their own countries, the report found record highs across all categories of displaced people and came with a sharp call from the high commissioner for a greater humanitarian effort to address the situation. The report's release followed a series of high-profile incidents in Europe and the Middle East that highlighted the dangers faced by many refugees fleeing war and persecution and drew the world's attention to the growing migrant crisis.

NUMBER OF DISPLACED PEOPLE REACHES HISTORIC PROPORTIONS

According to the UNHCR's report, the number of people displaced worldwide had grown to 59.5 million by the end of 2014, compared to 51.2 million at the end of 2013. This was the single-year largest increase ever recorded by the UNHCR and meant that an average of 42,500 people became refugees, asylum seekers, or internally displaced every day throughout 2014. The total number of displaced persons was also the highest it had been since World War II, and, if all of the refugees inhabited their own nation, it would constitute the twenty-fourth largest country in the world by population.

Among all displaced persons, there were 19.5 million refugees, 38.2 million people internally displaced, and 1.8 million awaiting responses to their asylum claims. By comparison, the UNHCR recorded 16.7 million refugees, 33.3 million internally displaced persons, and 1.2 million asylum seekers in 2013. About 14.4 million of the 2014 refugees fall under UNHCR's mandate; the remainder was Palestinian refugees registered with the United Nations Relief and Works Agency for Palestine Refugees in the Near East. Nearly 14 million people became newly displaced in 2014.

The report also found that more than 1.66 million individual applications for asylum or refugee status were submitted in 157 countries or territories during the course of the year—the highest level ever recorded. Russia was the world's largest recipient of new individual asylum applications in 2014, receiving nearly 275,000 claims, followed by Germany, the United States, and Turkey. Notably, the UNHCR found that roughly 34,000 asylum applications had been filed by unaccompanied or separated children in 82 countries, primarily Afghanistan, Eritrea, Syria, and Somalia. Indeed, the report found that 51 percent of the world's refugees in 2015 were children, compared to 41 percent in 2009.

The UNHCR cited at least fifteen conflicts across Africa, the Middle East, Europe, and Asia that had begun or reignited in the past five years and were contributing to the growing rate of displacement, noting that ongoing instability in countries such as Afghanistan and Somalia were not only causing people to leave but also preventing millions from returning home. In fact, only 126,800 refugees were able to return to their home countries in 2014, the lowest return rate in thirty-one years; half these refugees returned to the Democratic Republic of the Congo, Mali, or Afghanistan. Displacements had generally been caused by armed conflicts, generalized violence, or human rights violations in various countries. The report found that the war in Syria has been the biggest contributor to the growth in displacement since 2011, with the country producing 7.6 million internally displaced people and nearly 4 million refugees in 2014. Afghanistan and Somalia are the next biggest sources of refugees, with 2.59 million and 1.1 million, respectively.

The report also explored trends in refugees' locations, finding that nearly 86 percent of refugees are currently living in regions or countries that are less developed, with those countries ranked by the United Nations as least developed housing 25 percent of all global refugees in 2014. Among refugees for which the UNHCR had location data, roughly 3.5 million were living in planned and managed camps, with another 487,000 living in self-settled camps. Approximately 300,000 were living in a collective center, and about 112,000 were in a "reception" or "transit" camp. Individual or private housing was found to be the most popular among refugees, with about 7.6 million people living in such accommodations.

REGIONAL TRENDS

Europe experienced the greatest growth in the number of displaced people—an increase of 51 percent—due largely to continued conflict in the Ukraine and the high number of Syrian refugees who fled to Turkey. More than 6.7 million displaced people were living in Europe by the end of 2014, including nearly 1.6 million Syrian refugees who arrived in Turkey— the country that hosted the highest number of refugees within its borders. Germany and Sweden received the highest number of asylum applications among European countries.

The number of displaced people in the Middle East and North Africa grew by 19 percent in 2014, fueled primarily by the Syrian civil war. Approximately 7.6 million Syrians had been displaced within their own country while another 3.9 million had fled abroad, mostly to Turkey, Lebanon, and Jordan. In addition to the displaced Syrians, roughly 2.6 million people were displaced within Iraq and more than 300,000 were displaced in Libya, following the Islamic State of Iraq and the Levant (ISIL) militants' continued attacks in those countries. Sub-Saharan Africa saw a 17 percent increase in displaced people, including 3.7 million refugees and 11.4 million internally displaced people, 4.5 million of whom were newly displaced. Ethiopia became the largest refugee-hosting country in Africa in 2014. Asia experienced a 31 percent increase in displacement, with Iran and Pakistan among the world's top four refugee-hosting countries.

Displacement in the Americas increased by 12 percent. Colombia continued to have one of the world's largest internally displaced populations at 6 million people. The United States received 44 percent more asylum claims in 2014 than in 2013, namely due to people fleeing violence or persecution in Central America.

THE CRISIS IN CONTEXT

The UNHCR released its report amid growing international alarm over the hundreds of thousands of refugees attempting dangerous journeys to European countries. According to the UNHCR, a record 219,000 refugees and asylum seekers crossed the Mediterranean

Sea in 2014, or "almost three times the previously known high of about 70,000, which took place in 2011 during the 'Arab Spring.'" That number was dwarfed in 2015, with more than 750,000 "detected migrants" arriving in Europe by sea by November 2015, according to the International Organization for Migration (IOM).

In many cases, these refugees took extreme measures to reach Europe, with some sailing in flimsy rubber dinghies or small wooden boats. IOM reported that in 2015 more than 2,800 migrants died trying to cross the Central Mediterranean from Libya and Tunisia, and another 606 people died en route from other Mediterranean crossing locations. This included a widely reported incident that occurred in April when a boat carrying approximately 800 migrants capsized off the coast of Libya. Overcrowding was suspected to have been a contributing factor to the accident.

European countries were struggling to manage this influx, with some bearing a greater burden than others, particularly Italy, Germany, Greece, and Hungary. According to Eurostat, the statistical office of the European Union, Germany had received more than 331,000 asylum applications from migrants by the end of October 2015, while Hungary had received more than 143,000 claims. In a number of instances, the Italian military rescued hundreds of refugees from flimsy or overcrowded boats in the Mediterranean.

The UNHCR's findings were also echoed by entities including the Institute for Economics and Peace. Days before the UNHCR published its report, the global think tank issued its updated Global Peace Index, which found that refugees and internally displaced people account for 1 percent of the world's population and concluded that the world has, on average, become more violent since 2007.

"We are witnessing a paradigm change, an unchecked slide into an era in which the scale of global forced displacement as well as the response required is now clearly dwarfing anything seen before," said United Nations High Commissioner for Refugees António Guterres. "With huge shortages of funding and wide gaps in the global regime for protecting victims of war, people in need of compassion, aid and refuge are being abandoned. For an age of unprecedented mass displacement, we need an unprecedented humanitarian response and a renewed global commitment to tolerance and protection for people fleeing conflict and persecution."

—Linda Fecteau Grimm

Following is a press release from the United Nations High Commissioner for Refugees (UNHCR) on June 18, 2015, summarizing its annual Global Trends report on the worldwide refugee situation; and portions of the UNHCR Global Trends report, also released on June 18, 2015.

UNHCR Announces Increase in Refugees Worldwide

June 18, 2015

Wars, conflict and persecution have forced more people than at any other time since records began to flee their homes and seek refuge and safety elsewhere, according to a new report from the UN refugee agency.

UNHCR's annual Global Trends Report: World at War, released on Thursday (June 18), said that worldwide displacement was at the highest level ever recorded. It said the number of people forcibly displaced at the end of 2014 had risen to a staggering 59.5 million compared to 51.2 million a year earlier and 37.5 million a decade ago. . . .

Globally, one in every 122 humans is now either a refugee, internally displaced, or seeking asylum. If this were the population of a country, it would be the world's 24th biggest.

"We are witnessing a paradigm change, an unchecked slide into an era in which the scale of global forced displacement as well as the response required is now clearly dwarfing anything seen before," said UN High Commissioner for Refugees António Guterres.

Since early 2011, the main reason for the acceleration has been the war in Syria, now the world's single-largest driver of displacement. Every day last year on average 42,500 people became refugees, asylum seekers, or internally displaced, a four-fold increase in just four years.

"It is terrifying that on the one hand there is more and more impunity for those starting conflicts, and on the other there is seeming utter inability of the international community to work together to stop wars and build and preserve peace," Guterres added.

The UNHCR report detailed how in region after region, the number of refugees and internally displaced people is on the rise. In the past five years, at least 15 conflicts have erupted or reignited: eight in Africa (Côte d'Ivoire, Central African Republic, Libya, Mali, northeastern Nigeria, Democratic Republic of Congo, South Sudan and this year in Burundi); three in the Middle East (Syria, Iraq, and Yemen); one in Europe (Ukraine) and three in Asia (Kyrgyzstan, and in several areas of Myanmar and Pakistan).

"Few of these crises have been resolved and most still generate new displacement," the report noted, adding that in 2014 only 126,800 refugees were able to return to their home countries—the lowest number in 31 years.

Meanwhile, decades-old instability and conflict in Afghanistan, Somalia and elsewhere means that millions of people remain on the move or—as is increasingly common—stranded for years on the edge of society as long-term internally displaced or refugees. . . .

HALF OF ALL REFUGEES ARE CHILDREN

The Global Trends report detailed that in 2014 alone 13.9 million people became newly displaced—four times the number of the previous year. Worldwide there were 19.5 million refugees (up from 16.7 million in 2013), 38.2 million were displaced inside their own countries (up from 33.3 million in 2013), and 1.8 million people were awaiting the outcome of claims for asylum (against 1.2 million in 2013).

Most alarmingly, however, it showed that over half the world's refugees are children.

"With huge shortages of funding and wide gaps in the global regime for protecting victims of war, people in need of compassion, aid and refuge are being abandoned," warned Guterres. "For an age of unprecedented mass displacement, we need an unprecedented humanitarian response and a renewed global commitment to tolerance and protection for people fleeing conflict and persecution."

Syria is the world's biggest producer of both internally displaced people (7.6 million) and refugees (3.88 million at the end of 2014). Afghanistan (2.59 million) and Somalia (1.1 million) are the next biggest refugee source countries.

Almost nine out of every 10 refugees (86 per cent) are in regions and countries considered economically less developed.

EUROPE (UP 51%)

. . . In the EU, the biggest volume of asylum applications was in Germany and Sweden. Overall, forced displacement numbers in Europe totalled 6.7 million at the end of the year, compared to 4.4 million at the end of 2013, and with the largest proportion of this being Syrians in Turkey and Ukrainians in the Russian Federation.

MIDDLE EAST AND NORTH AFRICA (UP 19%)

Syria's ongoing war, with 7.6 million people displaced internally, and 3.88 million people displaced into the surrounding region and beyond as refugees, has alone made the Middle East the world's largest producer and host of forced displacement. Adding to the high totals from Syria was a new displacement of least 2.6 million people in Iraq and 309,000 newly displaced in Libya.

SUB-SAHARAN AFRICA (UP 17%)

. . . In all, sub-Saharan Africa saw 3.7 million refugees and 11.4 million internally displaced people, 4.5 million of whom were newly displaced in 2014. The 17 per cent overall increase excludes Nigeria, as methodology for counting internal displacement changed during 2014 and it could not be reliably calculated. Ethiopia replaced Kenya as the largest refugee-hosting country in Africa and the fifth largest worldwide.

ASIA (UP 31%)

Long one of the world's major displacement producing regions, the number of refugees and internally displaced people in Asia grew by 31 per cent in 2014 to 9 million people. Continuing displacement was also seen in and from Myanmar in 2014, including of Rohingya from Rakhine state and in the Kachin and Northern Shan regions. Iran and Pakistan remained two of the world's top four refugee hosting countries.

AMERICAS (UP 12%)

The Americas also saw a rise in forced displacement. The number of Colombian refugees dropped by 36,300 to 360,300 over the year, although mainly because of a revision in the numbers of refugees reported by Venezuela. Colombia continued, nonetheless to have one of the world's largest internally displaced populations, reported at 6 million people and with 137,000 Colombians being newly displaced during the year. With more people fleeing gang violence or other forms of persecution in Central America, the United States saw 36,800 more asylum claims than in 2013, representing growth of 44 per cent. . . .

SOURCE: United Nations High Commissioner for Refugees. "Worldwide displacement hits all-time high as war and persecution increase." June 18, 2015. www.unhcr.org/558193896.html.

UN Releases Global Trends Report on Refugees

June 18, 2015

[All footnotes, tables, figures, maps, and infographics, and in-text references to them, have been omitted.]

I. INTRODUCTION

The year 2014 has seen continuing dramatic growth in mass displacement from wars and conflict, once again reaching levels unprecedented in recent history. One year ago, UNHCR announced that worldwide forced displacement numbers had reached 51.2 million, a level not previously seen in the post-World War II era. Twelve months later, this figure has grown to a staggering 59.5 million, roughly equaling the population of Italy or the United Kingdom. . . .

. . . In addition to the ongoing crisis in the Syrian Arab republic, new conflicts in the Central African Republic, South Sudan, Ukraine, and Iraq, among others, have caused suffering and massive displacement. As a consequence, the combined number of refugees and internally displaced persons protected/assisted by UNHCR in 2014 increased by 11.0 million persons, reaching a record high of 46.7 million persons by year end.

It is not just the scale of global forced displacement that is disconcerting but also its rapid acceleration in recent years. For most of the past decade, displacement figures ranged between 38 million and 43 million persons annually. Since 2011, however, when levels stood at 42.5 million, these numbers have grown to the current 59.5 million—a 40 percent increase within a span of just three years. Such growth poses challenges to finding adequate responses to these crises, increasingly leading to the multiple displacement of individuals or secondary movements in search of safety. In Europe, more than 219,000 refugees and migrants crossed the Mediterranean Sea during 2014. That's almost three times the previously known high of about 70,000, which took place in 2011 during the 'Arab spring' . . . UNHCR has received information of over 3,500 women, men, and children reported dead or missing in the Mediterranean Sea during the year, clearly demonstrating how dangerous and unpredictable this situation has become.

While 2.9 million persons sought refuge abroad, mostly in neighbouring countries, 11.0 million were displaced within the borders of their countries. In addition, a record high of nearly 1.7 million persons lodged asylum claims on an individual basis during 2014. Conflict and persecution thus forced an average of 42,500 persons per day to leave their homes in 2014. This compares to 32,200 one year ago and constitutes a four-fold increase since 2010 (10,900).

The war in the Syrian Arab republic, entering into its fourth year in 2014, was a major cause for the global increase. With at least 7.6 million Syrians estimated to be displaced within their country at year end, global forced displacement levels were heavily impacted by this one country. . . . The escalating crisis in the Syrian Arab republic resulted in Turkey becoming the world's largest refugee-hosting country, a ranking that had been occupied by Pakistan for more than a decade. . . .

Globally, only 126,800 refugees were able to return to their country of origin during the year, the lowest annual level in three decades. In contrast, UNHCR submitted 103,800 refugees for resettlement in 2014, some 10,000 more than in 2013. Nevertheless, the number of refugees considered to be in protracted situations was 6.4 million at year end.

Today, more than half of the world's refugees are children, a figure that has increased consistently. The number of unaccompanied or separated children filing an asylum application during the year also continued to increase, surpassing the figure of 34,000 for the first time since UNHCR started systematically collecting such information in 2006. In previous years, this figure had never exceeded 25,000. . . .

II. Refugee Population

The global number of refugees under UNHCR's mandate, including persons in refugee-like situations, was estimated at 14.4 million at year end, some 2.7 million more than at the end of 2013 (+23%). This was the highest level since 1995, when an estimated 14.9 million persons were considered to be refugees at year end. . . .

Some 1.55 million Syrian refugees were newly registered and granted temporary protection during the year, mainly in neighbouring countries, while an additional 96,100 were granted international protection on an individual basis. Armed conflict, human rights violations, and violence also heavily affected sub-Saharan Africa, where hundreds of thousands fled their country in 2014, notably from South Sudan, the Central African Republic, Eritrea, the Democratic Republic of the Congo, and Somalia. While 283,500 individuals fled outbreaks of violence in Pakistan and sought refuge in Afghanistan, the same is true for hundreds of thousands of Ukrainians who fled to the Russian Federation and other countries in Europe. Further increases in global refugee figures result from revisions of refugee estimates in the Islamic republic of Iran, as explained further below. . . .

[The following section providing further details about the refugee population has been omitted.]

Countries of Asylum

The year 2014 was marked by a shift in the balance of both the main hosting and source countries of refugees, provoked by a combination of the Syrian crisis and large-scale displacement across parts of Africa. Turkey emerged as the largest refugee-hosting country in 2014, replacing Pakistan, which has occupied this rank for more than a decade. The driving factor behind the rankings of the world's four main refugee-hosting countries is the relatively recent Syrian crisis, together with the world's largest protracted refugee situation—Afghanistan. Together, Turkey, Pakistan, Lebanon, and the Islamic republic of Iran hosted more than 5.2 million or 36 per cent of all refugees worldwide.

The top 10 refugee-hosting countries combined hosted 57 per cent of all refugees under UNHCR's mandate, with eight of these witnessing at times dramatic increases in their respective refugee figures during the year. One million Syrian refugees were registered in Turkey over the course of the year and granted temporary protection by the Government there. Combined with other refugee populations, the total number of refugees in Turkey stood at almost 1.6 million, making it for the first time the world's largest refugee-hosting country. . . .

[The following section containing additional data from refugee-hosting countries has been omitted.]

Countries of Origin

By the end of 2014, the Syrian Arab republic had become the world's top source country of refugees, overtaking Afghanistan, which has held this position for more than three decades. With Somalia as the third-largest source country, these three countries together accounted for 7.6 million or more than half (53%) of all refugees under UNHCR's responsibility at the end of 2014. While Afghanistan and Somalia were listed among this top three for a number of years, the Syrian Arab republic did not feature among even the top 30 source countries just three years ago. This turnaround clearly demonstrates the rapid deterioration of the situation in that country. . . .

Developing Countries are Shouldering the Responsibility

Developing regions have continued to receive millions of new refugees—and, during the past few years, in increasing numbers. Two decades ago, developing regions were hosting about 70 per cent of the world's refugees. By the end of 2014, this proportion had risen to 86 per cent—at 12.4 million persons, the highest figure in more than two decades. The Least Developed Countries alone provided asylum to 3.6 million refugees or 25 per cent of the global total.

Comparing the size of a refugee population to the Gross Domestic Product (Purchasing Power Parity)—the GDP (PPP)—per capita or the national population size provides a different perspective. When the number of refugees per 1 USD GDP (PPP) per capita is high, the relative contribution and effort made by countries, in relation to their national economy, can also be considered to be high.

In 2014, the 30 Countries with the largest number of refugees per 1 USD GDP (PPP) per capita were all members of developing regions, and included 18 Least Developed Countries. More than 5.9 million refugees, representing 42 per cent of the world's refugees, resided in countries whose GDP (PPP) per capita was below USD 5,000.

Ethiopia has the highest number of refugees in relation to its national economy during the year, hosting 440 refugees per 1 USD GDP (PPP) per capita. Pakistan was second with 316 refugees per 1 USD GDP (PPP) per capita, followed by Chad (203), Uganda (195), Kenya (190), and Afghanistan (155). The developed country with the highest number of refugees in relation to its national economy was the Russian Federation, in 34th place, with nine refugees per 1 USD GDP (PPP) per capita.

These rankings change when the number of refugees is compared to the national population of the host country. Here, the Syrian crisis displays its full effect, with Lebanon and Jordan continuing to occupy the first two places. Lebanon tops the list with 232 refugees per 1,000 inhabitants, followed by Jordan (87), Nauru (39), Chad (34), and Djibouti (23). In other words, in Lebanon almost one in four inhabitants was a refugee at the end of 2014.

III. Durable Solutions for Refugees

Protecting and finding durable solutions for refugees are core mandates of UNHCR. Hence, durable solutions remain an integral part of UNHCR's mission. This mandate is affirmed by both the 1951 Convention relating to the Status of Refugees as well as UNHCR's Executive Committee. This is in addition to regional instruments, which have strongly backed the mandate of finding permanent solutions to the plight of refugees.

The need for cooperation among signatory states to find such permanent solutions is enshrined in the 1951 Convention and other similar instruments. . . .

Return of Refugees

When a climate of national protection is fully restored, refugees can typically return voluntarily to their country of origin in safety and dignity. It may be tempting, then, to assume that the total number of returnees can measure the safety conditions in their place of origin. In principle, however, the processes of voluntary return involve many actors and stakeholders. It is not uncommon that civil wars, political instability, and general levels of insecurity prevent or limit the number of refugee returns in a particular country or specific location of return. . . .

. . . When conditions in the country of origin are deemed to be right and safe, UNHCR in collaboration with its partners promotes and facilitates the voluntary return of refugees. These processes can range from registration and screening to repatriation agreements and packages, transportation arrangements or reception in countries of origin. During the course of the repatriation processes, particular attention is paid to returnees with specific needs in order to ensure that their requisite protection, assistance, and care are provided. . . .

Of the three traditional durable solutions, voluntary repatriation ranks the highest in numerical terms. Available data indicate that, over the past four decades, the number of refugee returns has always been higher than the total number of resettled refugees. However, with the number of refugee returns currently at a 30-year low, resettlement as both burden-sharing and a protection tool is increasingly gaining ground. . . .

During 2014, a total 126,800 refugees returned to their country of origin, virtually all of them with UNHCR assistance. This is the lowest number recorded since 1983, when 103,000 refugees returned during the year. The 2014 figure is also significantly below the level observed one year earlier (414,600). Clearly, wars and the general political insecurity witnessed around the world in recent years have contributed to the prevailing trends. . . .

[The following sections detailing resettlement and local integration have been omitted.]

IV. INTERNALLY DISPLACED PERSONS

. . . The Internal Displacement Monitoring Centre estimated the global number of persons displaced by armed conflict, generalized violence, or human rights violations at the end of 2014 to be some 38.2 million. This is unprecedented since 1989, the first year for which global statistics on IDPs are available.

The number of IDPs, including those in IDP-like situations, who benefited from UNHCR's protection and assistance activities stood at 32.3 million at the end of 2014. This was not only the highest figure on record—and 8.3 million more than at the end of 2013 (23.9 million)—but it also constituted a five-fold increase since the introduction of the inter-agency cluster approach in January 2006. Where UNHCR was engaged with IDP populations during the year, offices reported an estimated 8.6 million newly displaced persons, particularly in Iraq, the Syrian Arab republic, the Democratic Republic of the Congo, Ukraine, South Sudan, and Pakistan. Among those countries where UNHCR was operational, some 1.8 million IDPs returned home during the reporting period, about one quarter of them with UNHCR's assistance . . .

Several years of civil war and armed conflict in the Syrian Arab republic brought the number of IDPs in that country to an estimated 7.6 million persons by the end of 2014, the highest number worldwide. . . .

[The remaining section containing additional data about internally displaced persons has been omitted.]

V. Asylum Seekers

The deteriorating humanitarian situation in a number of countries throughout the year is clearly reflected in the statistical data on individuals lodging asylum applications during the reporting period. More than 1.66 million individual applications for asylum or refugee status were submitted to states or UNHCR in 157 countries or territories during 2014, the highest level ever recorded. While the provisional 2014 figure constituted a 54 per cent increase in asylum claims globally compared to 2013 (1.08 million), the increase in industrialized countries was an estimated 45 percent of the provisional total of 1.66 million asylum claims, an estimated 1.47 million were initial applications lodged in 'first instance' procedures. The remaining 189,000 claims were submitted at second instance, including with courts or other appellate bodies.

[The remaining section containing additional data about asylum applications and decisions, and VI regarding stateless persons, have been omitted.]

VII. Other Groups or Persons of Concern

UNHCR has continued to extend its protection or assistance activities to individuals it considers to be 'of concern' but who do not fall into any of the previous population categories. . . .

The number of persons in this category stood at more than 1 million by year end. One fifth of this number was made up of Afghans—former refugees who continue to face economic and security challenges in the course of reintegration. . . . The situation is similar for the 109,000 former Congolese refugees who have returned from the Republic of Congo and who continue to be assisted by UNHCR and its partners.

This category also included former Angolan refugees whose refugee status had ended as a result of cessation in 2012 but whose local integration continued to be monitored by UNHCR. . . . An increasing number of host communities directly or indirectly affected by displacement are also included among those considered to be others of concern to UNHCR, as is the case for Uganda (180,000 persons).

[The following sections containing additional demographic and location data on displaced persons, as well as the report's appendix with detailed data tables, have been omitted.]

Source: United Nations High Commissioner for Refugees. "UNHCR Global Trends Report: World at War." June 18, 2015. http://unhcr.org/556725e69.html.

OTHER HISTORIC DOCUMENTS OF INTEREST

U.S. President and Attorney General Respond to Mass Shootings

JUNE 18, JULY 22, NOVEMBER 28, AND DECEMBER 3, 2015

As in years prior, 2015 was marred by multiple mass shootings across the United States. Although there is no official definition of the phrase "mass shooting," it is generally considered to mean four or more people fatally shot during one incident. Using this meaning, in 2015, there were a total of twenty-seven mass shootings in the United States according to GunViolenceArchive.org. Each incident brought the question about gun ownership back to the forefront of public debate, especially as the 2016 presidential campaign season kicked off and candidates used the events to support their views on gun rights. A number of the shooting incidents brought about renewed discussion of issues including racism, abortion rights, and legal immigration. Late in 2015, Senate Democrats unveiled legislation that would provide greater assurances that those purchasing guns were actually permitted to do so. By the close of the year, the bill had not yet passed out of committee.

MASS SHOOTINGS IN THE UNITED STATES

According to James Alan Fox, a criminology professor at Northeastern University and scholar on the subject of mass killings, since the 1980s, a minimum of four fatalities per shooting event has generally been accepted as the baseline to define a mass shooting. Such a definition has many detractors; however, criminal justice specialists argue that by reducing the number of fatalities required to qualify as a mass shooting, events such as domestic violence, armed robbery, and gang violence, would have to be included, which would add a large number to the statistics.

The Congressional Research Service reports that mass shootings have increased slightly, with an average of 20.2 shootings per year from 2004 to 2008, and 22.4 per year from 2009 to 2013. According to Professor Fox, such data can be manipulated depending on which years are taken into account in the averages. "The only increase has been in fear, and in the perception of an increase," he told *The New York Times*. He indicated that the number of mass shootings has likely remained steady for decades and the shootings themselves seem more prevalent due to our twenty-four hour news cycle and the advent of the Internet.

Based on Federal Bureau of Investigation (FBI) data, on average, mass shootings happen every two weeks, and account for only 1 percent of total gun deaths in the United States. Most federal data does not take into account shootings in some states such as Florida because of poor reporting standards, so it is widely accepted that the average number of gun-related deaths per year is somewhat underestimated. A majority—53 percent—of mass shootings are family related, according to an analysis of FBI data by *USA Today*, and 57 percent of those killed knew the attacker. According to Everytown for Gun Safety, an organization that advocates for stricter gun control, from 2009 to mid-2015, 11 percent of mass shootings were carried out by someone noted by authorities to have shown signs of mental illness prior to the attack.

CHARLESTON CHURCH SHOOTING

On the evening of June 17, Dylann Roof took part in a prayer service at the Emanuel African Methodist Episcopal Church in Charleston, South Carolina, before opening fire, killing nine and injuring one. All the victims were African American. Roof was arrested on June 18 after his father and uncle contacted police, and he was charged with nine counts of murder the following day. Roof pleaded not guilty on July 31, although unconfirmed reports indicated that he told investigators that he committed the shooting for racial reasons. The Department of Justice indicted Roof on thirty-three federal hate crimes and weapons charges. According to Attorney General Loretta Lynch, Roof was "fanning racial flames and exacting revenge" when he "decided to seek out and murder African Americans because of their race." It was determined in September that Roof would face the death penalty, but his attorneys said that he would agree to plead guilty if the maximum sentence was reduced to life in prison without parole. Roof's trial is scheduled for July 2016.

The mass shooting in Charleston sparked not only an increase in the debate about gun rights, but also brought to the forefront continuing racial tensions in the South. Roof's manifesto and multiple photos that were found on his computer featured the Confederate battle flag. The flag had flown on South Carolina statehouse grounds for decades, and after the shooting it quickly became a rallying cry for those who felt it was a relic of a period in the state's history that should not be celebrated. In early July, the South Carolina House and Senate voted for the removal of the Confederate flag from display outside the capitol. It was taken down on July 10.

PLANNED PARENTHOOD SHOOTING

Throughout 2015, the future funding of Planned Parenthood was debated in the halls of Congress and across the nation. The organization again found itself in the headlines on November 27, 2015, when a shooting occurred at a Colorado Springs, Colorado, facility. There, three were killed and two were injured. A standoff with the suspect, Robert Lewis Dear Jr., lasted five hours before he agreed to surrender and allow those trapped inside to leave. Dear was arrested in connection with the shooting and charged with first-degree murder. Dear did not enter a formal guilty or not guilty plea; however, during his December hearing, he spoke out during court proceedings and said he was "guilty" and a "warrior for the babies." According to those who know Dear, he was deeply religious and an ardent opponent of abortion.

Again, the November shooting became a focal point for gun rights activists and gun supporters alike. Many government officials equated the shooting to a form of domestic terrorism. Attorney general Lynch called the attack "a crime against women receiving healthcare services." In a statement on the shooting, President Barack Obama said the nation "can't let [these attacks] become normal. If we truly care about this—if we're going to offer up our thoughts and prayers again . . . then we have to do something about the easy accessibility of weapons of war on our streets to people who have no business wielding them. Period. Enough is enough."

County Employees Killed at Holiday Party

On December 2, county employees were holding a holiday party at the Inland Regional Center in San Bernardino, California. Syed Rizwan Farook, an environmental inspector for the county health department and one of the attendees, reportedly left after a dispute with another colleague. He returned with his wife, Tashfeen Malik, and opened fire, killing fourteen and injuring twenty-two before fleeing the scene. The pair was later killed in a shootout with police.

In a testimony before the Senate Judiciary Committee, FBI director James Comey said that the couple had been planning a terror attack before Malik received her K-1 visa to come to the United States from Saudi Arabia as Farook's fiancée. Attorney General Lynch said the attack had "a single, repugnant purpose: to harm, frighten and intimidate anyone who believes in open and tolerant societies; in free and democratic governments, and in the right of every human being to live in peace, security and freedom."

When the FBI announced that Malik had a connection with the Islamic State of Iraq and the Levant (ISIL), the rhetoric in relation to the shooting quickly changed. Presidential candidate Donald Trump said that the United States should bar any Muslims from entering the country, even if they are legal U.S. residents. Although many of his fellow Republicans rebuked the use of such racist rhetoric, they also increased calls for the temporary halting of a program that has allowed refugees coming from the Middle East to receive expedited visas. President Obama indicated that such ideas played into the hands of ISIL. "Terrorists like ISIL are trying to divide us along lines of religion and background," the president said, adding, "Across the country, Americans are reaching out—to their Muslim friends, neighbors and co-workers—to let them know we're here for each other. . . . That's the message I hope every Muslim–American hears: That we're all part of the same American family."

Gun Control Debate Rages On

After each of the mass shootings in 2015, Democrats and Republicans alike have again broached the issue of gun control. Republicans, on the one hand, have held fast to the idea that personal freedom and gun ownership supersede stricter gun controls. Some have even suggested that allowing law-abiding citizens to have guns could stop mass shootings, and there was some evidence being circulated in media outlets of such instances.

Democrats, on the other hand, continue to call for stricter gun control, at times pointing to the lower rates of gun deaths in other industrialized nations. For example, in 2012, the most recent year for which comparable statistics are available, the United Kingdom had 0.1 gun murders per 100,000, while the United States had 2.9. Following a mass shooting at a community college in Oregon in October, during which ten were killed, Senate Democrats unveiled a plan that would include closing the loopholes in gun background checks, expanding the background check database, and increasing regulations on illegal gun purchases. The bill echoed earlier attempts at control, namely the Manchin–Toomey bill of 2013 that followed the 2012 shooting at Sandy Hook Elementary School in Newtown, Connecticut, during which twenty-seven people, many of them young children, were killed. That bipartisan attempt at gun control failed, and, ultimately, the October legislation did not come to the floor for a vote in 2015. It is unlikely that the bill will pass in the Republican-controlled House and Senate, particularly as the 2016 elections draw near.

—Heather Kerrigan

Following are a statement by President Barack Obama on June 18, 2015, following the mass shooting in Charleston, South Carolina; a July 22, 2015, statement by Attorney General Loretta Lynch following federal indictments against the Charleston shooter; a November 28, 2015, statement by President Obama on the Planned Parenthood shooting in Colorado Springs, Colorado; and a statement by the president on December 3, 2015, following the San Bernardino, California, mass shooting.

President Obama Responds to Shooting in Charleston

DOCUMENT

June 18, 2015

Good afternoon, everybody. This morning I spoke with, and Vice President Biden spoke with, Mayor Joe Riley and other leaders of Charleston to express our deep sorrow over the senseless murders that took place last night.

Michelle and I know several members of Emanuel AME Church. We knew their pastor, Reverend Clementa Pinckney, who, along with eight others, gathered in prayer and fellowship and was murdered last night. And to say our thoughts and prayers are with them and their families and their community doesn't say enough to convey the heartache and the sadness and the anger that we feel.

Any death of this sort is a tragedy. Any shooting involving multiple victims is a tragedy. There is something particularly heartbreaking about the death happening in a place in which we seek solace and we seek peace, in a place of worship.

And Mother Emanuel is, in fact, more than a church. This is a place of worship that was founded by African Americans seeking liberty. This is a church that was burned to the ground because its worships—worshipers worked to end slavery. When there were laws banning all-Black church gatherings, they conducted services in secret. When there was a nonviolent movement to bring our country closer in line with our highest ideals, some of our brightest leaders spoke and led marches from this church's steps. This is a sacred place in the history of Charleston and in the history of America.

The FBI is now on the scene with local police, and more of the Bureau's best are on the way to join them. The Attorney General has announced plans for the FBI to open a hate crime investigation. We understand that the suspect is in custody. And I'll let the best of law enforcement do its work to make sure that justice is served.

Until the investigation is complete, I'm necessarily constrained in terms of talking about the details of the case. But I don't need to be constrained about the emotions that tragedies like this raise. I've had to make statements like this too many times. Communities like this have had to endure tragedies like this too many times. We don't have all the facts, but we do know that, once again, innocent people were killed in part because someone who wanted to inflict harm had no trouble getting their hands on a gun.

Now is the time for mourning and for healing. But let's be clear: At some point, we as a country will have to reckon with the fact that this type of mass violence does not happen in other advanced countries. It doesn't happen in other places with this kind of frequency. And it is in our power to do something about it. I say that recognizing the politics in this town fore-close a lot of those avenues right now. But it would be wrong for us not to acknowledge it. And at some point, it's going to be important for the American people to come to grips with it and for us to be able to shift how we think about the issue of gun violence collectively.

The fact that this took place in a Black church obviously also raises questions about a dark part of our history. This is not the first time that Black churches have been attacked. And we know that hatred across races and faiths pose a particular threat to our democracy and our ideals. The good news is, I am confident that the outpouring of unity and strength and fellowship and love across Charleston today from all races, from all faiths, from all places of worship indicates the degree to which those old vestiges of hatred can be over-come. That certainly was Dr. King's hope just over 50 years ago, after four little girls were killed in a bombing in a Black church in Birmingham, Alabama.

He said, "They lived meaningful lives," and "they died nobly." "They say to each of us," Dr. King said, "Black and White alike, that we must substitute courage for caution. They say to us that we must be concerned not merely with [about]* who murdered them, but about the system, the way of life, the philosophy which produced the murderers. Their death says to us that we must work passionately and unrelentingly for the realization of the American Dream.

"And if one will hold on, he will discover that God walks with him, and that God is able to lift you from the fatigue of despair to the buoyancy of hope, and transform dark and desolate valleys into sunlit paths of inner peace."

Reverend Pinckney and his congregation understood that spirit. Their Christian faith compelled them to reach out not just to members of their congregation or to members of their own communities, but to all in need. They opened their doors to strangers who might enter a church in search of healing or redemption.

Mother Emanuel church and its congregation have risen before—from flames, from an earthquake, from other dark times—to give hope to generations of Charlestonians. And with our prayers and our love, and the buoyancy of hope, it will rise again now as a place of peace.

Thank you.

*White House correction.

Source: Executive Office of the President. "Remarks on the Shootings in Charleston, South Carolina." June 18, 2015. *Compilation of Presidential Documents* 2015, no. 00439 (June 18, 2015). https://gpo.gov/fdsys/pkg/DCPD-201500439/pdf/DCPD-201500439.pdf.

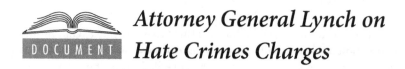

Attorney General Lynch on Hate Crimes Charges

July 22, 2015

Attorney General Lynch released the following statement after the federal grand jury released its indictment against Dylann Storm Roof:

"Good afternoon and thank you for coming.

"I am joined here today by Vanita Gupta, the head of the department's Civil Rights Division and Mark Giuliano, Deputy Director of the FBI.

"We are here today to announce that a federal grand jury in South Carolina has returned a 33-count indictment against Dylann Storm Roof, charging him with federal hate crimes and firearms charges for killing and attempting to kill African-American parishioners at Emanuel African Methodist Episcopal Church in Charleston, South Carolina, because of their race and in order to interfere with their exercise of their religion.

"As set forth in the indictment, several months prior to the tragic events of June 17, Roof conceived of his goal of increasing racial tensions throughout the nation and seeking retribution for perceived wrongs he believed African Americans had committed against white people.

"To carry out these twin goals of fanning racial flames and exacting revenge, Roof further decided to seek out and murder African Americans because of their race. An essential element of his plan, however, was to find his victims inside of a church, specifically an African-American church, to ensure the greatest notoriety and attention to his actions.

"As alleged, Roof set forth the evening of June 17, 2015 to carry out this plan and drove to the Emanuel African Methodist Episcopal Church in Charleston, South Carolina, known as "Mother Emanuel." Mother Emanuel was his destination specifically because it was a historically African-American church of significance to the people of Charleston, of South Carolina and the nation.

"On that summer evening, Dylann Roof found his targets, African Americans engaged in worship. Met with welcome by the ministers of the church and its parishioners, he joined them in their bible study group. The parishioners had bibles. Dylann Roof had his 45 caliber glock pistol and eight magazines loaded with hollow point bullets. And as set forth in the indictment, while the parishioners of Mother Emanuel were engaged in religious worship and bible study, Dylann Roof drew his pistol and opened fire on them, ultimately killing nine church members.

"As you know, the state of South Carolina is also prosecuting Roof for the murders, attempted murders and firearms offenses he is alleged to have committed. We commend the state authorities for their tremendous work and quick response. It is important to note, however, that South Carolina does not have a hate crimes statute and as a result, the state charges do not reflect the alleged hate crime offenses presented in the federal indictment returned today.

"The federal indictment returned today charges Roof with nine murders and three attempted murders under the Matthew Shepard and James Byrd Hate Crimes Prevention Act. This federal hate crimes law prohibits using a dangerous weapon to cause bodily injury, or attempting to do so, on the basis of race or color. The Shepard Byrd Act was enacted specifically to vindicate the unique harms caused by racially motivated violence.

"Roof is also charged with nine murders and three attempted murders under a second federal hate crimes statute that prohibits the use or threat of force to obstruct any person's free exercise of their religious beliefs.

"Finally, Roof has been charged with multiple counts of using a firearm in the commission of these racially motivated murders and attempted murders.

"For these crimes, Roof faces penalties of up to life imprisonment or the death penalty. No decision has been made on whether to seek the death penalty in this case. The department will follow our usual rigorous protocol to thoroughly consider all factual and legal issues relevant to that decision, which will necessarily involve counsel for the defendant

Roof. In addition, consultation with the victims' families is an important part of this decision making process and no decision will be made before conferring with them.

"The family members of those killed at Emanuel AME and the survivors were informed of these federal charges earlier today.

"I also note that this indictment contains allegations and is not evidence of the defendant's guilt.

"This federal grand jury indictment follows an announcement I made on June 18, 2015, that the Department of Justice was conducting a hate crime investigation into the shooting incident at Emanuel AME. Immediately following the shooting, experienced prosecutors from the U.S. Attorney's Office in South Carolina and the Civil Rights Division began working closely with the FBI, ATF and state and local law enforcement officials including the South Carolina Law Enforcement Division—or SLED—Charleston Police and the Solicitor's Office for the Ninth Circuit of South Carolina, in thoroughly investigating these crimes. I would like to [thank] the many state and federal law enforcement officials for their dedication and hard work to ensure that this investigation was conducted thoroughly and expeditiously. I would also like to thank South Carolina U.S. Attorney Bill Nettles for his and his office's tremendous efforts on this case, as well as the dedicated attorneys from the Civil Rights Division.

"In particular, I would like to thank Charleston Solicitor Scarlett Wilson for being such a cooperative and effective partner in this matter. We have a strong working relationship with Solicitor Wilson and her office and we look forward to our continued collaboration as these parallel state and federal prosecutions work their way through their respective court systems.

"Questions?"

SOURCE: U.S. Department of Justice. "Attorney General Lynch Statement Following the Federal Grand Jury Indictment Against Dylann Storm Roof." July 22, 2015. www.justice.gov/opa/pr/attorney-general-lynch-statement-following-federal-grand-jury-indictment-against-dylann-storm.

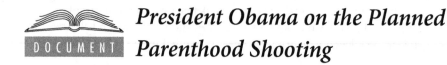

President Obama on the Planned Parenthood Shooting

November 28, 2015

The last thing Americans should have to do, over the holidays or any day, is comfort the families of people killed by gun violence, people who woke up in the morning and bid their loved ones goodbye with no idea it would be for the last time. And yet, 2 days after Thanksgiving, that's what we are forced to do again.

We don't yet know what this particular gunman's so-called motive was for shooting 12 people, or for terrorizing an entire community, when he opened fire with an assault weapon and took hostages at a Planned Parenthood center in Colorado. What we do know is that he killed a cop in the line of duty, along with two of the citizens that police officer was trying to protect. We know that law enforcement saved lives, as so many of them do every day, all across America. And we know that more Americans and their families had fear forced upon them.

This is not normal. We can't let it become normal. If we truly care about this—if we're going to offer up our thoughts and prayers again, for God knows how many times, with a truly clean conscience—then we have to do something about the easy accessibility of weapons of war on our streets to people who have no business wielding them. Period. Enough is enough.

May God bless Officer Garrett Swasey and the Americans he tried to save, and may He grant the rest of us the courage to do the same thing.

SOURCE: Executive Office of the President. "Statement on the Shootings in Colorado Springs, Colorado." November 28, 2015. *Compilation of Presidential Documents* 2015, no. 00845 (November 28, 2015). https://gpo.gov/fdsys/pkg/DCPD-201500845/pdf/DCPD-201500845.pdf.

President Obama on the San Bernardino Killings

December 3, 2015

Yesterday a tragedy occurred in San Bernardino, and as I said in the immediate aftermath, our first order of business is to send our thoughts and prayers to the families of those who have been killed and to pray for a speedy recovery for those who were injured during this terrible attack.

I had a chance to speak with Mayor Davis of San Bernardino, and I thanked law enforcement in that city for their timely and professional response. I indicated to Mayor Davis that the entire country is thinking about that community and thanked him and his office for the way that they've been able to manage an extraordinarily difficult situation with calm and clarity and very much appreciated the coordination that's been taking place between local law enforcement and the FBI investigators.

At this stage, we do not yet know why this terrible event occurred. We do know that the two individuals who were killed were equipped with weapons and appeared to have access to additional weaponry at their homes. But we don't know why they did it. We don't know at this point the extent of their plans. We do not know their motivations.

And I just received a briefing from FBI Director Comey, as well as Attorney General Lynch, indicating the course of their investigation. At this point, this is now a FBI investigation. That's been done in cooperation and consultation with local law enforcement. It is possible that this was terrorist related, but we don't know. It's also possible that this was workplace related. And until the FBI has been able to conduct what are going to be a large number of interviews, until we understand the nature of the workplace relationship between the individual and his superiors—because he worked with the organization where this terrible shooting took place—until all the social media and electronic information has been exploited, we're just not going to be able to answer those questions.

But what I can assure the American people is, we're going to get to the bottom of this and that we are going to be vigilant, as we always are, in getting the facts before we issue any decisive judgments in terms of how this occurred.

More broadly, as I said yesterday, we see the prevalence of these kinds of mass shootings in this country, and I think so many Americans sometimes feel as if there's nothing we can do about it. We are fortunate to have an extraordinary combination of law enforcement and intelligence and military that work every single day to keep us safe. But we can't just leave it to our professionals to deal with the problem of these kinds of horrible killings. We all have a part to play.

And I do think that, as the investigation moves forward, it's going to be important for all of us—including our legislatures—to see what we can do to make sure that when individuals decide that they want to do somebody harm, we're making it a little harder for them to do it. Because right now it's just too easy. And we're going to have to, I think, search ourselves as a society to make sure that we can take basic steps that would make it harder—not impossible, but harder—for individuals to get access to weapons. So there will be, I think, a press conference later today led by the Attorney General. Director Comey will continue to brief not only the press, but also Members of Congress about the course of the investigation. Our expectation is, is that this may take some time before we're able to sort it all through. There may be mixed motives involved in this, which makes the investigation more complicated. But rest assured that we will get to the bottom of this.

And in the meantime, once again, I want to offer our deepest condolences to those who've been affected by this terrible tragedy. And for those who've been injured, we hope that they get well quickly and that they're able to be back together with their families.

Thank you very much, everybody.

SOURCE: Executive Office of the President. "Remarks Following a Meeting With Members of the National Security Team on the Shootings in San Bernardino, California." December 3, 2015. *Compilation of Presidential Documents* 2015, no. 00863 (December 3, 2015). https://gpo.gov/fdsys/pkg/DCPD-201500863/pdf/DCPD-201500863.pdf.

OTHER HISTORIC DOCUMENTS OF INTEREST

FROM THIS VOLUME

FROM PREVIOUS *HISTORIC DOCUMENTS*

Supreme Court Upholds Affordable Care Act Subsidies

JUNE 25, 2015

Ever since the Patient Protection and Affordable Care Act (ACA) passed in 2010, its opponents have been relentless in their efforts to either repeal it or prevent its full implementation. The attacks were political—by February 2015, House Republicans had held fifty-six votes to repeal the law—and legal—in 2012, the first of three legal challenges to the ACA reached the Supreme Court but lost when a divided court upheld the law in a close 5–4 vote. Similarly, in 2014, the Supreme Court upheld the Act's birth control mandate 5–4. One year later, the third legal challenge to the ACA made it to the Supreme Court in *King v. Burwell* where, on June 25, 2015, the Court again, this time by a larger 6–3 majority, upheld the ACA against its challengers.

Chief Justice John G. Roberts Jr. wrote both the 2012 and 2015 majority decisions. The first case upheld the ACA against a challenge to its central mandate that all qualified taxpayers must buy insurance. By contrast, *King v. Burwell* concerned a challenge to the ACA's provision of tax credits or subsidies, intended to make insurance more affordable, and turned on the interpretation of a single phrase in the voluminous law: "an Exchange established by the State." Specifically, challengers argued that the plain language of six words in one provision of the Act could only be read as limiting those tax credits to people living in one of the sixteen states that created its own insurance exchange, and did not allow credits to those living in any of the thirty-four states that opted to rely on the federal exchange rather than create their own. In upholding the law against this challenge, the Chief Justice interpreted the meaning of those words within the context of the overall Act, ruling that the subsidies form a central part of the Act's architecture such that to deny their nationwide application would bring about "the type of calamitous result that Congress plainly meant to avoid."

THE STRUCTURE AND LEGAL HISTORY OF THE ACA

Three major reforms lie at the heart of the ACA, which was designed to expand the number of people covered by individual health insurance. These three reforms were designed to interlock in such a way that to omit any one of them would make the entire foundation of the Act collapse.

The first reform guaranteed coverage to everyone, regardless of their preexisting medical conditions. In the past, this kind of requirement in state laws had led people to wait until they were sick before purchasing insurance. When a larger percentage of the insured pool is sick, prices go up. Higher prices lead more people to drop insurance until they get sick or injured and need coverage. This, in turn, leads to still higher prices in what has been colorfully described as an "economic death spiral."

The second and third reforms were added by the ACA specifically to prevent the death spiral that had doomed previous reform efforts. To bring more healthy people onto the insurance rolls, the second reform of the ACA mandates coverage, requiring that everyone must buy insurance or pay a penalty, unless the cost of buying the insurance is more than 8 percent of the individual's income. The third reform provides for tax credits and subsidies to help individuals afford insurance if their household income is between 100 and 400 percent of the federal poverty line.

In addition to the three main reforms, the ACA also requires the creation of an "exchange" in each state. In essence, an exchange is an online marketplace where people can compare and purchase insurance plans and learn whether they qualify for tax credits. The ACA gives all states the opportunity to establish their own exchanges, but also provides that if a state chooses not to establish an exchange, then the federal government, through the Department of Health and Human Services (HHS), will establish "such exchange within the state."

ANOTHER CHALLENGE TO THE ACA REACHES THE SUPREME COURT

King v. Burwell, the third ACA case to reach the Supreme Court, involved a challenge to part of the law's third reform: the subsidies offered through tax credits to low income households in order to purchase health insurance. The case turned on the meaning of six words in Section 36B, which provides that tax credits "shall be allowed" for any "applicable taxpayer" if the taxpayer has enrolled in an insurance plan through "*an Exchange established by the State.*" The challengers to the ACA argue that this language plainly and unambiguously limits the provision of tax credits to those who purchase insurance on a state-run exchange and that states using the federal exchange do not qualify.

Currently, sixteen states and the District of Columbia have established their own exchanges. The remaining thirty-four states have elected to use the federally established exchange. According to the Kaiser Family Foundation, if tax credits were abolished from all states using the federal exchange, an estimated 6.4 million people would lose a total of $1.7 billion in subsidies. This would raise the cost of insurance to a larger percentage of their income, pushing virtually them all outside the pool of people mandated to purchase insurance. It is likely that most of these people, particularly those who are young and healthy, would drop their coverage, thus disrupting the individual insurance markets.

SUPREME COURT UPHOLDS LEGALITY OF SUBSIDIES

Chief Justice Roberts's majority opinion was joined by the Court's four liberal justices in its entirety. Additionally, Justice Anthony M. Kennedy signed on with the majority, making it a solid 6–3 opinion. Justice Antonin Scalia filed a dissenting opinion that was joined by Justices Clarence Thomas and Samuel Alito Jr.

Chief Justice Roberts blamed the ambiguity at the core of this case on the "unfortunate reality" that the ACA "contains more than a few examples of inartful drafting" and "does not reflect the type of care and deliberation that one might expect of such significant legislation." Nevertheless, he described the Court's role to "do our best" to interpret the words of the statute "in their context and with a view to their place in the overall statutory scheme." He also recognized that the challengers had strong arguments about the "plain meaning" of the words, but asserted that what may seem obvious in isolation, may turn out to be "untenable in light of [the statute] as a whole."

The Court reached an initial conclusion that the words at issue—"an Exchange established by the State"—were ambiguous after a technical examination of the frequently complicated language used throughout the entire statute. The words "federal" and "state" exchanges were used equivalently with no meaningful difference throughout the Act, according to the majority opinion. In fact, many other provisions of the ACA would be rendered meaningless, unnecessary, or redundant if the words were read to exclude the federal exchange. For example, lengthy provisions discuss the role and treatment of individuals who were due tax credits under the federal exchanges, but those individuals would not exist if the challengers' limited reading was the correct one. Other sections defined the word "exchange" itself to mean all exchanges, both state and federal.

Once finding that the words at issue were ambiguous, the Chief Justice's majority opinion turned to an examination of the broader structure of the law to determine which interpretation best fit within the overall statutory scheme. He described the three major interlocking reforms of the ACA: guaranteed coverage regardless of preexisting conditions, requirement to maintain health insurance, and the availability of tax credits to those who cannot afford the insurance. These reforms, together, were designed to "broaden the health insurance risk pool to include healthy individuals, which will lower health insurance premiums." The Chief Justice accepted that these reforms interlock in such a way that to remove one would have a cascading effect that could well collapse the entire health care structure.

Under the challengers' reading of the statute, no tax credits would be available to people in the majority of states that rely on the federal exchange. This would greatly reduce the pool of people who earn enough money to be required to purchase insurance in those states. It would also undermine both the mandated coverage aspect of the Act and the tax credit reforms, and could, the Court argued, "push a state's individual insurance market into a death spiral." The Court found it to be "implausible that Congress meant the Act to operate in this manner." Had Congress wanted the entire viability of the Act to turn on six words, it is also unlikely that they would have buried them in a subsection of the tax code and not used a more prominent and logical method to make this clear, the majority wrote.

Looking to the role of the Supreme Court in a democracy, the Chief Justice emphasized the importance of respecting the legislature and taking care "not to undo what it has done." In the case of the ACA, Congress sought "to improve health insurance markets, not to destroy them." To interpret the Act in a way that is consistent with this goal, the Court ruled that tax credits must be available to those who qualify, regardless of whether they purchase insurance on state or federal exchanges.

In a characteristically strongly worded dissent, Justice Scalia said the majority's decision to replace the ACA's clear words "Exchange established by the State" and instead read in their place "Exchange established by the State or Federal Government" is "of course quite absurd, and the Court's 21 pages of explanation make it no less so." He colorfully described the majority's reasoning as "interpretive jiggery-pokery" and suggested that the Court has worked so hard to uphold the ACA that it should henceforth be referred to by the name "SCOTUScare."

IMPACT OF THE DECISION

The Supreme Court's ruling that the health care law provides for nationwide tax subsidies to help lower-income people afford health insurance was generally received as a sweeping victory for the Obama administration's signature legislation. In a statement, President Barack Obama asserted that the ACA "is here to stay."

There are, however, still other cases challenging different aspects of the ACA working their way through the lower courts. The closest to reaching the Supreme Court, *Sissel v. HHS*, challenges the constitutionality of the entire law based on what the challengers argue were faulty procedures relied on to pass it initially. The case focuses on the Origination Clause of the Constitution, which reads: "All Bills for raising revenue shall originate in the House of Representatives." The District Court for the District of Columbia rejected the suit finding both that the bill enacting the individual mandate was not a "bill for raising revenue" and that it had originated in the House of Representatives, although in a somewhat formulaic way. This was upheld by the appellate court, but, on October 26, 2015, the Pacific Legal Foundation (the conservative legal organization litigating the case) asked the Supreme Court to hear its appeal and strike down the ACA in its entirety.

—Melissa Feinberg

Following is the edited text of the U.S. Supreme Court's decision in King v. Burwell, *in which the Court upheld the constitutionality of Affordable Care Act subsidies by a 6–3 vote.*

DOCUMENT   *King v. Burwell*

June 25, 2015

[Footnotes have been omitted.]

No. 14-114

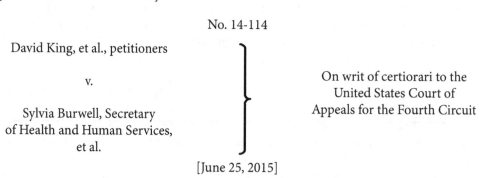

David King, et al., petitioners	On writ of certiorari to the
v.	United States Court of
Sylvia Burwell, Secretary of Health and Human Services, et al.	Appeals for the Fourth Circuit

[June 25, 2015]

CHIEF JUSTICE ROBERTS delivered the opinion of the Court.

The Patient Protection and Affordable Care Act adopts a series of interlocking reforms designed to expand coverage in the individual health insurance market. First, the Act bars insurers from taking a person's health into account when deciding whether to sell health insurance or how much to charge. Second, the Act generally requires each person to maintain insurance coverage or make a payment to the Internal Revenue Service. And third, the Act gives tax credits to certain people to make insurance more affordable.

In addition to those reforms, the Act requires the creation of an "Exchange" in each State—basically, a marketplace that allows people to compare and purchase insurance plans. The Act gives each State the opportunity to establish its own Exchange, but provides that the Federal Government will establish the Exchange if the State does not.

This case is about whether the Act's interlocking reforms apply equally in each State no matter who establishes the State's Exchange. Specifically, the question presented is whether the Act's tax credits are available in States that have a Federal Exchange.

[Section I, detailing the Act's history and describing the reforms, has been omitted.]

II

The Affordable Care Act addresses tax credits in what is now Section 36B of the Internal Revenue Code. That section provides: "In the case of an applicable taxpayer, there shall be allowed as a credit against the tax imposed by this subtitle . . . an amount equal to the premium assistance credit amount." 26 U. S. C. §36B(a). Section 36B then defines the term "premium assistance credit amount" as "the sum of the *premium assistance amounts* determined under paragraph (2) with respect to all *coverage months* of the taxpayer occurring during the taxable year." §36B(b)(1) (emphasis added). Section 36B goes on to define the two italicized terms—"premium assistance amount" and "coverage month"—in part by referring to an insurance plan that is enrolled in through "an Exchange established by the State under [42 U. S. C. §18031]." 26 U. S. C. §§36B(b)(2)(A), (c)(2)(A)(i).

The parties dispute whether Section 36B authorizes tax credits for individuals who enroll in an insurance plan through a Federal Exchange. Petitioners argue that a Federal Exchange is not "an Exchange established by the State under [42 U. S. C. §18031]," and that the IRS Rule therefore contradicts Section 36B. The Government responds that the IRS Rule is lawful because the phrase "an Exchange established by the State under [42 U. S. C. §18031]" should be read to include Federal Exchanges.

When analyzing an agency's interpretation of a statute, we often apply the two-step framework announced in *Chevron*, 467 U. S. 837. Under that framework, we ask whether the statute is ambiguous and, if so, whether the agency's interpretation is reasonable. *Id.*, at 842–843. This approach "is premised on the theory that a statute's ambiguity constitutes an implicit delegation from Congress to the agency to fill in the statutory gaps." *FDA v. Brown & Williamson Tobacco Corp.*, 529 U. S. 120, 159 (2000). "In extraordinary cases, however, there may be reason to hesitate before concluding that Congress has intended such an implicit delegation." *Ibid.*

This is one of those cases. The tax credits are among the Act's key reforms, involving billions of dollars in spending each year and affecting the price of health insurance for millions of people. Whether those credits are available on Federal Exchanges is thus a question of deep "economic and political significance" that is central to this statutory scheme; had Congress wished to assign that question to an agency, it surely would have done so expressly. *Utility Air Regulatory Group v. EPA*, 573 U. S. ___, ___ (2014) (slip op., at 19) (quoting *Brown & Williamson*, 529 U. S., at 160). It is especially unlikely that Congress would have delegated this decision to the IRS, which has no expertise in crafting health insurance policy of this sort. See *Gonzales v. Oregon*, 546 U. S. 243, 266–267 (2006). This is not a case for the IRS.

It is instead our task to determine the correct reading of Section 36B. If the statutory language is plain, we must enforce it according to its terms. *Hardt v. Reliance Standard Life Ins. Co.*, 560 U. S. 242, 251 (2010). But oftentimes the "meaning—or ambiguity—of certain words or phrases may only become evident when placed in context." *Brown & Williamson*, 529 U. S., at 132. So when deciding whether the language is plain, we must read the words "in their context and with a view to their place in the overall statutory scheme. *Id.*, at 133 (internal quotation marks omitted). Our duty, after all, is "to construe statutes, not isolated provisions." *Graham County Soil and Water Conservation Dist. v. United States ex rel. Wilson*, 559 U. S. 280, 290 (2010) (internal quotation marks omitted).

A

We begin with the text of Section 36B. As relevant here, Section 36B allows an individual to receive tax credits only if the individual enrolls in an insurance plan through "an Exchange established by the State under [42 U. S. C. §18031]." In other words, three things must be true: First, the individual must enroll in an insurance plan through "an Exchange." Second, that Exchange must be "established by the State." And third, that Exchange must be established "under [42 U. S. C. §18031]." We address each requirement in turn.

First, all parties agree that a Federal Exchange qualifies as "an Exchange" for purposes of Section 36B. Section 18031 provides that "[e]ach State shall . . . establish an American Health Benefit Exchange . . . for the State." §18031(b)(1). Although phrased as a requirement, the Act gives the States "flexibility" by allowing them to "elect" whether they want to establish an Exchange. §18041(b). If the State chooses not to do so, Section 18041 provides that the Secretary "shall . . . establish and operate *such Exchange* within the State." §18041(c)(1) (emphasis added).

By using the phrase "such Exchange," Section 18041 instructs the Secretary to establish and operate the same Exchange that the State was directed to establish under Section 18031. See Black's Law Dictionary 1661 (10th ed. 2014) (defining "such" as "That or those; having just been mentioned"). In other words, State Exchanges and Federal Exchanges are equivalent—they must meet the same requirements, perform the same functions, and serve the same purposes. Although State and Federal Exchanges are established by different sovereigns, Sections 18031 and 18041 do not suggest that they differ in any meaningful way. A Federal Exchange therefore counts as "an Exchange" under Section 36B.

Second, we must determine whether a Federal Exchange is "established by the State" for purposes of Section 36B. At the outset, it might seem that a Federal Exchange cannot fulfill this requirement. After all, the Act defines "State" to mean "each of the 50 States and the District of Columbia"—a definition that does not include the Federal Government. 42 U. S. C. §18024(d). But when read in context, "with a view to [its] place in the overall statutory scheme," the meaning of the phrase "established by the State" is not so clear. *Brown & Williamson*, 529 U. S., at 133 (internal quotation marks omitted).

After telling each State to establish an Exchange, Section 18031 provides that all Exchanges "shall make available qualified health plans to qualified individuals." 42 U. S. C. §18031(d)(2)(A). Section 18032 then defines the term "qualified individual" in part as an individual who "resides in the State that established the Exchange." §18032(f)(1)(A). And that's a problem: If we give the phrase "the State that established the Exchange" its most natural meaning, there would be *no* "qualified individuals" on Federal Exchanges. But the Act clearly contemplates that there will be qualified individuals on *every* Exchange. As we just mentioned, the Act requires all Exchanges to "make available qualified health plans to qualified individuals"—something an Exchange could not do if there were no such individuals. §18031(d)(2)(A). And the Act tells the Exchange, in deciding which health plans to offer, to consider "the interests of qualified individuals . . . in the State or States in which such Exchange operates"—again, something the Exchange could not do if qualified individuals did not exist. §18031(e)(1)(B). This problem arises repeatedly throughout the Act.

See, *e.g.,* §18031(b)(2) (allowing a State to create "one Exchange . . . for providing . . . services to both qualified individuals and qualified small employers," rather than creating separate Exchanges for those two groups).

These provisions suggest that the Act may not always use the phrase "established by the State" in its most natural sense. Thus, the meaning of that phrase may not be as clear as it appears when read out of context. . . .

The upshot of all this is that the phrase "an Exchange established by the State under [42 U. S. C. §18031]" is properly viewed as ambiguous. The phrase may be limited in its reach to State Exchanges. But it is also possible that the phrase refers to *all* Exchanges—both State—at least for purposes of the tax credits. If a State chooses not to follow the directive in Section 18031 that it establish an Exchange, the Act tells the Secretary to establish "such Exchange." §18041. And by using the words "such Exchange," the Act indicates that State and Federal Exchanges should be the same. But State and Federal Exchanges would differ in a fundamental way if tax credits were available only on State Exchanges—one type of Exchange would help make insurance more affordable by providing billions of dollars to the States' citizens; the other type of Exchange would not.

The conclusion that Section 36B is ambiguous is further supported by several provisions that assume tax credits will be available on both State and Federal Exchanges. For example, the Act requires all Exchanges to create outreach programs that must "distribute fair and impartial information concerning . . . the availability of premium tax credits under section 36B." §18031(i)(3)(B). The Act also requires all Exchanges to "establish and make available by electronic means a calculator to determine the actual cost of coverage after the application of any premium tax credit under section 36B." If tax credits were not available on Federal Exchanges, these provisions would make little sense. . . .

The Affordable Care Act contains more than a few examples of inartful drafting. (To cite just one, the Act creates three separate Section 1563s. See 124 Stat. 270, 911, 912.) Several features of the Act's passage contributed to that unfortunate reality. Congress wrote key parts of the Act behind closed doors, rather than through "the traditional legislative process." Cannan, A Legislative History of the Affordable Care Act: How Legislative Procedure Shapes Legislative History, 105 L. Lib. J. 131, 163 (2013). And Congress passed much of the Act using a complicated budgetary procedure known as "reconciliation," which limited opportunities for debate and amendment, and bypassed the Senate's normal 60-vote filibuster requirement. *Id.,* at 159–167. As a result, the Act does not reflect the type of care and deliberation that one might expect of such significant legislation. . . .

Anyway, we "must do our best, bearing in mind the fundamental canon of statutory construction that the words of a statute must be read in their context and with a view to their place in the overall statutory scheme." *Utility Air Regulatory Group,* 573 U. S., at ___ (slip op., at 15) (internal quotation marks omitted). After reading Section 36B along with other related provisions in the Act, we cannot conclude that the phrase "an Exchange established by the State under [Section 18031]" is unambiguous.

B

Given that the text is ambiguous, we must turn to the broader structure of the Act to determine the meaning of Section 36B. "A provision that may seem ambiguous in isolation is often clarified by the remainder of the statutory scheme . . . because only one of the permissible meanings produces a substantive effect that is compatible with the rest of the law." *United Sav. Assn. of Tex. v. Timbers of Inwood Forest Associates, Ltd.*, 484 U. S. 365, 371 (1988). Here, the statutory scheme compels us to reject petitioners' interpretation because it would destabilize the individual insurance market in any State with a Federal Exchange, and likely create the very "death spirals" that Congress designed the Act to avoid. . . .

As discussed above, Congress based the Affordable Care Act on three major reforms: first, the guaranteed issue and community rating requirements; second, a requirement that individuals maintain health insurance coverage or make a payment to the IRS; and third, the tax credits for individuals with household incomes between 100 percent and 400 percent of the federal poverty line. In a State that establishes its own Exchange, these three reforms work together to expand insurance coverage. The guaranteed issue and community rating requirements ensure that anyone can buy insurance; the coverage requirement creates an incentive for people to do so before they get sick; and the tax credits—it is hoped—make insurance more affordable. Together, those reforms "minimize . . . adverse selection and broaden the health insurance risk pool to include healthy individuals, which will lower health insurance premiums." 42 U. S. C. §18091(2)(I).

Under petitioners' reading, however, the Act would operate quite differently in a State with a Federal Exchange. As they see it, one of the Act's three major reforms—the tax credits—would not apply. And a second major reform—the coverage requirement—would not apply in a meaningful way. As explained earlier, the coverage requirement applies only when the cost of buying health insurance (minus the amount of the tax credits) is less than eight percent of an individual's income. 26 U. S. C. §§5000A(e)(1)(A), (e)(1)(B)(ii). So without the tax credits, the coverage requirement would apply to fewer individuals. And it would be a *lot* fewer. In 2014, approximately 87 percent of people who bought insurance on a Federal Exchange did so with tax credits, and virtually all of those people would become exempt. . . . If petitioners are right, therefore, only one of the Act's three major reforms would apply in States with a Federal Exchange.

The combination of no tax credits and an ineffective coverage requirement could well push a State's individual insurance market into a death spiral. One study predicts that premiums would increase by 47 percent and enrollment would decrease by 70 percent. E. Saltzman & C. Eibner, The Effect of Eliminating the Affordable Care Act's Tax Credits in Federally Facilitated Marketplaces (2015). Another study predicts that premiums would increase by 35 percent and enrollment would decrease by 69 percent. L. Blumberg, M. Buettgens, & J. Holahan, The Implications of a Supreme Court Finding for the Plaintiff in King vs. Burwell: 8.2 Million More Uninsured and 35% Higher Premiums (2015). And those effects would not be limited to individuals who purchase insurance on the Exchanges. Because the Act requires insurers to treat the entire individual market as a single risk pool, 42 U. S. C. §18032(c)(1), premiums outside the Exchange would rise along with those inside the Exchange. . . .

It is implausible that Congress meant the Act to operate in this manner. . . . Congress made the guaranteed issue and community rating requirements applicable in every State in the Nation. But those requirements only work when combined with the coverage requirement and the tax credits. So it stands to reason that Congress meant for those provisions to apply in every State as well. . . .

[Section C, which contains information on the applicability of tax credits to state and federal exchanges, has been omitted.]

D

Petitioners' arguments about the plain meaning of Section 36B are strong. But while the meaning of the phrase "an Exchange established by the State under [42 U. S. C. §18031]" may seem plain "when viewed in isolation," such a reading turns out to be "untenable in light of [the statute] as a whole." *Department of Revenue of Ore. v. ACF Industries, Inc.*, 510 U. S. 332, 343 (1994). In this instance, the context and structure of the Act compel us to depart from what would otherwise be the most natural reading of the pertinent statutory phrase.

Reliance on context and structure in statutory interpretation is a "subtle business, calling for great wariness lest what professes to be mere rendering becomes creation and attempted interpretation of legislation becomes legislation itself." *Palmer v. Massachusetts, 308 U. S. 79, 83 (1939).* For the reasons we have given, however, such reliance is appropriate in this case, and leads us to conclude that Section 36B allows tax credits for insurance purchased on any Exchange created under the Act. Those credits are necessary for the Federal Exchanges to function like their State Exchange counterparts, and to avoid the type of calamitous result that Congress plainly meant to avoid.

* * *

In a democracy, the power to make the law rests with those chosen by the people. Our role is more confined—"to say what the law is." *Marbury v. Madison*, 1 Cranch 137, 177 (1803). That is easier in some cases than in others. But in every case we must respect the role of the Legislature, and take care not to undo what it has done. A fair reading of legislation demands a fair understanding of the legislative plan.

Congress passed the Affordable Care Act to improve health insurance markets, not to destroy them. If at all possible, we must interpret the Act in a way that is consistent with the former, and avoids the latter. Section 36B can fairly be read consistent with what we see as Congress's plan, and that is the reading we adopt.

The judgment of the United States Court of Appeals for the Fourth Circuit is

Affirmed.

JUSTICE SCALIA, with whom JUSTICE THOMAS and JUSTICE ALITO join, dissenting.

The Court holds that when the Patient Protection and Affordable Care Act says "Exchange established by the State" it means "Exchange established by the State or the Federal Government." That is of course quite absurd, and the Court's 21 pages of explanation make it no less so.

[Section I, outlining the case background, has been omitted.]

II

The Court interprets §36B to award tax credits on both federal and state Exchanges. It accepts that the "most natural sense" of the phrase "Exchange established by the State" is an Exchange established by a State. *Ante*, at 11. (Understatement, thy name is an opinion on the Affordable Care Act!) Yet the opinion continues, with no semblance of shame, that "it is also possible that the phrase refers to all Exchanges—both State and Federal." *Ante*, at 13. (Impossible possibility, thy name is an opinion on the Affordable Care Act!) The Court claims that "the context and structure of the Act compel [it] to depart from what would otherwise be the most natural reading of the pertinent statutory phrase." *Ante*, at 21.

I wholeheartedly agree with the Court that sound interpretation requires paying attention to the whole law, not homing in on isolated words or even isolated sections. Context always matters. Let us not forget, however, *why* context matters: It is a tool for understanding the terms of the law, not an excuse for rewriting them.

Any effort to understand rather than to rewrite a law must accept and apply the presumption that lawmakers use words in "their natural and ordinary signification." *Pensacola Telegraph Co. v. Western Union Telegraph Co.*, 96 U. S. 1, 12 (1878). Ordinary connotation does not always prevail, but the more unnatural the proposed interpretation of a law, the more compelling the contextual evidence must be to show that it is correct. Today's interpretation is not merely unnatural; it is unheard of. Who would ever have dreamt that "Exchange established by the State" means "Exchange established by the State *or the Federal Government*"? Little short of an express statutory definition could justify adopting this singular reading.

Yet the only pertinent definition here provides that "State" means "each of the 50 States and the District of Columbia." 42 U. S. C. §18024(d). Because the Secretary is neither one of the 50 States nor the District of Columbia, that definition positively contradicts the eccentric theory that an Exchange established by the Secretary has been established by the State.

Far from offering the overwhelming evidence of meaning needed to justify the Court's interpretation, other contextual clues undermine it at every turn. To begin with, other parts of the Act sharply distinguish between the establishment of an Exchange by a State and the establishment of an Exchange by the Federal Government. . . . Provisions such as these destroy any pretense that a federal Exchange is in some sense also established by a State.

Reading the rest of the Act also confirms that, as relevant here, there are *only* two ways to set up an Exchange in a State: establishment by a State and establishment by the Secretary. . . .

Making matters worse, the reader of the whole Act will come across a number of provisions beyond §36B that refer to the establishment of Exchanges by States. Adopting the Court's interpretation means nullifying the term "by the State" not just once, but again and again throughout the Act. . . .

It is bad enough for a court to cross out "by the State" once. But seven times?

Congress did not, by the way, repeat "Exchange established by the State under [§18031]" by rote throughout the Act. Quite the contrary, clause after clause of the law uses a more general term such as "Exchange" or "Exchange established under [§18031]." See, *e.g.*, 42 U. S. C. §§18031(k), 18033; 26 U. S. C. §6055. It is common sense that any speaker who says "Exchange" some of the time, but "Exchange established by the State" the rest of the time, probably means something by the contrast.

Equating establishment "by the State" with establishment by the Federal Government makes nonsense of other parts of the Act. . . . How could a State control the type of electronic interface used by a federal Exchange? The Act allows a State to control contracting decisions made by "an Exchange established by the State." §18031(f)(3). Why would a State get to control the contracting decisions of a federal Exchange? The Act also provides "Assistance to States to establish American Health Benefit Exchanges" and directs the Secretary to renew this funding "if the State . . . is making progress . . . toward . . . establishing an Exchange." §18031(a). Does a State that refuses to set up an Exchange still receive this funding, on the premise that Exchanges established by the Federal Government are really established by States? It is presumably in order to avoid these questions that the Court concludes that federal Exchanges count as state Exchanges only "for purposes of the tax credits." *Ante*, at 13. (Contrivance, thy name is an opinion on the Affordable Care Act!). . . .

Faced with overwhelming confirmation that "Exchange established by the State" means what it looks like it means, the Court comes up with argument after feeble argument to support its contrary interpretation. None of its tries comes close to establishing the implausible conclusion that Congress used "by the State" to mean "by the State or not by the State."

The Court emphasizes that if a State does not set up an Exchange, the Secretary must establish "such Exchange." §18041(c). It claims that the word "such" implies that federal and state Exchanges are "the same." *Ante*, at 13. To see the error in this reasoning, one need only consider a parallel provision from our Constitution: "The Times, Places and Manner of holding Elections for Senators and Representatives, shall be prescribed in each State by the Legislature thereof; but the Congress may at any time by Law make or alter *such Regulations*." Art. I, §4, cl. 1 (emphasis added). Just as the Affordable Care Act directs States to establish Exchanges while allowing the Secretary to establish "such Exchange" as a fallback, the Elections Clause directs state legislatures to prescribe election regulations while allowing Congress to make "such Regulations" as a fallback. Would anybody refer to an election regulation made by Congress as a "regulation prescribed by the state legislature"? Would anybody say that a federal election law and a state election law are in all respects equivalent? Of course not. The word "such" does not help the Court one whit. The Court's argument also overlooks the rudimentary principle that a specific provision governs a general one. Even if it were true that the term "such Exchange" in §18041(c) implies that federal and state Exchanges are the same in general, the term "established by the State" in §36B makes plain that they differ when it comes to tax credits in particular.

The Court's next bit of interpretive jiggery-pokery involves other parts of the Act that purportedly presuppose the availability of tax credits on both federal and state Exchanges. *Ante*, at 13–14. It is curious that the Court is willing to subordinate the express words of the section that grants tax credits to the mere implications of other provisions with only tangential connections to tax credits. One would think that interpretation would work the other way around. In any event, each of the provisions mentioned by the Court is perfectly consistent with limiting tax credits to state Exchanges. . . . What stops a federal Exchange's outreach program from fairly and impartially telling customers that no tax credits are available? A third provision requires an Exchange to report information about each insurance plan sold—including level of coverage, premium, name of the insured, and "amount of any advance payment" of the tax credit. 26 U. S. C. §36B(f)(3). What stops a federal Exchange's report from confirming that no tax credits have been paid out?

The Court persists that these provisions "would make little sense" if no tax credits were available on federal Exchanges. *Ante*, at 14. Even if that observation were true, it would show only oddity, not ambiguity. Laws often include unusual or mismatched provisions . . . . It is entirely natural for slight mismatches to occur when, as here, lawmakers draft "a single statutory provision" to cover "different kinds" of situations . . . .

Roaming even farther afield from §36B, the Court turns to the Act's provisions about "qualified individuals." *Ante*, at 10–11. Qualified individuals receive favored treatment on Exchanges, although customers who are not qualified individuals may also shop there. See *Halbig v. Burwell*, 758 F. 3d 390, 404–405 (CADC 2014). The Court claims that the Act must equate federal and state establishment of Exchanges when it defines a qualified individual as someone who (among other things) lives in the "State that established the Exchange," 42 U. S. C. §18032(f)(1)(A). Otherwise, the Court says, there would be no qualified individuals on federal Exchanges, contradicting (for example) the provision requiring every Exchange to take the "interests of qualified individuals" into account when selecting health plans. *Ante*, at 11 (quoting §18031(e)(1)(b)). Pure applesauce. . . . There is no need to rewrite the term "State that established the Exchange" in the definition of "qualified individual," much less a need to rewrite the separate term "Exchange established by the State" in a separate part of the Act.

Least convincing of all, however, is the Court's attempt to uncover support for its interpretation in "the structure of Section 36B itself." *Ante*, at 19. The Court finds it strange that Congress limited the tax credit to state Exchanges in the formula for calculating the amount of the credit, rather than in the provision defining the range of taxpayers eligible for the credit. Had the Court bothered to look at the rest of the Tax Code, it would have seen that the structure it finds strange is in fact quite common. Consider, for example, the many provisions that initially make taxpayers of all incomes eligible for a tax credit, only to provide later that the amount of the credit is zero if the taxpayer's income exceeds a specified threshold. See, *e.g.,* 26 U. S. C. §24 (child tax credit); §32 (earned-income tax credit); §36 (first-time-homebuyer tax credit). Or consider, for an even closer parallel, a neighboring provision that initially makes taxpayers of all States eligible for a credit, only to provide later that the amount of the credit may be zero if the taxpayer's State does not satisfy certain requirements. See §35 (health-insurance-costs tax credit). One begins to get the sense that the Court's insistence on reading things in context applies to "established by the State," but to nothing else . . . .

The Court has not come close to presenting the compelling contextual case necessary to justify departing from the ordinary meaning of the terms of the law. Quite the contrary, context only underscores the outlandishness of the Court's interpretation. Reading the Act as a whole leaves no doubt about the matter: "Exchange established by the State" means what it looks like it means.

III

For its next defense of the indefensible, the Court turns to the Affordable Care Act's design and purposes . . . . The Court reasons that Congress intended these three reforms to "work together to expand insurance coverage"; and because the first two apply in every State, so must the third. *Ante*, at 16.

This reasoning suffers from no shortage of flaws. To begin with, "even the most formidable argument concerning the statute's purposes could not overcome the clarity [of] the statute's text." *Kloeckner v. Solis*, 568 U. S. ___, ___, n. 4 (2012) (slip op., at 14, n. 4). Statutory design and purpose matter only to the extent they help clarify an otherwise ambiguous provision. Could anyone maintain with a straight face that §36B is unclear? To mention just the highlights, the Court's interpretation clashes with a statutory definition, renders words inoperative in at least seven separate provisions of the Act, overlooks the contrast between provisions that say "Exchange" and those that say "Exchange established by the State," gives the same phrase one meaning for purposes of tax credits but an entirely different meaning for other purposes, and (let us not forget) contradicts the ordinary meaning of the words Congress used. On the other side of the ledger, the Court has come up with nothing more than a general provision that turns out to be controlled by a specific one, a handful of clauses that are consistent with either understanding of establishment by the State, and a resemblance between the tax-credit provision and the rest of the Tax Code. If that is all it takes to make something ambiguous, everything is ambiguous.

Having gone wrong in consulting statutory purpose at all, the Court goes wrong again in analyzing it. The purposes of a law must be "collected chiefly from its words," not "from extrinsic circumstances." *Sturges v. Crowninshield*, 4 Wheat. 122, 202 (1819) (Marshall, C. J.). . . .

The Court protests that without the tax credits, the number of people covered by the individual mandate shrinks, and without a broadly applicable individual mandate the guaranteed-issue and community-rating requirements "would destabilize the individual insurance market." *Ante*, at 15. If true, these projections would show only that the statutory scheme contains a flaw; they would not show that the statute means the opposite of what it says. Moreover, it is a flaw that appeared as well in other parts of the Act . . . .

Similarly, the Department of Health and Human Services originally interpreted the Act to impose guaranteed-issue and community-rating requirements in the Federal Territories, even though the Act plainly does not make the individual mandate applicable there. *Ibid.*; see 26 U. S. C. §5000A(f)(4); 42 U. S. C. §201(f). . . . The Department changed its mind a year later, after what it described as "a careful review of [the] situation and the relevant statutory language." . . . How could the Court pronounce it "implausible" for Congress to have tolerated instability in insurance markets in States with federal Exchanges, *ante*, at 17, when even the Government maintained until recently that Congress did exactly that in American Samoa, Guam, the Northern Mariana Islands, Puerto Rico, and the Virgin Islands?

Compounding its errors, the Court forgets that it is no more appropriate to consider one of a statute's purposes in isolation than it is to consider one of its words that way . . . . A State would have much less reason to take on these burdens if its citizens could receive tax credits no matter who establishes its Exchange. (Now that the Internal Revenue Service has interpreted §36B to authorize tax credits everywhere, by the way, 34 States have failed to set up their own Exchanges. *Ante*, at 6.) So even if making credits available on all Exchanges advances the goal of improving healthcare markets, it frustrates the goal of encouraging state involvement in the implementation of the Act. *This* is what justifies going out of our way to read "established by the State" to mean "established by the State or not established by the State"?

Worst of all for the repute of today's decision, the Court's reasoning is largely self-defeating. The Court predicts that making tax credits unavailable in States that do not set up their own Exchanges would cause disastrous economic consequences there. If that is so, however, wouldn't one expect States to react by setting up their own Exchanges? And wouldn't that outcome satisfy two of the Act's goals rather than just one: enabling the Act's reforms to work and promoting state involvement in the Act's implementation? The Court protests that the very existence of a federal fallback shows that Congress expected that some States might fail to set up their own Exchanges. *Ante*, at 19. . . .

IV

Perhaps sensing the dismal failure of its efforts to show that "established by the State" means "established by the State or the Federal Government," the Court tries to palm off the pertinent statutory phrase as "inartful drafting." *Ante*, at 14. This Court, however, has no free-floating power "to rescue Congress from its drafting errors." *Lamie v. United States Trustee*, 540 U. S. 526, 542 (2004) (internal quotation marks omitted). Only when it is patently obvious to a reasonable reader that a drafting mistake has occurred may a court correct the mistake . . . .

Let us not forget that the term "Exchange established by the State" appears twice in §36B and five more times in other parts of the Act that mention tax credits. What are the odds, do you think, that the same slip of the pen occurred in seven separate places? No provision of the Act—none at all—contradicts the limitation of tax credits to state Exchanges . . . .

V

The Court's decision reflects the philosophy that judges should endure whatever interpretive distortions it takes in order to correct a supposed flaw in the statutory machinery. That philosophy ignores the American people's decision to give *Congress* "[a]ll legislative Powers" enumerated in the Constitution. Art. I, §1. They made Congress, not this Court, responsible for both making laws and mending them. This Court holds only the judicial power—the power to pronounce the law as Congress has enacted it. We lack the prerogative to repair laws that do not work out in practice, just as the people lack the ability to throw us out of office if they dislike the solutions we concoct. We must always remember, therefore, that "[o]ur task is to apply the text, not to improve upon it." *Pavelic & LeFlore v. Marvel Entertainment Group, Div. of Cadence Industries Corp.*, 493 U. S. 120, 126 (1989).

Trying to make its judge-empowering approach seem respectful of congressional authority, the Court asserts that its decision merely ensures that the Affordable Care Act operates the way Congress "meant [it] to operate." *Ante*, at 17. First of all, what makes the Court so sure that Congress "meant" tax credits to be available everywhere? Our only evidence of what Congress meant comes from the terms of the law, and those terms show beyond all question that tax credits are available only on state Exchanges. More importantly, the Court forgets that ours is a government of laws and not of men. That means we are governed by the terms of our laws, not by the unenacted will of our lawmakers. "If Congress enacted into law something different from what it intended, then it should amend the statute to conform to its intent." *Lamie, supra*, at 542. In the meantime, this Court "has no roving license . . . to disregard clear language simply on the view that . . . Congress 'must have intended' something broader." *Bay Mills*, 572 U. S., at ___ (slip op., at 11).

Even less defensible, if possible, is the Court's claim that its interpretive approach is justified because this Act "does not reflect the type of care and deliberation that one might expect of such significant legislation." *Ante*, at 14–15. It is not our place to judge the quality of the care and deliberation that went into this or any other law. A law enacted by voice vote with no deliberation whatever is fully as binding upon us as one enacted after years of study, months of committee hearings, and weeks of debate. Much less is it our place to make everything come out right when Congress does not do its job properly. It is up to Congress to design its laws with care, and it is up to the people to hold them to account if they fail to carry out that responsibility.

Rather than rewriting the law under the pretense of interpreting it, the Court should have left it to Congress to decide what to do about the Act's limitation of tax credits to state Exchanges. If Congress values above everything else the Act's applicability across the country, it could make tax credits available in every Exchange. If it prizes state involvement in the Act's implementation, it could continue to limit tax credits to state Exchanges while taking other steps to mitigate the economic consequences predicted by the Court. If Congress wants to accommodate both goals, it could make tax credits available everywhere while offering new incentives for States to set up their own Exchanges. And if Congress thinks that the present design of the Act works well enough, it could do nothing. Congress could also do something else altogether, entirely abandoning the structure of the Affordable Care Act. The Court's insistence on making a choice that should be made by Congress both aggrandizes judicial power and encourages congressional lassitude.

Just ponder the significance of the Court's decision to take matters into its own hands. The Court's revision of the law authorizes the Internal Revenue Service to spend tens of billions of dollars every year in tax credits on federal Exchanges. It affects the price of insurance for millions of Americans. It diminishes the participation of the States in the implementation of the Act. It vastly expands the reach of the Act's individual mandate, whose scope depends in part on the availability of credits. What a parody today's decision makes of Hamilton's assurances to the people of New York: "The legislature not only commands the purse but prescribes the rules by which the duties and rights of every citizen are to be regulated. The judiciary, on the contrary, has no influence over . . . the purse; no direction . . . of the wealth of society, and can take no active resolution whatever. It may truly be said to have neither FORCE nor WILL but merely judgment." The Federalist No. 78, p. 465 (C. Rossiter ed. 1961).

***

Today's opinion changes the usual rules of statutory interpretation for the sake of the Affordable Care Act. That, alas, is not a novelty. In *National Federation of Independent Business v. Sebelius*, 567 U. S. ___, this Court revised major components of the statute in order to save them from unconstitutionality. The Act that Congress passed provides that every individual "shall" maintain insurance or else pay a "penalty." 26 U. S. C. §5000A. This Court, however, saw that the Commerce Clause does not authorize a federal mandate to buy health insurance. So it rewrote the mandate-cum-penalty as a tax. 567 U. S., at ___–___ (principal opinion) (slip op., at 15–45). The Act that Congress passed also requires every State to accept an expansion of its Medicaid program, or else risk losing *all* Medicaid funding. 42 U. S. C. §1396c. This Court, however, saw that the Spending Clause does not authorize this coercive condition. So it rewrote the law to withhold only the *incremental* funds associated with the Medicaid expansion. 567 U.S., at ___–___ (principal opinion) (slip op., at 45–58). Having transformed two major parts of the law, the Court today has turned its attention to a third. The Act that Congress passed makes tax credits available only on an "Exchange established by the State." This Court, however, concludes that this limitation would prevent the rest of the Act from working as well as hoped. So it rewrites the law to make tax credits available everywhere. We should start calling this law SCOTUScare.

Perhaps the Patient Protection and Affordable Care Act will attain the enduring status of the Social Security Act or the Taft-Hartley Act; perhaps not. But this Court's two decisions on the Act will surely be remembered through the years. The somersaults of statutory interpretation they have performed ("penalty" means tax, "further [Medicaid] payments to the State" means only incremental Medicaid payments to the State, "established by the State" means not established by the State) will be cited by litigants endlessly, to the confusion of honest jurisprudence. And the cases will publish forever the discouraging truth that the Supreme Court of the United States favors some laws over others, and is prepared to do whatever it takes to uphold and assist its favorites.

I dissent.

SOURCE: U.S. Supreme Court. *King v. Burwell*. 576 U.S.__(2015). www.supremecourt.gov/opinions/14pdf/14-114_qol1.pdf.

OTHER HISTORIC DOCUMENTS OF INTEREST

FROM PREVIOUS *HISTORIC DOCUMENTS*

Supreme Court Legalizes Same-Sex Marriage Nationwide

JUNE 26, 2015

In a historic opinion given on June 26, 2015, the U.S. Supreme Court ruled that same-sex couples have the same constitutionally protected right to marry that opposite-sex couples have. The closely divided 5–4 decision, *Obergefell v. Hodges,* came on the two-year anniversary of the Court's last major decision involving gay rights. That decision, *U.S. v. Windsor*, overturned the Defense of Marriage Act (DOMA), a law that had specifically denied federal marriage benefits to same-sex couples who had been legally married, but it did not directly address the broader issue of whether same-sex couples have a right to marry. In the two years since the *Windsor* opinion, the right to marry had spread across the country, led largely by the edict of lower federal courts, voter initiatives, and state legislation, such that by the time of the 2015 opinion, same-sex marriage was already legal in thirty-six states and the District of Columbia. At the same time, public opinion polling documented rapidly changing attitudes, showing a majority of Americans approving of such marriages. Following the landmark decision in *Obergefell,* all states were required to allow same-sex couples to marry.

Justice Anthony Kennedy wrote the majority opinion in this case, also having written the opinions in many of the Court's decisions expanding the legal rights of homosexual individuals. He was joined by the more liberal members of the Court: Justices Ruth Bader Ginsburg, Stephen Breyer, Sonia Sotomayor, and Elena Kagan.

THE COURT REVIEWS THE HISTORY OF MARRIAGE

Before addressing the particulars of the case before it, the majority first noted the history of marriage in soaring, romantic language. Justice Kennedy wrote, "The lifelong union of a man and a woman always has promised nobility and dignity to all persons, without regard to their station in life." To the religious, it is "sacred," and to the secular, he continued, it offers a "unique fulfillment." Marriage, Kennedy wrote, rises "from the most basic human needs" and "is essential to our most profound hopes and aspirations." He discussed the centrality of marriage "since the dawn of history," citing historic figures from Confucius to Cicero.

Those opposing same-sex marriage point out that this long history has been based on an understanding that marriage is a union between a man and a woman. The majority opinion found that, for the respondents, the allowance of same-sex marriage "would demean a timeless institution if the concept and lawful status of marriage were extended to two persons of the same sex." Justice Kennedy rejected this historical argument, asserting instead that "far from seeking to devalue marriage, the petitioners seek it for themselves because of their respect—and need—for its privileges and responsibilities. And their immutable nature dictates that same-sex marriage is their only real path to this profound commitment."

The majority then reviewed ways that our understanding of marriage has not been static but has gone through deep transformations over time. For example, marriages were once arranged by parents based on political, religious, and financial concerns, only changing to the idea of a voluntary contract between a man and a woman several hundred years ago. The changing status of women throughout history has impacted marriage profoundly as centuries-old doctrines that designate married women as legal property of their husbands have been cast aside. These changes, Justice Kennedy argued, have only "strengthened, not weakened, the institution of marriage."

The opinion then ran quickly through the changes in our country's experience with, and understanding of, same-sex rights. Until the mid-20th century, same-sex intimacy was condemned as immoral and was considered a crime in many states. An amicus brief from the Organization of American Historians described the experience of gays and lesbians as "prohibited from most government employment, barred from military service, excluded under immigration laws, targeted by police, and burdened in their rights to associate." Until recently, homosexuality was defined as a mental disorder by the psychiatric community. The first Supreme Court case to address the legal status of gay people was *Bowers v. Hardwick* in 1986, which upheld the right of states to criminalize homosexual intimacy. The Supreme Court reversed this decision in 2003 with the case *Lawrence v. Texas*, in an opinion written by Justice Kennedy.

In 2003, Massachusetts became the first state to hold that its state constitution guaranteed same-sex couples the right to marry. After that ruling, additional states legalized same-sex marriage either through legislatures, referendums, or judicial opinions. Other states amended their state constitutions to make it clear that they did not support rights to same-sex marriage. In the 2013 *Windsor* case, the Supreme Court, in another opinion penned by Justice Kennedy, invalidated DOMA in language that did not address the constitutionality of same-sex marriage directly, but strongly implied that it would uphold these marriages shortly. After that case, challenges to state laws and constitutions that barred same-sex couples from the institution of marriage were filed in almost every federal court in the country. Most reached the conclusion that excluding same-sex couples from marriage violates the U.S. Constitution. Justice Kennedy took the unusual step of attaching citations to all these cases to the end of his opinion as Appendix 1. Because the Sixth Circuit, encompassing Michigan, Kentucky, Ohio, and Tennessee, ruled the other way, there was a split in the courts, so the Supreme Court granted *certiorari* to resolve the issue nationwide.

STATES MAY NOT LAWFULLY REFUSE RECOGNITION OF SAME-SEX MARRIAGE

The central legal question in this case is whether the Fourteenth Amendment to the Constitution requires states to license a marriage between two people of the same sex. There are two clauses in this amendment that could form the foundation of the answer. The first is the Due Process Clause, which says that no state shall "deprive any person of life, liberty, or property without due process of law." This clause, writes Justice Kennedy, has been interpreted as protecting "fundamental liberties," extending to "certain personal choices central to individual dignity and autonomy, including intimate choices that define personal identity and beliefs."

In addressing whether the fundamental liberties arguments apply to the petitioners in this case, Justice Kennedy made clear his view that the Constitution is a living document that must evolve with societal changes, a view strongly opposed by the dissent, who are generally characterized as strict constructionists relying only on the views of the drafters to interpret the Constitution. Justice Kennedy wrote that those who developed and ratified the Constitution and Fourteenth Amendment "did not presume to know the extent of freedom in all of its dimensions, and so they entrusted to future generations a charter protecting the right of all persons to enjoy liberty as we learn its meaning."

Marriage has long been recognized as a fundamental right under the Due Process Clause. Justice Kennedy cited many such cases including *Loving v. Virginia*, the 1967 case that invalidated laws against interracial marriage in which the Court held marriage to be "one of the vital personal rights essential to the orderly pursuit of happiness." The *Obergefell* opinion goes on to explore the various rationales that courts have given over time for finding marriage to be such an important institution, and it found that all the same principles apply equally whether the couples involved be "opposite-sex" or "same-sex." For example, the intimate decisions involving whether to get married or whom to marry are "among life's momentous acts of self-definition" and deeply implicate an individual's "personal autonomy." One Supreme Court case from 1987 held that the right to marriage was so essential that it could not be denied to convicted prisoners because marriage dignifies couples who "wish to define themselves by their commitment to each other." Another justification for the importance placed on marriage is that it safeguards children and families, although Justice Kennedy was clear that this does not mean that the right to marry can in any way be conditioned on procreation. He talked about the permanency and stability so important to children and afforded and protected by marriage. Marriage laws that deny this to hundreds of thousands of children currently being raised by same-sex couples "harm and humiliate the children" who "suffer the stigma of knowing their families are somehow lesser."

The Equal Protection Clause of the Fourteenth Amendment is closely related to the Due Process Clause, and the Court here ruled that under them both, same-sex couples may not be deprived of the right and liberty that comes from marriage. In the 1970s, the Court relied on the Equal Protection clause to invalidate many of the marriage laws that imposed a legally subordinate role to women, showing, Justice Kennedy wrote, that "the Equal Protection Clause can help to identify and correct inequalities in the institution of marriage, vindicating precepts of liberty and equality under the Constitution."

Finally, Justice Kennedy addressed some of the leading objections raised by his opinion. The dissent chose to frame the issue in this case as whether the Constitution recognizes a "new" right called the "right to same-sex marriage" rather than whether same-sex couples may exercise the same "right to marry" exercised by opposite-sex couples. He argued that such an approach has been rejected in the past, since the Supreme Court did not ask whether the Constitution protects a "right to interracial marriage," a "right of inmates to marry," or a "right of fathers with unpaid child support duties to marry." Rather, these precedents all found no justification to exclude these parties from the "right to marry."

FOUR DISSENTING OPINIONS

The four more conservative members of the Court—Chief Justice John Roberts Jr., Justice Antonin Scalia, Justice Clarence Thomas, and Justice Samuel Alito—dissented from the majority opinion. Each wrote his own separate dissenting opinion in tones that *The New York Times* described as "ranging from resigned dismay to bitter scorn."

The dissenters' arguments shared a common theme: the Court's judicial activism had usurped the role of the democratic process to create by fiat a brand new right. Chief Justice Roberts marked his strong disagreement by, for the first time in his ten years on the bench, reading from his dissent in open court. He argued that, even though the majority had strong points to make based in social policy and fairness, it is not the court's role to order "the transformation of a social institution that has formed the basis of human society for millennia." "Just who do we think we are?" Justice Roberts asked. "[T]his Court is not a legislature. Whether same-sex marriage is a good idea should be of no concern to us." He did not, however, begrudge the genuine celebrations of the supporters of marriage inclusion. "Celebrate the achievement of a desired goal. Celebrate the opportunity for a new expression of commitment to a partner. Celebrate the availability of new benefits. But do not celebrate the Constitution. It had nothing to do with it."

The three other dissenting opinions shared Chief Justice Roberts's views. Justice Scalia described the majority decision as "a threat to American democracy," robbing citizens of "the freedom to govern themselves." In caustic language, he criticized the lofty style of Justice Kennedy's opinion for being "as pretentious as its content was egotistic." The majority opinion, he wrote, "discovered" a new "fundamental right" that had been "overlooked by every person alive at the time of ratification, and almost everyone else in the time since."

REACTION TO THE HISTORIC RULING AND ITS IMPACT

Immediately after the release of the opinion, huge crowds waving rainbow flags celebrated on the sidewalk in front of the Supreme Court. President Barack Obama read a statement from the White House Rose Garden calling the ruling "a victory for America," affirming that "when all Americans are truly treated as equal, we are more free." The named plaintiff, Jim Obergefell, reacted to the ruling, saying it "affirms what millions across the country already know to be true in our hearts: that our love is equal."

The decision nullified bans on same-sex marriage in all fifty states and required states to begin issuing marriage licenses. Kim Davis, a county clerk in Kentucky, received national attention for refusing to issue licenses to same-sex couples, despite the Supreme Court's ruling, based on her religious beliefs. Her case illustrated what most legal commenters predict will be the next wave of litigation involving gay marriage: arguments that religious liberty protected by the First Amendment will be in conflict with same-sex marriage. President Obama's statement included a reference to the many people who oppose same-sex marriage "based on sincere and deeply held beliefs" and called on Americans to "recognize different viewpoints; revere our deep commitment to religious freedom." In his opinion, Justice Kennedy emphasized that the "First Amendment ensures that religious organizations and persons are given proper protection as they seek to teach the principles that are so fulfilling and so central to their lives and faiths, and to their own deep aspirations to continue the family structure they have long revered." In his dissent, Justice Thomas, however, dismissed this language as a "weak gesture," and Chief Justice Roberts responded similarly that "people of faith can take no comfort in the treatment they receive from the majority today." The chief justice added that "hard questions arise when people of faith exercise religion in ways that conflict with the new right to same-sex marriage."

—Melissa Feinberg

Following is the edited text of the Supreme Court's decision in Obergefell v. Hodges, *in which the Court ruled in a 5–4 decision that the Constitution provides same-sex couples the right to marry.*

DOCUMENT   *Obergefell v. Hodges*

June 26, 2015

[Footnotes have been omitted.]

James Obergefell, et al., petitioners	Nos. 14-556, 14-562, 14-571, and 14-574
v.	
Richard Hodges, Director, Ohio Department of Health, et al.	
Valeria Tanco, et al., petitioners	
v.	
Bill Haslam, Governor of Tennessee, et al.	On writs of certiorari to the United States Court of Appeals for the Sixth Circuit
April Deboer, et al., petitioners	
v.	
Rick Snyder, Governor of Michigan, et al.	
Gregory Bourke, et al., petitioners	
v.	
Steve Beshear, Governor of Kentucky	[June 26, 2015]

JUSTICE KENNEDY delivered the opinion of the Court.

The Constitution promises liberty to all within its reach, a liberty that includes certain specific rights that allow persons, within a lawful realm, to define and express their identity. The petitioners in these cases seek to find that liberty by marrying someone of the same sex and having their marriages deemed lawful on the same terms and conditions as marriages between persons of the opposite sex.

[Sections I and II, containing the background of the case and the history of Supreme Court rulings on same-sex rights, have been omitted.]

III

Under the Due Process Clause of the Fourteenth Amendment, no State shall "deprive any person of life, liberty, or property, without due process of law." The fundamental liberties protected by this Clause include most of the rights enumerated in the Bill of Rights. See *Duncan v. Louisiana*, 391 U. S. 145, 147–149 (1968). In addition these liberties extend to certain personal choices central to individual dignity and autonomy, including intimate choices that define personal identity and beliefs. See, *e.g., Eisenstadt v. Baird*, 405 U. S. 438, 453 (1972); *Griswold v. Connecticut*, 381 U. S. 479, 484–486 (1965).

The identification and protection of fundamental rights is an enduring part of the judicial duty to interpret the Constitution. That responsibility, however, "has not been reduced to any formula." *Poe v. Ullman*, 367 U. S. 497, 542 (1961) (Harlan, J., dissenting). Rather, it requires courts to exercise reasoned judgment in identifying interests of the person so fundamental that the State must accord them its respect. See *ibid.* That process is guided by many of the same considerations relevant to analysis of other constitutional provisions that set forth broad principles rather than specific requirements. History and tradition guide and discipline this inquiry but do not set its outer boundaries. See *Lawrence, supra,* at 572. That method respects our history and learns from it without allowing the past alone to rule the present.

The nature of injustice is that we may not always see it in our own times. The generations that wrote and ratified the Bill of Rights and the Fourteenth Amendment did not presume to know the extent of freedom in all of its dimensions, and so they entrusted to future generations a charter protecting the right of all persons to enjoy liberty as we learn its meaning. When new insight reveals discord between the Constitution's central protections and a received legal stricture, a claim to liberty must be addressed.

Applying these established tenets, the Court has long held the right to marry is protected by the Constitution. In *Loving v. Virginia*, 388 U. S. 1, 12 (1967), which invalidated bans on interracial unions, a unanimous Court held marriage is "one of the vital personal rights essential to the orderly pursuit of happiness by free men." The Court reaffirmed that holding in *Zablocki v. Redhail*, 434 U. S. 374, 384 (1978), which held the right to marry was burdened by a law prohibiting fathers who were behind on child support from marrying. The Court again applied this principle in *Turner v. Safley*, 482 U. S. 78, 95 (1987), which held the right to marry was abridged by regulations limiting the privilege of prison inmates to marry. Over time and in other contexts, the Court has reiterated that the right to marry is fundamental under the Due Process Clause. See, *e.g., M. L. B. v. S. L. J.*, 519 U. S. 102, 116 (1996); *Cleveland Bd. of Ed. v. LaFleur*, 414 U. S. 632, 639–640 (1974); *Griswold, supra,* at 486; *Skinner v. Oklahoma ex rel. Williamson*, 316 U. S. 535, 541 (1942); *Meyer v. Nebraska*, 262 U. S. 390, 399 (1923).

It cannot be denied that this Court's cases describing the right to marry presumed a relationship involving opposite-sex partners. The Court, like many institutions, has made assumptions defined by the world and time of which it is a part. This was evident in *Baker v. Nelson*, 409 U. S. 810, a one-line summary decision issued in 1972, holding the exclusion of same-sex couples from marriage did not present a substantial federal question.

Still, there are other, more instructive precedents. This Court's cases have expressed constitutional principles of broader reach. In defining the right to marry these cases have identified essential attributes of that right based in history, tradition, and other constitutional liberties inherent in this intimate bond. See, *e.g., Lawrence*, 539 U. S., at 574; *Turner, supra*, at 95; *Zablocki, supra*, at 384; *Loving, supra*, at 12; *Griswold, supra*, at 486. And in assessing whether the force and rationale of its cases apply to same-sex couples, the Court must respect the basic reasons why the right to marry has been long protected. See, e.g., *Eisenstadt, supra*, at 453–454; *Poe, supra*, at 542–553 (Harlan, J., dissenting).

This analysis compels the conclusion that same-sex couples may exercise the right to marry. The four principles and traditions to be discussed demonstrate that the reasons marriage is fundamental under the Constitution apply with equal force to same-sex couples.

A first premise of the Court's relevant precedents is that the right to personal choice regarding marriage is inherent in the concept of individual autonomy. This abiding connection between marriage and liberty is why *Loving* invalidated interracial marriage bans under the Due Process Clause. See 388 U. S., at 12; see also *Zablocki, supra*, at 384 (observing *Loving* held "the right to marry is of fundamental importance for all individuals"). Like choices concerning contraception, family relationships, procreation, and childrearing, all of which are protected by the Constitution, decisions concerning marriage are among the most intimate that an individual can make. See *Lawrence, supra*, at 574. Indeed, the Court has noted it would be contradictory "to recognize a right of privacy with respect to other matters of family life and not with respect to the decision to enter the relationship that is the foundation of the family in our society." *Zablocki, supra*, at 386.

Choices about marriage shape an individual's destiny. As the Supreme Judicial Court of Massachusetts has explained, because "it fulfils yearnings for security, safe haven, and connection that express our common humanity, civil marriage is an esteemed institution, and the decision whether and whom to marry is among life's momentous acts of self-definition." Goodridge, 440 Mass., at 322, 798 N. E. 2d, at 955.

The nature of marriage is that, through its enduring bond, two persons together can find other freedoms, such as expression, intimacy, and spirituality. This is true for all persons, whatever their sexual orientation. See *Windsor*, 570 U. S., at ___–___ (slip op., at 22–23). There is dignity in the bond between two men or two women who seek to marry and in their autonomy to make such profound choices. Cf. *Loving, supra*, at 12 ("[T]he freedom to marry, or not marry, a person of another race resides with the individual and cannot be infringed by the State").

A second principle in this Court's jurisprudence is that the right to marry is fundamental because it supports a two-person union unlike any other in its importance to the committed individuals. This point was central to *Griswold v. Connecticut*, which held the Constitution protects the right of married couples to use contraception. . . . And in *Turner*, the Court again acknowledged the intimate association protected by this right, holding prisoners could not be denied the right to marry because their committed relationships satisfied the basic reasons why marriage is a fundamental right. The right to marry thus dignifies couples who "wish to define themselves by their commitment to each other." Marriage responds to the universal fear that a lonely person might call out only to find no one there. It offers the hope of companionship and understanding and assurance that while both still live there will be someone to care for the other. . . .

A third basis for protecting the right to marry is that it safeguards children and families and thus draws meaning from related rights of childrearing, procreation, and education. . . . Under the laws of the several States, some of marriage's protections for children and families are material. But marriage also confers more profound benefits. By giving recognition and legal structure to their parents' relationship, marriage allows children "to understand the integrity and closeness of their own family and its concord with other families in their community and in their daily lives." *Windsor, supra*, at ___ (slip op., at 23). Marriage also affords the permanency and stability important to children's best interests. See Brief for Scholars of the Constitutional Rights of Children as *Amici Curiae* 22–27.

As all parties agree, many same-sex couples provide loving and nurturing homes to their children, whether biological or adopted. And hundreds of thousands of children are presently being raised by such couples. . . . Most States have allowed gays and lesbians to adopt, either as individuals or as couples, and many adopted and foster children have same-sex parents, see id., at 5. This provides powerful confirmation from the law itself that gays and lesbians can create loving, supportive families.

Excluding same-sex couples from marriage thus conflicts with a central premise of the right to marry. Without the recognition, stability, and predictability marriage offers, their children suffer the stigma of knowing their families are somehow lesser. They also suffer the significant material costs of being raised by unmarried parents, relegated through no fault of their own to a more difficult and uncertain family life. The marriage laws at issue here thus harm and humiliate the children of same-sex couples. . . .

Fourth and finally, this Court's cases and the Nation's traditions make clear that marriage is a keystone of our social order. . . . The States have contributed to the fundamental character of the marriage right by placing that institution at the center of so many facets of the legal and social order.

As the State itself makes marriage all the more precious by the significance it attaches to it, exclusion from that status has the effect of teaching that gays and lesbians are unequal in important respects. It demeans gays and lesbians for the State to lock them out of a central institution of the Nation's society. Same-sex couples, too, may aspire to the transcendent purposes of marriage and seek fulfillment in its highest meaning.

The limitation of marriage to opposite-sex couples may long have seemed natural and just, but its inconsistency with the central meaning of the fundamental right to marry is now manifest. With that knowledge must come the recognition that laws excluding same-sex couples from the marriage right impose stigma and injury of the kind prohibited by our basic charter.

The right to marry is fundamental as a matter of history and tradition, but rights come not from ancient sources alone. They rise, too, from a better informed understanding of how constitutional imperatives define a liberty that remains urgent in our own era. Many who deem same-sex marriage to be wrong reach that conclusion based on decent and honorable religious or philosophical premises, and neither they nor their beliefs are disparaged here. But when that sincere, personal opposition becomes enacted law and public policy, the necessary consequence is to put the imprimatur of the State itself on an exclusion that soon demeans or stigmatizes those whose own liberty is then denied. Under the Constitution, same-sex couples seek in marriage the same legal treatment as opposite-sex couples, and it would disparage their choices and diminish their personhood to deny them this right.

[Additional discussion about equal protection has been omitted.]

IV

There may be an initial inclination in these cases to proceed with caution—to await further legislation, litigation, and debate. . . .

Yet there has been far more deliberation than this argument acknowledges. There have been referenda, legislative debates, and grassroots campaigns, as well as countless studies, papers, books, and other popular and scholarly writings. There has been extensive litigation in state and federal courts. See Appendix A, *infra*. Judicial opinions addressing the issue have been informed by the contentions of parties and counsel, which, in turn, reflect the more general, societal discussion of same-sex marriage and its meaning that has occurred over the past decades. As more than 100 *amici* make clear in their filings, many of the central institutions in American life—state and local governments, the military, large and small businesses, labor unions, religious organizations, law enforcement, civic groups, professional organizations, and universities—have devoted substantial attention to the question. This has led to an enhanced understanding of the issue—an understanding reflected in the arguments now presented for resolution as a matter of constitutional law. . . .

The dynamic of our constitutional system is that individuals need not await legislative action before asserting a fundamental right. The Nation's courts are open to injured individuals who come to them to vindicate their own direct, personal stake in our basic charter. An individual can invoke a right to constitutional protection when he or she is harmed, even if the broader public disagrees and even if the legislature refuses to act. The idea of the Constitution "was to withdraw certain subjects from the vicissitudes of political controversy, to place them beyond the reach of majorities and officials and to establish them as legal principles to be applied by the courts." *West Virginia Bd. of Ed. v. Barnette*, 319 U. S. 624, 638 (1943). This is why "fundamental rights may not be submitted to a vote; they depend on the outcome of no elections." *Ibid.* It is of no moment whether advocates of same-sex marriage now enjoy or lack momentum in the democratic process. The issue before the Court here is the legal question whether the Constitution protects the right of same sex couples to marry.

[A brief review on earlier similar cases before the Court has been omitted.]

Finally, it must be emphasized that religions, and those who adhere to religious doctrines, may continue to advocate with utmost, sincere conviction that, by divine precepts, same-sex marriage should not be condoned. The First Amendment ensures that religious organizations and persons are given proper protection as they seek to teach the principles that are so fulfilling and so central to their lives and faiths, and to their own deep aspirations to continue the family structure they have long revered. The same is true of those who oppose same-sex marriage for other reasons. In turn, those who believe allowing same sex marriage is proper or indeed essential, whether as a matter of religious conviction or secular belief, may engage those who disagree with their view in an open and searching debate. The Constitution, however, does not permit the State to bar same-sex couples from marriage on the same terms as accorded to couples of the opposite sex.

V

These cases also present the question whether the Constitution requires States to recognize same-sex marriages validly performed out of State. As made clear by the case of Obergefell and Arthur, and by that of DeKoe and Kostura, the recognition bans inflict substantial and continuing harm on same-sex couples.

Being married in one State but having that valid marriage denied in another is one of "the most perplexing and distressing complication[s]" in the law of domestic relations. *Williams v. North Carolina*, 317 U. S. 287, 299 (1942) (internal quotation marks omitted). Leaving the current state of affairs in place would maintain and promote instability and uncertainty. For some couples, even an ordinary drive into a neighboring State to visit family or friends risks causing severe hardship in the event of a spouse's hospitalization while across state lines. In light of the fact that many States already allow same-sex marriage—and hundreds of thousands of these marriages already have occurred—the disruption caused by the recognition bans is significant and ever-growing.

As counsel for the respondents acknowledged at argument, if States are required by the Constitution to issue marriage licenses to same-sex couples, the justifications for refusing to recognize those marriages performed elsewhere are undermined. See Tr. of Oral Arg. on Question 2, p. 44. The Court, in this decision, holds same-sex couples may exercise the fundamental right to marry in all States. It follows that the Court also must hold—and it now does hold—that there is no lawful basis for a State to refuse to recognize a lawful same-sex marriage performed in another State on the ground of its same-sex character.

* * *

No union is more profound than marriage, for it embodies the highest ideals of love, fidelity, devotion, sacrifice, and family. In forming a marital union, two people become something greater than once they were. As some of the petitioners in these cases demonstrate, marriage embodies a love that may endure even past death. It would misunderstand these men and women to say they disrespect the idea of marriage. Their plea is that they do respect it, respect it so deeply that they seek to find its fulfillment for themselves. Their hope is not to be condemned to live in loneliness, excluded from one of civilization's oldest institutions. They ask for equal dignity in the eyes of the law. The Constitution grants them that right.

The judgment of the Court of Appeals for the Sixth Circuit is reversed.

It is so ordered.

[The appendices have been omitted.]

CHIEF JUSTICE ROBERTS, with whom JUSTICE SCALIA and JUSTICE THOMAS join, dissenting.

Petitioners make strong arguments rooted in social policy and considerations of fairness. They contend that same-sex couples should be allowed to affirm their love and commitment through marriage, just like opposite-sex couples. That position has undeniable appeal; over the past six years, voters and legislators in eleven States and the District of Columbia have revised their laws to allow marriage between two people of the same sex.

But this Court is not a legislature. Whether same-sex marriage is a good idea should be of no concern to us. Under the Constitution, judges have power to say what the law is, not what it should be. The people who ratified the Constitution authorized courts to exercise "neither force nor will but merely judgment." The Federalist No. 78, p. 465 (C. Rossiter ed. 1961) (A. Hamilton) (capitalization altered).

Although the policy arguments for extending marriage to same-sex couples may be compelling, the legal arguments for requiring such an extension are not. The fundamental right to marry does not include a right to make a State change its definition of marriage. And a State's decision to maintain the meaning of marriage that has persisted in every culture throughout human history can hardly be called irrational. In short, our Constitution does not enact any one theory of marriage. The people of a State are free to expand marriage to include same-sex couples, or to retain the historic definition.

Today, however, the Court takes the extraordinary step of ordering every State to license and recognize same-sex marriage. Many people will rejoice at this decision, and I begrudge none their celebration. But for those who believe in a government of laws, not of men, the majority's approach is deeply disheartening. Supporters of same-sex marriage have achieved considerable success persuading their fellow citizens—through the democratic process—to adopt their view. That ends today. Five lawyers have closed the debate and enacted their own vision of marriage as a matter of constitutional law. Stealing this issue from the people will for many cast a cloud over same-sex marriage, making a dramatic social change that much more difficult to accept.

The majority's decision is an act of will, not legal judgment. The right it announces has no basis in the Constitution or this Court's precedent. . . . Just who do we think we are?

It can be tempting for judges to confuse our own preferences with the requirements of the law. But as this Court has been reminded throughout our history, the Constitution "is made for people of fundamentally differing views." *Lochner v. New York*, 198 U. S. 45, 76 (1905) (Holmes, J., dissenting). . . .

Understand well what this dissent is about: It is not about whether, in my judgment, the institution of marriage should be changed to include same-sex couples. It is instead about whether, in our democratic republic, that decision should rest with the people acting through their elected representatives, or with five lawyers who happen to hold commissions authorizing them to resolve legal disputes according to law. The Constitution leaves no doubt about the answer.

[The body of Chief Justice Roberts's dissent has been omitted.]

If you are among the many Americans—of whatever sexual orientation—who favor expanding same-sex marriage, by all means celebrate today's decision. Celebrate the achievement of a desired goal. Celebrate the opportunity for a new expression of commitment to a partner. Celebrate the availability of new benefits. But do not celebrate the Constitution. It had nothing to do with it.

I respectfully dissent.

JUSTICE SCALIA, with whom JUSTICE THOMAS joins, dissenting.

I join THE CHIEF JUSTICE's opinion in full. I write separately to call attention to this Court's threat to American democracy.

The substance of today's decree is not of immense personal importance to me. The law can recognize as marriage whatever sexual attachments and living arrangements it wishes, and can accord them favorable civil consequences, from tax treatment to rights of inheritance. Those civil consequences—and the public approval that conferring the name of marriage evidences—can perhaps have adverse social effects, but no more adverse than the effects of many other controversial laws. So it is not of special importance to me what the law says about marriage. It is of overwhelming importance, however, who it is that rules me. Today's decree says that my Ruler, and the Ruler of 320 million Americans coast-to-coast, is a majority of the nine lawyers on the Supreme Court. The opinion in these cases is the furthest extension in fact—and the furthest extension one can even imagine—of the Court's claimed power to create "liberties" that the Constitution and its Amendments neglect to mention. This practice of constitutional revision by an unelected committee of nine, always accompanied (as it is today) by extravagant praise of liberty, robs the People of the most important liberty they asserted in the Declaration of Independence and won in the Revolution of 1776: the freedom to govern themselves.

[The body of Justice Scalia's dissent has been omitted.]

***

Hubris is sometimes defined as o'erweening pride; and pride, we know, goeth before a fall. The Judiciary is the "least dangerous" of the federal branches because it has "neither Force nor Will, but merely judgment; and must ultimately depend upon the aid of the executive arm" and the States, "even for the efficacy of its judgments." *[The Federalist No. 78, pp. 522, 523 (J. Cooke ed. 1961) (A. Hamilton).]* With each decision of ours that takes from the People a question properly left to them—with each decision that is unabashedly based not on law, but on the "reasoned judgment" of a bare majority of this Court—we move one step closer to being reminded of our impotence.

JUSTICE THOMAS, with whom JUSTICE SCALIA joins, dissenting.

The Court's decision today is at odds not only with the Constitution, but with the principles upon which our Nation was built. Since well before 1787, liberty has been understood as freedom from government action, not entitlement to government benefits. The Framers created our Constitution to preserve that understanding of liberty. Yet the majority invokes our Constitution in the name of a "liberty" that the Framers would not have recognized, to the detriment of the liberty they sought to protect. Along the way, it rejects the idea—captured in our Declaration of Independence—that human dignity is innate and suggests instead that it comes from the Government. This distortion of our Constitution not only ignores the text, it inverts the relationship between the individual and the state in our Republic. I cannot agree with it.

I

The majority's decision today will require States to issue marriage licenses to same-sex couples and to recognize same-sex marriages entered in other States largely based on a constitutional provision guaranteeing "due process" before a person is deprived of his "life, liberty, or property." I have elsewhere explained the dangerous fiction of treating the Due Process Clause as a font of substantive rights. *McDonald v. Chicago*, 561 U. S. 742, 811–812 (2010) (THOMAS, J., concurring in part and concurring in judgment). It distorts the constitutional text, which guarantees only whatever "process" is "due" before a person is deprived of life, liberty, and property. U. S. Const., Amdt. 14, §1. Worse, it invites judges to do exactly what the majority has done here—"'roa[m] at large in the constitutional field' guided only by their personal views" as to the 'fundamental rights'" protected by that document. *Planned Parenthood of Southeastern Pa. v. Casey*, 505 U. S. 833, 953, 965 (1992) (Rehnquist, C. J., concurring in judgment in part and dissenting in part) (quoting *Griswold v. Connecticut*, 381 U. S. 479, 502 (1965) (Harlan, J., concurring in judgment)).

By straying from the text of the Constitution, substantive due process exalts judges at the expense of the People from whom they derive their authority.
[The body of Justice Thomas' dissent has been omitted.]

***

Our Constitution—like the Declaration of Independence before it—was predicated on a simple truth: One's liberty, not to mention one's dignity, was something to be shielded from—not provided by—the State. Today's decision casts that truth aside. In its haste to reach a desired result, the majority misapplies a clause focused on "due process" to afford substantive rights, disregards the most plausible understanding of the "liberty" protected by that clause, and distorts the principles on which this Nation was founded. Its decision will have inestimable consequences for our Constitution and our society. I respectfully dissent.

JUSTICE ALITO, with whom JUSTICE SCALIA and JUSTICE THOMAS join, dissenting.

Until the federal courts intervened, the American people were engaged in a debate about whether their States should recognize same-sex marriage. The question in these cases, however, is not what States *should* do about same-sex marriage but whether the Constitution answers that question for them. It does not. The Constitution leaves that question to be decided by the people of each State.

I

The Constitution says nothing about a right to same-sex marriage, but the Court holds that the term "liberty" in the Due Process Clause of the Fourteenth Amendment encompasses this right. Our Nation was founded upon the principle that every person has the unalienable right to liberty, but liberty is a term of many meanings. For classical liberals, it may include economic rights now limited by government regulation. For social democrats, it may include the right to a variety of government benefits. For today's majority, it has a distinctively postmodern meaning.

To prevent five unelected Justices from imposing their personal vision of liberty upon the American people, the Court has held that "liberty" under the Due Process Clause should be understood to protect only those rights that are "'deeply rooted in this Nation's history and tradition.'" *Washington v. Glucksberg*, 521 U. S. 701, 720–721 (1997). And it is beyond dispute that the right to same-sex marriage is not among those rights. . . .

For today's majority, it does not matter that the right to same-sex marriage lacks deep roots or even that it is contrary to long-established tradition. The Justices in the majority claim the authority to confer constitutional protection upon that right simply because they believe that it is fundamental.

[Section II has been omitted, and contained further discussion on the majority opinion.]

III

Today's decision usurps the constitutional right of the people to decide whether to keep or alter the traditional understanding of marriage. The decision will also have other important consequences.

It will be used to vilify Americans who are unwilling to assent to the new orthodoxy. In the course of its opinion, the majority compares traditional marriage laws to laws that denied equal treatment for African-Americans and women. *E.g., ante*, at 11–13. The implications of this analogy will be exploited by those who are determined to stamp out every vestige of dissent.

Perhaps recognizing how its reasoning may be used, the majority attempts, toward the end of its opinion, to reassure those who oppose same-sex marriage that their rights of conscience will be protected. *Ante*, at 26–27. We will soon see whether this proves to be true. I assume that those who cling to old beliefs will be able to whisper their thoughts in the recesses of their homes, but if they repeat those views in public, they will risk being labeled as bigots and treated as such by governments, employers, and schools.

The system of federalism established by our Constitution provides a way for people with different beliefs to live together in a single nation. If the issue of same-sex marriage had been left to the people of the States, it is likely that some States would recognize same-sex marriage and others would not. It is also possible that some States would tie recognition to protection for conscience rights. The majority today makes that impossible. By imposing its own views on the entire country, the majority facilitates the marginalization of the many Americans who have traditional ideas. Recalling the harsh treatment of gays and lesbians in the past, some may think that turnabout is fair play. But if that sentiment prevails, the Nation will experience bitter and lasting wounds.

Today's decision will also have a fundamental effect on this Court and its ability to uphold the rule of law. If a bare majority of Justices can invent a new right and impose that right on the rest of the country, the only real limit on what future majorities will be able to do is their own sense of what those with political power and cultural influence are willing to tolerate. Even enthusiastic supporters of same-sex marriage should worry about the scope of the power that today's majority claims.

Today's decision shows that decades of attempts to restrain this Court's abuse of its authority have failed. A lesson that some will take from today's decision is that preaching about the proper method of interpreting the Constitution or the virtues of judicial self-restraint and humility cannot compete with the temptation to achieve what is viewed as a noble end by any practicable means. I do not doubt that my colleagues in the majority sincerely see in the Constitution a vision of liberty that happens to coincide with their own. But this sincerity is cause for concern, not comfort. What it evidences is the deep and perhaps irremediable corruption of our legal culture's conception of constitutional interpretation.

Most Americans—understandably—will cheer or lament today's decision because of their views on the issue of same-sex marriage. But all Americans, whatever their thinking on that issue, should worry about what the majority's claim of power portends.

SOURCE: U.S. Supreme Court. *Obergefell v. Hodges*. 576 U.S.___(2015). http://www.supremecourt.gov/opinions/14pdf/14-556_3204.pdf.

OTHER HISTORIC DOCUMENTS OF INTEREST

FROM PREVIOUS *HISTORIC DOCUMENTS*

Eurogroup and International Monetary Fund Respond to Greek Debt Default

JUNE 27 AND 30, AND AUGUST 14, 2015

Greece's debt crisis worsened on June 30, 2015, when its government defaulted on debt repayments due to be made to the International Monetary Fund (IMF). The IMF and the European Union (EU) have been Greece's primary creditors since the first bailout package was agreed to in 2010 to keep Greece inside the eurozone, comprised of the EU's countries who share a common currency. The 2015 default occurred because negotiations between Greece and its eurozone partners for a replacement third bailout program had broken down days earlier. The new program would require major reforms of the Greek economy and more cuts in public spending, both of which were difficult for the Greek public to accept. The crisis was short-lived, however, when a third program was agreed to by mid-August. The new deal held out the possibility that Greece may be granted some debt relief if it fully implements the reform package.

TROUBLED EUROZONE MEMBERSHIP

Greece joined the eurozone in 2001, a few months before the euro notes and coins went into circulation. Since then, eurozone membership has grown from twelve countries to nineteen out of the EU's twenty-eight member states. Greece's membership has been the most problematic of all from the outset, mainly because of the poor state of its public finances. Since being founded as a modern state in 1829, the Greek government has consistently run up deficits and amounted large debts. The problem became more acute, however, after its economy began to contract sharply following the 2008 global financial crisis.

No country has left the eurozone since its creation and there was strong political pressure to do whatever it took to keep Greece inside. Even while Greece chafed at the austerity measures imposed by its eurozone partners, its citizens were generally anxious that Greece stay an EU and eurozone member. A eurozone exit—or a Grexit, as it was dubbed in the press—could be devastating for Greece because it would likely cause a sudden devaluation of whatever national currency it reintroduced, combined with soaring inflation and a commensurate drop in living standards.

In January 2015, a new chapter in Greek–EU relations was opened when parliamentary elections were won by the far-left Syriza party, which competed on an antiausterity platform. A showdown with its EU counterparts was inevitable, especially since Greece's bailout program with the EU was expiring. The two key Greek political figures in the drama that unfolded over the next eight months were the newly elected prime minister, Alexis Tsipras, and his finance minister, Yanis Varoufakis.

On the EU side, the dominant figure was Wolfgang Schäuble, the finance minister of Germany. As the EU's largest economy by far, Germany was Greece's biggest creditor, having provided loans of €56 billion ($61.5 billion) out of Greece's total debts of €323 billion. Schauble became deeply unpopular with Greeks because he kept urging the EU to hold firm in demanding that Greece follow through on commitments made under previous bailout programs agreed to between 2010 and 2012. Crucially, Schäuble opposed the Greek government's demand that the country be granted so-called debt relief, meaning that some of its debts should be written off. Schäuble's detractors accused him of deliberately trying to drive Greece out of the eurozone by adopting such an intransigent stance.

Schäuble's strongest supporters in defending his hardline view were other northern European eurozone members, notably The Netherlands and Finland. By contrast France and Italy, Greece's second and third largest creditors, which were led by socialist governments, were more receptive to Athens' argument that endless austerity had killed Greece's economic recovery. Even though the Greek government had cut public spending since 2009, Greece's debt-to-GDP ratio kept increasing because its economy continued contracting. The Greek economy shrank around 20 percent since 2009, unemployment rose to 25 percent, and the public debt increased to 177 percent of GDP. Across the Atlantic, both the IMF, which was a significant creditor of Greece, having loaned €32 billion, and the United States advised the European Union to restructure or relieve Greece's debts because they had become unsustainable.

GREECE CALLS FOR REFERENDUM

Greece's eurozone bailout program is managed by an institution called the European Stability Mechanism, which was established during the first eurozone debt crisis from 2009 to 2011. The Greek program expired at the end of 2014, but in February 2015, EU leaders decided to extend it until the end of June to give time for a replacement program to be negotiated with the Greek government. Relationships grew increasingly fractious as the weeks went by and the creditor nations continued to refuse to bow to Prime Minister Tsipras's demands that debt relief be a part of the discussion. On June 26, negotiations were broken off. Tsipras decided to put the EU's most recent offer directly to the Greek people in a referendum to be held on July 5. His EU counterparts strongly disapproved of this move.

Meanwhile, with the EU financial support expiring at the end of June, Greece found itself unable to make a debt repayment to the IMF of €1.2 billion Special Drawing Rights (a supplementary international reserve asset)—about $1.66 billion—that it was scheduled to make by June 30. The IMF announced that Greece was consequently in arrears, which marked the first time that a developed country had defaulted on debt repayments to the IMF. As the crisis escalated, the Greek government moved to avoid a flight of capital from the country by ordering banks to shut their doors and limiting the amount of money that account holders could withdraw from ATM machines to €60 per day. The government meanwhile, in the hastily called referendum, urged voters to reject the EU offer, which they did by a margin of 61 percent to 39 percent.

FRAUGHT NEGOTIATIONS RESULT IN BAILOUT

Buoyed by the referendum victory, Prime Minister Tsipras returned to the negotiating table demanding more concessions. During a summit in Brussels on July 12, eurozone leaders laid out the broad parameters of a compromise. They entailed keeping Greece inside the eurozone by providing further financial aid in return for Greece undertaking fiscal, structural, and economic reforms. The guidelines adopted by the leaders were fleshed out in negotiations conducted in the coming weeks, and on August 14 the new deal was unveiled by the eurozone finance ministers. Jeroen Dijsselbloem, the president of the Eurogroup (the institution that convenes eurozone ministers for regular meetings), hailed the deal as a major breakthrough. "We commended the Greek authorities on the strong commitment shown in the last week in the normalization of working methods," he said.

The new financial envelope provided to Greece amounted to €86 billion. Of this, €25 billion would be available on demand—if necessary—to recapitalize Greece's financially strapped banks. Another major takeaway was the establishment of a €50 billion privatization fund, to be supervised by EU institutions, through which Greece would agree to beef up an existing program to privatize state-owned assets. A portion of the proceeds from these privatizations was to be used to repay debts, a portion to recapitalize banks, and a portion to be invested in the economy.

Deficit targets were another key component of the agreement. Since the Syriza-led coalition government had taken power in January, Greece's economy slipped back into recession as investors lost confidence in the country's future given the fraught bailout negotiations. In response, the eurozone ministers decided to recalibrate Greece's targets, giving it a goal of transitioning from having a primary deficit of 0.25 percent of GDP for 2015 to a primary surplus of 3.5 percent in 2018.

On the hot button issue of debt relief, both sides could claim a victory of sorts. The eurozone ministers said that Greece's debt should be made sustainable "without nominal haircuts," meaning they were willing to consider giving Greece more time to repay debts and lower interest rates but would not write off debts entirely. But Athens could point to another clause where the eurozone left open a possibility of debt relief once the initial review of the program was completed when the EU would take a new look at Greece's "gross financing needs."

As for the reforms being demanded of Greece, the priorities included stepping up the fight against tax evasion to boost state coffers, trimming back public pensions, opening up labor and product markets for more investment, and depoliticizing the public sector. As for Greece's banking sector, it was to be recapitalized by a so-called bail-in mechanism, whereby bond-holders, but not depositors, would be asked to contribute financial support. On August 19, the worst of the crisis seemed to have passed when the first tranche of money from the €86 billion bailout, €26 billion, was unlocked.

In the second half of 2015, the tensions between Athens and its EU counterparts had eased considerably. The Greek parliament made some of the structural reforms demanded of it, although there was still much work to be done. One major issue of concern for the banking sector was what to do about an estimated €100 billion of nonperforming loans that were clogging up the system. The details of reforming the pension system also needed to be finalized, specifically what increases in social security contributions should employers and employees be asked to make. As reward for such efforts, the Greek government was pushing for the EU to complete a prompt—and positive—review of the program's implementation. This would pave the way, it hoped, for the discussion about debt relief that it had been demanding for so long. The European Commission, the EU's executive arm, indicated that the review would be completed in early 2016.

Meanwhile, the IMF held discussions with Greece and the eurozone about whether it should participate in the EU's third bailout program for Greece. The IMF's own financial assistance program for Greece is set to expire in early 2016. While the EU and IMF have partnered since 2010 in providing financial support to prop up Greece, as well as Portugal and Ireland, the relationship has had its difficulties. The IMF has consistently urged the EU to ease up on austerity and consider debt relief for Greece. Some eurozone members have scoffed back at the IMF that it is easier for it to make such recommendations for leniency given that the IMF only owns 10 percent of Greek debt compared to 70 percent owned by the EU. The EU maintains that the IMF's continued participation in the Greek program is indispensable. The IMF remains noncommittal, saying it will wait until the first review of the program is completed before making a decision on its participation.

—Brian Beary

Following is a statement from the Eurogroup released on June 27, 2015, regarding negotiations with Greece to prevent default; a statement from the IMF on June 30, 2015, marking Greece's official default; and two documents from August 14, 2015, one the text of the remarks by Eurogroup president Jeroen Dijsselbloem announcing the agreement between Greece and the European Union to provide Greece with a bailout, and second a statement from Eurogroup on the agreement with Greece.

DOCUMENT

Eurogroup Remarks on Failed Negotiations with Greece

June 27, 2015

Since the 20 February 2015 agreement of the Eurogroup on the extension of the current financial assistance arrangement, intensive negotiations have taken place between the institutions and the Greek authorities to achieve a successful conclusion of the review. Given the prolonged deadlock in negotiations and the urgency of the situation, institutions have put forward a comprehensive proposal on policy conditionality, making use of the given flexibility within the current arrangement.

Regrettably, despite efforts at all levels and full support of the Eurogroup, this proposal has been rejected by the Greek authorities who broke off the programme negotiations late on the 26 June unilaterally. The Eurogroup recalls the significant financial transfers and support provided to Greece over the last years. The Eurogroup has been open until the very last moment to further support the Greek people through a continued growth-oriented programme.

The Eurogroup takes note of the decision of the Greek government to put forward a proposal to call for a referendum, which is expected to take place on Sunday July 5, which is after the expiration of the programme period. The current financial assistance arrangement with Greece will expire on 30 June 2015, as well as all agreements related to the current Greek programme including the transfer by euro area Member States of SMP and ANFA equivalent profits.

The euro area authorities stand ready to do whatever is necessary to ensure financial stability of the euro area.

[1] Supported by all members of the Eurogroup except the Greek member.

IMF Releases Statement on Greek Default

June 30, 2015

Mr. Gerry Rice, Director of Communications at the International Monetary Fund (IMF), made the following statement today regarding Greece's financial obligations to the IMF due today:

"I confirm that the SDR 1.2 billion repayment (about EUR 1.5 billion) due by Greece to the IMF today has not been received. We have informed our Executive Board that Greece is now in arrears and can only receive IMF financing once the arrears are cleared.

"I can also confirm that the IMF received a request today from the Greek authorities for an extension of Greece's repayment obligation that fell due today, which will go to the IMF's Executive Board in due course."

Eurogroup President on Agreement with Greek Government

August 14, 2015

Good evening and welcome to this press conference. We have just finished the Eurogroup meeting and we've come to a positive conclusion on the proposals by the institutions. All the intense work of the last week has paid off and let me here also extend my thanks to the teams of the institutions and the team of the Greek government that had worked so hard these last months to reach an agreement. We also have reached agreement at the political level in the Eurogroup. We had a very constructive and good atmosphere. Of course there were differences, but we have managed to solve the last issues. We have issued a statement outlining the details of our agreement. I will therefore mention only the main elements.

First, we welcomed the agreement that was reached between Greece and the institutions on policy conditionality. It is to our mind in line with the key objectives set by the euro summit on 12 July, and if implemented with determination—of course it always boils down to determination—it will allow the Greek economy to return to sustainable growth.

Secondly, we commended the Greek authorities on the strong commitment shown in the last weeks in the normalisation of working methods with the institutions. I think that was very helpful to have a good and fruitful process and also we've seen important and determined legislative steps over the past weeks and days even, in Greece, and that has helped in the process of rebuilding trust; and many of the colleagues in the Eurogroup made that point.

Thirdly, on the policy conditionality, we welcomed the broad scope of the policy measures contained in the Memorandum of Understanding (MoU), as agreed. It's a comprehensive and ambitious reform package, it addresses the main challenges both on reaching sound public finances to return to growth, but also structural policy frameworks to enhance competitiveness. And finally it safeguards financial stability; it deals with the issues with the banks.

On the latter point, there will be later this year, this autumn, an asset quality review and stress test, and on the basis of that, recapitalisation will take place. In that process the bail-in instrument will apply for senior bondholders, whereas the bail-in of depositors is explicitly excluded. You will find this in our statement.

Fourthly, the Eurogroup underlined that a significantly strengthened privatisation programme is a part of the new ESM programme. Therefore it is important that the independent fund which will be set up will be established in Greece at the latest by end-2015. It will be under the supervision of the relevant European institutions. It will take on board the privatisation of state assets and the proceeds of this fund will, for the first €25 billion, completely be used to repay debt and for the second part of the target of €50 billion, it will be 50/50: 50% to repay debt and 50% can be reinvested. This fund will be set up before the end of the year. Proposals have to be made already at the latest by end October 2015. The ownership of this fund will be transferred as soon as possible after the recapitalisation of the banks has taken place later this year.

Fifth, on prior actions. We welcomed, as I already said, the comprehensive set of prior actions that has been legislated by the Greek authorities. The most recent prior actions legislated have been positively assessed by the institutions and I think this demonstrates that programme ownership has been picked up seriously and constructively by the Greek government.

The overall financing envelope of the agreed ESM programme will amount to €86 billion. This includes a €25 billion bank buffer, which can be available if needed to address potential bank recapitalisation and resolution costs. This money will, later on, after the first review as I said, be transferred to segregated account in the ESM. Whether it is needed will be decided of course after the assessment of the banks and the stress test later this year.

On debt sustainability—and this is of course the key issue—a debt sustainability assessment has been provided by the Commission, in a strong liaison with the ECB. The analysis basically concludes that debt sustainability can be achieved through a far-reaching and credible reform programme—I think we have that in front of us—and debt-related measures without nominal haircuts, because that was made explicit in the euro summit statement of 12 July. The Eurogroup stands ready to consider, after the positive completion of the first programme review, possible additional measures to ensure gross financing needs remaining at a sustainable level. "Gross financing needs" is the debt service approach that we will take when we look at the debt sustainability. We will do that after the successful completion of the first review.

Finally, we welcomed the intention of the IMF Board to consider further financial support for Greece. They will do so in the autumn. We stressed that such IMF involvement for the Eurogroup is indispensable. We welcomed the positive assessment of IMF staff of the policy conditionality contained in the MoU. For the IMF Board to consider further financial support, there are two issues that are crucial and we realise and accept that. First of all there needs to be a full specification of fiscal, structural and financial sector reforms; and secondly that debt sustainability is ensured. On those reforms, just to mention one is the pension reform and we have again underlined that at the latest in October there has to be clarity on those pension reforms from the side of the Greek government, in agreement with the institutions.

Finally, as regards the next steps, the necessary elements are all in place now to launch the relevant national procedures to get the formal approval of the ESM financial assistance programme. We expect that the ESM Board of Governors which will take the formal decision will be in a position to approve the proposal on Wednesday, 19 August, by the end of the day; and that it would also unlock the initial fist [sic] tranche of the programme.

That will be all from me. I will now give the floor to Vice-President Dombrovskis and to Klaus Regling.

SOURCE: Council of the European Union. "Remarks by J. Dijsselbloem following the Eurogroup meeting of 14 August 2015." August 14, 2015. © European Union, 2015. www.consilium.europa.eu/press-releases-pdf/2015/8/40802201775_en_635755053000000000.pdf.

Eurogroup Welcomes Agreement with Greece

August 14, 2015

The Eurogroup welcomes the agreement that has been reached between Greece and the European Institutions, with input from the IMF, on the policy conditionality underlying the new ESM macroeconomic adjustment programme. The Eurogroup commends the Greek authorities for their demonstrated strong commitment as shown by the normalisation of the working methods with the Institutions and the conduct of the negotiations in a determined and swift manner. This agreement is in line with the parameters and key objectives set by the Euro summit on 12 July and provides a comprehensive framework for restoring the Greek economy to a sustainable path.

The Eurogroup welcomes the wide scope of the policy measures contained in the Memorandum of Understanding (MoU), which, if implemented with determination, will address the main challenges facing the Greek economy. We are confident that decisive and as swift as possible implementation of the reform measures as spelled out in the MoU will allow the Greek economy to return to a sustainable growth path based on sound public finances, enhanced competitiveness, high employment and financial stability.

Greece will target a medium-term primary surplus of 3.5% of GDP with a fiscal path of primary balances of -0.25% in 2015, 0.5% in 2016, 1.75% in 2017 and 3.5% in 2018 to be achieved notably through upfront parametric fiscal reforms supported by measures to strengthen tax compliance and fight tax evasion. Greece will undertake an ambitious reform of the pension system aimed at ensuring its sustainability, efficiency and fairness. It will specify policies to fully compensate for the fiscal impact of the Constitutional Court ruling on the 2012 pension reform and to implement the zero deficit clause or mutually agreeable alternative measures by October 2015. Greece has furthermore committed to key labour and product market reforms to open up the economy to investment and competition, as well as to modernise and depoliticise the public sector. With regard to the financial sector, Greece has committed to take decisive measures to safeguard stability, including a recapitalisation of the banks as required, measures to enhance the insolvency framework and a significant improvement of the governance of the banks and the Hellenic Financial Stability Fund (HFSF). Following the results of the Asset Quality Review and Stress Tests before the end of the year, the bail in instrument will apply for senior debt bondholders whereas bail in of depositors is excluded. The Eurogroup stresses that the agreed conditionality needs to be further specified as requested by the IMF a matter of priority, in particular in the areas of pension reforms and financial sector strategy and governance, in agreement with the three Institutions in time for the completion of the first review under the ESM programme. Moreover, Greece will take urgently needed steps to tackle the non-performing loan (NPL) problem in the banking sector. Given the magnitude of the problem, we urge the authorities to develop all necessary instruments to that end, including opening the market for NPL servicing and disposal with the appropriate safeguards to protect vulnerable debtors and exploring the possibility of a bad bank.

Compliance with the conditionality of the MoU will be monitored by the Commission in liaison with the ECB and together with the IMF, as foreseen in Article 13(7) of the ESM Treaty.

The Eurogroup stresses that a significantly strengthened privatisation programme is a cornerstone of the new ESM programme. The Eurogroup welcomes the Greek authorities' commitment to adopt new legislation to ensure transparent privatisation procedures and adequate asset sale pricing, according to OECD principles and standards on the management of State Owned Enterprises (SOEs). To ensure a more ambitious privatisation process, an independent fund will be established in Greece under the supervision of the relevant European institutions by end-2015 and encompass the privatisation of independently valuated state assets, while avoiding fire sales. The Eurogroup expects the Greek government to endorse the plan for this fund by the end of October 2015 so that it can be operational by the end of the year. Its task will be to quickly identify, transfer over the lifetime of the programme, and manage valuable Greek assets through privatisation and other means, including minority shareholdings and to increase their value on a professional basis. This will include the shares in Greek banks after their recapitalisation, thus also enhancing banks' governance. This should ensure that a targeted value of EUR 50 bn can be realised, by putting the assets on the market, of which EUR 25bn will be used for the repayment of recapitalization of banks and other assets and 50% of every remaining euro (i.e. 50% of EUR 25bn) will be used for decreasing the debt to GDP ratio and the remaining 50% will be used for investments. The legislation to establish the Fund shall be adopted in agreement with European institutions.

The Eurogroup appreciates that the Greek authorities have taken additional important legislative steps over the last few days. This supports the gradual process of rebuilding trust, demonstrating the authorities policy resolve and programme ownership. Those steps include notably additional fiscal measures on the tax and expenditure side, legislation on early retirement as well as an extensive set of actions in relation to the financial sector and product markets. In addition, in line with the Eurogroup statement of 16 July, the Greek authorities took measures to adjust and complete the legislation adopted on 15 July 2015. The authorities have also repealed a number of provisions backtracking on previous programme commitments.

The Eurogroup welcomes that the implementation of those prior actions has been assessed positively by the Institutions. The Greek authorities have confirmed their intention to complete by September the follow up actions identified by the Institutions, including the need to bring the adopted household insolvency law in line with the proposal of the Institutions.

Based on the assessment of the Institutions, the ESM financial assistance facility agreement will cover an amount of up to EUR 86 bn. This includes a buffer of up to EUR 25 bn for the banking sector in order to address potential bank recapitalisation and resolution costs.

The first tranche under the ESM programme of EUR 26 bn will consist of two sub-tranches. The first sub-tranche of EUR 10 bn will be made available immediately in a segregated account at the ESM for bank recapitalisation and resolution purposes. The second sub-tranche of EUR 16 bn will be disbursed to Greece in several instalments, starting with a first disbursement of EUR 13 bn by 20 August, followed by one or more further disbursements in the autumn subject to the implementation of key milestones based on measures outlined in the MoU and to be specified by the European Institutions and agreed by the EWG.

A second tranche for banking recapitalisation and resolution needs of up to EUR 15 bn can be made available after the first review and no later than 15 November, subject to the completion of the planned Asset Quality Review and Stress Test and the implementation of the financial sector deliverables of the review. These funds will initially be transferred to the segregated ESM account and can be released upon the agreement of the ESM Board of Directors.

The debt sustainability assessment was conducted by the Commission, in liaison with the ECB, as foreseen in Article 13(1) of the ESM Treaty. The analysis concludes that debt sustainability can be achieved through a far-reaching and credible reform programme and additional debt related measures without nominal haircuts. In line with the Euro summit statement of 12 July, the Eurogroup stands ready to consider, if necessary, possible additional measures (possible longer grace and repayment periods) aiming at ensuring that Greece's gross financing needs remain at a sustainable level. These measures will be conditional upon full implementation of the measures agreed in the ESM programme and will be considered after the first positive completion of a programme review. The Eurogroup reiterates that nominal haircuts on official debt cannot be undertaken.

The Eurogroup considers the continued programme involvement of the IMF as indispensable and welcomes the intention of the IMF management to recommend to the Fund's Executive Board to consider further financial support for Greece once the full specification of fiscal, structural and financial sector reforms has been completed and once the need for additional measures has been considered and an agreement on possible debt relief to ensure debt sustainability has been reached. Resulting policy conditionality will be a shared one as the policy conditionality underlying the ESM macroeconomic adjustment programme is developed in parallel to the one of the IMF. Once approved, the full re-engagement of the IMF is expected to reduce subsequently the ESM financing envelope accordingly. The Eurogroup welcomes the positive assessment of IMF staff of the policy conditionality contained in the MoU as confirmed by the IMF Managing Director and looks forward to an IMF programme based on the latter.

The Eurogroup considers that the necessary elements are now in place to launch the relevant national procedures required for the approval of the ESM financial assistance.

The Eurogroup expects that the ESM Board of Governors will be in a position to authorise the European Commission signing the MoU on behalf of the ESM and approve the proposal for a financial assistance facility agreement by 19 August, subject to completion of national procedures, and thereby unlock the initial tranche of up to EUR 26 bn.

SOURCE: Council of the European Union. "Eurogroup statement on the ESM programme for Greece." August 14, 2015. © European Union, 2015. www.consilium.europa.eu/en/press/press-releases/2015/08/14-eurogroup-statement.

OTHER HISTORIC DOCUMENTS OF INTEREST

FROM THIS VOLUME

FROM PREVIOUS HISTORIC DOCUMENTS

Supreme Court Rejects Environmental Protection Agency Mercury Limits

JUNE 29, 2015

In late 2011, the Environmental Protection Agency (EPA) passed a bold environmental air quality rule designed to limit, for the first time, the toxic mercury emissions from coal-fired power plants. These power plants are the single largest source of manmade mercury pollution, which scientific studies have repeatedly identified as a dangerous neurotoxin, especially damaging to pregnant women and children. Industry groups and twenty-three states challenged the rule in the courts, arguing that its implementation imposed punishing costs on the utilities and that the EPA had not adequately taken these costs into account when it started its regulatory process. The challengers, including the National Federation of Independent Business, argued that the rule is among the costliest regulations ever issued. Nevertheless, in the years it took for the case to work its way to the Supreme Court, most of the 800 power companies subject to the rule had made the changes necessary to comply with its requirements. On June 29, 2015, in a blow to the administration's efforts to control dangerous air pollution, the Supreme Court in *Michigan v. EPA* agreed with the rule's challengers. In a 5–4 decision, Justice Antonin Scalia wrote that the EPA erred at the very onset of its rulemaking "when it deemed cost irrelevant" to its initial determination to regulate the power companies.

EPA Emission Regulations

In 1990, Congress amended the Clean Air Act directing the EPA to start regulating the emission from fossil fuel-fired power plants of mercury and over 180 other "hazardous air pollutants" if the agency found such regulation to be "appropriate and necessary." The agency completed a health study in 1998, showing that mercury released from power plants causes "substantial health harm." As a powerful neurotoxin, even small amounts of mercury are harmful to brain and nervous systems. When mothers are exposed to mercury during pregnancy, their children "have exhibited a variety of developmental neurological abnormalities," and an estimated 7 percent of women of childbearing age are exposed to unsafe levels of mercury. Based on the health study and additional data, in 2000, the EPA found that regulating power plant emissions satisfied the "appropriate and necessary" standard. According to an EPA statement, such regulation was "appropriate" because the power plants present "significant hazards to public health and the environment" and that technology is readily available to reduce these emissions. It was "necessary" because no other laws would be able to address these hazards. The EPA chose not to factor in the cost of limiting mercury emissions at this stage of its review, stating that "costs should not be considered" when determining whether to regulate power plant mercury emissions, but explicitly noting that, as the rulemaking proceeds and levels are determined, "the effectiveness and costs of controls will be examined."

In 2012, the EPA reaffirmed its determination that regulating mercury emissions was "appropriate and necessary" and started setting what the statute refers to as "floor standards." This is done by dividing the nation's power plants into categories based on their type and technology. The agency then created benchmarks by requiring the power plants in each group to match the emissions levels already achieved by the best-performing members of the same group. Due to a finding that it would not be cost-effective, the EPA, in almost all instances, did not require any more stringent standards than those already achieved by some plants prior to any regulation. After the benchmarking concluded, the EPA conducted a formal cost-benefit study, which found that the benefits achieved by the regulation were more than nine times the costs borne by the power plants and included as many as 11,000 fewer premature deaths a year and far more avoided illnesses.

On December 16, 2011, the EPA released its regulations—the first ever national standards to reduce mercury from the 600 coal-fired power plants, which were the dominant sources of environmental mercury. Many of the nation's power plants had already adopted the technology to control their emissions, but by requiring all to use the available technologies, a new higher standard could be held. The rule was expected to greatly reduce environmental mercury and modernize an aging fleet of power plants, many over fifty years old. The rule forces power plants to install and operate equipment that scrubs mercury and fine particulate matter from smoke stacks. The EPA estimated the expected annualized cost of compliance for the power plants to be $9.6 billion, with mercury controls accounting for roughly $2 billion of that total.

Court Finds the EPA Erred When it Started Rulemaking

The outcome of *Michigan v. EPA* turned on the meaning of a single word: appropriate. The Clean Air Act, which authorizes the EPA to regulate hazardous air pollutants, directs the agency to begin regulating if it "finds such regulation is appropriate and necessary." Justice Scalia, joined by Chief Justice John Roberts Jr. and Justices Anthony Kennedy, Clarence Thomas, and Samuel Alito Jr., objected to the EPA's approach, which "gave cost no thought at all, because it considered cost irrelevant to its initial decision to regulate." He ruled that the EPA was acting outside its authority when it did not consider costs at the outset.

Even giving due deference to the agency interpretation of the statute it administers, Justice Scalia concluded that the EPA "strayed far beyond those bounds when it read §7412(n)(1) to mean that it could ignore cost when deciding whether to regulate power plants." The term "appropriate" is a "'broad and all-encompassing term that naturally and traditionally includes consideration of all the relevant factors,'" he wrote, and although the term encompasses some flexibility, it does not give an agency the power to "'entirely fail to consider an important aspect of the problem' when deciding whether regulation is appropriate." Justice Scalia reviewed case law showing that agencies have long treated cost as a centrally relevant factor in rulemaking. "Against the backdrop of this established administrative practice," he wrote, "it is unreasonable to read an instruction to an administrative agency to determine whether 'regulation is appropriate and necessary' as an invitation to ignore cost." This failure could not be cured by the fact that the EPA did conduct thorough cost-benefit analyses later in determining what the standard should be for mercury emissions. "The question before us," Justice Scalia wrote, "is the meaning of the 'appropriate and necessary' standard that governs the initial decision to regulate." That standard, he concludes, encompasses cost.

Three justices joined with Justice Elena Kagan in a strong dissenting opinion that decried the ruling as "a decision that deprives the American public of the pollution control measures that the responsible Agency, acting well within its delegated authority, found would save many, many lives." Justice Kagan did not disagree with the majority that evaluating costs is an important part of rulemaking, writing, "[L]et there be no doubt about this—that EPA's power plant regulation would be unreasonable if '[t]he Agency gave cost no thought *at all.*'" However, she asserted, "that is just not what happened here." For over a decade, the EPA repeatedly took costs into account as it set emission limits. It just did not measure costs at "the opening bell" when it could not have done so with any accuracy. She described the majority's view as "peculiarly blinkered" when it held the rule to be invalid "because EPA did not explicitly analyze costs at the very first stage of the regulatory process . . . even though EPA later took costs into account again and again and . . . so on."

Justices Scalia and Kagan drew opposite conclusions from the same sports car metaphor. According to Justice Scalia, "[b]y EPA's logic, someone could decide whether it is 'appropriate' to buy a Ferrari without thinking about cost, because he plans to think about cost later when deciding to upgrade the sound system." This is "witty but wholly inapt," according to Justice Kagan, who began by pointing out that emissions limits are not a luxury good, and elaborated, "[a] better analogy might be to a car owner who decides without first checking prices that it is 'appropriate and necessary' to replace her worn-out brake-pads, aware from prior experience that she has ample time to comparison-shop and bring that purchase within her budget."

ULTIMATE IMPACT OF THE COURT'S DECISION

Political opponents of the EPA regulation and industry organizations cheered the ruling. House majority leader Kevin McCarthy, R-Calif., said in a statement, "The Supreme Court's decision today vindicates the House's legislative actions to rein in bureaucratic overreach and institute some common sense in rulemaking." This sentiment was echoed by the U.S. Chamber of Commerce's reaction to the decision, describing it as clarifying that the "EPA cannot turn a blind eye when it imposes massive costs on our economy in return for minimal environmental benefit. The decision affirms the common sense principle that Congress requires agencies to consider the consequences of regulations that they impose on businesses and consumers." The stock prices of coal companies even ticked upward briefly after the ruling.

The practical impact of the decision, however, is likely to be much more narrow than contemplated by headlines describing the Supreme Court as "throwing out" or "blocking" the mercury standards, both because many companies have already complied with the rule and because of the limited legal impact of the decision. In the three years since the EPA's rule regulating power company mercury emissions was first promulgated, most of the power plant operators have installed the technology necessary to cut mercury and other toxic emissions. Following the ruling, EPA spokesperson Melissa Harrison said, "EPA is disappointed that the Court did not uphold the rule, but this rule was issued more than three years ago, investments have been made and most plants are already well on their way to compliance."

Supporters of the rule were relieved that the Court did not challenge the EPA's authority to limit emissions at all, but instead held that it did not follow the rules properly when it initially decided that rulemaking was appropriate and necessary. The Court focused on how and when the agency evaluated costs, but it did not strike down the rule; the decision only required that the EPA go through the exercise of rewriting parts of the rule and making a new threshold determination that it is "appropriate" to regulate mercury from power plants, but this time taking compliance costs into consideration. This should not pose a problem for the EPA because it already conducted a thorough cost-benefit analysis, which determined that the rule will create health benefits of $37 billion to $90 billion per year, many times the $9.6 billion in estimated annual costs. Vickie Patton, general counsel for the Environmental Defense Fund, said that "while today's decision is a setback, EPA has ample information to swiftly address the Court's concerns." Whether it can get a revision in place before the end of the Obama administration is an open question.

The mercury regulations at issue in this case were part of a series of Clean Air Act regulations recently passed by the EPA, forming the centerpiece of the Obama administration's environmental legacy. In April 2014, in *EPA v. EME Homer City Generation*, the Supreme Court, in a 6–2 decision, upheld the first of these regulations—the Cross-State Air Pollution Rule. This rule was aimed at protecting downwind states from the harmful air pollution that is emitted by distant power plants and then blows across state borders. It limits the sulfur dioxide and oxides of nitrogen pollution emitted from coal-fired power plants across twenty-eight eastern states. More recently, in August 2015, the EPA released its final Clean Power Plan, designed to limit greenhouse gas emissions from power plants. The carbon limits in the plan are expected to shut down more than half the nation's aging coal-fired power plants, but the plan is likely to face further court challenges.

—Melissa Feinberg

Following is the edited text of the Supreme Court's ruling in Michigan v. EPA, *in which the Court ruled 5–4 against the Environmental Protection Agency's mercury regulations.*

DOCUMENT   *Michigan v. EPA*

June 29, 2015

[Footnotes have been omitted.]

Michigan, et al., petitioners	Nos. 14-46 and 14-49
v.	
Environmental Protection Agency, et. al.	
Utility Air Regulatory Group, petitioner	
v.	On writs of certiorari to the United States Court of Appeals for the District of Columbia Circuit
Environmental Protection Agency, et. al.	
National Mining Association, petitioner	
v.	
Environmental Protection Agency, et. al.	

[June 29, 2015]

JUSTICE SCALIA delivered the opinion of the Court.

The Clean Air Act directs the Environmental Protection Agency to regulate emissions of hazardous air pollutants from power plants if the Agency finds regulation "appropriate and necessary." We must decide whether it was reasonable for EPA to refuse to consider cost when making this finding.

[Section I, containing case background, has been omitted.]

II

Federal administrative agencies are required to engage in "reasoned decisionmaking." *Allentown Mack Sales & Service, Inc. v. NLRB*, 522 U. S. 359, 374 (1998) (internal quotation marks omitted). "Not only must an agency's decreed result be within the scope of its lawful authority, but the process by which it reaches that result must be logical and rational." *Ibid.* It follows that agency action is lawful only if it rests "on a consideration of the relevant factors." *Motor Vehicle Mfrs. Assn. of United States, Inc. v. State Farm Mut. Automobile Ins. Co.*, 463 U. S. 29, 43 (1983) (internal quotation marks omitted).

EPA's decision to regulate power plants under §7412 allowed the Agency to reduce power plants' emissions of hazardous air pollutants and thus to improve public health and the environment. But the decision also ultimately cost power plants, according to the Agency's own estimate, nearly $10 billion a year. EPA refused to consider whether the costs of its decision outweighed the benefits. The Agency gave cost no thought *at all*, because it considered cost irrelevant to its initial decision to regulate.

EPA's disregard of cost rested on its interpretation of §7412(n)(1)(A), which, to repeat, directs the Agency to regulate power plants if it "finds such regulation is appropriate and necessary." The Agency accepts that it *could* have interpreted this provision to mean that cost is relevant to the decision to add power plants to the program. Tr. of Oral Arg. 44. But it chose to read the statute to mean that cost makes no difference to the initial decision to regulate. See 76 Fed. Reg. 24988 (2011) ("We further interpret the term 'appropriate' to not allow for the consideration of costs"); 77 Fed. Reg. 9327 ("Cost does not have to be read into the definition of 'appropriate'").

We review this interpretation under the standard set out in *Chevron U. S. A. Inc. v. Natural Resources Defense Council, Inc.*, 467 U. S. 837 (1984). Chevron directs courts to accept an agency's reasonable resolution of an ambiguity in a statute that the agency administers. *Id.*, at 842–843. Even under this deferential standard, however, "agencies must operate within the bounds of reasonable interpretation." *Utility Air Regulatory Group v. EPA*, 573 U. S. ___, ___ (2014) (slip op., at 16) (internal quotation marks omitted). EPA strayed far beyond those bounds when it read §7412(n)(1) to mean that it could ignore cost when deciding whether to regulate power plants.

A

The Clean Air Act treats power plants differently from other sources for purposes of the hazardous-air-pollutants program. Elsewhere in §7412, Congress established cabined criteria for EPA to apply when deciding whether to include sources in the program. It required the Agency to regulate sources whose emissions exceed specified numerical thresholds (major sources). It also required the Agency to regulate sources whose emissions fall short of these thresholds (area sources) if they "presen[t] a threat of adverse effects to human health or the environment . . . warranting regulation." §7412(c)(3). In stark contrast, Congress instructed EPA to add power plants to the program if (but only if) the Agency finds regulation "appropriate and necessary." §7412(n)(1)(A). One does not need to open up a dictionary in order to realize the capaciousness of this phrase. In particular, "appropriate" is "the classic broad and all-encompassing term that naturally and traditionally includes consideration of all the relevant factors." 748 F. 3d, at 1266 (opinion of Kavanaugh, J.). Although this term leaves agencies with flexibility, an agency may not "entirely fai[l] to consider an important aspect of the problem" when deciding whether regulation is appropriate. *State Farm, supra,* at 43.

Read naturally in the present context, the phrase "appropriate and necessary" requires at least some attention to cost. One would not say that it is even rational, never mind "appropriate," to impose billions of dollars in economic costs in return for a few dollars in health or environmental benefits. In addition, "cost" includes more than the expense of complying with regulations; any disadvantage could be termed a cost. EPA's interpretation precludes the Agency from considering any type of cost—including, for instance, harms that regulation might do to human health or the environment. The Government concedes that if the Agency were to find that emissions from power plants do damage to human health, but that the technologies needed to eliminate these emissions do even more damage to human health, it would *still* deem regulation appropriate. See Tr. of Oral Arg. 70. No regulation is "appropriate" if it does significantly more harm than good.

There are undoubtedly settings in which the phrase "appropriate and necessary" does not encompass cost. But this is not one of them. Section 7412(n)(1)(A) directs EPA to determine whether "*regulation* is appropriate and necessary." (Emphasis added.) Agencies have long treated cost as a centrally relevant factor when deciding whether to regulate. Consideration of cost reflects the understanding that reasonable regulation ordinarily requires paying attention to the advantages *and* the disadvantages of agency decisions. It also reflects the reality that "too much wasteful expenditure devoted to one problem may well mean considerably fewer resources available to deal effectively with other (perhaps more serious) problems." *Entergy Corp. v. Riverkeeper, Inc.,* 556 U. S. 208, 233 (2009) (BREYER, J., concurring in part and dissenting in part). Against the backdrop of this established administrative practice, it is unreasonable to read an instruction to an administrative agency to determine whether "regulation is appropriate and necessary" as an invitation to ignore cost. . . .

B

EPA identifies a handful of reasons to interpret §7412(n)(1)(A) to mean that cost is irrelevant to the initial decision to regulate. We find those reasons unpersuasive.

EPA points out that other parts of the Clean Air Act expressly mention cost, while §7412(n)(1)(A) does not. But this observation shows only that §7412(n)(1)(A)'s broad reference to appropriateness encompasses *multiple* relevant factors (which include but are not limited to cost); other provisions' specific references to cost encompass just cost. It is unreasonable to infer that, by expressly making cost relevant to other decisions, the Act implicitly makes cost irrelevant to the appropriateness of regulating power plants. . . . Other parts of the Clean Air Act also expressly mention environmental effects, while §7412(n)(1)(A) does not. Yet that did not stop EPA from deeming environmental effects relevant to the appropriateness of regulating power plants. . . .

Turning to the mechanics of the hazardous-air pollutants program, EPA argues that it need not consider cost when first deciding *whether* to regulate power plants because it can consider cost later when deciding *how much* to regulate them. The question before us, however, is the meaning of the "appropriate and necessary" standard that governs the initial decision to regulate. And as we have discussed, context establishes that this expansive standard encompasses cost. Cost may become relevant again at a later stage of the regulatory process, but that possibility does not establish its irrelevance at *this* stage. In addition, once the Agency decides to regulate power plants, it must promulgate certain minimum or floor standards no matter the cost (here, nearly $10 billion a year); the Agency may consider cost only when imposing regulations beyond these minimum standards. By EPA's logic, someone could decide whether it is "appropriate" to buy a Ferrari without thinking about cost, because he plans to think about cost later when deciding whether to upgrade the sound system. . . .

EPA persists that Congress treated power plants differently from other sources because of uncertainty about whether regulation of power plants would still be needed after the application of the rest of the Act's requirements. That is undoubtedly *one* of the reasons Congress treated power plants differently; hence §7412(n)(1)(A)'s requirement to study hazards posed by power plants' emissions "after imposition of the requirements of [the rest of the Act]." But if uncertainty about the need for regulation were the only reason to treat power plants differently, Congress would have required the Agency to decide only whether regulation remains "necessary," not whether regulation is "appropriate *and* necessary." In any event, EPA stated when it adopted the rule that "Congress did not limit [the] appropriate and necessary inquiry to [the study mentioned in §7412(n)(1)(A)]." 77 Fed. Reg. 9325. The Agency instead decided that the appropriate-and-necessary finding should be understood in light of all three studies required by §7412(n)(1), and as we have discussed, one of those three studies reflects concern about cost.

C

The dissent does not embrace EPA's far-reaching claim that Congress made costs altogether irrelevant to the decision to regulate power plants. Instead, it maintains that EPA need not "explicitly analyze costs" before deeming regulation appropriate, because other features of the regulatory program will on their own ensure the cost effectiveness of regulation. *Post*, at 2 (opinion of KAGAN, J.). This line of reasoning contradicts the foundational principle of administrative law that a court may uphold agency action only on the grounds that the agency invoked when it took the action. *SEC v. Chenery Corp.*, 318 U. S 80, 87 (1943). When it deemed regulation of power plants appropriate, EPA said that cost was *irrelevant* to that determination—not that cost-benefit analysis would be deferred until later. Much *less* did it say (what the dissent now concludes) that the consideration of cost at subsequent stages will ensure that the costs are not disproportionate to the benefits. What it said is that cost is irrelevant to the decision to regulate.

That is enough to decide these cases. But for what it is worth, the dissent vastly overstates the influence of cost at later stages of the regulatory process.

[A discussion of the costs has been omitted.]

D

Our reasoning so far establishes that it was unreasonable for EPA to read §7412(n)(1)(A) to mean that cost is irrelevant to the initial decision to regulate power plants. The Agency must consider cost—including, most importantly, cost of compliance—before deciding whether regulation is appropriate and necessary. We need not and do not hold that the law unambiguously required the Agency, when making this preliminary estimate, to conduct a formal cost-benefit analysis in which each advantage and disadvantage is assigned a monetary value. It will be up to the Agency to decide (as always, within the limits of reasonable interpretation) how to account for cost.

Some of the respondents supporting EPA ask us to uphold EPA's action because the accompanying regulatory impact analysis shows that, once the rule's ancillary benefits are considered, benefits plainly outweigh costs. The dissent similarly relies on these ancillary benefits when insisting that "the outcome here [was] a rule whose benefits exceed its costs." *Post*, at 16. As we have just explained, however, we may uphold agency action only upon the grounds on which the agency acted. Even if the Agency *could* have considered ancillary benefits when deciding whether regulation is appropriate and necessary—a point we need not address—it plainly did not do so here. In the Agency's own words, the administrative record "utterly refutes [the] assertion that [ancillary benefits] form the basis for the appropriate and necessary finding." 77 Fed. Reg. 9323. The Government concedes, moreover, that "EPA did not rely on the [regulatory impact analysis] when deciding to regulate power plants," and that "[e]ven if EPA had considered costs, it would not necessarily have adopted . . . the approach set forth in [that analysis]." Brief for Federal Respondents 53–54.

* * *

We hold that EPA interpreted §7412(n)(1)(A) unreasonably when it deemed cost irrelevant to the decision to regulate power plants. We reverse the judgment of the Court of Appeals for the D. C. Circuit and remand the cases for further proceedings consistent with this opinion.

It is so ordered.

[The concurring opinion of Justice Thomas has been omitted.]

JUSTICE KAGAN, with whom JUSTICE GINSBURG, JUSTICE BREYER, and JUSTICE SOTOMAYOR join, dissenting.

. . . . Despite that exhaustive consideration of costs, the Court strikes down EPA's rule on the ground that the Agency "unreasonably . . . deemed cost irrelevant." *Ante*, at 15. On the majority's theory, the rule is invalid because EPA did not explicitly analyze costs at the very first stage of the regulatory process, when making its "appropriate and necessary" finding. And that is so even though EPA later took costs into account again and again and . . . so on. The majority thinks entirely immaterial, and so entirely ignores, all the subsequent times and ways EPA considered costs in deciding what any regulation would look like.

. . . . That context matters. The Agency acted well within its authority in declining to consider costs at the opening bell of the regulatory process given that it would do so in every round thereafter—and given that the emissions limits finally issued would depend crucially on those accountings. Indeed, EPA could not have measured costs at the process's initial stage with any accuracy. And the regulatory path EPA chose parallels the one it has trod in setting emissions limits, at Congress's explicit direction, for every other source of hazardous air pollutants over two decades. The majority's decision that EPA cannot take the same approach here—its micromanagement of EPA's rulemaking, based on little more than the word "appropriate"—runs counter to Congress's allocation of authority between the Agency and the courts. Because EPA reasonably found that it was "appropriate" to decline to analyze costs at a single stage of a regulatory proceeding otherwise imbued with cost concerns, I respectfully dissent.

[The remainder of the dissent has been omitted.]

SOURCE: U.S. Supreme Court. *Michigan v. EPA*. 576 U.S.___(2015). www.supremecourt.gov/opinions/14pdf/14-46_bqmc.pdf.

OTHER HISTORIC DOCUMENTS OF INTEREST

FROM THIS VOLUME

- United Nations Climate Change Conference Reaches Historic Agreement, p. 656

FROM PREVIOUS *HISTORIC DOCUMENTS*

- Supreme Court Rules on EPA's Authority to Regulate Carbon Dioxide Emissions, *2011*, p. 293
- EPA Inspector General on Mercury Pollution Regulations, *2005*, p. 95
- National Academy of Public Administration and EPA on Clean Air Regulations, *2003*, p. 173

Supreme Court Rules on Use of Execution Drug

JUNE 29, 2015

Three death row inmates facing imminent execution in Oklahoma challenged the specific combination of drugs that the state planned to use in its lethal injection. They argued that the use of one of the drugs made it unacceptably likely that the inmates would suffer extreme pain before they died, in violation of the Eighth Amendment's ban on cruel and unusual punishment. One of the traditional drugs long-used in executions has in recent years become almost impossible for states to procure, so they have turned instead to more experimental and untested combinations of lethal drugs. The drug at issue in this case, midazolam, had been used in several highly publicized botched executions where inmates who were supposed to be unconscious called out in pain, and it took far longer than intended for them to die. In the case of *Glossip v. Gross*, decided by a narrow 5–4 vote, Justice Samuel Alito Jr. wrote the opinion upholding the use of Oklahoma's lethal injection cocktail, including the controversial drug. The inmates, he wrote, failed both to prove that the execution protocol entails a substantial risk of severe pain and to identify an available alternative that entails less risk of pain. The next day Oklahoma announced that it would resume lethal injection executions using the challenged drug.

LETHAL INJECTION IN THE UNITED STATES

When the Constitution and the Bill of Rights were first adopted, capital punishment, primarily by hanging, was an accepted form of punishment. Starting in the late 1880s, many states changed their method of execution to electrocution, which, at the time, was considered more scientific and humane. This continued as the predominate execution method until the Supreme Court put a stop to the death penalty in 1967, only to reverse the decision in 1976. After this hiatus, lethal injection became the most prevalent method of carrying out a death sentence. It was adopted by Oklahoma in 1977, and as of 2015 is the method used in thirty-six states.

As practiced in the vast majority of these states, lethal injection involves the use of three different drugs. The latter two drugs cause death by paralyzing the inmate and stopping the heart. On their own, these two drugs would cause intense burning and extreme pain, so the first drug injected is intended to keep the inmate in a deep, coma-like unconsciousness. For most of the history of lethal injection, this important first drug has been a fast-acting barbiturate sedative, primarily sodium thiopental. In the 2008 Supreme Court case *Base v. Rees*, a plurality of the Court ruled that this three-drug cocktail does not violate the Eighth Amendment. The plurality recognized that the second and third drugs can cause intense pain, but said that the first drug would render the prisoner deeply unconscious, thus preventing the experience of the pain.

Changing economics and antideath penalty political activism have limited the availability of that first drug from pharmaceutical companies. The only American manufacturer of sodium thiopental ceased all domestic production in 2009, resuming production in Italy, where the Italian government prohibited the sale for use in lethal injections. Unwilling to face legal action in Italy, this company stopped manufacturing sodium thiopental entirely in 2011. States turned to an alternative barbiturate manufactured in Denmark, another antideath penalty country that quickly shut down the supply. While manufacturers are available in India and other countries, none has yet met the high standards set by the Food and Drug Administration (FDA) for importation of a foreign drug and are therefore illegal to bring into the United States.

Unable to find a dependable supply of proven death penalty drugs, Oklahoma and several other states have experimented with alternative combinations of drugs never used before in lethal injections. In particular, these states turned to a sedative called midazolam, which has not yet been approved by the FDA as effective for achieving a coma-like state. This was the drug used in three botched executions in 2014: Dennis McGuire in Ohio, Clayton Lockett in Oklahoma, and Joseph Wood in Arizona. These three executions involved problems getting the prisoners into the deeply unconscious state, leading to prolonged deaths and indications of conscious suffering. Lockett woke up during his execution; he writhed and moaned and said that the drugs were not working. Twelve other executions using the drugs at issue in this case did not appear to have any significant problems.

Four death row inmates in Oklahoma challenged the constitutionality of the state's execution protocols, arguing that use of the midazolam sedative led to an unacceptably high risk that the death would involve unbearable pain and suffering in violation of the Eighth Amendment. These four men—Charles Warner, Richard Glossip, John Grant, and Benjamin Cole—had all been convicted of murder and sentenced to death by Oklahoma juries. They went to court asking for a preliminary injunction to halt their executions while they brought a case to prove that the state's planned use of this drug poses "substantial and constitutionally intolerable risks." Such preliminary injunctions are appropriate only when the petitioner can establish a likelihood that they will ultimately succeed on the merits of the case. After holding an evidentiary hearing, the district court denied their request for an injunction and concluded that the inmates had failed to prove that midazolam is ineffective. Rather, the court found that if properly used in high doses, it can be an appropriate drug. The Court of Appeals for the Tenth Circuit agreed, and the case was appealed to the Supreme Court. In January 2015, one of the inmates, Warner, was executed. (It was later revealed in October 2015 that the state had used the wrong drug to stop Warner's heart.) The Supreme Court agreed to hear the appeal and stayed the executions of the remaining three petitioners until their appeal could be resolved.

SUPREME COURT APPROVES USE OF CONTROVERSIAL EXECUTION DRUG

Justice Alito wrote the majority opinion in this case, joined by Chief Justice John Roberts Jr. and Justices Anthony Kennedy, Antonin Scalia, and Clarence Thomas. He reviewed the lower court's reliance on expert testimony and the safeguards recently put into place before concluding that the court did not commit a clear error when it found that midazolam is "highly likely to render a person unable to feel pain during an execution." More controversially, he added a new rule for those challenging methods of execution. These challengers must, he wrote, "satisfy their burden of establishing that any risk of harm was substantial when compared to a known and available alternative method of execution." In his view, it is the death row inmates who must "identify a known and available alternative method of execution that entails a lesser risk of pain." The petitioners cannot meet this burden, according to the majority, because "Oklahoma has been unable to procure those drugs despite a good-faith effort to do so."

The principal dissent, written by Justice Sonia Sotomayor and joined by the three remaining justices, criticized the majority for turning "aside petitioners' plea that they at least be allowed a stay of execution while they seek to prove midazolam's inadequacy." She described the requirement that the petitioners prove the availability of an alternative means for their own executions as "wholly novel." Her dissent cites past cases that interpreted the Eighth Amendment as "categorically" prohibiting cruel and unusual punishments, and she argued that the majority's opinion changes this meaning by making a decision about whether or not an execution method violates the Eighth Amendment conditional dependent on the alternatives that are available at the time. Justice Sotomayor wrote: "A method of execution that is intolerably painful—even to the point of being the chemical equivalent of burning alive—will, the Court holds, be unconstitutional if, and only if, there is a 'known and available alternative' method of execution."

In other opinions, Justices Breyer and Scalia engaged in a battle over the ongoing existence of the death penalty itself. Joined only by Justice Elena Kagan, Justice Breyer dissented from the majority opinion but expressed his willingness to go beyond the facts of the case at hand. "Rather than try to patch up the death penalty's legal wounds one at a time," he wrote, "I would ask for full briefing on a more basic question: whether the death penalty violates the Constitution." In a lengthy opinion, including numerous charts and maps, Justice Breyer argued that the way the death penalty is administered today is rife with constitutional defects. Specifically, his dissent detailed evidence of racial and geographic inequities that prove an arbitrary application of the death penalty; evidence of lengthy delays in executing death row inmates, which undermines the deterrent value of the death penalty; and evidence that innocent individuals have been executed. "How long are we going to have this conversation," he asked.

Justice Scalia, joined by Justice Thomas, spoke from the bench to rebut Justice Breyer, calling his argument a "rewriting of the Eighth Amendment," which is "full of internal contradictions and (it must be said) gobbledy-gook."

Oklahoma Places Executions on Hold

Shortly after the opinion was released, Oklahoma announced that it would resume executions using lethal injection. Execution dates were set for Glossip, Cole, and Grant. As Glossip's October execution date approached, he petitioned for a delay based on newly discovered evidence of his innocence. Despite the efforts of supporters ranging from celebrity activist Susan Sarandon to Pope Francis, his appeals were rejected. But, within the hour of Glossip's execution, Oklahoma governor Mary Fallin ordered a surprise thirty-seven-day stay of execution. When prison officials had opened the box of lethal drugs in preparation for Glossip's execution, they discovered that they had received the wrong third drug in the three-drug protocol, which is designed to stop the prisoner's heart. The governor issued a stay to address issues raised by the last-minute substitution. Later, Oklahoma's highest criminal court agreed unanimously to halt all scheduled executions until the conclusion of an ongoing state investigation of its execution drug protocols. Currently, all executions are on hold until an undetermined date in 2016.

The Supreme Court agreed to hear four additional death penalty cases in its 2014–2015 term. In oral arguments in the first of these cases, which involved challenges to the instructions Kansas trial judges give to juries in death penalty cases, Justice Scalia continued his death penalty feud with Justice Breyer. When questioning one of the lawyers, Justice Scalia stated, "Kansans, unlike our Justice Breyer, do not think the death penalty is unconstitutional and indeed very much favor it."

—Melissa Feinberg

Following is the edited text of the Supreme Court's decision in Glossip v. Gross, *in which the Court ruled 5–4 to uphold the use of a controversial lethal injection drug known as midazolam.*

DOCUMENT   *Glossip v. Gross*

June 29, 2015

[Footnotes have been omitted.]

No. 14-7955

Richard E. Glossip, et al.,
petitioners

v.

Kevin J. Gross, et al.

On writ of certiorari to
the United States Court of
Appeals for the Tenth Circuit

[June 29, 2015]

JUSTICE ALITO delivered the opinion of the Court.

Prisoners sentenced to death in the State of Oklahoma filed an action in federal court under Rev. Stat. §1979, 42 U. S. C. §1983, contending that the method of execution now used by the State violates the Eighth Amendment because it creates an unacceptable risk of severe pain. They argue that midazolam, the first drug employed in the State's current three-drug protocol, fails to render a person insensate to pain. After holding an evidentiary hearing, the District Court denied four prisoners' application for a preliminary injunction, finding that they had failed to prove that midazolam is ineffective. The Court of Appeals for the Tenth Circuit affirmed and accepted the District Court's finding of fact regarding midazolam's efficacy.

For two independent reasons, we also affirm. First, the prisoners failed to identify a known and available alternative method of execution that entails a lesser risk of pain, a requirement of all Eighth Amendment method-of-execution claims. See *Baze v. Rees*, 553 U. S. 35, 61 (2008) (plurality opinion). Second, the District Court did not commit clear error when it found that the prisoners failed to establish that Oklahoma's use of a massive dose of midazolam in its execution protocol entails a substantial risk of severe pain.

[Sections I, II, and III, containing the background on the case and providing a brief history of the death penalty in the United States, have been omitted.]

IV

Our first ground for affirmance is based on petitioners' failure to satisfy their burden of establishing that any risk of harm was substantial when compared to a known and available alternative method of execution. In their amended complaint, petitioners proffered that the State could use sodium thiopental as part of a single-drug protocol. They have since suggested that it might also be constitutional for Oklahoma to use pentobarbital. But the District Court found that both sodium thiopental and pentobarbital are now unavailable to Oklahoma's Department of Corrections. The Court of Appeals affirmed that finding, and it is not clearly erroneous. On the contrary, the record shows that Oklahoma has been unable to procure those drugs despite a good-faith effort to do so.

Petitioners do not seriously contest this factual finding, and they have not identified any available drug or drugs that could be used in place of those that Oklahoma is now unable to obtain. Nor have they shown a risk of pain so great that other acceptable, available methods must be used. Instead, they argue that they need not identify a known and available method of execution that presents less risk. But this argument is inconsistent with the controlling opinion in *Baze*, 553 U. S., at 61, which imposed a requirement that the Court now follows.

Petitioners contend that the requirement to identify an alternative method of execution contravenes our pre-*Baze* decision in *Hill v. McDonough*, 547 U. S. 573 (2006), but they misread that decision. The portion of the opinion in *Hill* on which they rely concerned a question of civil procedure, not a substantive Eighth Amendment question. In *Hill*, the issue was whether a challenge to a method of execution must be brought by means of an application for a writ of habeas corpus or a civil action under §1983. *Id.*, at 576. We held that a method-of-execution claim must be brought under §1983 because such a claim does not attack the validity of the prisoner's conviction or death sentence. *Id.*, at 579–580. The United States as *amicus curiae* argued that we should adopt a special pleading requirement to stop inmates from using §1983 actions to attack, not just a particular means of execution, but the death penalty itself. To achieve this end, the United States proposed that an inmate asserting a method-of-execution claim should be required to plead an acceptable alternative method of execution. *Id.*, at 582. We rejected that argument because "[s]pecific pleading requirements are mandated by the Federal Rules of Civil Procedure, and not, as a general rule, through case-by-case determinations of the federal courts." *Ibid. Hill* thus held that §1983 alone does not impose a heightened pleading requirement. *Baze*, on the other hand, addressed the substantive elements of an Eighth Amendment method-of-execution claim, and it made clear that the Eighth Amendment requires a prisoner to plead and prove a known and available alternative. Because petitioners failed to do this, the District Court properly held that they did not establish a likelihood of success on their Eighth Amendment claim.

Readers can judge for themselves how much distance there is between the principal dissent's argument against requiring prisoners to identify an alternative and the view, now announced by JUSTICES BREYER and GINSBURG, that the death penalty is categorically unconstitutional. *Post*, p. ___ (BREYER, J., dissenting). The principal dissent goes out of its way to suggest that a State would violate the Eighth Amendment if it used one of the methods of execution employed before the advent of lethal injection. *Post*, at 30–31. And the principal dissent makes this suggestion even though the Court held in *Wilkerson* that this method (the firing squad) is constitutional and even though, in the words of the principal dissent, "there is some reason to think that it is relatively quick and painless." *Post*, at 30. Tellingly silent about the methods of execution most commonly used before States switched to lethal injection (the electric chair and gas chamber), the principal dissent implies that it would be unconstitutional to use a method that "could be seen as a devolution to a more primitive era." *Ibid.* If States cannot return to any of the "more primitive" methods used in the past and if no drug that meets with the principal dissent's approval is available for use in carrying out a death sentence, the logical conclusion is clear. But we have time and again reaffirmed that capital punishment is not *per se* unconstitutional. See, e.g., *Baze*, 553 U. S., at 47; id., at 87–88 (SCALIA, J., concurring in judgment); *Gregg*, 428 U. S., at 187 (joint opinion of Stewart, Powell, and Stevens, JJ.); *id.*, at 226 (White, J., concurring in judgment); *Resweber*, 329 U. S., at 464; *In re Kemmler*, 136 U. S., at 447; *Wilkerson*, 99 U. S., at 134–135. We decline to effectively overrule these decisions.

V

We also affirm for a second reason: The District Court did not commit clear error when it found that midazolam is highly likely to render a person unable to feel pain during an execution. We emphasize four points at the outset of our analysis. First, we review the District Court's factual findings under the deferential "clear error" standard. This standard does not entitle us to overturn a finding "simply because [we are] convinced that [we] would have decided the case differently." *Anderson v. Bessemer City*, 470 U. S. 564, 573 (1985).

Second, petitioners bear the burden of persuasion on this issue. *Baze*, supra, at 41. Although petitioners expend great effort attacking peripheral aspects of Dr. Evans' testimony, they make little attempt to prove what is critical, *i.e.*, that the evidence they presented to the District Court establishes that the use of midazolam is sure or very likely to result in needless suffering.

Third, numerous courts have concluded that the use of midazolam as the first drug in a three-drug protocol is likely to render an inmate insensate to pain that might result from administration of the paralytic agent and potassium chloride. See, *e.g.*, 776 F. 3d 721 (case below affirming the District Court); *Chavez v. Florida SP Warden*, 742 F. 3d 1267 (affirming the District Court); *Banks v. State*, 150 So. 3d 797 (Fla. 2014) (affirming the lower court); *Howell v. State*, 133 So. 3d 511 (Fla. 2014) (same); *Muhammad v. State*, 132 So. 3d 176 (Fla. 2013) (same). (It is noteworthy that one or both of the two key witnesses in this case—Dr. Lubarsky for petitioners and Dr. Evans for respondents—were witnesses in the *Chavez*, *Howell*, and *Muhammad* cases.) "Where an intermediate court reviews, and affirms, a trial court's factual findings, this Court will not 'lightly overturn' the concurrent findings of the two lower courts." *Easley v. Cromartie*, 532 U. S. 234, 242 (2001). Our review is even more deferential where, as here, multiple trial courts have reached the same finding, and multiple appellate courts have affirmed those findings. Cf. *Exxon Co., U. S. A. v. Sofec, Inc.*, 517 U. S. 830, 841 (1996) (explaining that this Court "'cannot undertake to review concurrent findings of fact by two courts below in the absence of a very obvious and exceptional showing of error'" (quoting *Graver Tank & Mfg. Co. v. Linde Air Products Co.*, 336 U. S. 271, 275 (1949))).

Fourth, challenges to lethal injection protocols test the boundaries of the authority and competency of federal courts. Although we must invalidate a lethal injection protocol if it violates the Eighth Amendment, federal courts should not "embroil [themselves] in ongoing scientific controversies beyond their expertise." *Baze*, *supra*, at 51. Accordingly, an inmate challenging a protocol bears the burden to show, based on evidence presented to the court, that there is a substantial risk of severe pain.

[Parts A, B, and C of Section V, further detailing the petitioners' arguments, have been omitted.]

VI

For these reasons, the judgment of the Court of Appeals for the Tenth Circuit is affirmed. It is so ordered.

JUSTICE SCALIA, with whom JUSTICE THOMAS joins, concurring.

I join the opinion of the Court, and write to respond to JUSTICE BREYER's plea for judicial abolition of the death penalty.

Welcome to Groundhog Day. The scene is familiar: Petitioners, sentenced to die for the crimes they committed (including, in the case of one petitioner since put to death, raping and murdering an 11-month-old baby), come before this Court asking us to nullify their sentences as "cruel and unusual" under the Eighth Amendment. They rely on this provision because it is the only provision they *can* rely on. They were charged by a sovereign State with murder. They were afforded counsel and tried before a jury of their peers—tried twice, once to determine whether they were guilty and once to determine whether death was the appropriate sentence. They were duly convicted and sentenced. They were granted the right to appeal and to seek postconviction relief, first in state and then in federal court. And now, acknowledging that their convictions are unassailable, they ask us for clemency, as though clemency were ours to give.

The response is also familiar: A vocal minority of the Court, waving over their heads a ream of the most recent abolitionist studies (a superabundant genre) as though they have discovered the lost folios of Shakespeare, insist that *now*, at long last, the death penalty must be abolished for good. Mind you, not once in the history of the American Republic has this Court ever suggested the death penalty is categorically impermissible. The reason is obvious: It is impossible to hold unconstitutional that which the Constitution explicitly *contemplates*. The Fifth Amendment provides that "[n]o person shall be held to answer for a capital . . . crime, unless on a presentment or indictment of a Grand Jury," and that no person shall be "deprived of life . . . without due process of law." Nevertheless, today JUSTICE BREYER takes on the role of the abolitionists in this long-running drama, arguing that the text of the Constitution and two centuries of history must yield to his "20 years of experience on this Court," and inviting full briefing on the continued permissibility of capital punishment, *post*, at 2 (dissenting opinion). Historically, the Eighth Amendment was understood to bar only those punishments that added "'terror, pain, or disgrace'" to an otherwise permissible capital sentence. *Baze v. Rees*, 553 U. S. 35, 96 (2008) (THOMAS, J., concurring in judgment). Rather than bother with this troubling detail, JUSTICE BREYER elects to contort the constitutional text. Redefining "cruel" to mean "unreliable," "arbitrary," or causing "excessive delays," and "unusual" to include a "decline in use," he proceeds to offer up a white paper devoid of any meaningful legal argument. Even accepting JUSTICE BREYER's rewriting of the Eighth Amendment, his argument is full of internal contradictions and (it must be said) gobbledy-gook. . . .

Capital punishment presents moral questions that philosophers, theologians, and statesmen have grappled with for millennia. The Framers of our Constitution disagreed bitterly on the matter. For that reason, they handled it the same way they handled many other controversial issues: they left it to the People to decide. By arrogating to himself the power to overturn that decision, JUSTICE BREYER does not just reject the death penalty, he rejects the Enlightenment.

[The concurring opinion of Justice Thomas has been omitted.]

JUSTICE BREYER, with whom JUSTICE GINSBURG joins, dissenting.

For the reasons stated in JUSTICE SOTOMAYOR's opinion, I dissent from the Court's holding. But rather than try to patch up the death penalty's legal wounds one at a time, I would ask for full briefing on a more basic question: whether the death penalty violates the Constitution.

The relevant legal standard is the standard set forth in the Eighth Amendment. The Constitution there forbids the "inflict[ion]" of "cruel and unusual punishments." Amdt. 8. The Court has recognized that a "claim that punishment is excessive is judged not by the standards that prevailed in 1685 when Lord Jeffreys presided over the 'Bloody Assizes' or when the Bill of Rights was adopted, but rather by those that currently prevail." *Atkins v. Virginia*, 536 U. S. 304, 311 (2002). Indeed, the Constitution prohibits various gruesome punishments that were common in Blackstone's day. See 4 W. Blackstone, Commentaries on the Laws of England 369–370 (1769) (listing mutilation and dismembering, among other punishments).

Nearly 40 years ago, this Court upheld the death penalty under statutes that, in the Court's view, contained safeguards sufficient to ensure that the penalty would be applied reliably and not arbitrarily. See *Gregg v. Georgia*, 428 U. S. 153, 187 (1976) (joint opinion of Stewart, Powell, and Stevens, JJ.); *Proffitt v. Florida*, 428 U. S. 242, 247 (1976) (joint opinion of Stewart, Powell, and Stevens, JJ.); *Jurek v. Texas*, 428 U. S. 262, 268 (1976) (joint opinion of Stewart, Powell, and Stevens, JJ.); but cf. *Woodson v. North Carolina*, 428 U. S. 280, 303 (1976) (plurality opinion) (striking down mandatory death penalty); *Roberts v. Louisiana*, 428 U. S. 325, 331 (1976) (plurality opinion) (similar). The circumstances and the evidence of the death penalty's application have changed radically since then. Given those changes, I believe that it is now time to reopen the question.

In 1976, the Court thought that the constitutional infirmities in the death penalty could be healed; the Court in effect delegated significant responsibility to the States to develop procedures that would protect against those constitutional problems. Almost 40 years of studies, surveys, and experience strongly indicate, however, that this effort has failed. Today's administration of the death penalty involves three fundamental constitutional defects: (1) serious unreliability, (2) arbitrariness in application, and (3) unconscionably long delays that undermine the death penalty's penological purpose. Perhaps as a result, (4) most places within the United States have abandoned its use.

I shall describe each of these considerations, emphasizing changes that have occurred during the past four decades. For it is those changes, taken together with my own 20 years of experience on this Court, that lead me to believe that the death penalty, in and of itself, now likely constitutes a legally prohibited "cruel and unusual punishmen[t]."

[Sections I, II, III, and IV, further describing the key points of the dissenting opinion, have been omitted.]

V

I recognize a strong counterargument that favors constitutionality. We are a court. Why should we not leave the matter up to the people acting democratically through legislatures? The Constitution foresees a country that will make most important decisions democratically. Most nations that have abandoned the death penalty have done so through legislation, not judicial decision. And legislators, unlike judges, are free to take account of matters such as monetary costs, which I do not claim are relevant here. See, *e.g.*, Berman, Nebraska Lawmakers Abolish the Death Penalty, Narrowly Overriding Governor's Veto, Washington Post Blog, Post Nation, May 27, 2015) (listing cost as one of the reasons why Nebraska legislators recently repealed the death penalty in that State); cf. California Commission on the Fair Administration of Justice, Report and Recommendations on the Administration of the Death Penalty in California 117 (June 30, 2008) (death penalty costs California $137 million per year; a comparable system of life imprisonment without parole would cost $11.5 million per year), online at http://www.ccfaj.org/rr dp-official.html; Dáte, The High Price of Killing Killers, Palm Beach Post, Jan. 4, 2000, p. 1A (cost of each execution is $23 million above cost of life imprisonment without parole in Florida).

The answer is that the matters I have discussed, such as lack of reliability, the arbitrary application of a serious and irreversible punishment, individual suffering caused by long delays, and lack of penological purpose are quintessentially judicial matters. They concern the infliction—indeed the unfair, cruel, and unusual infliction—of a serious punishment upon an individual. I recognize that in 1972 this Court, in a sense, turned to Congress and the state legislatures in its search for standards that would increase the fairness and reliability of imposing a death penalty. The legislatures responded. But, in the last four decades, considerable evidence has accumulated that those responses have not worked.

Thus we are left with a judicial responsibility. The Eighth Amendment sets forth the relevant law, and we must interpret that law. See *Marbury v. Madison*, 1 Cranch 137, 177 (1803); Hall, 572 U. S., at ___ (slip op., at 19) ("That exercise of independent judgment is the Court's judicial duty"). We have made clear that "'the Constitution contemplates that in the end our own judgment will be brought to bear on the question of the acceptability of the death penalty under the Eighth Amendment.'" *Id.*, at ___ (slip op., at 19) (quoting *Coker v. Georgia*, 433 U. S. 584, 597 (1977) (plurality opinion)); see also *Thompson v. Oklahoma*, 487 U. S. 815, 833, n. 40 (1988) (plurality opinion).

For the reasons I have set forth in this opinion, I believe it highly likely that the death penalty violates the Eighth Amendment. At the very least, the Court should call for full briefing on the basic question.

With respect, I dissent.

[Justice Breyer's tables and graphics have been omitted.]

[The dissenting opinion of Justice Sotomayor has been omitted.]

SOURCE: U.S. Supreme Court. *Glossip v. Gross*. 576 U.S.__(2015). http://www.supremecourt.gov/opinions/14pdf/14-7955_aplc.pdf.

OTHER HISTORIC DOCUMENTS OF INTEREST

California Passes Law to Require Vaccinations for Public School Students

JUNE 30, 2015

Spurred by a measles outbreak that began in December 2014 in Southern California and sickened 150 individuals, on June 30, Governor Jerry Brown signed into law a bill that would require all children entering the public school system to be vaccinated, even if such vaccinations violated a parent's personal or religious beliefs. Brown faced sharp criticism from anti-vaccine groups that argued that he was forcing parents to do something against their will that they believed could harm their child. Pro-vaccinators, however, celebrated the governor's decision, noting that vaccinating a greater number of children would help prevent the spread of disease. The new law would make California only the third in the nation to deny religious exemption waivers for vaccines, and the thirty-second to deny vaccine exemptions on grounds of personal or moral beliefs.

MEASLES OUTBREAK FORCES ACTION

In 2012, Governor Brown signed into law a bill that required parents seeking a "personal belief" exemption from vaccination to first receive consultation from a healthcare professional about the risks and benefits of vaccines. Those seeking an exemption on religious grounds were not included in the law. Despite the new regulations, vaccination rates, particularly in California's most affluent areas, continued to fall. In fall 2014, approximately 3 percent, or around 13,500, of California kindergarteners were not vaccinated and held a personal belief exemption, up from less than 1 percent a few years earlier. A total 80,000 public school students held such exemptions. According to state epidemiologist Dr. Gil Chavez, in some schools, vaccination rates were 50 percent or lower, creating an environment in which disease could quickly spread.

In December 2014, a measles outbreak linked to Disneyland in Southern California quickly spread throughout the west, infecting 150 people, some of whom required hospitalization. Many of those who contracted the highly contagious disease had not been vaccinated against it, either because they disagreed on personal or religious grounds or because they were too young for the combination measles-mumps-rubella (MMR) vaccine. The outbreak was declared over in April 2015, but the situation led state Senate and Assembly members to formulate legislation that would remove vaccination exemptions for children in public schools.

SB 277 Introduced, Debated

SB 277 was first introduced in the Senate in April 2015. It instantly raised public ire, specifically from affluent individuals who had begun refusing to vaccinate their children on personal grounds. The raucous public debate reached a fever pitch when State Sen. Richard Pan, a Democrat, who coauthored the bill, had to be given additional security after he received a number of threatening phone calls and e-mail from those who opposed the legislation. He continued to press on against critics, even after he was compared to a Nazi who should be hung, stating that "SB 277 is about freedom; freedom from deadly contagions that are now preventable because of vaccines."

Those who did not support the legislation did so primarily because of questions about the safety of vaccines. Specifically, a number of cases have been debated in the courts that the MMR vaccine can cause autism. This belief has been widely disputed by those in the medical community, and in February 2009, a special federal court found no evidence to suggest such link. In 2013, the Institute of Medicine conducted a comprehensive study on vaccine safety and found them to be "among the most safe and effective public health interventions to prevent serious disease and death." Even so, vaccination rates have continued to decline across the country. In some states, vaccine refusal and the spacing out of vaccinations beyond what is recommended has meant that usage in these areas is comparable to that in developing, conflict-ridden nations.

The anti-SB 277 campaign was led partially by the California Coalition for Vaccine Choice, whose website states that the law "eliminates a parent's right to exempt their children from one, some, or all vaccines," a procedure that it calls "risk-laden." Additionally, the group states that the vaccine mandate forces students to "lose their State Constitutional right for a free and appropriate education in public and private K–12 schools."

The National Vaccine Information Center (NVIC) also opposed the proposed legislation. The nonprofit organization is dedicated to educating the public about vaccines to prevent "vaccine injuries and deaths." The group said that the government should not be permitted to decide for parents which vaccines their children should receive. Barbara Loe Fisher, NVIC president, said that the bill "fails to value the health and educational needs of vulnerable children," by arguing that doctors rarely distribute medical exemptions for vaccinations, which under SB 277 would be the only acceptable means to opt out of vaccination. During testimony before California's Senate Education Committee, Dawn Richardson, NVIC's director of advocacy said, "SB 277 is based on the faulty assumption that denying partially or unvaccinated children an education produces an overall desirable outcome for the state of California. The bottom line is SB 277 needs to be opposed because it isolates, marginalizes and punishes healthy California children whose parents don't agree with all government mandated vaccines by extorting an education with vaccination."

Supporters of the law, including the California Medical Association (CMA), American Academy of Pediatrics, California, California Immunization Coalition, Vaccinate California, and Health Officers Association of California, argued that the health benefits of immunizations far outweigh any concerns. "Immunizations have been a cornerstone of medical advancements in this century, eliminating the fear of death and permanent disability from diseases that once threatened communities across the world," said CMA president Luther Cobb.

Supporters stated that an important health benefit of vaccines is what is known as herd immunity, the notion that when a majority of a population is vaccinated against a specific disease, it has less chance to spread and infect those in the group. And in response to anti-vaccinators concerned about potential health risks, supporters pointed to research conducted by the National Institutes of Health which has found on numerous occasions that strict exemption policies at the state level increase vaccination rates and that higher vaccination rates lead to lower levels of disease and outbreaks.

SB 277 Passes State Senate and Assembly

Despite public opposition, the state Senate passed SB 277 by a vote of 25–11 on May 14. During the first week of June, the body passed an amended version that would make it easier for families to obtain a medical exemption by allowing doctors to take family history into account. On June 9, a California state Assembly committee approved SB 277, thus sending it for a full vote on the Assembly floor. "This is fundamentally a bill about public health. Every child deserves the right to go to school in a safe and healthy environment," Democratic assemblymember Rob Bonta, chairman of the committee, said following the 12–6 party line vote. Assemblymember Marie Waldron, a Republican, voted against the measure in committee, saying that "informed consent is a human right" and that the bill could result in a "loss of freedom." Assemblymember Mike Gatto, a Democrat, stated that he would vote against the bill on the floor because it would allow the state the ability to "[infringe] on the rights of children to attend school."

On June 25, the bill passed the full Assembly with by a vote of 46–31. In response, Cobb said with the governor's signature, the law would help keep preventable disease from spreading. "We've seen with this recent epidemic that rates of immunization are low enough that epidemics can be spread now," adding that "reasons for failing to immunize people . . . are based on unscientific and untrue objections, and it's just a good public-health measure." On June 29, the Senate voted 24–14 to approve the Assembly's version of the bill and pass it to the governor's desk for signature.

Governor Signs Legislation

Just one day after final Senate passage, on June 30 Governor Brown signed SB 277 into law, stating that "the science is clear that vaccines dramatically protect children against a number of infectious and dangerous diseases." He added, "While it's true that no medical intervention is without risk, the evidence shows that immunization powerfully benefits and protects the community."

Under the new law, which goes into effect in 2016, children will not be permitted to enroll in school if they have not received the appropriate vaccinations. The mandatory vaccine law would not apply to home-based private schools, students in independent study programs that do not include classroom-based education, and special education and related services. Additionally, the law would still allow an exemption for those children who can obtain a medical reason from a doctor about why they should not be vaccinated. Those children who are already enrolled in school and who had a personal belief exemption prior to the close of 2015 would be permitted to remain in public school until seventh grade, at which point the parent would have to vaccinate or homeschool the child. Unvaccinated children with personal belief exemptions in public daycare facilities would be permitted to remain in the public school system until kindergarten.

—Heather Kerrigan

Following is the text of California Senate Bill 277, signed into law by Governor Jerry Brown on June 30, 2015; and the text of Governor Brown's statement about the newly signed legislation also on June 30, 2015.

DOCUMENT   *California's SB 277 Signed Into Law*

June 30, 2015

Senate Bill No. 277

CHAPTER 35

An act to amend Sections 120325, 120335, 120370, and 120375 of, to add Section 120338 to, and to repeal Section 120365 of, the Health and Safety Code, relating to public health.

[Approved by Governor June 30, 2015. Filed with Secretary of State June 30, 2015.]

BILL TEXT

THE PEOPLE OF THE STATE OF CALIFORNIA DO ENACT AS FOLLOWS:

SECTION 1.   Section 120325 of the Health and Safety Code is amended to read:
120325. In enacting this chapter, but excluding Section 120380, and in enacting Sections 120400, 120405, 120410, and 120415, it is the intent of the Legislature to provide:

(a) A means for the eventual achievement of total immunization of appropriate age groups against the following childhood diseases:

(1) Diphtheria.

(2) Hepatitis B.

(3) Haemophilus influenzae type b.

(4) Measles.

(5) Mumps.

(6) Pertussis (whooping cough).

(7) Poliomyelitis.

(8) Rubella.

(9) Tetanus.

(10) Varicella (chickenpox).

(11) Any other disease deemed appropriate by the department, taking into consideration the recommendations of the Advisory Committee on Immunization Practices of the United States Department of Health and Human Services, the American Academy of Pediatrics, and the American Academy of Family Physicians.

(b) That the persons required to be immunized be allowed to obtain immunizations from whatever medical source they so desire, subject only to the condition that the immunization be performed in accordance with the regulations of the department and that a record of the immunization is made in accordance with the regulations.

(c) Exemptions from immunization for medical reasons.

(d) For the keeping of adequate records of immunization so that health departments, schools, and other institutions, parents or guardians, and the persons immunized will be able to ascertain that a child is fully or only partially immunized, and so that appropriate public agencies will be able to ascertain the immunization needs of groups of children in schools or other institutions.

(e) Incentives to public health authorities to design innovative and creative programs that will promote and achieve full and timely immunization of children.

SEC. 2.   Section 120335 of the Health and Safety Code is amended to read:
120325. (a) As used in this chapter, "governing authority" means the governing board of each school district or the authority of each other private or public institution responsible for the operation and control of the institution or the principal or administrator of each school or institution.

(b) The governing authority shall not unconditionally admit any person as a pupil of any private or public elementary or secondary school, child care center, day nursery, nursery school, family day care home, or development center, unless, prior to his or her first admission to that institution, he or she has been fully immunized.

The following are the diseases for which immunizations shall be documented:

(1) Diphtheria.

(2) Haemophilus influenzae type b.

(3) Measles.

(4) Mumps.

(5) Pertussis (whooping cough).

(6) Poliomyelitis.

(7) Rubella.

(8) Tetanus.

(9) Hepatitis B.

(10) Varicella (chickenpox).

(11) Any other disease deemed appropriate by the department, taking into consideration the recommendations of the Advisory Committee on

Immunization Practices of the United States Department of Health and Human Services, the American Academy of Pediatrics, and the American Academy of Family Physicians.

(c) Notwithstanding subdivision (b), full immunization against hepatitis B shall not be a condition by which the governing authority shall admit or advance any pupil to the 7th grade level of any private or public elementary or secondary school.

(d) The governing authority shall not unconditionally admit or advance any pupil to the 7th grade level of any private or public elementary or secondary school unless the pupil has been fully immunized against pertussis, including all pertussis boosters appropriate for the pupil's age.

(e) The department may specify the immunizing agents that may be utilized and the manner in which immunizations are administered.

(f) This section does not apply to a pupil in a home-based private school or a pupil who is enrolled in an independent study program pursuant to Article 5.5 (commencing with Section 51745) of Chapter 5 of Part 28 of the Education Code and does not receive classroom-based instruction.

(g) (1) A pupil who, prior to January 1, 2016, submitted a letter or affidavit on file at a private or public elementary or secondary school, child day care center, day nursery, nursery school, family day care home, or development center stating beliefs opposed to immunization shall be allowed enrollment to any private or public elementary or secondary school, child day care center, day nursery, nursery school, family day care home, or development center within the state until the pupil enrolls in the next grade span.

(2) For purposes of this subdivision, "grade span" means each of the following:

(A) Birth to preschool.

(B) Kindergarten and grades 1 to 6, inclusive, including transitional kindergarten.

(C) Grades 7 to 12, inclusive.

(3) Except as provided in this subdivision, on and after July 1, 2016, the governing authority shall not unconditionally admit to any of those institutions specified in this subdivision for the first time, or admit or advance any pupil to 7th grade level, unless the pupil has been immunized for his or her age as required by this section.

(h) This section does not prohibit a pupil who qualifies for an individualized education program, pursuant to federal law and Section 56026 of the Education Code, from accessing any special education and related services required by his or her individualized education program.

SEC. 3.   Section 120338 is added to the Health and Safety Code, to read:
120338. Notwithstanding Sections 120325 and 120335, any immunizations deemed appropriate by the department pursuant to paragraph (11) of subdivision (a) of Section 120325 or paragraph (11) of subdivision (b) of Section 120335, may be mandated before a pupil's first admission to any private or public elementary or secondary school, child care center, day nursery, nursery school, family day care home, or development center, only if exemptions are allowed for both medical reasons and personal beliefs.

SEC. 4.   Section 120365 of the Health and Safety Code is repealed.

SEC. 5.   Section 120370 of the Health and Safety Code is amended to read:
120370. (a) If the parent or guardian files with the governing authority a written statement by a licensed physician to the effect that the physical condition of the child is such, or medical circumstances relating to the child are such, that immunization is not considered safe, indicating the specific nature and probable duration of the medical condition or circumstances, including, but not limited to, family medical history, for which the physician does not recommend immunization, that child shall be exempt from the requirements of Chapter 1 (commencing with Section 120325, but excluding Section 120380) and Sections 120400, 120405, 120410, and 120415 to the extent indicated by the physician's statement.

(b) If there is good cause to believe that a child has been exposed to a disease listed in subdivision (b) of Section 120335 and his or her documentary proof of immunization status does not show proof of immunization against that disease, that child may be temporarily excluded from the school or institution until the local health officer is satisfied that the child is no longer at risk of developing or transmitting the disease.

SEC. 6.   Section 120375 of the Health and Safety Code is amended to read:
120375. (a) The governing authority of each school or institution included in Section 120335 shall require documentary proof of each entrant's immunization status. The governing authority shall record the immunizations of each new entrant in the entrant's permanent enrollment and scholarship record on a form provided by the department. The immunization record of each new entrant admitted conditionally shall be reviewed periodically by the governing authority to ensure that within the time periods designated by regulation of the department he or she has been fully immunized against all of the diseases listed in Section 120335, and immunizations received subsequent to entry shall be added to the pupil's immunization record.

(b) The governing authority of each school or institution included in Section 120335 shall prohibit from further attendance any pupil admitted conditionally who failed to obtain the required immunizations within the time limits allowed in the regulations of the department, unless the pupil is exempted under Section 120370, until that pupil has been fully immunized against all of the diseases listed in Section 120335.

(c) The governing authority shall file a written report on the immunization status of new entrants to the school or institution under their jurisdiction with the department and the local health department at times and on forms prescribed by the department. As provided in paragraph (4) of subdivision (a) of Section 49076 of the Education Code, the local health department shall have access to the complete health information as it relates to immunization of each student in the schools or other institutions listed in Section 120335 in order to determine immunization deficiencies.

(d) The governing authority shall cooperate with the county health officer in carrying out programs for the immunization of persons applying for admission to any school or institution under its jurisdiction. The governing board of any school district may use funds, property, and personnel of the district for that purpose. The governing authority of any school or other institution may permit any licensed physician or any qualified registered nurse as provided in Section 2727.3 of the Business and Professions Code to administer immunizing agents to any person seeking admission to any school or institution under its jurisdiction.

SOURCE: California Legislature. "Senate Bill No. 227." Signed into law June 30, 2015. https://leginfo.legislature.ca.gov/faces/billTextClient.xhtml?bill_id=201520160SB277.

Governor Brown Issues Signing Statement on Vaccine Legislation

DOCUMENT

June 30, 2015

To the Members of the California State Senate:

SB 277 has occasioned widespread interest and controversy—with both proponents and opponents expressing their positions with eloquence and sincerity. After carefully reviewing the materials and arguments that have been presented, I have decided to sign this bill.

The science is clear that vaccines dramatically protect children against a number of infectious and dangerous diseases. While it's true that no medical intervention is without risk, the evidence shows that immunization powerfully benefits and protects the community.

The Legislature, after considerable debate, specifically amended SB 277, to exempt a child from immunizations whenever the child's physician concludes that there are "circumstances, including but not limited to, family medical history, for which the physician does not recommend immunization."

Thus, SB 277, while requiring that school children be vaccinated, explicitly provides an exception when a physician believes that circumstances—in the judgment and sound discretion of the physician—so warrant.

SOURCE: Office of the Governor of California. "SB 277 Signing Message." June 30, 2015. www.gov.ca.gov/docs/SB_277_Signing_Message.pdf.

OTHER HISTORIC DOCUMENTS OF INTEREST

FROM PREVIOUS *HISTORIC DOCUMENTS*

July

National Transportation Safety Board Responds to Deadly Amtrak Crash

JULY 8, 2015

On May 12, 2015, an Amtrak train derailed in Philadelphia, killing eight passengers. According to investigators, the train was traveling at a high rate of speed heading into a dangerous curve prior to the accident. In response, on July 8, 2015, the National Transportation Safety Board (NTSB) issued safety recommendations to both the Federal Railroad Administration (FRA) and the National Railroad Passenger Corporation (Amtrak). The recommendations included improving data collection through the implementation of both inward- and outward-facing video and audio recording equipment in locomotive control compartments. The NTSB considers the recording devices essential to monitoring safety violations to prevent crashes and in reconstructing a timeline of events in the case of a rail accident. Although there was no indication in the Philadelphia crash that the operator had been using an electronic device, the NTSB said that the installation of recording devices could help monitor whether train operators are violating railroad policies.

DERAILMENT OF TRAIN 188

On May 12, 2015, Amtrak passenger train 188, en route from Washington, D.C., to New York City, derailed near Frankford Junction in Philadelphia, Pennsylvania. The NTSB recovered the event recorder from the wreckage, which showed acceleration—rather than a gradual deceleration—into a steeply curved area of track with a speed restriction of fifty miles per hour and the manual application of the emergency brake when the train reached 106 miles per hour just prior to the derailment. The crash killed eight passengers and more than 200 of the 243 passengers and crew on board were injured. The site of the train 188 derailment occurred in the same section of track where an earlier fatal derailment in 1943 killed seventy-nine people.

During an initial press conference following the crash, the NTSB stated that if Automatic Train Control (ATC) had been activated on this section of track the accident would have likely been avoided. Though trains remain under manual control, ATC systems are able to warn the operator to apply brakes when a train exceeds the maximum speed for a portion of track. A signal alerts the engineer, but if the train operator fails to reduce the speed, ATC reduces a train's speed automatically. This system was installed and active on the southbound portion of the curve where the derailment occurred, but not on the northbound section of track because the risk was said by rail officials to be minimal due to the close proximity of the Philadelphia station where speeds remain restricted while trains depart the station.

The engineer of train 188 was interviewed by investigators shortly after the accident and claimed to remember little of the events leading up to the crash. The engineer handed over his cell phone to the authorities for use in the investigation. It was suspected that the engineer may have been distracted by use of a personal electronic device, but the NTSB later reported that there was no evidence that the engineer had either texted or made or received a call during the time period in question. The NTSB was also able to rule out train malfunction and track abnormalities.

NTSB Response

On May 19, 2015, the FRA issued an emergency order to Amtrak requiring modification of its ATC system to enforce the passenger train speed restrictions on the section of track where the derailment occurred. The emergency order also required Amtrak to identify other curves on the Northeast Corridor with a more than twenty-mile-per-hour drop in the authorized approach speed. The identified curves were to be assessed for added signage and possible implementation of ATC, with a twenty-day deadline to design an action plan for those additional warnings.

Separate recommendations released by the NTSB in July 2015, addressed to both the FRA and Amtrak, call for the installation and activation of equipment to record audio and video of locomotive control compartments. The use of similar recording devices on aircraft has been proven helpful to reconstruct events leading up to accidents rather than relying only on crew or passenger interviews for information. It is the NTSB's belief that the implementation of such recording devices, both inward and outward facing, would provide for greater overall passenger rail safety. Recording equipment would also allow management oversight of policies prohibiting personal cell phone usage in an industry where it is difficult to directly monitor employees. The NTSB's July recommendations reiterate and expand on similar recommendations it made in February 2010 regarding the use of recording devices. The FRA did not act on the earlier NTSB advice for a variety of reasons, including cost and disagreement regarding whether such recording devices are truly useful.

The NTSB has repeatedly recommended the use of audio and/or video recorders as far back as in 1996 when a train crashed in Silver Spring, Maryland. The NTSB reports twelve rail accidents between 1996 and 2013 where the lack of recording equipment hindered its investigation (see Table I). In the recommendations to the FRA, the NTSB also cited two rail investigations that have been aided positively by recording equipment. In these cases, the recording equipment helped provide an accurate timeline and corroborate information presented by the engineer.

Though the recommendations set forth by the NTSB following the derailment of passenger train 188 focus primarily on the installation of both inward and outward audio and video recording devices, during a congressional hearing the NTSB also called for increased use of ATC and Positive Train Control (PTC). The universal application of ATC has been long advocated by the NTSB, as has upgraded automatic braking systems. Currently, the sections of track with ATC are reviewed by private rail operators and upgrades are implemented based on a risk analysis. Congress mandated the implementation of PTC, an upgrade to the current automatic braking system, by December 31, 2015.

During testimony before the U.S. Senate Committee on Commerce, Science, and Transportation, NTSB vice chairman T. Bella Dinh-Zarr commented on the May 12, 2015, derailment of Amtrak train 188 and stated that use of PTC or ATC would have prevented the derailment. Her testimony strongly advocated the NTSB's position that the deadline for PTC activation not be extended. In her testimony, Dinh-Zarr stated, "Since 2004, in the 30

PTC-preventable freight and passenger rail accidents that the NTSB investigated, 69 people died, more than 1,200 were injured, and damages totaled millions of dollars."

Despite the NTSB's opposition, the deadline for this congressionally required upgrade was extended to 2018 following threats by some of the nation's largest commuter rail service providers to discontinue or limit service if the deadline was not extended. The extension was prompted largely by financial concerns from the private sector, because the installation of PTC is not federally funded. Though plans to install this automated system are scheduled to move forward, the implementation of PTC across the entire U.S. rail system has not been popular with some rail engineers and unions. Railroad engineers are reluctant to convert to a system that is more automatic, allowing for less experienced individuals to operate with the same amount of autonomy as more seasoned operators.

NTSB RELEASES DOCUMENTS

On February 1, 2016, the NTSB released hundreds of pages of its findings, although none reached a conclusion about the cause of the derailment. With the document release were two transcripts of interviews conducted with train operator Brandon Bostian. In the transcripts, Bostian remembers accelerating the train up to eighty miles-per-hour and then braking when he felt the sharp curve approaching. He reported thinking, "Well, this is it, I'm going over." NTSB investigators have been focusing on the possibility that Bostian lost situational awareness prior to the crash, and the possibility has been floated that a rock was thrown at the windshield and distracted Bostian. The segment of track on which the derailment occurred frequently had been a target of rock-throwing vandals, and the train assistant conductor reported to the NTSB that he heard Bostian say that the train hit something shortly before the crash. The NTSB is continuing its analysis of the evidence available, is expected to hold a formal hearing in April, and will make a draft report of its findings available around the one-year anniversary of the crash.

—Sarah Gall

Following are two safety recommendations released by the National Transportation Safety Board (NTSB) on July 8, 2015, including the February 23, 2010, recommendations referenced therein, following a deadly Amtrak train derailment.

NTSB Safety Recommendations R-10-1 and R-10-2

July 8, 2015

[All footnotes have been omitted.]

The Honorable Sarah Feinberg
Acting Administrator
Federal Railroad Administration
Washington, DC 20590

About 9:21 p.m. on May 12, 2015, Amtrak passenger train 188 derailed at milepost 81.62 near Frankfort Junction in Philadelphia, Pennsylvania. The tracks in the area of the derailment have a 4-degree curve with a permanent speed restriction of 50 mph. Event recorder data indicated the train was traveling 106 mph when the engineer made an emergency brake application; soon afterward, the train derailed at the curve. There were 250 passengers and 8 Amtrak employees on board. Eight passengers died, and more than 200 passengers were treated for injuries.

Background

The National Transportation Safety Board (NTSB) has long advocated the use of recording devices inside locomotive cabs as an aid in accident investigations and for use by transportation management in efficiency testing and performance monitoring programs. Our initial recommendation for "voice recorders" came as a result of our investigation into the 1996 collision of a Maryland Rail Commuter (MARC) train—operated by CSX Transportation (CSXT)—and an Amtrak train near Silver Spring, Maryland. Eleven people died, including all three CSXT operating crewmembers. We reiterated this safety recommendation in our investigation of the 1999 Bryan, Ohio, railroad accident where there were no surviving crewmembers. However, the Federal Railroad Administration (FRA) stated that no action would be taken to implement the recommendation. Since the FRA's refusal to act on the recommendation of in-cab audio recorders, the NTSB has investigated additional accidents in which audio recorders would have provided information to help determine probable cause and improve safety. . . . As a result, in issuing recommendations to the FRA after investigating this accident, the NTSB included a recommendation to require the installation of inward-facing video recorders in all controlling locomotive cabs and cab car operating compartments.

However, the benefit of recording audio and images of operating crew members is not limited to investigations. These recordings could help railroad management prevent accidents by identifying safety issues before they lead to injuries and loss of life by using them to develop valuable training tools. . . . Discussing the strong safety case for a requirement for inward-facing cameras in locomotives, the NTSB noted that:

> [I]n all too many accidents, the individuals directly involved are either limited in their recollection of events or, as in the case of the Chatsworth accident, are not available to be interviewed because of fatal injuries. In a number of accidents the NTSB has investigated, a better knowledge of crewmembers' actions before an accident would have helped reveal the key causal factors and would perhaps have facilitated the development of more effective safety recommendations.

Accordingly, the NTSB enhanced its earlier recommendation and called for the FRA to require the installation, in control compartments, of "crash- and fire-protected inward- and outward-facing audio and image recorders capable of providing recordings [for at least 12 hours] to verify that train crew actions are in accordance with rules and procedures that are essential to safety as well as train operating conditions." The NTSB also recommended that the FRA "[r]equire that railroads regularly review and use in-cab audio and image recordings . . . to verify that train crew actions are in accordance with rules and procedures that are essential to safety."

... The NTSB recognizes the significant privacy concerns regarding the public disclosure of audio and image recordings. Congress also has been sensitive to the public disclosure of these sensitive data and information after transportation accidents. For this reason, in 1990, it enacted confidentiality protections that prohibit the NTSB from publicly disclosing aviation cockpit voice recordings and from prematurely disclosing transcripts of oral communications by flight crewmembers. In 2000, it enacted similar confidentiality protections prohibiting the disclosure of aviation cockpit video recordings and surface vehicle voice or video recordings, as well as premature disclosure of aviation cockpit video transcripts and surface vehicle voice or video transcripts of oral communications of train employees or other surface transportation operating employees. Congress also precluded litigants from using discovery to obtain cockpit and surface vehicle recordings and transcripts in any judicial proceeding.

Audio and image recorders in locomotives and cab car operating compartments are critically important because they could assist NTSB investigators and others with understanding what happened in a train before an accident.... The Amtrak 188 accident in Philadelphia is only the latest example where the engineer's recollection of events is limited, and inward-facing recorders could have provided valuable information as NTSB determines the probable cause of this tragic accident. The following table lists rail accidents in which the NTSB recommended the use of audio and/or image recorders in the cab. In almost all cases, the NTSB's investigations were hampered by the lack of audio and/or image data.

Table 1 Damages incurred in previous accidents.

Location	Date	Fatalities	Injuries	Damages/Costs
Silver Spring, MD	Feb. 16, 1996	11	26	$7.5 million
Bryan, Ohio	Jan. 17, 1999	2		$5.3 million
Gunter, TX	May 19, 2004	1	4	$2.1 million
Macdona, TX	June 28, 2004	3	32	$5.85 million
Anding, MS	July 10, 2005	4		$10.1 million
Texarkana, AR	Oct. 15, 2005	1		$2.3 million
Chatsworth, CA	Sept. 12, 2008	25	102	$12 million
Two Harbors, MN	Sept. 30, 2010		5	$8.1 million
Red Oak, Iowa	April 17, 2011	2		$8.7 million
Goodwell, OK	June 24, 2012	3		$14.8 million
Chaffee, MO	May 25, 2013		2	$11 million
Bronx, NY	Dec. 1, 2013	4	59	$9 million
Total:		**56**	**230**	**$96.75 million**

[Table footnotes have been omitted.]

Recently, two NTSB rail investigations were aided by inward-facing audio and image recorders. In a 2013 accident in which a Bay Area Rapid Transit train struck roadway workers, a digital audio and video recorder was mounted above the operator's seat in the lead car. It was positioned to record the operator and the car control panel. The information gathered from the recording helped verify the accident sequence and provided an accurate timeline of events. In a second case, a Metrolink commuter train collided with a truck tractor on February 24, 2015, in Oxnard, California. The Metrolink locomotive was equipped with inward- and outward-facing audio and image recorders. Although the investigation is ongoing, the information provided by the inward-facing audio and image recorder has been critical in corroborating the engineer's description of events.

The need for recorded information—including audio and images—for operational and safety oversight is an important issue across transportation modes. The NTSB has made recommendations in aviation that address this issue for large transport category aircraft operations, as well as helicopter emergency services operations. Similarly, the NTSB issued recommendations for heavy commercial highway vehicles to require that motor carrier operators use recorded information for operational and safety oversight.

Recommendations

The NTSB continues to believe inward- and outward-facing audio and image recorders improve the quality of accident investigations and provide the opportunity for proactive steps by railroad management to improve operational safety. We have been encouraged by the inclusion of these recommendations in previously proposed rail safety legislation, and we hope this can be part of a rail safety legislative proposal that may be considered by this Congress. We are also encouraged that two Class I railroads and some commuter railroads have proceeded with installing in-cab audio and image recorder devices in their locomotives. Although we will continue to address the recommendation to individual railroads, we believe the FRA should take the lead on this important safety initiative. Because of this, the National Transportation Safety Board reiterates the following recommendations to the Federal Railroad Administration:

R-10-1

Require the installation, in all controlling locomotive cabs and cab car operating compartments, of crash- and fire-protected inward- and outward-facing audio and image recorders capable of providing recordings to verify that train crew actions are in accordance with rules and procedures that are essential to safety as well as train operating conditions. The devices should have a minimum 12-hour continuous recording capability with recordings that are easily accessible for review, with appropriate limitations on public release, for the investigation of accidents or for use by management in carrying out efficiency testing and system-wide performance monitoring programs.

R-10-2

Require that railroads regularly review and use in-cab audio and image recordings (with appropriate limitations on public release), in conjunction with other performance data, to verify that train crew actions are in accordance with rules and procedures that are essential to safety.

We are also making three recommendations to Amtrak pertaining to the installation of inward- and outward-facing audio and image recorders.

Chairman HART, Vice Chairman DINH-ZARR, and Members SUMWALT and WEENER concurred in these recommendations.

[Instructions for sending a response to the recommendations have been omitted.]

Safety Recommendation
Date: February 23, 2010

The Honorable Joseph C. Szabo
Administrator
Federal Railroad Administration
[Address omitted]

About 4:22 p.m., Pacific daylight time, on Friday, September 12, 2008, westbound Southern California Regional Rail Authority (SCRRA) Metrolink train 111, consisting of one locomotive and three passenger cars, collided head on with eastbound Union Pacific Railroad (UP) freight train LOF65–12 (Leesdale Local) near Chatsworth, California. The Metrolink train derailed its locomotive and lead passenger car; the UP train derailed its 2 locomotives and 10 of its 17 cars. The force of the collision caused the locomotive of train 111 to telescope into the lead passenger coach by about 52 feet. The accident resulted in 25 fatalities, including the engineer of train 111. Emergency response agencies reported transporting 102 injured passengers to local hospitals. Damages were estimated to be in excess of $12 million.

The National Transportation Safety Board determined that the probable cause of this accident was the failure of the Metrolink engineer to observe and appropriately respond to the red signal aspect at Control Point (CP) Topanga because he was engaged in prohibited use of a wireless device, specifically text messaging, that distracted him from his duties. Contributing to the accident was the lack of a positive train control system that would have stopped the Metrolink train short of the red signal and thus prevented the collision.

... [D]uring at least part of the time that he could have been, and should have been, observing the signal at CP Topanga, the engineer was likely reading an incoming text message, formulating a response, and entering that response into his wireless device.

[Additional details regarding the engineer's text messaging activity have been omitted.]

TRAIN 111 ENGINEER'S PATTERN OF WIRELESS DEVICE USE

The investigation revealed that, between about 6:05 a.m. and 4:22 p.m. on the day of the accident, the engineer sent or received a total of 95 text messages. During the time periods (morning and evening shifts) that he was responsible for operating a train, he sent 21 text messages, received 20 text messages, and made four outgoing telephone calls. The investigation further revealed that this amount of activity was not unusual for this engineer. . . .

The *General Code of Operating Rules* and Connex operating rules forbid non-work-related and non-emergency use of personal wireless devices by operating crewmembers. In fact, the train 111 engineer was in violation of Connex operating rules simply by having his wireless device in the locomotive cab and turned on while he was at the controls of the locomotive or cab control car. . . .

The engineer was well aware that he was violating company rules with regard to his use of a wireless device. In 2006, as part of an efficiency test, he was found to have his cell phone turned on in his briefcase. He said that he had forgotten to turn it off when he went on duty, but he was documented at that time as having failed to comply with company safety rules. Only about a month before the accident, the conductor on the engineer's train saw the engineer using his cell phone, and he reminded him of the prohibition. . . . The NTSB concludes that the Metrolink engineer was aware that he was violating company safety rules when he used his cell phone to make calls or to send and receive text messages while on duty, but he continued the practice nonetheless.

LEESDALE LOCAL CONDUCTOR'S USE OF WIRELESS DEVICE

. . . The records indicate that the conductor of the Leesdale Local sent or received a total of 41 text messages while on duty, with 35 of these being sent or received during the time the conductor's report shows that the train was moving. His last outgoing text message was received and logged by the Verizon network at 4:20 p.m., about the time his train exited tunnel 27 and about 2 minutes before the collision.

Although the conductor was in the cab of the locomotive at the time he sent his last text message before the accident, he was not at the controls. . . . The NTSB therefore concludes that, although the conductor of the Leesdale Local violated operating rules . . . any distraction caused by such use did not cause or contribute to this accident.

[Additional details regarding history of safety infractions committed by Train 111 engineer have been omitted.]

EFFICIENCY TESTING AND MANAGEMENT OVERSIGHT

. . . [T]he engineer habitually used his cell phone at times when he knew that any distraction from the task at hand could have serious safety consequences. Further, by actively encouraging and facilitating access by unauthorized persons to the locomotive cab, he created a situation that could pose another serious safety risk.

As acknowledged during the public hearing on this accident, the nature of rail operations makes enforcement of certain operating rules extremely difficult, if not impossible. Metrolink trains, as is common with other passenger trains, have only the engineer in the operating compartment. No reasonable method exists for management, by personal observation, to determine whether the engineer (or other crewmember) boards the train with a personal wireless device in his or her possession, and once the train leaves a station, no mechanism is currently in place to determine whether the device is in use.

. . . The engineer clearly took advantage of the privacy afforded by the locked locomotive cab to freely and repeatedly use his cell phone in violation of railroad operating rules. Even though this engineer and conductor had worked together 5 days a week, two shifts per day, for the previous 5 months, the conductor was not aware of the extent to which the engineer was using his wireless device while aboard the train. It is therefore unlikely that routine efficiency testing would ever have identified the scope of the engineer's violations with regard to wireless devices.

Similarly, the engineer's permitting of unauthorized persons to occupy the operating compartment of his locomotive stood a very low likelihood of being discovered through ordinary management supervision or efficiency testing. The engineer was familiar enough with his route and with the scope of management's oversight to be able to violate the rules without discovery. He had already allowed his rail fan friends one "ride-along" earlier in the week, and he knew where, when, and how they could again board his train undetected on the evening of the accident.

After the accident, Metrolink stiffened the penalty for unauthorized use of wireless devices by crewmembers on moving trains. Such violations will now result in immediate termination of employment. Similarly, with the issuance of Emergency Order 26, the Federal Railroad Administration (FRA) has raised violations involving the use of wireless devices to the Federal level. But making the violation more serious or the penalty more severe does not address the difficulty in identifying violators. With regard to both cell phone use and allowing unauthorized persons into his train's operating compartment, the train 111 engineer obviously had a high degree of confidence that his actions would not be detected.

As shown in the case of the conductor of the Leesdale Local, who also made inappropriate use of a wireless device to send a text message only minutes before the collision, even having other crewmembers present is an insufficient deterrent against such use.

The NTSB therefore concludes that, because of the privacy afforded by a locomotive cab or train operating compartment, routine efficiency testing and performance monitoring practices are inadequate to determine whether or to what extent engineers or other crewmembers may not be complying with safety rules such as those regarding use of wireless devices or allowing access by unauthorized persons.

In-Cab Audio and Image Recording Devices

The engineer in this accident was able to conceal his inappropriate behavior. . . . The NTSB believes that the only reasonable and reliable mechanism for making such observations is an in-cab audio and image recorder that will capture a crewmember's activities while in the train operating compartment.

The NTSB has long supported the installation of audio recording devices in locomotive cabs and train operating compartments. . . .

As a result of its investigation of the collision between a Maryland Rail Commuter train and an Amtrak train near Silver Spring, Maryland, on February 16, 1996, in which no operating crewmembers survived, the NTSB was unable to determine whether certain crewmember activities leading up to the accident may have contributed to the accident. Consequently, the NTSB made the following recommendation to the FRA:

R-97-9

Amend 49 Code of Federal Regulations Part 229 to require the recording of train crewmembers' voice communications for exclusive use in accident investigations and with appropriate limitations on the public release of such recordings.

After its investigation of another railroad accident with no surviving crewmembers that occurred in 1999 in Bryan, Ohio, the NTSB reiterated Safety Recommendation R-97-9 to the FRA. The FRA responded that it has reluctantly come to the conclusion that this recommendation should not be implemented at the present time. . . . [The] FRA appreciates that, as time passes and other uses are found for recording media that may create synergies with other public and private purposes, the Board's recommendation may warrant re-examination.

Based on this response and further meetings, the NTSB classified Safety Recommendation R-97-9—"Closed—Unacceptable Action."

Since the refusal by the FRA to act on the recommendation regarding in-cab recorders, the NTSB has continued to investigate accidents in which such recorders would have provided valuable information to help determine probable cause and develop safety recommendations. Most recently, as a result of its investigation of a July 10, 2005, collision of two CN freight trains in Anding, Mississippi, the NTSB made the following safety recommendation to the FRA:

R-07-3

Require the installation of a crash- and fire-protected locomotive cab voice recorder, or a combined voice and video recorder, (for the exclusive use in accident investigations and with appropriate limitations on the public release of such recordings) in all controlling locomotive cabs and cab car operating compartments. The recorder should have a minimum 2-hour continuous recording capability, microphones capable of capturing crewmembers' voices and sounds generated within the cab, and a channel to record all radio conversations to and from crewmembers.

. . . The FRA indicated in its response to the NTSB's recommendation that the subject of in-cab video and audio recordings had been discussed at a meeting of the Railroad Safety Advisory Committee Locomotive Working Group. Pending more information about those discussions, Safety Recommendation R-07-3 was classified—"Open—Acceptable Response" on July 31, 2009.

As is clear from the wording of Safety Recommendations R-97-9 and R-07-3, the NTSB's emphasis up to this point has been on the use of audio and/or image recordings as a tool of accident investigation. But this accident demonstrates that audio-only in-cab recordings that may be reviewed only after an accident do not represent the most effective use of recorder technology for accident prevention. . . .

The presence, in addition to audio recording capability, of in-cab image recording capability would have been the only means available to have determined exactly what actions the engineer was taking during the accident trip. These images would have revealed the engineer's text messaging activities even absent any sounds that could have been captured by an audio recorder. Similarly, any entry into the locomotive or train operating compartment by unauthorized persons would be evident on image recorders.

. . . The NTSB has long advocated the use of recorded audio and images not only after an accident has occurred, but routinely, as part of management's efficiency testing and performance monitoring programs. In the same way that railroad operating employees are continually tested on signal compliance or speed control, audio and image recordings of engineers and other crewmembers could be reviewed at random to verify compliance with safety rules and procedures. In particular, this information could allow railroads to identify noncompliant behaviors and pursue corrective action before an accident occurs. . . . Regular review of in-cab audio and image recordings would give managers insight into other potential safety issues or unsafe operating practices that may not be revealed by any other means and of which the crews themselves may be unaware. Action could then be taken to address these issues through changes in rules, operating practices, or employee training programs.

[Repeated information regarding managerial oversight has been omitted.]

Therefore, the National Transportation Safety Board makes the following recommendations to the Federal Railroad Administration:

Require the installation, in all controlling locomotive cabs and cab car operating compartments, of crash- and fire-protected inward- and outward-facing audio and image recorders capable of providing recordings to verify that train crew actions are in accordance with rules and procedures that are essential to safety as well as train operating conditions. The devices should have a minimum 12-hour continuous recording capability with recordings that are easily accessible for review, with appropriate limitations on public release, for the investigation of accidents or for use by management in carrying out efficiency testing and systemwide performance monitoring programs. (R-10-1)

Require that railroads regularly review and use in-cab audio and image recordings (with appropriate limitations on public release), in conjunction with other performance data, to verify that train crew actions are in accordance with rules and procedures that are essential to safety. (R-10-2)

The National Transportation Safety Board has also reclassified the following safety recommendation previously issued to the Federal Railroad Administration:

R-07-3

Require the installation of a crash- and fire-protected locomotive cab voice recorder, or a combined voice and video recorder, (for the exclusive use in accident investigations and with appropriate limitations on the public release of such recordings) in all controlling locomotive cabs and cab car operating compartments. The recorder should have a minimum 2-hour continuous recording capability, microphones capable of capturing crewmembers' voices and sounds generated within the cab, and a channel to record all radio conversations to and from crewmembers.

Because Safety Recommendation R-10-1, issued as a result of this accident investigation, expands upon and reinforces the intent of Safety Recommendation R-07-3, that recommendation, which was previously classified—"Open—Acceptable Response," is reclassified—"Closed—Unacceptable Action/Superseded."

[Instructions for sending a response to the recommendations have been omitted.]

Chairman HERSMAN, Vice Chairman HART, and Member SUMWALT concurred in these recommendations. Chairman Hersman filed a concurring statement, in which Vice Chairman Hart and Member Sumwalt joined, which is attached to the final Railroad Accident Report.

SOURCE: National Transportation Safety Board. "R-10-1 and -2 (Reiteration)." July 8, 2015. www.ntsb .gov/safety/safety-recs/RecLetters/R-10-001-002.pdf.

NTSB Safety Recommendations R-15-28 through 30

July 8, 2015

[All footnotes have been omitted.]

Mr. Joseph H. Boardman
President and Chief Executive Officer
National Railroad Passenger Corporation
[Address omitted.]

[Introductory paragraph detailing the NTSB's mission has been omitted.]

Based on the NTSB's ongoing investigation of the derailment of the National Railroad Passenger Corporation (Amtrak) passenger train 188 on May 12, 2015, we are issuing safety recommendations that address the installation of inward- and outward-facing audio and image recorders in this letter. We appreciate that Amtrak has installed outward-facing cameras and has announced plans to install inward-facing video cameras in some locomotive cabs and cab car operating compartments. However, the installed outward-facing cameras are not fire and crash protected, and Amtrak's announcement does not address the technical specification for the inward-facing cameras, a plan or schedule for installation, how Amtrak intends to use the recorded images, or the need to record in-cab audio in addition to video. Facts supporting the NTSB's recommendations are presented below.

[Factual information, background information, and a table detailing damages incurred in previous accidents, repeated from recommendations to the FRA dated July 8, 2015, have been omitted.]

Recommendations

. . . . In a May 26, 2015, press release, Amtrak announced it will install inward-facing video cameras in its ACS-64 locomotives that operate on the Northwest corridor by the end of 2015. Amtrak also announced it is developing a plan to install inward-facing cameras on the rest of the fleet. The NTSB is encouraged by this statement, but believes that additional requirements for a complete inward and outward-facing audio and image recorder system are necessary. Because of this, the National Transportation Safety Board makes the following recommendations to the National Railroad Passenger Corporation:

> Install, in all controlling locomotive cabs and cab car operating compartments, crash- and fire-protected inward- and outward-facing audio and image recorders capable of providing recordings to verify that train crew actions are in accordance with rules and procedures that are essential to safety as well as train operating conditions. The devices should have a minimum 12-hour continuous recording capability with recordings that are easily accessible for review, with appropriate limitations on public release, for the investigation of accidents or for use by management in carrying out efficiency testing and systemwide performance monitoring programs. (R-15-28)

> Semi-annually, issue a public report detailing Amtrak's progress in installing crash- and fire-protected inward- and outward-facing audio and image recorders. The report should include the number of locomotives and cab car operating compartments that have been equipped with the recorders, as well as the number of locomotives and cab car operating compartments in Amtrak's fleet that still lack those devices. (R-15-29)

> Regularly review and use in-cab audio and image recordings in conjunction with other performance data to verify crewmember actions are in accordance with rules and procedures that are essential to safety. (R-15-30)

We are also reiterating recommendations R-10-1 and R-10-2, which require inward- and outward-facing audio and image recorders, to the Federal Railroad Administration.

Chairman HART, Vice Chairman DINH-ZARR, and Members SUMWALT and WEENER concurred in these recommendations.

[Instructions for sending a response to the recommendations have been omitted.]

SOURCE: National Transportation Safety Board. "R-15-28 through -30." July 8, 2015. www.ntsb.gov/safety/safety-recs/recletters/R-15-028-030.pdf.

OTHER HISTORIC DOCUMENTS OF INTEREST

FROM PREVIOUS *HISTORIC DOCUMENTS*

- GAO Testimony On Amtrak, *1994*, p. 197

Governor Haley and NAACP on Agreement to Remove Confederate Flag

JULY 9 AND 11, 2015

The existence of the Confederate flag on the grounds of the statehouse in South Carolina has long been a lightning rod for those who view the flag as a symbol of black oppression and racism. Efforts have been made both within and outside the state to encourage the flag's removal, including an economic boycott of the state by the National Association for the Advancement of Colored People (NAACP). The ultimate catalyst for removal of the flag was the murder of nine African Americans at a church in Charleston in June 2015, allegedly by a man who supported the white supremacist movement and frequently appeared in photos with a Confederate flag. Ultimately, after strong pressure from across the country, the South Carolina legislature voted in July to have the flag removed, but debate continued nationwide regarding what purpose the flag serves in modern society.

HISTORY OF THE CONFEDERATE FLAG

The Confederate flag in its current iteration was never an official flag of the Confederacy during the Civil War. The "rebel flag," or "stars and bars" as it is alternately known, was the battle flag of Gen. Robert E. Lee's Northern Virginia army and did not become closely affiliated with the Confederacy as a whole until after the end of the war. Even then, it was primarily used during events commemorating those who lost their lives in defense of the South.

It was not until the 1940s when the flag became what some individuals, especially people of color, consider synonymous with racism. The Dixiecrat Party adopted the flag in 1948 as a symbol of its party's resistance to the federal government. A key policy position of the party at the time was the continuation of segregation, especially as the federal government made attempts to integrate schools and public facilities. Two years after the landmark *Brown v. Board of Education* decision in which the Supreme Court ruled segregation in public schools unconstitutional, Georgia became the first state to incorporate the battle flag into its official state flag, although it was revised in 2001 to reduce the Confederate imagery. Alabama, Arkansas, and Florida adopted symbols from the Confederate flag into their state flags, while Mississippi still includes an emblem of the Confederate flag in its state flag. Florida, Georgia, Louisiana, Mississippi, and South Carolina all have laws banning the desecration of the Confederate flag, although a Supreme Court ruling protecting burning a flag as a First Amendment right supersedes these laws.

In recent history, the flag has been frequently used by the Ku Klux Klan and other white supremacist organizations, leading many to view it as a symbol of black oppression. Others, however, view the flag as a symbol of Southern pride. A national CNN/ORC poll conducted in late June 2015 showed that of those Americans surveyed, 57 percent believe the flag is a symbol of Southern pride while 33 percent believe it is representative of racism. The poll showed a stark divide between black and white respondents, with 72 percent of blacks believing the flag is synonymous with racism, while only 25 percent of whites shared that opinion.

GOVERNOR HALEY, LEGISLATORS WORK FOR FLAG REMOVAL

In South Carolina, the first state to secede from the Union before the start of the Civil War, the Confederate flag was not flown at the state capitol until 1961 when it was raised during a ceremony commemorating the Battle of Fort Sumter. In 1962, the legislature approved a resolution to keep the flag on statehouse grounds but did not indicate a time for the flag's removal. Many prominent African Americans have alleged that the decision to raise and keep the flag at the capitol was related more to Southern dissatisfaction with the growing civil rights movement and less to the 100-year anniversary of the start of the Civil War. James Forman Jr., a Yale Law School professor, wrote, "The flag has been adopted knowingly and consciously by government officials seeking to assert their commitment to black subordination." *Washington Post* columnist Eugene Robinson called the 1961 raising of the flag "a middle finger directed at the federal government."

The flag remained in place on the statehouse dome until 2000, when lawmakers responded to a challenge from the NAACP. At that time, the legislature voted to remove the Confederate flag from the capitol building and instead place a smaller version of the flag at a monument for Confederate soldiers located on statehouse grounds. The flag was affixed directly to the pole without a pulley system, meaning it could not be raised or lowered, but could only be removed. And, according to the agreement that moved the flag to the monument, removal would require a two-thirds vote in the state legislature. Because the legislature denied the request of the NAACP to remove the flag completely, the group announced that it would boycott the state and encouraged its supporters to do so as well. That year, hundreds of conferences were relocated from South Carolina, tourism suffered, and North Carolina saw an economic increase because businesses moved from South Carolina across its border.

Three days after the Charleston church shooting, South Carolina governor Nikki Haley joined Sen. Lindsey Graham, R-S.C., Sen. Tim Scott, R-S.C., and former governor Mark Sanford to call for the flag's removal. "Today, we are here in a moment of unity in our state, without ill will, to say it is time to move the flag from the capitol grounds," Haley said during a press conference, adding that the flag remains "an integral part of our past" but "does not represent the future." Haley said it was her hope "that by removing a symbol that divides us, we can move our state forward in harmony, and we can honor the nine blessed souls who are now in heaven." Haley had previously avoided the question of whether the flag should be banned, calling it a "sensitive issue."

The South Carolina legislature adjourned on June 4, but because it had failed to pass a budget compromise, it was coming back into session on June 23. At that point, the legislature could determine whether to extend its session to take up the flag debate. Haley promised that if the legislature failed to do so, she would use her executive power to call them back into session. Public figures from across the nation encouraged the legislature to vote to remove the flag as soon as possible both to honor those killed in the Charleston church shooting and help the state move forward. White House spokesperson Josh Earnest said the president believes the flag "should be taken down and placed in a museum where it belongs."

CONFEDERATE FLAG REMOVED FROM STATEHOUSE GROUNDS

When it met on June 23, the legislature agreed to schedule a debate on removal of the Confederate flag. Debate began in the state Senate on July 6, and although it was heated at times, the flag removal bill swiftly passed by a vote of 37–3 and moved on to the House, where it bypassed committee and went directly to the floor for a vote on July 9.

Following thirteen hours of emotional debate and the introduction of sixty-eight amendments aimed at stalling a vote, on July 9, the South Carolina House voted 94–20 to remove the Confederate flag from statehouse grounds. Those who voted against the measure said they did so because they found removal of the flag to mean that the state was ignoring a painful yet integral part of its history that it should not repeat, and because they saw the flag as a remembrance of those who lost their lives defending South Carolina. Prior to the signing ceremony on July 9, Haley stated, "We're a state that believes in tradition. We're a state that believes in history. We're a state that believes in respect." She added, "We will bring [the flag] down with dignity, and we will make sure it is put in its rightful place."

On July 10, hundreds turned out for a ceremony at the statehouse for the removal of the flag. Although she did not speak at the event, during an interview shortly before the flag was taken down, Haley stated, "No one should ever drive by the statehouse and feel pain. No one should ever drive by the statehouse and feel like they don't belong." As part of the agreement to remove the flag from statehouse grounds, lawmakers said that the state would build a display to house the flag at a museum near the capitol building. The decision to spend $5.3 million to expand the statehood museum to create a space for the flag drew ire from many across the state.

Less than one week after the flag came down, members of the Ku Klux Klan and Black Panthers held competing protests outside the state capitol. Governor Haley urged residents to "[stay] away from the disruptive, hateful spectacle members of the Ku Klux Klan hope to create." An estimated 2,000 attended the two protests, which were controlled by statehouse police. Five were arrested and less than two dozen were injured during the protests.

NATIONWIDE IMPACT OF THE SOUTH CAROLINA DECISION

Following the lowering of the flag, NAACP president Cornell William Brooks said in a statement that "a symbolic stain of racism has been dismissed from the state Capitol grounds," adding that the flag "should be studied and no longer honored." Brooks also noted that the group would vote to end its fifteen-year economic boycott of the state, which had prohibited the group from tourism and spending in South Carolina. On July 11, the NAACP passed a resolution that welcomed the actions of the South Carolina legislature, but also "clearly recognize[d] that there are still battles to be fought in other states and jurisdictions where emblems of hate and oppression continue to be celebrated."

The NCAA, which had stood in solidarity with the NAACP, announced a similar decision. "With this impending change, and consistent with our policy, South Carolina may bid to host future NCAA championships once the flag no longer flies at the State House grounds," NCAA Board of Governors chair Kirk Schultz said shortly before the flag was removed.

Following the removal of the flag in South Carolina, online sales of Confederate flag merchandise increased. On Amazon.com, for instance, in the twenty-four hours after the flag came down Confederate flags were the top three selling items on the site. In response, a number of retailers including Amazon.com, eBay, Kmart, Sears, Target, and Wal-Mart announced that they would no longer sell products featuring the Confederate flag. Warner Bros. stated that it would no longer produce toy replicas of the General Lee car from its 1970s–1980s show *The Dukes of Hazzard*, which features the Confederate flag on its roof.

Other Southern states began considering how to deal with their own Confederate memorials and symbols. In Alabama, Governor Robert Bentley ordered four Confederate flags to be permanently removed from statehouse grounds, while governors in Maryland, North Carolina, and Virginia followed Texas's lead and moved to prohibit license plates featuring the Confederate flag. Mississippi's U.S. senators called on state leadership to consider revising the state flag to remove the Confederate imagery, while one Democratic representative from the state introduced legislation to ban the Mississippi flag in its current form from House office buildings and the House side of the U.S. Capitol building.

—Heather Kerrigan

Following is the text of a statement from South Carolina governor Nikki Haley on July 9, 2015, following a vote by the state House of Representatives to remove the Confederate flag from statehouse grounds; a statement from NAACP national and state leaders on July 9, 2015, welcoming the removal of the flag; and a NAACP resolution from July 11, 2015, ending the group's fifteen-year economic boycott of the state.

Governor Haley Remarks on Confederate Flag Removal

July 9, 2015

Governor Nikki Haley today issued the following statement:

"Today, as the Senate did before them, the House of Representatives has served the State of South Carolina and her people with great dignity. I'm grateful for their service and their compassion. It is a new day in South Carolina, a day we can all be proud of, a day that truly brings us all together as we continue to heal, as one people and one state."

SOURCE: Office of the Governor of South Carolina. "Statement From Gov. Nikki Haley." July 9, 2015. http://governor.sc.gov/News/Pages/RecentNews.aspx.

NAACP Leaders React to Removal of Confederate Flag

July 9, 2015

Today, the South Carolina House of Representatives voted 94–20 to remove the Confederate battle flag from public spaces including state Capitol grounds. Later today, Governor Nikki

Haley is expected to sign the bill into law. In light of this monumental victory, the NAACP released the following statement:

By President Cornell William Brooks, NAACP President & CEO:

"The NAACP applauds the South Carolina legislature for voting to remove the Confederate Battle flag—one of the longest standing symbols of hatred and exclusion—from public spaces and state Capitol grounds today. The confederate battle flag as a symbolic stain of racism has been dismissed from the state Capitol grounds and may now be deposited to a museum. This flag should be studied and no longer honored. This legislative decision affirms the 15 years of collective advocacy of the NAACP on both the national and state level to bring down the flag, in particular our 15 year economic boycott of the state that was joined by the NCAA and UAW. As we head to Philadelphia for our 106th Annual Convention this Saturday, we can now consider an emergency resolution to lift the economic boycott of the state. Today, South Carolina ushers the state and our country into a new era—one of unity and inclusion at a time of such profound tragedy. By removing the flag, South Carolina not only denounces an odious emblem of a bygone era but also honors the lives of nine students of scripture who were gunned down in a church, including that of Rev. Clementa Pinckney, the former South Carolina state senator. We applaud Governor Nikki Haley for her leadership and moral courage by changing her position and supporting the flag removal in the aftermath of tragedy. This decision will make South Carolina more welcoming and affirming of all people irrespective of their skin color."

By Dr. Lonnie Randolph, NAACP South Carolina State Conference President:

"Today, the South Carolina legislature did the right thing—one that is profoundly American—by taking down the Confederate battle flag. I applaud South Carolina state senators, members of the House of Representatives and Governor Nikki Haley for their commitment and support to the citizens of South Carolina and the citizens of this country. Fifteen years ago, the NAACP launched longstanding boycott against the state until the battle flag came down."

Source: National Association for the Advancement of Colored People. "NAACP Applauds South Carolina State Legislature for Voting to Remove Confederate Battle Flag." July 9, 2015. www.naacp .org/press/entry/naacp-applauds-south-carolina-state-legislature-for-voting-to-remove-confed.

NAACP Approves Resolution to End Economic Boycott of South Carolina

July 11, 2015

WHEREAS, the Confederate Battle Flag is a symbol of racial, ethnic and religious hatred, oppression, and murder which offends untold millions of people; and

WHEREAS, on June 17, 2015, nine members of the Emmanuel AME Church including their Pastor were gunned down as they were studying their Bible in their House of Worship by an individual driven by a hatred which was fueled by the Confederate Battle Flag and all that it stands for; and

WHEREAS, [i]n 1999, as a result of the insistence of the State of South Carolina to continue to fly the Confederate flag on the grounds of the state capitol, the NAACP called for a boycott of the state South Carolina; and

WHEREAS, [i]n 2000 the NAACP reiterated its condemnation of the [C]onfederate battle flag and the [C]onfederate battle emblem being flown over, being displayed in or on any public site or space building, or any emblem, flag standard or as part of any public communication; and

WHEREAS, as a result of the NAACP boycott, the South Carolina State Conference of NAACP Branches, led by the courageous and tenacious leadership of President Dr. Lonnie Randolph was, at times, degraded but never defeated; and

WHEREAS, had the South Carolina State Conference of NAACP Branches chosen at any point to prematurely end the boycott, it would have easily given strength and support to those elements within society who wanted to perpetuate the hatred and history of oppression associated with the Confederate flag; and

WHEREAS, on Friday, July 10, 2015, the flag was removed permanently from the Capitol grounds as a result of actions taken by the South Carolina Senate, the [S]outh Carolina House of Representatives, and the South Carolina Governor; and

WHEREAS, while removal of the flag was clearly a victory for the NAACP and a defeat for promoters of hate, the NAACP clearly recognizes that there are still battles to be fought in other states and jurisdictions where emblems of hate and oppression continue to be celebrated; and

WHEREAS, removal of the confederate flag is not going to solve most of the severe tangible challenges facing our nation, including discrimination in our criminal justice system, economic system, employment, education, housing, health care, or other barriers to full and equal protection under law and full first-class citizenship, but it does symbolize an end to the reverence of and adherence to values that support racially-based chattel slavery and the hatred which has divided our country for too long.

THEREFORE BE IT RESOLVED that the NAACP ends its boycott of South Carolina.

SOURCE: National Association for the Advancement of Colored People. "Resolution: NAACP Ends Boycott of South Carolina." July 11, 2015. www.naacp.org/blog/entry/resolution-naacp-ends-boycott-of-south-carolina.

OTHER HISTORIC DOCUMENTS OF INTEREST

FROM THIS VOLUME

New Horizons Spacecraft
Reaches Pluto

JULY 14 AND NOVEMBER 9, 2015

In July 2015, the United States achieved three space exploration firsts with the National Aeronautics and Space Administration's (NASA) New Horizons mission: the first exploration of Pluto, the first exploration of a world so far from Earth, and the first country to send a space probe to every planet in the solar system. The spacecraft collected countless images and observations of Pluto and its five moons during a six-month study period, transmitting data that changed scientists' understanding of the bodies' makeup and geologic history.

MISSION TO PLUTO

Pluto was discovered on February 18, 1930, by Clyde Tombaugh, a researcher at the Lowell Observatory in Flagstaff, Arizona, who was searching for a "Planet X" that scientists thought existed at the edge of the solar system. While classified as a planet in 1930, Pluto was reclassified as a dwarf planet by the International Astronomical Union in August 2006 because it had not "cleared its neighboring region of other objects"—one of three criteria for a body to be classified as a full-size planet.

Pluto was still considered a planet when NASA conceived of and launched the New Horizons mission, which centered on a flyby of the world and its five moons, two of which were discovered by the Hubble Space Telescope while the New Horizons spacecraft was in flight. The mission's primary objective was to explore the evolution of icy dwarf planets like Pluto and other objects in the Kuiper Belt, an outer region of the solar system populated by icy objects that contain information about the early formation of the solar system. New Horizons was also part of a series of missions—such as Cassini's exploration of Saturn and the Mars rovers—meant to inform NASA's longer-term plan to send astronauts to Mars in the 2030s.

The New Horizons spacecraft was roughly the size of a piano and weighed about 1,000 pounds. Its payload included seven instruments designed to produce color, composition, and thermal maps; analyze the composition and structure of Pluto's atmosphere and search for atmospheres around other objects; examine Pluto's interaction with solar winds; and measure the amount of space dust hitting the spacecraft during its voyage. New Horizons also carried a small aluminum canister containing the remains of Tombaugh, who'd passed away in 1997 at the age of 90. In addition, the spacecraft contained a 2004 Florida state quarter, which depicted a space shuttle as part of its design. The quarter was symbolic of Florida's role in space exploration but also served a purpose: engineers used it as a spin-balance weight for the spacecraft. Johns Hopkins University's Applied Physics Laboratory designed, built, and operated the spacecraft and helped manage the mission, while the Southwest Research Institute led the mission, science team, payload operations, and encounter science planning.

New Horizons launched from the Cape Canaveral Air Force Station in Florida on January 19, 2006, beginning its approximately decade-long journey to Pluto.

A Visit to Jupiter

New Horizons's voyage also included a flyby of Jupiter and its moons, which helped the mission team gain flyby experience before reaching Pluto and gave the spacecraft a gravity boost to help it along its journey. The flyby began in January 2007, with the spacecraft making its closest approach to the planet's surface—at a distance of 1.4 million miles—on February 28. New Horizons captured stunning photos of volcanic activity on Io, one of Jupiter's moons, as well as a motion-picture sequence of a volcanic eruption. The spacecraft also took incredibly detailed photos of Jupiter's high-altitude clouds and provided the first close-up images of lightning near the planet's poles. After completing the flyby, the spacecraft went into hibernation mode until December 2014, shortly before it began its approach to Pluto.

Pluto Study Begins

New Horizons's study of Pluto was scheduled to take six months and began on January 15, 2015. The spacecraft took its first color photo of Pluto and its moon Charon on April 9, which, according to NASA, was the first color image of Pluto ever captured by a spacecraft approaching the dwarf planet. New Horizons was 71 million miles away at the time. NASA also released a color movie showing Pluto and Charon in orbit that was created from a series of color images the spacecraft took between May 29 and June 3.

On July 14, after traveling for nearly ten years and across approximately 3 billion miles, New Horizons made its closest approach to Pluto, traveling past the dwarf planet at nine miles per second from a distance of 7,750 miles above the surface. The spacecraft sent a signal back to flight control that evening to confirm that it had survived the flyby—a signal that took four hours and 25 minutes to reach Earth. "We are in lock with telemetry from the spacecraft," said Alice Bowman, mission operations manager. "We have a healthy spacecraft, we have recorded data from the Pluto system, and we are outbound from Pluto." NASA released the first zoomed-in image of Pluto the following day. Where previous images had been lacking in detail and showed the surface as only a blur of colors, the New Horizons image clearly showed diverse terrain, ranging from wide smooth areas to lumpy regions and huge mountains.

The spacecraft began its full data download on September 5, a process expected to take as long as sixteen months, and new details of the dwarf planet and its composition began to emerge. Among the discoveries was the observation of a bright, heart-shaped formation on Pluto's surface that spanned approximately 1,000 miles near its equator. Informally dubbed the Tombaugh Region, the formation comprised frozen plains as well as a mountainous area. The lack of impact craters in the plains area was also an interesting discovery because the mission team expected that the surface would have been hit by at least some objects from the Kuiper Belt. This observation implied that Pluto's surface was less than 100 million years old—relatively young in the solar system's 4.5 billion-year-old history—and still geologically active. Close-up examination of the Tombaugh Region's mountains bolstered this hypothesis, as evidence suggested they had also formed within the last 100 million years. The mountains, some with elevations as high as 11,000 feet, also led scientists to speculate that there could be water on Pluto. They knew Pluto's surface was covered with nitrogen ice, methane ice, and carbon monoxide ice, but these materials are too soft to form mountains, prompting scientists to hypothesize that the mountains' bedrock must be made of water ice.

Indeed, New Horizons found evidence of a wide range of surface ages on Pluto, from ancient to intermediate to relatively young. This was an important discovery for the mission team because it demonstrated that geologic activity on icy worlds is not dependent on tidal heating. Scientists previously thought Pluto would be similar to Neptune's moon Triton, the surface of which is also free of impact craters due to ongoing geological activity. That activity had been attributed to Neptune's gravitational pull, which, by acting on Triton on a regular basis, heated Triton's interior and powered its geological change. However, there is no larger body pulling on Pluto with its gravity, challenging scientists' initial hypothesis.

Other noted findings included evidence of two potential ice volcanoes on the surface. Unlike Earth volcanoes, these would spew water ice, nitrogen, ammonia, or methane if they erupted. One of the formations, called Wright Mons, is approximately ninety miles high and if confirmed to be a volcano would be the largest such feature discovered in the outer solar system. Images show only one crater on Wright Mons, leading scientists to believe that it too formed relatively recently and that it could have been active late in Pluto's history.

New Horizons also found evidence of widespread past and present glacial activity on the surface, including networks of eroded valleys and formations similar to those in Yellowstone National Park. In addition, the spacecraft identified blue hazy layers in Pluto's atmosphere, which scientists believe to be a photochemical smog resulting from sunlight acting on methane and other molecules in the atmosphere—a more complex finding than they anticipated. "Pluto has greatly exceeded our expectations in diversity of landforms and processes—processes that continue to the present," said Alan Howard, a professor at the University of Virginia and scientific collaborator with the New Horizons's Geology, Geophysics, and Imaging team.

Beyond Pluto's surface, New Horizons took the first clear pictures of moons Nix and Hydra and found a system of chasms on Charon that are larger than the Grand Canyon. The spacecraft also found an area of cliffs and troughs on Charon, which imply that the moon's crust had been fractured, likely because of internal activity. Additionally, New Horizons found that Pluto's moons are unlike any others in the solar system in that they do not rotate synchronously, that is, with one side always facing the dwarf planet. They were also found to spin much faster than other moons and are very wobbly in their orbits.

"The exploration of Pluto and its moons by New Horizons represents the capstone event to 50 years of planetary exploration by NASA and the United States," said NASA administrator Charles Bolden. "Once again we have achieved a historic first. The United States is the first nation to reach Pluto, and with this mission has completed the initial survey of our solar system, a remarkable accomplishment that no other nation can match."

The Next Horizon

Following its successful flyby, New Horizons continued on its journey beyond Pluto and into the Kuiper Belt. The spacecraft will next travel to a body found by the Hubble Space Telescope in 2014 that is known as 2014 MU69. Located roughly 1 billion miles from Pluto, MU69 is barely 1 percent of the dwarf planet's size, but about ten times larger than average-sized comets. "Although this flyby probably won't be as dramatic as the exploration of Pluto we just completed, it will be a record-setter for the most distant exploration of an object ever made," wrote Alan Stern, New Horizons principal investigator, in a blog post for *Sky & Telescope Magazine*.

New Horizons is expected to reach MU69 in 2019.

—Linda Fecteau Grimm

Following is the text of a July 14, 2015, press release from the National Aeronautics and Space Administration (NASA) marking New Horizons's approach to Pluto; and the text of a November 9, 2015, press release from NASA announcing some of the discoveries made by New Horizons.

DOCUMENT   *New Horizons Reaches Pluto*

July 14, 2015

NASA's New Horizons spacecraft is at Pluto.

After a decade-long journey through our solar system, New Horizons made its closest approach to Pluto Tuesday, about 7,750 miles above the surface—roughly the same distance from New York to Mumbai, India—making it the first-ever space mission to explore a world so far from Earth.

"I'm delighted at this latest accomplishment by NASA, another first that demonstrates once again how the United States leads the world in space," said John Holdren, assistant to the President for Science and Technology and director of the White House Office of Science and Technology Policy. "New Horizons is the latest in a long line of scientific accomplishments at NASA, including multiple missions orbiting and exploring the surface of Mars in advance of human visits still to come; the remarkable Kepler mission to identify Earth-like planets around stars other than our own; and the DSCOVR satellite that soon will be beaming back images of the whole Earth in near real-time from a vantage point a million miles away. As New Horizons completes its flyby of Pluto and continues deeper into the Kuiper Belt, NASA's multifaceted journey of discovery continues."

"The exploration of Pluto and its moons by New Horizons represents the capstone event to 50 years of planetary exploration by NASA and the United States," said NASA Administrator Charles Bolden. "Once again we have achieved a historic first. The United States is the first nation to reach Pluto, and with this mission has completed the initial survey of our solar system, a remarkable accomplishment that no other nation can match."

Per the plan, the spacecraft currently is in data-gathering mode and not in contact with flight controllers at the Johns Hopkins University Applied Physics Laboratory (APL) in Laurel, Maryland. Scientists are waiting to find out whether New Horizons "phones home," transmitting to Earth a series of status updates that indicate the spacecraft survived the flyby and is in good health. The "call" is expected shortly after 9 p.m. EDT tonight.

The Pluto story began only a generation ago when young Clyde Tombaugh was tasked to look for Planet X, theorized to exist beyond the orbit of Neptune. He discovered a faint point of light that we now see as a complex and fascinating world.

"Pluto was discovered just 85 years ago by a farmer's son from Kansas, inspired by a visionary from Boston, using a telescope in Flagstaff, Arizona," said John Grunsfeld, associate administrator for NASA's Science Mission Directorate in Washington. "Today, science takes a great leap observing the Pluto system up close and flying into a new frontier that will help us better understand the origins of the solar system."

New Horizons' flyby of the dwarf planet and its five known moons is providing an up-close introduction to the solar system's Kuiper Belt, an outer region populated by icy objects ranging in size from boulders to dwarf planets. Kuiper Belt objects, such as Pluto, preserve evidence about the early formation of the solar system.

New Horizons principal investigator Alan Stern of the Southwest Research Institute (SwRI) in Boulder, Colorado, says the mission now is writing the textbook on Pluto.

"The New Horizons team is proud to have accomplished the first exploration of the Pluto system," Stern said. "This mission has inspired people across the world with the excitement of exploration and what humankind can achieve."

New Horizons' almost 10-year, three-billion-mile journey to closest approach at Pluto took about one minute less than predicted when the craft was launched in January 2006. The spacecraft threaded the needle through a 36-by-57 mile (60 by 90 kilometers) window in space—the equivalent of a commercial airliner arriving no more off target than the width of a tennis ball.

Because New Horizons is the fastest spacecraft ever launched—hurtling through the Pluto system at more than 30,000 mph, a collision with a particle as small as a grain of rice could incapacitate the spacecraft. Once it reestablishes contact Tuesday night, it will take 16 months for New Horizons to send its cache of data—10 years' worth—back to Earth.

New Horizons is the latest in a long line of scientific accomplishments at NASA, including multiple rovers exploring the surface of Mars, the Cassini spacecraft that has revolutionized our understanding of Saturn and the Hubble Space Telescope, which recently celebrated its 25th anniversary. All of this scientific research and discovery is helping to inform the agency's plan to send American astronauts to Mars in the 2030's.

"After nearly 15 years of planning, building, and flying the New Horizons spacecraft across the solar system, we've reached our goal," said project manager Glen Fountain at APL. "The bounty of what we've collected is about to unfold."

APL designed, built and operates the New Horizons spacecraft and manages the mission for NASA's Science Mission Directorate. SwRI leads the mission, science team, payload operations and encounter science planning. New Horizons is part of NASA's New Frontiers Program, managed by the agency's Marshall Space Flight Center in Huntsville, Alabama.

Follow the New Horizons mission on Twitter and use the hashtag #PlutoFlyby to join the conversation. Live updates also will be available on the mission Facebook page.

SOURCE: National Aeronautics and Space Administration. "NASA's Three-Billion-Mile Journey to Pluto Reaches Historic Encounter." July 14, 2015. www.nasa.gov/press-release/nasas-three-billion-mile-journey-to-pluto-reaches-historic-encounter.

 *New Horizons Discoveries Yield Extensive Information*

DOCUMENT

November 9, 2015

[All graphics have been omitted.]

From possible ice volcanoes to twirling moons, NASA's New Horizons science team is discussing more than 50 exciting discoveries about Pluto at this week's 47th Annual Meeting of the American Astronomical Society's Division for Planetary Sciences in National Harbor, Maryland.

"The New Horizons mission has taken what we thought we knew about Pluto and turned it upside down," said Jim Green, director of planetary science at NASA Headquarters in Washington. "It's why we explore—to satisfy our innate curiosity and answer deeper questions about how we got here and what lies beyond the next horizon."

For one such discovery, New Horizons geologists combined images of Pluto's surface to make 3-D maps that indicate two of Pluto's most distinctive mountains could be cryovolcanoes—ice volcanoes that may have been active in the recent geological past.

"It's hard to imagine how rapidly our view of Pluto and its moons are evolving as new data stream in each week. As the discoveries pour in from those data, Pluto is becoming a star of the solar system," said mission Principal Investigator Alan Stern of the Southwest Research Institute in Boulder, Colorado. "Moreover, I'd wager that for most planetary scientists, any one or two of our latest major findings on one world would be considered astounding. To have them all is simply incredible."

The two cryovolcano candidates are large features measuring tens of miles or kilometers across and several miles or kilometers high.

"These are big mountains with a large hole in their summit, and on Earth that generally means one thing—a volcano," said Oliver White, New Horizons postdoctoral researcher at NASA's Ames Research Center in Moffett Field, California. "If they are volcanic, then the summit depression would likely have formed via collapse as material is erupted from underneath. The strange hummocky texture of the mountain flanks may represent volcanic flows of some sort that have traveled down from the summit region and onto the plains beyond, but why they are hummocky, and what they are made of, we don't yet know."

While their appearance is similar to volcanoes on Earth that spew molten rock, ice volcanoes on Pluto are expected to emit a somewhat melted slurry of substances such as water ice, nitrogen, ammonia, or methane. If Pluto proves to have volcanoes, it will provide an important new clue to its geologic and atmospheric evolution.

"After all, nothing like this has been seen in the deep outer solar system," said Jeffrey Moore, New Horizons Geology, Geophysics and Imaging team leader, at Ames.

PLUTO'S LONG HISTORY OF GEOLOGIC ACTIVITY

Pluto's surface varies in age—from ancient, to intermediate, to relatively young—according to another new finding from New Horizons.

To determine the age of a surface area of the planet, scientists count crater impacts. The more crater impacts, the older the region likely is. Crater counts of surface areas on Pluto indicate that it has surface regions dating to just after the formation of the planets of our solar system, about four billion years ago.

But there also is a vast area that was, in geological terms, born yesterday—meaning it may have formed within the past 10 million years. This area, informally named Sputnik Planum, appears on the left side of Pluto's "heart" and is completely crater-free in all images received, so far.

New data from crater counts reveal the presence of intermediate, or "middle-aged," terrains on Pluto, as well. This suggests Sputnik Planum is not an anomaly—that Pluto has been geologically active throughout much of its more than 4-billion-year history.

"We've mapped more than a thousand craters on Pluto, which vary greatly in size and appearance," said postdoctoral researcher Kelsi Singer, of the Southwest Research Institute (SwRI) in Boulder, Colorado. "Among other things, I expect cratering studies like these to give us important new insights into how this part of the solar system formed."

Locations of more than 1,000 craters mapped on Pluto by NASA's New Horizons mission indicate a wide range of surface ages, which likely means Pluto has been geologically active throughout its history.

BUILDING BLOCKS OF THE SOLAR SYSTEM

Crater counts are giving the New Horizons team insight into the structure of the Kuiper Belt itself. The dearth of smaller craters across Pluto and its large moon Charon indicate the Kuiper Belt, which is an unexplored outer region of our solar system, likely had fewer smaller objects than some models had predicted.

This leads New Horizons scientists to doubt a longstanding model that all Kuiper Belt objects formed by accumulating much smaller objects—less than a mile wide. The absence of small craters on Pluto and Charon support other models theorizing that Kuiper Belt objects tens of miles across may have formed directly, at their current—or close to current—size.

In fact, the evidence that many Kuiper Belt objects could have been "born large" has scientists excited that New Horizons' next potential target—the 30-mile-wide (40–50 kilometer wide) KBO named 2014 MU69—which may offer the first detailed look at just such a pristine, ancient building block of the solar system.

PLUTO'S SPINNING, MERGED MOONS

The New Horizons mission also is shedding new light on Pluto's fascinating system of moons, and their unusual properties. For example, nearly every other moon in the solar system—including Earth's moon—is in synchronous rotation, keeping one face toward the planet. This is not the case for Pluto's small moons.

Pluto's small lunar satellites are spinning much faster, with Hydra—its most distant moon—rotating an unprecedented 89 times during a single lap around the planet. Scientists believe these spin rates may be variable because Charon exerts a strong torque that prevents each small moon from settling down into synchronous rotation.

Another oddity of Pluto's moons: scientists expected the satellites would wobble, but not to such a degree.

Most inner moons in the solar system keep one face pointed toward their central planet; this animation shows that certainly isn't the case with the small moons of Pluto, which behave like spinning tops. Pluto is shown at center with, in order from closest to farthest orbit, its moons Charon, Styx, Nix, Kerberos and Hydra.

"Pluto's moons behave like spinning tops," said co-investigator Mark Showalter of the SETI Institute in Mountain View, California.

Images of Pluto's four smallest satellites also indicate several of them could be the results of mergers of two or more moons.

Data from NASA's New Horizons mission indicates that at least two—and possibly all four—of Pluto's small moons may be the result of mergers between still smaller moons. If this discovery is borne out with further analysis, it could provide important new clues to the formation of the Pluto system.

"We suspect from this that Pluto had more moons in the past, in the aftermath of the big impact that also created Charon," said Showalter.

Source: National Aeronautics and Space Administration. "Four Months after Pluto Flyby, NASA's New Horizons Yields Wealth of Discovery." November 9, 2015. www.nasa.gov/press-release/four-months-after-pluto-flyby-nasa-s-new-horizons-yields-wealth-of-discovery.

OTHER HISTORIC DOCUMENTS OF INTEREST

FROM THIS VOLUME

FROM PREVIOUS *HISTORIC DOCUMENTS*

August

Texas Voter ID Law Struck Down

AUGUST 5, 2015

In 2013, the U.S. Supreme Court, in an important and controversial opinion, held a major provision of the Voting Rights Act of 1965 to be unconstitutional. Prior to this decision, certain states with a long, proven history of voter discrimination were required by Section 5 of the Voting Rights Act to obtain preclearance from a federal court before they could make changes to their voting laws. The Supreme Court, in *Shelby City v. Holder*, held that the formula used to determine which states were subject to preclearance was unconstitutional. Chief Justice John G. Roberts Jr., writing for a divided court, declared, "Things have changed in the South," and as such he held that it was no longer constitutional to require some states to get preapproval of voting law changes based only on past conduct. Within hours of this decision, states that had been under the preclearance requirement rushed to make changes to their voting laws that had previously been blocked, and anti-voter ID advocates were left wondering whether a weakened Voting Rights Act had any teeth.

Texas was one of the first states to act. Once free of the need to get approval before changing voter laws, the state immediately passed the strictest voter photo ID requirement in the country. On August 5, 2015, one day before the fiftieth anniversary of the Voting Rights Act of 1965, the U.S. Court of Appeals for the Fifth Circuit relied on the historic civil rights law to strike down the new law. It was the first time since the *Shelby* decision that a federal appeals court had relied on the Voting Rights Act to rule against a voter ID law. The three-judge panel held unanimously in *Veasey v. Abbott* that the Texas law violated Section 2 of the Voting Rights Act. This section was not at issue in the recent Supreme Court case and bans voting laws that disproportionately burden minority voters' opportunity to participate in the political process.

The Texas Voter ID Law

Prior to 2010, only two states had strict photo identification requirements. After the 2010 elections, however, many state legislatures passed new laws that impacted the ease of voting, some of which have been struck down by the courts for various reasons. Going into the 2016 presidential election year, according to the National Conference of State Legislatures, currently thirty-three states have voter identification laws in force, nine of which strictly require photo identifications. Proponents of these laws argue that requirements are needed to prevent in-person voter fraud and to increase confidence in the election process. Opponents note that there is no empirical evidence that this kind of fraud exists in any significant way to justify the increased burdens placed on the right to vote. Rather, these critics argue that the laws are a modern equivalent of the poll tax, designed to suppress the turnout of young and minority voters.

In 2011, Texas passed SB 14, one of the strictest photo ID laws in the country. At the time, Texas was one of several states subject to Section 5 of the Voting Rights Act requiring federal preclearance of any new voting law. In 2012, a federal court in D.C. found that SB 14 would make it significantly more difficult for minority citizens to vote and denied approval of the new law. This is where the story would have ended, but, in *Shelby* in 2013, the U.S. Supreme Court struck down Section 5 of the Voting Rights Act, finding that the formula relied on to determine which states were subject to preclearance was constitutionally faulty. Only hours later, Texas attorney general Greg Abbott announced that Texas would implement the formerly defunct SB 14.

With the implementation of SB 14, Texas required voters to present one of a limited number of forms of identification at the polls, including an unexpired Texas driver's license; an unexpired U.S. military photo ID card; an unexpired U.S. passport or photo citizenship certificate; a concealed handgun license; or a special election ID certificate issued by the Department of Public Safety obtained with a combination of driver's license, certified birth certificate, or U.S. citizenship papers with two forms of supporting identification. The state would not accept college student identifications, voter registration cards, workplace photo IDs, utility bills, or photo IDs from any other federal public or private entity. Although the strict voter ID law does, like all states, allow religious accommodations and disability exemptions, it does not exempt voters who are elderly, indigent, or in nursing homes.

The law was challenged in federal district court by, among others, the Texas NAACP and the Mexican American Legislative Caucus (MALC) of the Texas House of Representatives. The suit was brought under Section 2 of the Voting Rights Act, which prohibits "voting qualification or prerequisite to voting . . . which results in a denial or abridgement of the right of any citizen . . . to vote on account of race or color." Section 2 was amended by Congress in 1986 to make clear that a violation of Section 2 need only require a showing of "discriminatory effect" on the voting rights of minority citizens. After the eight-day trial of *Veasey v. Perry*, at which dozens of expert and lay witnesses testified, Judge Nelva Gonzales Ramos, on October 9, 2014, struck down the law in a sweeping 147-page decision. The court ruled that "SB 14 creates an unconstitutional burden on the right to vote, has an impermissible discriminatory effect against Hispanics and African-Americans, and was imposed with an unconstitutional discriminatory purpose. The Court further holds that SB 14 constitutes an unconstitutional poll tax."

Just weeks before the November 2014 elections, Judge Gonzales Ramos entered a permanent injunction against the enforcement of SB 14 and ordered the state to go back to enforcing the rules that were in place before the passage of the new voter ID rules. The State of Texas appealed the decision to the federal appellate court, which granted the state's motion to stay the lower court's ruling during the appeals process. The plaintiffs appealed the stay on emergency motions to the U.S. Supreme Court, where they were denied. Justice Ruth Bader Ginsburg famously stayed up all night to write a strong dissenting opinion to the court's order permitting the Texas Voter ID laws to go into effect just before the November 2014 election.

Appellate Court Rules in *Veasey v. Abbott*

On August 5, 2015, the Fifth Circuit Court of Appeals upheld what it referred to as the district court's "well-supported" findings that SB 14 had a discriminatory effect on minority voting rights in violation of Section 2 of the Voting Rights Act. The district court had correctly, according to the appellate court, based its conclusion on two findings. First, it found evidence of a stark racial disparity between those Texas voters who have the necessary ID to satisfy the requirements of SB 14 and those who do not. Experts testified that 608,470 registered voters in Texas, 4.5 percent of all voters, lack the adequate identification to vote under the strict ID law. Further, of these voters, Hispanic voters were 195 percent and Black voters were 305 percent more likely than white voters to lack the necessary identification. These findings were corroborated by survey evidence.

Second, the court concluded that SB 14 "worked in concert with Texas's legacy of state-sponsored discrimination to bring about this disproportionate result." To reach this conclusion, the court examined various factors that had been previously endorsed as relevant by the Supreme Court to conclude that the racial disparity is a product of "current or historical conditions of discrimination." Among the factors reviewed by the court was evidence that past discrimination in education, employment, and health outcomes hinder the ability of minority groups to participate effectively in the political process. The court relied on the district court findings that 29 percent of African Americans and 33 percent of Hispanics in Texas live below the poverty line, compared to only 12 percent of Anglos. Unemployment rates as well as high school and college graduation rates are also significantly lower among minority groups in Texas.

Not only was there evidence that past discrimination had led to disproportionately large percentages of minority voters living in poverty, but the district court had substantial expert testimony that those living in poverty were much more likely to lack the forms of ID required by SB 14 because they are less likely to own cars and need drivers' licenses or to need ID for obtaining credit or other financial services. Circumstances make it further difficult because often low income wage earners with no paid leave must forego income to take the time to travel to a processing site to get the photo identification. For a voter without access to a vehicle, it can take more than three hours to travel to the nearest location issuing the IDs.

Although the appellate court agreed with Judge Gonzales Ramos that SB 14 had a discriminatory effect on minority voting rights and violated Section 2, the decision was not completely supportive of the district court's sweeping decision. Judge Gonzales Ramos had found that the voter ID law was passed with the purpose of discriminating against minority voters. The Fifth Circuit held that much of the evidence relied on to make this judgment was based too far in the past and that this was an error. Without the finding of intent to discriminate, the remedy for a violation of Section 2 would be to refashion the voter ID law only as much as needed to remedy the specific violation, while a finding of intent would require striking down the entire law. Further, a finding that the voter law was passed with the intent of discriminating could serve as the justification to once again subject Texas to the preclearance requirements of Section 5 of the Voting Rights Act.

Impact of the Court's Decision

After the ruling, Texas attorney general Ken Paxton announced, "Texas will continue to fight for its voter ID requirement to ensure the integrity of elections in the Lone Star State." Just a few weeks later, his office filed papers asking for a review and reconsideration of the opinion in *Veasey v. Abbott* by the full bench of the Fifth Circuit Federal Appeals Court. He also asked to be able to continue enforcing the voter ID law while the case is being appealed and signaled that he intends to appeal to the U.S. Supreme Court.

It is unclear what rules will be in place at voting booths in Texas while the next high-turnout national presidential election approaches. Currently North Carolina is awaiting a ruling on its law, which is in many ways similar to that of Texas. By contrast, other states are working to make it easier to vote. California and Oregon, for instance, have passed laws calling for automatic voter registration at the DMV.

Veasey v. Abbott has the potential to be the first court decision relating to the Voting Rights Act to reach the Supreme Court since it struck down Section 5, and there is keen interest in whether the Supreme Court intends to further limit the scope and application of the historic Voting Rights Act.

—Melissa Feinberg

Following are excerpts from the Fifth Circuit ruling in Veasey v. Abbott *in which the court ruled on August 5, 2015, to strike down Texas' voter ID law.*

DOCUMENT   *Veasey v. Abbott*

August 5, 2015

[All footnotes have been omitted.]

IN THE UNITED STATES COURT OF APPEALS
FOR THE FIFTH CIRCUIT

MARC VEASEY, et al., Plaintiffs—Appellees
TEXAS ASSOCIATION OF HISPANIC COUNTY JUDGES AND COUNTY
COMMISSIONERS, Intervenor Plaintiffs—Appellees
v.
GREG ABBOTT, in his Official Capacity as Governor of Texas; CARLOS CASCOS,
Texas Secretary of State; STATE OF TEXAS; STEVE MCCRAW, in his Official Capacity
as Director of the Texas Department of Public Safety, Defendants—Appellants

Appeal from the United States District Court for the Southern District of Texas

Before STEWART, Chief Judge, HAYNES, Circuit Judge, and BROWN, District Judge
(*sitting by designation).

HAYNES, Circuit Judge:
    In 2011, Texas ("the State") passed Senate Bill 14 ("SB 14"), which requires individuals to present one of several forms of photo identification in order to vote. Plaintiffs filed suit challenging the constitutionality and legality of the law. The district court held that SB 14 was enacted with a racially discriminatory purpose, has a racially discriminatory effect, is a poll tax, and unconstitutionally burdens the right to vote.
    We VACATE and REMAND the Plaintiffs' discriminatory purpose claim for further consideration in light of the discussion below. If on remand the district court finds that SB 14 was passed with a discriminatory purpose, then the law must be invalidated. However, because the finding on remand may be different, we also address other arguments raised by the Plaintiffs. We AFFIRM the district court's finding that SB 14 has a discriminatory

effect in violation of Section 2 of the Voting Rights Act and remand for consideration of the proper remedy. We VACATE the district court's holding that SB 14 is a poll tax and RENDER judgment in the State's favor. Because the same relief is available to Plaintiffs under the discriminatory effect finding affirmed herein, under the doctrine of constitutional avoidance, we do not address the merits of whether SB 14 unconstitutionally burdens the right to vote under the First and Fourteenth Amendments. We therefore VACATE this portion of the district court's opinion and DISMISS Plaintiffs' First and Fourteenth Amendment claims.

[Sections I and II, containing the factual background and standing in the case, have been omitted.]

III. Discussion

A. Discriminatory Purpose

The State appeals the district court's judgment that SB 14 was passed with a discriminatory purpose in violation of the Fourteenth and Fifteenth Amendments and Section 2 of the Voting Rights Act. We review this determination for clear error; as the district court did, we apply the framework articulated in *Village of Arlington Heights v. Metropolitan Housing Development Corp.*, 429 U.S. 252, 265–68 (1977), which remains the proper analytical framework for these kinds of cases. "If the district court's findings are plausible in light of the record viewed in its entirety, we must accept them, even though we might have weighed the evidence differently if we had been sitting as a trier of fact." However, if the district court committed an error of law in making its fact findings in this case, we may set aside those fact findings and remand the case for further consideration. In the words of the Supreme Court, when the district court's "findings are infirm because of an erroneous view of the law, a remand is the proper course unless the record permits only one resolution of the factual issue." Although the district court properly cited the *Arlington Heights* framework, we conclude that some "findings are infirm," necessitating a remand on this point.

"Proof of racially discriminatory intent or purpose is required to show a violation of the Equal Protection Clause." However, "[r]acial discrimination need only be one purpose, and not even a primary purpose, of an official action for a violation to occur." *Arlington Heights* enumerated a multi-factor analysis for evaluating whether a facially neutral law was passed with a discriminatory purpose, and courts must perform a "sensitive inquiry into such circumstantial and direct evidence of intent as may be available." The appropriate inquiry is not whether legislators were aware of SB 14's racially discriminatory effect, but whether the law was passed *because of* that disparate impact. Importantly, although discriminatory effect is a relevant consideration, knowledge of a potential impact is not the same as intending such an impact.

The Court articulated the following non-exhaustive list of factors to guide courts in this inquiry: (1) "[t]he historical background of the decision . . . particularly if it reveals a series of official actions taken for invidious purposes," (2) "[t]he specific sequence of events leading up to the challenged decision," (3) "[d]epartures from normal procedural sequence," (4) "substantive departures . . . particularly if the factors usually considered important by the decisionmaker strongly favor a decision contrary to the one reached," and (5) "[t]he legislative or administrative history . . . especially where there are contemporary statements by members of the decision making body, minutes of its meetings, or reports." "Once racial discrimination is shown to have been a 'substantial' or 'motivating' factor behind enactment of the law, the burden shifts to the law's defenders to demonstrate that the law would have been enacted without this factor." If the law's defenders are unable to carry this burden, the law is invalidated.

The State's stated purpose in passing SB 14 centered on protection of the sanctity of voting, avoiding voter fraud, and promoting public confidence in the voting process. No one questions the legitimacy of these concerns as motives; the disagreement centers on whether there were impermissible motives as well. We recognize that evaluating motive, particularly the motive of dozens of people, is a difficult enterprise. We recognize the charged nature of accusations of racism, particularly against a legislative body, but we also recognize the sad truth that racism continues to exist in our modern American society despite years of laws designed to eradicate it.

[Additional discussion about the discriminatory effect of SB 14 has been omitted.]

B. Discriminatory Effect

If the district court again finds discriminatory purpose on remand, then it would not need to address effect. However, because the result could be different on remand and because the district court addressed, and the parties fully briefed, discriminatory effect, we now turn to consideration of it. Plaintiffs allege that SB 14 has a discriminatory effect in violation of Section 2 of the Voting Rights Act, which proscribes any "voting qualification or prerequisite to voting or standard, practice, or procedure . . . which results in a denial or abridgement of the right of any citizen . . . to vote on account of race or color." 52 U.S.C. § 10301(a). Unlike discrimination claims brought pursuant to the Fourteenth Amendment, Congress has clarified that violations of Section 2(a) can "be proved by showing discriminatory effect alone." *Thornburg v. Gingles*, 478 U.S. 30, 35 (1986); *see also* 52 U.S.C. § 10301(b).

To satisfy this "results test," Plaintiffs must show not only that the challenged law imposes a burden on minorities, but that "a certain electoral law, practice, or structure interacts with social and historical conditions to cause an inequality in the opportunities enjoyed by black and white voters to elect their preferred representatives." *Gingles*, 478 U.S. at 47.

[Evaluation of the Voting Rights Act, Section 2, has been omitted.]

1. DISPARATE IMPACT

The district court found that 608,470 registered voters, or 4.5% of all registered voters in Texas, lack SB 14 ID. Of those, 534,512 voters did not qualify for a disability exemption from SB 14's requirements. The latter figure, which was derived by comparing the Texas Election Management System with databases containing evidence of who possesses SB 14 ID, is known as the "No-Match List."

Plaintiffs' experts then relied on four distinct methods of analysis to determine the races of those on the No-Match List. Those included: (1) ecological regression analysis, (2) a homogenous block group analysis, (3) comparing the No-Match List to the Spanish Surname Voter Registration list, and (4) reliance upon data provided by Catalist LLC, a company that compiles election data. The ecological regression analysis performed by Dr. Stephen Ansolabehere, an expert in American electoral politics and statistical methods in political science, which compared the No-Match List with census data, revealed that Hispanic registered voters and Black registered voters were respectively 195% and 305% more likely than their Anglo peers to lack SB 14 ID. According to Dr. Ansolabehere, this disparity is "statistically significant and highly unlikely to have arisen by chance." The block group analysis yielded similar results, and other experts arrived at similar conclusions. These statistical analyses of the No-Match List were corroborated by a survey of over 2,300 eligible Texas voters, which concluded that Blacks were 1.78 times more likely than Whites, and Latinos 2.42 times more likely, to lack SB 14 ID. Even the study performed by the State's expert, which the district court found suffered from "severe methodological oversights," found that 4% of eligible White voters lacked SB 14 ID, compared to 5.3% of eligible Black voters and 6.9% of eligible Hispanic voters. The district court thus credited the testimony and analyses of Plaintiffs' three experts, each of which found that SB 14 disparately impacts African-American and Hispanic registered voters in Texas. . . .

The district court likewise concluded that SB 14 disproportionately impacted the poor. It credited expert testimony that 21.4% of eligible voters earning less than $20,000 per year lack SB 14 ID, compared to only 2.6% of voters earning between $100,000 and $150,000 per year. Those earning less than $20,000 annually were also more likely to lack the underlying documents to get an EIC. Dr. Jane Henrici, an anthropologist and professorial lecturer at George Washington University, explained that:

> [U]nreliable and irregular wage work and other income . . . affect the cost of taking the time to locate and bring the requisite papers and identity cards, travel to a processing site, wait through the assessment, and get photo identifications. This is because most job opportunities do not include paid sick or other paid leave; taking off from work means lost income. Employed low-income Texans not already in possession of such documents will struggle to afford income loss from the unpaid time needed to get photo identification.

Furthermore, the court found that the poor are less likely to avail themselves of services that require ID, such as obtaining credit and other financial services. They are also less likely to own vehicles and are therefore more likely to rely on public transportation. As a result, the poor are less likely to have a driver's license and face greater obstacles in obtaining photo identification. Even obtaining an EIC poses an obstacle—the district court credited evidence that hundreds of thousands of voters face round-trip travel times of 90 minutes or more to the nearest location issuing EICs. Of eligible voters without access to a vehicle, a large percentage faced trips of three hours or more to obtain an EIC.

. . . We conclude that the district court did not reversibly err in determining that SB 14 violates Section 2 by disparately impacting minority voters.

Foremost, the State disputes the propriety of using statistical analyses to determine the racial composition of the No-Match List. . . .

[Elaborations on the effects of this disparate impact have been omitted.]

2. THE SENATE FACTORS

We next consider the district court's finding that SB 14 "produces a discriminatory result that is actionable because [it] . . . interact[s] with social and historical conditions in Texas to cause an inequality in the electoral opportunities enjoyed by African-Americans and Hispanic voters." The district court found Senate Factors 1, 2, 5, 6, 7, 8, and 9 probative.

(a) Senate Factor 1: History of Official Discrimination

[T]he district court again found that Texas's history of discrimination in voting acted in concert with SB 14 to limit minorities' ability to participate in the political process. We repeat Shelby County's admonishment that "history did not end in 1965," 133 S. Ct. at 2628, and emphasize that contemporary examples of discrimination are more probative than historical examples. Even discounting this factor and the district court's analysis of it, however, we conclude that the other factors support its finding that SB 14 has a discriminatory effect.

[Senate Factor 2 (b), discussing racially polarized voting, has been omitted.]

(c) Senate Factor 5: Effects of Past Discrimination

Next, the district court appraised "[t]he extent to which minority group members bear the effects of past discrimination in areas such as education, employment, and health, which hinder their ability to participate effectively in the political process." The disparity in education, employment, and health outcomes between Anglos, African-Americans, and Hispanics is manifest by fact that the 29% of African-Americans and 33% of Hispanics in Texas live below the poverty line compared to 12% of Anglos. The unemployment rate for Anglos is also significantly lower. At trial, the court found that 6.1% of Anglos were unemployed compared to 8.5% of Hispanics and 12.8% of African-Americans. Furthermore, 91.7% of Anglo 25-year-olds in Texas have graduated from high school, compared to 85.4% of African-Americans, and only 58.6% of Hispanics. Anglos are also significantly more likely to have completed college—33.7% of Anglos hold a bachelor's degree, compared to 19.2% of African-Americans and 11.4% of Hispanics. Finally, the district court credited testimony that African-Americans and Hispanics are more likely than Anglos to report being in poor health, and to lack health insurance.

According to the district court, "[t]hese socioeconomic disparities have hindered the ability of African-Americans and Hispanics to effectively participate in the political process. Dr. Ansolabehere testified that these minorities register and turnout for elections at rates that lag far behind Anglo voters." This is significant because the inquiry in Section 2 cases is whether the vestiges of discrimination act in concert with the challenged law to impede minority participation in the political process. The district court concluded in the affirmative, and the State does not contest these underlying factual findings on appeal.

The district court credited expert testimony that tied these disparate educational, economic, and health outcomes to Texas's history of discrimination. According to Dr. Vernon Burton, a professor with an expertise in race relations, past state-sponsored employment discrimination and Texas's maintenance of a "separate but equal" education system both contributed to the unequal outcomes that presently exist. Although *Brown v. Board of Education* (1954), mandated desegregated schools in 1954, Dr. Burton testified that Texas maintained segregated schools until roughly 1970. . . .

[Senate Factor 6 (d) discussing racial appeals in political campaigns has been omitted.]

(e) Senate Factor 7 and Factor 8: Minority Public Officials and Responsiveness to Minority Needs

The extent to which minority candidates are elected to public office also contextualizes the degree to which vestiges of discrimination continue to reduce minority participation in the political process. The district court found that African-Americans comprise 13.3% of the population in Texas, but only 1.7% of all Texas elected officials are African-American. Similarly, Hispanics comprise 30.3% of the population but hold only 7.1% of all elected positions. . . .

The district court also found that Texas's history of discrimination, coupled with SB 14's effect on minorities in Texas, demonstrated a lack of responsiveness to minority needs by elected officials. . . .

(f) Factor 9: Tenuousness of Policies Underlying the Law

Finally, the district court concluded that the policies underlying SB 14's passage were tenuous. While increasing voter turnout and safeguarding voter confidence are legitimate state interests, the district court found that "the stated policies behind SB 14 are only tenuously related to its provisions." While in-person voting fraud is rare and mail-in fraud is comparatively much more common, SB 14's voter ID restrictions would only combat the former.

The district court likewise found that concerns about undocumented immigrants and non-citizens voting were misplaced. It credited testimony that undocumented immigrants are unlikely to vote as they try to avoid contact with government agents for fear of being deported. At least one Representative voting for SB 14 conceded that he had no evidence to substantiate his fear of undocumented immigrants voting. Additionally, the district court found that SB 14 would not prevent non-citizens from voting, since non-citizens can legally obtain a Texas driver's license or concealed handgun license, two forms of SB 14 ID. . . .

(g) Discriminatory Effect Conclusion

Given its findings regarding SB 14's disparate impact and the Senate Factors, the district court held that SB 14 acted in concert with current and historical conditions of discrimination to diminish African-Americans' and Hispanics' ability to participate in the political process. Contrary to the State's assertion, we conclude that the district court performed the "intensely local appraisal" required by *Gingles*. It clearly delineated each step of its analysis, finding that:

> (1) SB 14 specifically burdens Texans living in poverty, who are less likely to possess qualified photo ID, are less able to get it, and may not otherwise need it; (2) a disproportionate number of Texans living in poverty are African-Americans and Hispanics; and (3) African-Americans and Hispanics are more likely than Anglos to be living in poverty because they continue to bear the socioeconomic effects caused by decades of racial discrimination.

The district court thoroughly evaluated the "totality of the circumstances," each finding was well-supported, and the State has failed to contest many of the underlying factual findings. Furthermore, the district court's analysis comports with the Supreme Court's recent instruction that "a disparate-impact claim that relies on a statistical disparity must fail if the plaintiff cannot point to a defendant's policy or policies causing that disparity." *Inclusive Communities*, 135 S. Ct. at 2523. The district court here acknowledged this principle and tethered its holding to two findings. First, the court found a stark, racial disparity between those who possess or have access to SB 14 ID, and those who do not. Second, it applied the Senate Factors to assess SB 14 worked in concert with Texas's legacy of state-sponsored discrimination to bring about this disproportionate result.

As such, we conclude that the district court did not clearly err in determining that SB 14 has a discriminatory effect on minorities' voting rights in violation of Section 2 of the Voting Rights Act. . . .

[Additional discussion of the plaintiffs' arguments has been omitted.]

IV. Conclusion

For the reasons stated above, we VACATE the district court's judgment that SB 14 was passed with a racially discriminatory purpose and REMAND for further consideration of Plaintiffs' discriminatory purpose claims, using the proper legal standards and evidence. We VACATE the district court's holding that SB 14 is a poll tax under the Fourteenth and Twenty-Fourth Amendments and RENDER judgment for the State on this issue. We need not and do not address whether SB 14 unconstitutionally burdens the right to vote under the First and Fourteenth Amendments; therefore, we VACATE the district court's judgment on that issue and DISMISS those claims. We AFFIRM the district court's finding that SB 14 violates Section 2 of the Voting Rights Act through its discriminatory effects and REMAND for consideration of the appropriate remedy.

Finally, on remand, the district court should: (1) give further consideration to its discriminatory purpose findings as specified herein; and (2) if the district court does not find that SB 14 was imposed with a discriminatory purpose, consider what remedy it should grant due to SB 14's discriminatory effect in violation of Section 2 of the Voting Rights Act, taking account of any impact of SB 983 and this opinion. We leave it to the district court in the first instance to decide whether any additional evidence may be proffered on the matters remanded.

SOURCE: U.S. Court of Appeals for the Fifth Circuit. *Veasey v. Abbott*. No. 14-41127. www.ca5.uscourts. gov/opinions/pub/14/14-41127-CV0.pdf.

OTHER HISTORIC DOCUMENTS OF INTEREST

FROM PREVIOUS *HISTORIC DOCUMENTS*

- District Court Rules on Texas Voter ID Law, *2012*, p. 401

Republicans and Democrats Hold First 2016 Presidential Election Debates

---

AUGUST 6 AND OCTOBER 14, 2015

The 2016 U.S. presidential race got into full swing during the summer of 2015 with the first debates between candidates. The Republicans held their first debate on August 6 in Cleveland, Ohio, and the Democrats on October 13 in Las Vegas, Nevada. The dominant story of the campaign was the meteoric rise of world-famous, wealthy real estate developer Donald Trump, who emerged as a clear frontrunner in the Republican race. Trump's brash, colorful style set him apart from his competitors, especially former Florida Governor Jeb Bush, the party establishment favorite who was frontrunner until Trump entered the fray, sending Bush's poll numbers plummeting. On the Democratic side, former Secretary of state Hillary Clinton fought to maintain her position as frontrunner after left-leaning Democrats rallied behind Bernie Sanders, a self-described democratic socialist and Independent U.S. senator from Vermont. Sharp differences between the Democratic and Republican presidential lineups were exposed during the debates. The Democrats comprised a handful of seasoned politicians sparring with each other in relatively restrained and respectful tones, while the Republican debates were a scrappier affair, with seventeen candidates from diverse backgrounds competing for airtime.

The Rise of Trump: Early Front Runners Knocked Off Course

In the first half of 2015, Jeb Bush, a son and brother of two past presidents, was modestly successful at solidifying his place as the party frontrunner. But enthusiasm levels were muted among Republicans faced with the prospect of selecting another member of the Bush political dynasty as their nominee. Jeb's brother, George W. Bush, left the White House in 2009 and did so amid a sea of discontent over the protracted military engagement in Iraq and the faltering state of the economy, which at that time was plunging into deep recession. Jeb attempted to distance himself from his brother by effectively saying that the Iraq War was a mistake.

Prior to Trump's entrance, Bush's main rival was thought to be Sen. Marco Rubio, R-Fla. Bush and Rubio had much in common. Both were fluent Spanish-speaking Floridians with strong ties to the Latino community, Rubio via his Cuban parents and Bush via his Mexican-born wife. This background was seen as valuable given that Latinos are an increasingly large share of the electorate. Republicans recalled painfully how their 2012 nominee, Mitt Romney, won only a quarter of the Latino vote, a significant factor in his defeat by President Obama. A third candidate whose star was in the ascendant, Texas Sen. Ted Cruz, was born in Canada to a Cuban father and an American mother. But unlike Bush and Rubio, Cruz firmly opposed giving undocumented migrants a path to permanent residency—a big priority for many Latino voters—and appealed instead to the anti-immigrant wing of the party.

The race for the nomination had thus been following a fairly conventional course until June when a figure from entirely outside of the Republican Party and the political world entered the fray: Donald Trump, the larger-than-life New York property tycoon and television celebrity. As early as 2011, Trump gave occasional hints that he might seek the presidency. Political analysts at the time were unsure whether to take his comments seriously. Trump ultimately declined to mount a campaign against incumbent President Barack Obama, who was comfortably reelected in November 2012. Then on June 16, 2015, two days after he celebrated his sixty-ninth birthday, Trump ended the speculation by announcing that he would in fact seek the Republican nomination for 2016.

Overnight, the dynamics of the presidential race changed. Although he had never stood for elected office before, Trump proved to be a fast learner of the art of political campaigning. He leveraged his nationwide name recognition and deployed his television presenting skills on the debate stages, at increasingly large rallies, and in media interviews. Despite lacking any support from the Republican Party leadership, within a few weeks of his announcement Trump was leading Bush, Cruz, and Rubio in the opinion polls. Analysts remarked that Trump's popularity was partly due to his having emerged from the media and business world, and partly due to the general public's consistently dipping respect for career politicians in recent years. Aware of this trend, Trump heralded his outsider status as one of his greatest assets. He argued that he would get things done because he was not weighed down by party political baggage and could do deals with all sides.

Trump also had a penchant for making sensationalist comments which, coupled with his at times crude manners and shallow knowledge of policy, led pundits to predict his popularity would soon wane. But they were proved wrong as Trump maintained his lead in polls through summer and fall. Perhaps the biggest firestorm Trump raised was his reaction to Islamist-inspired terrorist shootings in San Bernardino, California, on December 2. Fourteen people were killed in the shooting, and Trump responded by calling for a ban on all Muslims entering the United States to prevent further attacks. While he drew near universal criticism for his comments, including from fellow Republicans, Trump refused to back down and continued to ride high in the polls.

REPUBLICANS DEBATE IN CLEVELAND

The first 2016 Republican presidential debate featured seventeen candidates, more than for any other party race in the history of U.S. presidential elections. The lineup included:

- Jeb Bush, former governor of Florida
- Ben Carson, retired neurosurgeon
- Chris Christie, governor of New Jersey
- Ted Cruz, U.S. senator from Texas
- Carly Fiorina, former chief executive of tech giant Hewlett-Packard
- Lindsay Graham, U.S. senator from South Carolina
- Jim Gilmore, former governor of Virginia
- Mike Huckabee, former governor of Arkansas

- Bobby Jindal, governor of Louisiana
- John Kasich, governor of Ohio
- Rand Paul, U.S. senator from Kentucky
- George Pataki, former governor of New York
- Rick Perry, former governor of Texas
- Marco Rubio, U.S. senator from Florida
- Rick Santorum, former U.S. senator from Pennsylvania
- Donald Trump, property tycoon and television personality
- Scott Walker, governor of Wisconsin

Three of the seventeen—Carson, Fiorina, and Trump—were political outsiders, having built up their careers in the private sector. This was indicative of the rising dissatisfaction among the ranks of Republican voters with their professional politicians, the so-called party elite. Polls often put the combined vote of these three outsider candidates as high as 50 percent of Republican voters.

With so many candidates in the field, Fox News, who hosted the first debate, decided to hold one debate at prime time for ten candidates who were polling the highest and an "undercard" debate preceding the main event for the other seven. Some undercard candidates grumbled about this, alleging that the metric— recent opinion polls—used to split the candidates into two camps was flawed.

Trump, who was participating in his first formal political debate, quickly delivered verbal fireworks in a testy exchange with one of the moderators, Megyn Kelly. She questioned Trump over remarks he previously made referring to women as "fat pigs, dogs, slobs, and disgusting animals." Trump replied that he was "kidding" and quipped that the remark was directed at "only Rosie O'Donnell," a liberal-minded television personality, comedienne, and activist. Trump then deftly wove his overarching campaign themes in, saying, "I don't frankly have time for total political correctness. And to be honest with you, this country doesn't have time either. This country is in big trouble. We don't win anymore. We lose to China. We lose to Mexico both in trade and at the border. We lose to everybody." The exchange with Kelly further confirmed Trump's tendency not to apologize for previous crude remarks he made or to moderate his tone in response to criticisms. Trump harbored residual resentment against Kelly for her line of questioning, sparking a mini-feud between them that led to his boycotting the next debate that Kelly moderated in January 2016.

The first debate revealed how divided Republican candidates are on immigration. Bush said, "I believe that the great majority of people coming here illegally have no other options. They want to provide for their family." Bush argued in favor of "a path to earned legal status," which, he explained, was "not amnesty…which means you pay a fine and do many things over an extended period of time." Adopting a similarly immigrant-friendly stance, Rubio argued for opening up more channels to legal immigration. Rubio noted that most people who cross the U.S.–Mexican border were not actually from Mexico but rather from Central American countries such as Guatemala, El Salvador, and Honduras. A lot of people were trying to immigrate legally to the United States, Rubio said, but they were unable to because of how restrictive United States immigration laws are.

Cruz used the immigration policy discussion to try to score points against Bush and Rubio, claiming that "a majority of the candidates have supported amnesty. I have never supported amnesty and I led the fight against Chuck Schumer's gang of eight amnesty legislation in the Senate." Rubio co-sponsored that bill, which failed to become law because it could not muster majority support in the Republican-led House of Representatives.

Trump took a strident anti-immigrant stance by doubling down on remarks he made earlier in the summer about Mexican immigrants. Trump had alleged that they were "bringing drugs, bringing crime. They're rapists and some, I assume, are good people." He reiterated his support for building a border wall between the U.S. and Mexico to keep out illegal immigrants. Trump also noted, "If it weren't for me, you wouldn't even be talking about illegal immigration." It was indeed true that Trump's prioritizing of the issue made immigration a central theme of the campaign. He seemed to benefit from vocalizing the topic since surveys showed that Republican voters perceived him as being the strongest of the candidates on combating illegal immigration.

Another debate highlight was a spat between Senator Paul and Governor Christie over the U.S. National Security Agency (NSA)'s mass surveillance programs that were put in place in the wake of the September 11, 2001, terrorist attacks. Paul, a passionate libertarian, said, "I want to collect more records from terrorists, but less records from innocent Americans," arguing that the NSA was constitutionally bound to obtain warrants from judges in order to conduct surveillance activity. Christie defended the NSA mass surveillance programs as justified in the face of the terrorist threat. "I was appointed U.S. Attorney by President Bush on September 10, 2001, and the world changed enormously the next day . . . this is not theoretical to me. I went to the funerals," he said, referring to the victims of the 9/11 attacks. The exchange exposed the persistent split among Republicans between an anti-government wing that opposes giving federal authorities access to citizens' private data, and a national security wing that supports giving government whatever tools it says it needs to fight terrorism.

Other candidates sought to differentiate themselves from the pack. Ohio governor Kasich set himself apart from his more socially conservative rivals by saying that he had attended a wedding of a gay friend and would love and accept his daughter were she gay. Although he said little during the debate, Carson's concluding remark, "I'm the only one to separate Siamese twins," went over well with the audience. Carson's soft-spoken manner and apolitical background was an asset at first and he shot to second place in polls. But after deadly Islamic terrorist attacks—Paris in November and San Bernardino in December—his weak grasp of foreign policy was perceived as a liability and his poll numbers faded.

In the undercard debate, Fiorina came across as especially strong and articulate. Trumpeting how she came to head of Hewlett-Packard, the largest tech company in the world, worth $90 billion, Fiorina said, "The highest calling of leadership is to challenge the status quo." She was quick to criticize the frontrunner Trump, whom the moderator referred to as "the elephant that is not in the room tonight," saying that "since [Trump] has changed his mind on amnesty, on healthcare and on abortion, I would just ask, what are the principles by which he will govern?" Among the others, Santorum was notable for stressing his fervent anti-abortion credentials, while Graham spoke of the need to make America more energy independent and "to break the strangle hold" that foreign fossil fuel producers enjoy. While Fiorina was hailed by many as the winner of the undercard debate, she failed to maintain momentum and her campaign soon faded.

Republican National Committee chairman Reince Priebus called the first debate "the most inclusive in the history of either party" and said that it showed the Party's "deep bench of candidates." Having seventeen different viewpoints on the stage, according to Priebus, was "a stark contrast with the Democratic Party establishment, which will coronate their nominee with hardly any say from voters," adding that the nation's future would be better secured under one of the Republican contenders than under Hillary Clinton. In particular, Priebus said, while Clinton wants to increase the power of government and "stifle innovation," Republicans instead want to reduce spending and find innovative ways to grow the economy that best suits the needs of the American people.

SANDERS AND CLINTON VIE IN LAS VEGAS

In early 2015, many progressive-minded Democrats hoped that Sen. Elizabeth Warren of Massachusetts would run for president. But after Warren declined to do so, they rapidly coalesced around Sanders. Aged seventy-three, Sanders was the oldest of the combined twenty-two Republican and Democratic candidates to participate in the first debates. Other Democrats had hoped that Vice President Joe Biden, an esteemed, popular figure in the party, would challenge Clinton. However, Biden spent much of 2015 grieving his son's untimely death from cancer, and on October 21 definitively declined to run.

Five candidates appeared on stage at the first Democratic debate:

- Lincoln Chafee, former governor of Rhode Island

- Hillary Clinton, former secretary of state, U.S. senator, and first lady

- Martin O'Malley, former governor of Maryland and mayor of Baltimore

- Bernie Sanders, U.S. senator from Vermont

- Jim Webb, former U.S. senator from Virginia

Viewers had the opportunity to see frontrunners Clinton and Sanders lay out their core policy agendas. Top priorities for Sanders included further tightening regulations in the banking sector, changing the laws on financing political campaigns to stamp out corruption, and phasing out fossil fuels. Clinton's priorities included tax hikes for the wealthy, tax decreases for the middle-class, tighter restrictions on gun sales (a rare case where Clinton was politically more to the left than Sanders), and stronger worker rights such as paid leave and equal pay for women. "I'm a progressive who likes to get things done," Clinton said, when asked by CNN moderator Anderson Cooper to define her political identity.

Clinton consolidated her frontrunner status by delivering a convincing performance, displaying detailed knowledge of policy issues, and remaining calm and composed in exchanges. The evening's unlikely highlight came when Sanders defended Clinton when she was under sustained fire from Republicans for installing a private server for her emails while serving as secretary of state from 2009 to 2013. "The American people are sick and tired of hearing about your damn emails," Sanders said, turning to a beaming Clinton who appeared visibly relieved. The exchange was a good illustration of how Democratic candidates tended to be more respectful of each other and loath to make personal attacks in contrast to their Republican counterparts. Faced with a larger number of rivals, the Republican candidates were more prone to attacking one another in a bid to winnow down the field of candidates. Clinton did score a hit against Sanders after he cited

Denmark's strong welfare state as a potential role model for the country. "We are not Denmark. I love Denmark. We are the United States of America," Clinton said.

The remaining candidates failed to make such an impactful showing. Chafee blamed his poor performance on his federal political greenness evidenced by a now-regretted 1999 Senate vote for a bill that made banks bigger. And Webb's hardline stance on foreign policy seemed at odds with Democrat orthodoxy. At one point, Webb lambasted President Obama for approving the recently concluded international deal concerning Iran's nuclear program, on ice since Iran's Islamic revolution of 1979, and which may now help normalize U.S. relations with Tehran. O'Malley performed somewhat better, outlining concrete policy ideas in areas including gun safety, climate change, immigration, and raising the minimum wage. But he failed to gain traction in the subsequent months, and remained stuck between 1 percent and 2 percent in national polls.

Democratic National Committee chair Debbie Wasserman Schultz said the first Democratic debate proved that there is a great divide between the two parties and their nominees. "Our candidates laid out their vision for continuing our economic progress," she said, while "the Republicans have and will likely continue to treat their debates like a reality TV show, continue to snipe at one another, showcasing their divisive and offensive policies." Schultz did not respond to RNC critics who said that the primaries were little more than a coronation of Clinton. Instead, she celebrated what was the most-watched Democratic debate in history and congratulated the candidates for their positive messaging about their ideas for America, including increasing the minimum wage, ensuring equal pay for women, instituting gun control, making higher education more affordable, fixing the immigration system, and fighting climate change. According to Schultz, the Democratic candidates were able to accomplish in one debate what the Republicans could not accomplish over "nearly 10 hours of debate"

CANDIDATES BOW OUT

Chafee and Webb dropped out of the presidential race shortly after the first debate. Five Republicans—Graham, Jindal, Pataki, Perry, and Walker—withdrew from the race between September and December due to low poll ratings.

By the end of 2015, eight presidential debates had been held, five Republican and three Democratic. Clinton and Trump remained the frontrunners for their respective parties, each enjoying leads of around ten percentage points in most polls. All eyes were turning to Iowa and New Hampshire, the states to hold the first primaries in early February 2016. Among Democrats, Sanders continued gaining ground on Clinton. On the Republican side, Cruz succeeded in separating himself from the rest of the pack to emerge as the biggest threat to Trump's chance to clinch the nomination.

—Brian Beary

Following is a press release from the Republican National Committee on August 6, 2015, remarking on the first Republican presidential primary debate; and a statement from the Democratic National Committee on October 14, 2015, following the Democrat's first presidential primary debate.

RNC Issues Statement on First Republican Presidential Debate

August 6, 2015

RNC Chairman Reince Priebus released the following statement following the first Republican presidential primary debates:

"Tonight, the country saw a diverse and dynamic Republican Party. We are blessed to have so many candidates that bring with them a range of experiences and a wealth of ideas to strengthen our country. There should be no doubt that the Republican Party's nomination process will be a true competition, and voters will be the ones who decide our nominee. It's a stark contrast with the Democratic Party establishment, which will coronate their nominee with hardly any say from voters.

"We're proud to have a deep bench of candidates, and we're grateful that tonight's debates were the most inclusive in the history of either party. Americans had the chance to hear from seventeen candidates. One thing is certain: our candidates all offer a better vision for the future than Hillary Clinton. While Clinton wants to spend more of Americans' money to grow the government, Republicans want to let Americans keep more of their money to grow the economy. While Clinton wants to stifle innovation, Republicans want to empower entrepreneurs young and old to discover new ways to improve the lives of American families.

"With more debates to come, we look forward to continuing to make this contrast. Voters will have many more opportunities to hear from our candidates and decide which one is best equipped to defeat Hillary Clinton and lead the country toward a bright future."

SOURCE: Republican National Committee. "RNC Statement on First Republican Presidential Primary Debates." August 6, 2015. www.gop.com/rnc-statement-on-first-republican-presidential-primary-debate.

DNC Chair Responds to First Democratic Presidential Primary Debate

October 14, 2015

DNC Chair Rep. Debbie Wasserman Schultz released the following statement today in response to the first Democratic Debate in Las Vegas:

"I congratulate all of our Democratic candidates for President, for the American people are surely the winners of last night's debate. On that stage, they saw and heard from our party's candidates, one of whom will go on to be the 45th President of the United States, based on the substance of their policies and their vision for moving our nation forward.

"In just two and a half hours of debate, our Democratic candidates covered more serious topics and bold ideas than the GOP candidates could muster in nearly 10 hours of debate. By a long shot.

"The contrast between each party's candidates, values and policies was demonstrated in stark terms last night. Our candidates laid out their vision for continuing our economic progress through increasing the minimum wage and ensuring equal pay for women and made clear their priorities for our future through their support for combatting climate change, enacting gun violence prevention measures, making college more affordable and fixing our broken immigration system.

"The Republicans have and will likely continue to treat their debates like a reality TV show, continuing to snipe at one another, showcasing their divisive and offensive policies—policies that would take away access to health care and kick immigrants out of our country; and roll back progress for middle class families and hardworking Americans by enacting the same old, tired trickle-down economics that preceded an economic collapse and failed in the past.

"I'm thrilled that this debate set a record for the most watched Democratic debate in history and proud of our candidates for their commitment to a substantive debate that drew a clear contrast for voters on the choice they will have in the 2016 general election.

"Thank you to CNN, Facebook, the Nevada Democratic Party and the incredible, unionized staff of the Wynn hotel for helping put on an incredible, record-setting debate for our candidates and for the American people. As we move forward into the 2016 cycle, I look forward to our future debates and additional events and opportunities for our candidates to get their message out and connect with voters."

SOURCE: Democratic National Committee. "DNC Chair Statement on the First Democratic Debate." October 14, 2015. www.democrats.org/Post/dnc-chair-statement-on-the-first-democratic-debate.

OTHER HISTORIC DOCUMENTS OF INTEREST

FROM PREVIOUS *HISTORIC DOCUMENTS*

Kentucky Court Rules
on Clerk's Refusal to Issue
Same-Sex Marriage Licenses

AUGUST 12, 2015

In the days following the landmark Supreme Court ruling in *Obergefell v. Hodges,* which recognized a fundamental and constitutionally protected right of same-sex couples to marry, thousands of gay couples flooded the offices of registrars across the country seeking marriage licenses. In one county in Kentucky, however, these couples and all others were turned away empty-handed. Kim Davis, the county clerk in Rowan County, Kentucky, to avoid issuing licenses to gay applicants, opted to stop issuing marriage licenses entirely. In the federal court case that ensued, she argued that her sincerely held religious faith would be violated if she were to issue marriage licenses to same-sex couples. Federal trial judge David L. Bunning rejected this notion in *Miller v. Davis,* ruling that, while Davis is "certainly free to disagree" with the Supreme Court opinion, "that does not excuse her from complying with it." Her appeals to the Sixth Circuit Court of Appeals and then to the Supreme Court were rejected, and when she defied Judge Bunning's order and continued to turn away couples seeking marriage licenses, she spent five days in jail for contempt of court. She was released only after pledging that she would not interfere with any of her deputy clerks who issued marriage licenses although she continued to refuse to issue the licenses herself. Her standoff with the federal courts generated tremendous media attention and several Republican presidential candidates trumpeted her cause and even visited her in jail.

CLERK REFUSES MARRIAGE LICENSE ISSUANCE

Rowan County is a small rural county in northeastern Kentucky with a population of 23,655. Davis was elected to the position of county clerk in January 2015, and she had plenty of prior experience in the office. Her mother had been county clerk for the previous thirty-seven years, and Davis had worked as her deputy for almost thirty years. Davis described experiencing a religious conversion in 2011 and joined an Apostolic Pentecostal congregation where she worships several times a week. In keeping with the tenets of this faith, she stopped cutting her hair and wearing makeup and adopted a modest form of dress. Her religious beliefs led her, within hours of the Supreme Court decision on June 26 holding that states are constitutionally required to recognize same-sex marriage, to announce that the Rowan County Clerk's Office would no longer issue marriage licenses at all. Citing her religious beliefs, she said in a statement that "it is not a light issue for me. It is a heaven or hell decision."

The governor of Kentucky, Steve Beshear, issued orders for all county clerks to implement the Supreme Court decision and to begin issuing marriage licenses to same-sex couples. He later addressed religious concerns expressed by county clerks as follows: "You can continue to have your own personal beliefs but, you're also taking an oath to fulfill the duties prescribed by law, and if you are at that point to where your personal convictions tell you that you simply cannot fulfill your duties that you were elected to do, then obviously an honorable course to take is to resign and let someone else step in who feels that they can fulfill those duties." Aware of these directives, Davis, nevertheless, expressed her plans to implement a "no marriage licenses" policy for the remaining three and a half years of her term as Rowan County clerk.

FEDERAL JUDGE ORDERS DAVIS TO ISSUE MARRIAGE LICENSES

Four couples who had been denied marriage licenses in Rowan County filed for injunctive relief in federal court on July 1, 2015. They were represented by the American Civil Liberties Union (ACLU) of Kentucky, which filed the lawsuit against Davis in her role as county clerk, seeking an order that she comply with the mandate from the Supreme Court's *Obergefell v. Hodges* ruling. Davis was represented in court by a Florida-based law firm, Liberty Counsel, which argued that requiring her to approve the plaintiffs' marriages would violate her constitutionally protected freedom of religion. The case was assigned to federal district court Judge Bunning of the U.S. District Court for the Eastern District of Kentucky who held two days of hearings on the matter. Judge Bunning described the case as one presenting a conflict of two important American liberties: the fundamental right to marry and the right to free exercise of religion. "Each party," he wrote, "seeks to exercise one of these rights, but in doing so, they threaten to infringe upon the opposing party's rights."

On August 12, 2015, Judge Bunning ruled in favor of the couples who were seeking to marry and ordered Davis, in her official capacity as Rowan County clerk, to stop applying her "no marriage licenses" policy to future marriage license requests. To reach this conclusion, he found that her refusal to issue licenses infringes on the plaintiff's fundamental right to marry and serves no compelling state interest. He rejected her argument that "protecting her religious freedom" was a sufficient state interest, finding countervailing interests on the part of the state, particularly the state's interest in upholding the rule of law. "Our form of government," he wrote, "will not survive unless we, as a society, agree to respect the U.S. Supreme Court's decisions, regardless of our personal opinions." He added that Davis is "certainly free to disagree with the Court's opinion, as many Americans likely do, but that does not excuse her from complying with it. To hold otherwise would set a dangerous precedent."

Further, he found the governor's order to the county clerks to start processing same-sex marriage licenses to be facially neutral and generally applicable and not aimed at suppressing religious freedom. As such, it only needs to be rationally related to a legitimate state interest to survive constitutional scrutiny. Serving the state interest in upholding the rule of law is sufficient, he found, to support the governor's directive. He also rejected Davis's argument that forcing her to issue marriage licenses that bear her "imprimatur and authority" as Rowan County clerk would violate her constitutional rights by forcing her to endorse same-sex marriage, a message she finds objectionable. He disputed whether the clerk's role of certifying that certain information is accurate on a form is really the same as requiring the clerk to condone or endorse same-sex marriage. "Davis is simply being asked to signify that couples meet the legal requirements to marry. The state is not asking her to condone same-sex unions on moral or religious grounds, nor is it restricting her from engaging in a variety of religious activities," the judge ruled.

Davis Appeals the Judge's Order

Although the district court ruled against Davis, the judge gave her until August 31 for his order to take effect. She immediately filed an appeal to the U.S. Court of Appeals for the Sixth Circuit and asked for the district judge's order to be stayed pending the appeal. The Sixth Circuit, in a unanimous ruling, rejected her request to extend the stay. To qualify for a stay, Davis would have had to meet a legal standard that required her to show likelihood that she would ultimately prevail in her case. The Appeals Court found "little or no likelihood" that she would succeed on the merits of her case. "It cannot be defensibly argued that the holder of the Rowan County Clerk's office . . . may decline to act in conformity with the United States Constitution as interpreted by a dispositive holding of the United States Supreme Court," the appeals court wrote.

She then took her case directly to the Supreme Court, petitioning for an emergency order to allow her to continue refusing to grant marriage licenses. Her motion gave the high court its first opportunity to weigh in on whether the freedom of religion clause of the First Amendment could shelter those who object to the increased recognition of rights for gay citizens. On August 31, 2015, just as the temporary two-week stay of the federal trial court judge's order was expiring, the Supreme Court declined to grant the stay, with no dissent noted.

Davis Jailed for Contempt of Court

On September 1, 2015, the plaintiffs returned to the clerk's office to again apply for marriage licenses. Despite being under a court order to grant the licenses, Davis turned the couples away, saying that she was acting "under God's authority." Judge Bunning ordered Davis as well as her six deputy clerks into his court for a contempt hearing on September 3, 2015. On the stand, Davis repeated her belief that "marriage is between one man and one woman" and said that she had no choice but to refuse licenses to same-sex couples. "The court cannot condone the willful disobedience of its lawfully issued order," Judge Bunning replied. "If you give people the opportunity to choose which orders they follow, that's what potentially causes problems." He ordered her taken into custody for contempt of court and said she would remain in jail until she was prepared to comply with the court's order to issue marriage licenses.

Davis' staff had also been ordered to attend the hearing, where five out of the six deputy clerks agreed to start issuing marriage licenses. The sixth was Davis's son, Nathan. Although he refused to issue licenses, he agreed not to interfere with other deputies. The deputy clerks reopened the offices on September 4 and began to issue marriage licenses. They are under a continuing requirement to submit status reports to the court every two weeks confirming their compliance with court orders. After five days in jail, Judge Bunning lifted his contempt of court finding and ordered Davis's release from detention. According to his order, "Davis shall not interfere in any way, directly or indirectly, with the efforts of her deputy clerks to issue marriage licenses to all legally eligible couples. If Defendant Davis should interfere in any way with their issuance, that will be considered a violation of this Order and appropriate sanctions will be considered."

Davis returned to work on September 14, 2015, and, while she will not issue licenses herself, she agreed not to interfere with the work of her deputy clerks. She did change the license form, replacing her name with language to the effect that the licenses are being issued under the authority of the federal court. Although Kentucky law requires that marriage licenses be authorized by the county clerk, both the governor and the attorney general of Kentucky have said the licenses are valid and will be recognized by the state.

DAVIS GAINS NATIONWIDE ATTENTION

After serving time in jail for her beliefs and garnering massive public attention to her cause, Davis became to many Christian conservatives the face of religious opposition to same-sex marriage and a symbol of the fight against an overreaching federal government. Republican presidential candidate Mike Huckabee called her case a "criminalization of Christianity," and he offered to go to jail in her place. Another politician running for the Republican presidential nomination, Sen. Ted Cruz, R-Texas, issued a statement when Davis was jailed, saying that "those who are persecuting Kim Davis believe that Christians should not serve in office . . . or, if Christians do serve in public office, they must disregard their religious faith—or be sent to jail." Several commentators noted comparisons between Davis and George C. Wallace, the segregationist governor of Alabama who famously stood in the doorway of the University of Alabama in 1963 to prevent the entry of two black students in defiance of a court order.

Part of the reason why so much attention was focused on Davis may be that she was one of very few such clerks nationwide who refused to issue same-sex licenses. This was the point Marc Solomon, national campaign director of Freedom to Marry, made when he described the focus on the Davis case to the *New York Times* as "a tempest in a teapot." He continued, "If the big backlash and the mass resistance that our opponents promised is one clerk from a county of under 25,000 people, I think we're in very good shape."

—Melissa Feinberg

Following is the U.S. District Court for the Eastern District of Kentucky decision in the case of Miller v. Davis, *in which the court ruled on August 12, 2015, that Rowan County clerk Kim Davis must issue marriage licenses to same-sex couples.*

DOCUMENT   *Miller v. Davis*

August 12, 2015

[All footnotes have been omitted.]

CIVIL ACTION NO. 15-44-DLB

APRIL MILLER, et al. PLAINTIFFS
vs.
KIM DAVIS, individually and in her official capacity, et al. DEFENDANTS

****

I. Introduction

This matter is before the Court on Plaintiffs' Motion for Preliminary Injunction. Plaintiffs are two same-sex and two opposite-sex couples seeking to enjoin Rowan County Clerk Kim Davis from enforcing her own marriage licensing policy. On June 26, 2015, just hours after the U.S. Supreme Court held that states are constitutionally required to recognize same-sex marriage, Davis announced that the Rowan County Clerk's Office would no longer issue marriage licenses to any couples. See *Obergefell v. Hodges*, 135 S. Ct. 2584 (2015). Davis, an Apostolic Christian with a sincere religious objection to same-sex marriage, specifically sought to avoid issuing licenses to same-sex couples without discriminating against them. Plaintiffs now allege that this "no marriage licenses" policy substantially interferes with their right to marry because it effectively forecloses them from obtaining a license in their home county. Davis insists that her policy poses only an incidental burden on Plaintiffs' right to marry, which is justified by the need to protect her own free exercise rights. . . .

At its core, this civil action presents a conflict between two individual liberties held sacrosanct in American jurisprudence. One is the fundamental right to marry implicitly recognized in the Due Process Clause of the Fourteenth Amendment. The other is the right to free exercise of religion explicitly guaranteed by the First Amendment. Each party seeks to exercise one of these rights, but in doing so, they threaten to infringe upon the opposing party's rights. The tension between these constitutional concerns can be resolved by answering one simple question: Does the Free Exercise Clause likely excuse Kim Davis from issuing marriage licenses because she has a religious objection to same-sex marriage? For reasons stated herein, the Court answers this question in the negative.

II. Factual and Procedural Background

[Background with regard to plaintiffs and other clerk's duties has been omitted.]

. . . Under Kentucky law, county clerks are also responsible for issuing marriage licenses. . . . The marriage license section has the following components:

(a) *An authorization statement of the county clerk issuing the license for any person or religious society authorized to perform marriage ceremonies to unite in marriage the persons named;*

(b) *Vital information for each party . . . ; and*

(c) *The date and place the license is issued, and the signature of the county clerk or deputy clerk issuing the license.*

Davis does not want to issue marriage licenses to same-sex couples because they will bear the above-mentioned authorization statement. She sees it as an endorsement of same-sex marriage, which runs contrary to her Apostolic Christian beliefs. . . .

In the wake of *Obergefell*, Governor Beshear issued the following directive to all county clerks:

Effective today, Kentucky will recognize as valid all same sex marriages performed in other states and in Kentucky. In accordance with my instruction, all executive branch agencies are already working to make any operational changes that will be necessary to implement the Supreme Court decision. . . .

He has since addressed some of the religious concerns expressed by some county clerks:

> You can continue to have your own personal beliefs but, you're also taking an oath to fulfill the duties prescribed by law, and if you are at that point to where your personal convictions tell you that you simply cannot fulfill your duties that you were elected to do, th[e]n obviously an honorable course to take is to resign and let someone else step in who feels that they can fulfill those duties.

Davis is well aware of these directives. Nevertheless, she plans to implement her "no marriage licenses" policy for the remaining three and a half years of her term as Rowan County Clerk.

III. STANDARD OF REVIEW

A district court must consider four factors when entertaining a motion for preliminary injunction:

(1) whether the movant has demonstrated a strong likelihood of success on the merits;

(2) whether the movant would suffer irreparable harm;

(3) whether an injunction would cause substantial harm to others; and

(4) whether the public interest would be served by the issuance of such an injunction . . .

IV. ANALYSIS

[Section A detailing the clerk's official duties has been omitted.]

B. Plaintiffs' Motion for Preliminary Injunction

1. Plaintiffs' likelihood of success on the merits

a. The fundamental right to marry

. . . If a state law or policy "significantly interferes with the exercise of a fundamental right[, it] cannot be upheld unless it is supported by sufficiently important state interests and is closely tailored to effectuate only those interests." *Zablocki v. Redhail*, 434 U.S. 374, 388 (1978). A state substantially interferes with the right to marry when some members of the affected class "are absolutely prevented from getting married" and "[m]any others, able in theory to satisfy the statute's requirements[,] will be sufficiently burdened by having to do so that they will in effect be coerced into forgoing their right to marry." *Id.* at 387. . . .

The state action at issue in this case is Defendant Davis' refusal to issue any marriage licenses. Plaintiffs contend that Davis' "no marriage licenses" policy significantly interferes with their right to marry because they are unable to obtain a license in their home county. Davis insists that her policy does not significantly discourage Plaintiffs from marrying because they have several other options for obtaining licenses: (1) they may go to one of the seven neighboring counties that are issuing marriage licenses; (2) they may obtain licenses from Rowan County Judge Executive Walter Blevins; or (3) they may avail themselves of other alternatives being considered post-*Obergefell*.

Davis is correct in stating that Plaintiffs can obtain marriage licenses from one of the surrounding counties; thus, they are not totally precluded from marrying in Kentucky. However, this argument ignores the fact that Plaintiffs have strong ties to Rowan County. They are long-time residents who live, work, pay taxes, vote and conduct other business in Morehead. Under these circumstances, it is understandable that Plaintiffs would prefer to obtain their marriage licenses in their home county. And for other Rowan County residents, it may be more than a preference. The surrounding counties are only thirty minutes to an hour away, but there are individuals in this rural region of the state who simply do not have the physical, financial or practical means to travel.

This argument also presupposes that Rowan County will be the only Kentucky county not issuing marriage licenses. While Davis may be the only clerk currently turning away eligible couples, 57 of the state's 120 elected county clerks have asked Governor Beshear to call a special session of the state legislature to address religious concerns related to same-sex marriage licenses. If this Court were to hold that Davis' policy did not significantly interfere with the right to marry, what would stop the other 56 clerks from following Davis' approach? What might be viewed as an inconvenience for residents of one or two counties quickly becomes a substantial interference when applicable to approximately half of the state. . . .

Having considered Davis' arguments in depth, the Court finds that Plaintiffs have one feasible avenue for obtaining their marriage licenses—they must go to another county. Davis makes much of the fact that Plaintiffs are able to travel, but she fails to address the one question that lingers in the Court's mind. Even if Plaintiffs are able to obtain licenses elsewhere, why should they be required to? The state has long entrusted county clerks with the task of issuing marriage licenses. It does not seem unreasonable for Plaintiffs, as Rowan County voters, to expect their elected official to perform her statutorily assigned duties. And yet, that is precisely what Davis is refusing to do. Much like the statutes at issue in *Loving* and *Zablocki*, Davis' "no marriage licenses" policy significantly discourages many Rowan County residents from exercising their right to marry and effectively disqualifies others from doing so. The Court must subject this policy apply heightened scrutiny.

b. The absence of a compelling state interest

When pressed to articulate a compelling state interest served by her "no marriage licenses" policy, Davis responded that it serves the State's interest in protecting her religious freedom. The State certainly has an obligation to "observe the basic free exercise rights of its employees," but this is not the extent of its concerns. In fact, the State has some priorities that run contrary to Davis' proffered state interest. Chief among these is its interest in preventing Establishment Clause violations. See U.S. Const. amend. I (declaring that "Congress shall make no law respecting the establishment of religion"). Davis has arguably committed such a violation by openly adopting a policy that promotes her own religious convictions at the expenses of others. In such situations, "the scope of the employees' rights must [ ] yield to the legitimate interest of governmental employer in avoiding litigation."

The State also has a countervailing interest in upholding the rule of law. See generally *Papachristou v. City of Jacksonville*, 405 U.S. 156, 171 (1972) ("The rule of law, evenly applied to minorities as well as majorities, . . . is the great mucilage that holds society together."). Our form of government will not survive unless we, as a society, agree to respect the U.S. Supreme Court's decisions, regardless of our personal opinions. Davis is certainly free to disagree with the Court's opinion, as many Americans likely do, but that does not excuse her from complying with it. To hold otherwise would set a dangerous precedent.

For these reasons, the Court concludes that Davis' "no marriage licenses" policy likely infringes upon Plaintiffs' rights without serving a compelling state interest. Because Plaintiffs have demonstrated a strong likelihood of success on the merits of their claim, this first factor weighs in favor of granting their request for relief.

2. Potential for irreparable harm to Plaintiffs

. . . The Court is not aware of any Sixth Circuit case law explicitly stating that a denial of the fundamental right to marry constitutes irreparable harm. However, the case law . . . suggests that the denial of constitutional rights, enumerated or unenumerated, results in irreparable harm. It follows that Plaintiffs will suffer irreparable harm from Davis' "no marriage licenses" rule, absent injunctive relief. Therefore, this second factor also weighs in favor of granting Plaintiffs' Motion.

3. Potential for substantial harm to Kim Davis

a. The right to free exercise of religion

The First Amendment provides that "Congress shall make no law respecting an establishment of religion, or prohibiting the free exercise thereof." This Free Exercise Clause "embraces two concepts—freedom to believe and freedom to act." *[citation omitted.]* "The first is absolute but, in the nature of things, the second cannot be." Therefore, "[c]onduct remains subject to regulation for the protection of society."

Traditionally, a free exercise challenge to a particular law triggered strict scrutiny. See, e.g., *Sherbert v. Verner*, 374 U.S. 398, 407 (1963). A statute would only be upheld if it served a compelling government interest and was narrowly tailored to effectuate that interest. *Id.* However, the U.S. Supreme Court has retreated slightly from this approach. See *Emp't Div., Dep't of Human Res. of Oregon v. Smith*, 494 U.S. 872 (1990); *Church of the Lukumi Babalu Aye, Inc. v. City of Hialeah*, 508 U.S. 520 (1993). While laws targeting religious conduct remain subject to strict scrutiny, "[a] law that is neutral and of general applicability need not be justified by a compelling governmental interest even if the law has the incidental effect of burdening a particular religious practice." *Babalu*, 508 U.S. at 532; see also *Smith*, 494 U.S. at 880 (stating further that an individual's religious beliefs do not "excuse him from compliance with an otherwise valid law prohibiting conduct that the State is free to regulate"). . . .

For purposes of this inquiry, the state action at issue is Governor Beshear's post-*Obergefell* directive, which explicitly instructs county clerks to issue marriage licenses to same-sex couples. Davis argues that the Beshear directive not only substantially burdens her free exercise rights by requiring her to disregard sincerely-held religious beliefs, it does not serve a compelling state interest. She further insists that Governor Beshear could easily grant her a religious exemption without adversely affecting Kentucky's marriage licensing scheme, as there are readily available alternatives for obtaining licenses in and around Rowan County.

This argument proceeds on the assumption that Governor Beshear's policy is not neutral or generally applicable, and is therefore subject to strict scrutiny. However, the text itself supports a contrary inference. Governor Beshear first describes the legal impact of the Court's decision in *Obergefell,* then provides guidance for all county clerks in implementing this new law. His goal is simply to ensure that the activities of the Commonwealth are consistent with U.S. Supreme Court jurisprudence. . . .

The Beshear directive certainly serves the State's interest in upholding the rule of law. However, it also rationally relates to several narrower interests identified in *Obergefell.* By issuing licenses to same-sex couples, the State allows them to enjoy "the right to personal choice regarding marriage [that] is inherent in the concept of individual autonomy" and enter into "a two-person union unlike any other in its importance to the committed individuals." 135 S. Ct. at 2599-2600. It also allows same-sex couples to take advantage of the many societal benefits and fosters stability for their children. Id. at 2600-01. Therefore, the Court concludes that it likely does not infringe upon Davis' free exercise rights.

b. The right to free speech

[Discussion about the free speech clause of the First Amendment has been omitted.]

Davis contends that this directive violates her free speech rights by compelling her to express a message she finds objectionable. Specifically, Davis must issue marriage licenses bearing her "imprimatur and authority" as Rowan County Clerk to same-sex couples. Davis views such an act as an endorsement of same-sex marriage, which conflicts with her sincerely-held religious beliefs.

As a preliminary matter, the Court questions whether the act of issuing a marriage license constitutes speech. Davis repeatedly states that the act of issuing these licenses requires her to "authorize" same-sex marriage. A close inspection of the KDLA marriage licensing form refutes this assertion. The form does not require the county clerk to condone or endorse same-sex marriage on religious or moral grounds. It simply asks the county clerk to certify that the information provided is accurate and that the couple is qualified to marry under Kentucky law. Davis' religious convictions have no bearing on this purely legal inquiry.

The Court must also acknowledge the possibility that any such speech is attributable to the government, rather than Davis. The State prescribes the form that Davis must use in issuing marriage licenses. She plays no role in composing the form, and she has no discretion to alter it. Moreover, county clerks' offices issue marriage licenses on behalf of the State, not on behalf of a particular elected clerk. . . .

[Additional discussion of Davis's argument and the Kentucky Religious Freedom Act have been omitted.]

V. CONCLUSION

District courts are directed to balance four factors when analyzing a motion for preliminary injunction. In this case, all four factors weigh in favor of granting the requested relief. Accordingly, for the reasons set forth herein,

IT IS ORDERED that Plaintiffs' Motion for Preliminary Injunction against Defendant Kim Davis, in her official capacity as Rowan County Clerk, is hereby granted.

IT IS FURTHER ORDERED that Defendant Kim Davis, in her official capacity as Rowan County Clerk, is hereby preliminarily enjoined from applying her "no marriage licenses" policy to future marriage license requests submitted by Plaintiffs.

This 12th day of August, 2015.

Signed by: David L. Bunning, United States District Judge

SOURCE: U.S. District Court Eastern District of Kentucky Northern Division at Ashland. *Miller v. Davis.* Civil Action No. 14-44-DLB.

OTHER HISTORIC DOCUMENTS OF INTEREST

FROM THIS VOLUME

Greek Prime Minister Calls for Election Following Bailout

AUGUST 21, 2015

After a dramatic summer showdown with his European Union (EU) counterparts over his country's third bailout program, Greek prime minister Alexis Tsipras on August 20 called new elections to give Greek citizens an opportunity to deliver their verdict on the deal. With Greeks suffering severely from five years of EU- and International Monetary Fund (IMF)–imposed austerity policies aimed at lowering the national debt, Tsipras had promised when elected in January 2015 an end to austerity. Having failed to achieve this in July's bailout deal, some thought he would be punished at the polls. But by running a skillful campaign that stressed the pros of the bailout package, while acknowledging its imperfections, Tsipras and his Syriza party convincingly won the September 20 elections. Many Greeks gave him credit for having negotiated hard with the EU for six months and for bringing those talks to a successful conclusion. Despite facing continuing economic hardship, the public seemed resigned to implementing further austerity policies as a price worth paying for remaining inside the EU's single currency area, the eurozone.

TSIPRAS DEFENDS IMPERFECT DEAL

Greece had been forced to renegotiate the terms of the EU and IMF's financial support programs, which have prevented the country from going bankrupt, because the existing programs, first crafted in 2010, were due to expire at the end of June 2015. Brinksmanship in the run-up to that expiry deadline inflicted further pain on the Greeks as the uncertainty over the talks' outcome pushed the country's economic growth forecasts downward again. In addition, in late June and early July, the Syriza-led coalition government, to prevent a rush on the banks, put limits on how much money its citizens could withdraw from their bank accounts each day. On top of that, Tsipras infuriated his EU counterparts by holding a referendum on July 6 on the EU's latest offer for a third bailout deal and urged his compatriots to vote no to the deal, which they did by 61.3 percent.

Less than a week after the referendum, Tsipras concluded the bailout negotiations at a summit of eurozone leaders on July 12. His critics were quick to point out that the final bailout package, worth €86 billion ($93 billion), had more stringent terms attached to it than the offer in June that Tsipras had successfully persuaded the Greek people to reject. Nevertheless, he managed to secure the Greek parliament's approval for the deal, with 229 voting in favor and 64 against. The bailout deal received the support of the main center-left and center-right parties of Greece, respectively PASOK and New Democracy. By contrast, 32 parliamentarians from Tsipras's own left-wing Syriza party voted against it in protest over the government having signed on to more austerity policies. Their defection was followed shortly afterward by the formation of a new party, Popular Unity, comprised mainly of ex-Syriza supporters opposed to the new bailout.

Tsipras made a lengthy address to the Greek people on August 21, deploying his considerable rhetorical skills to justify his course of action. "During the last few months we all experienced difficult and dramatic moments," he said. "The pressure, the blackmail, the ultimatums, the financial asphyxiation led to a situation without precedent." He assured them that "today, this difficult phase conclusively ends with the ratification of the agreement, the disbursement of the first installment of the 23 billion euros and the payment of the country's obligations both abroad and at home."

Showing a candor that the voters seemed to appreciate, he said, "I want to be completely honest with you. We did not achieve the agreement that we were hoping to achieve prior to January's elections." Nevertheless, Tsipras pointed to some areas where he argued that the government had gained some concessions in the negotiations. He cited an end to job cuts in the public sector, a reduction in the amount of budgetary surplus the government is required to run, and a more gradual pace of privatizing public assets to pay off some of the national debt.

Looking to the future, he highlighted what he thought would be the key upcoming issues for discussion between Greece and its bailout partners. He vowed to fight to prevent a liberalization of collective redundancies in the private sector, an improvement in the legal protections for public property, and an eventual write-down of some of Greece's debt. Debt relief is the single greatest long-term goal for Greece because it has amassed a national debt that is nearly double the size of its economy and one that many economists say it will never be able to fully pay off. The third bailout deal, while offering no immediate debt relief, does include a pledge to revisit the question at a later date.

The conclusion of the negotiations marked a turning point. Henceforth, the focus of the government's energies turned toward implementing the program and improving the health of the Greek economy for the long haul. Tax evasion has long been endemic in Greece, and it has contributed to the soaring debt. "This fight to finally have those who have been perennially benefiting to also pay" and "the fight against tax evasion, for a fair and stable tax system" were among the challenges Tsipras cited. Striking an optimistic note in concluding his address, he said, "We have not yet experienced the positive outcomes that lie ahead, trapped until now by the pressures of the negotiation."

ECONOMIC CONTRACTION CONTINUES

The economic indicators for Greece show little sign of improvement in the near-term. Having suffered economic contraction for five successive years, Greece experienced a brief resurgence of growth in 2014 (0.8 percent) before slipping back into recession in 2015. Since 2008, the gross domestic product (GDP) per capita of Greeks has declined from around €29,000 to €16,000, while the nation's unemployment rate has increased from 8 percent to 27 percent. Prodded by austerity programs, the government's deficits have gradually diminished. However, the continual shrinkage in the economy's size has meant that the debt-to-GDP ratio has kept increasing, from 109 percent in 2008 at the start of the financial crisis to 197 percent in 2015. One bright spot has been that inflation has remained consistently low due to Greece's eurozone membership, where inflation has been low for more than a decade.

The economic depression has had a devastating impact on ordinary Greeks, as many news articles published on the topic attest. The UK's *Guardian* newspaper, for example, quoted Christos, a twenty-seven-year-old master's graduate in transport engineering, who now works in a coffee shop. Commenting on the July referendum, Christos explained that "the 'no' vote was a way for Greeks to express their feelings to Europe. There's a certain happiness that the no vote has been heard." Nikos Aggelakis, a seventy-year-old corner shop manager in Athens, said of the quarter where he manages his shop: "This area used to be very lively, people were outside having a stroll, going for a drink, buying flowers, but in the last few years things have just been getting worse and worse."

With youth unemployment as high as 70 percent, there is talk of a "lost generation" of young Greeks who have known nothing but austerity for their entire young adulthood. Yet throughout the negotiations process, a majority of Greeks have remained in favor of their government negotiating another bailout deal with the EU and IMF, viewing it as a better alternative to being forced to exit the eurozone.

Alexandra Galani, a twenty-five-year-old Greek, called the bailout "a necessary evil," adding that "it would be a disaster to return to the drachma, not even our grandchildren would have enough to eat." Abandoning the euro would likely trigger a sharp devaluation of whatever national currency the government adopted to replace it. This would make Greek exports more competitive in global markets, but it would also further lower living standards for Greeks because imported goods would become more expensive and thus more difficult to obtain.

Given that Tsipras's Syriza party had been elected on a stridently antiausterity platform, it was unsurprising that some of its members defected over the new bailout deal. High-profile party figures who left included the former finance minister, Yanis Varoufakis, and the speaker of the parliament, Zoe Konstantopoulou. Varoufakis, who had become well known in Europe as a key negotiator during the bailout negotiations in the first half of 2015, likened the deal to the way in which the 1919 Treaty of Versailles overly harshly punished Germany after World War I, which sowed the seeds for subsequent conflict. Konstantopoulou criticized Tsipras for calling the September election before he had held a Syriza party congress.

In Greek politics, the largest center-right party for many years is New Democracy, which elected a new leader, Vangelis Meimarakis, in the run-up to the election. So did the Greek socialist party PASOK, which put Fofi Gennimata at the helm. For many years PASOK had been the largest party of the political in Greece until Syriza, which had its roots in far-left communist ideology, eclipsed it during the debt crisis. The Syriza defectors formed a new party, Popular Unity, led by Panagiotis Lafazanis, which took its name from a 1970 alliance of leftist Chilean leader Salvador Allende. Other parties competing in the election included the communist party, the far-right Golden Dawn, the popular right Independent Greeks, and two centrist parties, Potami and EK.

Syriza Wins Again

While polls predicted a tight race between New Democracy and Syriza for first place, to the surprise of many, Tsipras's Syriza easily won, taking 35.5 percent. This gave it 145 of the 300 seats parliament because, under Greek electoral law, the party that wins the most votes gains a fifty-seat bonus. However, Syriza was still five seats shy of an overall majority, and Tsipras had to find a coalition partner. He chose to revive the partnership that he had forged with the Independent Greeks in January, with the latter having won ten seats, which secured a working majority for the coalition.

One remarkable feature about the results was how slightly voting shares for parties had changed from January's elections. Thus, New Democracy came in second place winning seventy-five seats, followed by Golden Dawn with eighteen seats, PASOK took seventeen, the communist party fifteen, Potami eleven, Independent Greeks ten, and EK nine. In a kind of moral victory for Tsipras, the Popular Unity party received no seats because they only won 2.9 percent of votes, just under the 3 percent electoral threshold that must be cleared to gain representation in the parliament. The voter turnout rate was 56.6 percent, down 7 percentage points since January, a signal of the Greeks' weariness at going to the polls, this being the sixth election for them in as many years.

As eyes turned to the reelected government's willingness to implement the terms of the July bailout deal, new battle lines started to be drawn: tax rates for farmers and private remedial schools, reform of the pensions system, and what to do with a glut of nonperforming home mortgages that has left the banking sector severely weakened. After winning a slim victory in parliament on a package of reforms on October 17, Tsipras sketched out the path ahead. "There are no new measures here," he said. "There are difficult measures that we all knew about."

—Brian Beary

Following is the text of Greek prime minister Alexis Tsipras's August 21, 2015, address in which he explains his decision for snap elections following a new bailout from the European Union.

DOCUMENT   *Tsipras Calls Snap Election*

August 21, 2015

[F]ellow Greek citizens,

During the last few months we all experienced difficult and dramatic moments.

The tough negotiation with the creditors was a difficult challenge for both the government and the country.

The pressure, the blackmail, the ultimatums, the financial asphyxiation led to a situation without precedent.

We all lived through this.

However, we did so with patience, composure, and the endurance of our people.

The determination of our people, as recorded by the referendum.

The decision to change, to change the country, to change all that led us to the crisis and the deterioration of social conditions.

Let's be clear:

Without this popular determination the creditors would have either completely imposed their will.

Or they would have led us to destruction.

This determination was present at each stage of the negotiations.

This determination reinforced our resolve, as we battled on a daily basis against the often-irrational demands and threats of the creditors.

Today, this difficult phase conclusively ends with the ratification of the agreement, the disbursement of the first instalment of the 23 billion euros and the payment of the country's obligations both abroad and at home.

The economy will receive a boost. The market will normalize. The banks will soon return to regular activity.

Of course, this is not the end of the difficult situation that we have been facing for the last five years.

It is my conviction, however, that it can be—through consistent work and effort on all of our parts—the beginning of the end of this difficult situation.

The decisive step towards stabilizing the financing of our economy.

A beginning that won't be easy, but that will hold prospects and possibilities.

As long as society is fully behind this.

Calm and determined, as during these past months.

My fellow Greek citizens,

I want to be completely honest with you.

We did not achieve the agreement that we were hoping to achieve prior to January's elections.

We also did not experience the reaction that we had been anticipating.

In this battle we made concessions.

But we obtained a deal that—given the overwhelmingly negative conditions in Europe and the fact that we inherited the absolute attachment of the country to the memoranda terms—was the best that one could achieve.

We are obliged to adhere to this agreement but, at the same time, we will fight to minimize its negative consequences.

Based on the interests of the majority.

In order to reclaim, as soon as possible, our sovereignty against our creditors.

Without accepting their interpretations as infallible truths.

Without accepting horizontal cuts, the destruction of labor, the permanent decimation of the weakest social forces.

And we have already proven that we can do this, that we can persist and achieve a lot of things.

Consider the position of the partners prior to this agreement:

A five-month extension of the previous programme, full implementation of the previous government's commitments and then new prerequisites.

At this time, following the referendum, we have an approved three-year deal, with secure funding.

Also bear in mind that the partners were asking for the immediate abolition of EKAS, the privatization of IPTO and of the secondary tier of the PPC.

The above were not accepted—a win for us on these issues.

The partners were also asking for the implementation of a zero deficit clause concerning the supplementary funds.

In the agreement there is an explicit reference regarding equivalent measures and we are ready to take up the charge on this.

Also, the restoration of labor relations and the prevention of the liberalization of collective redundancies in the private sector is our unwavering goal, and I believe we will achieve it.

The redundancies in the public sector are now a thing of the past and the school guards, the cleaners and the universities' administrative staff have been restored to their positions.

There is no longer a 5 euro fee in the hospitals, while the recruitment process for 4,500 medical and nursing staff that are direly needed is moving ahead through the Supreme Council for Civil Personnel Selection (ASEP).

Let us also not forget that we have agreed upon dramatically smaller surpluses than the previous government, so that the fiscal adjustment—the required measures—is lower by 20 billion euros.

Furthermore, the new loan agreement is not subject to the colonial nature of English law that the Greek governments agreed upon in previous agreements, but rather is governed by European and international law, allowing our country to maintain all the privileges and immunities that safeguard public property.

And finally, this is the first time that the procedure concerning the write-down of the Greek debt has been determined in such an explicit and unequivocal manner, which is perhaps the most crucial aspect to solving the Greek problem.

We gained considerable ground but this does not mean that we achieved what we, and the people, expected.

My fellow Greek citizens,

Now that this difficult cycle has reached its end,

And contrary to the usual stance of many who unfortunately believe that they are entitled to keep their positions, their seats, their offices regardless of the conditions and circumstances

I feel a deep moral and political obligation for you to judge all that I have done.

Both the positive results and the mistakes.

Both the successes and the missteps.

That is why I have decided to go to the President of the Republic shortly, to submit my resignation, as well as the resignation of the government.

The scope of the popular mandate that I received on 25th January has been exhausted.

And now the sovereign people must express their opinion once more.

You, through your vote, will determine whether we represented the country with the determination and courage required during the difficult negotiations with the creditors.

You, through your vote, will decide whether the agreement achieved provides the conditions to overcome the crisis, for the economy to recover and for us to finally begin the efforts to put an end to the memoranda and the resultant harsh conditions.

You, through your vote, will decide who should lead Greece—and how—in this difficult, but at last promising, path ahead of us.

Who can better negotiate the debt write-down, and how that can be done.

Who can move forward—and how—at a confident and steady pace, with the necessary, deep, progressive reforms that the country needs.

Finally, you will judge all of us through your vote.

Those of us that consistently fought for our country, both here and abroad, so that Greece would not to find itself at gunpoint.

And those that claimed that Greece should receive loans, i.e. a memorandum, but in drachmas—as a matter of ideological consistency—who converted the majority that the people gave us, the first government of the Left in the country, into a parliamentary minority.

As well as those from the old political system and those colluding with their efforts, who during these past months called on us and pressed us, in line with the strictest creditors' demands, to sign anything that was placed in front of us.

By even slandering our resistance as alleged stalling.

My fellow Greek citizens,

I rely on your judgment with a clear conscience.

Proud of the efforts made by my government, and my own.

During this entire period, I strived to remain faithful to what we had promised.

We negotiated decisively and persistently, and stayed the course.

We withstood pressures and blackmail.

It is true that we pushed matters to the brink for the people and the economy.

However, we also turned the Greek case into a global issue.

We turned the resistance of our people into an incentive of struggle for other European peoples.

And Europe will not be the same following these difficult six months.

The notion that an end must finally be put to austerity is gaining ground.

The differences among the democratic and progressive European forces are being increasingly felt.

And we, Greece, with a prestige and a scope much larger than our size, played, and are playing, a leading role in the forthcoming changes.

Greece will be at the forefront of the discussion concerning Europe's future.

Yesterday, I submitted a written request to the President of the European Parliament that the European Parliament, as an institution with direct democratic legitimacy, play an active role in the Greek program.

Transparency, open democratic debate, democratic accountability and impact assessment will be an integral part from now on of the implementation of our agreement with the partners.

My fellow Greek citizens,

During this period, despite the tough negotiation and the difficult conditions, we also managed to engage in a different way of governing.

The one hundred-instalment regulation, the measures on the humanitarian crisis, the opening of ERT, the bill concerning the broadcasting frequencies, the law regarding immigrants, the decisive intervention to stop the environmental crime in Skouries, and dozens of other measures and initiatives are proof of our commitment to governing in a new way.

These actions also attest to our decision to change the country with courage and confidence, by capitalizing on social support for reform objectives.

We still have many battles ahead, this time within the country.

The fight against collusion and corruption, which we have already commenced.

The fight to finally have those who have been perennially benefiting to also pay, a group that no one has dared touch until now.

The battle for justice to be applied to those who until now have been above the law.

The fight against tax evasion, for a fair and stable tax system.

The mother of all battles—to change the state mechanism so that it becomes more effective.

Friendlier towards citizens.

Unfriendly towards political favors, partisanship and corruption.

And all of this requires a clear mandate and a strong government to firmly hold the course without wavering.

And above all, it requires the support of society.

The support of those who want changes in line with democracy, progressive reforms, transparency and justice.

My fellow Greek citizens,

I remain optimistic, despite the difficulties.

I believe that we have not yet experienced the positive outcomes that lie ahead, trapped until now by the pressures of the negotiation.

I will ask for the vote of the Greek people in order for us to govern and apply all aspects of our governmental programme.

More experienced, better prepared, more practical, but always committed to the ultimate goal of a free, democratic, and socially just Greece, we will remain dedicated and consistent as we face the new conditions.

I assure you, I will not forfeit nor will we forfeit our ideas and values.

Regardless of the difficulties.

And I invite all of you, together, to calmly and decisively fight for a better future for our country.

In these difficult times, we must hold on to—and champion—what matters most: our country and our democracy.

Thank you.

SOURCE: Prime Minister of the Hellenic Republic. "Prime Minister Alexis Tsipras' State Address." August 21, 2015. www.primeminister.gov.gr/english/2015/08/21/prime-minister-alexis-tsipras-state-address.

OTHER HISTORIC DOCUMENTS OF INTEREST

September

New Prehuman Species Discovered in South Africa

SEPTEMBER 10, 2015

On September 10, 2015, an international team of sixty scientists joined with the South African government to announce what was widely described as a remarkable discovery: more than 1,500 fossils belonging to a previously unknown human ancestor. Called *Homo naledi,* the new species had characteristics similar to both modern humans and their earlier apelike ancestors, a combination that perplexed the broader scientific community and generated speculation that it could be the "missing link" in humans' evolutionary history. While the fossils are still being analyzed, many believe they will have a significant impact on current understanding of where humans came from.

A LUCKY TIP AND AN UNUSUAL JOB POSTING

The team that made the discovery was led by Lee Berger, a professor at the University of the Witwatersrand in South Africa and a National Geographic Society explorer-in-residence. Berger was well-known among paleontologists and anthropologists, having made headlines in 2010 with another discovery of fossils in a cave near Johannesburg. Berger had determined those fossils also belonged to a new species, which he named *Australopithecus sediba*—a species that geologists concluded lived between 1.78 million and 1.95 million years ago. The *Australopithecus* genus is generally applied to species that are close relatives of humans but display more primitive, apelike characteristics than species in the *Homo* genus.

In 2013, Berger received a tip about a possible find in the Rising Star Cave, a popular site for caving expeditions roughly thirty miles northwest of Johannesburg. The cave was also within the Cradle of Humankind World Heritage Site—a location that earned this name because of its wealth of fossilized hominid remains. Two cavers had happened upon a small cavern filled with fossils, pictures of which they sent to Pedro Boshoff, a geologist and former student of Berger. Boshoff in turn alerted Berger, who recognized that the fossils were not human and immediately began pursuing funding to explore the cavern.

Funded by the National Geographic Society and supported by the University of the Witwatersrand and South Africa's Department of Science and Technology, Berger assembled a sixty-person team of international scientists, including six particularly slender women. The fossils had been discovered in a chamber that could only be accessed by climbing a steep rock face called the Dragon's Back and dropping down a long vertical shoot that narrowed to a gap about 7.5 inches wide. Berger posted an advertisement on Facebook looking for people who had a background in paleontology or archaeology, caving experience, could travel to South Africa immediately, and most important, could fit through the chute. Out of sixty applicants, Berger selected a team of six women who he nicknamed "underground astronauts."

The team set up camp and first entered the cave in November 2013. The women worked in two-hour shifts in teams of three, communicating with the rest of the team via cameras and roughly two miles of fiber optic cables. Over the course of three weeks, and a few additional days in March, the women used paintbrushes and toothpicks to extract more than 1,550 fossil elements—the single largest fossil hominid find in Africa. Berger then gathered a team of 30 "early career scientists" and twenty senior scientists who had helped him evaluate his 2010 find to analyze the new discovery during a six-week workshop in Johannesburg that began in March 2014.

Homo naledi Revealed

On September 10, 2015, Berger and his team published two papers on their findings in the scientific journal *eLife* and announced their discovery with South African officials during a ceremony at the Cradle of Humankind Visitor Center. "These discoveries underline the fact that, despite our individual differences in appearance, language, beliefs, and cultural practices, we are bound together by a common ancestry," said Cyril Ramaphosa, deputy president of South Africa. "Today, we unearth our past. Today, we catch a glimpse of our future."

The team concluded that the fossils were from about fifteen different individuals who spanned various age groups, from infancy to late adulthood. While they had anticipated that the remains would belong to an apelike ancestor such as *Australopithecus*, they determined the fossils to be more human overall and belonging to a new species that they dubbed *Homo naledi*. Naledi means "star" in a local South African language.

Homo naledi, they said, was a slender creature that stood upright, was approximately 4.5–5 feet tall, and probably weighed no more than about 100 pounds. While it had an apelike pelvis, it also had relatively long legs and flat feet very similar to modern humans. This suggested they were good long-distance walkers—a notable characteristic of the *Homo* genus. Its shoulders were also apelike, but its hands had the same wrist and palm as human hands, which is typically indicative of a tool-using species. However, it had curved fingers like an ape and its first thumb bone had unique ridges for the muscles that draw it close to the hand, meaning they had a powerful grip and were also climbers. Its skull was similar to that of modern humans, though it had a more pronounced brow bone and a brain about two-thirds smaller. It also had small, human-like teeth. Although *Homo naledi* exhibited a mix of both primitive and more evolved traits, it was classified in the *Homo* genus largely because of the shape of its skull, smaller teeth, long legs, and more modern feet. "The message we're getting is of an animal right on the cusp of the transition from *Australopithecus* to *Homo*," Berger told *National Geographic*. "Everything that is touching the world in a critical way is like us. The other parts retain bits of their primitive past."

This mix of characteristics led to some speculation as to whether *Homo naledi* was the "missing link" scientists had been looking for in the evolutionary cycle between modern humans and their apelike ancestors. There is a roughly million-year gap in the fossil record between ancestors in the australopithecines group, which are primitive and apelike, and *Homo erectus*, an early human that made fire, wielded tools, traveled on foot, and had large brains and body proportions similar to those of modern humans. Paleoanthropologist Louis Leakey discovered a species in 1964 that he dubbed *Homo habilis* given his and his colleagues' belief that it had been a tool-wielding creature.

However, there was some disagreement in the scientific community about whether *Homo habilis* really belonged to the *Homo* genus or would be more accurately classified as *Australopithecus*. By the time of Berger's discovery, scientists had largely moved on from the idea of finding a fossil that directly linked *Homo sapiens* to early ancestors. "The human tree is quite bushy, so the idea of a 'missing link' between humans and apes is kind of a Victorian-era idea, and we like to shy away from that," said Steven Churchill, human paleontologist at Duke University and one of the expedition's leaders. Berger himself described *Homo naledi* as more of a "bridge" between bipedal primates and humans.

Berger's team also concluded that *Homo naledi* appeared to have intentionally deposited the bodies of the dead in the remote chamber. While some questioned this theory, the team said they had ruled out a number of other possibilities. There was no damage or trace of injury on the fossils and only a few bird and rodent bones in the chamber, making it unlikely a predator or other creature had dragged the bodies into the crevice. There were no signs of water that could have moved the bodies into the crevice, or any signs of rubble, plant material, or other debris that may have washed in along with them. Furthermore, the team did not find any evidence, such as tools or other items, in the cave to suggest that *Homo naledi* was living there. This was a unique and potentially significant discovery, because it implied funerary behavior and symbolic thinking that scientists had previously only associated with later species of humans who had lived within the past 200,000 years.

At the time of publication, the team had not yet dated the fossils and the geology of the cave did not provide them with many clues. Geologists believe the cave is at most 3 million years old, but it is also possible that the fossils are younger and even less than 100,000 years old. If the latter is true, it could have a major impact on current understanding of the human evolutionary timeline because it would suggest that *Homo naledi* existed at the same time as more evolved human species.

THE SEARCH CONTINUES

Following the team's announcement, the fossils were put on display at the Cradle of Humankind Visitor Center until October 11. Berger's team also uploaded scans and 3D models of all of the fossil fragments to an open database widely available online, and encouraged others to help study the items.

"It's not only remarkable, it's also rather weird. But nonetheless, the fossils are important," said Bernard Wood, a paleoanthropologist at The George Washington University. "Intellectually, it's a real puzzle. And I think it's going to take scientists quite a time to get their heads around what the real significance of these discoveries is."

Berger's team continues to search the chamber as well as other parts of Rising Star Cave for more fossils, in addition to several other sites in South Africa.

—Linda Fecteau Grimm

Following is a press release from the Republic of South Africa's Department of Science and Technology on September 10, 2015, congratulating the scientists who worked on the team that discovered the new prehuman species; and a statement by Deputy President Cyril Ramaphosa of South Africa, also on September 10, 2015, on the historic discovery.

South African Government Congratulates Team on Discovery of New Species

September 10, 2015

Government has welcomed the discovery of a new hominin species by the University of the Witwatersrand (Wits) at the Cradle of Humankind World Heritage Site, 50 km northwest of Johannesburg.

The discovery of the new species in the Homo lineage, which may have engaged in funerary practices, is unparalleled in the history of South Africa's palaeosciences.

The Rising Star Expedition, which is responsible for the research, has made a significant contribution to the successful implementation of the Palaeosciences Strategy of the Department of Science and Technology (DST) and South Africa's standing in this research field.

The Minister of Science and Technology, Naledi Pandor, said the DST was pleased with the research results of the team, led by Prof. Lee Berger of the Wits Evolutionary Studies Institute, and that it looked forward to more output from the site.

Consisting of more than 1,550 numbered fossil elements, the discovery is the single largest fossil hominin find yet made on the continent of Africa. The initial discovery was made in 2013 in a cave known as Rising Star.

The fossils, which have yet to be dated, lay in a chamber about 90 metres (some 100 yards) from the cave entrance, accessible only through a chute so narrow that a special team of very slender individuals needed to be recruited to retrieve them.

"The palaeosciences are one of the scientific areas earmarked in DST strategies for exploitation, owing to South Africa's geographic advantage in this area," said the Minister.

Also speaking on Thursday, 10 September, at the Cradle of Humankind where the announcement was made, Deputy President Cyril Ramaphosa said that the discovery would encourage humankind to further ponder the scope of human existence all over the world.

"These discoveries underline the fact that, despite our individual differences in appearance, language, beliefs and cultural practices, we are bound together by a common ancestry," he said.

Deputy President Ramaphosa said that government had fulfilled its international responsibility to the United Nations Educational, Scientific and Cultural Organization to protect, preserve and showcase the Cradle of Humankind Visitor Centre in Maropeng, where this new discovery will be on display for a month, from 11 September to 11 October 2015.

"Within our own age, the scientific achievements of these underground 'astronauts' give us hope that we may have the means to overcome the modern-day challenges of hunger, social exclusion and underdevelopment," he added.

Wits said the discovery would shed light on the origins and diversity of the Homo genus. The new species, Homo naledi, appears to have intentionally deposited the bodies of its dead in a remote cave chamber, behaviour previously thought limited to humans.

The finds are described in two papers published in the scientific journal *eLife* and reported in the cover story of the October issue of *National Geographic* (http://natgeo.org/naledi) and a *NOVA/National Geographic* special (#NalediFossils). An international team of scientists took part in the research.

Dr Gansen Pillay, Deputy CEO of the NRF, said, "The South African Strategy for the Paleosciences provides an explicit roadmap that includes government's vision to protect, preserve and generate knowledge in this critical scientific area. Central to the Strategy is the mandate of the NRF, namely, the development of excellent human capital and contributing to the knowledge economy through new knowledge generation. It was therefore natural for the NRF to be involved in this project. We are excited about its findings and we congratulate the team."

SOURCE: Republic of South Africa Department of Science and Technology. "Government congratulates Wits on discovery of new hominin species." September 10, 2015. © 2011–Current, Department: Science & Technology, Republic of South Africa. All rights reserved. www.dst.gov.za/index.php/media-room/communiques/1501-department-of-science-and-technology-congratulates-wits-on-discovery-of-new-hominin-species.

South African Deputy President Remarks on New Species

September 10, 2015

Esteemed Guests,
Members of the Media,
Ladies and Gentlemen,

Today will be written into the history books as one of those moments in which the world learnt something new and remarkable.

The discovery of a new species of primitive hominin in our own genus reveals much about our ancestors.

In time, it may reveal much about ourselves.

This find will generate interest from beyond the scientific community.

It will inspire poets and writers to revisit Africa's rich oral traditions, and to imagine ways to retell the story of our common ancestry.

It will encourage us to enquire further about the whole scope of human existence, the world around us, and the world before us.

We expect that it will catch the imagination and stimulate the interest of people across the world—people who are excited about knowledge and learning.

We are delighted that discoveries that we would never have imagined have been found here at the southern tip of the African continent.

Maropeng, the visitor centre to the Cradle of Humankind World Heritage Site, was opened almost 10 years ago.

At the time we said that this would become an iconic place, a place of pilgrimage, a place belonging to the people of South Africa, Africa and the world, the place where our collective umbilical cord is buried.

We did not imagine then that a new species would be unearthed telling us more about our human journey than we knew before.

We now know that research in the Cradle of Humankind will yield yet more information for decades to come.

Ladies and Gentlemen,

The legendary Professor Philip Tobias, a stalwart of the University of the Witwatersrand, is no longer with us.

But I am quite sure he would have reminded us that these finds again underline the fact that Africa, our continent, is the home of great scientific discoveries, the home of our humanity, the home of our culture.

These discoveries underline the fact that despite our individual differences in appearance, language, beliefs and cultural practices, we are bound together by a common ancestry.

Government has fulfilled its international responsibility to UNESCO to protect, preserve and showcase this site of outstanding universal value to the world.

On behalf of the people of South Africa, I invite the world to visit the Cradle of Humankind Visitor Centre, Maropeng where this new find will be on display for one month.

This discovery is the result of outstanding research by a large team of collaborators from across the world.

This research was conducted by the Evolutionary Studies Institute at the University of Witwatersrand, host to the Department of Science and Technology and the National Research Foundation Centre of Excellence in the Palaeosciences.

We wish to congratulate the Vice-Chancellor of Wits University Professor Adam Habib, Professor Lee Berger, Professor Paul Dirks, Professor John Hawks and all those who have been involved in bringing the world this historic moment.

There was once a period in Africa's history where our ancestors existed in a capricious, precarious environment that demanded innovation, adaptation and resolve.

Within our own age, the scientific achievements of these 'underground astronauts' give us hope that we may have the means to overcome modern day challenges of hunger, social exclusion and underdevelopment.

These achievements give us hope that we may preserve the species and achieve shared prosperity.

These men and women of science are not only interested in our past. They are interested too in our future.

They are interested in what makes us who we are, where we have come from, and where we are capable of going.

Today, we unearth our past.

Today, we catch a glimpse of our future.

I thank you.

Census Bureau Reports on Poverty in the United States

SEPTEMBER 16, 2015

In September 2015, the U.S. Census Bureau released its official annual estimate of poverty and income in the United States alongside the supplemental measure of these statistics, which takes into account, among other things, safety net programs. Both the official and supplemental measures showed no statistically significant change in the poverty rate or number of those in poverty from 2013 to 2014. Even so, economists said the fact that these numbers remained stagnant while more and more jobs were added to the economy was a sign that income inequality was continuing to grow and government safety net programs were likely not helping lift Americans out of poverty as intended. One bright spot in the report, however, was the growing number of Americans with health insurance, which was likely directly related to the 2010 Affordable Care Act.

RATE AND NUMBER OF AMERICANS IN POVERTY REMAINS UNCHANGED

Since the Federal Reserve Board of Governors announced the official end of the recession in 2009, the economy has gradually continued to improve. Unemployment reached a peak of 10 percent in October 2009 and had fallen to 5 percent by December 2015, its lowest level since April 2008. Although many positive improvements have been made, when the Census Bureau released its annual *Income and Poverty in the United States* report, it showed no statistically significant change in the official poverty rate from 2013 to 2014. In 2013, the percentage of those in poverty was 14.5 percent, while in 2014 it was 14.8 percent, or 46.7 million people. The 2014 report marked the fourth consecutive year the Census Bureau had not detected a statistically significant change in the number of those in poverty.

The 2014 poverty threshold for a family of four was $24,230 and $12,071 for an individual. Overall, number and type of families in poverty did not show a significant change from 2013 to 2014. By age group, those under 18 had a 21.1 percent poverty rate, the 18 to 64 group was 13.5 percent, and those 65 and older were 10 percent. None of the four Census regions showed a statistically significant difference from 2013, either. In the South, which continued to have the highest poverty rate of the four regions, 16.5 percent, or 19.5 million people, were in poverty. In the Midwest, 13 percent, or 8.7 million people, lived in poverty. The Northeast had a 12.6 percent poverty rate, or 7 million individuals, and the West had a 15.2 percent poverty rate, or 11.4 million individuals.

No statistically significant change was recorded in the poverty rate among all racial groups: non-Hispanic whites had a poverty rate of 10.1 percent, while blacks had a rate of 26.2 percent, Hispanics a rate of 23.6 percent, and Asians a rate of 12 percent. The poverty rate for blacks continued to be approximately two and a half times higher than that of non-Hispanic whites. The only significant change evidenced by Census data was the increase of 3.4 percent in the number of black children in poverty.

The number of shared households, those with one or more additional non-householder, spouse, or partner, had reached 23.9 million by spring 2015, still higher than 19.7 million prior to the start of the recession in 2007; however, that number did not mark a statistically significant change from 2014. According to the Census Bureau, the 6.5 million young adults between the ages of 25 and 34 who lived with their parents in spring 2015 have an official poverty rate of 7.2 percent. However, if poverty is determined based solely on the individual's income, the poverty rate is closer to 39.4 percent.

Median household income was $53,657 in 2014, which again was not a statistically significant difference from 2013. The Census Bureau reported that this could be linked to an increase in nontraditional households, which typically have lower incomes than family households. Ten percent of American households had an income of less than $12,280 in 2014, while 5 percent were at the opposite end of the spectrum, above $206,570.

SUPPLEMENTAL POVERTY MEASURE ALSO REMAINS UNCHANGED

The official Census estimate of poverty does not account for food stamps, cash assistance, tax credits, and a variety of other government support systems, all of which can have a significant impact on the number of Americans considered impoverished. The official estimate also does not account for children under the age of 15 who are unrelated to anyone in their household. In 2010, the Census released its first supplemental poverty report, which was hailed as a more accurate method for determining the number of Americans living in poverty by taking into account government assistance programs and expenses such as health insurance, child care, housing, job expenses including transportation, and nontraditional children, such as those in foster care.

For the first time in 2015, the Census Bureau released both its official poverty estimate and the supplemental report at the same time. While the official report recorded a poverty rate of 14.8 percent, the supplemental report calculated a slightly higher total at 15.3 percent of American families living in poverty, or 48.4 million individuals. This, however, was not a statistically significant change from 2013. While the totals calculated by the official and supplemental reports are somewhat similar in many areas, the biggest difference in the supplemental report relates to children. The official poverty measure found 21.5 percent of children in poverty, while the supplemental measure only reported 16.7 percent.

According to Jane Waldfogel of Columbia University, although the supplemental report also found little change in the poverty and income data from 2013 to 2014, there were some indications that certain safety net programs are helping move some Americans out of poverty. Waldfogel told NPR, "[T]he most important anti-poverty program for families with children are the refundable tax credits, the earned income tax credit and the child tax credit, and together, those are reducing child poverty by about 7 percentage points this year."

Both the official and supplemental reports still have their critics, who believe that the data does not represent an accurate picture of Americans in poverty. Robert Rector, a senior research fellow at the conservative Heritage Foundation said that low-income Americans typically spend $2.30 for every dollar brought in. However, this "doesn't mean they are chowing down on filet mignon or not working hard to make ends meet. But they are working hard to put food on the table, keep the car running and stay in the apartment they have," but they are not necessarily hungry and homeless, he said.

Stagnant Income and Poverty Rates Plague America

While economic recovery continues, it is still not resulting in the gains—or hitting all segments of the economy—that many had hoped. "Despite decent employment growth in 2014, the persistent high unemployment yielded no improvements in wages and no improvement in the median incomes of working-age households or any reduction in poverty," said Lawrence Mishel, president of the liberal Economic Policy Institute, following the release of the Census report. "Anyone wondering why people in this country are feeling so ornery need look no further than this report," he added.

The data served as yet another call to action for Republicans and Democrats in Congress to again push their differing policies that they believed could best pull people out of poverty and create a thriving middle class. Rep. Paul Ryan, D-Wis., said it was time to "help people move from welfare into work and self-sufficiency," instead of "just treating the symptoms of poverty."

The call to action was perhaps even more pronounced with the upcoming 2016 presidential election. Both leading Democratic candidates, former secretary of state Hillary Clinton and Sen. Bernie Sanders of Vermont, cited income inequality as key tenets of their campaign platforms. Clinton touted a "fairness economy" that would be based on equal pay for men and women, an increase in taxes for the wealthiest Americans, and expanded social services. She said that increasing wages "for hard-working Americans so they can afford a middle class life" is "my mission from the first day I'm president to the last." Sanders's plan included progressive estate taxes, an increase in the federal minimum wage, greater spending on infrastructure to create blue collar jobs, trade deal revisions, a youth jobs program, pay equality, Medicare for all, and tuition-free higher education. Criticizing their counterpart's ideologies as akin to what they consider the failed policies of President Barack Obama, many Republican presidential contenders spoke of increased self-sufficiency through a reduction of government benefits. Leading Republican contender Donald Trump proposed raising taxes on the wealthiest Americans but reducing corporate taxes, which he believes will stimulate greater job creation and investment in the American economy.

Health Insurance Coverage on the Rise

When the Census Bureau releases its annual figures on income and poverty, it also reports on health insurance coverage. And while most of the Census poverty and income findings had no statistically significant year-over-year increase from 2013 to 2014, Americans experienced significant gains in health insurance coverage during that timeframe. In 2014, 10.4 percent, or 33 million, of Americans were without health insurance, a decrease of 2.9 percent from 2013. Minority and lower-income Americans experienced the greatest increase in the number of insured.

The decrease in the number of uninsured Americans was attributed to the ongoing implementation of the Affordable Care Act (ACA). Census data showed that every state experienced a decrease in the number of uninsured, but those states that chose to expand Medicaid under the ACA had the greatest declines. Massachusetts had the lowest uninsured rate at 3.3 percent while Texas had the highest at 19.1 percent.

—Heather Kerrigan

Following are excerpts from the U.S. Census Bureau report on poverty in the United States, released on September 16, 2015; and excerpts from the U.S. Census Bureau supplemental poverty report also released on September 16, 2015.

Census Bureau Report
on Poverty in the United States

September 16, 2015

[All portions of the report not corresponding to poverty have been omitted.]

[Tables, graphs, and footnotes, and references to them, have been omitted.]

POVERTY IN THE UNITED STATES

HIGHLIGHTS

- In 2014, the official poverty rate was 14.8 percent. There were 46.7 million people in poverty. Neither the poverty rate nor the number of people in poverty was statistically different from the 2013 estimates.

- For the fourth consecutive year, the number of people in poverty at the national level was not statistically different from the previous year's estimates.

- The 2014 poverty rate was 2.3 percentage points higher than in 2007, the year before the most recent recession.

- The 2014 poverty rates for most demographic groups examined were not statistically different from the 2013 rates. Poverty rates went up between 2013 and 2014 for only two groups: people with a bachelor's degree or more and married-couple families.

- For most groups, the number of people in poverty did not show a statistically significant change. The number of people in poverty increased for unrelated individuals, people aged 18 to 64 with a disability, people with at least a bachelor's degree, and married-couple families.

- The poverty rate in 2014 for children under age 18 was 21.1 percent. The poverty rate for people aged 18 to 64 was 13.5 percent, while the rate for people aged 65 and older was 10.0 percent. None of these poverty rates were statistically different from the 2013 estimates.

RACE AND HISPANIC ORIGIN

The poverty rate for non-Hispanic Whites was 10.1 percent in 2014, lower than the poverty rates for other racial groups. Non-Hispanic Whites accounted for 61.8 percent of the total population and 42.1 percent of the people in poverty. For non-Hispanic Whites, neither the poverty rate nor the number of people in poverty experienced a statistically significant change between 2013 and 2014.

For Blacks, the 2014 poverty rate was 26.2 percent and there were 10.8 million people in poverty. For Asians, the 2014 poverty rate was 12.0 percent, which represented 2.1 million people in poverty. Among Hispanics, the 2014 poverty rate was 23.6 percent and there were 13.1 million people in poverty. None of these estimates were statistically different from the 2013 estimates.

Age

In 2014, 13.5 percent of people aged 18 to 64 (26.5 million) were in poverty compared with 10.0 percent of people aged 65 and older (4.6 million) and 21.1 percent of children under age 18 (15.5 million). Children represented 23.3 percent of the total population and 33.3 percent of the people in poverty. None of these age groups experienced a statistically significant change in the number or rate of people in poverty between 2013 and 2014.

Related children are people under age 18 related to the householder by birth, marriage, or adoption who are not themselves householders or spouses of householders. The poverty rate and the number in poverty for related children under age 18 were 20.7 percent and 15.0 million in 2014, not statistically different from the 2013 estimates. For related children in families with a female householder, 46.5 percent were in poverty, compared with 10.6 percent of related children in married-couple families.

The poverty rate and the number in poverty for related children under age 6 were 23.5 percent and 5.5 million in 2014, not statistically different from the 2013 estimates. About 1 in 5 of these children were in poverty in 2014. More than half (55.1 percent) of related children under age 6 in families with a female householder were in poverty. This was more than four times the rate of their counterparts in married-couple families (11.6 percent).

Sex

In 2014, 13.4 percent of males and 16.1 percent of females were in poverty. Neither poverty rate showed a statistically significant change from its 2013 estimate.

Gender differences in poverty rates were more pronounced for those aged 65 and older. The poverty rate for women aged 65 and older was 12.1 percent while the poverty rate for men aged 65 and older was 7.4 percent. The poverty rate for women aged 18 to 64 was 15.3 percent while the poverty rate for men aged 18 to 64 was 11.6 percent. For children under age 18, the poverty rate for girls (21.1 percent) was not statistically different from the poverty rate for boys (21.2 percent).

Nativity

Of all people, 86.6 percent were native-born and 13.4 percent were foreign-born. The 2014 poverty rate and the number in poverty for the native born and the foreign born were not statistically different from 2013; 14.2 percent and 38.9 million for the native born and 18.5 percent and 7.8 million for the foreign born. Within the foreign-born population, 46.8 percent were naturalized U.S. citizens, while the remaining were not citizens of the United States. The poverty rates in 2014 were 11.9 percent for the foreign-born naturalized citizens and 24.2 percent for those who were not U.S. citizens, neither statistically different from 2013.

REGION

None of the four regions experienced a significant change in the poverty rate or the number in poverty between 2013 and 2014. In 2014, the poverty rate and the number in poverty were 12.6 percent and 7.0 million for the Northeast, 13.0 percent and 8.7 million for the Midwest, 16.5 percent and 19.5 million for the South, and 15.2 percent and 11.4 million for the West (Table 3). The South continued to have a higher poverty rate than the other three regions.

RESIDENCE

Inside metropolitan statistical areas, the poverty rate and the number of people in poverty were 14.5 percent and 38.4 million in 2014. Among those living outside metropolitan statistical areas, the poverty rate and the number in poverty were 16.5 percent and 8.2 million in 2014. Neither group experienced a statistically significant change in the poverty rates or the number in poverty between 2013 and 2014.

The 2014 poverty rate and the number of people in poverty for those living inside metropolitan areas, but not in principal cities, were 11.8 percent and 19.7 million. Among those who lived in principal cities, the 2014 poverty rate and the number in poverty were 18.9 percent and 18.7 million. Neither group experienced a statistically significant change in the poverty rates or the number in poverty between 2013 and 2014.

Within metropolitan areas, people in poverty were more likely to live in principal cities in 2014. While 37.3 percent of all people living in metropolitan areas lived in principal cities, 48.7 percent of poor people in metropolitan areas lived in principal cities.

WORK EXPERIENCE

In 2014, 6.9 percent of workers aged 18 to 64 were in poverty. The poverty rate for those who worked full time, year round was 3.0 percent, while the poverty rate for those working less than full time, year round was 15.9 percent. None of these rates were statistically different from the 2013 poverty rates.

Among those who did not work at least 1 week in 2014, the poverty rate and the number in poverty were 33.7 percent and 16.4 million in 2014, not statistically different from the 2013 estimates (Table 3). Those who did not work in 2014 represented 24.7 percent of all people aged 18 to 64, compared with 61.7 percent of people aged 18 to 64 in poverty.

DISABILITY STATUS

In 2014, for people aged 18 to 64 with a disability, the poverty rate was 28.5 percent, not statistically different from 2013, whereas the number of people aged 18 to 64 with a disability increased from 4.0 million in 2013 to 4.4 million 2014. For people aged 18 to 64 without a disability, the poverty rate and number in poverty were 12.3 percent and 22.1 million, neither statistically different from the previous year estimates.

Among people aged 18 to 64, those with a disability represented 7.9 percent of all people compared with 16.6 percent of people aged 18 to 64 in poverty.

EDUCATIONAL ATTAINMENT

In 2014, 28.9 percent of people aged 25 and older without a high school diploma were in poverty. The poverty rate for those with a high school diploma but with no college was

14.2 percent, while the poverty rate for those with some college but no degree was 10.2 percent. None of these rates were statistically different from the 2013 poverty rates.

Among people with at least a bachelor's degree, the poverty rate and the number in poverty were 5.0 percent and 3.4 million in 2014, up from 4.4 percent and 3.0 million in 2013. People with at least a bachelor's degree in 2014 represented 32.5 percent of all people aged 25 and older, compared with 13.7 percent of people aged 25 and older in poverty.

FAMILIES

In 2014, the family poverty rate and the number of families in poverty were 11.6 percent and 9.5 million, neither statistically different from the 2013 estimates. For married-couple families, both the poverty rate and the number in poverty increased to 6.2 percent and 3.7 million in 2014, up from 5.7 percent and 3.4 million in 2013. The poverty rate for families with a female householder was 30.6 percent in 2014, not statistically different from 2013, while the number in poverty decreased to 4.8 million in 2014 down from 5.2 million in 2013. For families with a male householder, neither the poverty rate nor the number in poverty showed any statistical change between 2013 and 2014. For families with a male householder, 15.7 percent were in poverty in 2014. This represented 1.0 million families in 2014.

DEPTH OF POVERTY

Categorizing a person as "in poverty" or "not in poverty" is one way to describe his or her economic situation. The income-to-poverty ratio and the income deficit or surplus describe additional aspects of economic well-being. While the poverty rate shows the proportion of people with income below the relevant poverty threshold, the income-to-poverty ratio gauges the depth of poverty and shows how close a family's income is to its poverty threshold. The income-to-poverty ratio is reported as a percentage that compares a family's or an unrelated person's income with the applicable threshold. For example, a family with an income-to-poverty ratio of 125 percent has income that is 25 percent above its poverty threshold.

The income deficit or surplus shows how many dollars a family's or an individual's income is below (or above) their poverty threshold. For those with an income deficit, the measure is an estimate of the dollar amount necessary to raise a family's or a person's income to their poverty threshold.

RATIO OF INCOME TO POVERTY

Table 5 presents the number and the percentage of people with specified income-to-poverty ratios—those below 50 percent of poverty ("Under 0.50"), those below 125 percent of poverty ("Under 1.25"), those below 150 percent of poverty ("Under 1.50"), and those below 200 percent of poverty ("Under 2.00").

In 2014, 20.8 million people reported family income below one-half of their poverty threshold. They represented 6.6 percent of all people and 44.6 percent of those in poverty. About 1 in 5 people (19.4 percent) had family income below 125 percent of their threshold, about 1 in 4 people (24.1 percent) had family income below 150 percent of their poverty threshold, while approximately 1 in 3 (33.4 percent) had family income below 200 percent of their threshold.

Of the 20.8 million people with family income below one-half of their poverty threshold, 6.8 million were children under age 18, 12.5 million were aged 18 to 64, and 1.5 million were aged 65 and older. The percentage of people aged 65 and older with income below 50 percent of their poverty threshold was 3.2 percent, less than one-half the percentage of the total population at this poverty level (6.6 percent).

The demographic makeup of the population differs at varying degrees of poverty. In 2014 children represented:

- 23.3 percent of the overall population.

- 20.0 percent of the people with income above 200 percent of their poverty threshold.

- 27.3 percent of people with income between 100 percent and 200 percent of their poverty threshold.

- 32.8 percent of the population below 50 percent of their poverty threshold.

By comparison, people aged 65 and older represented:

- 14.6 percent of the overall population.

- 4.8 percent of the people with income above 200 percent of their poverty threshold.

- 17.6 percent of the people between 100 percent and 200 percent of their poverty threshold.

- 7.1 percent of people below 50 percent of their poverty threshold.

Income Deficit

The income deficit for families in poverty (the difference in dollars between a family's income and its poverty threshold) averaged $10,137 in 2014, which was not statistically different from the inflation-adjusted 2013 estimate. The average income deficit was larger for families with a female householder ($10,662) than for married-couple families ($9,474).

For families in poverty, the average income deficit per capita for families with a female householder ($3,194) was higher than for married-couple families ($2,565). For unrelated individuals, the average income deficit for those in poverty was $6,826 in 2014. The $6,552 deficit for women was lower than the $7,183 deficit for men.

Shared Households

Shared households are defined as households that include at least one "additional" adult, a person aged 18 or older, who is not the householder, spouse or cohabiting partner of the householder. Adults aged 18 to 24 who are enrolled in school are not counted as additional adults.

In 2015, the number and percentage of shared households remained higher than in 2007, prior to the recession. In 2007, there were 19.7 million shared households, representing 17.0 percent of all households; by 2015, there were 23.9 million shared households, representing 19.2 percent of all households.

Between 2014 and 2015, however, the changes in the number and percentage of shared households were not statistically significant. The changes in the number and percentage of adults residing in shared households were also not statistically significant.

In 2015, an estimated 11.1 million adults aged 25 to 34 were additional adults in someone else's household. Of these young adults, 6.5 million lived with their parents. The changes in the number and percentage of young adults living in their parent's household between 2014 and 2015 were not statistically significant.

It is difficult to assess the precise impact of household sharing on overall poverty rates. In 2014, adults aged 25 to 34 living with their parents had an official poverty rate of 7.2 percent (when the entire family's income is compared with the threshold that includes the young adult as a member of the family). However, if poverty status was determined using only the young adult's own income, 39.4 percent of those aged 25 to 34 would have been below the poverty threshold for a single person under age 65. Moreover, although 7.3 percent of families including at least one adult child of the householder aged 25 to 34 were poor, 13.1 percent of those families would have had incomes below poverty if the young adult were not living in the household.

Source: U.S. Census Bureau. "Income and Poverty in the United States: 2014." September 16, 2015. www .census.gov/content/dam/Census/library/publications/2015/demo/p60-252.pdf.

Census Bureau Report on Supplemental Poverty Measures

September 16, 2015

[All figures, tables, graphics, and references to them, have been omitted.]

[Only the sections related to poverty estimates, poverty rates, and the effect of non-cash benefits have been included below.]

Poverty Estimates for 2014: Official and SPM

The measures presented in this study use the 2015 CPS ASEC income information that refers to calendar year 2014 to estimate SPM resources. These are the same data used for the preparation of official poverty statistics and reported in DeNavas-Walt and Proctor (2015). The SPM thresholds for 2014 are based on out-of-pocket spending on basic needs (FCSU). Thresholds use 5 years of quarterly data from the CE; the thresholds are produced at the BLS. Expenditures on shelter and utilities are determined for three housing tenure groups. The three groups include owners with mortgages, owners without mortgages, and renters. The thresholds used here include the value of Supplemental Nutrition Assistance Program (SNAP) benefits in the measure of spending on food. The American Community Survey (ACS) data on rents paid are used to adjust the SPM thresholds for differences in spending on housing across geographic areas.

The two measures use different units of analysis. The official measure of poverty uses the census-defined family that includes all individuals residing together who are related by birth, marriage, or adoption and treats all unrelated individuals over the age of 14 independently. For the SPM, the "family unit" includes all related individuals who live at the same address, as well as any co-resident unrelated children who are cared for by the family (such as foster children), and any cohabiters and their children. These units are referred to as *SPM Resource Units*. Selection of the unit of analysis for poverty measurement implies that members of that unit share income or resources with one another.

SPM thresholds are adjusted for the size and composition of the SPM Resource Unit relative to the two-adult-two-child threshold using an equivalence scale. The official measure adjusts thresholds based on family size, number of children and adults, as well as whether or not the householder is aged 65 or over. The official poverty threshold for a two-adult-two-child family was $24,008 in 2014. The SPM thresholds vary by housing tenure and are higher for owners with mortgages and renters than the official threshold. These two groups comprise about 76 percent of the total population. The official threshold increased by $384 between 2013 and 2014. The SPM thresholds for renters increased from $25,144 in 2013 to $25,460 in 2014. Thresholds for homeowners, with or without mortgages, did not change significantly between 2013 and 2014.

SPM resources are estimated as the sum of cash income plus any federal government noncash benefits that families can use to meet their FCSU needs minus taxes (plus tax credits), work expenses, and out-of-pocket medical expenses.

POVERTY RATES: OFFICIAL AND SPM

Figure 1 shows poverty rates using the two measures for the total population and for three age groups: under 18 years, 18 to 64 years, and 65 years and over. Table 2 shows poverty rates for selected demographic groups. The percentage of the population that was poor using the official measure for 2014 was 14.8 percent (DeNavas-Walt and Proctor, 2015). For this study, including unrelated individuals under the age of 15 in the universe, the poverty rate was 14.9 percent. The SPM rate was 15.3 percent for 2014, significantly higher than the official rate. While, as noted, SPM poverty thresholds are generally higher than official thresholds, other parts of the measure also contribute to differences in the estimated prevalence of poverty in the United States.

In 2014, 48.4 million people were poor using the SPM definition of poverty, more than the 47.0 million using the official definition of poverty with our universe. While for most groups, SPM rates were higher than official poverty rates, the SPM shows lower poverty rates for children, individuals included in SPM Resource Units, Blacks, the native born, renters, those living outside metropolitan areas, residents of the Midwest and the South, those covered by only public health insurance, those not working, and individuals with a disability. Most other groups had higher poverty rates using the SPM, rather than the official measure. Official and SPM poverty rates for females, people in female householder units, people in homes without mortgages, and the uninsured were not statistically different. Note that poverty rates for those 65 years and over were higher under the SPM compared with the official measure. This partially reflects that the official thresholds are set lower for individuals with householders in this age group, while the SPM thresholds do not vary by age. . . .

THE SPM AND THE EFFECT OF CASH AND NONCASH
TRANSFERS, TAXES, AND OTHER NONDISCRETIONARY EXPENSES

This section moves away from comparing the SPM with the official measure and looks only at the SPM. This exercise allows us to gauge the effects of taxes and transfers and other necessary expenses using the SPM as the measure of economic well-being. The previous section characterized the poverty population using the SPM in comparison with the current official measure. This section examines in more detail the population defined as poor when using the SPM.

The official poverty measure takes account of cash benefits from the government, such as Social Security and Unemployment Insurance (UI) benefits, Supplemental Security Income (SSI), public assistance benefits, such as Temporary Assistance for Needy Families, and workers' compensation benefits, but does not take account of taxes or non-cash benefits aimed at improving the economic situation of the poor. Besides taking account of cash benefits and necessary expenses, such as MOOP expenses and expenses related to work, the SPM includes taxes and noncash transfers. The important contribution that the SPM provides is allowing us to gauge the effectiveness of tax credits and transfers in alleviating poverty. We can also examine the effects of the nondiscretionary expenses, such as work and MOOP expenses.

Table 4a shows the effect that various additions and subtractions had on the SPM rate in 2014, holding all else the same and assuming no behavioral changes. Additions and subtractions are shown for the total population and by three age groups. Additions shown in the table include cash benefits, also accounted for in the official measure, as well as non-cash benefits, included only in the SPM. This allows us to examine the effects of government transfers on poverty estimates. Because child support paid is subtracted from income, we also examine the effect of child support received on alleviating poverty. Child support payments received are counted as income in both the official measure and the SPM.

Removing one item from the calculation of SPM resources and recalculating poverty rates shows, for example, that without Social Security benefits, the SPM rate would have been 23.5 percent, rather than 15.3 percent. This means that, without Social Security bene-fits the number of people living below the poverty line would have been 74.4 million, rather than the 48.4 million people classified as poor with the SPM. Not including refundable tax credits (the Earned Income Tax Credit [EITC] and the refundable portion of the child tax credit) in resources, the poverty rate for all people would have been 18.4 percent, rather than 15.3 percent, all else constant. On the other hand, removing amounts paid for child support, income and payroll taxes, work-related expenses, and MOOP expenses from the calculation resulted in lower poverty rates. Without subtracting MOOP expenses from income, the SPM rate would have been 11.8 percent, rather than 15.3 percent: in numbers, this would be 37.4 million, rather than 48.4 million people classified as poor. . . .

. . . In 2014, not accounting for refundable tax credits would have resulted in a poverty rate of 23.8 percent for children, rather than 16.7 percent. Not subtracting MOOP expenses from the income of families with children would have resulted in a poverty rate of 13.5 percent. For the 65 years and over group, SPM rates increased by about 5.7 percentage points with the subtraction of MOOP expenses from income while Social Security bene-fits lowered poverty rates by 35.6 percentage points for the 65 and over group, from 50.0 percent to 14.4 percent.

. . . For most elements, effects of additions and subtractions between the 2 years were not statistically different, however, some items had small differences in their effect on poverty rates. SNAP and UI lowered SPM rates less in 2014 than in 2013, while refundable tax credits had a larger effect. MOOP had a smaller effect on SPM rates in 2014 than in the previous year, increasing SPM rates 3.5 percentage points, rather than 3.8 percentage points in 2013.

SUMMARY

This report provides estimates of the SPM for the United States. The results shown illustrate differences between the official measure of poverty and a poverty measure that takes account of noncash benefits received by families and nondiscretionary expenses that they must pay. The SPM also employs a new poverty threshold that is updated with information on expenditures for FCSU by the BLS. Results showed higher poverty rates using the SPM than the official measure for most groups.

The SPM allows us to examine the effects of taxes and noncash transfers on the poor and on important groups within the poverty population. As such, there are lower percentages of the SPM poverty populations in the very high and very low resource categories than we find using the official measure. Since noncash benefits help those in extreme poverty, there were lower percentages of individuals with resources below half the SPM threshold for most groups. In addition, the effect of benefits received from each program and taxes and other nondiscretionary expenses on SPM rates were examined.

These findings are similar to those reported in earlier work using a variety of experimental poverty measures that followed recommendations of the NAS poverty panel (Short et al., 1999 and Short, 2001). Experimental poverty rates based on the NAS panel's recommendations have been calculated every year since 1999. While SPM rates are available only from 2009, estimates are available for earlier years for a variety of experimental poverty measures, including the most recent for 2014. They include poverty rates that employ CE-based thresholds, as well as thresholds that increase each year from 1999 based on changes in the Consumer Price Index (similar to the official thresholds) and estimates that do not adjust thresholds for geographic differences in housing costs. However, the methods used for many of the elements in the experimental measures differ markedly from those in the SPM and, therefore, they are not considered to be comparable measures.

SOURCE: U.S. Census Bureau. "The Supplemental Poverty Measure: 2014." September 16, 2015. www .census.gov/content/dam/Census/library/publications/2015/demo/p60-254.pdf.

OTHER HISTORIC DOCUMENTS OF INTEREST

FROM THIS VOLUME

FROM PREVIOUS *HISTORIC DOCUMENTS*

People's Bank of China Remarks
on Market Downturn

SEPTEMBER 16 AND OCTOBER 27, 2015

Years of rapid growth in the Chinese economy created a precarious stock market situation, similar to that experienced in the United States prior to the Great Depression. In mid-2015, the stock market could no longer sustain the rapid investment being made despite slowing economic growth, and the Shanghai Composite, which is the nation's largest index, lost 40 percent of its value over the course of three months. The decline prompted quick, drastic action by the Chinese government, including devaluation of the country's currency and a prohibition on who could sell stocks. The impact of the Chinese stock market collapse rippled around the world, where major indices experienced declines. By early 2016, the Chinese stock market did not show any signs that it had restabilized.

PREDICTORS OF ECONOMIC COLLAPSE

Heading into 2015, many economic analysts were predicting a tumble in the Chinese stock market. The nation's economy had experienced rapid growth averaging an annualized rate of 9.1 percent from 1989 to 2014. In 2010, China overtook Japan to become the world's second largest economy. And in 2014, China took the number one spot from the United States in real purchasing power. The mainland's largest stock market, the Shanghai Composite Index, and its smaller counterpart, the Shenzhen, have kept pace, growing at an exponential rate alongside the nation's economy. But in 2014, the nation had its lowest growth rate in 24 years at 7.4 percent. For many Western nations, such growth rate would be considered abnormally high, but in China, a rapidly industrializing nation, it is well below normal. The Chinese government quickly entered damage control mode and attempted to reverse earlier rhetoric that any gross domestic product (GDP) below 8 percent would spark certain chaos in the economy by calling the 2014 rate "the new normal."

In November 2014, seeking to further stimulate growth in the economy—and in particular within the housing market, which had slowed—the Chinese government cut interest rates to record lows. As a result, the Shanghai Composite Index jumped substantially. Stock ownership is common among the Chinese public—80 percent of market investors are individuals, not funds—and as rates fell and stocks grew, more and more Chinese investors sought to increase their portfolios. Despite the high risk, many did this through margin trading, the practice of borrowing money from a broker to make stock purchases. Margin trading was one of the practices that led to the U.S. stock market crash of 1929.

A MULTITUDE OF CRASHES

The economic bubble, which had been building as more individual investors entered the market while corporate profits and the economy as a whole remained weak by Chinese standards, burst on June 12 when the Shanghai Composite lost nearly a third of its value before bouncing back. The late July stock market crash wiped out $3 trillion in investments. On August 24—dubbed Black Monday—Shanghai Composite equities closed down 8.5 percent, a drop that resulted in the loss of billions of dollars of investments. In total, from June 12 until late August, the Shanghai Index lost more than 40 percent of its value, despite intervention from the Chinese government. On August 27, the turmoil seemed to slow, when markets around the world rallied and the Shanghai Composite closed up 5.3 percent.

All these drops had a significant impact on investors, many of whom had more debt than equity primarily because of margin trading. This meant that a 30 percent drop in the market could mean a 60 percent loss for some investors. However, despite the 40 percent drop, the market was still up 60 percent over its 2014 value.

Although the impact sent shockwaves across China, international analysts noted that historically the Chinese stock market has been relatively volatile compared to those of the United States, United Kingdom, and Japan. The Chinese financial markets are far newer in comparison to the markets of other industrialized nations, and such drops in China will only even out as its financial markets continue to develop.

CURRENCY DEVALUATION

On August 11 and 12, in an attempt to stem the continuing economic damage, China devalued its currency. Such a move makes Chinese products cheaper on international markets, thus making the nation's exports more competitive. Such a decision, however, is also risky because it makes the nation look economically weak, which can cause investors to pull their money out of China and further hurt the overall economy. In the case of China's 2015 stock market crash, if the nation valued its currency in line with the market—rather than benchmarking it against the U.S. dollar—the value of the yuan likely would have naturally declined, which would make it look less volatile.

The United States has long accused the Chinese government of manipulating its currency in an effort to make itself more competitive in international exports markets, and in 2011, the U.S. Senate voted to give the Treasury new powers to take action against those nations suspected of devaluing their currencies. China faced swift global criticism for taking matters into its own hands as markets tumbled. Nations that export a large volume of goods to China—including Australia, Canada, and South Korea—saw the greatest immediate impact both in their financial markets and across various manufacturing sectors.

REACTION FROM THE CHINESE GOVERNMENT AND PUBLIC

In addition to devaluing its currency, the Chinese government undertook a number of methods to reign in control of its stock market, including giving money to brokerages to purchase stocks and ensure their liquidity, prohibiting those who own more than 5 percent of a company's total stock from selling shares, further cutting interest rates, and stopping new companies from being listed on the Shanghai Composite Index. Some individual companies voluntarily suspended the trading of their own stocks in July. The measures resulted in the freezing of assets of some of China's wealthiest citizens for at least six months.

To determine the various causes of the drop, the Chinese government launched an investigation into whether illegal short selling—the practice of selling stocks in hopes that their price will decline so that the original seller can repurchase them at a lower rate—was taking place. By Chinese law, only banks approved by the government can participate in this practice. Securities officials also began looking into rumor spreading, a crime that can result in up to three years in jail. Hundreds were arrested following the stock market collapse, including a magazine journalist who was convicted of rumor spreading, and a billionaire hedge fund manager who was found to be engaging in market manipulation.

The impact outside of mainland China was more limited because the Chinese mainland stock market allows only minimal foreign investment, estimated at 1 percent of the total value of the Shanghai Composite. The greatest concern was whether the deceleration of the Chinese economy and stock market slump would trigger another global financial crisis. A number of companies experienced declining revenue due to a fall in import demand for their products. Other corporations, such as U.S.-based Yum! Brands, Inc., saw a decrease in its sales in China. In the United States, the Dow fell 1,000 points at opening on August 24, its largest decrease ever, primarily due to China's failing stock market.

LATE 2015 INTEREST RATE DROP AND 2016 BUST

On October 27, the People's Bank of China announced that it would reduce interest rates from 4.6 percent to 4.35 percent to encourage additional economy growth. "Despite the recent difficulties such as stock market turbulence," a statement from the Bank began, "the State Council decided to take the most decisive step in liberalizing interest rates." The bank's deputy governor, Yi Gang, reported that reducing interest rates was "key to enhancing the efficiency of resource allocation" and "will be the most beneficial to China's economic development and people's livelihood." The October decision marked the sixth time interest rates had been reduced since November 2014, and international economists suggested that cuts and other tactics would likely soon be undertaken because, according to Eswar Prasad, the former head of the China division at the International Monetary Fund, "the measures taken so far have had limited traction in supporting growth." Ultimately, the October rate cut had little impact on the economy.

By mid-January 2016, the Chinese government reported a disappointing annualized GDP growth rate of 6.9 percent. The Shanghai Composite closed out 2015 up only 12.6 percent, and growth did not pick up in the new year. On January 4 and 7, the government temporarily halted all trading when the market fell 7 percent on opening on both days. Between January 4 and 15, the Shanghai Index fell 18 percent. Many other stock markets around the world declined as a result. In response, the government moved to put in place even more economic controls, including devaluing the national currency again to its lowest rate since March 2011, in an attempt to drive more money back into China.

—Heather Kerrigan

Following are financial statistics released by the People's Bank of China on September 16, 2015, about the state of the nation's economy in August; and an October 27, 2015, statement from the deputy governor of the People's Bank of China on the reduction of the deposit interest rate.

People's Bank of China
Releases August Market Statistics

September 16, 2015

1. Broad money rose by 13.3 percent and narrow money by 9.3 percent

At end-August, the broad money supply (M2) stood at 135.69 trillion yuan, increasing by 13.3 percent year-on-year, the same pace as a month earlier but up 0.5 percentage points from the same period last year. The narrow money supply (M1), at 36.28 trillion yuan, rose by 9.3 percent year-on-year, up 2.7 percentage points from a month earlier and 3.6 percentage points from the same period last year. The amount of currency in circulation (M0) was 5.91 trillion yuan, increasing by 1.8 percent year-on-year. The month saw a net money injection of 5.1 billion yuan.

2. RMB loans rose by 809.6 billion yuan while foreign currency loans fell by US$2 billion

At end-August, outstanding RMB and foreign currency loans totaled 97.05 trillion yuan, up 14.7 percent year-on-year. Outstanding RMB loans grew by 15.4 percent year-on-year to 91.08 trillion yuan, down 0.1 percentage points from a month earlier but up 2.1 percentage points from the same period last year. RMB loans increased by 809.6 billion yuan in August, 49 billion yuan more than the growth in the same period last year. By sector, household loans rose by 353 billion yuan, with short-term loans and medium and long-term (MLT) loans increasing by 67.5 billion and 285.5 billion yuan, respectively; loans to non-financial enterprises, government agencies and organizations grew by 421 billion yuan, with short-term loans, MLT loans and bill financing rising by 28.9 billion, 121.7 billion and 245.7 billion yuan, respectively; loans to non-banking financial institutions declined by 54.6 billion yuan. At end-August, outstanding foreign currency loans stood at US$934.8 billion, up 1.2 percent year-on-year. In August, lending in foreign currencies dropped by US$2 billion.

3. RMB deposits increased by 53.2 billion yuan and foreign currency deposits by US$27 billion

At end-August, the outstanding amount of RMB and foreign currency deposits was 138.32 trillion yuan, up 12.8 percent year-on-year. RMB deposits recorded an outstanding amount of 134.05 trillion yuan, rising by 13.0 percent year-on-year, down 0.4 percentage points from a month earlier and 0.7 percentage points from the same period last year. RMB deposits rose by 53.2 billion yuan in August, 372.3 billion yuan less than the growth in the same period last year. Specifically, household deposits and deposits of non-financial enterprises climbed by 186.5 billion and 667.3 billion yuan, respectively, while fiscal deposits and deposits of non-banking financial institutions slid by 159 billion and 795.6

billion yuan, respectively. At end-August, the outstanding amount of foreign currency deposits was US$667.4 billion, up 1.8 percent year-on-year. Foreign currency deposits increased by US$27 billion in August.

4. The monthly weighted average interbank lending rate and the monthly weighted average interest rate on bond pledged repo both stood at 1.79 percent

In August, lending, spot bond and bond repo transactions in the interbank RMB market totaled 53.28 trillion yuan. The average daily turnover was 2.54 trillion yuan, up 103.8 percent year-on-year. Specifically, the average daily turnover of interbank lending, spot bond and bond repo transactions posted year-on-year growth rates of 118.2 percent, 138.9 percent and 96.7 percent, respectively.

In August, the monthly weighted average interbank lending rate stood at 1.79 percent, up 0.28 percentage points from the previous month but down 1.38 percentage points from the same period last year. The monthly weighted average interest rate on bond pledged repo was 1.79 percent, up 0.36 percentage points from the previous month but down 1.32 percentage points from the same period last year.

5. RMB cross-border trade settlement reached 755.9 billion yuan and RMB settlement of direct investment 225.7 billion yuan

In August, RMB settlement of cross-border trade in goods, cross-border trade in services and other current account items, outward FDI and inward FDI amounted to 692.9 billion, 63 billion, 85.1 billion and 140.6 billion yuan, respectively.

NOTES

1. Data for the current period are preliminary figures.

2. Since October 2011, monetary aggregates have included deposits of housing provident fund centers and non-depository financial institutions' deposits with depository financial institutions.

3. Since August 2014, re-exports have been removed from trade in services statistics to be included in trade in goods, reducing the former and expanding the latter correspondingly.

4. The year-on-year M2 growth rate for the current month is calculated on a comparable basis.

5. Starting from 2015, deposits of non-banking financial institutions are included in RMB deposits, foreign currency deposits and deposits in RMB and foreign currencies; lending to non-banking financial institutions is included in RMB loans, foreign currency loans and loans in RMB and foreign currencies.

SOURCE: People's Bank of China. "Financial Statistics, August 2015." September 16, 2015. www.pbc.gov.cn/english/130721/2952271/index.html.

Statement on Reduction of Interest Rate in China

DOCUMENT

October 27, 2015

Editor's Note: The reduction of interest rates and reserve requirement ratio announced by the People's Bank of China on October 23 is an important measure adopted in response to the current macro-economic situation, as well as a pre-emptive, fine-tuning adjustment based on the price movements and liquidity situation. In addition, the central bank has announced to remove the deposit interest rate ceiling for commercial banks and rural credit cooperatives. As a result, interest rate controls have been basically lifted and the market-based interest rate reform has entered a new stage. Despite the recent difficulties such as stock market turbulence and the worrying signs in capital flows and foreign exchange, the State Council decided to take the most decisive step in liberalizing interest rates. This reflects the determination of the Chinese Government to press ahead with reforms. In this sense, the removal of the deposit interest rate ceiling has far reaching significance that warrants deeper and closer examination. Deputy Governor Yi Gang recently had a discussion on this issue with academic experts. Below is a summary of the Deputy Governor's key points.

1. A brief history of market-based interest rate reform. The market-based interest rate reform started more than two decades ago. In 1992, the Chinese Communist Party in its 14th National Congress proposed, for the first time, market-based resource allocation, i.e. to have the market play a fundamental role in resource allocation. Since then, our understanding of resource allocation has gradually shifted from focusing on market allocation of products to market allocation of factors of production. Seen from this perspective, the market-based interest rate reform has come a long way. At the operational level, with the lifting of controls over the inter-bank lending interest rates in 1996 as a start, the PBC has, since then, been advancing the market-based interest rate reform progressively. In 2003–2004, major steps were adopted to further liberalize the control over interest rates, with the ceiling of deposit interest rates raised and the floor of loan interest rates lowered. After this, due to the rapid buildup of foreign exchange reserves and the subsequent excessive liquidity supply, the focus of macro-economic management was shifted to sterilization of excess liquidity through quantitative tools and the pace of market-based interest rate reform slowed down somewhat. Since 2012–2013, the reform pace accelerated, leading to the removal of interest rate controls nowadays. Interest rate liberalization is an integral part of China's economic reform and an important step toward achieving market-based resource allocation. It is also a long and gradual process in which one step is taken after another following careful preparations.

2. Improving the pricing of factors of production is key to enhancing the efficiency of resource allocation. Allocation of financial resources or capital is closely related to the efficiency of resource allocation. In a traditional planned economy, consideration is usually given to where resources are to be allocated, for example to urbanization, to real estate sector, to infrastructure building, or to other areas. Ultimately, how resources are allocated is about efficiency. If efficiency is low, a lot will be wasted and the effects in terms of

supporting economic growth, increasing income, and building a well-off society will be poor. The core of enhancing allocation efficiency lies in getting the factor prices right. In economic theory, this is very clear. The general public may think otherwise since they are mainly concerned with where resources are allocated. But in fact, allowing the price mechanism to allocate capital to more efficient sectors of the economy will be the most beneficial to China's economic development and people's livelihood.

3. The market-based interest rate reform is an important way to diversify financial products. With economic development, there are more diversified demands for the allocation of financial resources. There are all kinds of enterprises, large-scale, small- and medium-sized, and micro businesses; there are state-owned, private, and foreign-invested enterprises. Their demands are different. As far as individuals' demands are concerned, people save for varying purposes, such as old-age support, children's wedding, and contingent uses, etc. Therefore, having interest rates determined by market supply and demand will provide a basis for more diversified financial products and differentiated interest rates to meet the varying demands of market participants.

When price is controlled, products supplied are all alike. In a planned economy, products are not diversified. The subsequent weak demands further contributes lack of variety of products supplied. In the 1980s, those Chinese visiting Russia found big department stores near the Red Square, and a street full of shops selling products from the central and eastern European countries that were members of the Council for Mutual Economic Assistance (CMEA). They favored those shops selling products from Yugoslavia and Poland, because market-based reforms started earlier in these countries and their products were more diversified. However, shops selling products from the CMEA members with a strongly planned economy only offered one kind of product with poor quality, although those shops were very large. Therefore, lack of product diversity is associated with the old days of a planned economy. The same applies to financial products. If prices of financial products are tightly controlled, products would lack variety, and as a result supply and demand would not be able to meet the needs of economic development and social progress. It is fair to say that interest rate liberalization is the main channel to meet the increasingly diversified financial demands and promote economic development.

4. Interest rate liberalization creates basic conditions for the transformation of monetary policy framework. There were very few types of financial products and no real monetary policy in the planned economy era. At the beginning of the transition period, the conduct of monetary policy inevitably relied more on quantitative instruments, and many called for acceleration of the transformation of the monetary policy framework. With the reform this time, we also talked about the transformation of monetary policy framework and improving the transmission mechanism. Path dependence might happen in this process. The existence of administrative controls will lead to dependence on such controls and the perception that the removal of controls will create chaos. Such a perception usually hinders reforms. Similar perceptions existed in 1980s when people were skeptic about the price reform.

In fact, progress of market-based interest rate reform provides basic conditions for transforming the monetary policy framework. Such progress also provides microeconomic foundations for the transmission of monetary policy, facilitating the transition towards price-based instruments. Looking at the microeconomic level, if interest rates are always controlled and determined by the central bank, commercial banks tend to rely on the rates set by the central bank. At the initial stage of interest rate liberalization, commercial banks still preferred to rely on the rates decided by the central bank due to their limited pricing capabilities and inadequate analysis of pricing mechanism. Even if you ask them to price their own interest rates, they would simply follow their peers. But it has been more than a decade since the interest rate reform in 2004, and substantial progress has been made. Commercial banks are relatively well-prepared now.

Nevertheless, there are still signs that commercial banks rely on administrative controls. For instance, if you go to a commercial bank branch for a mortgage loan, its sales person would show you the bank's preferential policies, and elaborate on how competitive these policies are compared with those of other commercial banks. But if you ask for a lower interest rate, the sales person would say no and explain that the interest rates are set by the central bank. This is quite interesting. Once commercial banks feel that something is difficult to explain, they will refer to the central bank, which demonstrates their reliance. If the administrative controls over interest rates are lifted, commercial banks will have to handle their competitive pressures in a more independent and market-based way.

5. Partial liberalization creates a dual-track price system and distorts the market. The price within the controlled track is usually lower and that outside the track is higher in such a system. When we first launched the market-based price reform in 1980s, steel was very costly in the market but the price within the controlled system was quite cheap. This caused speculation and arbitrage.

When commercial banks were first allowed to sell wealth management products, the interest rates on these products were very high, and savings products within the controlled track had relatively low interest rates. The price difference has narrowed as more products are offered outside the controlled track. Of course, during this process, there might be growing concerns that interest rate liberalization will push all interest rates higher towards the level of those on wealth management products. Actually this concern is unfounded because it is inconsistent with the supply and demand relationship of capital.

6. The substantial decline in the cost of information processing should also be flexibly reflected in interest rates. The pricing of deposit products and some credit products rely heavily on data processing cost. Information technology including computer system, network, internet, and cloud computing has had a huge impact on financial business, especially the cost of data processing. Therefore it's natural that such impact should be reflected in interest rates. Otherwise, it may be reflected in the other track of the dual-track system, which would cause many problems.

In terms of deposits, experiences of mature market economies such as the United States, United Kingdom, and Australia show that demand deposits or checking accounts involve a huge amount of information processing, which is very costly for the banking sector. Since customers may withdraw such deposits at any time, the banking sector did not pay interests on this category of deposits at first. A very important clause in Regulation Q of the United States banned interest payments on demand deposits by member banks of the Federal Reserve System. With the enhanced efficiency in information processing and the abolishment of Regulation Q in the late 1980's, banks began to pay small interests on demand deposits. In the United States, however, interest on demand deposits is very low. The interest rate on demand deposits in China is currently 0.35%, which is much higher than that in the United States.

The substantial fall of information processing cost is mainly a result of advances in electronic processing thanks to the development of computer science and networks. With the decline in information processing cost and competition from financial innovation initiated by internet companies such as third-party payment companies, some customers expect a higher return on deposits. Of course, in their early days such businesses offered products linked to money market funds and took advantage of the dual-track system. It can be expected that the evolution of competition in the future will be closely related to technological progress and changes in costs.

7. The market-based interest rate reform is not about leaving everything to the market. There will still be monetary policy adjustments and macro-prudential regulation. Interest rates are the outcome of resource allocation, determined by market supply and demand. At the same time, interest rates are also an important element of monetary policy and macro-economic management, as emphasized by the State Council on many occasions. From a micro perspective, the liberalization of interest rates can optimize resource allocation. From a macro perspective, the reform is not about leaving everything to the market. There will be monetary policy adjustment in line with counter-cyclical needs to make interest rates consistent with the direction of macro-economic management. More specifically, interest rates should be adjusted at different stages of national development and reflect the inflation cycle. As a result, more efforts should be paid to the improvement of the central bank's monetary policy framework and the improvement of transmission mechanism in the process of interest rate liberalization.

Meanwhile, regulation and self-regulation are also necessary for macro-prudential management. Some "teeth" are required to address certain abnormal market phenomenon. At the beginning of the global financial crisis, the U.S. Federal Reserve cut its policy rate to around zero and launched the first round of quantitative easing. The monetary condition became very accommodative. At that time, some banks on the verge of bankruptcy such as Washington Mutual and Wachovia offered deposit rates of 7%–8% or even above 10% to attract deposits. This reflected their desperation to attract new deposits to cover their deteriorating conditions. From the perspective of macro-prudential management and financial stability, this kind of behavior was destructive. So some "teeth" were needed to address these issues. Similar situation existed in China. During the Asian financial crisis, some insolvent small trust companies, securities companies, and credit cooperatives issued OTC debts with high interest rates to delay their closure. In fact, this kind of practices caused more troubles and became more difficult to handle.

For this reason, liberalization of interest rate both emphasizes the concept of market and resource allocation and requires macro-economic management. This involves knowledge of economic theory, which may create confusion in the general public. We hope that academic circles can spread knowledge of basic economics and help the general public understand this reform better. This way, some misunderstanding of the reform or incorrect opinions can be avoided. Of course, we will always keep an open mind when listening to all kinds of opinions. To sum up, it's not easy to make up the mind to push ahead with the market-based interest rate reform, and to achieve final success is no easy job either. I hope we can make joint efforts to support and help the financial sector in this process.

The growing Chinese economy calls for commensurate financial markets and products. Country experiences have shown that real economy can benefit from more developed financial markets and more efficient resource allocation that meet diversified demands. In today's interconnected global economy, an efficient and sound financial market is crucial, and letting market forces to determine interest rates is an unavoidable path toward that goal. As such, we have to strengthen the guidance and management of interest rates, remain vigilant on potential risks, and press ahead with the market-based interest rate reform steadfastly.

SOURCE: People's Bank of China. "On Removal of the Deposit Interest Rate Ceiling Dr. Yi Gang, Deputy Governor." October 27, 2015. www.pbc.gov.cn/english/130724/2969444/index.html.

OTHER HISTORIC DOCUMENTS OF INTEREST

FROM PREVIOUS *HISTORIC DOCUMENTS*

United Nations and Burkina Faso Leaders Remark on Coup

SEPTEMBER 17, 20, 23, AND 25, 2015

Burkina Faso, a nation long hampered by political turmoil, again experienced unrest in September 2015 when its transitional government was overthrown during a coup attempt. The Economic Community of West African States (ECOWAS) was able to secure the release of transitional government leaders less than one week after the coup began, and democratic elections were held within two months. Even so, international political analysts remain wary of how politically stable the nation will remain moving forward.

BUILDUP TO A COUP

Burkina Faso encompasses the former French colony of Upper Volta in western Africa and gained independence in 1960. Since then, it has witnessed a series of coups and counter-coups. In 1987, Thomas Sankara, the young president and noted Marxist Pan-Africanist revolutionary, died under suspicious circumstances and was succeeded by Blaise Compaoré, then viewed as Sankara's closest friend. Sankara, who gave the country its current name, translated in the local Mossi language as "The Land of Upright Men," remained a hero to generations of activists after his death.

Once in office, Compaoré called for a "rectification" of Sankara's revolution and proceeded to hold power for the next twenty-seven years, notwithstanding periodic challenges to his rule. Compaoré secured his place in power partly through the Regiment of Presidential Security (RSP), an elite military organization staffed with loyalists and charged with protecting the president. Under his tenure, the RSP was expanded to more than 1,200 members, forming an extrajudicial paramilitary group accountable only to the president. The RSP was traditionally given better weapons, benefits, and pay compared to the regular army, which it was intended to offset in case of a political crisis. Its role in society remained controversial, with troops accused of human rights abuses under the Compaoré government, notably during the protests to remove the president in 2014.

Burkina Faso's most recent bout of political instability deepened with the ouster of President Compaoré in October 2014. Compaoré had tried to alter the term limit of two consecutive five-year terms in order to stand for presidential elections scheduled for October 2015. The bid to change the constitution prompted widespread protests led by young activists aligned with *Balai Citoyen* (Citizen's Broom) and the *Collectif Anti-Référendum* (Anti-Referendum Collective). *Balai Citoyen* led some eighteen groups opposed to an indefinite extension of the president's tenure, culminating with the burning of the parliament building as the National Assembly met to consider the amendment.

Political opposition in recent years has been directed by young people. Almost two-thirds of the country's population is under the age of twenty-five; they are concerned about access to education and employment in a country where life prospects have traditionally been determined by a pervasive patronage system. Liberalization during the latter years of the Compaoré government, including municipal elections and greater media freedoms, afforded the opportunity for greater political organization as these protesters came of age.

Youth demonstrations preceded a loss of support for the government within the broader military, which took power after Compaoré resigned on October 31, 2014, calling for elections within ninety days. He later retreated to exile in the neighboring Ivory Coast, with former aides vying to succeed him. On November 1, General Honoré Traoré, the head of the military, declared himself leader of the government but was supplanted hours later by Yacouba Isaac Zida, the deputy leader of the RSP. Zida was then persuaded by the African Union (AU) to cede the presidency to the country's ambassador to the United Nations (UN), Michel Kafando. Zida then took office as prime minister and formed an interim government to lead the country until the next elections. A transitional charter was confirmed that month and prohibited both men from standing in the next elections, scheduled for October 11, 2015.

TENSIONS CONTINUE TO RISE

Political tensions rose from December 2014 in response to the prime minister's proposal that the RSP be integrated into the regular military, with pay cuts in line with average salaries. In February 2015, the RSP called for the prime minister to resign and blocked access to his office, forcing the government to postpone the decision to annul the regiment. The question of its future was expected to be decided by the National Reconciliation and Reform Commission later in the year. The RSP was also granted the right to nominate its own leader, Lt. Col. Joseph Moussa Céleste Coulibaly, following complaints that the prime minister had given one of his protégés oversight of the organization. These concessions provoked renewed protests by increasingly assertive civil groups led by *Balai Citoyen*, but they enabled the transition plan to otherwise proceed as planned in preparation for the October elections.

The specifics of the country's transition plan remained controversial in the run-up to the 2015 elections. Displaced loyalists of Compaoré particularly objected to the provision that prevented them from standing for political office. The National Reconciliation and Reform Commission also affirmed the earlier recommendation that the RSP be disbanded and integrated within the general military. This motion deepened disquiet within the old guard. Prime Minister Zida, who earlier had been perceived as a RSP loyalist due to his former leadership position with the group, endorsed the recommendations.

SHORT-LIVED COUP

Plans to dissolve the RSP precipitated a coup on September 16, 2015, in which the RSP stormed a cabinet meeting and placed President Kafando and the prime minister under arrest. The head of the RSP, Gilbert Diendéré, announced that he was head of the government under the auspices of a new National Democratic Council from September 17, 2015. Coincidentally, results from the May exhumation of the presumed remains of former president Thomas Sankara were also due to be published that day, possibly implicating members of the RSP in his 1987 assassination. In response to the attempted coup, Army Chief of Staff Pingrenoma Zagre encouraged "the people to maintain their trust in the National Armed Forces, who have been engaging with national and international actors since the early hours of this crisis, to search for a solution that will ensure for our nation, peace and security."

The coup was strongly rejected by international observers. In a joint statement with the African Union and ECOWAS, the UN called for humane treatment and immediate release of the detained leaders, as well as the prompt resumption of the transition process, which was pending completion weeks ahead of the new elections. Echoing civic groups, the UN also called for security and military forces, including the RSP, to recognize the authority of the civilian government. Rights groups had consistently called for the disbandment of the RSP as a prerequisite for a full democratic transition.

The coup provoked a resumption of public protests, which increased pressure upon the junta to engage with ECOWAS negotiators led by President Macky Sall of Senegal. Burkina Faso's traditional ethnic Mossi monarch, the *Mogho Naba*, also facilitated talks between the opposing sides, securing the release and reinstatement of the president and prime minister a week later on September 24. The UN praised the efforts of ECOWAS mediators in reversing the coup and pledged its support for the country's upcoming elections.

General Diendéré, who had earlier proclaimed his support for a civilian government, with the condition that existing RSP privileges be preserved, later admitted that he regretted staging its removal. The RSP was formally disbanded during the first full meeting of the reinstated transitional government on September 25; its assets were frozen on September 26 and its barracks were secured on October 1. The successful return of the government and unexpectedly peaceful dissolution of the RSP were seen as encouraging signs of growing institutional stability in Burkina Faso. Zida told his countrymen that "the construction of democracy not only for Burkina Faso but also for other countries is not an easy task," adding that "it is unimaginable and unthinkable that this people would allow itself to be ruled by coup plotters, wherever they come from." Later in December 2015, General Diendéré and other RSP members were formally charged with involvement in the deaths of Thomas Sankara and Norbert Zongo, a high-profile newspaper editor who was killed during the Compaoré government.

Successful Elections Held, Long-Term Stability in Question

The postponed national elections were ultimately held on November 29, and were marked by 60 percent turnout in the country's first peaceful leadership transition since 1960. Roch Marc Christian Kaboré, a former prime minister and founder of the new *Mouvement du Peuple pour le Progrès* (MPP; People's Movement for Progress), won the presidency and a legislative majority. Upon taking office, Kaboré pledged to continue strengthening Burkinabé institutions in a shift from personality-based government. He also promised to address the ongoing economic problems, endorsing "social democracy" with improved access to education and health care and employment initiatives, as well as anti-corruption measures. Paul Kaba Thieba was named as prime minister of a new eight-party government, also led by the MPP, in January 2016. The technocratic coalition is the first since independence to omit any military representatives.

Democracy in Burkina Faso will remain fragile in the intermediate future, given its long history of military interventions. Institutional credibility is a recent development and the culture of patronage will likely continue to govern expectations among some of the political class. Meanwhile, enduring poverty presents a medium-term political liability, with bolstered civil groups now able to demand accountability more effectively than under the previous government. The regional threat of Islamist militancy is also a concern following terrorist attacks on a hotel and café in the capital Ouagadougou by al Qaeda in the Islamic Maghreb (AQIM) in January 2016. Nevertheless, the negotiated restoration of the legitimate government has surprised political observers, who expected another military government given the depressingly familiar execution of the initial coup. Burkina Faso's subsequent success in holding free and fair elections has further increased the likelihood of a durable transition to democracy.

—Anastazia Clouting

Following are two press releases from the United Nations News Centre—the first, on September 17, 2015, calls for the immediate end to the coup in Burkina Faso and release of the nation's transitional leaders, while the second, released on September 23, 2015, welcomes the release of Burkina Faso's transitional government leaders and the end of the coup—and two press releases from the government of Burkina Faso on September 20 and 25, 2015, detailing the struggle to seat a government.

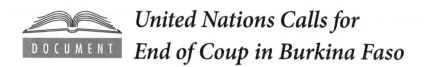

United Nations Calls for End of Coup in Burkina Faso

September 17, 2015

Secretary-General Ban Ki-moon and the United Nations human rights chief today spoke out against the coup d'état in Burkina Faso and called for the immediate release of the country's transitional leaders.

President Michel Kafando, Prime Minister Yacouba Isaac Zida and several Government ministers were detained on Wednesday by elements of the Régiment de sécurité présidentielle while they were at a meeting in the capital, Ouagadougou.

"The Secretary-General condemns in the strongest terms the coup d'état in Burkina Faso. He reiterates that all Burkinabé officials under detention must be released immediately and demands the resumption of the country's political transition, in accordance with Burkina Faso's Constitution and Transitional Charter," said a statement issued by Mr. Ban's spokesperson.

"The Secretary-General deplores the violence reported in the country and calls on the Burkinabé defence and security forces to exercise restraint and ensure respect for the human rights and security of all Burkinabé citizens. Those responsible for the coup d'état and its consequences must be held accountable."

High Commissioner for Human Rights Zeid Ra'ad Al Hussein said in a statement that he is "extremely concerned" at the military coup in Burkina Faso. "The arrest and detention of the President, the Prime Minister and two ministers of the Transitional Government by members of the Presidential Security Regiment is unacceptable."

He stressed that the detainees should be treated with dignity and humanity, and released immediately. "I also urge the coup leaders to avoid any use of force, particularly in the context of anti-coup demonstrations, and to respect the rights of the population to demonstrate peacefully."

The Secretary-General's Special Representative for West Africa, Mohamed Ibn Chambas, is presently in Ouagadougou and working closely with the Economic Community of West African States (ECOWAS), the African Union and other international partners to support and safeguard the transition in Burkina Faso.

The UN, ECOWAS, and AU issued a joint statement in which they demanded that the defense and security forces submit themselves to the political authority and in the current context, to the transitional authorities. They also reiterate their full support to the transition in this crucial period ahead of the elections scheduled for 11 October, and reaffirmed their determination to support the national authorities to ensure the successful completion of the transition process.

The members of the Security Council, in a statement issued to the press, condemned the detention "in the strongest terms" and demanded that the leaders be released safely and immediately.

"The members of the Security Council expressed their strong support to the transitional authorities of Burkina Faso and urged all actors to comply with the transitional calendar, notably the holding of free, fair and credible elections, scheduled for 11 October 2015."

Meanwhile, the Security Council, which was briefed on the latest developments by Under-Secretary-General for Political Affairs Jeffrey Feltman in a closed-door meeting, issued a statement to the press in which it strongly condemned "the unconstitutional and forceful seizure of power."

"The members of the Security Council urged the perpetrators to restore constitutional order and return power to the civilian transitional authorities without delay," said the statement.

SOURCE: United Nations. News Centre. "Condemning coup, UN officials call for immediate release of Burkina Faso's leaders." September 17, 2015. www.un.org/apps/news/story.asp?NewsID=51900#.Vq7jb7w6KCJ.

Burkina Faso Army Chief Responds to Ongoing Violence

September 20, 2015

In its difficult progress towards a new era of democracy, our country is again facing a crisis resulting in loss of human life.

I would therefore like, on behalf of the National Armed Forces and on my own behalf, to present our condolences to the families who were bereaved during the events in recent days.

I would also like to wish a speedy recovery to the injured.

The National Armed Forces reaffirm their attachment to Republican values, the basis of national brotherhood and cohesion.

I would like to remind National Armed Forces staff, that our mission is to guarantee the security of the population and to ensure the protection of persons and property.

In the current national context, I firmly condemn all acts of violence against the population and I urge all members of the military to keep in mind that they must perform their duties with professionalism.

In my capacity as Chief of Staff of the Armed Forces, I am asking the people to maintain their trust in the National Armed Forces, who have been engaging with national and international actors since the early hours of this crisis, to search for a solution that will ensure for our nation, peace and security.

God bless Burkina Faso.

Ouagadougou, September 19, 2015

Brigadier General Pingrenoma Zagre

Grand Officer of the National Order

SOURCE: Government of Burkina Faso. "Burkina Faso: Message from the Chief of Staff of the Armed Forces." September 20, 2015. Translated from French by SAGE Publishing. www.gouvernement.gov.bf/spip.php?article1552.

United Nations Welcomes End of Coup in Burkina Faso

September 23, 2015

Following a coup d'état last week in Burkina Faso, Secretary-General Ban Ki-moon today welcomed the reinstatement of President Michel Kafando and of the transitional institutions in the country.

In a statement, Mr. Ban commended the efforts undertaken by the Economic Community of West African States (ECOWAS) Authority of Heads of State and

Government, including the ECOWAS high-level mediation team, towards the early resolution of the political crisis.

President Kafando, Prime Minister Yacouba Isaac Zida and several Government ministers were detained one week ago and later released by elements of the Presidential Guard.

Today, the UN chief paid tribute to the excellent collaboration between the United Nations, the African Union, ECOWAS and other international partners to ensure the return to constitutional order in the country.

He stressed that the resumption of the transition process will enable Burkina Faso to hold presidential and legislative elections in accordance with the country's Constitution and Transitional Charter.

He also called on all national stakeholders to exercise restraint and to ensure respect for the physical integrity and human rights of all Burkinabé citizens.

Meanwhile, the Secretary-General's Special Representative for West Africa, Mohamed Ibn Chambas, will continue to work closely with regional and international partners to support national authorities in the lead-up to peaceful and transparent elections.

SOURCE: United. Nations News Centre. "Following coup d'etat in Bukina Faso, Ban welcomes reinstatement of President." September 23, 2015. www.un.org/apps/news/story.asp?NewsID=51950#.Vq7jfLw6KCJ.

Burkina Faso Acting Prime Minister Holds Press Conference on End of Coup

September 25, 2015

The first Council of Ministers enshrining the restoration of the Transitional Government, after General Diendéré's aborted coup, was held this Friday, September 25, 2015, at the premises of the Prime Ministry. At the end of the meeting, the Head of the Government, Yacouba Isaac ZIDA, gave a mini press conference to the journalists gathered before the steps of the prime minister's office.

WHAT WERE THE POINTS ADDRESSED DURING THIS COUNCIL OF MINISTERS?

First of all, it was a great pleasure for the members of the government to meet all together. It was an opportunity for us all to observe a minute of silence in memory of our compatriots killed during the recent events. I will take advantage of your microphones to once again give our most sincere condolences to the families of the victims. We obviously discussed the situation that our country has experienced in the past week. We have made important decisions towards resolving the crisis faced by the country, to restart the state apparatus, to give more serenity for the continuity of the administration, to give new impetus to the transition process so that our primary mission, which is organizing the elections, can be carried out in better conditions.

Is there a date for the elections?

For the moment, it is too early to decide a date. As I said, we are first and foremost concerned with making the country and the people safe again, as well as with getting the administration working again. You see that everything has been blocked for ten days. The electoral process will resume, but certainly in consultation with all stakeholders, we will be able to determine a date.

Did you discuss the Presidential Security Regimen?

The issue of the Presidential Security Regimen (PSR), we did talk about. You will have the results in the minutes of the Council of Ministers.

What decision was made, disarmament or dissolution?

Both disarmament and dissolution at the same time.

At what date?

Immediately!

There is a minister (Editor's Note: Sidi Paré, Minister for Security) who was absent from the Council of Ministers. Is his absence justified?

The minutes of the Council of Ministers will be more complete. You will have certain details. Please allow us to pass on this question.

Still the curfew?

Yes, still the curfew. You know that military units are deployed. They need this curfew to work, in order not to put the population more at risk. The curfew will continue for two or three days, until everything returns to normal.

And the call for a general strike?

Of course, the strike action was called following a requirement. We believe that we should be able to suspend the call for a strike action in the coming hours.

Why did you gather here and not at Kosyam? [Translator's note: Kosyam is the presidential palace of Burkina Faso]

We believe that we are here in a much calmer, much more serene setting after the events at Kosyam last week. It is not necessarily that there are problems at Kosyam. Until things get clearer, we prefer to be here, in a much more serene spirit for work.

HAVE YOU SUFFERED VIOLENCE?

No, I have not suffered violence.

WHAT LESSONS WILL YOU DRAW?

What I note, is that the construction of democracy not only for Burkina Faso but also for other countries is not an easy task. It is difficult and requires a lot of perseverance, because adversity is here. We need to be persistent to implement true democracy. It is the aspiration of our people. No one can imagine a people who would accept being governed by putschists. Especially the people of Burkina Faso that you know as well as I do: it is unimaginable and unthinkable that this people would allow itself to be ruled by coup plotters, wherever they come from.

HAS AN INVESTIGATION INTO GENERAL GILBERT DIENDÉRÉ BEEN OPENED?

We will set up a committee of inquiry which will work professionally in order to tell us who was a player, who did what, what is the degree of involvement of each person. Of course justice will do its duty after the findings of this investigation.

WILL THE BURKINA FASO CIVIL SERVANTS HAVE THEIR WAGES BY THE END OF THE MONTH?

Burkina Faso civil servants already have their salary. You can check. I think they have had their pay for at least seventy-two (72) hours.

WHERE IS GENERAL DIENDÉRÉ?

General Diendéré should currently be at camp Naaba Koom with his men.

DO YOU HAVE INFORMATION ON THE PSR'S WEAPONS INVENTORY?

Yes, the process is running normally.

DO YOU HAVE ASSURANCES THAT THERE IS NO MORE DANGER, WITH GENERAL DIENDÉRÉ AND HIS MEN IN THIS CAMP?

I can assure you that there will be no danger because all arrangements are being made so that all those involved will lay down their arms and that the process of disarming them and confining them to barracks may take place in better conditions. Those who will have to answer before the law, will do so. Those who should pursue a normal military career in other contexts, will continue. From my point of view, there is really no danger.

SOURCE: Government of Burkina Faso. "'The construction of democracy requires a lot of perseverance, because adversity is here!'" says Yacouba Isaac Zida." September 25, 2015. Translated from French by SAGE Publishing. www.gouvernement.gov.bf/spip.php?article1553.

OTHER HISTORIC DOCUMENTS OF INTEREST

FROM PREVIOUS *HISTORIC DOCUMENTS*

■ African Leaders Address Unrest in Burkina Faso, *2014*, p. 535

Japanese Parliament Considers Military Legislation

SEPTEMBER 18 AND 25, 2015

Japan, which has painted itself as a pacifist nation following defeat in World War II, has a constitutional policy that prohibits the formation of an official military body for defending the island and its allies. Since his selection as prime minister in December 2012, Shinzo Abe has pushed for a revision to the country's governing document that would allow for the development of a military force. According to the prime minister, such a body had become necessary in a time when North Korea continues to develop nuclear weapons and China threatens to take control of disputed territory. Opposition leaders in parliament— and many in the Japanese public—saw Abe's call for a military force as a concession to the United States, which they believed would ultimately call on Japan for combat assistance in fighting against terrorist organizations in the Middle East. On September 18, 2015, Japan's parliament voted to approve a package of eleven security measures backed by Abe that would allow for the creation of an official military force.

Japan's Peace Constitution

As adopted in 1947, Article 9 of Japan's constitution states, "Aspiring sincerely to an international peace based on justice and order, the Japanese people forever renounce war as a sovereign right of the nation and the threat or use of force as a means of settling international disputes." It continues, "To accomplish [this] aim . . . land, sea, and air forces, as well as other war potential, will never be maintained. The right of belligerency of the state will not be recognized." Without a military force, it was Japan's policy to use any diplomatic means necessary in the case of international disagreements or incursion.

Seven years after the constitution went into effect, Japan created a Self-Defense Force (JSDF) under the guise of the United Nation's right to self-defense. While not an official military body, it operates as more of a heavily armed police force. Many, including Prime Minister Abe, have questioned whether the UN right to self-defense extends to providing assistance in defense of Japan's allies. Abe has argued that assisting in such defense would allow the nation to strengthen its alliances and its own defense forces and carve out a larger international peacekeeping role for Japan. To date, when participating in international peacekeeping missions, Japan has been forced into a logistical role in noncombat areas.

Abe's Eleven Security Measures

Abe has long been a proponent of increasing the military's combat role, both during his first term as prime minister in 2006–2007 and following his reelection to the position in 2012. Abe argues that military self-defense would allow the country to better prepare and protect itself, particularly as neighboring nations have ramped up their own arsenals and nuclear technology. Since 2012, Abe has introduced a number of defense reforms, including an increase in the defense budget, the creation of a National Security Council, the development of an official security strategy, and changes in arms exports. In 2014, the prime minister, aware that he did not yet have support in parliament or among the general public, called for a reinterpretation of Article 9, instead of an official constitutional revision. On July 1, 2014, Abe's cabinet agreed to an interpretation of Article 9 that would allow Japan to take military action if one of its close allies was attacked and if such attack could result in a threat to Japan or its citizens. Abe's decision to circumvent parliament and the public by seeking approval only through his cabinet sparked outrage in parliament, amongst the Japanese public, and even abroad—Japanese ally South Korea indicated that Japan was ignoring the effect of World War II on many Asian nations. The United States, for its part, supported Abe's decision.

In 2015, Abe sought to formalize the reinterpretation by submitting a package of eleven security measures to parliament to permit the JSDF to enter into military combat assistance with its allies. According to the legislation, three primary factors must be met before the military would be involved in any conflict: use of force is restricted, all peaceful means have been exhausted, and the result of an attack against Japan or its allies must pose a threat to the Japanese people. In a national address, Abe said the measures would act as a deterrent to anyone who might attack Japan or its allies, and that the stipulations put in place would ensure that Japan does not enter military engagements with any frequency. Opponents, however, pointed to the concessions Japan has made to the United States since the end of World War II. Many expressed fear that the United States might coerce Japan into sending ground troops into the Middle East. "Japanese leaders are too weak to say no to the U.S.," said Tsuneo Watanabe, a senior fellow at the Tokyo Foundation.

Upper and Lower Houses Vote for Passage Despite Public Opposition

Abe's Liberal Democratic Party and its coalition partners hold comfortable majorities in both Houses of Parliament, all but guaranteeing that his security measures would easily pass. Japan's lower house took up the eleven security measures in June 2015. At one point, law scholars were called in to testify on the constitutionality of the bills. Setsu Kobayashi, a professor emeritus of constitutional law at Keio University, told lawmakers "Paragraph 2 of Article 9 does not grant any legal standing for military activities abroad." He called the package of security measures "a violation" of the nation's constitution.

A vote was called for July 16, 2015, in the lower house. An estimated 20,000 protesters lined the streets outside parliament chanting, "Don't send our children to war" and "Stop Abe's Recklessness." Polling conducted shortly before the lower house vote showed 61 percent of respondents disapproving of the security bills. The final moments of debate on the package of bills became raucous at times. Katsuya Okada, the leader of the largest opposition party in parliament, called it "a huge mistake to set aside a constitutional interpretation built up by governments for 70 years without sufficient public understanding and debate." Opposition lawmakers walked out of the chamber before the vote was held, and the bills passed handily. After the vote, Abe said the bills "are vital to protect the Japanese people's lives and prevent war" especially as "the security situation around Japan is getting tougher."

After passage, the package of bills passed to the upper house's special committee on security legislation. Committee members struggled for weeks to pass the legislation to a full vote of the upper house. Tens of thousands of protesters gathered outside the Diet on September 17, when the committee was expected to vote. Despite public opposition, Abe refused to back down, stating, "My determination for passage through this Diet session is unchanged," adding, "[a]fter the Diet passes current security legislation, the understanding (of the people) will surely spread as time passes by." Opposition lawmakers incited a brawl, which was broadcast live on television, when they attempted to physically block the chair of the committee from calling a vote. Ultimately, the measures passed out of committee and were taken up for consideration by the full upper house on September 18, 2015.

Debate in the upper house was tense. Taro Yamamoto, a member of an opposition part, said that the security measures would mean Japan would "absolutely be caught up in illegal American wars." Mizuho Fukushima, a member of the Social Democratic Party, said Japan "must not become accomplices to murder." Opponents attempted to introduce no-confidence and censure motions against Prime Minister Abe and staged filibuster-length speeches, but none of their efforts prevented a vote. The package of eleven security measures was ultimately passed at 2:00 a.m. on September 18, 2015.

During a press conference on September 18, the prime minister's Chief Cabinet Secretary reported that the legislation, while creating a military force, would not change Japan's pacifist ideology. "It remains entirely unchanged that Japan, as a peace-loving nation, will pursue peaceful solutions to global issues through diplomacy. Simultaneously, we believe that it is the responsibility of politics and the Government to secure the lives and peaceful daily lives of the Japanese people and ensure Japan's survival in the event of a contingency. For this reason, the Government submitted legislation that enables seamless responses. The passage of this legislation will not in any way change the Prime Minister's foreign policy of contributing to the peace and stability of the international community under the banner of 'Proactive Contribution to Peace,'" said Chief Cabinet Secretary Yoshihide Suga. Following passage less than one week later, Prime Minister Abe addressed reporters about the importance of the legislation. "Whether we like it or not, the security environment surrounding Japan is becoming increasingly severe," he said, adding that the measures were essential to ensuring the nation could "pass on a peaceful Japan to our children." Speaking to those the prime minister claimed were "fearmongering," Abe reiterated that the legislature had passed a "bill aimed at deterring war and contributing to peace and security of the world" and not a "war bill."

POSSIBLE IMPACT OF THE LEGISLATION

China and Japan have long been at odds over the East China Sea and South China Sea, primarily with regard to which nation maintains sovereignty over the area and therefore has the right to resource exploration. It is believed that the East China Sea, in particular, might have rich natural gas resources. In December, Japan announced that it would deploy thousands of troops and military vessels to an island in the East China Sea in an attempt to check China's military presence in the region. The nation also began ramping up its strategic partnerships with the Philippines and Vietnam and held joint military exercises with the Philippines army.

It is likely that the prime minister's security measures will be challenged in Japanese court. However, in the past the courts have been unwilling to overrule the government, so there is no indication that they would be tempted in this instance. Abe might also face voter backlash when upper house elections are held in July 2016. If the public chooses to vote out those who backed the security measures, Abe's government would be severely weakened. Such retaliation at the voting booth is not without precedent. In 1960, former prime minister and Abe's grandfather, Nobusuke Kishi, formed a pact with the United States that would allow U.S. and Japanese forces to fight together if Japan was attacked. Although the measure won support in parliament, it was so unpopular with the public that he was forced to resign one month later.

—Heather Kerrigan

Following is an excerpt from a press conference held on September 18, 2015, by Japan's chief cabinet secretary on security legislation under consideration by the nation's parliament; and an excerpt from Prime Minister Shinzo Abe's press conference on September 25, 2015, regarding passage of the security legislation.

Cabinet Secretary Remarks on Security Legislation

DOCUMENT

September 18, 2015

CHIEF CABINET SECRETARY SUGA: I would like to give an overview of the Cabinet meeting. The meeting approved 23 general and other measures, the promulgation of legislation, a cabinet order, and personnel decisions. With regard to statements by ministers, the Minister of Land, Infrastructure, Transport and Tourism made a statement concerning the Priority Plan for Social Infrastructure Development; Minister Arimura made a statement concerning the holding of the Autumn 2015 National Traffic Safety Campaign and the "Zero Traffic Accident Fatality Day"; the Chairperson of the National Public Safety Commission made a statement concerning the holding of the Autumn 2015 National Traffic Safety Campaign; and the Minister for Foreign Affairs made a statement concerning the emergency grant aid for transporting humanitarian supplies in Nepal and the emergency grant aid for the process to restore democracy in the Central African Republic.

(Abridged)

Q&As

(Abridged)

REPORTER: I have a related question. It is in connection with the security legislation. The Abe administration has underscored Japan's intention to contribute to the peace and stability of the international community with the Japan-U.S. Alliance as the cornerstone. Do you consider that the passage of the legislation will add a new bargaining chip to Japan's diplomatic strategy and strengthen its diplomacy?

CHIEF CABINET SECRETARY SUGA: First of all, the Government has endeavored to provide careful and easy to understand explanations regarding the significance and the necessity of the legislation during more than 100 hours of discussions that have taken place at the House of Representatives and the House of Councillors, respectively. The Government will continue to provide thorough explanations to gain the understanding of the people. As you can all see from the recent news reports, North Korea has repeatedly conducted ballistic missile tests and has made various intimations, including proceeding with its nuclear development and conducting nuclear tests. In the East China Sea, China has repeatedly intruded into Japan's territorial waters, and the number of Air Self-Defense Force scrambles against Chinese aircraft has reached a record high. Under such circumstances, it remains entirely unchanged that Japan, as a peace-loving nation, will pursue peaceful solutions to global issues through diplomacy. Simultaneously, we believe that it is the responsibility of politics and the Government to secure the lives and peaceful daily lives of the Japanese people and ensure Japan's survival in the event of a contingency. For this reason, the Government submitted legislation that enables seamless responses. The passage of this legislation will not in any way change the Prime Minister's foreign policy of contributing to the peace and stability of the international community under the banner of "Proactive Contribution to Peace." . . .

SOURCE: Prime Minister of Japan and His Cabinet. "Press Conference by the Chief Cabinet Secretary." September 18, 2015. http://japan.kantei.go.jp/tyoukanpress/201509/18_a.html.

DOCUMENT

Prime Minister Abe on Passage of Security Measures

September 25, 2015

The current ordinary session of the Diet is scheduled to end the day after tomorrow. Each of the bills introduced during the session with the aim of breaking through the rigid bedrock-like regulations that have for many long years been holding back Japan's growth have been enacted. These include the first agricultural cooperative reforms in 60 years, healthcare system reforms focused on the needs of patients, and electricity and gas business liberalization. Bills aimed at administrative reform, empowering women in the workplace, and revitalizing education have also been enacted. This latest ordinary session of the Diet, which at eight months has been the longest of the post-war era, was an historic one, involving the most drastic reforms since the end of World War II.

The Legislation for Peace and Security was also approved during the current session of the Diet. The tragedy of war must never again be repeated. The legislation will fortify our pledge to never again wage war—a pledge we have maintained over the 70 years since the end of World War II. I believe we have now constructed a strong foundation to this end.

Whether we like it or not, the security environment surrounding Japan is becoming increasingly severe. North Korea possesses several hundred ballistic missiles with a range that covers most of Japan's territory, and their development of nuclear weapons fitted to those missiles is becoming an ever more serious issue. The threat of terrorism is also spreading throughout the world. We need to think of ways we can pass on a peaceful Japan to our children. Making robust preparations enabling us to seamlessly respond to any situation, ensuring that the Japan–U.S. Alliance fully functions in the situation that Japan finds itself threatened, and clearly demonstrating this to the world, and preemptively preventing war to ensure regional peace and stability—these are the core issues the Legislation for Peace and Security addresses.

During more than 200 hours of deliberations in both the House of Representatives and the House of Councillors, we were able to share our sense of crisis about the severe reality of Japan's situation with opposition parties such as the Japan Innovation Party, the Assembly to Energize Japan, the Party for Future Generations, and the New Renaissance Party, and they in turn submitted their own concrete counterproposals. Instead of being merely an "opposition of resistance," they acted as a responsible opposition, looking squarely at the reality and clearly proclaiming their own policies and positions. As Members of the Diet with a mandate from their electorate, they demonstrated an extremely sincere attitude toward this matter, and I would like to express my heartfelt respect to them.

Following intense policy consultations, the Assembly to Energize Japan, the Party for Future Generations, and the New Renaissance Party assented to the Peace and Security Legislation. The agreement was predicated on the strengthening of democratic controls over the mobilization of the Self Defense Forces, including the requirement of prior Diet approval. This is a framework in which a democratically elected government making its decision with the comprehensive involvement of the parliament consisting of representatives of the people.

Neither I, nor any other Japanese citizen wish for war. There is no doubt about that. I would like to remark once again that, in Japan—a world-class model of a democratic nation—referring to such a bill as a "war bill" is baseless, fearmongering and entirely irresponsible.

If it truly were a "war bill," there would surely have been vocal opposition to it from around the world. We are however receiving messages of support for the legislation from a large number of countries. We have received strong support from countries in Southeast Asia such as the Philippines, which was a battlefield in World War II and countries with which we once fought such as the U.S. and European ones. I believe that these supports prove that the legislation is not a "war bill" but a bill aimed at deterring war and contributing to peace and security of the world.

The Government intends to continue working to carefully explain the legislation in order to gain the greater understanding of the public.

We will resolutely protect the lives and peaceful livelihoods of the Japanese people in any situation. To achieve this, it is vital that we strengthen the foundations of our national security while also striving harder than ever to push forward with peaceful diplomacy.

As early as tomorrow, I will be heading to New York to attend the U.N. General Assembly. The world constantly faces a range of challenges, not least the issue of Syrian refugees currently streaming into Europe. In times such as these, I would like to declare my strong determination to see that Japan contributes to global peace and prosperity. The U.N. General Assembly provides an ideal opportunity for heads of state from around the world to gather. I would like to hold as many summit meetings as I can while there. In autumn, I also hope to hold Japan's first trilateral summit meeting in three years with

China and the Republic of Korea. The Government will work harder than ever to enhance relations with neighboring countries such as China, the Republic of Korea, and Russia. We intend to work on proactively pursuing diplomacy that takes a panoramic perspective of the world map. . . .

[A Q&A session with assembled press has been omitted.]

SOURCE: Prime Minister of Japan and His Cabinet. "Press Conference by Prime Minister Shinzo Abe." September 25, 2015. http://japan.kantei.go.jp/97_abe/statement/201509/1213465_9928.html.

OTHER HISTORIC DOCUMENTS OF INTEREST

FROM PREVIOUS *HISTORIC DOCUMENTS*

Senators Speak on Proposed Abortion Ban

SEPTEMBER 22, 2015

Throughout 2015, Congressional Republicans proposed a variety of bills and riders to ban abortions after twenty weeks of pregnancy, the point at which some Republicans argued fetuses can feel pain. The biggest push to ban abortions after twenty weeks came in September in the Senate when Republicans introduced the House-passed Pain-Capable Unborn Child Protection Act. Democrats ultimately blocked the bill from a vote. While debate continued in the House and Senate, Planned Parenthood, a health care provider and pro-choice advocacy organization, was facing accusations that it was profiting from the sale of aborted fetal tissue, an issue that renewed debate over the necessity of the group's federal funding.

ULTRA-CONSERVATIVES DEFEATED IN JANUARY

Republicans won big during the November 2014 midterm elections, and took control of both the House and Senate for the first time since 2006. In January, the new Republican majority showed signs of internal divide when the House attempted to pass legislation banning federal Affordable Care Act (ACA) subsidies for health insurance plans that provide coverage for abortions. The ultra-conservative members of the party wanted to insert a rider with the bill that would ban women from receiving an abortion after twenty weeks of pregnancy. The initial proposal faced some backlash for its strict wording, but it was revised to include a provision allowing for abortion in instances of rape, incest involving a minor, or when the mother's life is in danger. However, to be able to seek an abortion under the legislation, a woman would be required to report her rape or incest to authorities.

Many women in the House GOP caucus took issue with the provision, noting that a victim of rape often fears reporting the incident. According to the Rape, Abuse, and Incest National Network, federal statistics from 2008 to 2012 indicate that only an estimated 40 percent of rapes are reported. In 2013, the Justice Department claimed the number to be closer to 35 percent. Unable to garner the votes necessary for passage, Republican leadership dropped the twenty-week ban shortly before the bill banning federal funding of abortions went for a vote on the floor. In response, Cecile Richards, the president of Planned Parenthood, called the abortion ban proposal "so dangerous, extreme and unpopular that House Republicans can't even get their membership lined up behind them."

On January 22, 2015, the forty-second anniversary of the Supreme Court's ruling in *Roe v. Wade*, which effectively legalized abortions, the House voted 242–179 to eliminate federal subsidies for health insurance plans that cover abortions. Speaker of the House John Boehner, R-Ohio, called the vote a cause for rejoicing. Because Republicans held only a slim majority in the Senate, they were unable to find enough support for the House measure to put it to a vote on the floor.

Twenty-Week Abortion Ban Renewed and Defeated

The twenty-week ban was taken up again in the House in May. The bill, known as the Pain-Capable Unborn Child Protection Act, was similar to that floated in January, but it dropped the earlier language about rape victims receiving an exemption only in instances in which the rape was reported after female Republican legislators raised concerns that such language might re-traumatize victims and push females away from the party during the 2016 presidential election. The bill did include language requiring any woman who was able to receive an exemption for an abortion to undergo counseling or medical care two days before the procedure. Additionally, two doctors would be required at each procedure, one to perform the abortion, and another to help the fetus survive if it was born alive. The woman receiving the abortion would be required to sign a consent form prior to the procedure being completed, acknowledging her understanding that an attempt will be made to deliver a live fetus, if at all possible.

Outlawing abortions at the twenty-week mark has been widely debated for many years. Some believe that it is the point at which a fetus can experience pain, but the American Congress of Obstetricians and Gynecologists has said that fetal pain is unlikely to be felt until at least the third trimester of pregnancy, which begins well after twenty weeks of pregnancy. According to the Centers for Disease Control and Prevention, an estimated 10,220 abortions took place in 2011, and 91.4 percent of all abortions occurred at or prior to thirteen weeks of pregnancy, while only 1.3 percent occurred at or after twenty-one weeks. Thirteen states already have bans in place for abortions after twenty weeks gestation.

During floor debate, Rep. Trent Franks, R-Ariz., the bill's sponsor, called late-term abortions "the greatest human rights atrocity in the United States today." He continued, "It shouldn't be such a hard vote. Protecting little pain-capable unborn children and their mothers is not a Republican issue, or a Democrat issue. It is a test of our basic humanity and who we are as a human family." Speaking in opposition to the bill, and specifically about its exemptions, Rep. Lois Frankel, D-Fla., said, "You want to talk about pain? Let's talk about the agony of a woman who's raped and again violated by unnecessary government intrusion." Planned Parenthood's Richards also spoke out against the legislation, stating, "In states that have passed laws like this, some women and their families have been put into unimaginable situations, needing to end a pregnancy for serious medical reasons, but unable to do so." The House ultimately passed the legislation on May 13, by a party-line vote of 242–184.

The bill did not come to the Senate floor until September, where it was unlikely to pass because Republicans would need at least some Democratic support to reach sixty votes for passage. Even if Republicans could find enough Democratic support, President Barack Obama had already promised to veto any such legislation that came to his desk. During debate, Sen. Dan Coats, R-Ind., said the bill gave the body "the opportunity to protect the unborn children in this country whose lives are being ended—in many cases brutally—at an age at which these children are capable of experiencing pain." Coats cited statistics that the later into a pregnancy a woman receives an abortion the more likely she is to die from complications. At 21 weeks, Coats said, "she is 91 times more likely to die from abortion than she was in the first trimester." Senate Majority Leader Mitch McConnell, R-Ky., cited polls indicating that men and women alike oppose abortion after twenty weeks. He added, "The fact is that we are now one of just seven nations— among them countries such as North Korea and China—that allow elective abortions at such a late stage. Can't we do better than this as a country?"

Sen. Dick Durbin, D-Ill., noted that the issue of religion as separate from matters of state was written into our founding documents, and had, he thought, been put to rest long ago. "For 47 years . . . we have had Supreme Court guidance on when the government can play a role in the decision about the termination of a pregnancy," Durbin stated. "Now there is an effort on the floor of the Senate to change that basic guidance from the *Roe v. Wade* decision. Each time we step into this question, into something which seems as clear as 'at 20 weeks we will draw a line and after that there cannot be a legal termination of pregnancy,' we find we are walking into an area of uncertainty."

Democrats filibustered the Republican attempt at passage and defeated the cloture vote 54–42, short of the sixty votes needed to move the legislation ahead. The bill was not reintroduced by the end of 2015.

Planned Parenthood Videos Raise Concern

In July 2015, a series of videos developed by the pro-life Center for Medical Progress surfaced, reportedly indicating that Planned Parenthood clinics were profiting from selling aborted fetus parts. In the videos, Deborah Nucatola, the group's senior director of medical services, discuss payments of $30 to $100 per patient for aborted fetal tissue. While the edited version of the video makes it appear that the group is after profits, in the unedited version, Nucatola states that "No one's going to see this as a money making thing," adding "our goal . . . is to give patients the option without impacting our bottom line. The messaging is this should not be seen as a new revenue stream, because that's not what it is."

The footage, which was secretly recorded during a lunch meeting, was called by former Texas governor Rick Perry "a disturbing reminder of the organization's penchant for profiting off the tragedy of a destroyed human life," while former HP CEO and Republican presidential candidate Carly Fiorina called it "profiting on the death of the unborn while telling women it's about empowerment." In contrast, a number of medical organizations that deal with biospecimens for research purposes said that it was unlikely Planned Parenthood could make any profit off of their sales, and that the compensation for human tissue was perfectly legal. U.S. law states that while the sale of organs for transplant is illegal, tissue donation from aborted fetuses is legal, as is compensation to offset the costs of storage and transport. According to Sherilyn Sawyer, the director of Harvard University and Brigham and Women's Hospital's biorepository, many hospitals receive in the range of $100 to $500 when providing tissue blocks that are no longer required for patient care to a research organization.

Although Richards apologized for the manner in which Nucatola spoke about "specimens" in the videos, the group released a statement that "we help patients who want to donate tissue for scientific research, and we do this just like every other high-quality health care provider does—with full, appropriate consent from patients and under the highest ethical and legal standards. There is no financial benefit for tissue donation for either the patient or for Planned Parenthood. In some instances, actual costs, such as the cost to transport tissue to leading research centers, are reimbursed, which is standard across the medical field."

A number of states initiated investigations into allegations that Planned Parenthood was illegally profiting from tissue sales, as did the House Oversight and Government Reform Committee. None of the investigations yielded any evidence of wrongdoing; however, the Texas investigation resulted in a felony indictment against David Daleiden, who developed the videos. Despite the lack of wrongdoing on the part of Planned Parenthood, on October 13, 2015, the group announced that it would no longer accept reimbursement for fetal tissue donations.

Allegations about Planned Parenthood renewed debate about whether the group should receive federal funds, and it became a cornerstone of the September 2015 budget crisis. Republicans wanted to pass a budget bill that contained language that would defund the group entirely, their concern being that federal funds are being given to an organization that offers abortion services, even though Planned Parenthood is legally barred from using federal funds to perform abortions. Sen. Susan Collins, R-Maine, said that she did not believe "there are 60 votes in the Senate for that approach, which will then say to the House that we really need a clean (funding bill) if we're going to avoid a shutdown." Sen. Ted Cruz, R-Texas, a candidate for the 2016 Republican presidential nomination, said the party needed to "stand for our principles, and our principles should not be surrendering to the Democrats." Ultimately, the Planned Parenthood provision was dropped by Senate leaders in order to avoid a federal shutdown.

—Heather Kerrigan

Following is the text of a floor statement delivered by Sen. Mitch McConnell, R-Ky., on September 22, 2015, in favor of a twenty-week abortion ban; and a statement by Sen. Dick Durbin, D-Ill., in opposition to the twenty-week abortion ban, also on September 22, 2015.

Sen. McConnell Speaks in Favor of Twenty-Week Abortion Ban

September 22, 2015

Mr. President, ask a family to show you the first picture of their child these days, and you are likely to get a black-and-white image with delicate fingers and tiny toes. Maybe it is their precious Christine. Maybe it is their little guy Brett. But one thing's for sure—that baby is their child.

Scientific advances like the sonogram are helping pull back the curtain on the mystery of life, they are helping foster a new spirit of compassionate protection for the most defenseless, and they are providing new opportunities to bridge old political divides.

We in this Chamber are never going to agree completely on the abortion question, but we should at least be able to agree that if an unborn child has reached the point where he or she can feel pain, that child's life deserves protection. Science is telling us that a child can reach this stage around 20 weeks—in other words, 5 months. This is when unborn children can react— even recoil—to stimuli an adult would recognize as painful. This is when doctors even administer fetal anesthesia during surgery.

As the *New England Journal of Medicine* study recently demonstrated, babies delivered at this age can survive outside the womb. So even if we differ on the larger abortion issue, can't we at least agree that children at this late stage of development deserve our protection? The American people seem to think so. Polls show that American women and American men oppose abortions after 5 months. The fact is that we are now one of just seven nations—among them countries such as North Korea and China—that allow elective abortions at such a late stage. Can't we do better than this as a country? The Pain-Capable Unborn Child Protection Act would allow America to finally join the ranks of the most civilized nations on this issue.

Just this past weekend in Louisville, hundreds of Kentuckians gathered to spread a message of dignity and hope. They marched for those who may not meet them. They marched for those who may not hear them. But I hope Americans across the country, including participants in the 37th annual Walk for Life, will be encouraged to know that their voices of humanity and of respect are finally being heard again in a Senate under new leadership.

The executive director of Kentucky Right to Life said the issue before us is "critical." She said, "We have worked tirelessly to give these defenseless babies some protection." Several States have already taken action to protect these children. So has the House of Representatives. Now it is up to each of us to show where we stand. We are seeing how science is changing this debate.

So what I am asking every colleague is this: Look in your hearts and help us stand up for the most innocent life, help us protect that beating heart in that sonogram.

SOURCE: Sen. Mitch McConnell. "Pain-Capable Unborn Child Protection Bill." *Congressional Record*, Vol. 161, No. 137. S. 6859. September 22, 2015. www.gpo.gov/fdsys/pkg/CREC-2015-09-22/pdf/CREC-2015-09-22-pt1-PgS6859-5.pdf.

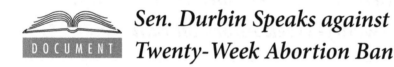

Sen. Durbin Speaks against Twenty-Week Abortion Ban

September 22, 2015

Mr. President, I would like to address the issue before the Senate. It relates to the divisive and controversial issue of abortion. It comes at an unusual moment in the history of the Congress.

This week, for the first time, the Pope will be addressing a joint session of Congress. It was 50 years ago when the first Pope visited the United States. The arrival of Pope Francis this week is a cause of great celebration to people from my State of Illinois and across this Nation because of their respect for his leadership of the Catholic Church. It calls to question, of course, the relationship between religion and our government.

This summer I finished a book called "Mayflower," which told the story of the Pilgrims coming to the United States, settling in in our country, looking for a new opportunity but looking more than anything for freedom of religious belief. They were followed by scores and thousands of others who came for the same reason.

My mother was an immigrant to this country, brought here at the age of 2. Her mother brought her and her sister and brother to our shores for a variety of reasons. But there is one thing that sticks out in that journey. Up in my office I have something that my grandmother carried across the ocean from Lithuania to the United States. It was a Roman Catholic prayer book written in Lithuanian. It was contraband in 1911 in Lithuania for her to possess it because the Russians were in control and the Russians were imposing the orthodox religion and making it difficult to practice the Catholic religion. I never knew my grandmother, but she was one brave lady to bring three kids across the ocean and stick in her bag that prayer book which meant so much to her, that prayer book which she could use in the United States of America without the government telling her she could not.

We have tried to strike the right balance between religion and our democracy from the beginning. I believe our Founding Fathers got it right. They said three things in the Constitution about religion: first, that each of us would have the freedom to worship as we choose or to choose not to worship; second, that the government would not choose a religion and that we would not have an official government religion; and third, that there would be no religious test for public office in America.

I thought those were settled principles, but this Presidential campaign suggests otherwise. We had the outrageous suggestion by a Republican Presidential candidate this last weekend that a Muslim should never serve as President of the United States. I would think that a man of his background and learning would at least take the time to understand our Constitution and the express provision which says that he is wrong, that there will never be a religious litmus test to serve in public office in the United States.

And now, this week on the floor of the Senate, we will have two votes on the issue of abortion. There was a time when this issue came before us frequently—not so much lately. It is a divisive and controversial issue; that is for sure. But this week the Republican Senate leadership has allowed two of their Presidential candidates to raise this issue on the floor of the Senate. It is no coincidence this issue comes before us the same week the Pope, the leader of the Catholic Church, will be addressing a joint session of Congress. It is more than a coincidence.

This particular bill relates to when a person can terminate a pregnancy. For 47 years, if I am not mistaken—maybe I have that calculation slightly wrong—we have had Supreme Court guidance on when the government can play a role in the decision about the termination of a pregnancy. Now there is an effort on the floor of the Senate to change that basic guidance from the *Roe v. Wade* decision. Each time we step into this question, into something which seems as clear as "at 20 weeks we will draw a line and after that there cannot be a legal termination of pregnancy," we find we are walking into an area of uncertainty.

I remember meeting many years ago, when we were debating this issue, a woman from Illinois. She was from the town of Naperville. In 1996 she told me a harrowing story of how legislation such as the bill before us would have impacted her. She learned late in her pregnancy that the child she was carrying could not survive outside the womb. Her doctors diagnosed her baby with at least nine major anomalies, including a fluid-filled cranium with no brain tissue. Sadly, she also had underlying medical conditions—personal conditions—that complicated her pregnancy even more. Doctors were concerned that if she went through with the pregnancy at that point, she ran the risk of never having another baby. With tears in her eyes, she told me how she and her husband agonized over the news and eventually decided it was best for them and their other children to terminate that pregnancy.

If the bill before us today—the 20-week abortion bill—had been the law of the land back then, sadly it would have jeopardized and endangered her health.

Well, 18 years later she came back to see me. I learned she was able to do what was best for her family in terminating that pregnancy. That was her decision with her doctor and her husband. But she was given a second chance. Soon after, she became pregnant again. This time she was thankful to give birth to a healthy baby boy. When she came to see me, she told me about her son Nick. She said he had become a star football player and had a bright future ahead of him.

If this bill had been the law of the land, this woman in Illinois—and others like her—would not even have had the choice to terminate a pregnancy for her own health protection and for the opportunity to have another baby. That is the challenge we face when we try to spell out in law all of the medical possibilities, limiting opportunities and decisions to be made by individuals under the most heartbreaking circumstances.

This bill has other issues. The fact that the rape and incest exceptions, which have largely been built into the law to this point, would be changed dramatically by this law raises questions as well. There is a requirement, as I understand it, in this law that victims of incest would have had to report to a law enforcement agency that crime of incest before they would even be able to terminate a pregnancy under these circumstances. That is not even realistic—to think some young child in a household, who has been exploited by another member of the family, would think to go to a law enforcement agency and report that other member of her family before they could qualify to terminate a pregnancy in this circumstance.

That shows the extremes this bill goes to. I hope we will defeat this measure. I sincerely hope the other Republican Presidential candidate, who is going to try to shut down the government over the funding of Planned Parenthood later in the week, does not prevail either. We need to move on to find other issues—not divisive issues but issues we can build a bipartisan consensus on to make this a stronger country.

We need to address the issue of funding our government and to accept the responsibilities to move forward in a bipartisan fashion. This bill does not do that.

I yield the floor.

SOURCE: Sen. Dick Durbin. "Pain-Capable Unborn Child Protection Act—Motion to Proceed." *Congressional Record*, Vol. 161, No. 137. S. 6860-61. September 22, 2015. www.gpo.gov/fdsys/pkg/CREC-2015-09-22/pdf/CREC-2015-09-22-pt1-PgS6860-4.pdf.

OTHER HISTORIC DOCUMENTS OF INTEREST

FROM PREVIOUS *HISTORIC DOCUMENTS*

Pope Francis Travels to the United States

SEPTEMBER 24 AND 26, 2015

In late September, Pope Francis, the widely revered head of the Catholic Church, made a visit to the United States, with stops in in Washington, D.C., Philadelphia, and New York. The pope was welcomed with great fanfare, in stark contrast to the first ever papal visit to the United States in 1965 when then-President Lyndon Johnson was forced to meet Pope Paul VI in a New York hotel because the nation had not yet established formal diplomatic ties with the Vatican. During his visit, the pope spoke at length about how the United States should harness its wealth and power to serve the neediest both within its own borders and around the world.

Multiple Stops in the United States

Pope Franciss's visit to the United States lasted just six days, but in that time he visited three major U.S. cities along the East Coast, offered prayers and mass, addressed the United Nations and the U.S. Congress, visited with the Catholic faithful, and dined with homeless Americans and politicians alike. The pope arrived from Cuba the evening of September 22, and the following day met with President Barack Obama before participating in a parade, holding a midday prayer with U.S. bishops, and canonizing a new saint. On September 24, the pope addressed a joint session of Congress and met with Speaker of the House John Boehner before flying to New York City for an evening prayer at St. Patrick's Cathedral. While in New York, the pope addressed the United Nations General Assembly, participated in a motorcade, held mass at Madison Square Garden, visited the 9/11 memorial for a prayer service, and visited a Catholic school. On September 26, the pope departed for Philadelphia, where, over the course of two days, he celebrated mass, visited Independence Hall, met with bishops, toured a correctional facility, and met with Vice President Joe Biden, before departing for Rome. Throngs of people from all over the world gathered outside wherever Francis was slated to be.

During his speech before the General Assembly, Pope Francis spoke about the greatest challenges facing the world today and offered solutions for solving them. Pope Francis said that there are a select few wealthy individuals who hoard resources and power, which leaves the poorest without a voice, even at the United Nations. "To enable these real men and women to escape from extreme poverty, we must allow them to be dignified agents of their own destiny," he said. He also said that bodies such as the United Nations often develop solutions that have no real basis in reality for those they seek to help, and no real means of enforcing decisions, whether the issue at hand is nuclear weapons or climate change. The pope stated that what the world needs is to find a new way to come together despite the issues that divide us.

A previously unannounced stop on Franciss's trip was made in Philadelphia, where the pope met with five victims of clergy sex abuse. In remarks released by the Vatican following the meeting, the pope said he was "deeply sorry for the times when you or your family spoke out, to report the abuse, but you were not heard or believed. Please know that the Holy Father hears you and believes you." He pledged, "Clergy and bishops will be held accountable when they abuse or fail to protect children." On his flight back to Rome, the pope further commented on the subject that has plagued the church for years. "We know the abuses are everywhere—in families, in the neighborhoods, in the schools, in the gyms," the pope said. "But when a priest abuses, it is very serious because the vocation of the priest is to make that boy, that girl grow toward the love of God, toward maturity and toward good. But instead of that, it squashed it," Francis said.

POPE SPEAKS BEFORE CONGRESS

Perhaps the most highly anticipated portion of Pope Franciss's visit was his speech before a joint session of Congress. Franciss's appearance made history as the first time the leader of the Catholic Church has addressed the House and Senate. During his speech, the pope encouraged compromise on domestic affairs and action to help those around the world who are suffering. Delivered in heavily-accented English, he spoke about many hot-button issues, including immigration, religious extremism, climate change, and European migrants.

The pope's primary message of working together to move forward also carried with it a running theme of the importance of the immigrant. "We, the people of this continent, are not fearful of foreigners, because most of us were once foreigners," the pope said. "I say this to you as the son of immigrants, knowing that so many of you are also descended from immigrants. Tragically, the rights of those who were here long before us were not always respected. For those peoples and their nations, from the heart of American democracy, I wish to reaffirm my highest esteem and appreciation." He also called on lawmakers to defend human life on a number of different fronts, including calling for the abolition of the death penalty, requesting assistance for European migrants, and asking Congress to work toward ending wars, instead of inciting them by selling weapons to those they know plan only to cause harm, just to make a profit. Francis also took on climate change deniers in Congress when he called "for a courageous and responsible effort . . . to avert the most serious effects of the environmental deterioration caused by human activity."

In concluding his speech, the pope called on Congress to seek "effective solutions rather than getting bogged down in discussions." In closing, he noted, "A nation can be considered great when it defends liberty as Lincoln did, when it fosters a culture which enables people to 'dream' of full rights for all their brothers and sisters, as Martin Luther King sought to do; when it strives for justice and the cause of the oppressed, as Dorothy Day did by her tireless work, the fruit of a faith which becomes dialogue and sows peace in the contemplative style of Thomas Merton."

CONTROVERSY SURROUNDING THE PAPAL VISIT

Prior to the pope's arrival at the White House for an event on the South Lawn before an estimated 15,000 people, there were reports that the White House and the Vatican had clashed over who received an invite to the event. On the White House guest list were an openly gay Episcopal bishop, an activist nun who has long been at odds with many positions of the Catholic Church, and a transgender rights advocate. Conservatives criticized the guest list as an attempt to politicize the papal visit, with Republican presidential candidate Mike Huckabee tweeting that Obama had made a "classless decision" that was an "insult to millions of Catholics." Both the White House and the Vatican downplayed such rhetoric, with the latter stating that the pope had met with members of the LGBT community before and stated that he would not judge them, and the former noting through press secretary Josh Earnest that "there is no plan or strategy that's been put in place to try to stage an event that will advance anybody's political agenda."

At the end of his time in Washington, D.C., Pope Francis met with controversial Kentucky clerk Kim Davis, who weeks earlier had made headlines when she was briefly jailed for refusing to issue marriage licenses to same-sex couples following the Supreme Court's ruling in *Obergefell v. Hodges*. Davis's attorney, Mat Staver, said that during the meeting Pope Francis thanked Davis for her courage and asked her to pray for him. The pope also presented Davis and her husband with two rosaries. The Vatican did not confirm the meeting—which caused an outrage in many circles around the country—until September 30. Francis was asked about his views on Davis during his return flight to Rome, and he noted his belief that conscientious objection is a human right, adding that "if a person does not allow others to be a conscientious objector, he denies a right."

CANONIZATION OF JUNIPERO SERRA

The greatest controversy during the pope's visit was his decision to canonize Junipero Serra, an 18th-century Spanish Franciscan monk who worked to evangelize Native Americans in California. The effort to canonize Serra began in the 1930s. His first of two required miracles occurred in the 1960s when a nun reported being cured of lupus after praying to Serra. He was later beatified by then-Pope John Paul II in 1988. In January 2015, Pope Francis announced that he would waive the requirement of a second miracle and would instead canonize Serra during his September visit to the United States, marking the first time a Hispanic had ever been named a saint. Although no explanation was offered by the Vatican about why Serra was being canonized without meeting traditional standards for sainthood, it was understood that the pope believed Serra deserved the distinction because of his evangelist work for the church.

The controversy surrounding Serra stems from his practices while working with native populations in the western United States, specifically corporal punishment and refusing to allow his followers to leave once they had entered his California missions. Many have equated his tactics to slavery and have indicated that the European diseases brought by Catholic missionaries including Serra were a major reason for population decline among Native Americans in the 18th century. "Canonizing Junipero Serra effectively condones and celebrates his use of imprisonment and torture to convert California Indians to Christianity," Valentin Lopez, the chair of a tribal band that had formerly lived in the San Juan Valley, wrote in a letter to California Gov. Jerry Brown. There have even been efforts undertaken to remove Serra's statue from the U.S. Capitol Building and replace it with a statue of the late astronaut Sally Ride.

Others viewed the pope's decision to grant sainthood to Serra as not an endorsement of his cruel treatment toward Native Americans, but rather as a larger statement to the United States regarding its current treatment of immigrant populations. "Our nation's origins are not just in 1776 in 13 English colonies with Washington and Jefferson," said Steven Hackel, a history professor at the University of California at Riverside and Serra scholar.

"I think their hope is that if Americans understand that they move toward a more sympathetic and embracing immigration policy," he added. Pope Francis himself has said that he believes Serra to be "one of the founding fathers of the United States."

Despite the controversy, Serra was canonized on September 23 at a mass at Catholic University in Washington, D.C., marking the first time an individual was awarded sainthood on U.S. soil. Pope Francis said Serra "was the embodiment of 'a Church which goes forth', a Church which sets out to bring everywhere the reconciling tenderness of God." Serra "was excited about blazing trails, going forth to meet many people, learning and valuing their particular customs and ways of life." Speaking to the questions about Serra's treatment of natives, Francis said that Serra "sought to defend the dignity of the native community, to protect it from those who had mistreated and abused it." These mistreatments, the pope added, "today still trouble us especially because of the hurt which they cause in the lives of many."

—Heather Kerrigan

Following is the text of Pope Francis's speech before a joint session of the U.S. Congress on September 24, 2015; a Vatican press release regarding the pope's canonization of Junipero Serra on September 24, 2015; and the text of the pope's speech delivered before the United Nations on September 26, 2015.

DOCUMENT   *Pope Francis Addresses U.S. Congress*

September 24, 2015

[Introduction to the address has been omitted.]

"I am most grateful for your invitation to address this Joint Session of Congress in 'the land of the free and the home of the brave'. I would like to think that the reason for this is that I too am a son of this great continent, from which we have all received so much and toward which we share a common responsibility.

"Each son or daughter of a given country has a mission, a personal and social responsibility. Your own responsibility as members of Congress is to enable this country, by your legislative activity, to grow as a nation. You are the face of its people, their representatives. You are called to defend and preserve the dignity of your fellow citizens in the tireless and demanding pursuit of the common good, for this is the chief aim of all politics. A political society endures when it seeks, as a vocation, to satisfy common needs by stimulating the growth of all its members, especially those in situations of greater vulnerability or risk. Legislative activity is always based on care for the people. To this you have been invited, called and convened by those who elected you.

"Yours is a work which makes me reflect in two ways on the figure of Moses. On the one hand, the patriarch and lawgiver of the people of Israel symbolises the need of peoples to keep alive their sense of unity by means of just legislation. On the other, the figure of Moses leads us directly to God and thus to the transcendent dignity of the human being. Moses provides us with a good synthesis of your work: you are asked to protect, by means of the law, the image and likeness fashioned by God on every human face.

"Today I would like not only to address you, but through you the entire people of the United States. Here, together with their representatives, I would like to take this opportunity to dialogue with the many thousands of men and women who strive each day to do an honest day's work, to bring home their daily bread, to save money and—one step at a time—to build a better life for their families. These are men and women who are not concerned simply with paying their taxes, but in their own quiet way sustain the life of society. They generate solidarity by their actions, and they create organisations which offer a helping hand to those most in need.

"I would also like to enter into dialogue with the many elderly persons who are a storehouse of wisdom forged by experience, and who seek in many ways, especially through volunteer work, to share their stories and their insights. I know that many of them are retired, but still active; they keep working to build up this land. I also want to dialogue with all those young people who are working to realise their great and noble aspirations, who are not led astray by facile proposals, and who face difficult situations, often as a result of immaturity on the part of many adults. I wish to dialogue with all of you, and I would like to do so through the historical memory of your people.

"My visit takes place at a time when men and women of good will are marking the anniversaries of several great Americans. The complexities of history and the reality of human weakness notwithstanding, these men and women, for all their many differences and limitations, were able by hard work and self-sacrifice—some at the cost of their lives—to build a better future. They shaped fundamental values which will endure forever in the spirit of the American people. A people with this spirit can live through many crises, tensions and conflicts, while always finding the resources to move forward, and to do so with dignity. These men and women offer us a way of seeing and interpreting reality. In honouring their memory, we are inspired, even amid conflicts, and in the here and now of each day, to draw upon our deepest cultural reserves.

"I would like to mention four of these Americans: Abraham Lincoln, Martin Luther King, Dorothy Day and Thomas Merton.

"This year marks the one hundred and fiftieth anniversary of the assassination of President Abraham Lincoln, the guardian of liberty, who laboured tirelessly that 'this nation, under God, [might] have a new birth of freedom'. Building a future of freedom requires love of the common good and cooperation in a spirit of subsidiarity and solidarity.

"All of us are quite aware of, and deeply worried by, the disturbing social and political situation of the world today. Our world is increasingly a place of violent conflict, hatred and brutal atrocities, committed even in the name of God and of religion. We know that no religion is immune from forms of individual delusion or ideological extremism. This means that we must be especially attentive to every type of fundamentalism, whether religious or of any other kind. A delicate balance is required to combat violence perpetrated in the name of a religion, an ideology or an economic system, while also safeguarding religious freedom, intellectual freedom and individual freedoms. But there is another temptation which we must especially guard against: the simplistic reductionism which sees only good or evil; or, if you will, the righteous and sinners. The contemporary world, with its open wounds which affect so many of our brothers and sisters, demands that we confront every form of polarisation which would divide it into these two camps. We know that in the attempt to be freed of the enemy without, we can be tempted to feed the enemy within. To imitate the hatred and violence of tyrants and murderers is the best way to take their place. That is something which you, as a people, reject.

"Our response must instead be one of hope and healing, of peace and justice. We are asked to summon the courage and the intelligence to resolve today's many geopolitical and economic crises. Even in the developed world, the effects of unjust structures and actions are all too apparent. Our efforts must aim at restoring hope, righting wrongs, maintaining commitments, and thus promoting the well-being of individuals and of peoples. We must move forward together, as one, in a renewed spirit of fraternity and solidarity, cooperating generously for the common good.

"The challenges facing us today call for a renewal of that spirit of cooperation, which has accomplished so much good throughout the history of the United States. The complexity, the gravity and the urgency of these challenges demand that we pool our resources and talents, and resolve to support one another, with respect for our differences and our convictions of conscience.

"In this land, the various religious denominations have greatly contributed to building and strengthening society. It is important that today, as in the past, the voice of faith continue to be heard, for it is a voice of fraternity and love, which tries to bring out the best in each person and in each society. Such cooperation is a powerful resource in the battle to eliminate new global forms of slavery, born of grave injustices which can be overcome only through new policies and new forms of social consensus.

"Here I think of the political history of the United States, where democracy is deeply rooted in the mind of the American people. All political activity must serve and promote the good of the human person and be based on respect for his or her dignity. 'We hold these truths to be self-evident, that all men are created equal, that they are endowed by their Creator with certain unalienable rights, that among these are life, liberty and the pursuit of happiness'. If politics must truly be at the service of the human person, it follows that it cannot be a slave to the economy and finance. Politics is, instead, an expression of our compelling need to live as one, in order to build as one the greatest common good: that of a community which sacrifices particular interests in order to share, in justice and peace, its goods, its interests, its social life. I do not underestimate the difficulty that this involves, but I encourage you in this effort.

"Here too I think of the march which Martin Luther King led from Selma to Montgomery fifty years ago as part of the campaign to fulfil his 'dream' of full civil and political rights for African Americans. That dream continues to inspire us all. I am happy that America continues to be, for many, a land of 'dreams'. Dreams which lead to action, to participation, to commitment. Dreams which awaken what is deepest and truest in the life of a people.

"In recent centuries, millions of people came to this land to pursue their dream of building a future in freedom. We, the people of this continent, are not fearful of foreigners, because most of us were once foreigners. I say this to you as the son of immigrants, knowing that so many of you are also descended from immigrants. Tragically, the rights of those who were here long before us were not always respected. For those peoples and their nations, from the heart of American democracy, I wish to reaffirm my highest esteem and appreciation. Those first contacts were often turbulent and violent, but it is difficult to judge the past by the criteria of the present. Nonetheless, when the stranger in our midst appeals to us, we must not repeat the sins and the errors of the past. We must resolve now to live as nobly and as justly as possible, as we educate new generations not to turn their back on our 'neighbours' and everything around us. Building a nation calls us to recognise that we must constantly relate to others, rejecting a mindset of hostility in order to adopt one of reciprocal subsidiarity, in a constant effort to do our best. I am confident that we can do this.

"Our world is facing a refugee crisis of a magnitude not seen since the Second World War. This presents us with great challenges and many hard decisions. On this continent, too, thousands of persons are led to travel north in search of a better life for themselves and for their loved ones, in search of greater opportunities. Is this not what we want for our own children? We must not be taken aback by their numbers, but rather view them as persons, seeing their faces and listening to their stories, trying to respond as best we can to their situation. To respond in a way which is always humane, just and fraternal. We need to avoid a common temptation nowadays: to discard whatever proves troublesome. Let us remember the Golden Rule: 'Do unto others as you would have them do unto you'.

"This Rule points us in a clear direction. Let us treat others with the same passion and compassion with which we want to be treated. Let us seek for others the same possibilities which we seek for ourselves. Let us help others to grow, as we would like to be helped ourselves. In a word, if we want security, let us give security; if we want life, let us give life; if we want opportunities, let us provide opportunities. The yardstick we use for others will be the yardstick which time will use for us. The Golden Rule also reminds us of our responsibility to protect and defend human life at every stage of its development.

"This conviction has led me, from the beginning of my ministry, to advocate at different levels for the global abolition of the death penalty. I am convinced that this way is the best, since every life is sacred, every human person is endowed with an inalienable dignity, and society can only benefit from the rehabilitation of those convicted of crimes. Recently my brother bishops here in the United States renewed their call for the abolition of the death penalty. Not only do I support them, but I also offer encouragement to all those who are convinced that a just and necessary punishment must never exclude the dimension of hope and the goal of rehabilitation.

"In these times when social concerns are so important, I cannot fail to mention the Servant of God Dorothy Day, who founded the Catholic Worker Movement. Her social activism, her passion for justice and for the cause of the oppressed, were inspired by the Gospel, her faith, and the example of the saints.

"How much progress has been made in this area in so many parts of the world! How much has been done in these first years of the third millennium to raise people out of extreme poverty! I know that you share my conviction that much more still needs to be done, and that in times of crisis and economic hardship a spirit of global solidarity must not be lost. At the same time I would encourage you to keep in mind all those people around us who are trapped in a cycle of poverty. They too need to be given hope. The fight against poverty and hunger must be fought constantly and on many fronts, especially in its causes. I know that many Americans today, as in the past, are working to deal with this problem.

"It goes without saying that part of this great effort is the creation and distribution of wealth. The right use of natural resources, the proper application of technology and the harnessing of the spirit of enterprise are essential elements of an economy which seeks to be modern, inclusive and sustainable. 'Business is a noble vocation, directed to producing wealth and improving the world. It can be a fruitful source of prosperity for the area in which it operates, especially if it sees the creation of jobs as an essential part of its service to the common good'. This common good also includes the earth, a central theme of the encyclical which I recently wrote in order to 'enter into dialogue with all people about our common home'. 'We need a conversation which includes everyone, since the environmental challenge we are undergoing, and its human roots, concern and affect us all'.

"In 'Laudato Si'", I call for a courageous and responsible effort to 'redirect our steps', and to avert the most serious effects of the environmental deterioration caused by human activity. I am convinced that we can make a difference and I have no doubt that the United States—and this Congress—have an important role to play. Now is the time for courageous actions and strategies, aimed at implementing a 'culture of care' and 'an integrated approach to combating poverty, restoring dignity to the excluded, and at the same time protecting nature'. 'We have the freedom needed to limit and direct technology'; 'to devise intelligent ways of . . . developing and limiting our power'; and to put technology 'at the service of another type of progress, one which is healthier, more human, more social, more integral'. In this regard, I am confident that America's outstanding academic and research institutions can make a vital contribution in the years ahead.

"A century ago, at the beginning of the Great War, which Pope Benedict XV termed a 'pointless slaughter', another notable American was born: the Cistercian monk Thomas Merton. He remains a source of spiritual inspiration and a guide for many people. In his autobiography he wrote: 'I came into the world. Free by nature, in the image of God, I was nevertheless the prisoner of my own violence and my own selfishness, in the image of the world into which I was born. That world was the picture of Hell, full of men like myself, loving God, and yet hating Him; born to love Him, living instead in fear of hopeless self-contradictory hungers'. Merton was above all a man of prayer, a thinker who challenged the certitudes of his time and opened new horizons for souls and for the Church. He was also a man of dialogue, a promoter of peace between peoples and religions.

"From this perspective of dialogue, I would like to recognise the efforts made in recent months to help overcome historic differences linked to painful episodes of the past. It is my duty to build bridges and to help all men and women, in any way possible, to do the same. When countries which have been at odds resume the path of dialogue—a dialogue which may have been interrupted for the most legitimate of reasons—new opportunities open up for all. This has required, and requires, courage and daring, which is not the same as irresponsibility. A good political leader is one who, with the interests of all in mind, seizes the moment in a spirit of openness and pragmatism. A good political leader always opts to initiate processes rather than possessing spaces.

"Being at the service of dialogue and peace also means being truly determined to minimize and, in the long term, to end the many armed conflicts throughout our world. Here we have to ask ourselves: Why are deadly weapons being sold to those who plan to inflict untold suffering on individuals and society? Sadly, the answer, as we all know, is simply for money: money that is drenched in blood, often innocent blood. In the face of this shameful and culpable silence, it is our duty to confront the problem and to stop the arms trade.

"Three sons and a daughter of this land, four individuals and four dreams: Lincoln, liberty; Martin Luther King, liberty in plurality and non-exclusion; Dorothy Day, social justice and the rights of persons; and Thomas Merton, the capacity for dialogue and openness to God.

Four representatives of the American people.

"I will end my visit to your country in Philadelphia, where I will take part in the World Meeting of Families. It is my wish that throughout my visit the family should be a recurrent theme. How essential the family has been to the building of this country! And how worthy it remains of our support and encouragement! Yet I cannot hide my concern for the family, which is threatened, perhaps as never before, from within and without. Fundamental relationships are being called into question, as is the very basis of marriage and the family. I can only reiterate the importance and, above all, the richness and the beauty of family life.

"In particular, I would like to call attention to those family members who are the most vulnerable, the young. For many of them, a future filled with countless possibilities beckons, yet so many others seem disoriented and aimless, trapped in a hopeless maze of violence, abuse and despair. Their problems are our problems. We cannot avoid them. We need to face them together, to talk about them and to seek effective solutions rather than getting bogged down in discussions. At the risk of oversimplifying, we might say that we live in a culture which pressures young people not to start a family, because they lack possibilities for the future. Yet this same culture presents others with so many options that they too are dissuaded from starting a family.

"A nation can be considered great when it defends liberty as Lincoln did, when it fosters a culture which enables people to 'dream' of full rights for all their brothers and sisters, as Martin Luther King sought to do; when it strives for justice and the cause of the oppressed, as Dorothy Day did by her tireless work, the fruit of a faith which becomes dialogue and sows peace in the contemplative style of Thomas Merton.

"In these remarks I have sought to present some of the richness of your cultural heritage, of the spirit of the American people. It is my desire that this spirit continue to develop and grow, so that as many young people as possible can inherit and dwell in a land which has inspired so many people to dream. God bless America!"

SOURCE: Holy See Press Office. Vatican Information Service. "The Pope at the United States Congress: political activity must promote the good of the person and be based on human dignity." September 24, 2015. http://visnews-en.blogspot.com/2015/09/the-pope-at-united-states-congress.html.

| DOCUMENT | *Pope Francis Canonizes Junipero Serra* |

September 24, 2015

Blessed Junipero Serra (1713–1784), known as the "Apostle of California", was canonised yesterday by Pope Francis during a solemn Mass celebrated in the National Shrine of the Immaculate Conception, the title under which, since 1847, the Virgin Mary is the patroness of the United States.

The new saint, born in Mallorca, Spain, was a missionary first in Mexico, where he learned the Pame language in order to teach the indigenous peoples the catechism and ordinary prayers, which he translated for them. He was also master of novices in the apostolic College of San Fernando. In 1767, the Jesuits were expelled from the missions of Baja California, which were entrusted to the Franciscans. Fr. Junipero was appointed Superior and arrived with 14 companions in the territory in 1760, where he founded the first mission of San Diego. He went on to found missions in Alta California: San Carlos de Monterrey, San Anselmo, San Gabriel and San Luis Obispo. In California alone he travelled 9,900 kilometres and 5,400 nautical miles to found new missions from which there derive the Franciscan names of Californian cities such as San Francisco, San Diego and Los Angeles. Serra was beatified by John Paul II in 1988.

In his homily the Pope cites St. Paul's words to the Philippians: "Rejoice in the Lord always! I say it again, rejoice!". "Paul tells us to rejoice; he practically orders us to rejoice. This command resonates with the desire we all have for a fulfilling life, a meaningful life, a joyful life. . . . Something deep within us invites us to rejoice and tells us not to settle for placebos which simply keep us comfortable. At the same time, though, we all know the struggles of everyday life. So much seems to stand in the way of this invitation to rejoice. Our daily routine can often lead us to a kind of glum apathy which gradually becomes a habit, with a fatal consequence: our hearts grow numb".

"We don't want apathy to guide our lives . . . or do we?" he continued. "We don't want the force of habit to rule our life . . . or do we? So we ought to ask ourselves: What can we do to keep our heart from growing numb, becoming anaesthetised? How do we make the joy of the Gospel increase and take deeper root in our lives? Jesus gives the answer. He said to his disciples then and he says it to us now: Go forth! Proclaim! The joy of the Gospel is something to be experienced, something to be known and lived only through giving it away, through giving ourselves away".

The spirit of the world "tells us to be like everyone else, to settle for what comes easy. Faced with this human way of thinking, 'we must regain the conviction that we need one another, that we have a shared responsibility for others and for the world'. It is the responsibility to proclaim the message of Jesus. For the source of our joy is 'an endless desire to show mercy, the fruit of our own experience of the power of the Father's infinite mercy'. Go out to all, proclaim by anointing and anoint by proclaiming. This is what the Lord tells us today. He tells us that a Christian finds joy in mission: Go out to people of every nation! A Christian experiences joy in following a command: Go forth and proclaim the good news! A Christian finds ever new joy in answering a call: Go forth and anoint!"

"Jesus sends His disciples out to all nations. To every people. We too were part of all those people of two thousand years ago. Jesus did not provide a short list of who is, or is not, worthy of receiving His message, His presence. Instead, He always embraced life as He saw it. In faces of pain, hunger, sickness and sin. In faces of the wounded, in thirst, weariness, doubt and pity. Far from expecting a beautiful life, smartly-dressed and neatly groomed, He embraced life as He found it. It made no difference whether it was dirty, unkempt, broken. Jesus said: Go out and tell the good news to everyone. Go out and in my name embrace life as it is, and not as you think it should be. Go out to the highways and byways, go out to tell the good news fearlessly, without prejudice, without superiority, without condescension, to all those who have lost the joy of living. Go out to proclaim the merciful embrace of the Father. Go out to those who are burdened by pain and failure, who feel that their lives are empty, and proclaim the 'folly' of a loving Father Who wants to anoint them with the oil of hope, the oil of salvation. Go out to proclaim the good news that error, deceitful illusions and falsehoods do not have the last word in a person's life. Go out with the balm which soothes wounds and heals hearts".

Mission is "never the fruit of a perfectly planned program or a well-organised manual. Mission is always the fruit of a life which knows what it is to be found and healed, encountered and forgiven. Mission is born of a constant experience of God's merciful anointing. The Church, the holy People of God, treads the dust-laden paths of history, so often traversed by conflict, injustice and violence, in order to encounter her children, our brothers and sisters. The holy and faithful People of God are not afraid of losing their way; they are afraid of becoming self-enclosed, frozen into elites, clinging to their own security. They know that self-enclosure, in all the many forms it takes, is the cause of so much apathy. So let us go out, let us go forth to offer everyone the life of Jesus Christ. The People of God can embrace everyone because we are the disciples of the One who knelt before his own to wash their feet.

"The reason we are here today is that many other people wanted to respond to that call. They believed that 'life grows by being given away, and it weakens in isolation and comfort'. We are heirs to the bold missionary spirit of so many men and women who preferred not to be 'shut up within structures which give us a false sense of security . . . within habits which make us feel safe, while at our door people are starving'. We are indebted to a tradition, a chain of witnesses who have made it possible for the good news of the Gospel to be, in every generation, both 'good' and 'new'".

"Today we remember one of those witnesses who testified to the joy of the Gospel in these lands, Fr. Junipero Serra. He was the embodiment of 'a Church which goes forth', a Church which sets out to bring everywhere the reconciling tenderness of God. Junipero Serra left his native land and its way of life. He was excited about blazing trails, going forth to meet many people, learning and valuing their particular customs and ways of life. He learned how to bring to birth and nurture God's life in the faces of everyone he met; he made them his brothers and sisters. Junipero sought to defend the dignity of the native community, to protect it from those who had mistreated and abused it. Mistreatment and wrongs which today still trouble us, especially because of the hurt which they cause in the lives of many people".

Father Serra "had a motto which inspired his life and work, a saying he lived his life by: siempre adelante! Keep moving forward! For him, this was the way to continue experiencing the joy of the Gospel, to keep his heart from growing numb, from being anaesthetised. He kept moving forward, because the Lord was waiting. He kept going, because his brothers and sisters were waiting. He kept going forward to the end of his life. Today, like him, may we be able to say: Forward! Let's keep moving forward!". . . .

Source: Holy See Press Office. Vatican Information Service. "The canonisation of Blessed Junipero Serra: Jesus has no 'shortlist' of people worthy of his message." September 24, 2015. http://visnews-en.blogspot .com/2015/09/the-canonisation-of-blessed-junipero.html.

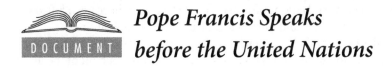

Pope Francis Speaks before the United Nations

September 26, 2015

[An introduction about the pope's remarks, provided by the Vatican Information Service, has been omitted.]

"Once again, following a tradition by which I feel honoured, the Secretary General of the United Nations has invited the Pope to address this distinguished assembly of nations. In my own name, and that of the entire Catholic community, I wish to express to you, Mr Ban Ki-moon, my heartfelt gratitude. I greet the Heads of State and Heads of Government present, as well as the ambassadors, diplomats and political and technical officials accompanying them, the personnel of the United Nations engaged in this 70th Session of the General Assembly, the personnel of the various programmes and agencies of the United Nations family, and all those who, in one way or another, take part in this meeting. Through you,

I also greet the citizens of all the nations represented in this hall. I thank you, each and all, for your efforts in the service of mankind.

"This is the fifth time that a Pope has visited the United Nations. I follow in the footsteps of my predecessors Paul VI, in 1965, John Paul II, in 1979 and 1995, and my most recent predecessor, now Pope Emeritus Benedict XVI, in 2008. All of them expressed their great esteem for the Organisation, which they considered the appropriate juridical and political response to this present moment of history, marked by our technical ability to overcome distances and frontiers and, apparently, to overcome all natural limits to the exercise of power. An essential response, inasmuch as technological power, in the hands of nationalistic or falsely universalist ideologies, is capable of perpetrating tremendous atrocities. I can only reiterate the appreciation expressed by my predecessors, in reaffirming the importance which the Catholic Church attaches to this Institution and the hope which she places in its activities.

"The United Nations is presently celebrating its seventieth anniversary. The history of this organised community of states is one of important common achievements over a period of unusually fast-paced changes. Without claiming to be exhaustive, we can mention the codification and development of international law, the establishment of international norms regarding human rights, advances in humanitarian law, the resolution of numerous conflicts, operations of peace-keeping and reconciliation, and any number of other accomplishments in every area of international activity and endeavour. All these achievements are lights which help to dispel the darkness of the disorder caused by unrestrained ambitions and collective forms of selfishness. Certainly, many grave problems remain to be resolved, yet it is also clear that, without all this international activity, mankind would not have been able to survive the unchecked use of its own possibilities. Every one of these political, juridical and technical advances is a path towards attaining the ideal of human fraternity and a means for its greater realisation.

"I also pay homage to all those men and women whose loyalty and self-sacrifice have benefited humanity as a whole in these past seventy years. In particular, I would recall today those who gave their lives for peace and reconciliation among peoples, from Dag Hammarskjöld to the many United Nations officials at every level who have been killed in the course of humanitarian missions, and missions of peace and reconciliation.

"Beyond these achievements, the experience of the past seventy years has made it clear that reform and adaptation to the times is always necessary in the pursuit of the ultimate goal of granting all countries, without exception, a share in, and a genuine and equitable influence on, decision-making processes. The need for greater equity is especially true in the case of those bodies with effective executive capability, such as the Security Council, the Financial Agencies and the groups or mechanisms specifically created to deal with economic crises. This will help limit every kind of abuse or usury, especially where developing countries are concerned. The International Financial Agencies are should care for the sustainable development of countries and should ensure that they are not subjected to oppressive lending systems which, far from promoting progress, subject people to mechanisms which generate greater poverty, exclusion and dependence.

"The work of the United Nations, according to the principles set forth in the Preamble and the first Articles of its founding Charter, can be seen as the development and promotion of the rule of law, based on the realisation that justice is an essential condition for achieving the ideal of universal fraternity. In this context, it is helpful to recall that the limitation of power is an idea implicit in the concept of law itself. To give to each his own, to cite the classic definition of justice, means that no human individual or group can consider itself absolute, permitted to bypass the dignity and the rights of other individuals or their social groupings. The effective distribution of power (political, economic, defence-related, technological, etc.) among a plurality of subjects, and the creation of a juridical system for regulating claims and interests, are one concrete way of limiting power. Yet today's world presents us with many false rights and—at the same time—broad sectors which are vulnerable, victims of power badly exercised: for example, the natural environment and the vast ranks of the excluded. These sectors are closely interconnected and made increasingly fragile by dominant political and economic relationships. That is why their rights must be forcefully affirmed, by working to protect the environment and by putting an end to exclusion.

"First, it must be stated that a true 'right of the environment' does exist, for two reasons. First, because we human beings are part of the environment. We live in communion with it, since the environment itself entails ethical limits which human activity must acknowledge and respect. Man, for all his remarkable gifts, which 'are signs of a uniqueness which transcends the spheres of physics and biology', is at the same time a part of these spheres. He possesses a body shaped by physical, chemical and biological elements, and can only survive and develop if the ecological environment is favourable. Any harm done to the environment, therefore, is harm done to humanity. Second, because every creature, particularly a living creature, has an intrinsic value, in its existence, its life, its beauty and its interdependence with other creatures. We Christians, together with the other monotheistic religions, believe that the universe is the fruit of a loving decision by the Creator, who permits man respectfully to use creation for the good of his fellow men and for the glory of the Creator; he is not authorised to abuse it, much less to destroy it. In all religions, the environment is a fundamental good.

"The misuse and destruction of the environment are also accompanied by a relentless process of exclusion. In effect, a selfish and boundless thirst for power and material prosperity leads both to the misuse of available natural resources and to the exclusion of the weak and disadvantaged, either because they are differently abled (handicapped), or because they lack adequate information and technical expertise, or are incapable of decisive political action. Economic and social exclusion is a complete denial of human fraternity and a grave offence against human rights and the environment. The poorest are those who suffer most from such offences, for three serious reasons: they are cast off by society, forced to live off what is discarded and suffer unjustly from the abuse of the environment. They are part of today's widespread and quietly growing 'culture of waste'.

"The dramatic reality [of] this whole situation of exclusion and inequality, with its evident effects, has led me, in union with the entire Christian people and many others, to take stock of my grave responsibility in this regard and to speak out, together with all those who are seeking urgently-needed and effective solutions. The adoption of the 2030 Agenda for Sustainable Development at the World Summit, which opens today, is an important sign of hope. I am similarly confident that the Paris Conference on Climatic Change will secure fundamental and effective agreements.

"Solemn commitments, however, are not enough, although they are certainly a necessary step toward solutions. The classic definition of justice which I mentioned earlier contains as one of its essential elements a constant and perpetual will: Iustitia est constans et perpetua voluntas ius sum cuique tribuendi. Our world demands of all government leaders a will which is effective, practical and constant, concrete steps and immediate measures for preserving and improving the natural environment and thus putting an end as quickly as possible to the phenomenon of social and economic exclusion, with its baneful consequences: human trafficking, the marketing of human organs and tissues, the sexual exploitation of boys and girls, slave labour, including prostitution, the drug and weapons trade, terrorism and international organised crime. Such is the magnitude of these situations and their toll in innocent lives, that we must avoid every temptation to fall into a declarationist nominalism which would assuage our consciences. We need to ensure that our institutions are truly effective in the struggle against all these scourges.

"The number and complexity of the problems require that we possess technical instruments of verification. But this involves two risks. We can rest content with the bureaucratic exercise of drawing up long lists of good proposals—goals, objectives and statistics—or we can think that a single theoretical and aprioristic solution will provide an answer to all the challenges. It must never be forgotten that political and economic activity is only effective when it is understood as a prudential activity, guided by a perennial concept of justice and constantly conscious of the fact that, above and beyond our plans and programmes, we are dealing with real men and women who live, struggle and suffer, and are often forced to live in great poverty, deprived of all rights.

"To enable these real men and women to escape from extreme poverty, we must allow them to be dignified agents of their own destiny. Integral human development and the full exercise of human dignity cannot be imposed. They must be built up and allowed to unfold for each individual, for every family, in communion with others, and in a right relationship with all those areas in which human social life develops—friends, communities, towns and cities, schools, businesses and unions, provinces, nations, etc. This presupposes and requires the right to education—also for girls (excluded in certain places)—which is ensured first and foremost by respecting and reinforcing the primary right of the family to educate its children, as well as the right of churches and social groups to support and assist families in the education of their children. Education conceived in this way is the basis for the implementation of the 2030 Agenda and for reclaiming the environment.

"At the same time, government leaders must do everything possible to ensure that all can have the minimum spiritual and material means needed to live in dignity and to create and support a family, which is the primary cell of any social development. In practical terms, this absolute minimum has three names: lodging, labour, and land; and one spiritual name: spiritual freedom, which includes religious freedom, the right to education and all other civil rights.

"For all this, the simplest and best measure and indicator of the implementation of the new Agenda for development will be effective, practical and immediate access, on the part of all, to essential material and spiritual goods: housing, dignified and properly remunerated employment, adequate food and drinking water; religious freedom and, more generally, spiritual freedom and education. These pillars of integral human development have a common foundation, which is the right to life and, more generally, what we could call the right to existence of human nature itself.

"The ecological crisis, and the large-scale destruction of biodiversity, can threaten the very existence of the human species. The baneful consequences of an irresponsible mismanagement of the global economy, guided only by ambition for wealth and power, must serve as a summons to a forthright reflection on man: 'man is not only a freedom which he creates for himself. Man does not create himself. He is spirit and will, but also nature'. Creation is compromised 'where we ourselves have the final word. . . . The misuse of creation begins when we no longer recognise any instance above ourselves, when we see nothing else but ourselves'. Consequently, the defence of the environment and the fight against exclusion demand that we recognise a moral law written into human nature itself, one which includes the natural difference between man and woman, and absolute respect for life in all its stages and dimensions.

"Without the recognition of certain incontestable natural ethical limits and without the immediate implementation of those pillars of integral human development, the ideal of 'saving succeeding generations from the scourge of war', and 'promoting social progress and better standards of life in larger freedom', risks becoming an unattainable illusion, or, even worse, idle chatter which serves as a cover for all kinds of abuse and corruption, or for carrying out an ideological colonisation by the imposition of anomalous models and lifestyles which are alien to people's identity and, in the end, irresponsible.

"War is the negation of all rights and a dramatic assault on the environment. If we want true integral human development for all, we must work tirelessly to avoid war between nations and peoples. To this end, there is a need to ensure the uncontested rule of law and tireless recourse to negotiation, mediation and arbitration, as proposed by the Charter of the United Nations, which constitutes truly a fundamental juridical norm. The experience of these seventy years since the founding of the United Nations in general, and in particular the experience of these first fifteen years of the third millennium, reveal both the effectiveness of the full application of international norms and the ineffectiveness of their lack of enforcement. When the Charter of the United Nations is respected and applied with transparency and sincerity, and without ulterior motives, as an obligatory reference point of justice and not as a means of masking spurious intentions, peaceful results will be obtained. When, on the other hand, the norm is considered simply as an instrument to be used whenever it proves favourable, and to be avoided when it is not, a true Pandora's box is opened, releasing uncontrollable forces which gravely harm defence-less populations, the cultural milieu and even the biological environment.

"The Preamble and the first Article of the Charter of the United Nations set forth the foundations of the international juridical framework: peace, the pacific solution of disputes and the development of friendly relations between the nations. Strongly opposed to such statements, and in practice denying them, is the constant tendency to the proliferation of arms, especially weapons of mass distraction, such as nuclear weapons. An ethics and a law based on the threat of mutual destruction—and possibly the destruction of all mankind—are self-contradictory and an affront to the entire framework of the United Nations, which would end up as 'nations united by fear and distrust'. There is urgent need to work for a world free of nuclear weapons, in full application of the non-proliferation Treaty, in letter and spirit, with the goal of a complete prohibition of these weapons.

"The recent agreement reached on the nuclear question in a sensitive region of Asia and the Middle East is proof of the potential of political good will and of law, exercised with sincerity, patience and constancy. I express my hope that this agreement will be lasting and efficacious, and bring forth the desired fruits with the cooperation of all the parties involved.

"In this sense, hard evidence is not lacking of the negative effects of military and political interventions which are not coordinated between members of the international community. For this reason, while regretting to have to do so, I must renew my repeated appeals regarding to the painful situation of the entire Middle East, North Africa and other African countries, where Christians, together with other cultural or ethnic groups, and even members of the majority religion who have no desire to be caught up in hatred and folly, have been forced to witness the destruction of their places of worship, their cultural and religious heritage, their houses and property, and have faced the alternative either of fleeing or of paying for their adhesion to good and to peace by their own lives, or by enslavement.

"These realities should serve as a grave summons to an examination of conscience on the part of those charged with the conduct of international affairs. Not only in cases of religious or cultural persecution, but in every situation of conflict, as in Ukraine, Syria, Iraq, Libya, South Sudan and the Great Lakes region, real human beings take precedence over partisan interests, however legitimate the latter may be. In wars and conflicts there are individual persons, our brothers and sisters, men and women, young and old, boys and girls who weep, suffer and die. Human beings who are easily discarded when our response is simply to draw up lists of problems, strategies and disagreements.

"As I wrote in my letter to the Secretary-General of the United Nations on 9 August 2014, 'the most basic understanding of human dignity compels the international community, particularly through the norms and mechanisms of international law, to do all that it can to stop and to prevent further systematic violence against ethnic and religious minorities' and to protect innocent peoples.

"Along the same lines I would mention another kind of conflict which is not always so open, yet is silently killing millions of people. Another kind of war experienced by many of our societies as a result of the narcotics trade. A war which is taken for granted and poorly fought. Drug trafficking is by its very nature accompanied by trafficking in persons, money laundering, the arms trade, child exploitation and other forms of corruption. A corruption which has penetrated to different levels of social, political, military, artistic and religious life, and, in many cases, has given rise to a parallel structure which threatens the credibility of our institutions.

"I began this speech recalling the visits of my predecessors. I would hope that my words will be taken above all as a continuation of the final words of the address of Pope Paul VI; although spoken almost exactly fifty years ago, they remain ever timely. I quote: 'The hour has come when a pause, a moment of recollection, reflection, even of prayer, is absolutely needed so that we may think back over our common origin, our history, our common destiny. The appeal to the moral conscience of man has never been as necessary as it is today. For the danger comes neither from progress nor from science; if these are used well, they can help to solve a great number of the serious problems besetting mankind. Among other things, human genius, well applied, will surely help to meet the grave challenges of ecological deterioration and of exclusion. As Paul VI said: 'The real danger comes from man, who has at his disposal ever more powerful instruments that are as well fitted to bring about ruin as they are to achieve lofty conquests'.

"The common home of all men and women must continue to rise on the foundations of a right understanding of universal fraternity and respect for the sacredness of every human life, of every man and every woman, the poor, the elderly, children, the infirm, the unborn, the unemployed, the abandoned, those considered disposable because they are only considered as part of a statistic. This common home of all men and women must also be built on the understanding of a certain sacredness of created nature.

"Such understanding and respect call for a higher degree of wisdom, one which accepts transcendence, self-transcendence, rejects the creation of an all-powerful elite, and recognises that the full meaning of individual and collective life is found in selfless service to others and in the sage and respectful use of creation for the common good. To repeat the words of Paul VI, 'the edifice of modern civilisation has to be built on spiritual principles, for they are the only ones capable not only of supporting it, but of shedding light on it'.

"El Gaucho Martin Fierro, a classic of literature in my native land, says: 'Brothers should stand by each other, because this is the first law; keep a true bond between you always, at every time—because if you fight among yourselves, you'll be devoured by those outside'. The contemporary world, so apparently connected, is experiencing a growing and steady social fragmentation, which places at risk 'the foundations of social life' and consequently leads to 'battles over conflicting interests'.

"The present time invites us to give priority to actions which generate new processes in society, so as to bear fruit in significant and positive historical events. We cannot permit ourselves to postpone 'certain agendas' for the future. The future demands of us critical and global decisions in the face of world-wide conflicts which increase the number of the excluded and those in need.

"The praiseworthy international juridical framework of the United Nations Organisation and of all its activities, like any other human endeavour, can be improved, yet it remains necessary; at the same time it can be the pledge of a secure and happy future for future generations. And so it will, if the representatives of the States can set aside partisan and ideological interests, and sincerely strive to serve the common good. I pray to Almighty God that this will be the case, and I assure you of my support and my prayers, and the support and prayers of all the faithful of the Catholic Church, that this Institution, all its member States, and each of its officials, will always render an effective service to mankind, a service respectful of diversity and capable of bringing out, for sake of the common good, the best in each people and in every individual. God bless you all".

Source: Holy See Press Office. Vatican Information Service. "Francis at the United Nations: critical and global decisions in the face of worldwide conflicts." September 26, 2015. http://visnews-en.blogspot.com/2015/09/francis-at-united-nations-critical-and.html.

OTHER HISTORIC DOCUMENTS OF INTEREST

FROM THIS VOLUME

FROM PREVIOUS *HISTORIC DOCUMENTS*

John Boehner Resigns and New House Speaker Is Elected

SEPTEMBER 25 AND OCTOBER 29, 2015

Shocking those both inside and outside his party, on September 25, 2015, Speaker of the House John Boehner, R-Ohio, announced that he would resign his leadership position and Congressional seat the following month. The move came amid deep dissatisfaction in Republican House ranks and belief that the Republican majority was not doing enough to subvert the power of the White House. After his announcement, Republicans struggled to choose a new speaker after the frontrunner dropped out of the race. Ultimately, just days before Boehner's departure, the House overwhelmingly elected Rep. Paul Ryan, R-Wis., the chair of the powerful House Ways and Means Committee, to assume the role of speaker.

BOEHNER'S SURPRISE RESIGNATION

Boehner, the son of a Cincinnati bar owner, frequently spoke about his blue-collar roots and his unlikely ascent from being one in a family of twelve children to Congress in 1990 to his election as Speaker of the House in 2011. Although Boehner oversaw the largest Republican majority since the late 1920s, his tenure in the powerful position was rife with challenges, in large part because House Republican members have become increasingly divided on their ideologies, reflecting a growing rift in the American public.

On the evening of September 24, 2015, Speaker Boehner told his chief of staff and his wife that he might announce his resignation the following morning. He had intended to make such an announcement two months later, on November 17, his birthday, with an official departure date set for the end of the year. However, political infighting and dissatisfaction with leadership within the Republican House ranks—and the threat of a no-confidence vote made by thirty Republicans—forced Boehner's hand. The morning of September 25, Boehner said that he went to his usual coffee shop and diner, at which point he had an overwhelming feeling that he was doing the right thing. When he returned to Capitol Hill, he called a closed door Republican caucus meeting, at which point he announced that he would resign the speakership, and his House seat, effective October 30.

Speaking at a press conference, Boehner said, "It had become clear to me that this prolonged leadership turmoil would do irreparable harm to the institution." Boehner, who became emotional at times, said the decision "isn't about me. It's about the people. It's about the institution." House Majority Leader Kevin McCarthy, R-Calif., who was widely rumored to be Boehner's replacement, said the Ohio congressman "will be missed because there is simply no one else like him. Now is the time for our conference to focus on healing and unifying to face the challenges ahead and always do what is best for the American people." Those in the Republican caucus meeting told media outlets that Boehner's announcement was met with shock, anger, and some tears. However, some of the more conservative members of the party, such as Kentucky's Rep. Tom Massie, said it was "time for new leadership."

After speaking with Boehner about his decision, President Barack Obama told the media that Boehner "has always conducted himself with courtesy and civility with me. He has kept his word when he made a commitment. He is somebody who has been gracious. And I think maybe most importantly, he's somebody who understands that in government . . . you don't get 100% of what you want, but you have to work with people who you disagree with—sometimes strongly—in order to do the people's business."

Boehner's announcement came just one week before an impending government shutdown predicated on the failure of both parties to reach an agreement on a budget. Boehner's resignation made it less likely that a shutdown would occur because Republicans and Democrats would now be more likely to agree to a clean short-term funding mechanism known as a continuing resolution (CR), and then work on a longer-term solution after Boehner's replacement was chosen.

House Republicans Struggle to Find a New Leader

Boehner was the first speaker to resign in the middle of a Congress since Rep. Jim Wright, D-Texas, who was pushed out in 1989 during an ethics scandal. As soon as Boehner's announcement was made public, the political jockeying began to choose his successor—who would need 218 votes in the House to ascend to the speakership—and the remainder of the leadership team. Rep. McCarthy was seen as the likely replacement; however, the most conservative Republican members did not believe a McCarthy-led House would mark the stark difference from Boehner that they were seeking. McCarthy had also struggled to balance the power between the most conservative wing of the party and its other members, and during his time as whip failed to deliver some key votes. In a letter sent to Republicans attempting to allay such fears, McCarthy wrote that he wants the party "to be much closer to the people we represent," adding, "[i]f elected speaker, I promise you that we will have the courage to lead the fight for our conservative principles and make our case to the American people."

Other names floated as possible contenders in the race included Rep. Ryan and Rep. Cathy McMorris Rodgers, R-Wash., both of whom declined to run, despite pressure from inside the House. A vote was set for the 247-member Republican caucus on October 8 to choose its candidate for speaker, who would then be voted on—along with a Democratic candidate—by the full House on October 29. If at that point the House could not agree, Boehner would remain speaker, and the process would continue until a new leader was chosen. The October 8 ballot was to feature three candidates—McCarthy, Rep. Jason Chaffetz, R-Utah, and Daniel Webster, R-Florida, a favorite of the Tea Party. Shortly before the vote, McCarthy unexpectedly withdrew himself from the running, canceling the vote and sending members scrambling to find replacements. Tea Party conservatives in the House said they would have refused to back McCarthy, which would have meant he would need strong Democratic support to reach the 218-vote threshold.

All eyes quickly turned to Ryan, who on October 8 again stated that he was "grateful for the encouragement I've received" but that he would "not be a candidate." However, one day later, the 2012 vice presidential nominee was rumored to be considering the job. The House recessed on October 9 for one week, returning to Washington on October 18 still without a clear contender for the nomination. The lack of a Republican candidate gave rise to discussion about whether a Democrat would ultimately be selected as speaker, or whether someone outside Congress would be selected, because there is nothing in the Constitution that requires the Speaker to be a current House member.

Under heavy pressure from his colleagues, on October 22, Ryan announced that he would seek the speakership. In an interview with CNN, Boehner explained that he used every tactic he could to encourage Ryan to take the job, including using "every ounce of Catholic guilt that I could on him." Ryan said in an interview that he ultimately accepted the nomination, despite his earlier resistance, because he "really felt like our party needed to unify."

RYAN CHOSEN AS NEW SPEAKER OF THE HOUSE

On October 28, the House Republican conference again met to choose their nominee for speaker. Ryan handily won with a reported 200 votes to Webster's forty-three, and one vote each for Rep. Marsha Blackburn, R-Tenn., and McCarthy. On October 29, Ryan faced off against former Speaker of the House Rep. Nancy Pelosi, D-Calif., during a vote of the full House. Ryan received 236 votes to Pelosi's 184. Three other candidates also received votes, including Webster who received nine, and former Secretary of State Colin Powell who received one. In total, nine Republicans did not vote for Ryan and three Democrats chose not to vote for Pelosi.

Speaking from the well of the House in his final address, Speaker Boehner tearfully called on his colleagues to "believe in the long, slow struggle. Believe in this country's ability to meet her challenges and to lead the world. And remember, you can't do a big job alone, especially this one." In assuming the speakership, Ryan reflected on the importance of the change being made. "The House is broken. We're not solving problems. We're adding to them, and I am not interested in laying blame. We are not settling scores. We are wiping the slate clean." Ryan spent a bulk of his speech calling on all House members to be more collaborative and to end the petty infighting that had plagued the body over the past several years. He said it would be a relief to the American public "if we finally got our acts together."

Five weeks after taking the helm of House Republican leadership, Ryan outlined his agenda for the party in the coming year. His number one goal, he said, "is to put together a complete alternative to the left's agenda." While specific policy details were left out, Ryan said that the Republican caucus would tackle an overhaul of the tax code, strengthen the military, develop international trade agreements, and further secure America from threats from terrorist groups such as the Islamic State of Iraq and the Levant (ISIL). While his colleagues have often attempted to rollback laws and Executive Orders signed by President Obama, Ryan indicated that while the party would not be cooperative on all White House proposals, he also did not intend to "undo what the president has done, as if we could time-travel back to 2009." Instead, the speaker's agenda was rooted in the future, and he encouraged his party to "show what we would do . . . looking forward to 2017 and beyond."

—Heather Kerrigan

Following is the text of a statement by former Speaker of the House John Boehner, R-Ohio, released on September 25, 2015, announcing his intent to resign his speakership; the text of Boehner's remarks on October 29, 2015, in his final speech before the House; and the text of a statement by Rep. Paul Ryan, R-Wis., on October 29, 2015, on his election to the position of Speaker of the House.

Rep. Boehner Resigns Speakership

September 25, 2015

House Speaker John Boehner (R-OH) today issued the following statement:

"My mission every day is to fight for a smaller, less costly, and more accountable government. Over the last five years, our majority has advanced conservative reforms that will help our children and their children. I am proud of what we have accomplished.

"The first job of any Speaker is to protect this institution that we all love. It was my plan to only serve as Speaker until the end of last year, but I stayed on to provide continuity to the Republican Conference and the House. It is my view, however, that prolonged leadership turmoil would do irreparable damage to the institution. To that end, I will resign the Speakership and my seat in Congress on October 30.

"Today, my heart is full with gratitude for my family, my colleagues, and the people of Ohio's Eighth District. God bless this great country that has given me—the son of a bar owner from Cincinnati—the chance to serve."

SOURCE: Office of the Speaker of the House. "Statement by House Speaker John Boehner." September 25, 2015. www.speaker.gov/press-release/statement-house-speaker-john-boehner.

Speaker Boehner Makes Final Address

October 29, 2015

My colleagues, I rise today to inform you that I will resign as Speaker of the House effective upon the election of my successor.

I will also resign as Representative of Ohio's Eighth District at the end of this month.

I leave with no regrets or burdens. If anything, I leave as I started—just a regular guy humbled by the chance to do a big job.

That's what I'm most proud of—that I'm still just me. . . .

But before I go, let me just express what an honor it is been to serve with all of you.

The people's House is, in my view, the great embodiment of the American idea.

Everyone comes from somewhere and is on some mission.

I come from a part of the world where we're used to working.

As far back as I can remember, I was working . . . going back to when I was eight or nine, throwing newspapers, working at my dad's bar on Saturdays from 5 am–2 pm for 2 dollars . . . TOTAL.

I never thought about it as coming up the easy way or the hard way.

It's just the Cincinnati way.

Our city takes its name from a great Roman general, Cincinnatus—a farmer who answered the call of his nation to lead, then surrendered his power and returned to his plow.

For me, it wasn't a farm—it was a small business.

And it wasn't so much a calling as it was a mission: to strive for a smaller, less costly, and more accountable government in Washington, DC.

How did we do?

Well, here are some facts. . . .

For the first time in nearly 20 years, we have made real entitlement reforms, saving trillions over the long term.

We have protected 99 percent of Americans from tax increases.

We are on track to save taxpayers $2.1 trillion over the next 10 years—the most significant spending reductions in modern history.

We have banned earmarks altogether.

We have protected this institution, and made it more open to the people.

And every day in this capital city, hundreds of kids from the toughest of neighborhoods are finally getting a decent education.

I am proud of these things.

But the mission is not complete, and the truth is, it may never be. . . .

One thing I came to realize is that this battle over the size and scope of government has been going on for more than 200 years.

And the forces of the status quo go to an awful lot of trouble to prevent change. Real change takes time.

That's certainly true for all the things I just mentioned.

Yes, freedom makes all things possible.

But patience is what makes all things real.

So believe in the long, slow struggle.

Believe in this country's ability to meet her challenges, and lead the world.

Believe in the decency of people to come together and do what can be done.

And remember, you can't do a big job alone, especially this one.

I'm grateful to my family. . . .

I'm grateful to my colleagues. . . .

I'm grateful to all the people who work in this institution . . . you've made me proud every day.

I'm grateful to my staff . . . I've always told them, you never leave Boehnerland, and that certainly goes for me too.

And I'm especially grateful to all my constituents and volunteers over the years. . . .

That includes a student at Miami University in Oxford, Ohio who was putting up signs for me during one of my very first campaigns in the early 90s.

His name was Paul Ryan.

I don't think he knew how to pronounce my name. . . .

But, as Cincinnatus understood, there's a difference between being asked to do something and being called to do something.

Paul is being called to serve, and I know he will serve that calling with grace and energy.

I wish him, and his family, all the best.

My colleagues, I've described my life as a chase for the American Dream.

That chase began at the bottom of a hill just off the main drag in Reading, Ohio.

At the top was a small house with a big family . . . a shining city in its own right.

The hill had twists. And it had turns. And even a few tears . . . nothing wrong with that.

But let me tell you, it was all just perfect.

Never forget, we are the luckiest people on the face of the Earth.

In America, you can do anything if you're willing to work hard and make the necessary sacrifices.

If you falter—and you will—you can just dust yourself off and keep on going.

Because hope always springs eternal.

And if you just do the right things for the right reasons, good things will happen.

And this, too, can really happen to you. . . .

SOURCE: Office of the Speaker of the House. "Farewell Address: This, Too, Can Really Happen to You." October 29, 2015. www.speaker.gov/press-release/farewell-address-too-can-really-happen-you.

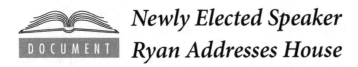

Newly Elected Speaker Ryan Addresses House

DOCUMENT

October 29, 2015

Thank you, Madam Leader. Before I begin, I want to thank the family and friends who flew in from Wisconsin and from all over to be here today. In the gallery, I have my mom, Betty; my sister, Janet; my brothers, Stan and Tobin; and more relatives than I can count. Most important of all, I want to recognize my wife, Janna, and our three kids: Liza, Charlie, and Sam.

I also want to thank Speaker Boehner. For almost five years, he led this House. And for nearly 25 years, he served it. Not many people can match his accomplishments: the offices he held, the laws he wrote. But what really sets John apart is he's a man of character—a true class act. He is, without question, the gentleman from Ohio. So please join me in saying, one last time, "Thank you, Mr. Speaker."

Now I know how he felt. It's not till you hold this gavel and stand in this spot and look out and see all 435 members of the House—as if all of America was sitting right in front of you. It's not till then that you feel it: the weight of responsibility, the gravity of the moment.

And standing here, I cannot help but think of something Harry Truman once said. The day after Franklin Roosevelt died and Truman became president, he told a group of reporters: "If you ever pray, pray for me now. . . . When they told me yesterday what had happened, I felt like the moon, the stars, and all the planets had fallen on me."

We all should feel that way. A lot is on our shoulders. So if you ever pray, pray for each other—Republicans for Democrats, Democrats for Republicans. And I don't mean pray for a conversion. Pray for a deeper understanding, because—when you're up here, you see it so clearly—wherever you come from, whatever you believe, we are all in the same boat.

I never thought I'd be the speaker. But early in my life, I wanted to serve in the House. I thought the place was exhilarating—because here, you could make a difference. If you had a good idea and worked hard, you could make it happen. You could improve people's lives. To me, the House represented the best of America: the boundless opportunity to do good.

But let's be frank: The House is broken. We are not solving problems. We are adding to them. And I am not interested in laying blame. We are not settling scores. We are wiping the slate clean. Neither the members nor the people are satisfied with how things are going. We need to make some changes, starting with how the House does business.

We need to let every member contribute—not once they have earned their stripes, but right now. I come at this job as a two-time committee chair. The committees should retake the lead in drafting all major legislation. If you know the issue, you should write the bill. Open up the process. Let people participate. And they might change their tune. A neglected minority will gum up the works. A respected minority will work in good faith. Instead of trying to stop the majority, they might try to become the majority.

In other words, we need to return to regular order. Now, I know that sounds like process. But it's actually a matter of principle. We are the body closest to the people. Every two years, we face the voters—and sometimes face the music. But we do not echo the people. We represent them. We are supposed to study up and do the homework that they cannot do. So when we do not follow regular order—when we rush to pass bills a lot of us do not understand—we are not doing our job. Only a fully functioning House can truly represent the people.

And if there were ever a time for us to step up, this would be that time. America does not feel strong anymore because the working people of America do not feel strong anymore. I'm talking about the people who mind the store and grow the food and walk the beat and pay the taxes and raise the family. They do not sit in this House. They do not have fancy titles. But they are the people who make this country work, and this House should work for them.

Here's the problem. They're working hard. They're paying a lot. They are trying to do right by their families. And they are going nowhere fast. They never get a raise. They never get a break. But the bills keep piling up—and the taxes and the debt. They are working harder than ever to get ahead. Yet they are falling further behind. And they feel robbed— cheated of their birthright. They are not asking for any favors. They just want a fair chance. And they are losing faith that they will ever get it. Then they look at Washington, and all they see is chaos.

What a relief to them it would be if we finally got our act together—what a weight off their shoulders. How reassuring it would be if we actually fixed the tax code, put patients in charge of their health care, grew our economy, strengthened our military, lifted people out of poverty, and paid down the debt. At this point, nothing could be more inspiring than a job well done. Nothing could stir the heart more than real, concrete results.

The cynics will scoff and say it's not possible. But you better believe we are going to try. We will not duck the tough issues. We will take them head on. We are going to do all we can so working people get their strength back and people not working get their lives back. No more favors for the few. Opportunity for all—that is our motto.

I often talk about the need for a vision. I'm not sure I ever said what I meant. We solve problems here—yes. We create a lot of them too. But at bottom, we vindicate a way of life. We show by our work that free people can govern themselves. They can solve their own problems. They can make their own decisions. They can deliberate, collaborate, and get the job done. We show self-government is not only more efficient and more effective; it is more fulfilling. In fact, we show it is that struggle, that hard work, the very achievement itself that makes us free.

That is what we do here. And we will not always agree—not all of us, not all of the time. But we should not hide our disagreements. We should embrace them. We have nothing to fear from honest differences honestly stated. If you have ideas, let's hear them. I believe a greater clarity between us can lead to a greater charity among us.

And there is every reason to have hope. When the first speaker took the gavel, he looked out at a room of 30 people, representing a nation of 3 million. Today, as I look out at you, we represent a nation of 300 million. So when I hear people say America does not have it—we are done, we are spent—I do not believe it. I believe, with every fiber of my being, we can renew the America Idea. Now, our task is to make us all believe.

My friends, you have done me a great honor. The people of this country have done all of us a great honor. Now, let's prove ourselves worthy of it. Let's seize the moment. Let's rise to the occasion. And when we are done, let us say we left the people—all the people—more united, happy, and free. Thank you.

SOURCE: Office of the Speaker of the House. "Speaker Ryan's Remarks to the House of Representatives." October 29, 2015. www.speaker.gov/press-release/speaker-ryans-remarks-house-representatives.

OTHER HISTORIC DOCUMENTS OF INTEREST

FROM PREVIOUS *HISTORIC DOCUMENTS*

October

U.S. and Doctors Without Borders Officials on Kunduz Airstrike and Troop Withdrawal

OCTOBER 3, 6, 7, AND 15, 2015

In September and October 2015, the fight against the Taliban in Afghanistan centered on the city of Kunduz, where Taliban forces had taken control. Over the course of two weeks, American troops supported Afghan forces to root out Taliban insurgents and retake the city. During this timeframe, a U.S. airstrike hit a Doctors Without Borders (*Médecins Sans Frontières*, or MSF) hospital, which the United States considered collateral damage incurred during operations, while international aid organizations condemned the attack as a war crime. Although civilian casualties inadvertently caused by coalition efforts account for a miniscule portion of those killed in the war in Afghanistan, each instance is given greater import because it reignites questions about whether foreign troops should still be in Afghanistan and it also serves as a rallying cry for insurgents, who use civilian deaths as a recruitment tool.

Less than two weeks after the airstrike in Afghanistan, President Barack Obama announced that he would scale back his earlier promises for a significant troop drawdown at the end of 2016, because of the continuing need in Afghanistan for U.S. forces. The move was welcomed by Afghan officials.

U.S. Airstrike Hits Doctors Without Borders Hospital

On October 3, an MSF-run hospital in Kunduz, Afghanistan, was hit by a U.S. airstrike. At least forty-two were killed in the attack, and thirty-seven were wounded. Fourteen of those killed were MSF staff, and three were children. According to those on the scene, the hospital was under attack for thirty to forty-five minutes and more than 100 patients and caretakers were inside the facility at the time. The facility was the only specialized trauma center in northeastern Afghanistan.

A statement from the U.S. military coalition indicated there was evidence that "insurgents . . . were directly firing upon U.S. service members" in the area which led to one American airstrike that hit a "medical facility." The statement did not indicate that multiple bombs hit the facility, as witnesses stated. Sayed Sarwar Hussaini, the spokesperson for Kunduz police, supported the U.S. version of events and said that there was evidence that Taliban fighters were in fact using the hospital as a staging ground for attacks, something MSF denied.

MSF and the United Nations immediately responded, with Zeid Ra'ad al-Hussein, the United Nations High Commissioner for Human Rights, stating that the attack was "tragic, inexcusable and, possibly, even criminal," while Meinie Nicolai, president of MSF, called the attack "abhorrent and a grave violation of international humanitarian law." Nicolai further rejected the U.S. notion that the "horrific loss of life will simply be dismissed as 'collateral damage.'" MSF called for an investigation to be carried out by the International Humanitarian Fact-Finding Commission into whether the U.S. airstrike constituted a breach of the Geneva Conventions. "This was not just an attack on our hospital—it was an attack on the Geneva Conventions. This cannot be tolerated. These Conventions govern the rules of war and were established to protect civilians in conflicts—including patients, medical workers and facilities. They bring some humanity into what is otherwise an inhumane situation," said Dr. Joanne Liu, MSF's international president. Afghan president Ashraf Ghani also said in a press release that "Afghan and foreign forces alike must put in serious efforts not to target public places in military operations."

Initially, it was unclear whether the United States knew that the facility was a hospital, or whether it was targeting the Taliban fighters who had reportedly been visiting the facility for treatment in the days leading up to the bombing. According to MSF, however, the hospital had given its precise GPS coordinates to the U.S. coalition multiple times to ensure the security of its staff and patients, most recently three days prior to the bombing. President Barack Obama promised that the Department of Defense would carry out an investigation into the bombing and that he "will await the results of that inquiry before making a definitive judgment as to the circumstances of this tragedy."

REPORTS ON AIRSTRIKE RELEASED

On November 5, MSF released its own review of the attack on the hospital in Kunduz. According to the report, the airstrikes began at 2:00 a.m., lasted for one hour and fifteen minutes, and were followed by shooting directed at those who were fleeing the facility. "Many staff describe seeing people being shot, most likely from the plane, as people tried to flee the main hospital building that was being hit with each airstrike," the report stated. According to the report, staff at the hospital made multiple attempts to contact the Afghan government and the Department of Defense to stop the attack. Despite claims by the U.S. government, the report indicated that "from all MSF accounts, there was no shooting from or around the Trauma Centre and the compound was in full MSF control with our rules and procedures fully respected." It did indicate that twenty Taliban fighters were in the facility at the time seeking treatment, but reiterated that it is the mission of MSF to treat all patients seeking care, regardless of their affiliation. In response to the report's release, Department of Defense spokesperson Capt. Jeff Davis said that the United States remained committed to repairing any damage done and was working "closely with MSF in identifying the victims, both those killed and wounded, so that we can conclude our investigations and proceed with follow-on actions to include condolence payments."

Less than three weeks later, the Department of Defense announced that its own internal investigation had concluded that "avoidable human error" was to blame in the bombing of the MSF facility. According to General John F. Campbell, the top American military commander in Afghanistan, the troops who carried out the bombing were using the gunship's targeting system, which initially pointed them to an empty field. Determining that was not the appropriate target, the troops instead turned to the nearest building, which happened to be the MSF hospital. Campbell said that a number of troops were suspended in relation to the findings. "This was a tragic but avoidable accident caused primarily by human error," Campbell said. "The medical facility was misidentified as a target by U.S.

personnel who believed they were striking a different building several hundred meters away where there were reports of combatants." The 3,000-page internal report was not released to the public.

In response to the Department of Defense announcement, Christopher Stokes, MSF's general director, said, "The U.S. version of events presented today leaves MSF with more questions than answers," and he added that "the frightening catalog of errors outlined today illustrates gross negligence on the part of U.S. forces and violations of the rules of war." In particular, the group disagreed with the timeline presented by the Department of Defense, which indicated that the bombing was called off at 2:37 a.m., seventeen minutes after a message was received from MSF. This sharply contradicts eyewitness reports that the attack lasted for more than an hour.

On December 9, MSF sent a petition to the White House asking President Obama to approve an independent investigation into the attack. "Only a full accounting by an independent, international body can restore our confidence in the commitments of the United States to uphold the laws of war, which prohibit such attacks on hospitals in the strongest terms," said Jason Cone, MSF-USA executive director, adding that "it is not sufficient for the perpetrators of attacks on medical facilities to be the only investigators." As of the end of 2015, the White House had not responded to the petition.

PRESIDENT OBAMA ANNOUNCES CHANGE IN TROOP STATUS IN AFGHANISTAN

In May 2014, President Obama announced from the Rose Garden his intent to reduce troop levels in Afghanistan to 1,000 by the end of 2016, down from a peak of 100,000, and that those remaining troops would be stationed primarily in Kabul where they would be responsible for training Afghan militia and assist in information gathering activities aimed at combatting terrorist cells. On October 15, 2015, Obama announced that, given the tenuous security situation in the nation, he would instead keep 5,500 troops in Afghanistan until 2017 in the cities of Kabul, Bagram, Jalalabad, and Kandahar. "Afghan forces are still not as strong as they need to be," the president said, adding that "the Taliban has made gains, particularly in rural areas, and can still launch deadly attacks in cities, including Kabul." The larger force will still be responsible for training and advising the Afghan army, but it will also play a larger role in counterterrorism efforts, including the use of drone strikes, and searching for al Qaeda and ISIL fighters. "I will not allow Afghanistan to be used as safe haven for terrorists to attack our nation again," Obama said.

According to the White House, the decision was made following months of meetings between Afghan officials, presidential advisers, and the National Security Council, and implementation was accelerated after the Taliban captured Kunduz, before the city was retaken by Afghan forces with the assistance of U.S. support. The president maintained that it was not his intent to keep America in an endless ground war in Afghanistan and that he would begin additional troop withdrawals as early as the security situation dictated. He also indicated that the decision to change the drawdown plan was "consistent with the overall vision that we've had" in Afghanistan. According to Obama, "we anticipated, as we were drawing down troops, that there would be times where we might need to slow things down or fill gaps in Afghan capacity. And this is a reflection of that."

Afghan officials welcomed the president's decision to leave a larger U.S. presence in the nation. Unlike his predecessor, President Ghani had been pushing for the United States to extend its troop presence and continue providing support to Afghan forces. "Our security [forces] have shown the will and capability to fight, but we still need the support of our allies, especially the United States," said Mohammad Daud Sultanzoy, an ally of Ghani.

—Heather Kerrigan

Following is an October 3, 2015, press release from Doctors Without Borders (MSF) detailing the attack on their hospital in Kunduz; a statement by Secretary of Defense Ash Carter on October 3, 2015, responding to the MSF hospital bombing; a press release on October 3, 2015, from Afghan president Ashraf Ghani expressing his sadness about the hospital bombing; an October 6, 2015, statement by Secretary of Defense Ash Carter expressing condolences to those impacted by the accidental airstrike; an October 7, 2015, speech by Dr. Joanne Liu, MSF's international president, calling for an independent investigation of the bombing; the text of a statement on October 10, 2015, from the Department of Defense announcing condolence payments for those affected by the hospital bombing; and an October 15, 2015, statement by President Barack Obama announcing the maintenance of troop levels in Afghanistan.

DOCUMENT

Doctors Without Borders Details Attack

October 3, 2015

At 2:10am on Saturday 3 October the Médecins Sans Frontières' (MSF) Trauma centre in Kunduz was hit several times during sustained bombing and was very badly damaged.

Three MSF staff are confirmed dead and more than 30 are unaccounted for. The medical team is working around the clock to do everything possible for the safety of patients and hospital staff.

"We are deeply shocked by the attack, the killing of our staff and patients and the heavy toll it has inflicted on healthcare in Kunduz," says Bart Janssens, MSF Director of Operations. "We do not yet have the final casualty figures, but our medical team are providing first aid and treating the injured patients and MSF personnel and accounting for the deceased. We urge all parties to respect the safety of health facilities and staff."

Since fighting broke out on Monday, MSF has treated 394 wounded. When the aerial attack occurred this morning we had 105 patients and their care-takers in the hospital and over 80 MSF international and national staff present.

MSF's hospital is the only facility of its kind in the whole north-eastern region of Afghanistan, providing free life- and limb-saving trauma care. MSF doctors treat all people according to their medical needs and do not make distinctions based on a patient's ethnicity, religious beliefs or political affiliation.

SOURCE: Medecins Sans Frontieres. "Afghanistan: MSF staff killed and hospital partially destroyed in Kunduz." October 3, 2015. www.msf.org/article/afghanistan-msf-staff-killed-and-hospital-partially-destroyed-kunduz.

Secretary of Defense
Responds to Hospital Bombing

October 3, 2015

Overnight I learned of a tragic incident involving a Doctors without Borders hospital in Kunduz, Afghanistan, that came under fire. The area has been the scene of intense fighting the last few days. U.S. forces in support of Afghan Security Forces were operating nearby, as were Taliban fighters.

While we are still trying to determine exactly what happened, I want to extend my thoughts and prayers to everyone affected.

A full investigation into the tragic incident is underway in coordination with the Afghan government. At this difficult moment, we will continue to work with our Afghan partners to try and end the ongoing violence in and around Kunduz.

SOURCE: U.S. Department of Defense. "Statement from Secretary of Defense Ash Carter on the Situation in Kunduz." October 3, 2015. www.defense.gov/News/News-Releases/News-Release-View/Article/621743/statement-from-secretary-of-defense-ash-carter-on-the-situation-in-kunduz.

Afghan President Expresses
Sorrow about Hospital Bombing

October 3, 2015

ARG, Kabul: Mohammad Ashraf Ghani, President of the Islamic Republic of Afghanistan, expresses his deep sorrow over the killing and wounding of civilians including the staff and doctors of Doctors without Borders as a result of the ongoing military operations in Kunduz Province.

The commander of Resolute Support Mission, General John Campbell in a telephone call to President Ghani, provided explanations about the incident and offered condolences to those affected. Both the President and Gen. Campbell agreed to launch a joint and thorough investigation.

The President said that the Afghan Security and Defense Forces and our allies in the Resolute Support Mission are obliged to ensure safety of civilians and exercise full precision in military operations.

President Ghani reiterates that the Afghan and foreign forces alike must put in serious efforts not to target public places in military operations.

SOURCE: Office of the President of the Islamic Republic of Afghanistan. "President Ghani expresses deep sorrow over killing of Civilians in Kunduz." October 3, 2015. http://president.gov.af/en/news/president-ghani-expresses-deep-sorrow-over-killing-of-civilians-in-kunduz.

Secretary Carter
Responds to Hospital Bombing

October 6, 2015

Today, Commander of U.S. forces in Afghanistan General John Campbell informed Congress that a U.S. military airstrike in Kunduz, Afghanistan, to support Afghan forces on the ground resulted in a mistaken attack on a Doctors Without Borders field hospital. Doctors Without Borders does important work all around the world, and the Department of Defense deeply regrets the loss of innocent lives that resulted from this tragic event. The investigation into how this could have happened is continuing, and we are fully supporting NATO and Afghanistan's concurrent investigations. We will complete our investigation as soon as possible and provide the facts as they become available. The U.S. military takes the greatest care in our operations to prevent the loss of innocent life, and when we make mistakes, we own up to them. That's exactly what we're doing right now. Through a full and transparent investigation, we will do everything we can to understand this tragic incident, learn from it, and hold people accountable as necessary.

SOURCE: U.S. Department of Defense. "Statement by Secretary of Defense Ash Carter on the Tragedy in Kunduz, Afghanistan." October 6, 2015. www.defense.gov/News/News-Releases/News-Release-View/Article/622041/statement-by-secretary-of-defense-ash-carter-on-the-tragedy-in-kunduz-afghanist.

Doctors Without Borders
Calls for Independent Investigation

October 7, 2015

On Saturday morning, MSF patients and staff killed in Kunduz joined the countless number of people who have been killed around the world in conflict zones and referred to as 'collateral damage' or as an 'inevitable consequence of war'. International humanitarian law is not about 'mistakes'. It is about intention, facts and why.

The US attack on the MSF hospital in Kunduz was the biggest loss of life for our organisation in an airstrike. Tens of thousands of people in Kunduz can no longer receive medical care now when they need it most. Today we say: enough. Even war has rules.

In Kunduz our patients burned in their beds. MSF doctors, nurses and other staff were killed as they worked. Our colleagues had to operate on each other. One of our doctors died on an improvised operating table—an office desk—while his colleagues tried to save his life.

Today we pay tribute to those who died in this abhorrent attack. And we pay tribute to those MSF staff who, while watching their colleagues die and with their hospital still on fire, carried on treating the wounded.

This was not just an attack on our hospital—it was an attack on the Geneva Conventions. This cannot be tolerated. These Conventions govern the rules of war and were established to protect civilians in conflicts—including patients, medical workers and facilities. They bring some humanity into what is otherwise an inhumane situation.

The Geneva Conventions are not just an abstract legal framework—they are the difference between life and death for medical teams on the frontline. They are what allow patients to access our health facilities safely and what allows us to provide healthcare without being targeted.

It is precisely because attacking hospitals in war zones is prohibited that we expected to be protected. And yet, ten patients including 3 children, and 12 MSF staff were killed in the aerial raids.

The facts and circumstances of this attack must be investigated independently and impartially, particularly given the inconsistencies in the US and Afghan accounts of what happened over recent days. We cannot rely on only internal military investigations by the US, NATO and Afghan forces.

Today we announce that we are seeking an investigation into the Kunduz attack by the International Humanitarian Fact-Finding Commission. This Commission was established in the Additional Protocols of the Geneva Conventions and is the only permanent body set up specifically to investigate violations of international humanitarian law. We ask signatory States to activate the Commission to establish the truth and to reassert the protected status of hospitals in conflict.

Though this body has existed since 1991, the Commission has not yet been used. It requires one of the 76 signatory States to sponsor an inquiry. Governments up to now have been too polite or afraid to set a precedent. The tool exists and it is time it is activated.

It is unacceptable that States hide behind 'gentlemen's agreements' and in doing so create a free for all and an environment of impunity. It is unacceptable that the bombing of a hospital and the killing of staff and patients can be dismissed as collateral damage or brushed aside as a mistake.

Today we are fighting back for the respect of the Geneva Conventions. As doctors, we are fighting back for the sake of our patients. We need you, as members of the public, to stand with us to insist that even wars have rules.

Source: Médecins Sans Frontières. "Afghanistan: Enough. Even war has rules." October 7, 2015. www .msf.org/article/afghanistan-enough-even-war-has-rules.

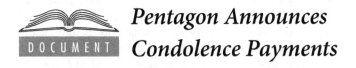

Pentagon Announces Condolence Payments

October 10, 2015

The Department of Defense believes it is important to address the consequences of the tragic incident at the Doctors Without Borders hospital in Kunduz, Afghanistan. One step the Department can take is to make condolence payments to civilian non-combatants injured and the families of civilian non-combatants killed as a result of U.S. military operations. Under the Commanders' Emergency Response Program (CERP), U.S. Forces-Afghanistan has the authority to make condolence payments and payments toward repair of the hospital. USFOR-A will work with those affected to determine appropriate payments. If necessary and appropriate, the administration will seek additional authority from the Congress.

Source: U.S. Department of Defense. "Statement from Pentagon Press Secretary Peter Cook on Kunduz Condolence Payments." October 10, 2015. www.defense.gov/News/News-Releases/News-Release-View/Article/622713/statement-from-pentagon-press-secretary-peter-cook-on-kunduz-condolence-payments.

DOCUMENT

President Obama Announces Change in Troop Levels in Afghanistan

October 15, 2015

Good morning. Last December, more than 13 years after our Nation was attacked by Al Qaida on 9/11, America's combat mission in Afghanistan came to a responsible end. That milestone was achieved thanks to the courage and the skill of our military, our intelligence, and civilian personnel. They served there with extraordinary skill and valor, and it's worth remembering especially the more than 2,200 American patriots who made the ultimate sacrifice in Afghanistan.

I visited our troops in Afghanistan last year to thank them on behalf of a grateful nation. I told them they could take great pride in the progress that they helped achieve. They struck devastating blows against the Al Qaida leadership in the tribal regions, delivered justice to Usama bin Laden, prevented terrorist attacks, and saved American lives. They pushed the Taliban back so the Afghan people could reclaim their communities, send their daughters to school, and improve their lives. Our troops trained Afghan forces so they could take the lead for their own security and protect Afghans as they voted in historic elections, leading to the first democratic transfer of power in their country's history.

Today, American forces no longer patrol Afghan villages or valleys. Our troops are not engaged in major ground combat against the Taliban. Those missions now belong to Afghans, who are fully responsible for securing their country.

But as I've said before, while America's combat mission in Afghanistan may be over, our commitment to Afghanistan and its people endures. As Commander in Chief, I will not allow Afghanistan to be used as safe haven for terrorists to attack our Nation again. Our forces therefore remain engaged in two narrow, but critical, missions: training Afghan forces and supporting counterterrorism operations against the remnants of Al Qaida. Of course, compared to the 100,000 troops we once had in Afghanistan, today fewer than 10,000 remain, in support of these very focused missions.

I meet regularly with my national security team, including commanders in Afghanistan, to continually assess, honestly, the situation on the ground, to determine where our strategy is working and where we may need greater flexibility. I have insisted consistently that our strategy focus on the development of a sustainable Afghan capacity and self-sufficiency. And when we've needed additional forces to advance that goal or we've needed to make adjustments in terms of our timetables, then we've made those adjustments. Today I want to update the American people on our efforts.

Since taking the lead for security earlier this year, Afghan forces have continued to step up. This has been the first fighting season where Afghans have largely been on their own. And they are fighting for their country bravely and tenaciously. Afghan forces continue to hold most urban areas. And when the Taliban has made gains, as is—as in Kunduz, Afghan forces backed by coalition support have been able to push them back. This has come at a very heavy price. This year alone, thousands of Afghan troops and police have lost their lives, as have many Afghan civilians. At the same time, Afghan forces are still not as strong as they need to be. They are developing critical capabilities: intelligence, logistics, aviation, command and control. And meanwhile, the Taliban has made gains, particularly in rural areas, and can still launch deadly attacks in cities, including Kabul. Much of this was predictable. We understood that as we transitioned, that the Taliban would try to exploit some of our movements out of particular areas and that it would take time for Afghan security forces to strengthen. Pressure from Pakistan has resulted in more Al Qaida coming into Afghanistan, and we've seen the emergence of an ISIL presence. The bottom line is, in key areas of the country, the security situation is still very fragile, and in some places, there is risk of deterioration.

Fortunately, in President Ghani and Chief Executive Abdullah, there is a national unity Government that supports a strong partnership with the United States. During their visit earlier this year, President Ghani and I agreed to continue our counterterrorism cooperation, and he has asked for continued support as Afghan forces grow stronger.

Following consultations with my entire national security team, as well as our international partners and Members of Congress, President Ghani, and Chief Executive Abdullah, I'm therefore announcing the following steps, which I am convinced offer the best possibility for lasting progress in Afghanistan.

First, I've decided to maintain our current posture of 9,800 troops in Afghanistan through most of next year, 2016. Their mission will not change. Our troops will continue to pursue those two narrow tasks that I outlined earlier: training Afghan forces and going after Al Qaida. But maintaining our current posture through most of next year, rather than a more rapid drawdown, will allow us to sustain our efforts to train and assist Afghan forces as they grow stronger, not only during this fighting season, but into the next one.

Second, I have decided that instead of going down to a normal Embassy presence in Kabul by the end of 2016, we will maintain 5,500 troops at a small number of bases, including at Bagram, Jalalabad in the east, and Kandahar in the south.

Again, the mission will not change. Our troops will focus on training Afghans and counterterrorism operations. But these bases will give us the presence and the reach our forces require to achieve their mission. In this sense, Afghanistan is a key piece of the network of counterterrorism partnerships that we need, from South Asia to Africa, to deal more broadly with terrorist threats quickly and prevent attacks against our homeland.

Third, we will work with allies and partners to align the steps I am announcing today with their own presence in Afghanistan after 2016. In Afghanistan, we are part of a 42-nation coalition, and our NATO allies and partners can continue to play an indispensable role in helping Afghanistan strengthen its security forces, including respect for human rights.

And finally, because governance and development remain the foundation for stability and progress in Afghanistan, we will continue to support President Ghani and the national unity Government as they pursue critical reforms. New provincial Governors have been appointed, and President Ghani is working to combat corruption, strengthen institutions, and uphold rule of law. As I told President Ghani and Chief Executive Abdullah yesterday, efforts that deliver progress and justice for the Afghan people will continue to have the strong support of the United States. And we cannot separate the importance of governance with the issues of security. The more effective these reforms happen, the better off the security situation is going to be. We also discussed American support of an Afghan-led reconciliation process. By now it should be clear to the Taliban and all who oppose Afghanistan's progress the only real way to achieve the full drawdown of U.S. and foreign troops from Afghanistan is through a lasting political settlement with the Afghan Government. And likewise, sanctuaries for the Taliban and other terrorists must end. And next week, I'll host Prime Minister Sharif of Pakistan, and I will continue to urge all parties in the region to press the Taliban to return to peace talks and to do their part in pursuit of the peace that Afghans deserve.

In closing, I want to speak directly to those whose lives are most directly affected by the decisions I'm announcing today. To the Afghan people, who have suffered so much: Americans' commitment to you and to a secure, stable, and unified Afghanistan, that remains firm. Our two nations have forged a strategic partnership for the long term. And as you defend and build your country, today is a reminder that the United States keeps our commitments.

And to our men and women in uniform: I know that this means that some of you will rotate back into Afghanistan. With the end of our combat mission, this is not like 2010, when nearly 500 Americans were killed and many more were injured. But still, Afghanistan remains dangerous; 25 brave Americans have given their lives there this year.

I do not send you into harm's way lightly. It's the most solemn decision that I make. I know the wages of war in the wounded warriors I visit in the hospital and in the grief of Gold Star families. But as your Commander in Chief, I believe this mission is vital to our national security interests in preventing terrorist attacks against our citizens and our Nation.

And to the American people: I know that many of you have grown weary of this conflict. As you are well aware, I do not support the idea of endless war, and I have repeatedly argued against marching into open-ended military conflicts that do not serve our core security interests.

Yet, given what's at stake in Afghanistan and the opportunity for a stable and committed ally that can partner with us in preventing the emergence of future threats and the fact that we have an international coalition, I am firmly convinced that we should make this extra effort. In the Afghan Government, we have a serious partner who wants our help. And the majority of the Afghan people share our goals. We have a bilateral security agreement to guide our cooperation. And every single day, Afghan forces are out there fighting and dying to protect their country. They're not looking for us to do it for them.

I'm speaking of the Afghan army cadet who grew up seeing bombings and attacks on innocent civilians who said, "Because of this, I took the decision to join the army, to try and save innocent people's lives." Or the police officer training to defuse explosives. "I know it's dangerous work," he says, but "I have always had a dream of wearing the uniform of Afghanistan, serving my people and defending my country."

Or the Afghan commando, a hardened veteran of many missions, who said, "If I start telling you the stories of my life, I might start crying." He serves, he said, because "the faster we bring peace, the faster we can bring education, and the stronger our unity will grow. Only if these things happen will Afghanistan be able to stand up for itself."

My fellow Americans, after so many years of war, Afghanistan will not be a perfect place. It's a poor country that will have to work hard on its development. There will continue to be contested areas. But Afghans like these are standing up for their country. If they were to fail, it would endanger the security of us all. And we've made an enormous investment in a stable Afghanistan. Afghans are making difficult, but genuine, progress. This modest, but meaningful, extension of our presence—while sticking to our current, narrow missions—can make a real difference. It's the right thing to do.

May God bless our troops and all who keep us safe. And may God continue to bless the United States of America.

The President's Afghanistan Policy

Q. Mr. President, can you tell us how disappointing this decision is for you? Is this a—can you tell us how disappointing this decision is for you?

The President. This decision is not disappointing. Continually, my goal has been to make sure that we give every opportunity for Afghanistan to succeed while we're still making sure that we're meeting our core missions.

And as I've continually said, my approach is to assess the situation on the ground, figure out what's working, figure out what's not working, make adjustments where necessary. This isn't the first time those adjustments have been made; this won't probably be the last.

What I'm encouraged by is the fact that we have a Government that is serious about trying to deliver security and the prospects of a better life for the Afghan people. We have a clear majority of the Afghans who want to partner with us and the international community to achieve those goals. We have a bilateral security arrangement that ensures that our troops can operate in ways that protect them while still achieving their mission. And we've always known that we had to maintain a counterterrorism operation in that region in order to tamp down any reemergence of active Al Qaida networks or other networks that might do us harm.

So this is consistent with the overall vision that we've had. And frankly, we anticipated, as we were drawing down troops, that there would be times where we might need to slow things down or fill gaps in Afghan capacity. And this is a reflection of that. And it's a dangerous area.

So part of what we're constantly trying to balance is making sure that Afghans are out there, they're doing what they need to do, but that we are giving them a chance to succeed and that we're making sure that our force posture in the area for conducting those narrow missions that we need to conduct, we can do so relatively safely. There are still risks involved, but force protection, the ability of our Embassies to operate effectively, those things all factor in.

And so we've got to constantly review these approaches. The important thing I want to emphasize, though, is, is that the nature of the mission has not changed. And the cessation of our combat role has not changed.

Now, the 25 military and civilians who were killed last year, that always weighs on my mind. And 25 deaths are 25 too many, particularly for the families of the fallen. But understand, relative to what was involved when we were in an active combat role and actively engaged in war in Afghanistan was a different, very different scenario.

So here, you have a situation where we have clarity about what our mission is. We've got a partner who wants to work with us. We're going to continually make adjustments to ensure that we give the best possibilities for success. And I suspect that we will continue to evaluate this going forward, as will the next President. And as conditions improve, we'll be in a position to make further adjustments.

But I'm absolutely confident this is the right thing to do. And I'm not disappointed because my view has always been, how do we achieve our goals while minimizing the strain and exposure on our men and women in uniform and make sure that we are constantly encouraging and sending a message to the Afghan people, this is their country, and they've got to defend it? But we're going to be a steady partner for them.

Okay? Thank you, everybody.

SOURCE: Executive Office of the President. "Remarks on United States Military Strategy in Afghanistan and an Exchange With Reporters." October 15, 2015. *Compilation of Presidential Documents* 2015, no. 00726 (October 15, 2015). www.gpo.gov/fdsys/pkg/DCPD-201500726/pdf/DCPD-201500726.pdf.

OTHER HISTORIC DOCUMENTS OF INTEREST

FROM PREVIOUS *HISTORIC DOCUMENTS*

United Nations, Israeli, and Palestinian Officials Remark on Wave of Terror

OCTOBER 8 AND 19, AND DECEMBER 13, 2015

Known as the Wave of Terror, in the fall of 2015, violence rocked Israel and Palestine. Hundreds on both sides were killed in uncoordinated attacks, many of which were perpetrated by teenagers spurred on by both hateful rhetoric from Israeli and Palestinian leaders and viral videos circulating around social media. The United Nations (UN) urged the leaders of the two nations to restart negotiations for a two-state solution and end Israeli occupation in Palestine, but by the close of 2015, each nation continued to blame the other for the ongoing violence and refused to concede.

Clash over the Temple Mount

The fall 2015 outbreak of violence started as a boiling-over of long-standing tensions about the Temple Mount in Jerusalem, considered to be the holiest site in Judaism and the third holiest for Muslims. Today, the al-Aqsa mosque stands on the location where Jews believe God spoke to Abraham. Israel currently controls access to the Temple Mount and the government believes that Palestinian visitors have often purposefully desecrated the site at the urging of their government. At times, Israel has tightened restrictions on who is able to visit the holy site, placing some of the most stringent controls on Palestinians. A visit in 2000 by former Israeli prime minister Ariel Sharon to the Temple Mount spurred an outbreak of violence known as the Second Intifada, during which forty-seven Palestinians were killed and nearly 2,000 were injured.

On September 13, 2015, Israeli police were called to the Temple Mount after reports of teenagers throwing pipe bombs from the mosque. Police raided the site to clear out those responsible, and a group of Palestinian youth barricaded themselves inside. Israeli police reportedly used tear gas and grenades to remove the Palestinians. According to Israeli prime minister Benjamin Netanyahu, the event was incited by Palestinian leadership who he said had spread "lies regarding our policy" about access to the Temple Mount. Palestinian Authority president Mahmoud Abbas gave his support to those who had been attacked on the Temple Mount by Israeli police, noting "every *shahid* [martyr] will reach paradise, and every injured person will be rewarded by God."

Following the incident, Israel attempted to calm tensions by limiting who could visit Temple Mount, which included the barring of all Israeli parliamentarians from the site. The nation passed a new law that gave security forces the right to shoot at protesters at the site when their own lives, or the lives of bystanders, were endangered. The law also instituted a minimum jail sentence for anyone throwing objects such as pipe bombs and Molotov cocktails, two frequent weapons used in the clashes at Temple Mount.

In a response in October, Abbas gave a speech stating that Jews should be barred from visiting the holy site. The United States blamed Abbas for inciting violence through such rhetoric.

SOCIAL MEDIA ROUSES YOUNG ATTACKERS

The fall 2015 uptick in violence was largely unorganized and was characterized by random instances of violence instead of consistent, well-orchestrated attacks. According to Israeli security officials, a majority of those arrested in relation to the attacks were not affiliated with any known terrorist organizations nor had they been previously arrested. This left security forces on both sides with little ability to stop the attacks in advance. In a speech, Netanyahu said the attacks were "mostly unorganized" and were "the result of wild and mendacious incitement by Hamas, the Palestinian Authority, several countries in the region and—no less and frequently much more—the Islamic movement in Israel."

Some international analysts questioned whether this had to do with the increasing rise of social media use in the Middle East to spread messages of hate and rally support. "You don't need something sophisticated," said Orit Perlov, a social media expert with the Institution for National Security Studies in Tel Aviv. "You just write the word 'it'an,' [which means] stab in Arabic, and then whoever has a knife in his house and wants to go, that's it." He added that although Israel and Palestine had arrested some known online instigators of violence, it did little good because "ideas are becoming immortal—you can take down pages but it will multiply itself."

Palestinian teenagers committed a number of attacks against Israelis with weapons such as small knives, potato peelers, and screwdrivers, indicating that there was little planning or foresight. According to Perlov, these young people could find countless videos of their countrymen being killed by Israelis, which were plastered all over social media and broadcast networks. In Palestinian society, those who defend the nation against Israelis are seen as martyrs. "There's a viral nature to these attacks," said Daniel Nisman, president of the Israeli security analysis firm Levantine Group. "One person goes out, they get killed, then they get glorified, it makes other people want to go out," adding, "you have a significant number of people who are willing to basically commit suicide attacks; they just don't have access to sophisticated weapons."

According to the Palestinian Authority, it was not only its citizens who had been called to action by social media. In a statement, the Palestinian Ministry of Information condemned those in Israel who had posted "a murder-glorifying hate song" following a spate of murders in Palestine in December. The Ministry asked "social media networks and different internet domains to delete the hate and incitement by the Israeli occupation terrorist gangs."

United Nations secretary general Ban Ki-moon said that he was "dismayed" by the number of young people in Palestine taking up arms. "I understand your frustration. I know your hopes for peace have been dashed countless times. You are angry at the continued occupation and expansion of settlements. Many of you are disappointed in your leaders and in us, the international community," Ban said. He called on young people in Palestine to put down their weapons and "to turn your frustration into a strong, but peaceful, voice for change. Demand that your leaders act responsibly to protect your future. Demand progress for a political solution—from your leaders, from Israeli leaders, and from the international community."

Rhetoric Continues to Enrage
Palestinians and Israelis; UN Seeks Peace

The continuing violence was also stoked by rhetoric from both Prime Minister Netanyahu and President Abbas. The former repeatedly referred to Palestinians as "terrorists" and continued to adhere to his promises that Israel would continue to build Jewish-only settlements in the disputed West Bank. In an unprecedented move, Netanyahu's government even temporarily barred Palestinians from visiting Jerusalem's Old City. Netanyahu also called on the Islamic Movement, a Palestinian group that runs religious services for Muslims in Israel, to be sanctioned for its role in the violence. According to Netanyahu, the group has accused Israel of plotting to take over Temple Mount, which the prime minister called an "absolute lie," adding that "we will rebuff them and we will defeat them." Abbas, however, continued to praise those who were "defending al-Aqsa" even while stating that his ultimate intent is to avoid violent confrontation with Israel. "We believe in peace and in peaceful people resistance. . . . We support our brothers who are protecting al-Aqsa who are suffering so much in order to protect it. We say to the Israeli government: stay away from our Muslim and Christian sites," Abbas said.

Deaths and injuries in the 2015 attacks unequally impacted Palestinians. During the first two weeks in October, twenty-seven Palestinians had been killed by Israeli security forces, while nearly 2,000 had been injured, according to the Palestinian Authority's Ministry of Health. In contrast, four Israelis had been killed while sixty-seven were injured. By late October, the United Nations estimated those figures to be closer to forty-seven Palestinians and seven Israelis killed, while 5,000 Palestinians and seventy Israelis had been injured.

Secretary General Ban called on leaders in Israel and Palestine to come to the table and reach an agreement that would put an end to the ongoing violence. "The status quo is only making things worse," Ban said. "We must, for the future of our children, turn back from this dangerous abyss, safeguard the two-state solution and lead people back onto the road towards peace." Jan Eliasson, the deputy secretary-general, added that if Palestine had a state of its own with a robust economy and employment opportunities for its citizens—which would only be brought about by the end of Israeli occupation—the Wave of Terror crisis may not have escalated as it did. A UN press release noted that Eliasson indicated that the violence "sharpened a sense of fear among Israelis who felt that their personal safety had been threatened and saw signs of growing anti-Semitism around the world and attempts that they believed aimed to delegitimize their country."

All these factors, combined with failed peace negotiations and an unwillingness of the two sides to come together to institute a lasting peace, created a scenario in which violence was almost certain to increase. In response to the UN's calls for action, Palestine renewed its requests that the body declare Israeli settlements in Palestine illegal, while Israel asked that the UN start holding Palestine responsible for the violence perpetrated by its citizens. The parties had last entered peace negotiations in 2014, using the United States as a mediator, and although some headway was made, the talks ultimately ended after the Hamas and Fatah political factions formed a coalition Palestinian government, which led Israel to end the talks because of Fatah's refusal to recognize the independent State of Israel.

—Heather Kerrigan

Following is the text of a statement delivered at an October 8, 2015, press conference by Israeli prime minister Benjamin Netanyahu remarking on the ongoing violence; the text of an October 19, 2015, statement by United Nations secretary general

Ban Ki-moon calling for the end of violence perpetrated by Israeli and Palestinian youth; and the text of a press release from the Palestinian Ministry of Information on December 13, 2015, calling on Israel to stop inciting Israeli settlers to commit violent acts against Palestinians.

Prime Minister Netanyahu
Denounces Palestinian Aggression

October 8, 2015

Prime Minister Benjamin Netanyahu, this evening (Thursday, 8 October 2015), issued the following statement at a press conference with Defense Minister Moshe Yaalon, Public Security Minister Gilad Erdan, IDF Chief-of-Staff Lt.-Gen. Gadi Eisenkot and Israel Police Acting Commissioner Bentzi Sau:

"This has been another difficult day for all of us, citizens of Israel. We are in the midst of a wave of terrorism. Terrorists that have been incited and who are riven with hate are trying to attack our people—babies, children, men and women, civilians and soldiers.

Our hearts—the hearts of the entire nation—are with the families of the victims whose lives were cut short by reprehensible murderers. In recent days and hours I have seen displays of heroism by soldiers, police and—no less—by civilians. I see this in Jerusalem, Kiryat Gat, Hebron, Petah Tikva, Tel Aviv and now in Afula.

Israelis are acting with bravery, composure and determination to neutralize and eliminate the terrorists. This requires extraordinary courage and resourcefulness and we are proud to be part of a country that has such citizens.

This vicious terrorism did not start today. It has accompanied the Zionist enterprise since its beginning. We have always known how to defeat the rioters and build up our country and so it will be now. The terrorists and the extremists behind them will achieve nothing. We will rebuff them and we will defeat them.

We are in the midst of a wave of terrorism with knives, firebombs, rocks and even live fire. While these acts are mostly unorganized, they are all the result of wild and mendacious incitement by Hamas, the Palestinian Authority, several countries in the region and—no less and frequently much more—the Islamic Movement in Israel, which is igniting the ground with lies regarding our policy on the Temple Mount and the purported changes that we want to make to the status quo. This is an absolute lie. We are also taking action against the inciters and the attackers.

The IDF, Israel Police and the ISA are working on all fronts—stakeouts, undercover, arrests, presence on the roads, guarding communities, operational entries into Palestinian towns, in-depth entries into neighborhoods in eastern Jerusalem and the demolition of terrorists' homes.

We have also sharpened open-fire against those who throw rocks and firebombs and we will impose minimum sentences on them and fines against minors. We have detained for investigation those who cooperated with the murderers in the Old City of Jerusalem. I demanded that the legal establishment close the shops of the merchants who either took part in this heinous act or stood aside.

Yesterday, I ordered that politicians—Jewish and Arab alike—be prevented from going up to the Temple Mount at this time. We do not need more matches to set the ground afire. We will take aggressive measures against the Islamic Movement in Israel and against other inciters. Nobody will be immune.

I would like to tell you, citizens of Israel, that we live in the Middle East and that the flames of radical Islam, which are burning the entire region, are also reaching us. But Israel is a very strong country and Israelis are a strong people. The measures that I have detailed, as well as others which I will not detail, are not an immediate, magical solution. But with persistence, thoroughness and determination, we will prove that terrorism does not pay—and we will defeat it.

I was asked today what I would say to a mother who fears to send her children outside. I would like to tell her—I would like to tell you, mother—your concerns are natural. They need not be overlooked nor should they be swept under the rug. We have a difficult situation now and we must show maximum alertness. Of course, we must also listen to instructions from the security forces and the authorities. But I would like to tell you something else: The security team that is sitting here—Prime Minister, Defense Minister, Public Security Minister, IDF Chief-of-Staff and the Israel Police Commissioner, and all other security elements—are doing our utmost to restore your security and that of your children, to all Israel."

SOURCE: Office of the Prime Minister of Israel. "PM Netanyahu's Press Conference Statement." October 8, 2015. www.pmo.gov.il/English/MediaCenter/Events/Pages/eventPressConference081015.aspx.

UN Secretary General
Calls for End to Youth Violence

October 19, 2015

Salaam Aleykum, Shalom!

Today, I would like to speak directly to the peoples of Israel and Palestine about the dangerous escalation in violence across the occupied Palestinian Territory and Israel, especially in Jerusalem. I am dismayed—as we all should be—when I see young people, children, picking up weapons and seeking to kill.

Let me be clear: violence will only undermine the legitimate Palestinian aspirations for statehood and the longing of Israelis for security.

To the youth of Palestine I say: I understand your frustration. I know your hopes for peace have been dashed countless times. You are angry at the continued occupation and expansion of settlements. Many of you are disappointed in your leaders and in us, the international community, because of our inability to end this occupation.

And to the leaders of Palestine I say: Harness the energy of your people in a peaceful way to make their dreams and aspirations a reality. You have the right to live a decent life in dignity, respect and freedom.

I know that this is your goal. It is also our goal. But it can only be reached by establishing a Palestinian state living side by side in peace with Israel, not through the violent acts we have been witnessing.

I urge the youth of Palestine—as the future of your people and society—to turn your frustration into a strong, but peaceful, voice for change. Demand that your leaders act responsibly to protect your future. Demand progress for a political solution—from your leaders, from Israeli leaders, and from the international community.

I am not asking you to be passive, but you must put down the weapons of despair.

To the leaders and people of Israel: Let me say, I appreciate your genuine concern about peace and security. I also understand the anger many Israelis feel.

When children are afraid to go to school, when anyone on the street is a potential victim, security is rightly your immediate priority. But walls, checkpoints, harsh responses by the security forces and house demolitions cannot sustain the peace and safety that you need and must have.

There is no so-called "security" solution. You—the people of Israel—as much as the Palestinian people, need to see a political horizon to break this cycle of violence and fear.

The United Nations stands by you. We will continue to support all efforts to create the conditions for a return to meaningful negotiations. In this we have never wavered.

And to all I say: do not allow the extremists on either side to use religion to further fuel the conflict. Palestinian and Israeli leaders: Stand firm against terror, violence and incitement. Demonstrate in both words and deeds that the historic status quo of holy sites in Jerusalem will be preserved.

Reaffirm your commitment to end the occupation and pursue a two-state solution by making changes on the ground.

Non-violence requires more courage and strength than violence. At this difficult time, let us say "enough is enough". Let us stop the posturing and brinkmanship. Let us stop mortgaging the future of both peoples and the region.

Let us get truly serious about reaching the only solution capable of durably stanching the bloodshed, the hatred and the fear of even greater conflict.

That is the courage and leadership the peoples of this holy land demand and deserve. Shukran jazeelan. Toda raba.

Thank you.

SOURCE: United Nations. "Secretary-General's video message to the Israeli and Palestinian people." October 19, 2015. www.un.org/sg/statements/index.asp?nid=9159.

Palestine Denounces Israeli Social Media Posts

December 13, 2015

The Ministry of Information denounces the support of Israeli PM Netanyahu for the terrorist incitement of Israeli settler gangs, while failing to take any action against the murderers of the Doma village Dawabsha family children who posted at social media networks a murder-glorifying hate song.

The Ministry considers that as incitement for the Israeli public to commit more of such crimes. The Ministry of Information considers Israel's failure to act against Israeli hate speech and incitement as a clear indication to the extent of Israel's interest in sponsoring terror and protecting settlers, while allowing them a free hand to commit more crimes; at a time when Israel's leaders are mouthing lies and inciting against the content of our media and social media networks.

The Ministry calls on the social media networks and different internet domains to delete the hate and incitement by the Israeli occupation terrorist gangs.

The Ministry also calls on the UN and the international community to take action for the immediate protection of our people against the Israeli settlers' terror fueled by shameful criminal incitement and the Israeli judiciary that leaves the murderers at large, ignoring the Palestinian blood, burning of children, and committing brutal atrocities.

SOURCE: Ministry of Information. State of Palestine. "Netanyahu government sponsors settlers' terror." December 13, 2015. http://minfo.ps/English/index.php?pagess=main&id=2613&butt=5.

OTHER HISTORIC DOCUMENTS OF INTEREST

FROM PREVIOUS *HISTORIC DOCUMENTS*

World Leaders Congratulate New Nepali Prime Minister and President

OCTOBER 12, 28, AND 29, AND NOVEMBER 2, 2015

Nepal, a landlocked nation in the Himalayas, has struggled to establish a permanent government and Constitution since becoming a republic in 2007. Its efforts have been hampered by attempts to balance the demands of the widely diverse sects within a nation where more than 100 languages are spoken, men hold supreme power, and a caste system has divided the population into haves and have nots. However, spurred by inaction following two devastating earthquakes in April and May, in September 2015, the interim Constituent Assembly approved a governing document and subsequently elected a new prime minister and president to guide its implementation.

INDIA APPROVES FIRST DEMOCRATIC CONSTITUTION

When Nepal changed its form of government from a monarchy to a republic in 2007, it was governed under an interim constitution, which was put in place to help a temporary Constituent Assembly fulfill its primary duty to write a permanent constitution. The body's work was to be completed by April 28, 2010, but disagreements over representation and provincial boundaries stalled negotiations, which led the Constituent Assembly to postpone the timeline by one year. In 2011, still unable to produce a final constitution, the body again postponed its deadline, this time to 2012. By May 2012, the Constituent Assembly dissolved because it was in a stalemate and could not effectively complete its work on a constitution that was acceptable to all parties involved. A second Nepalese Constituent Assembly was elected in November 2013, with the promise that a new constitution would be delivered to the Nepali people by 2014, with an effective date of January 22, 2015.

Sushil Koirala, head of the dominant Nepali Congress (NC) party, was chosen by the second Constituent Assembly as prime minister in 2014 to help usher a new constitution through parliament. He made a pledge at the time he accepted his seat to step down once the constitution had been adopted. Koirala was instrumental in bridging a number of disagreements between the various factions in the Second Constituent Assembly, but he could not force the group to maintain its timeframe for delivery of the governing document.

The spring 2015 earthquakes, which killed more than 9,000 Nepalis, were seen as a major catalyst for politicians to come together and end seven years of debate over the constitution. The final document, which passed the Constituent Assembly on September 17, 2015, with 507 of 601 members voting in favor, established seven secular states, a decision that was highly unpopular with ethnic minorities near the Indian border who believe that their power in the new government was being marginalized. Protests over this portion of the constitution led to the deaths of approximately forty demonstrators and police. Additional provisions in the constitution established a federal government that would have a bicameral parliament, while each individual state would have a unicameral parliament. A portion of the representatives to the lower house of the federal government would be elected through a simple majority, while others would be chosen through proportional representation, another concern of ethnic minorities who believed that their low-caste groups would be unlikely to gain enough seats in the Constituent Assembly to have a voice. The new constitution also sought to improve women's rights and defined human rights as fundamental in Nepali society.

Seeking to calm the concerns of ethnic minorities upon signing the nation's new constitution, President Ram Baran Yadav said, "Our country is multi-ethnic, multi-lingual, multi-religious and multi-cultural . . . this new document will safeguard the rights of all Nepali brothers and sisters." Koirala stated via Twitter that the new constitution was "an issue of pride for all Nepalis." It was the opinion of both the president and the prime minister that the document was still imperfect, but that it could be amended as required, and that an agreed-upon constitution was better than continuing without a governing document. With a constitution in place, Yadav called on the second Constituent Assembly to appoint a new prime minister, who would drive the formation of a permanent parliament and the implementation of the new governing document.

NEW PRIME MINISTER CHOSEN

Koirala made good on his pledge and resigned from his post on October 10. In a surprising move, however, shortly after announcing his resignation he also filed paperwork to run for reelection to the seat, which was strongly criticized by some NC members who thought the announcement could be detrimental to the party's hold on power. Koirala said he filed for reelection because the political parties were struggling to choose viable candidates for the office.

On October 11, the Constituent Assembly elected Koirala's opponent, Khadga Prasad Sharma Oli, the leader of the Communist Party of Nepal Unified Marxist-Leninist (UML). Oli received 338 votes to Koirala's 249, and his victory was secured in part through an agreement he signed promising to review the constitution in an effort to placate ethnic groups who did not support the redrawn provincial boundaries.

Oli first entered politics in 1970 as a member of the Nepal Communist Party, which was operating underground because of the monarchy's crackdown on its activities, and was jailed for fourteen years for his affiliation with the party. He had served in parliament since 1991 and held two ministerial positions—home minister and foreign minister—during this time. Oli's upbringing in eastern Nepal meant he was considered a member of the "high caste" that had regularly drawn the scorn of the minority Madhesi and Tharu sects. In a speech following his election, Oli pledged that although he is often viewed as "anti-Madhes, anti-Tharu, and called intolerant," he would "prove the allegations wrong by actions I will take." In forming his cabinet, Oli chose seven individuals and two deputy prime ministers from various political parties in an effort to appease the competing interest groups in the nation.

The new prime minister will have a number of challenges to tackle as he takes the helm of the government, including reviewing and potentially revising the new constitution as well as working to end violent protests carried out by ethnic Madhesis in the southern portion of the country, which have led to fuel shortages because India is unable to make deliveries. Oli will also need to continue rebuilding those areas that were devastated by two earthquakes in the spring of 2015. In June, the National Reconstruction Authority came into being and was tasked with allocating foreign and domestic donations to rebuild those areas hardest hit by the earthquakes. Political infighting within the group has stalled any progress, and the group has yet to distribute an estimated $4.4 billion in foreign donations.

NEPAL ELECTS FIRST FEMALE PRESIDENT

Following the appointment of a new prime minister, parliament met on October 29 to select a new Nepalese president. Yadav was elected to a two-year term in 2008, when the nation changed its form of government from a monarchy to a republic; however, his term was extended to 2015, because of the lengthy negotiations over the country's constitution.

Two candidates were considered for the presidency in 2015—Bidhya Devi Bhandari, deputy leader of the UML and a champion of women's rights, and Kul Bahadur Gurung, the leader of the Congress Party. Bhandari first entered the Nepalese political sphere after being elected to parliament when her husband, Madan, then leader of the UML, was killed in a suspicious car accident in 1993. Bhandari is credited with helping drive the movement that changed Nepal from a monarchy to a republic and held the position of defense minister from 2009 to 2011. Gurung previously served as a minister of education and had been jailed by the former monarchy for his attempts to install a democratic government in Nepal.

By a vote of 327–214, Bhandari was elected the nation's second president. Her election reflects an effort by the government to work toward moving Nepal away from a traditionally male-dominated society and came just one week after the election of Onsari Gharti as the nation's first female parliament speaker. In fact, Bhandari was instrumental in securing language in the new constitution that requires one-third of parliamentary seats to be held by women and a position for a woman on each government committee. But she drew criticism for another provision she pushed that would deny citizenship to the children of single mothers and women married to foreigners. In assuming the largely ceremonial role of president, Bhandari promised to champion women's rights and end the ongoing ethnic tensions. "I will do my best to protect the constitution and work for the country's development and prosperity," she said. Despite the challenges continuing to plague Nepal, there was hope that longtime allies Bhandari and Oli would work together to spur action in parliament.

—Heather Kerrigan

Following is an October 12, 2015, statement from the U.S. Embassy in Nepal congratulating Khadga Prasad Sharma Oli on his election as prime minister; an October 28, 2015, statement from the U.S. Embassy in Nepal congratulating Bidhya Devi Bhandari on her election as Nepal's president; an October 29, 2015, statement from the president of India congratulating Nepal on choosing leaders for its new government; and a November 2, 2015, press release from the Chinese Embassy welcoming the establishment of new leaders in Nepal.

DOCUMENT

U.S. Embassy Congratulates Prime Minister Oli

October 12, 2015

The United States congratulates Khadga Prasad Sharma Oli on his election as the Prime Minister of Nepal. We look forward to working with the Prime Minister on ongoing efforts to rebuild after the earthquake and to bring about a more prosperous, unified, and stable Nepal. The United States encourages all political stakeholders to fully engage in a democratic process that accommodates the aspirations of all Nepalis.

SOURCE: Embassy of the United States in Kathmandu Nepal. "Statement by Mark Toner, Deputy Spokesperson." October 12, 2015. http://nepal.usembassy.gov/pr-10-12-2015.html.

U.S. Embassy Congratulates President Bhandari

October 28, 2015

The United States congratulates Khadga Prasad Sharma Oli on his election as Prime Minister earlier this month and to Bidhya Devi Bhandari on her historic election as Nepal's first female President today. These elections follow the promulgation of a constitution and the formation of a new government, milestones in Nepal's democratic development that demonstrate the people of Nepal's commitment to democracy. The United States looks forward to continuing to partner with the people and government of Nepal as they build a more unified, stable, and prosperous country and rebuild after the devastating earthquake and its aftershocks earlier this year.

SOURCE: Embassy of the United States in Kathmandu, Nepal. "Statement by NSC Spokesperson Ned Price on the Election of a New Government in Nepal." October 28, 2015. http://nepal.usembassy.gov/pr-10-29-2015.html.

India's President Congratulates Bhandari

October 29, 2015

The President of India, Shri Pranab Mukherjee has congratulated Her Excellency Ms. Bidhya Devi Bhandari on her election as the President of Federal Democratic Republic of Nepal.

In his message to Her Excellency Ms. Bidhya Devi Bhandari, the President has said, "Please accept on behalf of the people and Government of India and on my own behalf, warm felicitations on your election as President of Nepal.

Your election comes at a critical juncture in Nepal's history. I am confident that under your guidance, the country will move towards peace, stability and development by accommodating the aspirations of all the Nepalese people.

India attaches the highest priority to further development of our close and multi-faceted relationship with Nepal. As a close friend and neighbour, India will continue to extend all possible assistance and cooperation in accordance with the priorities and wishes of the government and people of Nepal. I look forward to working with you towards further strengthening the understanding and cooperation between our two countries.

I would also like to avail of this opportunity to convey my best wishes for your personal health and well-being."

SOURCE: Government of India. Press Information Bureau. "President of India congratulates Ms. Bidhya Devi Bhandari on her election as President of Nepal." October 29, 2015. http://pib.nic.in/newsite/PrintRelease.aspx?relid=130050.

China Welcomes
New Nepali Leaders

November 2, 2015

On October 30, 2015, President Xi Jinping sent a message to Bidhya Devi Bhandari, congratulating her on assuming office as new President of Nepal.

Xi Jinping said in the congratulatory message that China always respects and supports the Nepalese people's independent choice of social system and development road, and believes that Nepal will start a new course in national development under the leadership of you and the Nepalese government. I attach great importance to the development of China-Nepal relations, and am willing to join efforts with you to promote China-Nepal comprehensive cooperative partnership of lasting friendship for constant development.

SOURCE: Embassy of the People's Republic of China in the United States. "Xi Jinping Sends Message Congratulating Bidhya Devi Bhandari on Assuming Office as New President of Nepal." November 2, 2015. www.china-embassy.org/eng/zgyw/t1311761.htm.

OTHER HISTORIC DOCUMENTS OF INTEREST

FROM THIS VOLUME

FROM PREVIOUS *HISTORIC DOCUMENTS*

American and Puerto Rican Leaders Remark on Island Nation's Default

OCTOBER 21 AND DECEMBER 1, 2015

In 2015, Puerto Rico faced a ballooning public debt that had grown from roughly 63 percent of the commonwealth's gross domestic product (GDP) in 2000 to 100 percent. It had accumulated approximately $72 billion worth of debt—more than each U.S. state except New York and California—largely in the form of municipal bonds. Unable to stimulate economic growth and feeling the pinch of various austerity measures, Puerto Rican officials sought congressional authorization to restructure the commonwealth's debt, warning that it could be forced to default on its obligations if the federal government failed to take action.

AN ECONOMIC "DEATH SPIRAL"

The roots of Puerto Rico's current financial crisis are often traced back to 2006, the year in which Congress repealed a federal tax credit that had exempted U.S. companies from paying taxes on income originated in U.S. territories. Puerto Rico's economy had grown rapidly under this program, particularly in the manufacturing sector. The tax credit's repeal prompted mainland companies to withdraw from the island, which, combined with high corporate taxes on domestic companies that had discouraged the development of Puerto Rican-based businesses, created a major void in the commonwealth's economy, leading to a period of contraction that drove up government deficits. That same year, the commonwealth endured a partial public shutdown after lawmakers failed to reach an agreement on financial measures that would enable Puerto Rico to pay off a $532 million line of credit needed to keep the government running. Lawmakers had been unable to agree on a spending plan since 2004, forcing the government to continue operating on its 2004 budget and ultimately leading to a $740 million budget shortfall.

Puerto Rico's economy has lagged ever since. The commonwealth's situation is in some ways uniquely challenging given its status as both an emerging, relatively poor island economy and a U.S. territory. For example, Puerto Rico must abide by U.S. minimum wage laws, which can make its businesses less appealing to investors than those of neighboring island economies because their wages, and therefore their costs, are much higher. Also, federal law requires that any goods transported between U.S. ports must be conducted by U.S.-built ships crewed by U.S. citizens and permanent residents. This effectively drives up import costs for the Puerto Rican government because foreign exporters cannot ship directly to the island; their goods must go to the mainland first.

In addition, only 40 percent of adult Puerto Ricans are employed or are actively seeking work, compared to 63 percent of U.S. adults. This discrepancy is due in large part to the fact that combined welfare and Medicaid benefits can be greater than the commonwealth's median family income. Roughly 45 percent of Puerto Ricans live in poverty, further straining public assistance programs. High energy costs also play a role in the commonwealth's economic challenges, as do increased taxes and spending cuts that have contributed to a 9 percent decrease in Puerto Rico's population since 2005 as citizens migrate to the United States in search of jobs and a better quality of life. This migration has in turn reduced Puerto Rico's tax base, further affecting revenue flows.

The commonwealth is also particularly reliant on deficit financing, issuing municipal bonds to help cover its bills. This is another instance in which Puerto Rico's situation is unique from that of U.S. states: all of its bonds are exempt from federal, state, or local taxes. This made the bonds particularly attractive to investors, creating a significant and steady demand for Puerto Rican bonds through 2013 and thereby facilitating the commonwealth's continual over-borrowing. Puerto Ricans themselves hold about $20 billion of the commonwealth's debt, and nearly 60 percent of the debt is held in Americans' retirement accounts. However, the more bonds Puerto Rico issued, the more interest payments it had to make to more bond holders. And the issuing of bonds became much more expensive for Puerto Rico in 2013 after a spike in unemployment and the biggest decrease in economic activity since 2010 shook investor confidence. As demand for the bonds fell, interest rates went up, and Standard & Poor's ultimately downgraded Puerto Rico's bonds to junk bond status in 2014—a designation reserved for the riskiest of bonds.

In an effort to address its debt, the Puerto Rican government imposed a new gross receipts tax, raised the retirement age, increased sales tax, and cut summer and Christmas bonuses for public workers. It also reinstated higher corporate tax rates, though a variety of tax breaks for different industries meant that few companies actually paid the top tax rates. The government also took several emergency measures to free up capital, including not paying tax refunds, selling assets from its worker's compensation fund, liquidating pension system assets, and suspending set-asides for future payments of general obligation bonds, which Puerto Rico is constitutionally obligated to repay. In addition, officials introduced a number of austerity measures to help reduce spending, such as reforming the government's largest pension fund from a defined benefit plan to a defined contribution plan, freezing collective bargaining agreements, cutting government employment through attrition and hiring freezes, and reducing expense by 20 percent. Yet these measures also had the effect of further cutting revenues and diminishing the government's capacity to repay creditors.

THE FIRST DEFAULT

On June 29, 2015, Puerto Rican governor Alejandro García Padilla declared during a televised address that the commonwealth's "public debt . . . is unpayable" and that a "unilateral and unplanned non-payment of obligations" loomed. He argued that allowing Puerto Rico to restructure its debt was the only way to avoid the current "death spiral." Padilla pointed to an analysis released earlier in the day by current and former International Monetary Fund staffers. Commissioned by Puerto Rico's Government Development Bank, the report found that the commonwealth's debt was actually larger than previously thought. The authors recommended several steps for addressing the crisis, including lowering minimum wage and government assistance amounts, as well as renegotiating the debt.

Just over one month later, Puerto Rico officially defaulted on its debt for the first time in its history when it failed to pay $58 million worth of a $483 million debt payment due on August 3. The decision to not pay this portion of the debt was strategic; it was owed to creditors—primarily credit unions and Puerto Rican citizens—at the commonwealth's Public Finance Corporation, which has less legal power than other creditors to sue Puerto Rico over a default. "This was a decision that reflects the serious concerns about the Commonwealth's liquidity in combination with the balance of obligations to our creditors and the equally important obligations to the people of Puerto Rico," said Melba Acosta Febo, president of the Government Development Bank.

CONGRESS, OBAMA ADMINISTRATION CONSIDER ASSISTANCE OPTIONS

Padilla's proposal to allow Puerto Rico to restructure its debt was not a new one. Resident Commissioner Pedro Pierluisi, Puerto Rico's only member of the House of Representatives, had introduced a bill in February 2015 seeking to give parts of the Puerto Rican government the ability to declare bankruptcy under Chapter 9 of the U.S. Bankruptcy Code. States can use Chapter 9 to allow their municipalities to declare bankruptcy, as demonstrated by the city of Detroit in 2013, but the code does not apply to Puerto Rico's municipalities and public corporations. The House Judiciary Committee held a hearing on the bill in February, but the legislation has not progressed since. It cannot advance without Republican votes, and Republicans generally do not support the Chapter 9 extension, arguing that there are other options available to Puerto Rico and that allowing the commonwealth to declare bankruptcy would be detrimental to American investors who hold its municipal bonds. The latter is a position shared by many investment fund managers who argue that providing the Chapter 9 option would violate the terms of investors' bond agreements and impose an unanticipated risk on bond holders.

On October 21, the White House released its own proposal for addressing Puerto Rico's financial crisis, calling on Congress to provide the commonwealth with an orderly debt restructuring option, either by extending Chapter 9 or by creating a new option, dubbed "Super Chapter 9," that would allow the commonwealth to restructure all its debt, including its general obligation bonds. The proposal also called for Congress to provide independent fiscal oversight to certify that Puerto Rico is implementing a recovery plan, reform the commonwealth's Medicaid program to ensure it provides better access to healthcare services, and enable Puerto Ricans to qualify for the Earned Income Tax Credit. "We have helped Puerto Rico attract job-creating investments, secure new funds to accelerate infrastructure projects, and lower energy costs on the island. These efforts are ongoing, but administrative actions cannot solve the crisis," said Treasury secretary Jacob Lew, National Economic Council director Jeff Zients, and Health and Human Services secretary Sylvia Matthews Burwell in a joint statement. "Without congressional action, Puerto Rico will face a long and difficult recovery that could have harmful consequences for the residents on the island and beyond."

Congress took up the issue of Puerto Rico's finances in earnest in December. The Senate Judiciary Committee held a hearing on December 1, presided over by Chairman Chuck Grassley, R-Iowa, to explore the causes of Puerto Rico's economic crisis and discuss possible solutions. In his opening remarks, Grassley acknowledged that Puerto Rico was facing a liquidity crisis and that factors such as the federal minimum wage mandate, a declining population, and attractive bond offerings had contributed to its fiscal situation. Yet he appeared to dismiss bankruptcy as an option. "Chapter 9 cannot bring about financial rehabilitation. It does not increase economic growth or alter the fundamental fiscal trajectory," he said. "The debt is a symptom of a bigger problem . . . Merely extending debt restructuring authority, absent tools to address the fundamental causes of the fiscal problem, is not a long-term solution that will help Puerto Rico." Testifying before the committee, Gov. Padilla challenged Sen. Grassley's argument by claiming that "a humanitarian crisis will envelop the 3.5 [million] American citizens on the island" if Congress did not give Puerto Rico restructuring authority. He noted that austerity measures had "caused further economic contraction" and could not bridge the gap in financing. "Putting Puerto Rico on a sustainable path in the long-term necessitates a legal framework to restructure all our liabilities," he added.

The following week, Sen. Orrin Hatch, R-Utah, and Rep. Sean Duffy, R-Wisc., each introduced a bill aimed at helping Puerto Rico. Sen. Hatch's bill included $3 billion in cash relief, reduced employee payroll taxes for five years, and required Puerto Rico to disclose more detailed information about its pension obligations. It also called for a federally appointed oversight board that would control the island's finances. Rep. Duffy's bill included provisions extending Chapter 9 to Puerto Rican cities and publicly owned institutions, and similarly called for a financial stability council to oversee the commonwealth's finances. At the same time, Puerto Rican officials sought to add a rider to Congress's omnibus spending bill that would allow for debt restructuring. The spending package passed without the measure, but House Speaker Paul Ryan, R-Wisc., acknowledged the issue's importance and asked committee leaders to come up with a plan to assist Puerto Rico by the end of March 2016.

A SECOND DEFAULT

On December 30, Gov. Padilla announced that Puerto Rico would default again, this time on a roughly $1 billion debt payment due on January 4, 2016. He noted that the biggest part of that payment—roughly $328 million owed in general obligation debts—would be paid. Half those funds would be provided by "clawing back" revenues from government agencies such as the highway and busing authorities.

Puerto Rico's next significant debt payment, totaling $1.9 billion, is due in July 2016. If the commonwealth continues to default, it could face legal challenges from its bond holders as well as an ongoing drop off of investor confidence. Padilla is scheduled to meet with creditors early in 2016 to discuss Puerto Rico's debt and explore the possibility of restructuring.

—Linda Fecteau Grimm

Following is the text of a statement from the U.S. Treasury Department on October 21, 2015, on the Obama administration's proposal to respond to Puerto Rico's imminent default; an opening statement from Sen. Chuck Grassley, R-Iowa, at the opening of a Senate Judiciary Committee hearing on Puerto Rico's fiscal crisis on December 1, 2015; and a statement by Puerto Rico governor Alejandro J. García Padilla, at the December 1, 2015, Senate Judiciary Committee hearing on Puerto Rico's default.

Treasury Department Announces Plan to Respond to Puerto Rico's Fiscal Crisis

DOCUMENT

October 21, 2015

WASHINGTON—U.S. Treasury Secretary Jacob J. Lew, National Economic Council Director Jeff Zients, and Health and Human Services Secretary Sylvia Mathews Burwell today released the following statement after the Obama Administration unveiled a detailed legislative outline to help Puerto Rico address its serious fiscal challenges. The Administration has worked extensively with Puerto Rican officials to find solutions to the Commonwealth's fiscal crisis, bringing the full capabilities of the Executive branch to bear in providing assistance to speed Puerto Rico's economic recovery. However, only Congress has the authority to provide Puerto Rico with the tools required to lay the foundation for the Commonwealth's recovery, and Congress must act.

"Puerto Rico, and the 3.5 million American citizens who call the island home, are facing a serious crisis that requires immediate congressional action. The Commonwealth has been mired in a decade long recession, during which more than 300,000 people left the island, the islands economy shrank and unemployment soared, and the Commonwealth's fiscal hole deepened. Puerto Rico has taken emergency actions to address these challenges, but those actions will be exhausted this winter. Puerto Rico has already taken significant steps to address its fiscal crisis, but more action is required.

"The Administration has been working with the Puerto Rico government to ensure that the Commonwealth is able to access all available, existing federal resources. We have helped Puerto Rico attract job-creating investments, secure new funds to accelerate infrastructure projects, and lower energy costs on the island. These efforts are ongoing, but administrative actions cannot solve the crisis. Only Congress has the authority to provide Puerto Rico with the necessary tools to address its near-term challenges and promote long-term growth.

"The proposal the Administration released today includes four central elements. First, Congress must provide Puerto Rico with an orderly restructuring regime to comprehensively address its financial liabilities by restructuring its debts. Second, Congress should provide independent fiscal oversight to certify that Puerto Rico adheres to the recovery plan it is implementing in a credible and transparent way. Third, Congress needs to reform the Commonwealth's Medicaid program and ensure that the program provides better access to healthcare services. Fourth, Congress should provide Puerto Rico with access to the Earned Income Tax Credit (EITC), a proven tool that has bipartisan support for rewarding work and supporting growth.

"Working together, Congress and the Administration can help Puerto Rico emerge from the current crisis. Without congressional action, Puerto Rico will face a long and difficult recovery that could have harmful consequences for the residents on the island and beyond."

SOURCE: U.S. Department of the Treasury. "Joint Statement by Treasury Secretary Jacob J. Lew, NEC Director Jeff Zients, and HHS Secretary Sylvia Mathews Burwell on the Obama Administration's Legislative Proposal to Address Puerto Rico's Urgent Fiscal Situation." October 21, 2015. www.treasury .gov/press-center/press-releases/Pages/jl0228.aspx.

Sen. Grassley Opens Hearing on Puerto Rico's Finances

December 1, 2015

Good morning. The purpose of today's hearing is to learn more about the origin of Puerto Rico's fiscal problems, and what's needed to help restore fiscal balance and economic growth. It's my hope that we'll have a valuable discussion based on facts, and informed by our witnesses' expertise.

Puerto Rico's debt crisis didn't happen overnight. It's been years in the making. Fundamentally, the starting point for any solution is to first identify the problem and understand its size and scope. Unfortunately, confusion reigns as Puerto Rico has failed to provide audited financial statements for the past two years.

What we do know is that for many years as Puerto Rico's economy suffered, debt and spending increased to the point where the Island lost investor confidence. Puerto Rico has defaulted on certain debt obligations, lost access to the normal markets, and now faces a liquidity crisis. The Governor and others have stated that the Island's current debt "is not payable."

Puerto Rico's economy has suffered for decades in part because of barriers to job creation and labor force participation. The federal minimum wage mandate, generous entitlement programs, bureaucratic red tape, and a bloated public sector have stifled business activity. This has a direct impact on Puerto Rico's residents, who are our fellow U.S. citizens. High unemployment rates have resulted in a declining population as Puerto Ricans have left the Island in search of jobs. A diminished population means lower tax revenues to fund government spending.

Despite these long-term economic challenges, for many years Puerto Rico maintained a balanced budget and high credit ratings on its debt. What, then, led to the fiscal crisis the Island faces today? While the economic challenges may be debatable, it's clear that since 2000, Puerto Rico's public debt has risen from 60 percent of GDP to now more than 100 percent. This is an indication of serious fiscal mismanagement.

Thanks to the highly attractive triple-tax exempt status of its bonds, it was easier for Puerto Rico to borrow and paper over deficits, rather than address financial shortcomings and economic realities in order to balance its budget. The consequence of this decision is an accumulation of approximately $72 billion of debt, arising from roughly 17 different debt issuers. This includes more than $18 billion in constitutionally protected general obligation debt. And, also around $24 billion in debt issued by public corporations, like the Puerto Rico Electric Power Authority (PREPA).

Moreover, because of its triple-tax exempt status, a wide array of investors own Puerto Rican bonds. According to Bloomberg, Puerto Ricans alone hold $20 billion of the debt. And nearly 60 percent of Puerto Rico's debt is held largely in the individual retirement accounts and 401(k)'s of regular folks throughout the U.S. I'm told that approximately 16,000 Iowans are invested in funds that hold PREPA bonds. These folks aren't vultures. They're middle-class Americans who probably knew little about Puerto Rico's finances. They simply invested in one of many tax-exempt municipal bond fund's containing Puerto Rico's bonds.

Notwithstanding all of this, we're told that Puerto Rico's debt needs to be restructured in order to address its fiscal challenges. Puerto Rico, though, lacks access to an orderly debt restructuring mechanism, like Chapter 9 of the bankruptcy code. Thus, Congress has been called upon to extend Chapter 9 to Puerto Rico's public corporations. Or to create a broad new bankruptcy regime, dubbed "Super Chapter 9," to restructure all debt, including the Island's constitutionally guaranteed general obligation bonds. According to a recent *New York Times* article, "advisers to the island's government have been urging the governor to default on the debt, saying that only a catastrophe would move Congress—especially Republicans—to help." I hope the Governor will tell us whether this is accurate. It would trouble me greatly if true.

This isn't the first time Congress has been asked to help address a situation like Puerto Rico now faces. In the past, we've provided help in a bipartisan way. During the 1990s, the District of Columbia faced its own fiscal crisis, as it was insolvent and unable to pay its bills. Congress worked with District and Clinton Administration officials to pass the District of Columbia Financial Responsibility and Management Assistance Act in 1995. We'll hear more about the response to that crisis and others from our witnesses today. I'll note that Congress considered extending Chapter 9 to the District of Columbia, but decided that there was "little practical significance or advantage to such a legislative gesture." As the committee report to the bill stated, "the issues facing the District of Columbia . . . require political and structural, as well as financial remediation."

One of the reasons extending Chapter 9 to the District was rejected is because it's designed primarily to restructure and decrease municipal debt. The idea being that relief from creditors is what's needed in order to gain a fresh start. But Chapter 9 cannot bring about financial rehabilitation. It does not increase economic growth or alter the fundamental fiscal trajectory. In short, Chapter 9 cannot address the root causes of fiscal problems, but instead pushes them off to future generations.

As for "Super Chapter 9," this is something that no State can do, and has been described as "unprecedented in the American context." It would be a bad idea, with negative consequences, for Congress to permit Puerto Rico to walk away from its constitutional debt obligations. Unlike other bonds, constitutional debt, whether issued by Puerto Rico or a State, has that government's full faith and credit commitment to repay the debt.

Let's not forget that Puerto Rico issued its bonds with the knowledge that Chapter 9 bankruptcy wasn't an option in the event of a default. Is it fair to retroactively change the rules at the expense of these investors, if other options exist for addressing Puerto Rico's debt problems? At the very least, this is an idea that should be at the end of the line, not the front.

The challenges Puerto Rico faces are great and require more than just short-term solutions that don't provide long-term relief. The debt is a symptom of a bigger problem. Merely extending debt restructuring authority, absent tools to address the fundamental causes of the fiscal problem, is not a long-term solution that will help Puerto Rico.

Puerto Rico has struggled to make the difficult decisions to cut spending and balance its budget.

If Congress is to act, then we must ensure that Puerto Rico has the tools to help itself out of this situation. Today's hearing can help us identify what may, or may not, need to be looked at for Puerto Rico to get its balance sheet back in order.

SOURCE: Senate Judiciary Committee. "Prepared Statement by Senator Chuck Grassley of Iowa, Chairman, Senate Judiciary Committee, Hearing on 'Puerto Rico's Fiscal Problems: Examining the Source and Exploring the Solution.'" December 1, 2015. www.judiciary.senate.gov/imo/media/doc/12-01-15%20Grassley%20Statement.pdf.

Puerto Rican Governor Testifies on His Nation's Fiscal Crisis

December 1, 2015

Chairman Grassley, Ranking Member Leahy and members of the Committee:

The consequences of a default without any legal framework to restructure our liabilities are so disastrous that for the past 6 months we have been executing emergency measures to continue meeting our obligations with our creditors and avoid a disruption of essential services to our citizens. These emergency measures are unsustainable.

The Commonwealth of Puerto Rico has so far avoided a major default with bondholders by executing emergency measures such as: not paying tax refunds; funding working capital needs by selling assets of the worker's compensation fund; advancing the liquidation of assets of our pension systems; stretching third-party payables to over $1.6 billion; suspending set-asides for the payment of general obligation bonds; and not paying the bonds of a subsidiary of the Government Development Bank for Puerto Rico ("GDB").

The emergency measures we are deploying are in addition to the austerity measures that Puerto Rico has been implementing over the last decade. Measures that have caused further economic contraction, limiting our ability to meet our obligations and causing massive outmigration. In the three years of my Administration alone we have, inter alia, reformed our largest pension fund from a defined benefit plan to a defined contribution plan, including for current employees; froze collective bargaining agreements, revenues measures that impacted the sales tax, the petroleum products tax and water rates; reduced government employment as a share of the population to an average lower than in the states through attrition and hiring freezes; and reduced expenses by twenty percent, the lowest spending level in a decade. The people of Puerto Rico have been the sole bearers of these burdens.

The depth of our debt crisis has been extensively documented. In June 29, 2015 we released a debt sustainability analysis commissioned from Dr. Anne Krueger, the former Chief Economist at the World Bank and First Deputy Director of the International Monetary Fund ("IMF") and other former IMF economists. That report was followed by the forensic accounting analysis by Conway MacKenzie dated August 25, 2015; the Puerto Rico Fiscal and Economic Growth Plan dated September 9, 2015; my written testimony for the U.S. Senate Committee on Energy and Natural Resources hearing titled "Puerto Rico: Economy, Debt and Options for Congress" held in October 22, 2015; and the Commonwealth of Puerto Rico Financial Information and Operating Data Report dated November 6, 2015. The five documents are enclosed. Various stakeholders have called for greater transparency with respect to the financial information of the Commonwealth. We can improve the availability of our financial data; however, equally true, is the fact that in no point in time has the Commonwealth provided as much financial information as we have currently disclosed. The reality and immediacy of the crisis has been validated by the U.S. Department of the Treasury and illustrated by the massive outmigration of our citizens.

The emergency measures and fiscal adjustments outlined above have so far stayed off a default. The actions, however, are having a devastating effect on our economy and on the Commonwealth's revenues: further diminishing our capacity to repay. The island is being suffocated by a vicious cycle of fiscal adjustments that decrease economic activity and revenues, which then require further fiscal adjustments. As the Puerto Rico Fiscal and Economic Growth Plan illustrates, over the next five years we project a financing gap of $28 billion. More austerity measures will not bridge that gap. Putting Puerto Rico on a sustainable path in the long-term necessitates a legal framework to restructure all our liabilities.

Given the absence of a restructuring mechanism we are trying to negotiate a resolution with a countless number of creditors. So far this type of voluntary process has not been encouraging. After more than a year of negotiation the Puerto Rico Electric Power Authority has not been able to reach an agreement with its creditors because of a single holdout. A holdout, I should add, that has extracted preferential treatment. This out of court restructuring process is yielding inequitable results for the debtor and a majority of the creditors. We need a restructuring process that is fair to all stakeholders, lowers electricity rates and promotes economic growth. The Commonwealth has no legal authority to restructure its debts or any legal recourse to defend its citizens from a default. Congress and the U.S. Courts have left the people of Puerto Rico bereft of any legal remedy. And the downward spiral of economic contraction and revenue declines is intensifying. In early November we revised our revenue forecast downward from $9.8 billion to $9.4 billion. Last month our revenues plummeted and, yesterday, we did a further downward revision to $9.2 billion.

In light of the rapidly deteriorating revenue situation, in accordance with Article 6, Section 8 of the Constitution of the Commonwealth of Puerto Rico, I ordered the "clawback" of revenues assigned to certain instrumentalities of the Commonwealth for the repayment of their debts. Together these instrumentalities have approximately $7 billion in bonds outstanding. In simple terms, we have begun to default on our debt in an effort to attempt to repay bonds issued with the full faith and credit of the Commonwealth and secure sufficient resources to protect the life, health, safety and welfare of the people of Puerto Rico.

Without a federally authorized legal framework, this will be the beginning of a very long and chaotic process. The choices ahead will become ever more difficult and potentially harmful to our economy, our stakeholders and our people. Let me be clear, if Congress does not provide Puerto Rico the authority to restructure all its liabilities a humanitarian crisis will envelop the 3.5 American citizens on the island. We are simply requesting rule of law. This costs nothing to the federal government. Give Puerto Rico the tools it needs to manage its crisis.

Thank you for your time and attention.

SOURCE: Senate Judiciary Committee. "Alejandro J. García Padilla, Governor of the Commonwealth of Puerto Rico, Written Testimony, U.S. Senate Committee on the Judiciary, Puerto Rico's Fiscal Problems: Examining the Source and Exploring the Solution." December 1, 2015. www.judiciary.senate.gov/imo/media/doc/Garcia-Padilla%20Testimony.pdf.

Testimony at Congressional Hearings on Benghazi Attack

OCTOBER 22, 2015

Following a 2012 attack on the U.S. consulate compound in Benghazi, Libya, in which four Americans were killed, the U.S. Congress launched a series of investigations into the incident, seeking to determine what motivated the attack and whether the State Department had failed to adequately protect consulate personnel. Seven congressional hearings and the State Department's own independent review concluded that the agency had not provided sufficient protection, and the State Department committed to implementing a number of recommended policy changes to help prevent a similar situation from occurring. Despite this extensive review, the House of Representatives called for the creation of a Select Committee on Benghazi to further probe the Obama administration's handling of the attack, setting up a political showdown between Republicans who claimed they needed more information and Democrats who accused them of politicizing the incident for electoral gain. The committee conducted dozens of private interviews and several public hearings throughout 2015, including an October hearing that drew more attention for committee members' partisan bickering than for the testimony of its sole witness, former secretary of state Hillary Clinton.

MAKING SENSE OF A TRAGEDY

U.S. ambassador to Libya Chris Stevens, Foreign Service officer Sean Smith, and security guards Tyrone Woods and Glen Doherty were killed during the attack on the Benghazi consulate on September 11. Questions about who was responsible for the incident and whether the State Department had been negligent in protecting the consulate immediately began to swirl. U.S. officials initially posited that the attack was connected to anti-American protests taking place across the Middle East following the release of a trailer for a film that depicted the Prophet Muhammad in a derogatory fashion. On September 15, the al Qaeda branch in Yemen claimed the attack was not a response to the film but retaliation for the June killing of Sheikh Abu Yahya al Libi, the organization's second in command. The Libyan government confirmed the same day that the attack had been preplanned.

The State Department quickly formed an independent commission, called the Accountability Review Board, to explore the root cause of the attack and determine whether the agency had failed to act in any way. The panel released its highly critical report in December 2012, finding that the department had ignored months of warnings from Ambassador Stevens about the need for additional security amid the deteriorating situation in Libya that followed the fall of Col. Muammar el-Qaddafi's government. The panel also took issue with the agency's decision to provide only a small force of trained U.S. military and security personnel for the compound, relying primarily on members of local Libyan militias for added protection. The report outlined twenty-nine recommendations aimed at addressing the State Department's security failings, including increasing security personnel in high-risk locations.

In a subsequent hearing before the Senate Foreign Relations Committee, Deputy Secretaries of State William Burns and Thomas Nides acknowledged the agency's errors and said they would accept all the commission's recommendations, noting that they had already begun implementing some of the changes. A month later, in January 2013, Clinton appeared before the same committee to offer her first testimony on the matter. Republicans sharply criticized her failure to respond to the consulate's warnings and accused the administration of misleading the public about the reasons for the attack. They were particularly incensed by comments UN ambassador Susan Rice made while appearing on Sunday talk shows following the attack, in which she continued to connect the film protests to the attack. In one of the most publicized moments of the hearing, Clinton drew further criticism from Republicans for her perceived lack of caring when she exclaimed, "What difference, at this point, does it make?"

The House of Representatives also held five hearings to investigate the attack, each concluding that, while the intelligence community had not received a specific threat to the Benghazi facility, the State Department had failed to provide enough protection, despite repeated requests for additional help.

SELECT COMMITTEE ON BENGHAZI FORMS

While most in Washington considered the Benghazi matter closed following this spate of hearings, the House of Representatives passed a bill in May 2014 creating the Select Committee on the Events Surrounding the 2012 Terrorist Attack in Benghazi, Libya. Democrats denounced the committee's formation as a politically motivated measure intended to hurt their party in the 2014 midterm elections and 2016 presidential race. The committee's Republican supporters countered that Congress needed more information to get a complete picture of the Benghazi incident and the Obama administration's related actions. They further accused Clinton of resisting scrutiny and blame for her role in the security lapses.

The bipartisan committee consists of seven Republican and five Democratic members of Congress and is chaired by Rep. Trey Gowdy, R-S.C. It is authorized to conduct a full investigation and issue a final report on all policies, decisions, and activities that led to the consulate attack, affected U.S. ability to prepare for the attack, and comprised the administration's efforts to respond to the attacks and rescue U.S. personnel. The committee was also directed to review the administration's internal and public communications about the attacks, efforts to find and prosecute attackers, and its compliance with congressional inquiries.

As of December 2015, the committee had held a total of four public hearings with State Department and intelligence community witnesses. An interim report released by the committee in May 2015 also indicated that the committee had conducted more than thirty private meetings and briefings with other executive branch officials, many of whom had not previously been questioned by Congress on the Benghazi attack. The committee also said it received tens of thousands of pages of e-mail and documents from the Obama administration for review, though the report lamented the administration's lengthy delays in transmitting the documents.

Throughout this period, Democrats continued to argue that the select committee and its investigations were a waste of taxpayer money, given that they had not revealed any new information, and that it was all for political show. And, once it was confirmed that Clinton would testify before the committee in October, they dismissed the committee as an effort to discredit the presidential candidate. Democratic claims suddenly appeared to hold water when, during an interview with Fox News on September 29, Rep. Kevin McCarthy, R-Calif., said, "Everybody thought Hillary Clinton was unbeatable, right? But we put together a Benghazi special committee, a select committee. What are her numbers today? Her numbers are dropping. Why? Because she's untrustable. But no one would have known any of that had happened had we not fought." Democrats immediately jumped on McCarthy's statement, saying it was proof that the sole purpose of the upcoming committee hearing was to damage Clinton. Clinton also weighed in, remarking, "When I hear a statement like that, which demonstrates unequivocally that this was always meant to be a partisan political exercise, I feel like it does a grave disservice and dishonors not just the memory of the four that we lost but of everybody who has served our country."

Roughly two weeks later, Rep. Richard Hanna, R-N.Y., told a local New York news channel that he thought there was "a big part of this investigation that was designed to go after people and an individual, Hillary Clinton," further feeding the controversy. Gowdy quickly came to his committee's defense, stating, "My team of investigators, drawn from the military, federal agencies and the congressional oversight and ethics committees, has worked hard, and in an above-board manner."

CLINTON APPEARS BEFORE THE SELECT COMMITTEE

On October 22, 2015, Clinton appeared before the committee to testify in what turned out to be a marathon hearing. Gowdy further defended the committee and the need for the hearing in his opening statement, claiming that previous investigations "were narrow in scope and either incapable or unwilling to access the facts and evidence necessary to answer all relevant questions" and that the panel was only seeking the truth. In her opening remarks, Clinton effectively summarized the testimony she had previously given to the Senate Foreign Relations Committee, noting her role in establishing the Accountability Review Board and overseeing the State Department's implementation of its recommendations. She also emphasized the importance of the United States' continued leadership in the Middle East, North Africa, and other regions around the globe, despite the inherent dangers. "Our men and women who serve overseas understand that we do accept a level of risk to represent and protect the country we love," she said. "But it is our responsibility to make sure they have the resources they need to do those jobs and to do everything we can to reduce the risks they face."

Over the next eleven hours, Clinton was questioned by Republicans for her response to the attack, with a focus on accusations that she ignored the consulate's security needs in the preceding months. Clinton largely remained calm and avoided any outbursts, though the hearing did include several notable, tense exchanges. In one such instance, Rep. Jim Jordan, R-Ohio, accused Clinton and Obama staff of trying to pin the incident on the controversial film because they knew admitting it was a terror attack would undermine the administration's strategy in Libya and claims that the United States was neutralizing al Qaeda. Clinton denied the allegation, saying that information about what had happened in Benghazi had been unclear immediately after the attack. "I'm sorry that it doesn't fit your narrative, Congressman, I can only tell you what the facts are," she said.

Late in the hearing, Jordan also probed Clinton on her use of a private e-mail address and server instead of an official State Department e-mail, questioning whether the committee could trust that she had turned over all e-mail related to Benghazi. Notably, the select committee's request for Benghazi-related e-mail had helped reveal Clinton's private e-mail system. Clinton responded by acknowledging that she had made a mistake by using her private e-mail, but she reiterated her previous statement that she had never sent or received classified information at that e-mail address and said she had publicly released her e-mail in an effort to be more transparent.

Clinton family friend and advisor Sidney Blumenthal also became an unexpected focus of the hearing. Republican committee members alleged that Clinton was too focused on reading and responding to Blumenthal's e-mail, which included his own memos on intelligence matters, when she should have been focused on the consulate's security. It was wrong, they argued, that Blumenthal should have access to her e-mail but not Ambassador Stevens and they questioned why she had never responded to more than 600 requests for added security in Benghazi but did respond to Blumenthal. Clinton noted that while Stevens had been in communication with her staff, he had not raised the security issues with them, instead taking the matter to the State Department's security team. She maintained that, while she was responsible for sending the Americans into Libya, she was not responsible for specific security requests, which fall under the purview of other State Department officials.

One of the most widely reported moments of the hearing did not involve Clinton at all. A disagreement between Gowdy and Rep. Elijah Cummings, D-Md., over whether the committee should release a transcript of its interview with Blumenthal devolved into a shouting match. Cummings, who came to Clinton's defense several times during the hearing, later commented, "We are better than using taxpayer dollars to try to destroy a campaign. That is not what America is all about." Rep. Adam Schiff, D-Mass., joined in Clinton's defense, accusing Gowdy of trying to lead the committee to a conclusion that would damage Clinton. Gowdy countered that the hearing was "not a persecution. I have reached no conclusions." Rep. Adam Smith, D-Wash., added to the critiques, noting that the Benghazi panel has "learned absolutely nothing" that had not already been uncovered.

Ultimately, the hearing failed to reveal new information, and the broad consensus in Washington was that Clinton had emerged unscathed. The committee has announced plans to continue interviewing another sixty current and former officials in the coming months.

—Linda Fecteau Grimm

Following is the opening statement by Rep. Trey Gowdy, R-S.C., chair of the Select Committee on Benghazi, on October 22, 2015, at the opening of the hearing; and the text of former secretary of state Hillary Clinton's statement for the record given during the October 22, 2015 hearing.

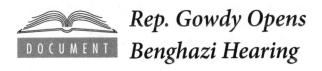

Rep. Gowdy Opens Benghazi Hearing

October 22, 2015

AS PREPARED FOR DELIVERY

Chris Stevens, Sean Smith, Glen Doherty and Tyrone Woods served our country with courage and with honor. They were killed under circumstances most of us could never imagine. Under cover of darkness, terrorists poured through the front gate of our facility and attacked our people and our property with machine guns, mortars and fire. . . .

We know what they gave us. What do we owe them? Justice for those who killed them. We owe their families our everlasting respect and gratitude. We owe them—and each other—the truth.

The truth about why we were in Libya.

The truth about what we were doing in Libya.

The truth about the escalating violence in Libya before we were attacked and these four men lost their lives.

The truth about requests for additional security.

The truth about requests for more personnel.

The truth about requests for more equipment.

The truth about where and why our military was positioned as it was on the anniversary of 9-11.

The truth about what was happening and being discussed in Washington while our people were under attack.

The truth about what led to the attacks.

The truth about what our government told the American people after the attacks.

Why were there so many requests for more security personnel and equipment, and why were those requests denied in Washington?

Why did the State Department compound in Benghazi not even come close to meeting proper security specifications?

What policies were we pursuing in Libya that required a physical presence in spite of the escalating violence?

Who in Washington was aware of the escalating violence in Libya?

What special precautions, if any, were taken on the anniversary of 9-11?

What happened in Washington after the first attack and what was the response to that attack?

What did the military do or not do?

What did our leaders in Washington do or not do and when?

Why was the American public given such divergent accounts of what caused these attacks?

And why is it so hard to get information from the very government these four men were representing and serving and sacrificing for?

Even after an Accountability Review Board and half a dozen congressional investigations, these and other questions still lingered. These questions lingered because those previous investigations were not thorough. These questions lingered because those previous investigations were narrow in scope and either incapable or unwilling to access the facts and evidence necessary to answer all relevant questions.

So the House of Representatives, including some Democrats, asked this Committee to write the final, definitive accounting of what happened in Benghazi. . . .

You will hear a lot about the Accountability Review Board today. Secretary Clinton mentioned the ARB more than 70 times in her previous testimony before Congress. But when you hear about the ARB you should also know State Department leadership hand-picked members of the ARB, the ARB never interviewed Secretary Clinton, the ARB never reviewed her emails and Secretary Clinton's top advisor was allowed to review and suggest changes to the ARB report before the public ever saw it. There is no transcript of ARB interviews, so it is impossible to know whether all relevant questions were asked and answered. And because there is no transcript it is impossible to cite ARB interviews with any particularity at all. That is not independent. That is not accountability. That is not a serious investigation.

You will hear there were previous congressional investigations into Benghazi. That is true. It should make you wonder why those previous investigations failed to interview so many witnesses and failed to access so many documents. If those previous congressional investigations really were serious and thorough, how did they miss Ambassador Stevens' emails? If those investigations were serious and thorough, how did they miss Secretary Clinton's emails? If those previous congressional investigations were serious and thorough, why did they fail to interview dozens of key State Department witnesses including agents on the ground, who experienced the terrorist attacks firsthand?

Just last month, three years after Benghazi, top aides finally returned documents to the State Department. A month ago, this Committee received 1500 new pages of Secretary Clinton's emails related to Libya and Benghazi. 3 years after the attacks. A little over two weeks ago, this Committee received roughly 1400 pages of Ambassador Stevens' emails. 3 years after the attacks.

It is impossible to conduct a serious, fact-centric investigation without access to the documents from the former Secretary of State, the Ambassador who knew more about Libya than anyone else, and testimony from witnesses who survived the attacks.

Madame Secretary, I understand some people—frankly in both parties—have suggested this investigation is about you. Let me assure you **why** it is not. . . . Not a single member of this Committee signed up for an investigation into you or your email system. We signed up because we wanted to honor the service and sacrifice of 4 people sent to a foreign land to represent us—who were killed—and do everything we can to prevent it from happening to others.

Our Committee has interviewed half a hundred witnesses, not a single one of them has been named Clinton until today. You were the Secretary of State for this country when our facility was attacked. So, of course this Committee is going to talk to you. You are an important witness, but you are just one important witness, among half a hundred important witnesses.

I understand you wanted to come sooner than today so let me be clear why that did not happen. You had an unusual email arrangement with yourself, which meant the State Department could not produce your emails to us.

You made exclusive use of personal email and a personal server. When you left the State Department you kept those public records to yourself for almost two years. You and your attorneys decided what to return and what to delete. Those decisions were your decisions, not ours. It was only in March of this year we learned of this email arrangement. Since we learned of your email arrangement we have interviewed dozens of witnesses, only one of whom was about your email arrangement, and that was a very short interview because he invoked his Fifth Amendment privilege against self-incrimination.

Making sure the public record is complete is what serious investigations do. So, it was important to gain access to Ambassador Stevens' emails, the emails of other Sr. leaders and witnesses, and it was important to gain access to your emails. Your emails are no more or less important than anyone else's. It just took longer to get them and garnered more attention in the process. . . .

There are certain characteristics that make our country unique in the annals of history. We are the greatest experiment in self-governance the world has ever known. And part of that self-governance includes self-scrutiny—even of the highest officials. Our country is strong enough to handle the truth. And our fellow citizens expect us to pursue the truth, wherever the facts take us.

So this committee is going to do what we pledged to do, and what should have been done long ago, which is interview the witnesses, examine the relevant evidence, and access the documents. We are going to pursue the truth in a manner worthy of the memory of the four men who lost their lives and worthy of the respect of our fellow citizens.

We are going to write that final, definitive accounting of what happened in Benghazi. We would like to do it with your help, but we are going to do it nonetheless. Because understanding what happened in Benghazi goes to the heart of who we are as a country and the promises we make to those we send into harm's way. They deserve the truth, the whole truth and nothing but the truth. The people we work for deserve the truth. The family and friends of those killed representing this country deserve the truth. There is no statute of limitations on that truth.

SOURCE: House of Representatives. The Select Committee on Benghazi. "Chairman Gowdy's Opening Statement." October 22, 2015. http://benghazi.house.gov/news/press-releases/chairman-gowdys-opening-statement.

Secretary Clinton
Testifies at Benghazi Hearing

October 22, 2015

The terrorist attacks in Benghazi, Libya on September 11, 2012 took the lives of four brave Americans: Ambassador Chris Stevens, Sean Smith, Glen Doherty, and Tyrone Woods.

I knew and admired Chris Stevens. He was one of our nation's most accomplished diplomats, previously serving in Syria, Egypt, Saudi Arabia, and Jerusalem during the second intifada.

I didn't have the privilege of meeting Sean Smith personally, but he was also a valued member of our State Department family. An Information Management officer, he was a veteran of the U.S. Air Force, and served in embassies and consulates in Pretoria, Baghdad, Montreal, and The Hague.

Tyrone Woods and Glen Doherty, who worked for the CIA and were killed at the Agency's outpost in Benghazi, were both former Navy SEALs and trained paramedics with distinguished records of service, including in Iraq and Afghanistan.

As you know, what happened in Benghazi has been scrutinized by an Accountability Review Board, seven previous Congressional investigations, multiple news organizations, and law enforcement and intelligence agencies. Along with other senior Obama administration officials, I also testified about this matter before both the Senate and the House. Today, I would like to summarize the statement I provided to the House Committee on Foreign Affairs on January 23, 2013.

First, the terrorist attacks in Benghazi are part of a broader strategic challenge to the United States and our partners in North Africa.

It's important we understand the context for this challenge, as we work together to protect our people and honor our fallen colleagues. Any clear-eyed examination of this matter must begin with this sobering fact: Since 1988, there have been 19 Accountability Review Boards investigating attacks on American diplomats and their facilities. Since 1977, 65 American diplomatic personnel have been killed by terrorists.

In addition to those who have been killed, we know what happened in Tehran, with hostages being taken in 1979; our embassy and Marine barracks bombed in Beirut in 1983; Khobar Towers in Saudi Arabia in 1996; our embassies in East Africa in 1998; consulate staff murdered in Jeddah, Saudi Arabia in 2004; the Khost attack in Afghanistan in 2009; and too many others.

But I also want to stress the list of attacks that were foiled, crises averted, and lives saved, is even longer. We should never forget that the security professionals get it right more than 99 percent of the time against difficult odds, because the terrorists only need to get it right once. That's why, like all my predecessors, I trusted the diplomatic security professionals with my life.

Administrations of both parties, in partnership with Congress, have made concerted and good-faith efforts to learn from the tragedies that have occurred, to implement recommendations from the review boards, to seek the necessary resources to better protect our people in a constantly-evolving threat environment.

In fact, of the nineteen Accountability Review Boards that have been held since 1988, only two have been made public. I want to stress that, because the two that have been made public, coming out of the East Africa embassy bombings, and this one regarding Benghazi, were honest attempts by the State Department, by the Secretary—Secretary Albright and myself—to be as transparent and open as possible.

We wanted to be sure that whatever these independent, non-partisan boards found would be made available to the Congress, and to the American people. Because as I said many times since September 11th, I take responsibility. And I was determined to leave the State Department and our country safer, stronger, and more secure.

Now, taking responsibility meant not only moving quickly in those first uncertain hours and days to respond to the immediate crisis, but also to make sure we were protecting our people and posts in high-threat areas across the region and the world.

It also meant launching an independent investigation to determine exactly what happened in Benghazi and to recommend steps for improvement. It also meant intensifying our efforts to combat terrorism, and support emerging democracies in North Africa and beyond.

Let me share briefly the lessons we have learned. First, let's start on the night of September 11th itself, and those difficult early days. I directed our response from the State Department and stayed in close contact with officials from across our government and the Libyan government.

So I did see firsthand what Ambassador Pickering and Chairman Mullen called "timely and exceptional coordination." No delays in decision-making, no denials of support from Washington, or from our military.

And I want to echo the review board's praise for the valor and courage of our people on the ground, especially our security professionals in Benghazi and Tripoli. The board said our response saved American lives in real time, and it did. The very next morning, I told the American people, "Heavily-armed militants assaulted our compound," and vowed to bring them to justice. And I stood later that day with President Obama as he spoke of an act of terror.

At this same time period, we were also seeing violent attacks on our embassies in Cairo, Sana'a, Tunis, and Khartoum, as well as large protests outside many other posts from India to Indonesia, where thousands of our diplomats serve. So I immediately ordered a review of our security posture around the world, with particular scrutiny for high-threat posts. And I asked the Department of Defense to join interagency security assessment teams, and to dispatch hundreds of additional Marine security guards.

I named the first Deputy Assistant Secretary of State for high-threat posts so that missions in dangerous places would get the attention they need. And we reached out to Congress, to help address physical vulnerabilities, including risks from fire, and to hire additional diplomatic security personnel, and Marine security guards.

Second, even as I took these steps, I quickly moved to appoint the Accountability Review Board, because I wanted them to come forward with their report before I left, because I felt the responsibility, and I wanted to be sure that I was putting in motion the response to whatever they found. . . . I accepted every one of their recommendations. Our Deputy Secretary for Management and Resources, Tom Nides, led a task force to ensure that all 29 were implemented quickly, and completely, as well as pursuing additional steps above and beyond the board. . . .

We also took a top to bottom look to rethink how we make decisions on where, when, and whether our people should operate in high-threat areas, and how we respond. We initiated an annual high-threat post review, chaired for the first time by the Secretary of State. And ongoing reviews by the deputy secretaries to ensure that pivotal questions about security reach the highest level. And we worked to regularize protocols for sharing information with Congress.

In addition to the immediate action we took, and the review board process, we moved on a third front: addressing the broader strategic challenge in North Africa, and the wider region. Benghazi did not happen in a vacuum. The Arab revolutions scrambled power dynamics, and shattered security forces across the region.

The United States must continue to lead, in the Middle East, in North Africa, and around the globe. When America is absent, especially from unstable environments, there are consequences. Extremism takes root, our interests suffer, and our security at home is threatened. That's why Chris Stevens went to Benghazi in the first place. I asked him to go. During the beginning of the revolution against Gadhafi, we needed somebody in Benghazi who could begin to build bridges with the insurgents and to begin to demonstrate that America would stand against Gadhafi.

Nobody knew the dangers, or the opportunities better than Chris. . . . He never wavered. He never asked to come home. He never said, let's shut it down, quit and go somewhere else, because he understood it was critical for America to be represented in that place, at that pivotal time.

So, we do have to work harder and better to balance the risks and the opportunities. Our men and women who serve overseas understand that we do accept a level of risk to represent and protect the country we love. They represent the best traditions of a bold and generous nation.

They cannot work in bunkers and do their jobs. But it is our responsibility to make sure they have the resources they need to do those jobs and to do everything we can to reduce the risks they face.

For me, this is not just a matter of policy, it's personal because I had the great honor to lead the men and women of the State Department and USAID—nearly 70,000 serving here in Washington and at more than 275 posts around the world. They get up, and go to work every day, often in difficult, and dangerous circumstances, thousands of miles from home, because they believe the United States is the most extraordinary force for peace and progress the earth has ever known. And when we suffer tragedies overseas, the number of Americans apply to the Foreign Service actually increases.

That tells us everything we know about the kind of patriots I'm talking about. They do ask what they can do for their country, and America is stronger for it. After traveling nearly a million miles and visiting 112 countries as Secretary of State, my faith in our country and our future is stronger than ever. Every time that blue and white airplane carrying the words "United States of America" touched down in some far off capital, I felt again the honor it was to represent the world's indispensable nation.

SOURCE: House of Representatives. The Select Committee on Benghazi. "Hillary Rodham Clinton, Statement for the Record, House Select Committee on Benghazi." October 22, 2015. http://benghazi .house.gov/sites/republicans.benghazi.house.gov/files/HRC%20Statement%20for%20the%20 Record%20-%20House%20Select%20Committee%20on%20Benghazi.pdf.

OTHER HISTORIC DOCUMENTS OF INTEREST

FROM THIS VOLUME

FROM PREVIOUS *HISTORIC DOCUMENTS*

November

Turkish President Remarks
on Party's Election Victory

NOVEMBER 2 AND 4, 2015

Following the election of a hung parliament in June, on August 24, 2015, refusing to form a coalition government, Turkish president Recep Tayyip Erdoğan called for snap elections to be held on November 1. The election took place as Turkey faced challenges on multiple fronts, including the ongoing rise of the Islamic State of Iraq and the Levant (ISIL), a flagging economy, and a collapsed ceasefire between the Turkish government and the Kurdistan Workers' Party (PKK). Despite polling in the lead up to the election, when the vote was tallied on November 1, Erdoğan's Justice and Development Party (AKP) won a comfortable majority of seats.

Turkish Voters Deliver Hung Parliament

When Turkish voters went to the polls on June 7, 2015, they did so with great uncertainty about the future of their state. ISIL was tightening its grip in neighboring Syria, forcing millions of Syrians into Turkey. The central government struggled to provide for the massive influx of refugees, and the Turkish public was often frustrated by violence perpetrated by ISIL supporters who came across the border with refugees and by the loss of jobs to Syrians who were willing to work for lower wages. In addition to the threat of ISIL, the Turkish government was still struggling to determine how best to deal with the PKK, a separatist movement that is considered a terrorist organization by both Turkey and a large number of Western nations. Erdoğan's government had last been engaged in successful ceasefire negotiations with the PKK in 2013.

During the June 7 elections, four parties won seats in Turkey's parliament. However, no party won an outright majority and therefore the ability to seat its own government. AKP, which had held power since 2002, won 258 seats, eighteen short of the total needed to form a government. The secular center-left Republican People's Party (CHP), considered the AKP's primary opposition, won 132 seats, while the right-wing National Movement Party (MHP) and the left-wing Kurdish People's Democratic Party (HDP) each took eighty seats.

On July 9, President Erdoğan asked the prime minister and current leader of the AKP, Ahmet Davutoğlu, to attempt to form a coalition government. Davutoğlu was given forty-five days to do so, after which point Erdoğan could choose either to extend the deadline or call for new elections. HDP and MHP refused to join any coalition government headed by AKP, which left Davutoğlu the option of negotiating only with the CHP. Negotiations lasted ten days before breaking down when CHP leader Kemal

Kiliçdaroğlu claimed that Davutoğlu had refused to negotiate a long-term solution and had instead advocated for a three-month interim government that would be replaced following early elections.

ERDOĞAN CALLS SNAP ELECTIONS

On August 18, Davutoğlu reported to Erdoğan that an agreement could not be reached with any of the major parties and, therefore, it planned to allow its mandate to form a government to expire. Erdoğan decided not to exercise his ability to extend the forty-five-day timeframe, and he also declined to give the CHP an opportunity to form a government despite a constitutional requirement to do so. Instead, Erdoğan announced on August 21 that he intended to call snap elections to break the hung parliament, saying that "as president, I know the scope of my authority and I am in a position where I need to use my powers all the way." An official announcement of a snap election was made August 24 at the conclusion of the forty-five-day window for AKP to form a coalition government. "A cabinet of ministers could not be established and it has become evident that, under current conditions, it cannot be formed," Erdoğan said. "Therefore, the decision to call repeat elections has become a necessity."

Erdoğan's critics considered the decision to hold new elections without offering CHP a chance to form a government to be an illegal attempt to ensure AKP's hold on power, instead of conceding to a coalition government. "The president is trampling all democratic precedents in a clear usurpation of the national will to prevent the CHP from forming a government that will relieve Turkey," Haluk Koç, a spokesperson for the CHP said of Erdoğan's decision. Based on Turkish opinion polls, analysts speculated that the outcome of the new election might be the same as the June vote, which would further weaken the AKP and potentially create a leadership vacuum. Concerns were also raised about the interim government that would be established by Davutoğlu tasked with overseeing the election and government operations until November 1. "A provisional government will not only be difficult to form, its legitimacy will also be deeply questioned and its effectiveness will be limited," a report from the Eurasia Group indicated, adding that such a government would be rife "with infighting resulting in a very tense and volatile period." The interim government was seated on August 28, with twelve positions allocated to AKP, twelve to independents, and two to HDP. The CHP and MHP refused to take part in the government.

AKP EMERGES VICTORIOUS

President Erdoğan set the new parliamentary election to be held on November 1 and vowed to respect the outcome, stating that the "election will be for continuity of stability and trust." When Turkish voters went to the polls in November, a renewed round of ceasefire negotiations between the government and PKK had collapsed, the Turkish economy was failing to make any large gains, and Turkish airstrikes against ISIL targets in Iraq and Syria had ramped up. Western governments hoped that the new round of elections would instill greater security and allow a new government to better assist on the global stage in the fight against ISIL, as well as assist in mitigating the flow of migrants into Europe, a journey that had claimed thousands of lives.

Elections for the 550 members of the Turkish parliament are done in a party-list proportional representation format, meaning that a party must win at least 10 percent of a vote nationwide to be allocated seats. Those parties that do not meet this threshold have their seats allocated to the winning party in each electoral district. A total of eighteen parties fielded candidates for the November election.

The lead up to the November election was marred by suppression of media coverage, which drew international attention, and violence against individual candidates and the various parties' headquarters. The AKP campaigned on creating more jobs and raising the minimum wage across the nation. The party also promised a rewrite of the constitution that would be more inclusive and democratic and offered greater protections for human rights. The CHP promised similar economic policies to those of the AKP, but it also said it would offer financial relief for students seeking secondary education and promised greater Internet freedoms. The MHP promised at least one job for each family, an increase in pension payments, and an end to university entrance exams to make it easier for more Turkish youth to attend college. The HDP used its campaign to call for renewed negotiations with the PKK and a return to peace.

Despite polls suggesting otherwise, the AKP won 49.5 percent of the vote, which translated into 316 seats, enough for Erdoğan's AKP to govern without the necessity of forming a coalition. The next closest vote getter was CHP, which won 134 seats, followed by HDP with fifty-nine seats, and MHP with forty-one seats. MHP's defeat at the polls was attributed to the party's refusal to participate in coalition negotiations with the AKP following the June parliamentary election, while HDP's loss was tied to ongoing violence perpetrated by the PKK.

Erdoğan said the vote reflected the idea that "the national will favored stability" and that at the polls "our nation said 'We do not want a coalition. We want to proceed with a single party government.'" Erdoğan said that the most important takeaway from the election was that the nation would benefit from a new constitution. While encouraging the parties in parliament to back the development of a new constitution, Erdoğan also suggested that the nation might consider giving more power to the executive to encourage faster decision making and action on a variety of issues.

Erdoğan called for the result of the election to "be respected by the whole world" but that he had "not seen such maturity." Erdoğan was referring to election monitors from the Organization for Security and Co-operation in Europe (OSCE), which said that violence in the southeastern portion of the country had impacted the election. "Physical attacks on party members, as well as the significant security concerns, particularly in the south-east . . . imposed restrictions on the ability to campaign," said Ignacio Sanchez Amor, the head of the OSCE observer mission, adding that there was evidence that media coverage of the parties and election had been stymied. The Parliamentary Assembly of the Council of Europe (PACE) also called the election process "unfair."

—Heather Kerrigan

Following are two press releases from the office of Turkish president Recep Tayyip Erdoğan on November 2 and 4, 2015, following the outcome of snap elections that left his AKP party in power.

Erdoğan Calls Vote Outcome a Statement on Stability

November 2, 2015

President Recep Tayyip Erdoğan performed the morning prayer at Eyüp Sultan Mosque. After chatting with citizens on his way out, President Erdoğan answered reporters' questions.

A reporter asked whether he was surprised by the outcome of election results. Recalling that the coalition talks did not yield any result, which led to resorting to the national will once again, President Erdoğan said: "The final decisive actor in our political world is the national will. And yesterday on November 1, the national will favored stability. Short-term developments showed the national will that there was no way out other than stability. I pray to Allah that the outcome may lead to beneficial developments for our country and our nation."

Underscoring that when you cannot control every part of the country, it would result in perilous plots, staged against the country, President Erdoğan said: "I always said; one nation, one flag, one homeland and one state. These points are a sine qua non for us. We need to enrich and further strengthen these points. We need to respond to these plots by protecting and upholding these points." Expressing his gratitude to the nation, President Erdoğan also thanked the nation for its democratic maturity.

"THE WHOLE WORLD SHOULD RESPECT THE RESULTS"

Recalling that foreign media outlets associated AK Party with President Erdoğan and said "Do not vote for Erdoğan", a reporter asked: "The majority of those, who vote for AK Party said 'President Erdoğan is carrying out a national struggle. Therefore, we have to support him.' Can we say that the outcome further strengthened your hand in this national struggle?" Noting that evaluations about him would not be right, President Erdoğan said: "Why is the world media taking such a close interest in Turkey while ignoring their own countries? Why don't they respect the national will? The national will elected me by 52%. They still have not respected that fact. This is thought-provoking. Ask them this: Is this your understanding of democracy? Why do not you respect 52%?"

Adding that a party won the power by 50% and the whole world should respect the results, President Erdoğan noted that he did not witness such a maturity in the world except for a few countries. President Erdoğan ended his statement by thanking the nation.

Source: Presidency of the Republic of Turkey. "National will favored stability." November 2, 2015. www.tccb.gov.tr/en/news/542/35824/national-will-favored-stability.html.

Erdoğan Suggests Writing of New Constitution

November 4, 2015

President Recep Tayyip Erdoğan hosted a luncheon at the Presidential Complex for some 400 mukhtars from Aydın, Balıkesir, Bilecik, Bolu, Denizli, Düzce, Eskişehir, Istanbul, Kocaeli, Konya and Yalova.

"WE HAVE NEVER REGARDED ANY APPROVING AUTHORITY OTHER THAN THE NATIONAL WILL"

Addressing his guests at the 14th Mukhtars' Meeting, President Erdoğan declared that he would continue to meet with mukhtars and maintain a strong relation with them. The President said: "As a citizen, coming from the heart of the nation, I have embraced it as a principle to walk my path with my people. That's why we have never regarded any approving authority other than the national will."

"THEY TRIED TO RETURN TURKEY TO THE CHAOTIC DAYS"

Wishing the newly-elected deputies success, President Erdoğan noted that most of the parties, elected into the Parliament on June 7, could not truly and correctly evaluate the outcome of the June 7 elections. The President said: "We witnessed, during this process, that the environment of peace and safety, restored and then maintained with great sacrifices during my 12-year-term as the PM, was put at risk. The separatist terrorist organization and a party, which clearly expressed that it relied on the terrorist organization, worked with all its strength to return Turkey to the chaotic days of bloodshed and tears."

"THE PARALLEL STATE STRUCTURE MOBILIZED ALL ITS MEANS AND CAPABILITIES TO ATTACK TURKEY'S ACHIEVEMENTS"

Stating that the parallel state structure mobilized all its means and capabilities to attack Turkey's achievements, President Erdoğan expressed that those, who deemed themselves as the "flagship of media" in Turkey, backed the treason, committed by the separatist and the parallel terrorist organizations and that a group from the business world also joined this choir.

"This complicated process of lies, slanders, hypocrisy, hubris, impudence and antagonism truly disturbed our nation," President Erdoğan said, adding that he took the country to elections in accordance with his constitutional powers after the coalition talks failed.

"THE NATION STOOD BESIDE THOSE DISPLAYING A LOCAL AND NATIONAL STANCE"

Declaring that, from now on, they would focus on the vision for a great and powerful Turkey to attain their 2023 goals and to solve the problems in the region, President Erdoğan said: "On November 1, our nation said 'We do not want a coalition. We want to proceed with a single party government.' Our nation clearly expressed that those, who embraced the methods of terrorist organizations instead of legitimate means of politics, were on the wrong path. The nation once again warned those, who resorted to violence and excessive acts, dominance of the majority by the minority, through their votes. The nation has rejected politics that would steer Turkey away from the environment of stability and safety."

Stating that the nation stood beside those displaying a local and national stance, President Erdoğan said: "The nation gave a loud and clear message to terror and terrorist organizations, to those that rely on terrorist organizations, to all kinds of parallel structures and to those who failed to demonstrate resistance and sense in the face of them."

"A NEW CONSTITUTION IS ONE OF THE MOST IMPORTANT MESSAGES OF THE ELECTION RESULTS"

President Erdoğan underscored that a new constitution was one of the most important messages of the election results, calling on the political parties to support the preparation of a new constitution.

Pointing out that a wide geography from the Balkans to the Middle East, from the Central Asia to Africa that tied their hopes to Turkey welcomed the election results with joy, President Erdoğan said: "Because as Turkey grows stronger, as Turkey advances on its path in a climate of stability and safety, our brothers look to the future with hope."

Mentioning the problems of the Syrian and Iraqi migrants, Turkey's attitude in the face of these problems and the panic witnessed in the EU countries, President Erdoğan said: "We have been through a War of Independence and we know what it means to fight for independence. We will continue to support our brothers and sisters fighting for their independence."

"THE PERIOD AHEAD OF TURKEY IS NOT A PERIOD FOR DISPUTE"

Underscoring that Turkey would resolutely continue its operations against the terrorist organization both inside the country and abroad until the terrorist organization laid down its arms, buried them in cement and all its members either surrounded or left the country, President Erdoğan said: "Our security forces will continue their operations until the terrorist organization's structures in the cities are brought down. The judicial and administrative investigations will also continue. The period ahead of Turkey is not a period for dispute. It is a period to get results. If we are to name this process, its name, from now on, is the National Unity and Brotherhood Process. We will not tolerate even the slightest threat against our unity, solidarity and brotherhood."

Making a clear distinction between the Kurds and the separatist terrorist organization, President Erdoğan said: "The officials of the People's Democratic Party say '2 thousand Kurds have been killed' in reference to the losses, sustained by the separatist terrorist organization. I am sorry but learn this first; this state would never fire upon its Kurdish citizens. It only fires upon terrorists. In our eyes, there is a clear distinction between the terrorists and the Kurdish people."

Expressing that they would soon finish Turkey's ongoing grand projects and add new projects to the list, President Erdoğan said that they would never give upon their goal to make Turkey one of the top 10 economies in the world.

"MAY THE NOV. 1 ELECTIONS YIELD BENEFICIAL RESULTS FOR OUR COUNTRY!"

"May the November 1 elections yield beneficial results for our country! I congratulate our political parties and deputies, the winners of a democratic competition. I offer my gratitude to each and every individual of our nation for their contributions to the manifestation of the national will," President Erdoğan said and he ended his speech as follows: "I thank each and every single one of you for honoring the Presidential Complex, the House of the Nation."

SOURCE: Presidency of the Republic of Turkey. "The nation has rejected politics that would steer Turkey away from the environment of stability and safety." November 4, 2015. www.tccb.gov.tr/en/news/542/35833/the-nation-has-rejected-politics-that-would-steer-turkey-away-from-the-environment-of-stability-and-safety.html.

OTHER HISTORIC DOCUMENTS OF INTEREST

FROM PREVIOUS *HISTORIC DOCUMENTS*

Justin Trudeau Sworn in
as Canadian Prime Minister

NOVEMBER 4, 2015

On August 2, 2015, Canadian prime minister Stephen Harper requested that Governor Gen. David Johnston dissolve parliament and prepare for a general election to be held on October 19. Though required by law to hold an election that October, Harper broke with Canadian tradition by calling the election in the summer, setting the stage for an unprecedented seventy-eight-day campaign—more than twice the typical campaign length. While seemingly set to advantage Harper's Conservative Party, a number of contentious issues ultimately led to a major electoral upset when the Liberal Party won more than half the seats in parliament and swept in a new prime minister, Justin Trudeau.

The Prospective Prime Ministers

Under Canada's parliamentary system, the leader of the political party that wins the most seats in the House of Commons during an election becomes the next prime minister. Harper had been in office since 2006, having led the Conservatives to two successive electoral victories in 2008 and 2011. The 2015 election was viewed by some as a referendum on Harper and his approach to governing, which his critics argued was both overly aggressive toward opponents and too focused on the Conservative Party's priority issues.

Among the opposition parties, Harper faced Liberal Party leader Justin Trudeau, the son of the late Pierre Trudeau, a two-term prime minister whose early popularity gave rise to the term "Trudeaumania." Justin Trudeau had been a teacher in Vancouver before winning election to the House of Commons in 2008. He became the Liberal Party's leader in 2013 and, at forty-three years old, would be Canada's second-youngest prime minister if his party succeeded in the general election.

Thomas Mulcair led the New Democratic Party, Canada's third mainstream and the most left-leaning, political party. At the time of the 2015 election, the New Democratic Party held the second most seats in parliament, making it the official opposition for the first time in party history. Gilles Duceppe of the Bloc Québécois, a social democratic and separatist party, and Elizabeth May of the Green Party were also engaged in the campaign, though their parties held only six parliamentary seats in 2015.

The Campaign Heats Up

From the beginning, the campaign was marked by issues surrounding Canada's economy, national security, and multiculturalism, in addition to corruption charges in the Senate.

The Senate had long been plagued by such allegations, especially since senators are appointed and the government in power often uses the positions as rewards. On June 9,

2015, the office of Auditor General Michael Ferguson released the findings of its review of 116 sitting and recently retired senators' expense accounts, reporting "irregularities" in more than 25 percent of them. Many of the issues highlighted in the report had to do with whether senators' claimed travel expenses were actually for business trips. Some reportedly expensed meals they had not paid for, while others claimed unjustified living expenses. All told, the questionable expenses totaled approximately C$840,000 ($602,000). The auditors recommended that the Senate send nine of these cases on to the police for possible criminal investigation, while the remaining instances were referred to an internal Senate body for further review.

The audit began in 2013 amid a dispute over expense claims submitted by four senators, three of whom Harper had appointed. Senate rules allow members who live more than 62 miles from Ottawa to claim living expenses while they are in the capital. Sen. Mike Duffy, a Harper appointee, had claimed his permanent residence was on Prince Edward Island, where he had a summer cottage, but for all other matters—including taxes—he listed his permanent residence as in Ottawa. He received C$90,000 in living expenses over four years, an amount that Conservatives said Duffy had repaid. However, it was later revealed that Harper's chief of staff had given Duffy a personal check to cover the reimbursement. The chief of staff resigned once the news broke, and Harper maintained he knew nothing of the check. Duffy went on trial for fraud and corruption in April 2015, which brought the issue back into the public eye shortly before the election.

Canada's stagnating economy was also a hotly debated campaign issue. Falling oil prices had dealt a blow to the country's energy industry, with the ongoing loss of manufacturing jobs and lagging exports of Canadian goods compounding the problem. Trudeau called for increased investment in infrastructure and running moderate budget deficits to help restimulate the economy, while Harper and Mulcair called for maintaining balanced budgets. The three parties were also divided on the Trans-Pacific Partnership (TPP), a free trade agreement involving twelve countries, including Canada. Harper claimed the agreement would be a tool for economic revitalization, but Mulcair said it would threaten thousands of jobs in the auto parts industry and refused to be bound by it. Trudeau expressed general support for free trade, though declined to take a position on TPP until the full text of the agreement became public.

The Harper government's handling of Syrian refugees was also a focus of the campaign. In September, it was revealed that the three-year-old Syrian boy found dead on a Turkish beach—photos of whom instantly went viral and prompted international outrage—was on his way to Canada with his family. The news brought increased attention to the government's slow processing of refugees. In January 2015, the government had promised to allow 10,000 Syrian refugees to enter Canada over a three-year period. By late August, the government had admitted approximately 1,000 Syrians, a figure that drew sharp criticism from aid groups and prospective refugee sponsors. On October 8, Minister of Citizenship and Immigration Chris Alexander confirmed in a statement that the prime minister's office had intervened in and slowed the process of reviewing Syrians' refugee claims—a highly unusual move. Alexander claimed the intervention was meant to ensure that Canadian security was not compromised and that refugees were sufficiently protected, although the applications had already been vetted through Canada's normal review process. Both Trudeau and Mulcair criticized Harper for this action.

National security was an important issue in the campaign, as well. In June, parliament approved a series of highly controversial antiterrorism measures put forth by Harper in the wake of a terrorist attack on Parliament Hill in October 2014. The new law lowered the threshold of evidence required to arrest someone suspected of terrorism, criminalized the promotion or advocacy of terrorism, expanded the no-fly list, permitted officials to seize or force a website to remove materials promoting or encouraging terrorist acts, and gave the Canadian Security Intelligence Service broad ability to "disrupt" suspected terror activity, whether that be by intercepting goods and financial transactions, interrupting a phone call, or other means. Opposition leaders characterized the law as vague and dangerous, and polls showed that more than half of Canadians opposed the measures. Along with Harper, Trudeau drew some criticism on this issue during the campaign because he voted for the law, though he promised to amend it if the Liberals won the election.

At the same time, Canada was contending with an increase in anti-Muslim sentiment, and Harper's advancement of related policy measures played a role in his shifting support. Back in 2011, Harper banned Muslim women from wearing the *niqab*, a face veil, during citizenship swearing-in ceremonies. One woman sued the government over the ban and won a favorable decision from the Federal Court of Appeal in September 2015. The court ruled that she had the right to wear religious headgear during the public ceremony after showing her face in private to verify her identity. Harper vowed to appeal the decision to Canada's Supreme Court and suggested he would consider applying similar rules to the federal civil service. Harper's actions contributed to a boost in the Conservatives' poll numbers, at the expense of the New Democratic Party. Then on October 2, the government introduced a new initiative to create a police hotline for Canadians to report "barbaric cultural practices," drawing widespread criticism from the press and the public. *The Globe and Mail* said the government was engaging in a "culture war fabricated to take voters' minds off the real and complex issues in this election," while the *Toronto Star* accused Harper of "relentlessly fanning hostility toward Muslims." A new hashtag, #BarbaricCulturalPractices, was created on Twitter, and Canadians used it both to sarcastically—for example, decrying the combination of socks and sandals—and seriously criticize Harper.

SHIFTING OUTLOOK TOWARDS LIBERALS

Amid these issues, Conservatives sought to portray Trudeau as inexperienced and ran negative ads with the slogan suggesting he was "Just not ready." Liberals later flipped the slogan and tried to use it to their advantage, proclaiming Trudeau as "Ready" in campaign ads.

Some analysts speculated that the longer campaign actually hurt Harper and the Conservatives, because it gave the public more time to get to know Trudeau and for Trudeau to overcome the low expectations Conservatives had set for him. For example, he exceeded expectations in the campaign's five debates, three of which covered a variety of topics while two focused specifically on the economy and foreign policy. At the same time, Harper appeared to grow increasingly unpopular with voters. Some attributed this dislike to Harper's long tenure in office; others noted that his policies had alienated various constituencies over the years, causing overall opposition to add up. Harper also made several decisions in the final days of the campaign that some viewed as desperate, including participating in an event with the scandal-racked former mayor of Toronto, Rob Ford.

LIBERALS SWEEP PARLIAMENT

Nearly 69 percent of Canadians turned out to vote on October 19. In a stunning upset, the Liberal Party won 184 of 338 seats in the election, marking an incredible turnaround for a party that had won only 34 seats in 2011. The Conservatives won 99 seats, down from 159 seats in the previous parliament. The New Democratic Party came in third with 44 seats, followed by Bloc Québécois with 10 seats and the Green Party with 1 seat. The results meant that Canada also had a new prime minister.

"Canadians have spoken," Trudeau said before an audience of supporters in Montreal. "You want a government with a vision and an agenda for this country that is positive and ambitious and hopeful. Well, my friends I promise you tonight that I will lead that government."

Harper conceded during a speech in Calgary and also resigned his leadership of the Conservative Party. "The disappointment you all so feel, is my responsibility and mine alone," he said.

A NEW GOVERNMENT

Trudeau and his new Cabinet were sworn in on November 4 at Rideau Hall in Ottawa. A small audience was invited to attend the ceremony in-person, but Trudeau also broke with tradition and invited the public onto the residence grounds, where they were able to watch the swearing-in on large screens. "We will be a government that governs for all Canadians and brings Canadians together," Trudeau said in a statement following the ceremony. "We will work tirelessly to honour the trust Canadians have given us, and together build an even better future for our children and grandchildren." The new prime minister also published an open letter to Canadians promising to bring real change to the government and calling for them to hold the government accountable to its commitments.

Trudeau said that when parliament returned in December, his first legislative priority would be lowering taxes for middle-income Canadians and raising taxes on the top 1 percent of earners. In addition, new Justice minister Joy Wilson-Raybould confirmed that she and the ministers of Health and Public Safety were working on legislation to decriminalize the possession of marijuana. Trudeau also promised to rebuild relationships with Canada's indigenous people and met with tribal chiefs during the Assembly of First Nations on December 7. Among other things, he pledged to invest in education programs and launch an investigation into the disappearance and murder of hundreds of indigenous women. Trudeau announced a major reform to the appointment process for senators in the early days of his administration as well, calling for a five-member board to select appointees.

—Linda Fecteau Grimm

Following is the text of Prime Minister Justin Trudeau's statement on November 4, 2015, shortly after his swearing-in ceremony; and the text of a letter from Trudeau to the Canadian people following the seating of his government on November 4, 2015.

Prime Minister Trudeau on His Swearing-in Ceremony

November 4, 2015

The Right Honourable Justin Trudeau, Prime Minister of Canada, today issued the following statement after the swearing-in of the 29th Ministry:

"Canadians from all across this country sent a message that it is time for real change, and I am deeply honoured by the faith they have placed in my team and me. Canadians chose a positive and optimistic plan for the future, and we will immediately begin implementing our plan for a strong middle class.

"Today we have the pleasure of introducing the team of extraordinary Canadians who will serve in the new Ministry. This strong, diverse, and experienced team will serve all Canadians, and for the first time in our country's history, there will be an equal number of women and men around the Cabinet table.

"Canadians expect to see their values and priorities reflected in their government, and we have listened closely to them. Canadians told us what kind of government they want, and we built the plan to make it happen.

"We are committed to investing in our economy, strengthening the middle class, and helping those working hard to join it. We will invest in job creation and broad-based prosperity to ensure every Canadian has a real and fair chance to succeed.

"We will shine more light on government to ensure it remains focused on the people it is meant to serve. Openness and transparency will be our constant companions, and we will work to restore Canadians' trust in their government and in our democracy. We are committed to the highest ethical standards and applying the utmost care in the handling of public funds.

"We will demonstrate national leadership and work with the provinces and territories to take real action on climate change and create the clean jobs of tomorrow.

"We will further strengthen our great country with a renewed, nation-to-nation relationship with Indigenous Peoples, based on a recognition of rights, respect, co-operation, and partnership. We will fulfil our sacred obligation to Canadian veterans and their families, who have given so much in service to our country. We are committed to both the security and safety of Canadians and the protection of their rights and freedoms. We will also reinvest in our cultural and creative industries and create an immigration system grounded in both compassion and economic opportunity.

"Canada is strong not in spite of its diversity, but because of it, and we are committed to bringing new leadership and a new tone to Ottawa. We also made a commitment to pursue our goals with a renewed sense of collaboration. Most importantly, we will be a government that governs for all Canadians and brings Canadians together.

"We will work tirelessly to honour the trust Canadians have given us, and together build an even better future for our children and grandchildren."

SOURCE: Office of the Prime Minister of Canada. "Statement by the Prime Minister of Canada Following the Swearing-in of the 29th Ministry." November 4, 2015. http://pm.gc.ca/eng/news/2015/11/04/statement-prime-minister-canada-following-swearing-29th-ministry. © Her Majesty the Queen in Right of Canada, 2016.

DOCUMENT

Prime Minister Trudeau Pens Open Letter to Canadians

November 4, 2015

My dear friends,

Today, I had the pleasure of introducing our team of extraordinary Canadians who will serve as Ministers in your new government. As a Canadian, you expect to see your values and priorities reflected in your government—and we have listened closely. Our strong, diverse, and experienced team will serve all Canadians, and—for the first time in our country's history—there will be an equal number of women and men around the Cabinet table.

Over the course of the campaign, we promised you a government that will bring real change—in both the things we do and the way we do them. We will immediately start implementing our plan for a strong and growing middle class. On Election Day, you sent a clear message, and you rightly expect us to fulfill our promises.

I am writing to you, today, to reaffirm my commitment to spend the next four years working hard to deliver on those promises. It is time for leadership that never seeks to divide Canadians, but takes every single opportunity to bring us together, including in Parliament.

We made a commitment to invest in growing our economy, strengthening our middle class, and helping those working hard to join it. We committed to fighting climate change and protecting our environment. We made a commitment to provide more direct help to those who need it by giving less to those who do not. We committed to public investment as the best way to spur growth, job creation, and economic prosperity. And we committed to a responsible, transparent fiscal plan for challenging economic times. We expect you to hold the government accountable for delivering these commitments.

Our country faces many real and immediate challenges—from a struggling middle class to the threat of climate change. If we are to overcome these obstacles, Canadians need to have faith in their government's honesty and willingness to listen. That is why we committed to set a higher bar for openness and transparency in Ottawa. Government and its information must be open by default. Simply put, it is time to shine more light on government to make sure it remains focused on the people it was created to serve—you.

But in order for you to trust your government, you need a government that will trust you. When we make a mistake—as all governments do—it is important that we acknowledge that mistake and learn from it. We know that you do not expect us to be perfect—but you expect us to work tirelessly, and to be honest, open, and sincere in our efforts to serve the public interest.

Before the election, we also made a commitment to bring new leadership and a new tone to Ottawa. Moving forward, we will pursue our goals and objectives with a renewed sense of collaboration. We fully understand and appreciate that partnerships with provincial, territorial, and municipal governments are vital to deliver the real, positive change that we promised you.

It is also time for a renewed, Nation-to-Nation relationship with Indigenous Peoples, one based on a recognition of rights, respect, co-operation, and partnership. Not only is this the right thing to do, but it is also a sure path to economic growth.

To close, I am deeply grateful to have this opportunity to serve you—and every Canadian across our great country. I am committed to leading an open, honest government that is accountable to Canadians, lives up to the highest ethical standards, brings our country together, and applies the utmost care and prudence in the handling of public funds.

Thank you for having faith in me. Thank you for putting your trust in our team.

We will not let you down.

Rt. Hon. Justin Trudeau, P.C., M.P.
Prime Minister of Canada

Source: Office of the Prime Minister of Canada. "Prime Minister Justin Trudeau's Open Letter to Canadians." November 4, 2015. http://pm.gc.ca/eng/news/prime-minister-justin-trudeaus-open-letter-canadians. © Her Majesty the Queen in Right of Canada, 2016.

Other Historic Documents of Interest

From this volume

- United Nations Issues Report Regarding the Ongoing Crisis in Syria, p. 583
- World Leaders Remark on ISIL Attacks, p. 608

From previous *Historic Documents*

- Canadian Officials on the Shutdown of Parliament, *2008*, p. 564

Taiwan's President Remarks on Historic Meeting with Chinese President

NOVEMBER 7, 2015

Chinese president Xi Jinping and Taiwanese president Ma Ying-jeou made history in November 2015 when they came together for the first meeting between leaders of the two governments since 1945. China and Taiwan's strained relations date back to 1949 when Chiang Kai-shek, leader of the Chinese nationalist political party, Kuomintang, was defeated in a civil war against Mao Zedong and the Communist Party and fled to the island to start a new government. Chiang claimed that the Communist government was illegitimate and that Taiwan, established as the Republic of China, was the mainland's rightful ruler, whereas the Communist People's Republic of China viewed Taiwan as a renegade province that belonged to the mainland. These competing claims have persisted through present day and continue to define political and economic relations between the two governments. Taiwan–China tensions have eased since Ma's election, but he has faced considerable criticism from the Taiwanese people, many of whom believe the island has become too economically dependent on China through Ma's actions, and his party's electoral prospects for 2016 appeared to be quickly eroding. The largely symbolic meeting between Ma and Xi was widely perceived to be a political play by both parties to shore up support for the Kuomintang at the expense of the Democratic Progressive Party (DPP), which has taken a stronger stance in favor of Taiwan's independence.

1992 CONSENSUS

Much of the recent tension between China and Taiwan in recent decades is connected to their 1992 Consensus, an agreement that states there is only one China, but allows the two governments to interpret that concept as they choose. China has sometimes reacted aggressively to perceived or potential violations of this agreement, including use of military force. In 1995 and 1996, for example, China launched several missiles over the Taiwan Strait—the 100-mile body of water separating the two—ahead of Taiwan's first direct presidential election in an effort to diminish support for then-President Lee Teng-hui, a strong advocate for the island's independence. Before Taiwan's next presidential election in 2000, Chinese premier Zhu Rongji offered a subtle threat during a press conference in an effort to undermine DPP candidate Chen Shui-ban. "Let me advise all these people in Taiwan. Do not just act on impulse at this juncture, which will decide the future course that China and Taiwan will follow. Otherwise, I'm afraid you won't get another opportunity to regret," he said. Then in 2005, China passed a law making Taiwan's secession illegal and threatening military action if the island government did not comply.

Other recent tensions have centered around China's construction of military facilities on the Paracels and Spratlys islands in the South China Sea. In a centuries-old disagreement, China, Taiwan, Malaysia, Brunei, Vietnam, and the Philippines have all made competing territorial claims on the region, which, in addition to having possible oil and gas reserves, is part of a major shipping route and home to fertile fishing grounds. There have been a number of maritime stand-offs between these countries, and tensions reached new heights in June 2015, following China's announcement that it had created seven new islands from seafloor sediment, upon which it had built ports, airstrips, radar facilities, and other military buildings. Also in 2015, China conducted a military exercise that included an assault on a building that looked very similar to the presidential office building in Taipei, setting off alarm in Taiwan that China could be planning a military invasion of the island.

China has also moved to push Taiwan out of the international community, starting with Taiwan's loss of its UN seat to China in 1971. China believes that Taiwan's international involvement would signify its legitimacy and could lead to the perception of the island government as a sovereign nation. While the Western world had allied with Chiang's government in the 1940s and refused to recognize China's Communist government, this alliance began to erode in earnest in 1979 after the United States, under President Richard Nixon, moved to normalize diplomatic relations with mainland China and opened an embassy in Beijing. The United States also signed a joint communiqué that read in part that "the Government of the United States of America acknowledges the Chinese position that there is but one China and Taiwan is part of China." Notably, the United States also passed the Taiwan Relations Act of 1979 to affirm its support for Taiwan's democratic system and continued conducting diplomatic relations with the government through a nonprofit called American Institute in Taiwan. The United States has provided ongoing military support for Taiwan since then to help prevent the breakout of a full-scale war in the Pacific.

Although the United States maintained relations with Taiwan, many other countries began to follow its example and recognize China as a legitimate government. China's promises to provide development aid and leveraging of its burgeoning population and emerging economy further motivated this change. More than thirty countries have since transitioned from pursuing diplomatic relations with Taiwan to engaging Beijing. Taiwan has attempted several times to regain its UN seat but has been opposed by the United States, Russia, and even the Taiwanese people. However, in May 2009, the Chinese government allowed Taiwan to observe the proceedings at the World Health Assembly under the name of "Chinese Taipei." This was the first time Taiwan had been granted observer status at a UN body since 1971 and was viewed by many as its reentry into world affairs.

EASING OF TENSIONS UNDER MA PRESIDENCY

To some extent, tensions between China and Taiwan have eased during Ma's presidency, in part because of his government's preservation of the status quo—not reunifying with China, but also not declaring independence. Ma has also been more willing to engage with China than some of his predecessors. The two governments have signed twenty agreements since Ma took office in 2008, which have helped increase trade between China and Taiwan by about 50 percent and also fueled tourism. About four million Chinese tourists visited Taiwan in 2014—a journey that had once been prohibited by the government.

However, Ma's approach to China has not always been favorably received by the Taiwanese people. In 2010, the two governments signed an Economic Cooperation Framework Agreement that cut tariffs on hundreds of Taiwanese exports to China and Chinese products entering Taiwan. The agreement was unanimously approved by Taiwan's Legislative Yuan, but thousands of citizens protested the deal, claiming it could flood the market with cheap Chinese products and would be an unwanted step toward reunification.

Support for Ma's economic policies further eroded during the global economic recession, which severely impacted Taiwan's economy. While Taiwan's economy had grown at a rapid pace since the 1990s with its production of high-end electronics components, that growth began to shrink in 2010 following the recession and as China's growth slowed. In five years, Taiwan's annual GDP growth fell from 12 percent to less than 4 percent, leading many to argue that the island had become too dependent on its biggest trading partner, China.

Then in June 2013, the two governments signed a service trade agreement that would open eighty Chinese industries and sixty-four Taiwanese industries to investment by each other and would purportedly help create thousands of jobs and generate hundreds of millions of dollars in export revenue for Taiwan. The agreement had to be ratified by the Legislative Yuan, where it faced strong opposition. In March 2014, the Kuomintang pushed the bill out of committee and onto the floor for consideration, prompting 200 activists to storm and occupy the legislature building in protest and another 500,000 people to demonstrate against the bill in the streets of Taipei. Led primarily by students, the protestors argued that the public had not been given sufficient time to review the agreement before it was pushed through the legislature and that Ma had not addressed their suspicions about the motives behind the deal. Calling themselves the Sunflower Movement, the protestors did not leave the building until Wang Jin-pyng, president of the Legislative Yuan, offered to pass a bill giving lawmakers more oversight of agreements with China.

Ma and the Kuomintang's faltering support led the party to a major defeat in 2014 in Taiwan's local elections—a loss considered a resounding public rejection of Ma's engagement with China. There is a deep distrust of China among the island's citizens, many of whom believe that any agreement or action involving the mainland that appears to help Taiwan is actually part of China's ongoing effort to take control of the island. Most do not want to reunify with China because they enjoy a better quality of life and have more political rights than those on the mainland, and they fear that reunification would erode those rights, as was true in Hong Kong after it rejoined China in 1997. They also increasingly identify as Taiwanese and not Chinese; polling conducted since the 1990s shows that the number of islanders who identify as Taiwanese has grown from nearly 18 percent in 1992 to 60 percent in 2015, while Chinese identification has fallen from just over 25 percent to about 3 percent. At the same time, polls show the majority of Taiwan's citizens want to maintain status quo relations with China.

XI AND MA MEET

Xi and Ma met on November 7, 2015, at the Shangri-La Hotel in Singapore. Ma had reportedly negotiated with the Chinese government for two years to secure the meeting. The talks began with a lengthy handshake and a photo op for media before both men gave opening remarks that were mostly broadcast live on Chinese TV; state-owned channels did not air Ma's statement or broadcast them later in the day.

Xi spoke first and acknowledged that the meeting was a historic step in opening new relations between the two governments. "We are seated together here today so that the tragedies of history will not be repeated, so that the gains from peaceful development across the strait will not be won and again lost, so that compatriots on both sides of the strait continue making peaceful and tranquil lives, and so that succeeding generations can share a beautiful future," he said. None of his remarks suggested that China would withdraw its claim to Taiwan. In fact, Xi noted that the people of China and Taiwan were "one family with blood that is thicker than water," and later stated, "We should use our actions to demonstrate to the world that Chinese people on both sides of the strait fully have the ability and wisdom to solve their own problems." Ma called for "both sides" to "respect each other's values and way of life" in his remarks. "Over the past 66 years, the two sides have developed as different systems. Turning military conflict into peaceful development has definitely not been an overnight effort," he added.

Details of Xi and Ma's discussion were not released, and the two reportedly did not reach any major new agreements. Some questioned why the two leaders would engage in this largely symbolic meeting at that particular time, prompting speculation that the encounter was timed to give the Kuomintang a boost before the 2016 elections. Ma's term will end in 2016, and it is widely expected that the DPP's Tsai Ing-wen will win the presidency and that the Kuomintang may not be able to maintain its hold on the legislature. Given Tsai's support for a more restrained approach to China and firmer stance in favor of Taiwan's independence, political observers question whether China–Taiwan relations will continue to warm once Ma leaves office, or if Tsai's administration will roll back some of his efforts. Observers also posit that these factors played a role in bringing China to the table, because the meeting provided an opportunity for the government to remind Taiwanese voters that it is beneficial to maintain a friendlier, more collaborative relationship with the mainland.

—Linda Fecteau Grimm

Following is the text of remarks delivered by Taiwanese president Ma Ying-jeou on November 7, 2015, following his meeting with Chinese president Xi Jinping.

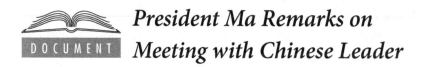

President Ma Remarks on Meeting with Chinese Leader

November 7, 2015

In my meeting with Mr. Xi, we exchanged views on cross-strait relations, peaceful development and the consolidation of the status quo of peace and prosperity. You must all be concerned about the atmosphere at the meeting. The meeting took place in a frank and very positive atmosphere. I found Mr. Xi to be pragmatic, flexible, and candid when discussing the issues. We hope that this spirit will be reflected in the handling of cross-strait relations.

Our discussions focused on several points.

The first point is the consolidation of the 1992 Consensus and the maintenance of peace across the Taiwan Strait. I told Mr. Xi that the consensus reached between the two sides in November 1992 was that the two sides of the Taiwan Strait insist on "one China," but differ as to what that means, and each side could express its interpretation verbally. This was the 1992 Consensus of "one China, respective interpretations." Our side's interpretation does not involve two Chinas; one China, one Taiwan; or Taiwan independence, as the Republic of China Constitution does not allow it. I also emphasized that sustainable peace and prosperity should be the common goal in the development of cross-strait relations. We will continue to consolidate the 1992 Consensus of "one China, respective interpretations" as the basis for relations, and maintain the status quo of peace and prosperity.

The second point is the reduction of hostility and peaceful handling of disputes. We told Mr. Xi that the people of Taiwan are especially concerned about security and dignity. We wanted Mr. Xi and mainland China to understand that we hope all disputes, whether they be political, military, social, cultural, legal, or of any other form, can be peacefully resolved, allowing both sides to experience mutual good will. I made special mention of the frustrations our people have had when participating in NGO activities, as well as the interventions our government has faced when taking part in regional economic integration and other international activities. We hope to see a reduction of hostility in these areas, especially with regard to our NGOs. I told Mr. Xi that these organizations comprise elite members and specialists, who have reacted quite strongly to these issues and the treatment they received. We hope there will be fewer such occurrences.

In response, Mr. Xi said he hopes these issues will be appropriately handled case by case.

I also stated that many people in Taiwan are concerned about mainland China's military deployments against Taiwan, including the Zhurihe base, with which we are all familiar and where missiles are deployed. Mr. Xi said that these deployments are in principle not targeted at Taiwan.

The third point is the expansion of cross-strait exchanges and mutual benefits. We emphasized that given the fact that Taiwan and mainland China have different social and economic systems, the two sides need sufficient time to engage in deeper exchanges. We also reiterated Taiwan's interest in participating in regional economic integration. The issue of which side joins first and which side joins later should not arise. Mr. Xi expressed willingness to discuss this issue and welcomed our participation in the Asian Infrastructure Investment Bank and mainland China's "one belt, one road" initiative.

The fourth point is the establishment of a cross-strait hotline. We believe that a hotline can be set up between the Mainland Affairs Council Minister and the Taiwan Affairs Office Minister, who can then exchange views on important or urgent issues. Mr. Xi stated that this matter could be promptly dealt with.

With regard to cultural and educational exchanges, I also expressed the hope that mainland China can allow more vocational college graduates to pursue higher education in Taiwan. I noted that our efforts over the past several years have met with limited success. As we from Taiwan know, our polytechnic universities have a shortage of students. I drew attention to the fact that Vietnam, Thailand, India, and Indonesia have been funding university lectures to pursue graduate studies at polytechnic institutes in Taiwan. We welcome these students. Before I took office, we had about 30,000 students from overseas studying in Taiwan. This year, the figure has increased to above 100,000. We intend to transform Taiwan into an Asia-Pacific center for higher education. I mentioned that mainland China has over a million vocational college graduates. Mr. Xi said he is willing to look into this matter. The vocational college graduates I refer to are like graduates from five-year junior colleges in Taiwan who then enroll in two-year programs at polytechnic colleges.

The fifth and final point is joint cooperation for cross-strait prosperity. I suggested that history has left behind several issues that the two sides cannot resolve overnight.

These issues must be handled pragmatically. If we deal rashly with some of the excessively sensitive issues, it will make things worse. The maintenance of cross-strait peace and stability is Taiwan's mainstream view. How cross-strait relations develop in the future will have to take into account the direction of public opinion. In particular, I reiterated that cross-strait relations should be built on the foundation of dignity, respect, sincerity, and good will, for only then can we narrow the psychological gap between the two sides.

I especially expressed the hope that the two sides can turn hostility into friendship and seek peace, not war.

After concluding his remarks, the president then opened the floor to questions from the media.

Following is a translation of the questions and responses in their entirety:

Q1: The media is calling this meeting a historic handshake. It seems that Mr. Xi responded to all the issues you brought up. But the point is, how will those responses be turned into concrete results in the future? In addition, your term in office will soon be coming to a close. President Ma, what expectations do you have for your successor?

President: Those are good questions. Today the leaders of the two sides of the Taiwan Strait have gotten together, but we couldn't really deal with overly technical issues. As such, we discussed principles and major issues. Any concord reached by the two sides, of course, is just an indicator. Let's take the 1992 Consensus as an example. This is the first time the leaders of the two sides discussed this issue since reaching that consensus in 1992. I just read to everyone, word by word, what the 1992 Consensus is, and why it reads "one China, respective interpretations." "Two Chinas," "one China, one Taiwan," and "Taiwan independence" will not be used in the Republic of China's interpretation of that consensus. The two sides have already discussed the 1992 Consensus for so many years, and this is the first time that the truth has been restored in the presence of the leaders from the two sides. That question came from Ho Zhen-zhung (何振忠) from the United Daily News (UDN). Originally, the term "one China, respective interpretations" was first used in the UDN on November 18, 1992.

As for the hotline, why does it connect Taiwan's Mainland Affairs Council (MAC) and the mainland's Taiwan Affairs Office (TAO), and not higher levels [of government]? We're starting there because there's already a hotline between the Straits Exchange Foundation (SEF) and the MAC at the deputy minister level. So now we'll set one up between the two ministers. We'll see how well it functions, and then see whether we need to make further adjustments.

Q2: The Taiwan public has expectations associated with "one China, respective interpretations." However, neither TAO Minister Zhang Zhijun (張志軍) nor Mr. Xi Jinping brought up "one China, respective interpretations." Is that disappointing? Do you feel that today's meeting was conducted based on equality and dignity?

President: I just pointed out that when the 1992 Consensus was formally confirmed on November 16, 1992, it specifically mentioned that both sides uphold the "one China" principle, but had different interpretations of that principle, which would be expressed in oral statements. Newspapers subsequently used the word "interpretation," and so everyone started to use that term. I just showed everyone a newspaper from that year, so it's quite clear. As for implementation, Mr. Xi has instructed the relevant agencies to discuss and research most of the issues, and the MAC will continue to follow up to see how things go. I emphasized that if the leadership doesn't make decisions, sometimes grass-roots elements will drag their feet.

Q3: You and Mr. Xi expressed hope to reduce hostility between the two sides, and you also mentioned that the Taiwan public is concerned about the deployment of missiles [on the mainland aimed at Taiwan]. Did you assert your position on removing those missiles?

President: I mentioned a bit earlier that their [mainland China's] deployment is a general, overall deployment program, not directed at the people of Taiwan. I think . . . I'm afraid that this is the first time that the leaders of the two sides have talked about this issue. At least I brought it up, and told him that the people in Taiwan are concerned. So I hope Mr. Xi will pay more attention to this issue.

Q4: During your discussions, did you raise the issue of Taiwan's marginalization with the mainland side, and mention Taiwan's desire to increase its participation in the international community?

President: I just talked about this on two different levels. One level concerns private NGOs. We have some civic groups that find it difficult to participate in international organizations. And I made a point to say that people in Taiwan have complained that they can't use their passports to get tour tickets of the United Nations. I explained that a small matter like that, if not handled correctly, can lead to a lot of dissatisfied people. On another level, the issue is our participation in international and regional economic integration. That's the governmental level, and we hope that it doesn't come down to an issue of who gets in first, since both sides are going to take part, and that would be advantageous to everyone. The participation of both sides in the World Trade Organization has benefited everyone, and we hope that's how things will be in the future. I also mentioned the Trans-Pacific Partnership (TPP) and the Regional Comprehensive Economic Partnership (RCEP), and let him know that issue is very important for both of us. So let's not look at these issues in terms of which side gets in first, as we should both participate.

Q5: President Ma, last year in an interview with the media you stated that when the leaders of the two sides meet, they should stabilize the concept of "1992 Consensus, respective interpretations," thus creating an "ultra-stable framework." Was that objective achieved through today's meeting?

President: I feel that it was helpful. First, the atmosphere today was good. Second, both sides were extremely positive about being able to hold today's meeting, and felt that this was a rare and historic opportunity. That's a very healthy and positive attitude. Both sides embrace the 1992 Consensus. Perhaps there are issues concerning how it's interpreted, but basically, the general direction is the same. If future presidents of the ROC, no matter who they are, can continue to promote the 1992 Consensus this way, I am confident that the status quo we have created can be maintained, and continue to move forward.

Q6: During the meeting when several substantive matters came up, did Mr. Xi directed related agencies to follow up? With regard to economic and trade cooperation and international organizations, when TAO Minister Zhang made remarks and mentioned the Asian Infrastructure Investment Bank, did he express hope that Taiwan would join under an appropriate name? Did Mr. Xi mention any concrete measures to be taken? Did you ask related agencies to become involved and was a concrete timetable set?

President: Yes. Mr. Xi stated that Taiwan would be able to participate in an appropriate manner and this was clarified in a concrete manner. About other things, like the NGO situation that I talked about, he said that they are willing to consider it as long as it doesn't create an impression of "two Chinas" or "one China, one Taiwan." We said that we weren't talking about any specific application, but we will sort out the various kinds of activities we want to participate in. Since Mr. Xi had made such statement, we hope this will come about. This is a task that the MAC and other related agencies will deal with once we return to Taiwan.

Q7: This Ma-Xi meeting is a milestone and opens a new chapter in the development of cross-strait relations. What type of prospects do you see for this new platform and new chapter?

President: I stated in the press conference I held two days ago that this meeting is not about an individual or a party. It is being held with Taiwan's future in mind and so that we can continue to interact with the mainland. In the future, the leader of Taiwan and the leader of the mainland should still have opportunities to replicate this type of meeting. In other words, my goal is for meetings between the leaders of the two sides to become normalized. Today was a first step. It is really quite odd that cross-strait relations have already reached this level, but that the cross-strait leaders have never met, isn't it? It should be a normal thing to meet at this time and take stock of the relevant issues, along with exchanging opinions candidly. That is my goal.

Q8: Although you indicated that you brought up the removal of missiles and "one China, respective interpretations" during the meeting, it doesn't seem that they were receptive. Do you feel that Mr. Xi actually responded to your requests?

President: I think for this topic at this meeting, the most important result was that we presented Mr. Xi with a detailed and fact-based explanation of the whys and wherefores of the 1992 Consensus and our position so that he can understand them. Mr. Xi noted that I have several decades of experience dealing with this topic. I figure it's about 27 or 28 years. Initially when the 1992 Consensus was reached, I was the MAC's deputy minister. And I've been talking about this issue consistently for so many years. Eight years ago, the 1992 Consensus had strayed a bit from its original track, and I urged both sides to simultaneously return to the 1992 Consensus. What do I mean by "simultaneously?" At that time, the mainland focused on "one China," while Taiwan focused on "respective interpretations." Consequently, the gap between the two sides was growing wider and wider. The consensus was originally something useful, but it wasn't utilized. It was not until I became president over seven years ago that we were able to bring the consensus back on course. The 1992 Consensus, of course, is not the same as signing an agreement or a treaty. Instead, it gives everyone some room for interpretation. That's not a bad thing. Cross-strait relations had been cut off for over 60 years. Now, just to be able to sit down and have a discussion was quite a feat. We will take it step by step, seeking common ground while respecting differences. Things we thought impossible in the past are now possible. Things we thought we were unable to do in the past we now can do, and things are continuing to develop. When I took office, no one thought that we would have an opportunity over the coming eight years to meet with the mainland's leader. We originally hoped to have a meeting at the annual APEC Economic Leaders' Meeting, but the mainland felt that was problematic. So today we are meeting in a third place. Both sides have exhibited a good deal of flexibility and a pragmatic attitude. That is what's most important, as once the correct attitude is in place, it becomes easier to discuss issues.

Q9: During the meeting, did you invite Mr. Xi to visit Taiwan?

President: Not yet. Let's take things step by step. Do you want me to invite him?

Q10: The 1992 Consensus was forged by semi-official organizations that were set up by each side and authorized to hold talks. Twenty-three years later, the leaders of the two sides have now held discussions and have also reached a consensus. Why should we continue with this 1992 Consensus instead of referring to it as the "2015 Consensus?"

President: Because I feel that the 1992 Consensus is a pretty good arrangement. Over the past seven years it's been quite clear. We can't have a new consensus each year, just like we make red wine every year. In principle, we should maintain the original 1992 Consensus and continue to give it new meaning by putting it into practice. That's the best way. It's like not being able to amend the constitution every day, and rely on interpretations instead. So in principle, I feel we should keep up with the times. Is the 1992 Consensus that we're talking about today completely the same as what we discussed 23 years ago? The results of putting it into practice show that it is extremely different now. Actually, the consensus has been able to steer the two sides toward peace and prosperity. I feel that this is a successful consensus. Perhaps each side views the consensus a bit differently, but that's not important. These differences can be overcome through ongoing negotiations. I think that in principle, the consensus is extremely viable.

Q11: Might there be a second Ma-Xi meeting before you leave office?

President: You may be getting ahead of yourself. Let's conclude this meeting first, evaluate it, follow up the implementation, and hope for some results. While I just said that a country's leader can't address overly detailed issues, it's inevitable that we broached a few. Let's see if there's new progress on some of these issues. If there is, then that's a success. As to whether I will invite him to Taiwan, I feel that we should take things gradually, step by step. We spent two years talking to get to today's meeting and now we made it happen. You could say that we are advancing with the times, and that the time was ripe.

Q12: When you shook hands, you unbuttoned your coat. Why? What was your frame of mind at the time?

President: I unbuttoned my coat because Western suits pull quite tight when you raise your hand. There was no special meaning. Did that create some sort of misunderstanding? I shouldn't think so. It was a good feeling, and we both gave a firm handshake.

Q13: Some people say that the last piece to the puzzle in your presidency has been to promote a cross-strait leaders' meeting. What goals do you have for your remaining time in office?

President: You've touched on a very important objective for this Ma-Xi meeting. Take for example things like the Cross-Strait Trade in Goods Agreement, the establishment of reciprocal representative offices, and allowing mainland passengers to transit in Taiwan on their way to other destinations. We hope to see some concrete results on all of these issues following this meeting. Why was this meeting held with only six months remaining in my term? Well, it's because I only have six months left in office. Mr. Xi still has over seven years left in his term. Relations between Taiwan and the mainland aren't going to end any time soon, and we still need to build good groundwork.

Over the past seven years, we have continued to build a foundation and create an ultra-stable framework for Taiwan and the mainland. That required a lot of attention and care. You can't just pay lip service and then wait for something to drop from the sky. That's not how the world works. We have put in a lot of work over the past seven years, but ultimately we have found a way to proceed. Everyone should just think: Is there another relationship in the world like the cross-strait relationship? There is none. It is extremely complex and involves internal issues, foreign relations, military matters, and economics. It's not at all easy. We need to cherish the gradual reconciliation that created this kind of situation.

Of course there will be some minor problems, but you have to think of ways to overcome them. You don't want these minor issues to impact the overall direction. That is the profound experience that I am taking away from this meeting, and I feel that Mr. Xi has the same intentions. I hope that this process can continue to move forward. Let's look at the big picture and not minor issues. I hope that in terms of overall direction and the overall situation, we're all on the same page, which will benefit both Taiwan and the mainland.

> Q14: Are you concerned about the results of today's Ma-Xi meeting? If Taiwan's next president doesn't accept the 1992 Consensus, will that have any impact?

> President: The two sides today have a clear consensus that the 1992 Consensus is the primary foundation that has allowed cross-strait relations to make tremendous advances over the past seven years, and created the most stable and peaceful cross-strait relations that we have seen in the past 66 years. Mr. Xi and I both hold this view. Everyone has clearly seen the developments of the past seven years. Without the 1992 Consensus, how would today be possible? Of course, not everyone is satisfied with the 1992 Consensus. But I feel that the most important thing is that it has paved the way for the achievements of the past seven years and has been tremendously effective.

Some friends in the international community have said that the substance of the 1992 Consensus seems to be quite vague, and joked that it is a masterpiece of ambiguity. However, regardless of whether it is ambiguous, what's most important is that it has been able to resolve problems. For example, before I came to Singapore I held a press conference in Taiwan where members of the media asked whether I would mention the "Republic of China" during the Ma-Xi meeting. And today, I said it during the meeting. Why can't we say anything about "two Chinas," "one China, one Taiwan," or "Taiwan independence?" Because the ROC Constitution doesn't permit it. I said "Republic of China," each and every word, in full. I took the firm position that an ROC president should take.

SOURCE: Embassy of the Republic of China (Taiwan) in St. Vincent and the Grenadines. "Opening remarks by President Ma at an international press conference following meeting with mainland Chinese leader Xi Jinping in Singapore (November 7, 2015)." Document post date November 25, 2015. www .taiwanembassy.org/VC/ct.asp?xItem=671270&ctNode=10047&mp=727.

OTHER HISTORIC DOCUMENTS OF INTEREST

FROM PREVIOUS *HISTORIC DOCUMENTS*

- China Unveils New Leadership, *2012*, p. 544
- Chen Shui-bian on His Reelection as President of Taiwan, *2004*, p. 259

United Nations Issues Report Regarding the Ongoing Crisis in Syria

NOVEMBER 11, 2015

By late 2015, the Arab Spring uprising in Syria, which began in 2011, had made little headway in toppling the government of President Bashar al-Assad. The failed state's civil war was entering its fifth year, and Syrians were fleeing the country in droves, undertaking dangerous journeys in an attempt to reach Europe. In response to the ongoing violence against civilians, a coalition led by the United States, France, and the United Kingdom launched targeted airstrikes against Assad strongholds. Despite its efforts to bring the warring factions to the table to implement a ceasefire, a number of international human rights agencies blamed the United Nations (UN) for not doing enough to both end the crisis and support the victims of Assad's brutal crackdown on his dissenters. In response, the UN published a report detailing its ongoing efforts in Syria and the challenges it faces in providing adequate humanitarian aid.

Syrian Civil War Enters Fifth Year

Syria was swept up in the pro-democracy Arab Spring movement in March 2011. What were peaceful demonstrations quickly devolved into violence after the arrest and torture of a group of teenagers accused of painting revolutionary slogans on school walls. Protesters were shot at by Assad's police forces, which triggered a nationwide movement calling for the president's resignation. When the demonstrators failed to gain ground, many turned to local militias for support and took up arms against the Assad regime. By 2012, these armed groups were fighting the government's security forces for key strongholds, including the capital city of Damascus.

A United Nations inquiry found that both the government and rebel fighters have committed war crimes including rape, murder, and torture, as well as potentially carried out massacres. These attacks have been heightened by the rise of the Islamic State of Iraq and the Levant (ISIL), which used the power vacuum in Syria to gain power and support. ISIL spread across Syria throughout 2014 and 2015, taking control of both rebel-held and government-held areas.

A number of nations have made attempts to work with the UN to encourage a political solution to the ongoing violence in Syria. In 2014, UN envoy Lakhdar Brahimi was unable to maintain the Geneva II talks—a UN-backed peace process aimed at facilitating a peaceful political transition—beyond two rounds because the Syrian government refused to address demands made by rebels, namely that Assad step down to allow for the creation of a democratic government. Brahimi's successor focused on instituting ceasefires in smaller areas of Syria and was able to end the fighting in al-Wair, a suburb outside of besieged Homs, in December 2015. Attempts to end the fighting pitted a number of nations against one another while Russia and Iran reportedly spent millions to arm Assad and his security forces. In contrast, the United States, United Kingdom, France, Qatar, Jordan, Turkey, and Saudi Arabia worked to support the opposition movement, but they stopped short of training and equipping these groups, despite plans to do so.

Ongoing Humanitarian Crisis

By the end of 2015, more than 200,000 Syrians had been killed in the violence and an estimated 11 million were displaced. More than 4.5 million of those displaced had fled Syria, primarily for neighboring Jordan, Turkey, and Lebanon. Another 10 percent attempted to make the treacherous journey to Europe, some on foot. According to the United Nations High Commissioner on Refugees, Turkey has borne the brunt of the refugee crisis, taking in an estimated 2.5 million refugees, followed by Lebanon and Jordan who took in more than 1 million and 600,000, respectively. In Europe, Germany received the greatest number of refugees, with an estimated 184,000 coming through its borders by the end of 2015. The UN estimates that $3.2 billion will be needed to help those inside Syria in 2016.

Despite the passage of three resolutions calling for an end to the attacks and an increase in aid for civilians, the UN claims its efforts in 2015 were largely hampered by the refusal of both the Assad regime and rebel groups to allow aid workers into the areas of greatest need. Even so, humanitarian agencies criticized the UN for failing Syrian citizens. "The bitter reality is that the Security Council has failed to implement its resolutions," said Jan Egeland, the secretary general for the Norwegian Refugee Council. "Parties to the conflict have acted with impunity and ignored the Security Council's demands, civilians are not protected and their access to relief has not improved," he added.

In response to its critics, the United Nations released a report on November 11, 2015, detailing the implementation of the three Security Council resolutions in question: 2139 (2014), 2165 (2014), and 2191 (2014). It found that pursuant to these resolutions, the UN has continued to work with its own humanitarian agencies—and their partners—to reach those Syrians most in need. According to the report, through October 2015, the World Food Program (WFP) had delivered food to more than four million Syrians, while the World Health Organization (WHO) provided supplies for 717,000 medical treatments. The United Nations Children's Emergency Fund (UNICEF) provided 5.3 million Syrians with clean water, health support, and educational assistance. The High Commissioner for Refugees provided 272,000 with protection services and relief items, while reproductive health and gender-based violence services were provided to 330,000 to the United Nations Population Fund. Additional services were provided by the International Organization for Migration (IOM), the Food and Agriculture Organization (FAO), and the United Nations Relief and Works Agency for Palestine Refugees in the Near East (UNRWA).

Despite such victories, the UN admitted in the report that "the delivery of humanitarian assistance to many of the 13.5 million people in need of assistance in the Syrian Arab Republic remained extremely challenging in many areas due to active conflict and insecurity and deliberate obstruction by the parties, including continuing burden-some administrative procedures." In particular, the UN expressed concern about 4.5 million Syrians who were living in hard-to-reach, primarily ISIL-controlled areas. UN bodies and their partners were also prevented from entering areas of active conflict between ISIL, Syrian opposition fighters, and Assad's security forces, in places such as Aleppo, Homs, and Hama, which had experienced the worst of the fighting. The Syrian government's security forces were also holding up some humanitarian aid deliveries, even though they had already been approved by the Syrian Ministry of Foreign Affairs. The UN report stated that these administrative requirements of the Assad regime ham-pered relief efforts and that at times it took as many as ten months to receive approval for a shipment.

The report also found that medical facilities in Syria continued to be the target of attacks by ISIL as well as Syrian opposition and government forces. This further hindered the ability of the UN and its partners to provide life-saving medical care. In a number of governorates, aid organizations have been prevented from delivering medical supplies and health personnel have been attacked and killed. According to the UN, in Syria "the funda-mental rules of international humanitarian and human rights law are being violated with little or no accountability. . . . Tragically, hundreds of civilians have been killed or injured in direct or indiscriminate attacks."

UN ENDORSES ROAD MAP FOR PEACE

In its November report on its work to provide humanitarian aid in Syria, the United Nations noted that it was encouraged by the unity of the international community, which met in Vienna, Austria, on October 30 to restart discussions on how to establish a politi-cal solution for Syria. In encouraging further action from UN member states, the report concluded, "Syrian civilians, including women and children, continue to bear the brunt of this conflict. The international community must come together to help Syrians find com-mon ground and stop the violence."

Building on these renewed negotiations, on December 18, 2015, the United Nations Security Council unanimously adopted Resolution 2254 that established an early January timeframe for talks to begin between Assad's government and opposition forces, which would be facilitated by the United Nations. The resolution also estab-lished a roadmap for political transition that was intended to begin with a ceasefire and would establish "credible, inclusive and non-sectarian governance" within six months. During the six-month process to develop a new Syrian government, a new constitution would also be drafted and a date for elections would be set for 2017. Secretary General Ban Ki-moon said the resolution "marks a very important step on which we must build," and "the United Nations stands ready to undertake these important tasks." By the end of 2015, no interested parties had taken action toward beginning the implementation of the UN roadmap.

—Heather Kerrigan

Following is the United Nations Security Council Report released on November 11, 2015, detailing the efforts of the United Nations to implement three of its 2014 reso-lutions on Syria.

UN Security Council Report on Implementation of Resolutions on Syria

November 11, 2015

[Footnotes have been omitted.]

I. INTRODUCTION

1. The present report is the twenty-first submitted pursuant to paragraph 17 of Security Council resolution 2139 (2014), paragraph 10 of Council resolution 2165 (2014) and paragraph 5 of Council resolution 2191 (2014), in which the Council requested me to report, every 30 days, on the implementation of the resolutions by all parties to the conflict in the Syrian Arab Republic. At the request of the Presidency of the Security Council, this report is submitted less than 30 days from the date of the previous report.

2. The information contained herein is based on the data available to the United Nations agencies on the ground from the Government of the Syrian Arab Republic and from open sources. Data from United Nations agencies and partners on their humanitarian deliveries have been reported for the period from 1 to 31 October 2015, where available.

II. MAJOR DEVELOPMENTS

A. Political/military

3. Widespread conflict and high levels of violence continued throughout the Syrian Arab Republic in October. Indiscriminate and disproportionate aerial bombings and ground attacks on places with a large civilian presence by Government forces, non-State armed opposition groups and designated terrorist groups continued to kill, injure, and displace civilians. The conduct of hostilities by all parties continued to be characterized by a widespread disregard for international humanitarian law and the obligation of all parties to protect civilians. While the United Nations has no independent means of verification, many sources report a continuation of the use of barrel bombs. The Syrian Network for Human Rights reported the use of 1,438 barrel bombs across the country in the month of October. On 9 November, a statement issued by the Syrian Ministry of Foreign Affairs and Expatriates gave assurances that the Syrian Arab Armed Forces do not and will not use indiscriminate weapons.

4. Heavy fighting continued to be reported in Damascus and Rif Dimashq governorates. Government forces carried out airstrikes in various areas of eastern Ghutah in Rif Dimashq. The town of Duma was hit repeatedly during the month, including on 29 October, when airstrikes hit the main field hospital in Duma, killing at least 15 civilians and injuring 50 others, many of whom were medical personnel. On 30 October, several airstrikes hit the al-Hal market in

Duma, killing at least 60 civilians and injuring 200 more. Elsewhere, according to reports received by the Office of the United Nations High Commissioner for Human Rights (OHCHR), over 30 civilians were killed and dozens injured in other attacks in eastern Ghutah during October, including in Ain Tarma, Hammura, Misraba and Harasta. Meanwhile, shelling in Marj temporarily displaced an estimated 1,400 families across eastern Ghutah and caused widespread destruction to critical infrastructure. In Darayya, OHCHR received reports that three people were killed between 25 and 29 October as a result of barrel bombs.

5. Non-State armed opposition groups continued to launch mortars and to shell Damascus city during the reporting period. OHCHR reported that on 1 October, a five year old child was killed when mortar rounds struck the rooftop of a residential building in Ish al-Werwer. On 13 October, the Embassy of the Russian Federation in the Mazra'a neighbourhood was hit, although no injuries were reported. On 14 October, a civilian was injured when a rocket struck an open area in the Mezzeh neighbourhood. On 17 October, one civilian was killed and seven injured when an improvised explosive device attached to a bicycle was detonated near a football pitch in Mezzeh. On 27 October, seven civilians were injured when mortar rounds hit Bab Tuma in old Damascus. Between 30 and 31 October, mortars struck several areas in Damascus, killing one civilian and injuring 12 others.

6. Fighting in Zabadani and Madaya, and in other areas in northwestern Rif Dimashq, as well as Fu'ah and Kafraya in Idlib governorate, decreased over the course of the reporting period following the ceasefire agreement reached in Istanbul, on 22 September 2015, with the facilitation of the Office of the United Nations Special Envoy for Syria. On 18 October, under the auspices of the agreement, a joint humanitarian convoy made up of United Nations personnel and other partners delivered assistance to Zabadani, Madaya and Buqayn, as well as to Fu'ah and Kafraya via a United Nations cross border operation through Turkey's Bab al-Hawa border crossing. The United Nations and its partners stand ready to immediately implement the remaining humanitarian elements of the agreement, including the delivery of additional humanitarian assistance and the evacuation of the wounded.

7. Intensified fighting between the parties continued in the northern governorates of the Syrian Arab Republic during the reporting period following ground and air offensives by the Government, supported by Russian-led airstrikes. In Hama and Idlib governorates, in October alone, an estimated 80,000 people were displaced by the fighting. Civilians were also killed and injured as a result of the fighting: for example, on 4 October, one civilian was killed and four wounded when Government forces dropped barrel bombs on a residential neighbourhood in Khan Shaykhun. OHCHR received reports that, on 26 October, a Government airstrike reportedly hit Kafr Nabel in Idlib, killing two civilians and injuring 10 others. On 20 October, a health clinic in Sarmin that is supported by a non-governmental organization was hit by an airstrike, killing two people and injuring at least 28 civilians. On 25 October, a field hospital in Latamnah, Hama, was reportedly hit by an air strike, killing six people.

8. In Aleppo governorate, fighting escalated between the parties to the south of Aleppo city, following an offensive by Government forces in early October. In response, non-State armed opposition groups staged a number of counter offensives in late October. Some 50,000 people were displaced as a result of the fighting. Civilians were also killed and injured as a result of the escalation in fighting around Aleppo by all parties to the conflict: for example, on 2 October, Government helicopters dropped a number of barrel bombs on Al-Bab, resulting in tens of casualties according to information received by OHCHR. On 7 October, at least four civilians were killed when Government jets struck a residential area in Daret Azza. On 16 October, Government airstrikes on the town of Kafr Karmin killed at least nine civilians, including five children.

9. Fighting also continued in Aleppo city during the reporting period, as Government forces and non-State armed opposition groups continued to shell the city, causing casualties among civilians. On 14 October, non-State armed opposition groups fired canister bombs on the neighbourhoods of Aziza and Maidan. OHCHR received reports that, on 16 October, non-State armed opposition groups fired improvised explosive devices at a Government-controlled residential neighbourhood of Aleppo, killing a woman and her child. On 20 October, mortars landed in two schools in Government-controlled areas of western Aleppo city, killing an estimated 19 civilians. Meanwhile, on 30 October, airstrikes took place on Al-Kalasah, Al-Fardous, Salaheddine, Al-Sheikh Maqsoud, Al-Bab and other areas controlled by non-State armed opposition groups inside and outside the city, reportedly killing more than 65 and injuring more than 100 people.

10. ISIL continued to launch attacks in various governorates during the reporting period. On 23 October, ISIL exerted its control over a stretch of the Homs-Damascus highway around Khanaser, cutting the main land access route for humanitarian and commercial actors to Aleppo city from within the Syrian Arab Republic. This resulted in an increase in commodity prices for the 700,000 people living in Government-controlled areas of western Aleppo city. The Government re-secured the highway at the start of November. Meanwhile, in northern Aleppo governorate, ISIL advanced south of Mare'a in early October, seizing a number of villages in the Handarat area of the Aleppo countryside, close to Aleppo city, and the major route between eastern Aleppo city and the Bab al-Salam border crossing with Turkey. As part of the offensive on 6 October, ISIL detonated a vehicle-borne improvised explosive device in Hritan, killing more than 20 people.

11. In Dayr al-Zawr governorate, ISIL continued its attacks on the Dayr al-Zawr city military airbase, although Government and Russian airstrikes reportedly blocked ISIL advances towards the military airbase over the last two weeks of October and also targeted other ISIL positions in Dayr al-Zawr and Raqqah. For example, on 18 October, two people were reported killed when Government airstrikes hit Mayadin town. On 19 October, at least three civilians, including one woman, were killed when Government jets hit the Aridi neighbourhood of Dayr al-Zawr city.

12. On 15 October, in Homs governorate, fighting continued in the northern countryside. OHCHR received reports that, on 15 October, Government forces reportedly dropped barrel bombs on Talbiseh, killing 15 civilians. Three additional aerial attacks on Talbiseh were reportedly carried out on 23 October,

killing 14 civilians, including six children. Meanwhile, six civilians were killed and 17 injured when Government forces struck Ghanto village on 26 October. On 27 October, Government forces hit the village of Halmoze, killing two civilians and wounding at least eight others. Separately, ISIL launched a sustained attack on central Homs in late October, which led to the capture of Mahin town by ISIL and the displacement of approximately 25,000 people.

13. In the Wa'r district of Homs city, multiple shellings and attacks from pro-Government forces were reported in October. For example, on 24 October, Government forces fired a mortar into the Wa'r district, damaging several houses. Since 31 August, pro-Government forces have closed all roads leading to Wa'r, and humanitarian supplies have not entered. However, on 31 October, local traders were allowed to bring in small quantities of food, and the Syrian Arab Red Crescent and Syrian non-governmental organizations delivered two small trucks full of medicines. Negotiations between the parties on a local agreement reportedly continue. On 3 November, the Office of the Special Envoy and the Office of the Resident and Humanitarian Coordinator conducted a cross-line mission to Wa'r and a submitted further request for an inter-agency convoy to Wa'r to the Syrian authorities.

14. Fighting in the southern governorates reported during October resulted in death and injury to civilians. In Dar'a governorate, Government airstrikes continued as did shelling between Government forces and non-State armed opposition groups. OHCHR received reports of several attacks with barrel bombs during the month, including an attack on Busra al-Sham on 21 October, which killed four children and two other civilians, and on Dael on 14 October which killed a pregnant woman and her one-year-old daughter. A child in the village of Barga was killed on 16 October by an explosive remnant of war. On 24 October, a vehicle-borne improvised explosive device was detonated by an unknown perpetrator around 300 meters from the national hospital in Tafas town in Dar'a.

15. Both Russian and United States-led coalition forces continued their operations in the Syrian Arab Republic throughout the month of October. On 8 October, an airstrike hit the Ferdous neighbourhood in the centre of Raqqah, hitting a vehicle and killing the driver and five of his family members, including one child. While Russian authorities and the United States-led coalition have acknowledged carrying out airstrikes in Raqqah governorate on that day, it is unclear who is responsible for this particular incident. In addition, OHCHR received a number of reports alleging that there had been civilian casualties as a result of airstrikes, in which reports the origin of the strikes could not, however, be adequately ascertained. On 3 October, an airstrike struck Ihsem in Idlib governorate, killing at least five civilians, including one woman and four children. A first responder was killed in a subsequent attack that took place soon after the first one and in the same area. On 9 October, airstrikes on Mayadin in Dayr al-Zawr governorate hit the area near Mayadin Hospital, killing one civilian who was in the vicinity. On 12 October, 12 civilians, including a child, were injured following an airstrike on Hayan, north-west of Aleppo. On 13 October, at least seven civilians were killed following an airstrike that hit a civilian area in Hayan. On 15 October, OHCHR received information that an airstrike hit a bakery, killing eight civilians and damaging a nearby mosque in Tir Mallah, Homs. On 15 October, a strike

allegedly hit a house in Ghanto, Homs, killing over 40 members of an extended family. On 27 October, multiple airstrikes in Asiya, al-Bawabiya, and Tel Hadiya in Aleppo governorate reportedly killed at least 22 civilians and injuring others.

16. Displacement continued throughout the Syrian Arab Republic in October. Over 190,000 people were displaced from various areas in Aleppo, Idlib, Hama, Homs, Rif Dimashq, Dayr al-Zawr, Raqqah and Dar'a governorates due to ongoing fighting.

17. Civilian infrastructure continued to be targeted during the reporting period. In Aleppo, the United Nations Children's Fund (UNICEF) recorded 10 days of water cuts during October (water remained cut as of 4 November), as well as persistent electricity cuts. On 23 October, a major water pipeline at Wadi Barada exploded, likely due to shelling in the vicinity and a general degradation of the pipes, resulting in the interruption of water supplies to parts of Damascus and to Qudsaya in Rif Dimashq.

18. There were developments regarding several local agreements during the reporting period. In Qudsaya, Rif Dimashq, reconciliation negotiations continued. According to reports, about 70 per cent of fighters in Qudsaya have surrendered their weapons and regularized their status through Government security branches; while the rest of fighters have so far refused to surrender their weapons. Government forces continued to close the main road to the district, with limited medical supplies, food or other assistance having reached the area in over two months. In Madamiyet, a separation wall with Darayya was built as part of an agreement with the representative of the Syrian Armed Forces in exchange for a promise to open the road leading to the town. However, restrictions on movement have reportedly not been lifted yet.

19. Following intense and constructive discussions in Vienna, the participants issued a joint communiqué encapsulating fundamental principles for a political solution and tasking the United Nations with the establishment of a negotiating process, bringing together the Government and the opposition as well as exploring modalities for a nationwide ceasefire to run in parallel with a renewed political process. The communiqué also stressed the importance of Syrian ownership of the political process.

B. Human rights

20. During the reporting period, OHCHR continued to receive allegations of arbitrary arrest and detention, sexual and gender-based violence, torture and other ill-treatment and deaths in custody as a result of torture or lack of medical care inside Government detention centres. OHCHR also received reports that Government intelligence personnel carried out house-to-house searches from 2 to 5 October in Damascus, Yabrud and Nubuk, arbitrarily detaining tens of people. OHCHR received reports that the Air Force Intelligence arrested a political activist affiliated with the Syrian Community Association on 23 October in Mabuja village in Homs governorate; his whereabouts is currently unknown.

21. Victims interviewed by OHCHR reported that they were subjected to torture and other ill-treatment at Military Intelligence Branches 291 and 215, and at

the Palestine Branch of Military Intelligence in Damascus, the Nayrab Military Airport, the Mezze Military Airport, Sidnaya prison and at the headquarters of the 4th Division in Damascus. Witnesses also spoke of other detainees, including women, being subjected to torture in these facilities.

22. ISIL carried out unlawful detentions of tens of young men in Dayr al-Zawr governorate during the reporting period, entering local markets and Internet cafes to determine whether any of those present were "spying". The detained men were taken to unknown locations. In Raqqah governorate, ISIL arrested a married couple in the Mashlab area on 5 October. They were accused of teaching mixed groups of male and female school children in their home. The whereabouts of the couple remains unknown.

23. ISIL continued to carry out executions of perceived spies and Government supporters without due process. On 10 October, three men accused of spying for the Government were executed in Palmyra. On 13 October, two men were publicly executed by gunfire, and a third man was executed in an isolated area; the three were also accused of spying for the Government. On 26 October, ISIL fighters tied three men to a pillar at one of the historical sites in Palmyra and detonated the pillars—the charges in their case were unknown. In Aleppo governorate, on 24 October, ISIL stoned two men to death in al-Bab town, north-east of Aleppo city, allegedly due to their sexual orientation. The execution took place after a summary "trial" in an ISIL-established court.

24. On 27 October, fighters with the Kurdish People's Protection Units detained four young men in Smehen village in al-Hasakah for the purpose of forcibly recruiting them into the group. The whereabouts of the men remains unknown.

25. On 3 October, fighters from Jaish al-Islam raided the detention centre in the Jabhat al-Nusra-established courthouse in Yalda in Rif Dimashq governorate and captured five "convicted" detainees, publicly executing them in Kishik Square. Jaish al-Islam stated that they were retaliating for the use of an improvised explosive device which targeted five of their members in Yalda earlier the same day, although no group had claimed responsibility for the incident.

26. Several media outlets reported in early November that, amid continued airstrikes by the Government, Jaish al-Islam used dozens of prisoners, both men and women, as human shields in Duma and eastern Ghuta. Reports indicate that the prisoners, many of whom may have been religious minorities, were placed in cages around heavily populated areas to deter further airstrikes in civilian areas. Some of the prisoners have allegedly been in captivity since 2013, when they were kidnapped from Government-held areas in eastern Ghouta.

C. HUMANITARIAN RESPONSE

27. United Nations humanitarian agencies and partners continued to reach millions of people in need in October through all modalities from within the Syrian Arab Republic and across borders pursuant to resolutions 2165 (2014) and 2191 (2014). The World Food Programme (WFP) delivered food assistance for over four million people in 12 governorates. The World Health Organization (WHO)

distributed medicines and supplies for 717,000 treatments in 10 governorates. UNICEF reached over 5.3 million people with multi-sector support, including 3.5 million with water, sanitation and hygiene support, over 2.4 million with health support and almost 180,000 with education support. The Office of the United Nations High Commissioner for Refugees (UNHCR) reached around 272,000 people with core relief items and protection services in 12 governorates. The United Nations Population Fund (UNFPA) delivered 330,000 reproductive health and gender-based violence services through implementing partners. The Food and Agriculture Organization of the United Nations (FAO) reached almost 20,000 people with food and agricultural assistance. The International Organization for Migration (IOM) delivered basic relief items for over 32,500 people. The United Nations Relief and Works Agency for Palestine Refugees in the Near East (UNRWA) provided support to more than 330,000 Palestine refugees. The Government of the Syrian Arab Republic continued to provide basic services to areas under its control as well as in many areas beyond its control.

28. Cross-border deliveries continued during the reporting period. As of 31 October, the United Nations and its implementing partners had sent 207 shipments—140 from Turkey and 67 from Jordan—to the Syrian Arab Republic under the terms of resolutions 2165 (2014) and 2191 (2014), including food assistance for over 2.4 million people; non-food items for 1.6 million people; medical supplies for almost four million treatments, as well as a number of surgical supply kits; and water and sanitation supplies for over one million people in Aleppo, Dar'a, Hama, Idlib, Ladhiqiyah and Qunaytirah governorates. In line with resolutions 2165 (2014) and 2191 (2014), the United Nations notified the Government of the Syrian Arab Republic in advance of each shipment, including the details of content, destination and number of beneficiaries.

29. The United Nations Monitoring Mechanism continued its operations in Jordan and Turkey. Since the start of operations, the Mechanism has monitored 207 United Nations humanitarian shipments consisting of 4,505 trucks, confirming the humanitarian nature of each and notifying the Syrian authorities after each shipment. The Mechanism continued to benefit from excellent cooperation with the Governments of Jordan and Turkey.

30. Three inter-agency convoys were completed during the month of October. On 8 October, the final phase of a three-part convoy to Hula in Homs was completed. A total of 60,000 people in hard-to-reach areas benefited from the convoy. Government authorities prohibited water, sanitation and hygiene items and some medical items from being loaded. On 18 October, humanitarian convoys of United Nations and other partners reached 10,000 people in Fu'ah and Kafraya, as well as some 20,000 people in Zabadani, Madaya and Buqayn with multi-sectoral assistance, including medical and surgical items.

31. United Nations agencies also undertook cross-line deliveries during the reporting period. For example, WFP reached over 12,000 people in non-State armed opposition group-controlled parts of Hama and Rif Dimashq governorates. FAO reached 3,000 people and distributed poultry packages in a cross-line delivery to Madimayet Elsham in Rif Dimashq. WHO provided 81,722 medical treatments through a local non-governmental organization partner across conflict

lines in Aleppo governorate, including the use of a haemodialysis machine and 100 dialysis sessions in Nubul subdistrict. On 28 October, UNICEF completed its second delivery of sodium hypochlorite to Raqqah; it is estimated that the supply will cover the water treatment needs for two million people for five months. Meanwhile, winter and education supplies for up to 12,000 people procured by UNICEF were delivered cross-line by the Syrian Arab Red Crescent to hard-to-reach locations in eastern Aleppo city during the last week of October. UNHCR undertook missions to Al Tall, Rif Dimashq, on 8 and 14 October, reaching some 5,000 people with basic relief items.

32. Both international and Syrian non-governmental organizations continued to deliver multi-sector assistance in the Syrian Arab Republic in October, including the provision of services, in line with previous months.

Humanitarian access

33. The delivery of humanitarian assistance to many of the 13.5 million people in need of assistance in the Syria Arab Republic remained extremely challenging in many areas due to active conflict and insecurity and deliberate obstruction by the parties, including continuing burdensome administrative procedures.

34. Access to the 4.5 million people living in hard-to-reach areas remained of critical concern. In October, United Nations agencies and partners reached 46 of the 147 hard-to-reach locations (31 per cent) overall. They reached 14 locations with food assistance for around 225,000 people, 18 locations with health support for over 130,000 medical treatments, 11 locations with water, sanitation and hygiene assistance for more than 50,000 people and 10 locations with relief items for almost 20,000 people. Nearly half of the people in hard-to-reach areas are in ISIL-controlled areas, to which the United Nations did not deliver assistance in October aside from water treatment materials provided by UNICEF.

35. Active conflict in several governorates hindered the effective delivery of humanitarian assistance, as well as people's access to essential services. For example, fighting and insecurity continued to prevent the delivery of life-saving food assistance to over 1.2 million people in parts of Rif Dimashq, rural Homs and rural Hama governorates in September. In Aleppo governorate, the western parts of Aleppo city remained inaccessible during the last week of October owing to the fact that ISIL had control over a stretch of the main Homs-Aleppo highway. As a result, in October, WFP was unable to deliver assistance for over 220,000 people in Aleppo. In response to the water crisis in Aleppo, UNICEF had been trucking clean drinking water to cover the needs of more than 700,000 people on a daily basis. However, reduced access to Aleppo as a result of ongoing fighting along access points to the south of the city forced UNICEF to temporarily downscale its water trucking operation to meet the needs of 200,000 people.

36. Deliberate interference and obstruction by the parties also continued to prevent aid delivery. For example, WFP continues to be unable to reach population in need in ISIL-controlled areas of the country, as all plans to deliver assistance to these areas have been suspended due to the inability to work independently and to monitor activities. This is preventing WFP assistance to an estimated 720,000

people in need of food assistance in almost all of Dayr al-Zawr and Raqqah governorates, parts of northern rural Aleppo and east rural Homs, as well as pockets in southern rural Hasakah and rural northwestern Hama governorates.

37. A limited number of humanitarian supplies went through the Nusaybin/Qamishli crossing in October. On 9 October, Turkish authorities gave approval for WFP to resume shipments via the crossing, while UNICEF was also approved to use the crossing to import $2.5 million in life-saving supplies. Syrian authorities had approved these shipments to cross the border in September. On 16 October, the Government of Turkey informed humanitarian operations that all such operations through the crossing would remain temporarily on hold due to persistent insecurity in the areas surrounding the border crossing. On an exceptional basis, since the trucks had already left the warehouse, 10 UNICEF trucks loaded with 4,800 family hygiene kits were allowed through on 19 October. UNICEF is waiting to move approximately 80 trucks full of life-saving supplies through the crossing.

38. As of 31 October, 27 out of the 88 inter-agency requests made in 2015 by the United Nations have been approved, in principle, by the Syrian Ministry of Foreign Affairs; 45 requests are pending approval; and three requests have been put on hold by the United Nations due to insecurity. The remaining 13 requests were submitted previously, but they are been subsumed by newer requests. Nine of the original request were put on hold by the United Nations due to insecurity and the other four requests, which went unanswered by the Government within a three-month time period, were resubmitted.

39. Of the 27 requests approved in principle by the Syrian Ministry of Foreign Affairs, 13 convoys have been completed. Of the remaining 14 requests approved in principle, seven have been unable to proceed due to the lack of approval from the Syrian Government security forces; two are held up due to a lack of agreement between the United Nations, the Syrian Arab Red Crescent and the Government on the access route; two are stalled by the lack of approval by non-State armed opposition groups for safe passage; and one remains pending the security situation. The remaining two requests approved in principle are under preparation. More than 282,000 beneficiaries in hard-to-reach and besieged locations could be reached if these convoys were able to proceed.

40. In addition to inter-agency convoys, a number of requests from United Nations agencies for single agency convoys remain pending, owing to insecurity, until approval is received from the Syrian authorities. WFP had 21 unapproved requests by the Syrian Government in several locations in Dar'a and Rif Dimashq governorates during the reporting period, preventing the delivery of assistance to 109,000 people. UNHCR had nine requests rejected on account of insecurity. Out of 69 individual requests made by UNICEF in 2015 to gain access to hard-to-reach areas, only six have been approved by the Syrian authorities.

41. All UNRWA operations in Yarmouk remained suspended during the reporting period. The most recent UNRWA mission inside Yarmouk was conducted on 28 March. On 31 October, the Al Marhama International Campaign, in cooperation with the charitable association for the relief of Palestinian people, completed the distribution of 448 food parcels and baby formula to civilians inside Yarmouk.

The distribution followed the delivery of 3,000 bags of bread to Yarmouk and Yalda on 21 and 25 October by the national commission for the relief of Palestinians in the Syrian Arab Republic. The passageway between Yarmouk and Yalda remains a volatile area. UNRWA was not permitted to conduct any missions to Yalda, Babila and Bayt Saham in October. Other humanitarian organizations have reportedly been allowed to continue their operations and to deliver assistance in these areas. The Syrian Arab Red Crescent mobile clinics continue to provide services in the three areas, visiting each location every third week. Meanwhile, in response to increasing prevalence of typhoid, UNICEF, in collaboration with the rural Damascus health directorate, distributed aqua tabs to Yalda, Babila and Bayt Saham and to the Yarmouk camp in October. The authorities have also continued to authorize a limited range of commercial goods to enter these areas on a daily basis.

42. No major changes in the administrative procedures required by the Syrian Government for the delivery of humanitarian assistance were reported in September. The current administrative procedures continued to delay or limit the delivery of assistance by United Nations agencies and United Nations partners. UNICEF reported that while the lead time for obtaining approvals from the Syrian authorities regarding the importation of regular humanitarian goods had improved, UNICEF still has two outstanding exemptions for health and nutrition supplies for 117,000 children that have been pending for more than two months. UNICEF also reported significant delays in the length of time taken to obtain approvals for the importation of information technology and telecommunications equipment (7 exemptions are pending between 3 and 10 months).

43. Progress continued to be made with regard to visas for United Nations staff members. In October, the Syrian Government approved 69 visas for United Nations staff, of which 38 were new visas and 31 were renewals. Over 95 per cent of the approved visas in October were granted within the agreed 15 working day review period. As of 31 October, 47 United Nations visa requests (either new visas or renewals) remained pending, 11 of which were beyond the agreed 15 working day review period. One visa application was rejected in October. The total number of visas rejected in 2015 is 40, exclusive of the four United Nations staff who were declared personae non grata in February 2015.

44. One international non-governmental organization was authorized to operate in October, bringing the total number of international non-governmental organizations authorized to operate in the Syrian Arab Republic to 16. International non-governmental organizations continued to face a series of administrative hurdles and restrictions that impact on their ability to operate. They remain restricted in their ability to partner with national humanitarian organizations, open sub-offices, conduct missions, join inter-agency convoys and undertake independent needs assessments. Fifteen visas for staff of international non-governmental organizations remain pending as of 31 October, 11 of which were submitted in September or October. Six visas were approved in October, including four that were submitted during the same month. The United Nations Resident and Humanitarian Coordinator continues to lead discussions with the Government regarding visas and the operating framework for international non-governmental organizations.

45. In October, two additional national non-governmental organizations, both in Damascus governorate, were authorized by the Government of the Syrian Arab Republic to partner with United Nations organizations. Overall, the number of national non-governmental organizations authorized to partner with United Nations organizations stands at 137. The organizations operate through 220 branches. Authorized national non-governmental organizations continue to operate under complex procedures in partnering with United Nations agencies.

Besieged areas

46. Of the 4.5 million people living in hard-to-reach areas, some 393,700 remained besieged in the Syrian Arab Republic. This includes some 200,000 people in Dary al-Zawr city who are besieged by ISIL; some 181,200 people who are besieged by the Syrian Government in various locations in eastern Ghutah, as well as Darayya and Zabadani in rural Damascus; and some 12,500 people who are besieged by non-State armed opposition groups and the Nusrah Front in Fu'ah and Kafraya in Idlib. The 26,500 people in Nubul and Zahra', in Aleppo governorate, are no longer considered to be besieged following consistent and credible reports that access to and from the enclave for people and commercial goods has significantly improved over the last three months, although access and protection concerns remain acute.

47. The parties to the conflict continued to entirely or heavily restrict access to besieged areas during the reporting period. During October, some 10,500 besieged people (2.7 per cent) were provided with food, health and basic relief assistance and some 16,700 besieged people (4.2 per cent) were provided with water, sanitation and hygiene assistance. The flow of commercial supplies through official routes remained largely blocked, leading to high prices for those commodities reaching besieged areas through unofficial and irregular supply lines. Freedom of movement remained heavily restricted, although certain groups, such as students and members of reconciliation councils, were occasionally allowed to leave from and return to some besieged areas.

48. In eastern Ghutah, Rif Dimashq, some 176,500 people are besieged in the following locations: Duma, Harasta, Arbin, Zamalka, Ain Tarma, Hammura, Jisrein, Kafr Batna, Saqba and Zabadini. No United Nations humanitarian assistance agency reached the besieged areas in eastern Ghutah during October, with the exception of UNICEF, which provided some 1,045 children with remedial education support in Duma.

49. In Zabadani, Rif Dimashq, some 500 people remain besieged by Government forces. On 18 October, the joint humanitarian convoy of United Nations personnel and other partners reached the city with food, basic relief items, water, sanitation and hygiene support and medicines.

50. In Darayya, Rif Dimashq, about 4,000 people remain besieged by Government forces. No United Nations assistance reached the areas during the reporting period. People in Darayya have not been assisted by the United Nations since October 2012.

51. In Fu'ah and Kafraya, Idlib governorate, some 12,500 people remain besieged by non-State armed opposition groups and the Nusra Front. On 18 October, the joint

humanitarian convoy of United Nations personnel and other partners reached Fu'ah and Kafraya with food, basic relief items, water, sanitation and hygiene support, and medicines for 10,000 people.

52. In the Government-controlled western neighbourhoods of Dayr al-Zawr city, some 200,000 people are besieged by ISIL. The number of people under siege has been reduced, however, as some people have managed to flee from the area. In partnership with the Syrian Arab Red Crescent, UNICEF provided water, sanitation and hygiene support to 6,195 people and psychosocial support to 720 children during the month of October. With approvals secured, plans remain for an emergency inter-agency United Nations airlift to deliver life-saving humanitarian assistance to the area, but thus far clashes in the vicinity of the military airport have prevented the operation from proceeding.

Free passage of medical supplies, personnel and equipment

53. While health-care facilities have special protected status under international humanitarian law, attacks on medical facilities continue unabated in the Syrian Arab Republic. During the reporting period, United Nations and health partners received reports—in the process of being verified by the United Nations and partner organizations—of 13 attacks on medical facilities and transport; eight on hospitals, two on other types of health facilities; and three on ambulances. Seven of the attacks took place in Hama governorate, three in Aleppo, two in Homs and one in Idlib governorate. All of the attacks were by airstrikes. As a result of the attacks, 11 people were reportedly killed, two of which were health staff, and approximately 40 people were injured.

54. Access to medical care continued to be restricted by insecurity and restrictions imposed by parties to the conflict, resulting in increased prices for medicines, a shortage of medical supplies in local markets, a reduction in pharmaceutical production and a shortage of qualified medical workers. The shortage of qualified medical staff and the degradation of essential services have further impacted access to adequate medical care. The availability of life-saving health services are of critical concern, in parts of Hasakah, Raqqah, Dayr al-Zawr, Dar'a, Idlib, Hama and Aleppo governorates, as well as the hard-to-reach and besieged areas of Rif Dimashq governorate.

55. In collaboration with the Ministry of Health, UNICEF and WHO supported the sixteenth national polio vaccination campaign, held from 18 to 22 October, during which 2.3 million children were vaccinated. All governorates were covered with the exception of Raqqah, Dayr al-Zawr and some parts of Idlib due to a combination of insecurity and restricted access imposed by the parties to the conflict. For example, because of the refusal of ISIL to allow the campaign to take place in the parts of Raqqah and Dayr al-Zawr governorates under their control, only 1.6 per cent of children under five were vaccinated in Raqqah and only 4.5 per cent of children in Dayr al-Zawr under five years of age were treated for the disease. Overall, some 500,000 children could not be vaccinated across the country due to access constraints.

56. In October, five new requests from WHO and one reminder were submitted to the Syrian authorities for approval to deliver supplies to 13 hard-to-reach parts of Rif

Dimashq, Hama, Dar'a, Aleppo, Dayr al-Zawr and Qunaytirah governorates. All requests have gone unanswered. In the meantime, United Nations and health sector partners continue to face extreme challenges in the delivery of medical supplies and the provision of preventative and curative services in ISIL-controlled areas.

Safety and security of staff and premises

57. A total of 30 United Nations staff members, 28 of whom are UNRWA staff, one from the United Nations Development Programme (UNDP), and one from UNICEF, continue to be detained or missing. The total number of humanitarian workers killed in the conflict since March 2011 is 81. This includes 17 staff members of the United Nations, 48 staff members and volunteers of the Syrian Arab Red Crescent, eight volunteers and staff members of the Palestinian Red Crescent Society and eight staff members of international non-governmental organizations. Of the 81, 15 have been killed since 1 January 2015.

III. OBSERVATIONS

58. Throughout the Syrian Arab Republic, the fundamental rules of international humanitarian and human rights law are being violated with little or no accountability. I repeat my call that the situation in the Syrian Arab Republic be referred to the International Criminal Court. Tragically, hundreds of civilians have been killed or injured in direct or indiscriminate attacks this month alone due to the continued use of explosive weapons in populated areas, including barrel bombs, shelling and car bombs. The use of explosive weapons in populated areas will have a severe long-term impact on the Syrian Arab Republic, resulting from the destruction of housing, essential infrastructure and services on which civilians depend. Furthermore, the use of these weapons is leaving deadly explosive remnants of war across the country. These will continue to pose a serious threat to Syrian civilians, particularly children, long after the hostilities have ended. I have taken note of the commitment by the Government of the Syrian Arab Republic to refrain from using indiscriminate weapons and expect this commitment to be translated into action.

59. Continued attacks against health-care facilities, transports and personnel and the denial of care to the wounded and sick continue to be of grave concern. Attacks on facilities, transports and personnel have a devastating multiplier effect, not only killing and injuring, but also leaving many people unable to get the treatment that they desperately need. Many Syrians are now unable to obtain even the most basic levels of care. Meanwhile, it is inhumane and unlawful that medicines and medical supplies continue to be prevented from reaching their intended beneficiaries. The protection and provision of medical care to the wounded and sick under all circumstances is clearly enshrined in international humanitarian law.

60. While the security situation is deteriorating, humanitarian access to those most in need is not improving. The level of access for humanitarian agencies to the 4.5 million people in hard-to-reach areas and their inability to obtain essential humanitarian supplies and services remains unacceptable. I must again urge the parties, and in particular the Government of the Syrian Arab Republic, to honour

their obligations under international humanitarian law and to act now. Security Council resolution 2139 (2014) leaves no room for interpretation or further negotiation. The parties must comply and facilitate the delivery of aid to civilians in need wherever they may be found in the Syrian Arab Republic.

61. In its resolution 2139 (2014), the Security Council also called upon the parties to lift the sieges of populated areas. This call has not been heard. It is shameful that nearly 400,000 people are being deliberately forced to live under siege conditions, largely without access to essential goods and services.

62. The scale of the devastation for the Syrian people has reached staggering proportions. There are now some 13.5 million people in need of some form of humanitarian or protection assistance, including some six million children. More than half of the people in the Syrian Arab Republic have been forced to leave their homes, and some 6.5 million people are internally displaced. Three out of every four Syrians is estimated to live in poverty. Health facilities, schools, markets and other essential services across the country are operating at reduced capacity, or are closed down. Living conditions for Syrians will only deteriorate further unless there is an end to the fighting.

63. I am encouraged that on 30 October, in Vienna, the international community finally re-engaged in the process of finding a political solution to the Syrian conflict. There is no military solution to this crisis. The Geneva communiqué remains the internationally agreed framework for a political settlement to the conflict, as reiterated by the Vienna communiqué. The latter is a first step in providing the opportunity for an expanded group of international stakeholders to further develop and elaborate this framework along the lines of the key principles of the Geneva communiqué. We need this type of renewed momentum, prompted by international re-engagement, in seeking a political settlement to the Syrian conflict. It is in this spirit that we should look at the Vienna communiqué as a promising development. I urge all parties to the conflict and the Member States with influence on those parties to further their engagement and spare no effort towards a political solution. As this report clearly highlights, Syrian civilians, including women and children, continue to bear the brunt of this conflict. The international community must come together to help Syrians find common ground and stop the violence.

SOURCE: United Nations Security Council. "Report of the Secretary-General on the implementation of Security Council resolutions 2139 (2014), 2165 (2014) and 2191 (2014)." November 11, 2015. www .securitycouncilreport.org/atf/cf/%7B65BFCF9B-6D27-4E9C-8CD3-CF6E4FF96FF9%7D/s_2015_ 862.pdf.

OTHER HISTORIC DOCUMENTS OF INTEREST

FROM THIS VOLUME

From previous *Historic Documents*

- United Nations–Brokered Syrian Peace Talks Conclude Without Agreement, *2014*, p. 31
- President Obama Remarks on the Conflict in Syria, *2013*, p. 411
- Lebanese Prime Minister on Impact of Syrian Civil War, *2013*, p. 69
- United Nations Fails to Take Action in Syria, *2012*, p. 81
- Arab Spring: Syrian Government's Violent Crackdown on Protests, *2011*, p. 168

Myanmar Holds Historic Election

NOVEMBER 13 AND 16, 2015

In November 2015, Myanmar took another step forward in its government reform efforts by holding a national, multiparty general election. The election would be the first since a military-backed civilian government was instated in 2011, ending a decades-long military dictatorship that oversaw the oppression and killing of thousands of its opponents. World-famous prodemocracy advocate Aung San Suu Kyi led the National League for Democracy to a resounding victory, inspiring hope among Myanmar's citizens that the government would continue to undergo major changes in the coming years.

Myanmar's Return to Democracy

Despite holding elections, Myanmar is not considered to be a full democracy because its military-drafted constitution requires that 25 percent of the seats in Myanmar's parliament, the Hluttaw, be given to unelected military representatives. These representatives also effectively hold veto power over any proposed constitutional changes, because the law requires 75 percent of Hluttaw members to approve such a change. The military also has the authority to select the leaders of Myanmar's Ministries of Defense, Home Affairs, and Border Affairs.

These laws are vestiges of the military dictatorship that governed Myanmar for nearly fifty years. The last time Myanmar had a truly democratically elected leader was in 1960, when Prime Minister U Nu resumed office following a brief caretaker government led by Gen. Bo Ne Win. Two years later, Ne Win led a coup d'état and seized power from U Nu, declaring that "parliamentary democracy was not suitable for Burma" and beginning decades of military rule that continually suppressed prodemocracy demonstrations.

The most notable example of this often-violent oppression occurred in 1988. Increasingly angered by the country's military rule, ongoing police brutality, economic mismanagement, and alleged government corruption, Myanmar's students initiated widespread prodemocracy demonstrations in March. What came to be known as the 8888 Uprising grew to involve ethnic minorities, Buddhists, Muslims, government workers, and other professionals, with protests drawing thousands of people. The military violently cracked down on protestors and imposed martial law in September, and by the end of the year an estimated 10,000 people—both soldiers and protestors—had been killed. The protests and the government's brutal response drew widespread attention from the global community, and the military faced significant pressure to hold a free and fair election. An election was held in May 1990, with the National League for Democracy (NLD), a prodemocracy party, receiving 60 percent of the vote and winning 392 of 485 available Hluttaw seats. However, the military junta annulled the results and many NLD members were imprisoned, including NLD leader Aung San Suu Kyi, who was placed under house arrest in 1989.

Nearly 20 years later, following extensive protests over the government's elimination of fuel subsidies and amid significant international pressure, the military announced that multiparty elections would be held in 2010. The military-backed Union Solidarity and Development Party (USDP) claimed it won 80 percent of the votes in that election, which was largely viewed as a sham. Yet the military hailed the election as a sign of Myanmar's transition to civilian democracy, officially dissolving the junta and swearing in former military commander and USDP leader U Thein Sein as president.

The new government instituted a number of reforms in the years following the 2010 election, which included freeing hundreds of political prisoners, removing thousands of names from the country's blacklist, abolishing a ban on public gatherings of more than five people, and allowing privately held newspapers. Suu Kyi was also released from house arrest in 2010 and the NLD reregistered as a political party ahead of Myanmar's 2012 by-elections held to fill Hluttaw seats vacated by parliamentarians' promotions to other posts. The NLD won 43 of the 45 contested seats, setting the stage for a political resurgence in 2015.

A Complicated Political Landscape

While 91 political parties had registered to participate in the 2015 election, the NLD and the USDP—two of the country's six major parties—were expected to win the most votes. Suu Kyi, who was elected to the Hluttaw during the 2012 by-elections, continued to lead her party throughout the campaign. She was the daughter of Aung San, a former premier who led the country to independence from British rule in the 1940s and also founded Myanmar's armed forces, the Tatmadaw, before he and several cabinet members were assassinated. Suu Kyi had left Myanmar to attend Oxford University, but returned in 1988 to care for her sick mother. She joined the fight to restore democracy amid the 8888 Uprising, making her first foray into the political arena during a speech before 500,000 protestors, and quickly became a potent symbol of the prodemocracy movement—a symbolism strengthened by the fifteen years Suu Kyi spent under house arrest.

The political and ethnic divisions within Myanmar provided a complicated context for the 2015 elections. Though the government and military are largely controlled by the majority Bamar ethnic group, the country has 135 official ethnicities. Seven of these groups have namesake states bordering neighbor countries and have continually clashed with the military, claiming persecution by the government and seeking greater autonomy. Despite government attempts to conduct peace talks, these groups continue to fight and voting was suspended in some regions due to security concerns.

The controversial treatment of another, unregistered ethnic minority—Rohingya Muslims—also shaped conversation around the election. Described by the United Nations as one of the world's most persecuted people, Rohingyas have been victimized by mass killings carried out by Rakhine Buddhists, and approximately 140,000 of them live in squalid displacement camps. Thousands of others have attempted to flee the country by boat, though many have died in the process. The government granted voting rights to the Rohingyas in 2010, and several of them were elected to the Hluttaw, but these rights were taken away ahead of the 2015 election, and Rohingyas were prohibited from registering as candidates. Suu Kyi, in particular, drew criticism for not speaking out against these abuses, and a number of international human rights organizations questioned whether any election could be considered free and fair if Myanmar did not extend voting rights to all its peoples.

The rise of Myanmar's radical Buddhist nationalism movement had an important influence on the election as well. What began in 2013 as a movement to boycott Muslim businesses and services had evolved into the Association for the Protection of Race and Religion, a group widely known as Ma Ba Tha. The organization advocates Buddhist supremacy and Buddhist-Muslim apartheid and has close ties to the USDP. Ma Ba Tha's influence was seen in legislation passed by the Hluttaw in July 2015 that forbade interfaith marriages, prohibited Buddhist women from changing their religion, restricted the number of children certain ethnic groups could have, and outlawed polygamy. USDP sought to position itself as a defender against perceived Islamic fundamentalism during the election, in an effort to capitalize on this growing anti-Muslim sentiment.

Conversely, the NLD was criticized by some for not including any Muslims among its list of parliamentary candidates and challenging the hardline Buddhists. Some also accused the party of hypocrisy as reports surfaced that several senior party officials were expelled for questioning party decisions, and candidates were banned from speaking to the media for a three-week period during the campaign.

ELECTION RESULTS FAVOR DEMOCRACY

The general election was held on November 8. International election observers, provided by the European Union, were stationed at polling locations across the country to help monitor the fairness of the election. Alexander Graf Lambsdorff, the chief observer, said teams had "reported very positively on the voting . . . with 95% rating the process a 'good' or 'very good.'"

When the votes were tallied, it was clear the NLD had won the election in a landslide. Out of 224 seats in the Hluttaw's Upper House, the NLD won 135 seats, the USDP won eleven, the military retained its fifty-six seats, and other smaller parties won twenty-two seats. In the Lower House, the NLD won 255 seats, compared to the USDP's thirty seats, the military's 110 seats, and the remaining thirty-eight seats won by other parties. While the NLD had been expected to do well in urban areas and regions where the Bamar majority is dominant, it won more seats than expected in rural parts of the country and regions where ethnic minorities are concentrated—areas where the USDP and ethnicity-based political parties, respectively, were expected to do well.

The victory gives the NLD control of the Hluttaw and the power to choose the next president. Suu Kyi cannot be considered because Myanmar's constitution disqualifies anyone who has "legitimate children" who have an "allegiance to a foreign power"; Suu Kyi's sons hold British passports. However, Suu Kyi said prior to the election that the new president would "have no authority" and "will act in accordance with the decisions of the party," suggesting she would maintain a strong influence on the next administration.

On November 12, President Sein issued a statement saying he would respect the election results, acknowledging that they reflected the people's will, and promising a peaceful transfer of power. Both he and Commander-in-Chief of Defense Services Sr. Gen. Min Aung Hlaing congratulated the NLD on its win and said they had agreed to Suu Kyi's request to meet to discuss national reconciliation. Sein reiterated this commitment during a meeting of more than 70 political party leaders on November 16. "I urge all the leaders of the political parties in attendance today, all political parties and citizens to work together to ensure a stable, peaceful, and prosperous Union of the Republic of Myanmar," he said. These overtures helped assuage concerns that Sein's government would attempt to ignore the election results and maintain control.

Suu Kyi, Sein, and Hlaing met on December 2 to discuss national reconciliation. While full details of the meetings have not been released, it was reported that Sein agreed to Suu Kyi's request that he ensure a peaceful transition of power. "This is the final victory of the reform process carried out by current government led by President Thein Sein, as there is no precedent in Myanmar for a government transferring power peacefully to an election winner," said Ye Htut, presidential spokesman. A similar agreement was reached with Hlaing. His office issued a statement saying that "both sides agreed to follow people's wish to collaborate for the country's stability, rule of law, national unity and development."

On February 1, 2016, the new Hluttaw members took their seats and the NLD's Win Myint was sworn in as speaker of the lower house. Htin Kyaw was sworn in as Myanmar's new president on March 30.

—Linda Fecteau Grimm

Following is the text of a press release from Myanmar president U Thein Sein's office on November 13, 2015, regarding national reconciliation following the electoral victory of the National League for Democracy (NLD); and the text of President Sein's speech on November 16, 2015, upon meeting with political parties following the general election.

Myanmar President Announces Intent to Meet with NLD Leaders

November 13, 2015

President U Thein Sein and Commander-in-Chief of Defence Services Senior General Min Aung Hlaing will hold talks with Daw Aung San Suu Kyi, the leader of the National League for Democracy, after the electoral process of the Union Election Commission has concluded.

In statements released by the President's Office and the Commander-in-Chief's Office yesterday in response to a request by the NLD leader to hold talks on national reconciliation, they said they will coordinate with the NLD to hold the talks when the electoral process is complete and will cooperate with the party for the stability of the country in post-election period.

The president and the commander-in-chief also congratulated the National League for Democracy for its leading position in the 2015 election results, with the NLD enjoying a landslide victory at the polls.

The commander-in-chief congratulated the families of the Tatmadaw and the entire Myanmar people for their voting discipline in this historic general election.

In the statement of the President's Office, the president promised a peaceful transfer of power within a set time frame and said he would respect the election results, which reflect the will of the people.

Daw Aung San Suu Kyi sent separate letters to President U Thein Sein, Commander-in-Chief of Defence Service Senior General Min Aung Hlaing and Pyithu Hluttaw Speaker Thura U Shwe Mann yesterday, requesting a meeting next week to address national reconciliation.

In her letters, she stressed the importance of the peaceful implementation of the desires of the people, which has been demonstrated in the election results.

Commander-in-Chief Senior General Min Aung Hlaing said yesterday at a meeting of the Tatmadaw's leading organising committee in Nay Pyi Taw that the army would assist in strengthening the country's multi-party democratic system, according to a report from the army's Myawady News Agency.

SOURCE: President's Office of the Republic of the Union of Myanmar. "Welcoming the new guard President, Commander-in-Chief to meet with NLD leader." November 13, 2015. www.president-office .gov.mm/en/?q=node/6138.

DOCUMENT

President Sein Speaks to Myanmar's Political Parties

November 16, 2015

I am delighted to meet once again with my colleagues, the leaders of the political parties. Since I initiated reforms, I have listened and implemented the advice given in meetings with political parties. Now, at this important time for the country, I meet with you all to ensure a smooth transition.

The 2015 general elections have now been successfully held. The international community has also congratulated the country on this achievement. As I had pledged, my government did everything possible under its authority to ensure that the elections were clean and free. We fulfilled this pledge. Holding clean and fair elections shows that our country's democratic transition is successfully moving forward. My government since taking office has implemented needed liberalization, media freedom, and governance to make it possible for the people to actively participate in politics. The role of political parties is also important, and I acknowledge their contributions today.

The elections, which are important for the transition after five years of implementing reforms, have now been successfully held. I acknowledge the Union Election Commission, political parties that participated, winning candidates, all the participants and voters for ensuring that the elections were peaceful, smooth and successful.

During the remainder of my government's term in office, existing laws, regulations, procedures, and guidance will continue to be upheld, and a smooth transition undertaken. In accordance with established procedures, I will send invitations for the convening of the second parliament. After parliament step by step carries out its work, transfer to the resulting new government will occur within the designated timeframe. I would like to stress that this work will be undertaken calmly, peacefully, and smoothly.

Within my government's five years in office, we have given our best efforts at implementing the required tasks. In particular, we fostered a new political culture of resolving issues through dialogue and negotiations between political forces. In the area of peace, we signed a nationwide ceasefire agreement (NCA) with eight Ethnic Armed Organizations (EAOs). We continue to strive for the inclusion of the remaining EAOs.

The importance of the agreement lies in the political guarantees for resolving armed conflict through political means, and together establishing a federal and democratic Union through political dialogue. The NCA is the best foundation for peace that we leave behind. Efforts are being made to begin political dialogue soon in accordance with the timeline provided in the NCA. I believe the next government will do its best to continue to build on this good foundation.

Elections are important in a democratic system, and they must be held on a regular basis. Under our country's system elections are held every five years. The people's decisions determine the results of the elections. There will be winning parties and losing parties. However, in a democratic system, just as the winning parties must work for the best interests of the people, the losing parties must ensure that the important democratic practice of checks and balances remains strong. Additionally, parties not elected to parliament must engage outside of it. This will ensure a healthy and lively democracy. Therefore, I urge all political parties to strive to ensure a strong system of checks and balances.

Since our country is undergoing transition, the success of this is not only the responsibility of the government, and parliament but also of all the political forces in the country. Therefore, the political parties have an important contribution to make towards the successful completion of the transition. Similarly, political parties also play a role in the peace process. In particular, all political forces will participate in their respective roles during political dialogue. Therefore, I remind political parties to make preparations to participate in political dialogue.

In every election, there will be winning and losing parties. The choices of the electorate may also change. No matter the changes, it is critical to continue development of the country while ensuring stability and peace. This is not only the duty of the government but also a responsibility of everyone.

Our country is taking the first steps on the democratic path, and is transitioning from an old to a new system. Therefore, the transition needs to occur methodically and delicately. Additionally, we need to consider our country's history and geo-politics. All these are important for our country's politics, economy, and the ongoing peace process. Those who will govern the country will need to pay attention to these issues.

As I pledged in my radio address aired before the elections, I firmly believe that the results of the elections truly reflect the will of the people. The transition after the elections needs to occur smoothly. Future elections will be better organized once the country is on the path to development and stability. All political forces have a role in achieving the goal of raising democratic standards.

During this important period, our abilities to reason, cooperate, and act with vision will be decisive.

In conclusion, I urge all the leaders of the political parties in attendance today, all political parties and citizens to work together to ensure a stable, peaceful, and prosperous Union of the Republic of Myanmar.

I invite the leaders of the political parties to discuss freely. I will respond with my comments.

Thank you.

SOURCE: President's Office of the Republic of the Union of Myanmar. "The full text of President U Thein Sein's speech at meeting with political parties in Yangon." November 16, 2015. www.president-office.gov.mm/en/?q=node/6148.

Other Historic Documents of Interest

World Leaders
Remark on ISIL Attacks

NOVEMBER 15, 16 AND 19, AND DECEMBER 11, 2015

On November 12, 2015, two suicide bombers detonated explosives in a suburb of Beirut, Lebanon, leaving upwards of forty dead. The next day, a series of suicide bombings and mass shootings were carried out in Paris and left 130 dead. Both events were orchestrated by the Islamic State of Iraq and the Levant (ISIL). The attacks raised alert levels around the world, and the manhunt for those linked to the event spread across Europe, centering in Brussels, Belgium, where one of the masterminds behind the Paris attack was thought to be living. While France chose to respond with ramped up airstrikes against ISIL strongholds in Iraq and Syria, in the United States, a debate over whether Syrian refugees should be allowed into the country began when it was learned that some of the Paris attackers had entered Europe with a wave of migrants from Syria.

Twin Bombings in Beirut

Lebanon, which shares a border with Syria, has been heavily impacted both by the influx of refugees fleeing the ongoing civil war in the country and the continuing violence perpetrated by ISIL, which used the power vacuum in Syria to gain strength. Lebanon itself has been internally destabilized by its inability to elect a president or seat a parliament since 2014, which has left it little heft to combat the growing ISIL threat.

On the evening of November 12, two suicide bombs were detonated in Bourj el-Barajneh, a suburb of Southern Beirut. The first went off outside a mosque, while the second, which was detonated nearby approximately five minutes later, went off outside a bakery and was intended to harm those who were responding to the first blast. It is believed that a third suicide bomber was killed during the second blast before he could detonate his vest. More than 200 were injured in the twin bombings, and an estimated forty-three were killed. Lebanese police quickly arrested six in connection with the attack, all of whom were of Syrian and Palestinian descent. ISIL claimed responsibility for the attack on a Twitter account, stating "Let the Shiite apostates know that we will not rest until we take revenge in the name of the Prophet."

Lebanese prime minister Tammam Salam called for unity following the bombings, which were the deadliest attacks in the nation since its civil war ended in 1990. Calling the attacks "unjustifiable" the prime minister called on those within Lebanon and around the world to unite against "plans to create strife." In the coming days, many in Lebanon expressed discontent because of the outpouring of support for those killed in the November 13 attacks in Paris that had not been similarly shown in Lebanon. In particular, many pointed to the decision of Facebook to activate a feature called Safety Check, which allows individuals to let their loved ones know during a disaster that they are safe, following the Paris attacks. The same feature was not activated after the bombings in Lebanon. "When my people died," wrote Lebanese doctor Elie Fares on his blog, "they did not send the world into mourning. Their death was but an irrelevant fleck along the international news cycle, something that happens in those parts of the world."

NIGHT OF TERROR IN PARIS

On the evening of November 13, a series of coordinated attacks took place in and around Paris. The attacks began in the Paris suburb of Saint-Denis at Stade de France, the national sports stadium, during an exhibition soccer match between France and Germany. There, three suicide bombings occurred outside the stadium within thirty minutes of each other. The suicide bombers, as well as one bystander, were killed. President François Hollande, who was in attendance at the game, was evacuated but asked that the match be continued, believing that the safety of fans could be better guaranteed inside the stadium. In footage played on national television of the match, two of the explosions from the suicide bombings can be heard, but no one on television or in the stadium reacts. At the conclusion of the game, fans were brought onto the field to await evacuation orders, and both the French and German soccer teams spent the night at the stadium.

At approximately 9:25 p.m., shooters opened fire on the Le Carillon café and adjacent restaurant, Le Petit Cambodge, in the center of Paris. Fifteen were killed by the gunmen who, according to eyewitnesses, shouted "Allahu Akbar" (God is great) during the attack. Less than ten minutes later, five were killed at Café Bonne Biere, another restaurant in the city center. An additional nineteen were killed during a shooting at the La Belle Equipe restaurant, followed by another suicide bombing at the Comptoir Voltaire café during which fifteen were injured.

Twenty minutes after the first café attack, another team of shooters opened fire inside the Bataclan Theater where an estimated 1,500 were in attendance for an Eagles of Death Metal concert. The siege lasted for twenty minutes, after which upward of sixty hostages were taken before police were able to gain control of the situation. A total of 130 were killed in the November attacks in Paris; eighty-nine were killed at the Bataclan theater alone. Seven of the nine attackers were killed either by police fire or suicide bomb. The attacks were the deadliest in France since World War II.

Speaking before France's parliament three days after the attack, President Hollande announced that "France is at war" and said that the nation would "respond with the cool determination that this vile attack against our country calls for." Hollande said that France was targeted because of its values and freedoms: "France, which values life, culture, sports, celebrations. France, which makes no distinction as to color, origin, background, religion. The France that the assassins wanted to kill was that of its young people in all their diversity. Most of the dead were under 30. Their names were Mathias, Quentin, Nick, Nohemi, Djamila, Hélène, Elodie, Valentin, and I've left out so many others! What was their only crime? Being alive." But he said, "Terrorists believe that free people will allow themselves to be intimidated by horror. That's not the case, and the French Republic has surmounted many other trials. It is still here, still alive and well."

In response to the attacks, France increased its airstrikes in Syria. On November 15, ten fighter jets carried out strikes that destroyed a suspected ISIL training facility and command center. Hollande also dispatched an aircraft carrier to the Persian Gulf containing dozens of planes to lend support to the air campaign. In a controversial move, Hollande announced a three-month state of emergency, which would permit house arrests and police searches, while restricting freedom of association by giving the government the opportunity to disband groups that appear to "present serious harm to the public order." According to Hollande, these "measures offer useful means to prevent terrorist acts."

Several countries in the traditionally fluid European Union (EU) instituted temporary border controls following the attack, even for those within the Schengen zone, the term used for the open border agreement between twenty-two European countries that does not require border checks or passports for those traveling from a Schengen member state. In light of the knowledge that nearly all the Paris attackers held EU passports, EU leaders held emergency meetings to determine whether more stringent border controls should be enacted. It was instead determined that the nations would develop a system to share passport data of those traveling within the Schengen zone. Some expressed concern that this might ultimately negate the purpose of Schengen, while others disagreed, including the leader of the National Front, Marine Le Pen, stating that, "the absence of national borders is criminal madness."

LOCKDOWN IN BRUSSELS

Based on information that the masterminds behind the Paris attacks might be in Belgium, from November 21 to November 25, the government imposed a strict lockdown in Brussels. Schools, restaurants, stores, and public transportation were shuttered while security forces combed streets and homes around the city to root out the perpetrators. During their searches, police called on the Belgian public not to post about police operations on social media, which led to an influx of Belgians posting cat pictures on Twitter. Police conducted more than twenty raids during the lockdown and made thirty-seven arrests. Four of those arrested had terrorism charges filed against them in relation to the Paris attack. The search did not locate Salah Abdeslam, a Belgian-born French national suspected of planning the attack from Brussels.

In a speech before parliament, Belgium prime minister Charles Michel said that the nation "must keep a cool head. This is a new chapter in the history of Europe. Faithless and lawless enemies who hide and strike with cowardice seek to impose a totalitarian model." Standing firm against ISIL terrorists, the prime minister said, "The freedom to believe or not to believe. The freedom to speak, debate, the freedom to caricature and criticize. The freedom to work, the freedom to go out, the freedom to love. In short, the freedom to live. For us, this is not negotiable."

U.S. GOVERNORS REFUSE REFUGEES WHILE CANADA WELCOMES THEM

In their investigation, Paris police learned that some of the attackers had likely entered the country during the Syrian refugee influx. Within days after the announcement, U.S. governors began refusing to allow Syrian refugees entering the United States to resettle within their borders. The Obama administration had promised to admit 10,000 Syrians over the course of a year, and 2,000 refugees had entered at the time of the Paris attacks. Ultimately, thirty Republican governors and one Democratic governor announced that they would not accept Syrian refugees, with only Colorado, Connecticut, Delaware, Hawaii, Pennsylvania, Vermont, and Washington stating that they still planned to welcome refugees. Alabama governor Robert Bentley, for example, said he would "oppose any attempt to relocate Syrian refugees to Alabama" because he would "not stand complicit to a policy that places the citizens of Alabama in harm's way." According to legal experts, the 1980 Refugee Act gave states little recourse in determining whether they would accept refugees. According to American University law professor Stephen Vladeck, "legally, states have no authority to do anything because the question of who should be allowed in this country is one that the Constitution commits to the federal government." The only power left to states would be to cut their funding for refugee resettlement which would make the process more difficult.

Republican presidential candidates also weighed in, suggesting that the United States should halt the refugee program until a better screening system could be devised that would help ensure that those with ties to ISIL were not entering the country. Presidential candidate Donald Trump suggested that all Muslims should be barred from entering the country, even those in the United States legally, until we could determine who did not have ties to terrorism or intent to harm the United States. President Obama told Americans that they "have to remember that many of these refugees are the victims of terrorism themselves" and that the United States "can welcome refugees who are desperately seeking safety and ensure our own security. We can and must do both."

In contrast to some U.S. leaders, newly elected prime minister Justin Trudeau pledged to allow 25,000 Syrian refugees to resettle in Canada. In welcoming the first group that arrived in his nation, the prime minister stated, "Let me reassure those coming to our country that our communities and all orders of government will work closely, together, to make it easier for you to adjust to these changes and become full participants in Canadian society. While it might be much colder outside than back home, I am sure that you will find warm welcomes from your neighbors." He added, "In the years to come, Canadians will look back with enormous pride on the contributions made by Syrian refugees and how they have made our country even better."

—Heather Kerrigan

Following is the text of a press release from the office of Governor Bob Bentley released on November 15, 2015, indicating his refusal to accept Syrian refugees; the text of French president François Hollande's speech before parliament on November 16, 2015, on the terror attacks in Paris; the text of remarks by President Barack Obama on November 16, 2015, regarding Syrian refugees entering the United States; the text of a speech by Belgium's Prime Minister Charles Michel on November 19, 2015, regarding efforts in Belgium to locate those responsible for the Paris attacks; and a statement from Canadian prime minister Justin Trudeau on December 11, 2015, welcoming Syrian refugees to his nation.

Alabama Governor Announces
Refusal to Accept Syrian Refugees

November 15, 2015

Governor Robert Bentley on Sunday announced he is refusing Syrian refugees relocating to Alabama.

"After full consideration of this weekend's attacks of terror on innocent citizens in Paris, I will oppose any attempt to relocate Syrian refugees to Alabama through the U.S. Refugee Admissions Program. As your Governor, I will not stand complicit to a policy that places the citizens of Alabama in harm's way," Governor Robert Bentley said.

The Alabama Law Enforcement Agency is working diligently with the FBI, DHS and federal intelligence partners to monitor any possible threats. Law enforcement presence has been increased at major gathering events in Alabama to further insure the safety of citizens. To date, there has been no credible intelligence of any terrorist threats in Alabama.

Alabama currently has one U.S. State Department approved refugee processing center in Mobile. There have been no Syrian refugees relocated in Alabama to date, though neighboring states have processed a number of refugees.

"The acts of terror committed over the weekend are a tragic reminder to the world that evil exists and takes the form of terrorists who seek to destroy the basic freedoms we will always fight to preserve. I will not place Alabamians at even the slightest, possible risk of an attack on our people. Please continue to join me in praying for those who have suffered loss and for those who will never allow freedom to fade at the hands of terrorists," Governor Bentley added.

SOURCE: Office of the Alabama Governor. "Governor Bentley Refuses Syrian Refugees Relocating to Alabama." November 15, 2015. http://governor.alabama.gov/newsroom/2015/11/governor-bentley-refuses-syrian-refugees-relocating-alabama.

President Hollande Addresses Parliament on Paris Attacks

November 16, 2015

Mr. President of the Congress,
Mr. President of the Senate,
Mr. Prime Minister,
Ladies and Gentlemen, Members of the Government,
Ladies and Gentlemen, Parliamentarians,

France is at war. The acts committed in Paris and near the Stade de France on Friday evening are acts of war. They left at least 129 dead and many injured. They are an act of aggression against our country, against its values, against its young people, and against its way of life.

They were carried out by a jihadist army, by Daesh, which is fighting us because France is a country of freedom, because we are the birthplace of human rights.

At this exceptionally solemn moment, I wanted to address a joint session of Parliament to demonstrate our national unity in the face of such an abomination and to respond with the cool determination that this vile attack against our country calls for.

In truth, our democracy has triumphed over much more fearsome enemies than these cowardly murderers. Our Republic is under no threat from these despicable killers.

I shall marshal the full strength of the State to defend the safety of its people. I know I can count on the dedication of police officers, gendarmes, service personnel, and you yourselves, our national representatives. You know what duty means and, when necessary, the spirit of sacrifice.

Terrorists believe that free people will allow themselves to be intimidated by horror. That's not the case, and the French Republic has surmounted many other trials. It is still here, still alive and well. Those who have sought to defy it have always been on the losing side of history. The same thing will be true this time. The French people are a staunch, tough, courageous people. They do not resign themselves, and when one of their children is thrown down, they rise up.

Those who wanted to destroy them by deliberately targeting innocents are cowards who fired on an unarmed crowd. It cannot be said that we are engaged in a war of civilizations, for these assassins do not represent one. We are in a war against jihadist terrorism that threatens the entire world, not just France.

In this war, which began some years ago, we are all aware that we need time, and that patience is every bit as necessary as the endurance and fierceness with which we will fight.

The enemy uses the vilest means in its attempts to kill. But it is not beyond capture, and more specifically, it is not out of reach.

So during this sad and difficult time, a time when our citizens have faced such horror, it is important to remain cool-headed. I appeal once again to all our compatriots to demonstrate those virtues that are a credit to our country: perseverance, unity, lucidity, dignity.

Today, our country is in mourning. We think about the innocent people who were cut down in Paris and in the outskirts of the city by armed killers. We think of their families who are experiencing the most inconsolable pain. We think about the hundreds of young people, young men and women, who were hit, wounded, traumatized by this terrible attack. As I speak, some of them are still fighting for their lives.

I applaud the work of our emergency rescue services, which have been mobilized since Friday. Our healthcare system had prepared for such an emergency situation, and it rose to the occasion, fulfilling its mission perfectly.

I also want to pay tribute to the security forces who are fully engaged in guaranteeing the safety of the French, as evidenced by the courage of those police officers who—when it came time to launch their assault on the Bataclan to free the hostages who were condemned to certain death without their intervention—once again showed determination and no thought for themselves.

On Friday, the terrorists' target was France as a whole. France, which values life, culture, sports, celebrations. France, which makes no distinction as to color, origin, background, religion. The France that the assassins wanted to kill was that of its young people in all their diversity. Most of the dead were under 30. Their names were Mathias, Quentin, Nick, Nohemi, Djamila, Hélène, Elodie, Valentin, and I've left out so many others! What was their only crime? Being alive.

What the terrorists were attacking was the France that is open to the world. Among the victims were several dozen of our foreign friends, representing 19 different nationalities.

Since Friday evening, I have been receiving messages of solidarity from heads of state and government around the globe. And the three colors of the French flag have adorned the most famous landmarks, reminding us that France has always been a beacon for humankind. And that when it is attacked, the whole world is thrown for a while into shadow.

Friday's acts of war were decided upon, planned and prepared in Syria. They were organized in Belgium and carried out on our soil with French complicity. Their objective was quite clear: to sow fear in order to divide us and to keep us from fighting terrorism in the Middle East.

We are facing an organization, Daesh, which has a territorial base, financial resources, and military capabilities. Since the beginning of the year, Daesh's terrorist army has struck in Paris, Denmark, Tunisia, Egypt, Lebanon, Kuwait, Saudi Arabia, Turkey, and Libya. Every day, it massacres and oppresses populations.

That is why the need to destroy Daesh concerns the whole international community. I have therefore asked the Council of Security to meet as soon as possible to adopt a resolution expressing our common will to combat terrorism.

Meanwhile, France will step up its operations in Syria.

Yesterday I ordered 10 French fighter jets to launch airstrikes on the Daesh stronghold of Raqqa. They destroyed a command center and a training camp. I want to congratulate the French pilots who successfully carried out this mission. I also want to thank our American allies who provided assistance in this operation. And I want to announce here, before Congress, that we will continue these strikes in the weeks to come. On Thursday, the Charles de Gaulle aircraft carrier will set sail for the eastern Mediterranean, which will triple our capacity to act. And we will act indefatigably and without respite.

Those who ordered the Paris attacks must know that far from undermining France's resolve, they further strengthened our determination to destroy them.

We are fighting terrorism wherever the very survival of States is under threat. That was the reason for my decision to intervene in Mali, and it still justifies the presence of our troops in the Sahel where Boko Haram carries out massacres, kidnappings, rapes, and murders. We are fighting terrorism in Iraq to allow the authorities of that country to restore their sovereignty throughout the entire country, and in Syria, where we are resolutely and tirelessly seeking a political solution, one that does not include Bashar al-Assad. But our enemy in Syria is Daesh.

There is no question of containing it. This organization must be destroyed, both to save the populations of Syria and Iraq, and those of Lebanon, Jordan, Turkey—all the neighboring countries. And to protect ourselves, to keep foreign fighters from coming to our country, as was the case on Friday, to commit terrorist acts.

But we must do more. Syria has become the largest breeding ground for terrorists that the world has ever known, and the international community—as I have noted more than once—is divided and incohesive. From the outset of the conflict, France has called for this unity, which is so necessary in order to act.

Today, we need more airstrikes, which we will carry out, and more support for those who are fighting Daesh, which we, France, will provide. But we need all those who can really combat this terrorist army to unite as part of a large, single coalition. That is what we are striving for.

In the next few days, I will therefore meet with President Obama and President Putin to unite our forces and to achieve a result which, at this point, has been put off for far too long.

France is speaking to everyone—to Iran, Turkey, the Gulf States. The Paris attacks occurred just as we were meeting with these countries in Vienna to find a political solution in Syria. Now, all of us—the neighboring countries, the major powers, but also Europe—must live up to our responsibilities.

I have asked the defense minister to take up this matter tomorrow with our European colleagues under article 42 (7) of the Treaty on European Union, the solidarity clause, which states that when one State is attacked, all the Member States shall have the obligation to provide aid and assistance because the enemy is not just France's enemy, it is Europe's enemy.

Europe cannot live in the belief that the crises around it have no effect on it. The refugee issue is directly linked to the wars in Syria and Iraq. The inhabitants of those countries, particularly those living in territories controlled by Daesh, are suffering hideously and they are fleeing. They are the victims of this same terrorist system.

That is why it is vital for Europe to offer a dignified welcome to those who are eligible for asylum and to send home those who are not. That requires effective protection for our external borders, which is not yet the case. France is working on it. We were the first to sound the alarm, and France and Germany are currently working to ensure that the countries facing an influx of refugees receive help. The first to receive help must be the countries of the region: Turkey, Jordan, and Lebanon. And if Europe does not control its external borders—we are seeing this before our very eyes—that means a return to national borders, when it's not walls and barbed wire.

That will mean the dismantling of the European Union.

It is also imperative for France's longtime demands to be implemented in Europe. I'm talking about controlling the arms trade, establishing coordinated and systematic border controls, and approving, before the end of 2015, what we call the European PNR, to track the return of jihadists and arrest them.

These are the demands that France will convey once again through the Interior Ministry to the meeting that will be held at our request on Friday.

Given the acts of war committed on our soil—coming in the wake of the attacks of January 7, 8 and 9, and in the wake of so many other crimes committed in recent years in the name of this same jihadist ideology—we must be merciless.

It hurts to say it, but we know that these were French people who killed other French people on Friday. Living here in our land are individuals who start out by committing crimes, become radicalized, and go on to become terrorists. Sometimes they leave to fight in Syria or Iraq.

Sometimes they form networks that provide training, in certain cases, or which help one another, with a view to carrying out terrorist acts at a time determined by their sponsors.

We have thwarted a number of these acts in the past few months, and now we know, alas, what the plot was, what the organization was, and what was being prepared in the course of those months.

It is therefore urgent for us to defend ourselves, on a long-term basis. What's at stake is the protection of our fellow citizens and our ability to live together.

Friday night, once we knew the terrible toll taken by the shootings, I convened the Council of Ministers. I ordered the immediate reestablishment of border controls and I proclaimed a state of emergency, as recommended by the Prime Minister.

It is now effective throughout France, and I expanded the ability to carry out police searches in every department of continental France. Last night, more than 104 people were placed under house arrest and there were 168 police searches. And there will be more.

But with the acts of war on November 13, the enemy has taken things to a new level. Democracy is capable of responding. Article 2 of the Declaration of the Rights of Man and of the Citizen affirms that safety and resistance against oppression are fundamental rights. So we must exercise them.

In accordance with these principles, we will provide the means to once again guarantee the safety of our fellow citizens.

I have decided that a bill prolonging the state of emergency for three months, adapting its content to the changes in threats and technologies, will be brought before Parliament on Wednesday.

Indeed, the law which governs the state of emergency of 3 April 1955 cannot really match the kind of technologies and threats we face today.

But it includes two exceptional measures: house arrest and police searches. These two measures offer useful means to prevent terrorist acts. I will ensure that they are fully implemented and strengthened.

The Prime Minister will therefore propose to Parliament that we adopt a comprehensive legal scheme for each of these provisions. And you, parliamentarians, I invite you to vote on them before the end of the week.

But we have to go beyond the emergency situation.

I have thought about this issue a lot. I honestly think that we must develop our constitution to allow the government authorities to take action against terrorism that incites war, in accordance with the rule of law.

Our Constitution currently has two specific schemes that are not appropriate for the situation we are in.

The first scheme involves Article 16 of the Constitution. It specifies that the regular functioning of public authorities be suspended. The president will then take such measures as warranted by the circumstances, overriding the distribution of the constitutional powers.

And then there's Article 36 of the Constitution, which relates to the state of siege. And this isn't appropriate either. A state of siege is decreed in situations of imminent peril resulting from a foreign war or an armed insurrection. In this situation, various powers are then transferred from the civil to the military authorities.

As you can see, neither of these systems is suited to the situation we find ourselves in. The regular functioning of the government authorities—and we are proving that today—has not been interrupted. Transferring power to the military authorities would be inconceivable. However, we are at war. But this war is a different kind of war, we are facing a new kind of adversary. A constitutional scheme is needed to deal with this emergency.

This was what was proposed in 2007 by the committee chaired by Edouard Balladur who looked at changes to our Constitution. He suggested changing Article 36 of our Constitution to include reference to a state of siege as well as a state of emergency, and his proposal was to allow a basic law to lay down the conditions in which these schemes will be used.

And I believe that this approach should be reintroduced. We need to have an appropriate tool to provide a framework for taking exceptional measures for a certain period without recourse to the state of siege and without compromising public freedoms.

This revision of the Constitution must be accompanied by other measures. The issue at stake is the deprivation of nationality. The deprivation of nationality should not result in making someone stateless, but we need to be able to strip French nationality from an individual found guilty of a terrorist act or other acts against a country's fundamental interests even if he was born a French person, if he has another nationality.

In the same way, we must be able to prohibit dual nationals from returning to our country if they constitute a terrorist threat, unless they agree to be closely monitored, as is the case in Britain.

We should be able to expel more rapidly foreigners who represent an especially serious threat to public order or the country's security, but we should do so in accordance with our international commitments.

I know that other proposals have been made to strengthen the surveillance of certain individuals, especially those who are on file. The government, in a spirit of national unity, will ask the Conseil d'Etat to look at whether these proposals are in accordance with our international commitments and our basic laws. That ruling will be made public and I will draw all the consequences.

We should think carefully about this decision. Our Constitution is a collective agreement. It unites all our citizens. It is a common rule. It includes principles; it has a preamble which shows that France is a state governed by the rule of law.

The Constitution is a common charter. It is a contract which unites all the citizens of the same country. And if the Constitution is a collective agreement, an essential agreement for living together, then the Constitution should include responses for combating those who want to undermine it, in the same way that groups and associations that incite hatred or incite others [to] carry out terrorism should be dissolved.

Ladies and gentlemen, parliamentarians, I ask you to think about the decision that I have taken. I will ask the Prime Minister to prepare this revision with you so that it can be adopted as soon as possible because we, or you, will extend the state of emergency beyond the 12-day period to three months. But after the state of emergency is lifted we must observe the rule of law in our efforts to combat terrorism.

And since the threat is going to continue and we will be involved in the fight against Daesh for a long time abroad and at home, I also decided to substantially strengthen the resources available to the justice system and the security forces.

Firstly, the investigation services and anti-terrorist judges should, within the context of judicial proceedings, be able to have recourse to the whole range of intelligence techniques offered by new technology, whose use is authorized, within an administrative context, through the intelligence law. Criminal proceedings should also, as far as possible, take account of the specific nature of the terrorist threat.

Secondly, the magistrates should have access to the most sophisticated investigation methods, notably in order to combat the trafficking of arms because terrorist acts are committed with these illegal weapons. Penalties will be significantly increased.

Lastly, in the face of violent terrorism, the self-defense of police officers and the conditions under which they can use their weapons should be addressed within the framework of the rule of law.

These various issues will be part of a major legislative project, which I will ask the prime minister to be conduct[ed] and initiate immediately, together with the ministers concerned—the Justice Minister, the Minister of the Interior—so that we do not lose any time before taking action.

These provisions will complement all the measures that have been adopted since 2012, that is to say two anti-terrorist laws, an intelligence law, the considerable strengthening of resources. But I am also aware that we need to further strengthen our resources because if we are at war, we cannot just use the provisions that we had a few years ago in the law on military planning and other texts, which were aimed at preserving the security of our citizens.

Five thousand additional jobs for police officers and gendarmes will be created within the next two years in order to bring the total to 10,000 security-related jobs over five years. This is a substantial effort that the government will assume within the budgetary context that you are aware of. But it will make it possible to restore the capacity of the internal security forces to 2007 levels.

The creation of these jobs will benefit the anti-terrorist services, the border police and, more generally, the country's overall security and will go hand in hand with the investment and equipment necessary to carry out the missions to combat terrorism.

Similarly, the Ministry of Justice will add 2,500 additional jobs in the prison service and the judiciary service. And I shouldn't forget the customs service, which will need an additional 1,000 employees in order [to] ensure border control, if necessary.

As for our armed forces, they are increasingly needed for operations abroad, which we will continue in order to ensure the necessary security of our compatriots. So there, too, I have decided that there will be no cutbacks in defense personnel until 2019. And this reorganization of our armed forces will benefit operational, cyber defense intelligence units. The government will, as swiftly as possible, submit a new plan for changes in defense personnel up to 2019.

I also want to make better use of defense reserves who are still being underused in our country, while we do have this resource. Reservists form a strong link between the nation and the army. They could in the future form a national guard that is trained and available.

All these budgetary decisions will be taken within the framework of the Finance Law, which is, at the moment, under discussion for 2016. They will necessarily result in extra spending, but under these circumstances, I believe that the security pact will have precedence over the stability pact.

So ladies and gentlemen, the faces of the dead, the wounded, the bereaved families, weigh heavily on my mind. This memory fuels an unwavering determination, which I know you share, to combat terrorism.

In my determination to combat terrorism, I want France to remain itself. The barbarians attacking it want to disfigure it. They will not succeed. They will not be able to disfigure it. They will never succeed in destroying the French soul. They will never prevent us from living, from living the way we want to, freely and fully, and we must demonstrate that with cool heads. And I'm thinking of the young people. I am thinking of those who feel wounded through all these victims and are wondering whether they can still live in a state governed by the rule of law.

We must continue, continue to work, to go out, to live, to influence the world and that is why the major climate conference event will not only still go ahead but will be a moment of hope and solidarity. A moment of hope because the future of the planet is at stake and a moment of solidarity, too, because, there will undoubtedly be more than 100 heads of state and government who will come here to negotiate a lasting, binding agreement, one which is differentiated so that we can all live and so that our children and grandchildren can continue to have the planet they will inherit. But they will also tell France, a country of freedom, how much the whole world stands in solidarity with it, and how much the whole world also needs to mobilize its efforts in order to combat terrorism.

In the same way, our democratic timetable will not be subject to blackmail by the terrorists. Regional elections will take place as planned and political life will come back into full operation. It's our duty to ensure that.

Mr. President of Congress, Mr. President of the Senate, ladies and gentlemen, parliamentarians, those who represent the entire nation, you represent it in all its diversity, in all its sensitivities and in its unity. You represent a free people, an invincible people, when it is united and comes together. It is our most precious asset. And we have to avoid any one-upmanship or excesses. That is our republican duty. By giving up the battle that the Republic should have been waging, it was able to distance itself from certain circumstances; we must ensure that this isn't the case today.

In the face of this new context of war, the Republic must equip itself with the means to eradicate terrorism, while upholding our values and without compromising the rule of law.

We will eradicate terrorism because the French want to continue to live together without fearing anything from their neighbors. We will eradicate terrorism because we are attached to freedom and to raising France's profile around the world. We will eradicate terrorism so that the movement of people and the mixing of cultures can continue and so that human civilization is enriched. We will eradicate terrorism so that France can continue to lead the way. Terrorism will not destroy France because France will destroy it.

Long live the French Republic and long live France.

SOURCE: Embassy of France in the United States. "Speech by the President of the Republic Before a Joint Session of Parliament." November 16, 2015. http://ambafrance-us.org/spip.php?article7169#06.

President Obama
on Syrian Refugees

November 16, 2015

The President. . . . Of course, much of our attention has focused on the heinous attacks that took place in Paris. Across the world, in the United States, American flags are at half-staff in solidarity with our French allies. We're working closely with our French partners as they pursue their investigations and track down suspects.

France is already a strong counterterrorism partner, and today we're announcing a new agreement. We're streamlining the process by which we share intelligence and operational military information with France. This will allow our personnel to pass threat information, including on ISIL, to our French partners even more quickly and more often, because we need to be doing everything we can to protect more attacks—protect against more attacks and protect our citizens. . . .

On the military front, our coalition is intensifying our airstrikes, more than 8,000 to date. We're taking out ISIL leaders, commanders, their killers. We've seen that when we have an effective partner on the ground, ISIL can and is pushed back. So local forces in Iraq, backed by coalition airpower, recently liberated Sinjar. Iraqi forces are fighting to take back Ramadi. In Syria, ISIL has been pushed back from much of the border region with Turkey. We've stepped up our support of opposition forces who are working to cut off supply lines to ISIL's strongholds in and around Raqqa. So, in short, both in Iraq and Syria, ISIL controls less territory than it did before. I made the point to my fellow leaders that if we want this progress to be sustained, more nations need to step up with the resources that this fight demands. . . .

On the humanitarian front, our nations agreed that we have to do even more, individually and collectively, to address the agony of the Syrian people. The United States is already the largest donor of humanitarian aid to the Syrian people, some $4.5 billion in aid so far. As winter approaches, we're donating additional supplies, including clothing and generators, through the United Nations. But the U.N. appeal for Syria still has less than half the funds needed. Today I'm again calling on more nations to contribute the resources that this crisis demands.

In terms of refugees, it's clear that countries like Turkey, Lebanon, and Jordan, which are already bearing an extraordinary burden, cannot be expected to do so alone. At the same time, all of our countries have to ensure our security. And as President, my first priority is the safety of the American people. And that's why, even as we accept more refugees—including Syrians—we do so only after subjecting them to rigorous screening and security checks.

We also have to remember that many of these refugees are the victims of terrorism themselves. That's what they're fleeing. Slamming the door in their faces would be a betrayal of our values. Our nations can welcome refugees who are desperately seeking safety and ensure our own security. We can and must do both.

Finally, we've begun to see some modest progress on the diplomatic front, which is critical because a political solution is the only way to end the war in Syria and unite the Syrian people and the world against ISIL. The Vienna talks mark the first time that all the key countries have come together—as a result, I would add, of American leadership—and reached a common understanding. With this weekend's talks, there's a path forward: negotiations between the Syrian opposition and the Syrian regime under the auspices of the United Nations; a transition toward a more inclusive, representative Government; a new Constitution, followed by free elections; and alongside this political process, a cease-fire in the civil war, even as we continue to fight against ISIL.

Now, these are obviously ambitious goals. Hopes for diplomacy in Syria have been dashed before. There are any number of ways that this latest diplomatic push could falter. And there are still disagreements between the parties, including, most critically, over the fate of Bashar Asad, who we do not believe has a role in Syria's future because of his brutal rule. His war against the Syrian people is the primary root cause of this crisis.

What is different this time, and what gives us some degree of hope, is that, as I said, for the first time, all the major countries on all sides of the Syrian conflict agree on a process that is needed to end this war. And so while we are very clear eyed about the very, very difficult road still head, the United States, in partnership with our coalition, is going to remain relentless on all fronts: military, humanitarian, and diplomatic. We have the right strategy, and we're going to see it through. So with that, I'm going to take some questions.

SOURCE: Executive Office of the President. "The President's News Conference in Belek, Turkey." November 16, 2015. *Compilation of Presidential Documents* 2015, no. 00815 (November 16, 2015). www .gpo.gov/fdsys/pkg/DCPD-201500815/pdf/DCPD-201500815.pdf.

Prime Minister of Belgium on Response to Paris Attacks

November 19, 2015

Mr Speaker,

Dear Colleagues,

Last Friday, three terrorist groups perpetrated an indiscriminate attack against innocent people. Innocents whose only sin was to be alive. Living in freedom.

This attack in the heart of Europe comes after many others: the Jewish museum in Brussels, *Charlie Hebdo*, Verviers and the Thalys train between Brussels and Paris.

These attacks took place in Paris, and were decided in Syria. They were carried out by Franco-Belgian cells.

129 people died, 350 people were wounded, some of whom are still fighting for their lives.

Women and men of 19 different nationalities. Our thoughts are with their families and friends. Our three compatriots who perished as a result of this barbaric act are also in our thoughts.

Mr Speaker,

Dear Colleagues,

We are outraged. We are sad. The terrorists are trying to destroy our values by spreading death. Our freedom to watch a concert or a football match or to relax sitting on a sidewalk cafe.

In this Parliament, we do not share the same ideological, political or philosophical beliefs. We represent the diversity of our people.

Let us now, more than ever, transcend our differences and join together.

More than ever, we must stand united behind our universal values.

Equality, separation of church and state, freedom of expression, tolerance and respect for others. . . .

These are and must remain the untouchable foundations of our democracy.

Fanaticism, just like racism, is a poison. A poison seeking to divide. A poison which must be destroyed.

The parliament and the government have a responsibility not to take this bait. It is the duty of all democrats to fight fanaticism and terrorism. Determined and ruthless. We shall fight the enemies of freedom with respect for the rule of law, adversarial procedures, presumption of innocence and the right to defence.

And let there be no doubt about this. We shall fight the enemies of freedom with respect for our constitutional state. That is the privilege of all democrats.

Growing fanaticism is not news. It is a known phenomenon that represents the greatest possible challenge to our democracy.

And maybe to our generation.

Chronology

On Friday evening, our authorities were mobilized to obtain as much information as possible in cooperation with the French authorities, enabling us to assess the situation hour by hour.

The CUTA, the Crisis Centre and the National Security Council immediately held the necessary meetings to take emergency, preliminary decisions.

Enhanced controls were set up at the French border, as well as in railway stations and airports.

Local police were immediately instructed to increase vigilance and to strengthen surveillance for public events.

A recommendation not to travel to Paris was issued.

Monday night, I once again convened the National Security Council to take note of a new assessment from the CUTA increasing the threat level to overall level 3.

The Crisis Centre proposed operational measures and informed all police districts.

We also recommended the cancellation of the Belgium-Spain football match. The next day, the German authorities made a similar decision.

Military presence has also been bolstered. Up to 300 additional military staff (in addition to the current 220) can be deployed. They have mainly been deployed in large cities, for static surveillance missions.

Ladies and gentlemen,

From the time of the implementation of the Government agreement, we committed to take initial steps in the fight against fanaticism and terrorism.

The *Charlie Hebdo* attacks and those foiled in Verviers accelerated and strengthened the decision process.

- The National Security Council is operational. It has met 14 times and many decisions have been taken.

- The army can now provide reinforcements to the police forces when the threat level so requires.

- The withdrawal of identity cards and passports for potential jihadist fighters is now planned.

- Belgian nationality may be stripped by a judge when convicting someone for terrorism.

- The CUTA has started the implementation of a dynamic register in which "foreign terrorist fighters" can be recorded.

- The possibilities of wiretapping and recording communications are extended in cases of terrorism.

- The strengthening of joint patrols in international trains has been decided upon.

- On the fiscal side, in 2015, EUR 200 million were earmarked to strengthen security investments and resources. These include special units. But that is not all. It was decided that a new wave of recruitment would be carried out. For instance, 45 new police officers have been hired for state security and 28 other recruitments are underway.

Mr. Speaker,

Dear Colleagues,

We have taken many strong measures in a few months. But it is not enough.
We must do more and we must do better.
We owe as much to our fellow citizens.
The government has given a strong signal.
400 million EUR are being made available for the fight against terrorism.
An amendment to the budget for 2016 will be submitted next week.
In addition to providing the necessary budget, the government intends to continue its action in four areas. We must:

1. **Eradicate the preaching of hate and calls to violence;**

2. **Focus efforts and resources specifically on individuals who are known to be potentially dangerous;**

3. **Strengthen the resources of our security forces;**

4. **Act at the international level.**

Dear Colleagues,

Eradicate the preaching of hate and calls to violence.

We note that calls to violence or terrorism are being trivialized.
This is unacceptable, and we must put an end to this.

The government will strengthen the legislative framework to condemn and/or identify preachers of hatred and terrorism.

We do not want extremist preachers in our country.

Preachers of hate can be placed under house arrest and deported. There is a legal basis for this.

Instructions will be provided to strictly apply these provisions. We request an immediate and general screening of all preachers present on our territory.

We must also fight hate crimes on websites. We will propose a law under which such sites can be closed down.

Freedom of worship is a constitutional right. However, places of worship cannot be spaces enabling the spread of jihadism. Such unauthorized, often clandestine, places of worship (mosques or cultural centres) must be dismantled.

There must also be transparency regarding the funding of mosques. This also applies to financing from abroad. The process for becoming a recognised mosque must be clarified.

Finally, the training of imams must be better supported in Belgium. These measures are necessary in order to avoid all forms of amalgamation.

The federal government wishes to consult with other states on this topic.

Specifically focusing efforts and resources on individuals identified as potentially dangerous.

The second area. We must focus the resources of our security services primarily on identifying jihadist sympathizers and monitoring them much better once they have been identified.

We will continue to strengthen the intelligence service. Through recruitment, facilities and legal resources (EUR 400 million made available).

Specifically, the CUTA has made significant progress in setting up a dynamic register aimed at putting Foreign Fighters on file. This file will improve the flow of information between the security authorities involved.

In the attacks or intended attacks, the terrorist cells were almost always linked to foreign fighters.

Preventing young people from travelling to combat areas or training camps is not enough. We must stop them from returning when they are not Belgians.

For us, the rule should be clear.

Jihadists returning to our country belong in prison.

For the other individuals on the threat analysis services' files, adversarial proceedings will be instituted to force them to wear an electronic bracelet. This will be part of an evidential process aimed at achieving de-radicalization and also improving public security.

Exchanges of information between intelligence services are vital in foiling attacks.

For the past several months, we have been preparing the introduction of NRP to control the identity of passengers in aircraft and high-speed trains.

This is aimed at preventing passengers from boarding if they are on file in a register of persons who represent a threat. Belgium will therefore apply this long-planned project at European level.

We will also develop an action plan to support regional and local authorities, in Molenbeek in particular, in their efforts aimed at improving security and life as a society.

The first preparatory meetings have already taken place. It will be necessary to develop prevention and repression as part of a cross-cutting approach.

The fight against all forms of crime, including against the illegal economy, must be a priority.

Strengthening the resources of our security services

The third area is the strengthening of our security services (police, justice and intelligence). In addition to the extra hires, it is also crucial to invest in new technologies such as voice recognition or ANPR cameras for number plate recognition.

Our security services have made the fight against arms trafficking a priority. However, the efforts must be stepped up even further.

In addition, the legislation on special investigation methods must be reviewed to expand the use of special investigation methods. For arms trafficking, for instance.

We must also better support our investigators. Specifically, house searches are currently prohibited between 9pm and 5am. We will abolish this time limitation in the context of terrorism. In the future, house searches will be able to be carried out 24 hours per day.

In addition, the limitation of administrative detention to 24 hours is an obstacle in terror investigations. We propose reviewing the Constitution aimed at extending this period from 24 to 72 hours.

We also note that prepaid mobile phone cards can be used to deceive our services. In the future, buying such cards anonymously shall no longer be possible.

Finally, we want to modernize procedures for security certificates and notices. Controls will be broadened, procedural deadlines will be shortened, and their time of validity will be reduced. This is targeted at the sensitive positions.

We also intend to evaluate and adapt, if necessary, the legislation relating to the concept of the "state of emergency". In very exceptional circumstances, the Government should be allowed, under supervision of the Parliament, to take exceptional and temporary measures to ensure public security.

Dear colleagues,

International action

This battle for security must be fought at home and abroad.

War and armed conflict in Syria, Libya and Iraq, as well as insecurity in the Sahel, and other areas, are destabilizing factors for Europe.

We have seen an unprecedented influx of refugees in Europe since the Second World War.

In line with international conventions, our country fully accepts its responsibilities. Thousands of places to house refugees were created.

The foundations of the European project are peace, free trade and the free movement of goods and people.

The strict and effective control of the external borders of the European Union is the corollary of the Schengen area. I am careful in using these words. The risk which we are facing is the collapse of the European project.

Solidarity between European countries is essential. However, it is not always self-evident.

The external borders of the European Union have to be strengthened urgently. It is vital for the future of Europe.

We must also work towards securing and stabilizing the European Union's neighbours.

We need to develop a strategic partnership with Turkey. Syrian refugees must be able to work in Turkey. And humanitarian assistance must be strengthened, not only in Turkey but also in Jordan and Lebanon for example. We must also work hard towards ensuring a more dignified and safe reception of refugees close to conflict zones.

Dear colleagues,

We must fight Daesh with total determination. This terror group controls a territory and has its own administration and funding. We must do more than simply stop its expansion. We must eradicate it. And again, we accept our responsibilities in this regard too.

Two weeks ago, we decided to mobilize the Leopold I frigate for an escort mission, as part of a defensive approach, for the Charles de Gaulle aircraft carrier. This mission was confirmed yesterday by the Government on the basis of Article 42.7 of the European Treaty.

We advocate a broad international coalition, preferably under a UN mandate. We are convinced that a Europe–USA–Russia–Iran political dialogue is as indispensable as it is urgent.

Dear colleagues,

In this international context, defining the strategic defence plan is an important issue for our security. It is necessary to establish our credibility on the international stage and solidarity with our allies. Our European roots and our commitment within NATO are and remain challenges of the utmost import to us.

This plan is well underway, and the final decisions, on the budget among other considerations, should soon be rendered.

Dear Colleagues,

These are the four areas and the specific measures that the government wishes to implement. However, this list is not exhaustive.

It can be added to and improved on the basis of operational proposals from our security services, as well as on the basis of a dialogue between the majority and the opposition.

All democrats must unite to strengthen our security.

I am taking the initiative of inviting our Minister-Presidents to draw up a coherent action plan.

The government is also requesting the authorization to set up a special parliamentary committee as part of the fight against terrorism.

The committee would enable all democrats to take and discuss initiatives and draft laws. The parliament is the beating heart of democracy. There is no better place in which to take action aimed at ensuring our security and safeguarding our freedoms.

CONCLUSION

Dear colleagues,

Over the past few days, I have been in contact with my counterparts in our neighbouring countries. I expressed our full support and the full cooperation of our services to the President of the Republic, Mr. François Hollande.

The Belgian and French judicial authorities have been working together closely as of Friday night.

An attack was prevented yesterday in Saint-Denis thanks to information provided by the Belgian teams. Our two countries have been cooperating closely in the fight against terrorism.

Speaking to British Prime Minister David Cameron, I confirmed our desire to set up exchanges of information between our services.

Also, I do not accept criticism denigrating our security services that are carrying out a difficult and tenacious task. I want to join with you in thanking our police forces, our intelligence agents, our magistrates, and our investigators for their courage and their mobilization.

Thanks to them, potentially tragic attacks in Saint-Denis or from Verviers have been thwarted.

Thanks to them, lives have been saved.

Thanks to them, in a few months, over 160 convictions for terrorist acts were rendered by the courts.

We fully accept our responsibilities and remain loyal to our partners.

Dear colleagues,

We must keep a cool head. This is a new chapter in the history of Europe.

Faithless and lawless enemies who hide and strike with cowardice seek to impose a totalitarian model.

The freedom to believe or not to believe.

The freedom to speak, debate, the freedom to caricature and criticize.

The freedom to work, the freedom to go out, the freedom to love.

In short, the freedom to live. For us, this is not negotiable.

We cannot accept any change in this respect.

The fight is not over.

We will not choose between safety and freedom.

We are proud of the universal values that we stand for.

We will not choose between the right to security and the exercise of freedoms. We want both. We want the one for the other.

There will be other threats, other attacks, and more suffering.

We will not give in to panic or to divisions or to amalgamations, nor to the spirit of revenge.

We will act with dignity and with an implacable will.

We will hold high our universal values. Those of Enlightenment and Human Rights.

We are standing strong and we will move forward.

SOURCE: Office of the Prime Minister of Belgium. "Fight against terrorism, the measures taken by the federal government and the speech of the Prime Minister." November 19, 2015. http://premier.be/en/fight-against-terrorism-measures-taken-federal-government-and-speech-prime-minister.

Prime Minister Trudeau Welcomes Syrian Refugees

December 11, 2015

The Prime Minister, Justin Trudeau, today issued the following statement after welcoming Syrian refugees to Canada late last night:

"Today, we welcome many Syrian refugees who were forced to flee their homeland because of war and conflict. Canada is doing the right thing by providing refuge for those so desperately seeking safety.

"This is a significant step in fulfilling our plan to bring 25,000 Syrian refugees to Canada in the coming months. It also demonstrates our commitment to refugee resettlement, which is part of Canada's proud humanitarian tradition.

"I know that, even for those facing extreme hardship, tragedy, and war in their country, leaving home is very difficult. The transition to a new life in a new country can be a very daunting process.

"Let me reassure those coming to our country that our communities and all orders of government will work closely, together, to make it easier for you to adjust to these changes and become full participants in Canadian society. While it might be much colder outside than back home, I am sure that you will find warm welcomes from your new neighbours.

"In the years to come, Canadians will look back with enormous pride on the contributions made by Syrian refugees and how they have made our country even better."

SOURCE: Office of the Prime Minister of Canada. "Statement by the Prime Minister of Canada on the Arrival of Syrian Refugees." December 11, 2015. http://pm.gc.ca/eng/news/2015/12/11/statement-prime-minister-canada-arrival-syrian-refugees. © Her Majesty the Queen in Right of Canada, 2016.

OTHER HISTORIC DOCUMENTS OF INTEREST

FROM THIS VOLUME

FROM PREVIOUS *HISTORIC DOCUMENTS*

Federal Court Rules on Obama Administration Immigration Plan

NOVEMBER 25, 2015

In the fall of 2014—following another failed congressional effort to pass comprehensive immigration reform legislation, and amid growing pressure from immigration advocates and fellow Democrats—President Barack Obama announced a series of executive actions that sought to address, in part, the presence of roughly 11 million illegal immigrants in the United States. Though heralded by some, the actions quickly drew heated criticism from Republicans in Congress and state officials who claimed the president had overstepped his constitutional boundaries. The Obama administration faced a series of legal challenges related to the actions throughout 2015, including a Texas-led lawsuit involving 26 states that culminated in a U.S. Court of Appeals for the Fifth Circuit ruling in November.

OBAMA ANNOUNCES DEFERRED ACTION PROGRAMS

Obama first announced the executive actions during a televised address on November 20, 2014, outlining a plan to allow approximately 4 million undocumented immigrants who were parents of U.S. citizens or legal permanent residents to remain in the United States temporarily, without threat of deportation, as long as they registered with the government and agreed to a background check. While registrants would not be permitted to vote or receive health insurance subsidies through Obamacare, they would be able to apply for a three-year work permit. Immigrants would only be eligible for this Deferred Action for Parents of Americans program if they had been in the United States for at least five years.

Obama also announced an expansion of the Deferred Action for Childhood Arrivals program, which he originally established by Executive Order in 2012. Under this program, the Department of Homeland Security would defer any enforcement actions against an individual for a period of two years if that individual met the following criteria: had been brought by his or her parents to the United States before the age of 16 and was currently younger than 31 years old; had continuously lived in the United States for at least five years; was either in school, had graduated high school or obtained a GED, or was an honorably discharged U.S. veteran; and had no criminal record and was not perceived as a threat to national security. Obama's 2014 actions extended the age cap of the program, changed the cutoff date for eligibility from pre-June 2007 arrivals to pre-January 2010 arrivals, and lengthened the timeframe for deferred deportations from two years to three.

In addition to these measures, Obama also implemented a Southern Border and Approaches Campaign Strategy, through which the Department of Homeland Security would be charged with commissioning three task forces focused on enhancing security of the southern maritime border, southern land border, and West Coast. The president also increased the number of visas available to skilled workers and spouses of green card holders, granted deferred deportations to some immediate relatives of U.S. citizens and legal permanent residents who "seek to enlist in the Armed Forces," and offered a discount to the first 10,000 immigrants who applied to the deferred deportation programs. Notably, Obama also signaled a shift in deportation priorities, calling for a focus on deporting those who have been convicted of felonies or "significant" misdemeanors.

The following day Obama issued two memos related to these actions to the heads of executive departments and agencies. One called for government officials to work with private and nonfederal public actors to develop recommendations for streamlining and improving the legal immigration system and to establish metrics to measure progress in implementing said recommendations. The other established the interagency White House Task Force on New Americans, which would work to identify and support successful state and local efforts to integrate immigrants and to determine how those efforts could be expanded and replicated.

STATES FILE LEGAL CHALLENGES

While praised by many immigration reform advocates and members of his own party, Obama's announcement quickly incited intense protest from congressional Republicans and a host of state and local elected officials who argued that the president did not have the authority to issue such actions. Their criticism soon led to legal challenges, including one lawsuit filed in November by Arizona's Maricopa County sheriff Joe Arpaio seeking to overturn the programs. Arpaio claimed the programs would encourage more people to enter the country illegally, which would in turn lead to more crime and create greater strain and higher costs for his office. The U.S. District Court for the District of Columbia rejected the suit, with Judge Beryl Howell writing, "The role of the Judiciary is to resolve cases and controversies properly brought by parties with a concrete and particularized injury—not to engage in policymaking better left to the political branches. The plaintiff's case raises important questions regarding the impact of illegal immigration on this nation, but the questions amount to generalized grievances which are not proper for the Judiciary to address."

In early December, then-Texas Attorney General and Governor-elect Greg Abbott filed a lawsuit against the government in the U.S. District Court for the Southern District of Texas. Twenty-three other states joined Texas in the suit, a number that grew to 25 by late January, with the additions of Tennessee and Nevada. The states argued that Obama was not following federal rulemaking requirements and that his programs would either force them to provide services to illegal immigrants or change their state laws to avoid doing so. For example, Texas claimed that the state would incur fees associated with providing driver's licenses and unemployment insurance to immigrants who were granted deferred actions. "Unilateral suspension of the Nation's immigration laws is unlawful," they wrote, adding that only the judiciary branch's "immediate intervention can protect the [states] from dramatic and irreparable injuries." Abbott also said it would not be the first time that Texas would be negatively impacted by Obama's immigration policies, claiming that the president's 2012 deferred action initiative had caused a major influx of Central Americans—including tens of thousands of unaccompanied children—to enter Texas illegally.

According to Pew Research Center, the states who filed the suit were home to about 46 percent of the undocumented immigrants who would potentially qualify for deportation relief. Of those, approximately half lived in Texas, with Florida hosting the next highest proportion. Some of the states had fewer than 5,000 residents who might qualify for the programs. In total, Pew reported that immigrants eligible for deportation relief comprise about 1.6 percent of the U.S. population, and 1.5 percent of the population in the states suing the government.

The Obama administration countered that the programs would only direct federal agents not to enforce deportation laws against a certain group of people and would simply be an expansion of an immigrant enforcement policy seeking to make more efficient use of limited resources—namely by focusing efforts on deporting criminals. They noted that the federal government has the resources to deport 400,000 immigrants a year and therefore must set priorities. Twelve states and the District of Columbia filed an amicus brief with the District Court in support of Obama's programs on January 12, writing in part, "The truth is that the directives will substantially benefit states, will further the public interest, and are well within the president's broad authority to enforce immigration law." The El Paso, Harris, and Dallas County Sheriffs' Offices and the Austin Police Department also expressed support for Obama's programs.

CONGRESSIONAL CHALLENGES

While the administration contended with Texas's lawsuit, it also faced legislative challenges to Obama's programs on Capitol Hill. On January 14, the House of Representatives voted to defund the programs through a measure attached to an appropriations bill providing continued funding for the Department of Homeland Security. However, the Senate failed twice to approve a similar measure and ultimately stripped the defunding provision from the appropriations bill they approved at the end of February. The House later accepted the revised bill and sent it on to Obama without any restrictions on his immigration programs.

Texas v. United States

On January 15, District Judge Andrew Hanen heard oral arguments in the case of *Texas v. United States.* In February, Hanen ruled against the government, ruling that allowing millions of illegal immigrants to remain in the United States lawfully would prove costly to the states and that the government had not followed proper procedures for enacting the new rules. He issued an injunction to prevent the programs from beginning until Texas's case was resolved.

The Obama administration quickly appealed this decision to the U.S. Court of Appeals for the Fifth Circuit, arguing that the states did not have the legal standing to sue the U.S. government over policies related to federal control of country's borders. The court denied the emergency request to lift the District Court's injunction on May 26, with Judge Jerry Smith writing that the administration was "unlikely to succeed on the merits of its appeal." Smith said that Texas had successfully established that the immigration programs would create a financial burden, writing that deferred deportation "triggers eligibility for federal and state benefits that would not otherwise be available." He also said that the programs went beyond "prosecutorial discretion," a legal concept in which a government with limited resources is allowed to set priorities for enforcement. The decision was a significant setback for the programs, because the Department of Homeland Security was scheduled to begin accepting applications and registering immigrants that month. The Fifth Circuit went on to hear oral arguments in the case in July.

On November 9, a three-judge panel ruled 2–1 against the government's appeal of the lower court's decision. The court said Obama's actions went beyond simply stating that the president would not deport immigrants because they also would allow individuals to be "lawfully present" in the United States. The Immigration and Naturalization Act of 1952 provides for how and when an immigrant can legally remain in the country, and the president does not have the power to unilaterally change that criteria. The court said that Obama's immigration plan "is foreclosed by Congress' careful plan; the program is 'manifestly contrary to the statute' and therefore was properly enjoined." Writing for the majority, Judge Smith added that Texas was in a strong legal position to bring the suit because it would indeed be harmed by new costs for issuing driver's licenses to immigrants and that the president had exceeded his authority by using his programs to grant benefits without congressional approval.

For the dissent, Judge Carolyn King wrote that the other judges had misstated the facts of the case and that Obama's memos contained "only guidelines for the exercise of prosecutorial discretion" and do not confer any benefits to accepted program applicants. "I would deem this case non-justiciable," she wrote, adding, "The policy decisions at issue in this case are best resolved not by judicial fiat, but via the political process."

Texas attorney general Ken Paxton praised the decision. "Today, the Fifth Circuit asserted that the separation of powers remains the law of the land, and the president must follow the rule of law, just like everybody else," he said. "Texas, leading a charge of 26 states, has secured an important victory to put a halt to the president's lawlessness." Program supporters expressed frustration and disappointment with the court. "Today's ruling is a slap in the face to the good people in America who have also been waiting for Congress and the courts to act with justice, humanity and common sense on the issue of immigration reform," said Angelica Salas, executive director for the Coalition for Humane Immigrant Rights of Los Angeles.

Obama administration lawyers had reportedly anticipated the negative outcome, yet had remained hopeful that the ruling would be issued in time to appeal the decision to the U.S. Supreme Court before the end of the president's term. "The Department of Justice remains committed to taking steps that will resolve the immigration litigation as quickly as possible in order to allow DHS to bring greater accountability to our immigration system by prioritizing the removal of the worst offenders, not people who have long ties to the United States and who are raising American children," said Patrick Rodenbush, spokesman for the Department of Justice.

The government filed its petition for certiorari, a legal brief asking the Court to review its case, with the Supreme Court on November 20. The Court agreed to take up the case on January 19, 2016, and heard oral arguments in April.

—Linda Fecteau Grimm

Following is the edited text of the Fifth Circuit Court of Appeals ruling in Texas v. United States *in which a three-judge panel ruled 2–1 against the Obama administration's plan for dealing with illegal immigrants currently in the United States.*

DOCUMENT

Texas v. United States

November 25, 2015

[Footnotes and appendices have been omitted.]

REVISED November 25, 2015

IN THE UNITED STATES COURT OF APPEALS
FOR THE FIFTH CIRCUIT

No. 15-40238

STATE OF TEXAS; STATE OF ALABAMA; STATE OF GEORGIA; STATE OF IDAHO; STATE OF INDIANA; STATE OF KANSAS;

STATE OF LOUISIANA; STATE OF MONTANA; STATE OF NEBRASKA; STATE OF SOUTH CAROLINA; STATE OF SOUTH DAKOTA;

STATE OF UTAH; STATE OF WEST VIRGINIA; STATE OF WISCONSIN;

PAUL R. LEPAGE, Governor, State of Maine;

PATRICK L. MCCRORY, Governor, State of North Carolina;

C. L. "BUTCH" OTTER, Governor, State of Idaho;

PHIL BRYANT, Governor, State of Mississippi;

STATE OF NORTH DAKOTA; STATE OF OHIO; STATE OF OKLAHOMA;

STATE OF FLORIDA; STATE OF ARIZONA; STATE OF ARKANSAS; ATTORNEY GENERAL BILL SCHUETTE; STATE OF NEVADA; STATE OF TENNESSEE,

Plaintiffs—Appellees,

versus

UNITED STATES OF AMERICA;

JEH CHARLES JOHNSON, Secretary, Department of Homeland Security;

R. GIL KERLIKOWSKE, Commissioner of U.S. Customs and Border Protection;

RONALD D. VITIELLO, Deputy Chief of U.S. Border Patrol, U.S. Customs and Border Protection;

SARAH R. SALDANA, Director of U.S. Immigration and Customs Enforcement;

LEON RODRIGUEZ, Director of U.S. Citizenship and Immigration Services,

Defendants—Appellants.

Appeal from the United States District Court for the Southern District of Texas

Before KING, SMITH, and ELROD, Circuit Judges.

JERRY E. SMITH, Circuit Judge:

The United States appeals a preliminary injunction, pending trial, forbidding implementation of the Deferred Action for Parents of Americans and Lawful Permanent Residents program ("DAPA"). Twenty-six states (the "states") challenged DAPA under the Administrative Procedure Act ("APA") and the Take Care Clause of the Constitution; in an impressive and thorough Memorandum Opinion and Order issued February 16, 2015, the district court enjoined the program on the ground that the states are likely to succeed on their claim that DAPA is subject to the APA's procedural requirements. . . .

The government appealed and moved to stay the injunction pending resolution of the merits. . . . Reviewing the district court's order for abuse of discretion, we affirm the preliminary injunction because the states have standing; they have established a substantial likelihood of success on the merits of their procedural and substantive APA claims; and they have satisfied the other elements required for an injunction.

[Section I.A. has been omitted and contains an overview the implementation of DAPA and DACA.]

B.

The states sued to prevent DAPA's implementation on three grounds. First, they asserted that DAPA violated the procedural requirements of the APA as a substantive rule that did not undergo the requisite notice-and-comment rulemaking. . . . Second, the states claimed that DHS lacked the authority to implement the program even if it followed the correct rulemaking process, such that DAPA was substantively unlawful under the APA. . . . Third, the states urged that DAPA was an abrogation of the President's constitutional duty to "take Care that the Laws be faithfully executed." . . .

[Summary of the District Court's ruling has been omitted.]

. . . On appeal, the United States maintains that the states do not have standing or a right to judicial review and, alternatively, that DAPA is exempt from the notice-and-comment requirements. The government also contends that the injunction, including its nationwide scope, is improper as a matter of law.

II.

"We review a preliminary injunction for abuse of discretion." A preliminary injunction should issue only if the states, as movants, establish

(1) a substantial likelihood of success on the merits, (2) a substantial threat of irreparable injury if the injunction is not issued, (3) that the threatened injury if the

injunction is denied outweighs any harm that will result if the injunction is granted, and (4) that the grant of an injunction will not disserve the public interest. . . .

III.

The government claims the states lack standing to challenge DAPA. As we will analyze, however, their standing is plain, based on the driver's-license rationale, so we need not address the other possible grounds for . . . .

A.

[Discussion of the legal precedent for establishing standing has been omitted.]

As we will show, DAPA would have a major effect on the states' fiscs, causing millions of dollars of losses in Texas alone, and at least in Texas, the causal chain is especially direct: DAPA would enable beneficiaries to apply for driver's licenses, and many would do so, resulting in Texas's injury.

Second, DAPA affects the states' "quasi-sovereign" interests by imposing substantial pressure on them to change their laws, which provide for issuing driver's licenses to some aliens and subsidizing those licenses. "[S]tates have a sovereign interest in 'the power to create and enforce a legal code.'" Pursuant to that interest, states may have standing based on (1) federal assertions of authority to regulate matters they believe they control, (2) federal preemption of state law, and (3) federal interference with the enforcement of state law, at least where "the state statute at issue regulate[s] behavior or provide[s] for the administration of a state program" and does not "simply purport to immunize [state] citizens from federal law." Those intrusions are analogous to pressure to change state law.

[Discussion of the legal precedent surrounding "quasi-sovereign" interests has been omitted.]

B.

At least one state—Texas—has satisfied the first standing requirement by demonstrating that it would incur significant costs in issuing driver's licenses to DAPA beneficiaries. . . .

If permitted to go into effect, DAPA would enable at least 500,000 illegal aliens in Texas to satisfy that requirement with proof of lawful presence or employment authorization. Texas subsidizes its licenses and would lose a minimum of $130.89 on each one it issued to a DAPA beneficiary. Even a modest estimate would put the loss at "several million dollars." . . .

Instead of disputing those figures, the United States claims that the costs would be offset by other benefits to the state. It theorizes that, because DAPA beneficiaries would be eligible for licenses, they would register their vehicles, generating income for the state, and buy auto insurance, reducing the expenses associated with uninsured motorists. The government suggests employment authorization would lead to increased tax revenue and decreased reliance on social services.

Even if the government is correct, that does not negate Texas's injury, because we consider only those offsetting benefits that are of the same type and arise from the same transaction as the costs. . . .

[Discussion of the precedent surrounding cost offsets has been omitted.]

C.

Texas has satisfied the second standing requirement by establishing that its injury is "fairly traceable" to DAPA. It is undisputed that DAPA would enable beneficiaries to apply for driver's licenses, and there is little doubt that many would do so because driving is a practical necessity in most of the state.

The United States urges that Texas's injury is not cognizable, because the state could avoid injury by not issuing licenses to illegal aliens or by not subsidizing its licenses. . . .

Indeed, treating the availability of changing state law as a bar to standing would deprive states of judicial recourse for many *bona fide* harms. For instance, under that theory, federal preemption of state law could never be an injury, because a state could always change its law to avoid preemption. But courts have often held that states have standing based on preemption. And states could offset almost any financial loss by raising taxes or fees. The existence of that alternative does not mean they lack standing.

[Discussion of the legal precedent surrounding preemption and the establishment of standing has been omitted.]

D.

Texas has satisfied the third standing requirement, redressability. Enjoining DAPA based on the procedural APA claim could prompt DHS to reconsider the program, which is all a plaintiff must show when asserting a procedural right. . . . And enjoining DAPA based on the substantive APA claim would prevent Texas's injury altogether.

[Section E. containing discussion of how the government's claim that Texas lacks standing is flawed has been omitted.]

IV.

Because the states are suing under the APA, they "must satisfy not only Article III's standing requirements, but an additional test: The interest [they] assert must be 'arguably within the zone of interests to be protected or regulated by the statute' that [they] say was violated." . . .

The interests the states seek to protect fall within the zone of interests of the INA. . . . With limited exceptions, unlawfully present aliens are "not eligible for any State or local public benefit." . . .

Contrary to the government's assertion, Texas satisfies the zone-of-interests test not on account of a generalized grievance but instead as a result of the same injury that gives it Article III standing—Congress has explicitly allowed states to deny public benefits to illegal aliens. . . .

V.

The government maintains that judicial review is precluded even if the states are proper plaintiffs. . . .

The United States relies on 8 U.S.C. § 1252(g) for the proposition that the INA expressly prohibits judicial review. But the government's broad reading is contrary to *Reno v. American-Arab Anti-Discrimination Committee ("AAADC")*, 525 U.S. 471, 482 (1999), in which the Court rejected "the unexamined assumption that § 1252(g) covers the universe of deportation claims—that it is a sort of 'zipper' clause that says 'no judicial review in deportation cases unless this section provides judicial review.'" The Court emphasized that § 1252(g) is not "a general jurisdictional limitation," but rather "applies only to three discrete actions that the Attorney General may take: her 'decision or action' to '*commence* proceedings, *adjudicate* cases, or *execute* removal orders.'" . . .

Congress has expressly limited or precluded judicial review of many immigration decisions, including some that are made in the Secretary's "sole and unreviewable discretion," but DAPA is not one of them.

Judicial review of DAPA is consistent with the protections Congress affords to states that decline to provide public benefits to illegal aliens. . . .

If 500,000 unlawfully present aliens residing in Texas were reclassified as lawfully present pursuant to DAPA, they would become eligible for driver's licenses at a subsidized fee. Congress did not intend to make immune from judicial review an agency action that reclassifies millions of illegal aliens in a way that imposes substantial costs on states that have relied on the protections conferred by § 1621.

[Further discussion of judicial review has been omitted.]

VI.

Because the interests that Texas seeks to protect are within the INA's zone of interests, and judicial review is available, we address whether Texas has established a substantial likelihood of success on its claim that DAPA must be submitted for notice and comment. . . .

A.

The government advances the notion that DAPA is exempt from notice and comment as a policy statement. We evaluate two criteria to distinguish policy statements from substantive rules: whether the rule (1) "impose[s] any rights and obligations" and (2) "genuinely leaves the agency and its decision makers free to exercise discretion." . . .

Although the DAPA Memo facially purports to confer discretion, the district court determined that "[n]othing about DAPA 'genuinely leaves the agency and its [employees] free to exercise discretion,'" a factual finding that we review for clear error. That finding was partly informed by analysis of the implementation of DACA, the precursor to DAPA.

Like the DAPA Memo, the DACA Memo instructed agencies to review applications on a case-by-case basis and exercise discretion, but the district court found that those statements were "merely pretext" because only about 5% of the 723,000 applications accepted for evaluation had been denied, and "[d]espite a request by the [district] [c]ourt, the [g]overnment's counsel did not provide the number, if any, of requests that were denied [for discretionary reasons] even though the applicant met the DACA criteria. . . ." The finding of pretext was also based on a declaration by Kenneth Palinkas, the president of the union representing the USCIS employees processing the DACA applications, that "DHS management has taken multiple steps to ensure that DACA applications are simply rubberstamped if the applicants meet the necessary criteria"; DACA's Operating Procedures, which "contain[] nearly 150 pages of specific instructions for granting or denying deferred action"; and some mandatory language in the DAPA Memo itself. In denying the government's motion for a stay of the injunction, the district court further noted that the President had made public statements suggesting that in reviewing applications pursuant to DAPA, DHS officials who "don't follow the policy" will face "consequences," and "they've got a problem." . . .

Instead of relying solely on the lack of evidence that any DACA application had been denied for discretionary reasons, the district court found pretext for additional reasons. It observed that "the 'Operating Procedures' for implementation of DACA contains nearly 150 pages of specific instructions for granting or recorded in a 'check the box' standardized form, for which USCIS personnel are provided templates. Certain denials of DAPA must be sent to a supervisor for approval[, and] there is no option for granting DAPA to an individual who does not meet each criterion." Dist. Ct. Op., 86 F. Supp. 3d at 669 (footnotes omitted). The finding was also based on the declaration from Palinkas that, as with DACA, the DAPA application process itself would preclude discretion: "[R]outing DAPA applications through service centers instead of field offices . . . created an application process that bypasses traditional in-person investigatory interviews with trained USCIS adjudications officers" and "prevents officers from conducting case-by-case investigations, undermines officers' abilities to detect fraud and national-security risks, and ensures that applications will be rubber-stamped."

[Sections B. and C. containing further discussion of the states' likelihood of success on the merits of their claim has been omitted.]

VII.

. . . "Federal governance of immigration and alien status is extensive and complex." *Arizona v. United States*, 132 S. Ct. at 2499. The limited ways in which illegal aliens can lawfully reside in the United States reflect Congress's concern that "aliens have been applying for and receiving public benefits from Federal, State, and local governments at increasing rates," 8 U.S.C. § 1601(3), and that "[i]t is a compelling government interest to enact new rules for eligibility and sponsorship agreements in order to assure that aliens be self-reliant in accordance with national immigration policy," § 1601(5).

In specific and detailed provisions, the INA expressly and carefully provides legal designations allowing defined classes of aliens to be lawfully present and confers eligibility for "discretionary relief allowing [aliens in deportation proceedings] to remain in the country." Congress has also identified narrow classes of aliens eligible for deferred action. . . . Entirely absent from those specific classes is the group of 4.3 million illegal aliens who would be eligible for lawful presence under DAPA were it not enjoined. . . .

Congress has enacted an intricate process for illegal aliens to derive a lawful immigration classification from their children's immigration status. . . . Although DAPA does not confer the full panoply of benefits that a visa gives, DAPA would allow illegal aliens to receive the benefits of lawful presence solely on account of their children's immigration status without complying with any of the requirements, enumerated above, that Congress has deliberately imposed. . . .

The INA authorizes cancellation of removal and adjustment of status if, *inter alia*, "the alien has been physically present in the United States for a continuous period of *not less than 10 years* immediately preceding the date of such application" and if "removal would result in *exceptional and extremely unusual hardship* to the alien's spouse, parent, or child, who is a citizen of the United States or an alien lawfully admitted for permanent residence." . . .

Instead of a ten-year physical-presence period, DAPA grants lawful presence to persons who "have continuously resided in the United States since before January 1, 2010," and there is no requirement that removal would result in exceptional and extremely unusual hardship. . . . Although the Secretary has discretion to make immigration decisions based on humanitarian grounds, that discretion is conferred only for particular family relationships and specific forms of relief—none of which includes granting lawful presence, on the basis of a child's immigration status, to the class of aliens that would be eligible for DAPA.

The INA also specifies classes of aliens eligible and ineligible for work authorization, including those "eligible for work authorization and deferred action"—with no mention of the class of persons whom DAPA would make eligible for work authorization. . . .

DAPA would dramatically increase the number of aliens eligible for work authorization, thereby undermining Congress's stated goal of closely guarding access to work authorization and preserving jobs for those lawfully in the country.

DAPA would make 4.3 million otherwise removable aliens eligible for lawful presence, employment authorization, and associated benefits, and "we must be guided to a degree by common sense as to the manner in which Congress is likely to delegate a policy decision of such economic and political magnitude to an administrative agency." DAPA undoubtedly implicates "question[s] of deep 'economic and political significance' that [are] central to this statutory scheme; had Congress wished to assign that decision to an agency, it surely would have done so expressly." But assuming *arguendo* that *Chevron* applies and that Congress has not directly addressed the precise question at hand, we would still strike down DAPA as an unreasonable interpretation that is "manifestly contrary" to the INA. . . .

[The following discussion, refuting the dissent's arguments that congressional inaction has given the government authority to implement DAPA, has been omitted.]

VIII.

The states have satisfied the other requirements for a preliminary injunction. They have demonstrated "a substantial threat of irreparable injury if the injunction is not issued." . . . DAPA beneficiaries would be eligible for driver's licenses and other benefits. . . . The district court found that retracting those benefits would be "substantially difficult—if not impossible," . . .

The harms the United States has identified are less substantial . . . Those alleged harms are vague, and the principles the government cites are more likely to be affected by the resolution of the case on the merits than by the injunction.

Separately, the United States postulates that the injunction prevents DHS from effectively prioritizing illegal aliens for removal. But the injunction "does not enjoin or impair the Secretary's ability to marshal his assets or deploy the resources of the DHS [or] to set priorities," . . . and any inefficiency is outweighed by the major financial losses the states face. . . .

IX.

The government claims that the nationwide scope of the injunction is an abuse of discretion and requests that it be confined to Texas or the plaintiff states. But the Constitution requires "an *uniform* Rule of Naturalization"; Congress has instructed that "the immigration laws of the United States should be enforced vigorously and *uniformly*"; and the Supreme Court has described immigration policy as "a comprehensive and *unified* system." . . .

The district court did not err and most assuredly did not abuse its discretion. The order granting the preliminary injunction is AFFIRMED.

KING, Circuit Judge, dissenting:

Although there are approximately 11.3 million removable aliens in this country today, for the last several years Congress has provided the Department of Homeland Security (DHS) with only enough resources to remove approximately 400,000 of those aliens per year. Recognizing DHS's congressionally granted prosecutorial discretion to set removal enforcement priorities, Congress has exhorted DHS to use those resources to "mak[e] our country safer." In response, DHS has focused on removing "those who represent threats to national security, public safety, and border security". . . .

Plaintiffs do not challenge DHS's ability to allow the aliens subject to the DAPA Memorandum. . . . Indeed, Plaintiffs admit that such removal decisions are well within DHS's prosecutorial discretion. Rather, Plaintiffs complain of the consequences of DHS's decision to use its decades-long practice of granting "deferred action" to these individuals, specifically that these "illegal aliens" may temporarily work lawfully for a living and may also eventually become eligible for some public benefits. Plaintiffs contend that these consequences and benefits must be struck down even while the decision to allow the "illegal aliens" to remain stands. But Plaintiffs' challenge cannot be so easily bifurcated. For the benefits of which Plaintiffs complain are not conferred by the DAPA Memorandum—the only policy being challenged in this case—but are inexorably tied to DHS's deferred action decisions by a host of unchallenged, pre-existing statutes and notice-and-comment regulations enacted by Congresses and administrations long past. Deferred action decisions, such as those contemplated by the DAPA Memorandum, are quintessential exercises of prosecutorial discretion. . . . Because all parties agree that an exercise of prosecutorial discretion itself is unreviewable, this case should be dismissed on justiciability grounds.

Even if this case were justiciable, the preliminary injunction, issued by the district court, is a mistake. If the Memorandum is implemented in the truly discretionary, case-by-case manner it contemplates, it is not subject to the APA's notice-and-comment requirements, and the injunction cannot stand. Although the very face of the Memorandum makes clear that it must be applied with such discretion, the district court concluded on its own—prior to DAPA's implementation, based on improper burden-shifting, and without seeing the need even to hold an evidentiary hearing—that the Memorandum is a sham, a mere "pretext" for the Executive's plan "not [to] enforce the immigration laws as to over four million illegal aliens." . . . That conclusion is clearly erroneous. The majority affirms and goes one step further today. It holds, in the alternative, that the Memorandum is contrary to the INA and substantively violates the APA. These conclusions are wrong. The district court expressly declined to reach this issue without further development, *id.* at 677, and the limited briefing we have before us is unhelpful and unpersuasive. For these reasons, as set out below, I dissent. . . .

[King's remaining discussion of the points of her dissent has been omitted.]

Source: U.S. Court of Appeals for the Fifth Circuit. *Texas v. United States.* No. 15-40238. Filed November 9, 2015. Revised November 25, 2015. www.ca5.uscourts.gov/opinions%5Cpub%5C15/15-40238-CV0.pdf.

OTHER HISTORIC DOCUMENTS OF INTEREST

December

Tunisian National Dialogue Quartet Awarded 2015 Nobel Peace Prize

DECEMBER 10, 2015

In 2015, the Norwegian Nobel Committee, the group tasked with awarding the annual Nobel Peace Prize, received more than 270 nominations, 205 of which were for individuals and the rest for organizations. Although the Nobel Committee does not release information on those nominated, speculation in the media centered on a group of high-profile individuals, including German chancellor Angela Merkel and Pope Francis. Ultimately, on October 10, 2015, the Committee announced that the award would go to the National Dialogue Quartet, an organization that came into being following Tunisia's Arab Spring uprising, and is credited with securing the country's fledgling democracy.

SPECULATION SURROUNDING NOBEL PEACE PRIZE

All five members of the Nobel Committee are appointed by the Norwegian parliament, although the intent is to keep the body's decisions free from political interference. In March 2015, the Norwegian Nobel Committee experienced an unexpected shakeup when, for the first time in its history, the group's chair was demoted. Thorbjørn Jagland held the position for six years and in that time had been involved in a number of controversies surrounding the Committee's choice of winners, most notably President Barack Obama, Chinese human rights activist Liu Xiaobo, and the European Union. In the case of Liu, the Chinese government froze some of its diplomatic relations with Norway in response to the award. Kaci Kullmann Five, the Committee's deputy chair, replaced Jagland.

Prior to the Committee's announcement of the winner of the 2015 Nobel Peace Prize, speculation focused primarily on Pope Francis for his work in social justice, as well as his efforts to broker an agreement between the United States and Cuba to renew diplomatic relations, and on Chancellor Merkel for allowing hundreds of thousands of refugees fleeing Syria into Germany. Other possible contenders included Mussie Zerai, an Eritrean advocate for refugees; Dmitry Muratov, the founder of an independent Russian newspaper; and Denis Mukwege, a gynecologist who has been floated as a possible contender for multiple years for his human rights work with rape victims in the Democratic Republic of Congo. Also widely discussed was a joint award to U.S. secretary of state John Kerry and Iranian foreign minister Mohammad Javad Zarif for their efforts securing the P5+1 agreement to restrict Iran's production of nuclear weapons.

On October 10, the Nobel Committee put speculation to rest when it announced that the Tunisian National Dialogue Quartet would be awarded the Nobel Peace Prize "for its decisive contribution to the building of a pluralistic democracy in Tunisia in the wake of the Jasmine Revolution of 2011." The Committee said it hoped that the award would "contribute towards safeguarding democracy in Tunisia and be an inspiration to all those who seek to promote peace and democracy in the Middle East, North Africa and the rest of the world." Tunisian president Beji Caid Essebsi said that the award was proof that the ongoing struggle in the nation is not all "dark and grim."

TUNISIA'S ARAB SPRING

The 2011 Arab Spring uprisings across the Middle East and Northern Africa were largely set in motion by protests in Tunisia against the government of President Zine al-Abidine Ben Ali. The protests began in December 2010 as localized demonstrations seeking to draw notice to income inequality in the nation. When those efforts failed to gain the president's attention, citizens turned to social media and took to the streets of the nation's capital of Tunis demanding both efforts to address income inequality and the implementation of democratic reforms that would make the government more inclusive of all sectors of Tunisian society.

In response to what became known as the Jasmine Revolution, President Ben Ali forced Internet outages across the nation. When protesters were undeterred, he then began promising new elections. He fired his interior minister, released demonstrators who had been jailed for their participation in the uprisings, and promised to investigate government corruption, create 300,000 jobs, and cut food prices. In his largest attempt to placate protesters, Ben Ali fired his entire cabinet. Even so, the demonstrations grew.

Without an end in sight, President Ben Ali declared a state of emergency and labeled demonstrators as "terrorists." According to the United Nations, an estimated 219 were killed in the ensuing violence; the Tunisian government estimated that number to be closer to seventy-eight. On January 14, 2011, Ben Ali made an unexpected announcement that he would temporarily step down from his position. He subsequently fled the country, ending his twenty-three-year reign.

A unity government was formed and sworn in days after Ben Ali's resignation. The new government allowed the participation of all political parties, but it quickly faced public backlash because of involvement of members of Ben Ali's Constitutional Democratic Rally (RCD) in key positions. The transitional cabinet was removed, and Prime Minister Mohamed Ghannouchi, who had been in his position since 1999, also stepped down because of public discontent over his earlier ties to Ben Ali. Ghannouchi was replaced by former foreign minister Beji Caid Essebsi, who effectively placed the nation in a state of emergency and gave government security forces permission to place anyone under house arrest without reason.

When the first elections of Arab Spring were held in Tunisia in October 2011, voters—who went to the polls in record numbers—gave the moderate Islamist Ennahda party, which had been banned under Ben Ali's rule, a 41 percent plurality in the Constituent Assembly. Less than two years after the election, the government had made little headway in instituting a lasting democracy and combating the rise of terrorism within its borders. The Islamists and secularists within the government were consistently at odds with each other, and the disagreements sometimes grew violent, as evidenced by the assassination of opposition leaders Mohamed Brahmi and Chokri Belaid in 2013.

The National Dialogue Quartet—a group made up of the Tunisian General Labor Union, the Tunisian Confederation of Industry, Trade and Handicrafts, the Tunisian Human Rights League, and the Tunisian Order of Lawyers—formed in the summer of

2013 in response to the ongoing political crisis. The Quartet acted as a mediator for the leaders of various political factions in the country and designed and negotiated a roadmap to establish Tunisia as a full-fledged democracy. This roadmap required that all three of the ruling parties give up their hold on power in favor of a new transitional government and new elections.

TUNISIAN NATIONAL DIALOGUE QUARTET ACCEPTS AWARD

In 2014, with the aid of the National Dialogue Quartet, the nation passed a constitution that was celebrated for its freedoms by Western nations and human rights groups alike. And the nation also held its first democrat presidential elections, during which Essebsi was elected. In presenting the Nobel Peace Prize, Five said that "Tunisia's path to democracy and rule of law since the Revolution of 2011 is remarkable for several reasons," including the ability to bridge differences between religious factions, the role and freedoms afforded to women, the peaceful transition for the new government, and the reflection of the importance of civil society.

In accepting the award, the Quartet said, "This tribute is not only to us. It is indeed a tribute to all Tunisian political players who adopted an approach of collective agreement, and succeeded in putting the interest of their homeland and their people above their narrow partisan interests." The Quartet acknowledged that their work was not easy and that at times they were forced to delay further action on the roadmap until consensus could be reached. But, they stated, "thanks to this consensual approach that we adopted and sponsored with the support of all elements of the civil society, the transition path was successfully completed."

Despite the fact that Tunisia emerged from Arab Spring as the strongest example of Middle Eastern democracy, the nation continues to struggle with fully democratic principles and a number of security issues. In March 2015, two dozen were killed in an attack on a museum in Tunis by Islamic extremists, and in June, thirty-eight foreign tourists were killed at a hotel in Sousse. At the time of the award, Tunisia was the largest contributor of foreign fighters to the Islamic State. During the Nobel lecture, Hassine Abassi, head of Tunisia's powerful General Labor Union, spoke to these ongoing challenges and noted that the nation was "well aware of all these difficulties, and fully aware of the challenges that lie ahead. We are determined to rely on ourselves in overcoming the difficulties, and we look forward to having the support of our friends all over the world."

Given these ongoing challenges, the award was not without its critics. Nobel Peace Prize Watch, a campaign aimed at ensuring the prize echoes the goals of liberating all nations from "weapons, warriors, and war," called the award "clearly outside the circle of recipients Nobel had in mind." Tunisian political scientist Hamdadi el-Aouni said that he did "not know what these people of the committee were thinking. I've just come back from Tunisia. There is no state, just total chaos. And there is certainly no peace there."

—Heather Kerrigan

Following is the text of the award presentation speech delivered by Nobel Committee chair Kaci Kullmann Five on December 10, 2015; and the text of the Nobel lecture delivered on December 10, 2015, by Hassine Abassi, Mohamed Fadhel Mahfoudh, Abdessatar Ben Moussa, and Ouided Bouchamaoui.

National Dialogue Quartet
Awarded 2015 Nobel Peace Prize

December 10, 2015

Your Majesties, Your Royal Highnesses, Laureate, Excellencies, Ladies and gentlemen,

The Norwegian Nobel Committee has decided to award the Nobel Peace Prize for 2015 to the Tunisian National Dialogue Quartet for its decisive contribution to the building of a pluralistic democracy in Tunisia in the wake of the Revolution of 2011.

It gives the Nobel Committee great pleasure to extend to the Quartet's representatives a warm welcome to this year's Peace Prize award ceremony: Hassine Abassi, Secretary General of the Tunisian General Labour Union (UGTT), Mohamed Fadhel Mahfoudh, President of the Tunisian Order of Lawyers (ONAT), Abdessatar Ben Moussa, President of the Tunisian Human Rights League (LTDH) and Ouided Bouchamaoui, President of the Tunisian Confederation of Industry, Trade and Handicrafts (UTICA).

Aux quatre représentants du Quartet, Lauréat du Prix Nobel de la Paix, je dis—soyez les bienvenus à Oslo!

The narrative underlying this year's Peace Prize is a dramatic one. It speaks to the core of Alfred Nobel's will and Nobel's vision of fraternity, disarmament and peace-building forums. Not because the Quartet has actively sought to promote disarmament, but because its work has led to a better platform for peace and non-violent resolution of conflicts. This is a story about building strong institutions to ensure justice and stability, and demonstrating the will to engage in dialogue and cooperation.

This year's prize is truly a prize for peace, awarded against a backdrop of unrest and war.

In the summer of 2013, Tunisia was on the brink of civil war. The Quartet's resolute intervention helped to halt the spiraling violence and put developments on a peaceful track. Tunisia was spared the horrors of civil war and instead established a constitutional system of government guaranteeing fundamental rights for the entire population, regardless of gender, political conviction or religious belief.

Ladies and gentlemen, this is an admirable accomplishment, and indeed worthy of a Nobel Prize!

The Quartet—receiving the Peace Prize as one entity, not as four organisations—represents different sectors and values in Tunisian society: working life, welfare, principles of the rule of law and human rights. This diversity gave the Quartet the moral authority to exercise its role as a mediator and driving force for peaceful democratic development in Tunisia. The Quartet has thus helped to lay the groundwork for national fraternity in the spirit of Alfred Nobel. The Committee hopes that this will serve as an example for other countries to follow, thereby fostering peace.

We live in turbulent times. In North Africa, the Middle East and Europe, millions of people are fleeing from war, oppression, suffering and terror. The causes of the refugee crisis are numerous and complex, and there are no simple solutions. But one thing is indisputable: if every country had done as Tunisia has done, and paved the way for dialogue, tolerance, democracy and equal rights, far fewer people would have been forced to flee. Tunisia has shown the world that Islamist and secular political movements can negotiate with one another to reach solutions in the country's best interests, if only they are willing to do so!

But there are also forces, dark forces, which for that very reason do not want Tunisia to succeed—which see the emergence of democracy and equal rights for all, including women, in an Arab Muslim country as a threat to their own ambitions for power, and as irreconcilable with their own extremist mind-set. This poses major security challenges for Tunisia. Security measures, states of emergency and ideological battles alone cannot solve these challenges. Economic and political reforms, not least a sustained effort to combat corruption, are also needed.

Let us take a closer look at the story behind this year's prize, and see just what makes it a Peace Prize in the truest sense.

The Arab Spring originated in Tunisia. To understand the causes of the uprising, it may help to quote the then 19-year-old Tunisian author Samar al-Mazghani, who shortly before the revolution described the paralysing hopelessness she felt in her home country under the Ben Ali dictatorship: "Here, we live with no dreams, or we dream with no life. . . . And our dreams are postponed until something happens to change this reality." That something occurred just months later: on 17 December 2010, the 26-year-old fruit and vegetable seller Mohamed Bouazizi set himself on fire in a desperate protest against the corruption and misrule that prevailed in his home town of Sidi Bouzid.

The tragic incident sparked long-suppressed anger among the inhabitants of Sidi Bouzid. Social media communicated news of what had happened, and the rage spread, culminating in nation-wide protests and demonstrations. Four weeks later, President Ben Ali, Tunisia's autocratic leader for many years, fled to Saudi Arabia. The dictator had experienced the truth of the old Tunisian saying, "The multitude is stronger than the king".

However, events gradually took a turn that aroused concern in Tunisia. The government, spearheaded by the Islamist party Ennahda, tried to insert provisions into the new constitution that would have had negative consequences for the status of women in society. Even before the revolution, Tunisian women had enjoyed greater freedom than women in other Arab countries. Now they wanted full equality, not reduced rights.

The situation gradually got worse. After two shocking political assassinations and the killing of eight Tunisian soldiers by terrorists, alongside large demonstrations against the government, many feared that the security situation was spiralling out of control. Peace was truly in jeopardy.

It was at this critical moment that the Quartet was established.

At the initiative of the Labour Union UGTT's Secretary General Hassine Abassi, the four organisations presented a joint proposal for resolving the national crisis. Their plan was to convince the 21 political parties in the Constituent Assembly to participate in a national dialogue under the oversight of the Quartet. The national dialogue was to be an egalitarian, compromise-oriented process, in which everyone would have a say, and each party would have the same number of votes, regardless of its size.

More specifically, the Quartet required the parties to sign an agreement—known as the "road map"—comprising three main points:

The sitting three-party government was to relinquish power.

A non-partisan technocratic government was to be appointed to govern the country until new parliamentary elections were held.

The Constituent Assembly of Tunisia was to complete its work by a specified deadline, and appoint an independent commission to prepare elections of a new parliament and a new president in the autumn of 2014.

The government initially rejected the Quartet's initiative, but after lengthy and difficult negotiations, the Quartet succeeded, slowly but surely, in bringing all the parties in Tunisia to the negotiation table. A decisive breakthrough was achieved when first two, and eventually all three, government parties agreed to step down as soon as the new constitution was adopted.

With the road map in place, the Constituent Assembly completed its demanding task within the stipulated time limit and in close cooperation with the Quartet and the other parties to the national dialogue process. Tunisia's new constitution was adopted on 26 January 2014. It is considered the most egalitarian and democratic constitution in the Arab world.

In accordance with the road map, the Troika government resigned and was replaced by a caretaker government. With that, the Quartet had fulfilled its self-defined mandate, and could conclude its role as mediator. The ultimate validation of the Quartet's historical effort came in the autumn of 2014, when the parliamentary and presidential elections were carried out. Both the technocratic government and the interim president resigned and were replaced by lawfully elected successors.

Ladies and gentlemen,

Tunisia's path to democracy and rule of law since the Revolution of 2011 is remarkable for several reasons.

First: Cooperation across religious divisions. Although Ennahda and the secular parties often stood on opposing sides during the work on the new constitution, they were compelled by the national dialogue process to negotiate and reach compromises in the best interests of Tunisian society as a whole, not just their own supporters. This gave the main religious parties part-ownership of the emerging democracy and the new constitution they were helping to shape. Those who claim that Islam and democracy are incompatible, or that Islamic and secular parties cannot work together for the good of society, need only look to Tunisia.

Second: The key role played by women. Women took the lead in the protests against political violence and against the attempts to introduce highly oppressive gender provisions in the new constitution. Without women's participation, the fruits of the Revolution could easily have been lost. Women must have the same opportunities as men to influence developments at every level of society if genuine democracy and lasting peace are to be achieved. If there is anyone who still doubts that this goal is attainable in Muslim and Arab countries, let him or her look to Tunisia.

Third: Peaceful transitions of power. Since the revolution in 2011 Tunisia has witnessed several shifts of government and presidents. Tunisian politicians and parties deserve credit for their willingness to accept the will of the people and the rules of democracy, even when this made it necessary for them to resign or step down in favour of their opponents.

Last, but not least: The crucial importance of civil society. When the constitutional process foundered and the government institutions and parties failed to resolve the political crisis, civil society organisations and representatives stepped in to assume national responsibility. There was no stronger symbol of this commitment than the

National Dialogue Quartet. But it did not stand alone. Other organisations also contributed, each in its own way. We can truly say, therefore, that the peace, democracy and constitutional state we now see are the work of the Tunisian people.

Dear Quartet,

The Norwegian Nobel Committee is aware that Tunisia faces major challenges, and that a great deal of work remains to be done. We hope that the Peace Prize will help to ensure that there is no return to the Tunisia that existed before democracy, before the revolution. And we hope, moreover, that the laws and institutions that the national dialogue process has helped create will be a foundation for lasting stability and progress. Or as the British-Irish politician Edmund Burke once advised another people, after another historic revolution: "Make the Revolution a parent of settlement, and not a nursery of future revolutions."

Tunisia's security challenges are urgent. They are all too familiar to us. They resemble our own. They are our own. In this time of terror, the threats against Tunisia and the Tunisian people are indistinguishable from the threats against other countries. They are the same forces that broke the peace this autumn with acts of terrorism in so many places, including Beirut, Ankara, in the airspace over the Sinai peninsula, and in Paris, Bamako and Tunis, and that recently murdered a Norwegian, a Chinese and a Russian hostage in Syria. Because the threat is essentially the same to us all, we must stand together to combat it.

For that very reason, this is the time to mobilise support for Tunisia and help to ensure that the democratisation process is continued and safeguarded. Among a great many other things, that means providing support for economic development and cooperation. The international community must assume its responsibility and invest in Tunisia.

Ladies and gentlemen,

One of the most important results of the national dialogue process is, without a doubt, the constitution of 26 January 2014. As I said earlier, it is the most democratic constitution in the entire Arab world. Members of the National Dialogue Quartet, it is easy for us Norwegians to appreciate the importance of this achievement. In the same year that you helped steer the constitutional process to a successful conclusion, the Norwegian people celebrated the 200th anniversary of their constitution. It was one of the most radical and democratic constitutions of its time, and we are still proud of it. It is the hope of the Norwegian Nobel Committee that, 200 years from now, the people of Tunisia will look back on the founding fathers and mothers of their constitution, including the National Dialogue Quartet, with the same sense of pride.

In closing, I would like to share with you that the boy you see on this year's Nobel diploma is intended by the artist to symbolise the uncertain future faced by young people today, especially all those who feel that they have no power or opportunity to influence it. This is a forceful, eloquent image. The expression on the young boy's face reflects a cry for hope for the future, for the opportunity to be seen and heard, take part in society, use his skills and live in peace and security.

We hope that this diploma will inspire the Quartet and all positive forces in Tunisia to continue their shared search for peaceful, forward-looking solutions, around the negotiation table, for the good of the nation.

And may the diploma remind us all of our obligation to the millions of children and young people who, while we are gathered here today, feel as if they are groping in the dark, with no hope or faith in the future. May these young people have the blindfold removed from their eyes and see a brighter future, a future in peace and freedom.

Inspired by this vision, I would like to conclude with the words of an earlier Peace Prize laureate, Martin Luther King, Jr.: "Darkness cannot drive out darkness; only light can do that. Hate cannot drive out hate; only love can do that."

SOURCE: The Nobel Foundation. "Award Ceremony Speech." December 10, 2015. Nobelprize.org. Nobel Media AB 2014. Accessed via web on March 21, 2016. © The Nobel Foundation 2015. Used with permission. www.nobelprize.org/nobel_prizes/peace/laureates/2015/presentation-speech.html.

DOCUMENT

National Dialogue Quartet Accepts Nobel Peace Prize

December 10, 2015

His Majesty,
Their Highnesses,
The respected members of the Nobel Committee,
Ladies and Gentlemen,

We, the National Dialogue Quartet, consisting of the Tunisian General Labour Union, the Tunisian Union of Industry Commerce and Handicrafts, the Tunisian National Bar Association, and the Tunisian League for the Defence of Human Rights, we are greatly honoured to be awarded the 2015 Nobel Peace Prize which is the culmination of a long relentless struggle on the path of national liberation, construction of democracy and promoting universal values and principles. We are pleased to extend our sincere thanks and gratitude to the Nobel Peace Prize Committee and the Norwegian Parliament who, by giving us this award, have highlighted the Tunisian experience to the whole world. This will certainly give us more impetus to carry on our work for the benefit of our country.

This tribute is not only to us. It is indeed a tribute to all Tunisian political players who adopted an approach of collective agreement, and succeeded in putting the interests of their homeland and their people above their narrow partisan interests. It is a tribute to Tunisian women and Tunisian young people who revolted against discrimination and exclusion, and even challenged death in defending their civil rights and their right for freedom, dignity and decent life. It is a tribute to thinkers, intellectuals, trade unionists, law professionals, civil society activists, and our brave soldiers and security forces whose vigilance, sacrifices and contributions have shaped the exceptional Tunisian experience, as they were the safety valve against all attempts to blow up our modernist society gains, and attempts to damage our civil State and the real merits targeted by our revolution.

Your Majesties,
Ladies and Gentlemen

Before talking about the National Dialogue experience, let us emphasize that our euphoria and pride in this historic occasion should not veil our grief, sorrow and outrage about what has happened in many parts of the world. A few days ago, our capital Tunis and before that, Sousse, Bardo Museum, Beirut, Paris, Sharm el-Sheikh and Bamako have witnessed barbaric and atrocious terrorist incidents in which hundreds of innocent people were killed. The feelings of compassion and sympathy cannot prevent the grief and agony of the families of victims and others who fell in other cities around the world.

The tribute paid by the international community to the Tunisian national dialogue process confirms indeed that we share the same universal values of human rights which underpin human rights and reject all forms of intellectual and ideological isolationism. The progress in confronting all threats and risks to us around the world requires more solidarity, the build-up of a lasting and fair partnership among the peoples of the world, and searching for serious solutions to the problems which many countries are facing because of poverty. We are today in urgent need of a dialogue between civilizations, and a peaceful coexistence within the context of diversity and variation. We are today in urgent need to make the fight against terrorism an absolute priority, which means constant coordination and cooperation among all nations to drain out its resources and disconnect it from its incubator environment. Today, we need to accelerate the elimination of hot spots all over the world, and particularly to find a solution for the Palestinian cause and enable the Palestinian people to exercise self-determination on their own land and build their independent state.

This occasion is a tribute to a country with a long history and a civilizational legacy spanning more than 3,000 years, a country shaped over time by successive civilizations and characterized by an inherent belief in peace and moderation.

This historic occasion, which coincides with the anniversary of the Universal Declaration of Human Rights, is a tribute to the spirit of an inspiring revolution that the Tunisians led five years ago to protect their legitimate rights, to defend their freedom and dignity, a revolution in which all Tunisians shouted with one voice, "The people want" ... "The people want the right to liberty" ... "The people want the right to dignity" ... "The people want the right to work".

These slogans did have a magical impact. They inspired various peoples to rise up and claim their legitimate rights, and express their rejection of autocracy, injustice and oppression.

Your Majesties,
Ladies and Gentlemen

On the 17th of December 2010, the Tunisian Revolution erupted against poverty and marginalisation, and against development options that established exclusion and injustice between different regions and different communities. Its slogans were to claim economic and social rights outlined in three main demands: Job Opportunity, Liberty and Social Justice. It was demonstrated in social movements and young people's sit-ins, which all demanded a solution to the problem of unemployment, and an elimination of marginalisation. They demanded the right to proper development, fair distribution of wealth, and equality.

However, this uprising took an express and direct political turn after the escape of the hierarchy of power. It demanded the dissolution of all structures of the ruling party, suspension of the old Constitution of 1959, and the departure of the whole existing government.

This situation left a great power vacuum that led the country into a serious crisis which could have had dire consequences. However, the established civil society—due to its deep roots in the community, its historic roles in the struggle for national independence and its unwavering support of the causes of its people—moved from the very first days to secure the fulfilment of the aims of the revolution. In order to steer the transitional process in a democratic and constitutional direction, the High Commission for Achieving the Goals of the Revolution was established. The High Commission brought together all political, civil and social views and the most prominent independent national leaders. This helped fill the vacuum successfully and paved the way for the Constituent Assembly Elections of 23 October 2011.

The start was rather frustrating, as the almost consensual political scene that the country witnessed before the Constituent Assembly Elections changed into a new reality overwhelmed by dangerous violations and practices that deepened the trend of political polarisation and created a lot of confusion and concern about the future of governance in the country. This resulted in intensified polarisation between political factions, and the emergence of tension and alienation in the Community. So, chaos and lawlessness dominated the scene, which encouraged undermining the prestige of the State, and spurred the predominance of smuggling gangs, parallel trading barons, terrorist groups and religious extremism. This resulted in the assassination of human rights activist and political martyr Mr. Chokri Belaid on 6 February 2013, followed by the assassination of the National Constituent Assembly Member, the martyr Mr. Mohammed Brahmi on 25 July of the same year, and resulted in the fall of many martyrs among the security forces and army soldiers. The Tunisian Citizen became confused because of the lack of security, the deterioration of social and economic conditions, and the dominance of chaos in several aspects of Tunisian life.

Because of this tense situation and the escalation of the people's uprising in Tunis and many Tunisian cities, and after disruption of the role of the Constituent Assembly when some opposition deputies suspended their participation, the National Dialogue Initiative was launched after our four institutions unanimously agreed to sponsor it. The political stakeholders agreed that they needed to move ahead, and accepted the invitation to sit at the dialogue table in order to achieve the necessary consensuses that would ensure the completion of the transitional process which already exceeded its deadlines. This is what actually happened when all groups and factions agreed to sign our Road Map.

Your Majesties,
Ladies and Gentlemen

The Road Map included a series of consensual solutions for the contentious points. It stated the following:

1. Acceptance to form a technocrat government of professional experts headed by an independent national figure. The members of the government were not to run in the upcoming elections. Moreover, the existing government had to pledge to step down as soon as the new technocrat government was appointed.

2. The National Constituent Assembly was to resume its functions and determine its mandate and the ending of its proceeding.

3. Commencement of consultations on the independent figure who would be entrusted to form the government.

4.   Agreement on a road map for completion of the transitional process that would set the timetable for the presidential and legislative elections. This timetable was to be announced to the general public after being signed by all parties. The roadmap agreement was to be issue[d] under an act adopted by the National Constituent Assembly in a special meeting. Besides, there should be a provisional organization and review of the public authorities.

The National Dialogue was not an easy process. Indeed, some of its rounds were so difficult that we were forced to suspend it for nearly one month, after it was not possible to reach consensus on some points mentioned in the Road Map. However, we did not give up and kept on working as a quartet. We contacted the political parties and managed to get them together at the dialogue table. Thanks to this consensual approach that we adopted and sponsored with the support of all elements of the civil society, the transition path was successfully completed. Eventually, a provisional government of independent professional experts was formed, and a new constitution for the country was drafted and approved with a high level of consensus. The Independent High Electoral Commission was elected, and the electoral law was issued which led to the holding of legislative and presidential elections, thus producing a new Parliament, a new President and a Government that won the confidence of the majority of the people's deputies.

Thanks to this spirit, we, the sponsoring quartet, realised that the special characteristics of the transitional period cannot be dealt with in accordance with the process of elections only, as these remain fragile and exposed to various setbacks. Instead, the transitional period should be backed by a consensual legitimacy. Hence, we sought to convince everyone that the majority approach in the transitional period, in a community that is still taking its first steps towards democracy, may involve disagreement, tension and aggravation. It should presumably be backed by a political approach which provides the most possible consensus, thus ensuring the country's unity and solidarity. It is an approach of consensus based on constructive dialogue. Such an approach in transitional periods is characterised in exceptional cases with a mutual alignment of the people's consensual legitimacy and the electoral legitimacy which could be weakened or corroded, so that each legitimacy would not cancel the other. However, such an approach to the transitional process requires minimum pre-requisites which are available in Tunisia, but unfortunately did not exist in other Arab Spring countries.

Consensus requires well-planned preparation, genuine willingness for dialogue, pre-agreed controls of work and a framework in which ideas and viewpoints are shared by various political factions. In particular, a sponsor trusted and appreciated by all parties concerned should undertake the task of running and deepening the dialogue until it achieves its objectives.

Your Majesties,
Ladies and Gentlemen

We are proud that the Tunisian National Dialogue experience has received such unprecedented international sympathy and appreciation. This prompts us to persevere in this approach and adopt it as a strategic option for the management of our political, economic, social and cultural affairs. This is why we look forward to setting this experience, after its completion, as a role model for other peoples that are today facing difficult transitional processes, so that lessons could be learned to help solv[e] their challenges in a similar way.

The successes achieved along the consensual transition path still need us to make tremendous efforts to fortify and consolidate them, so that they become a basis for new successes. We recognise that there are many challenges ahead of us, and there are still huge risks surrounding us.

At the political level, we are looking forward to completing the constituent path and organizing power and authority on a democratic basis, by finalizing the establishment of the remaining constitutional institutions necessary to consolidate liberties and resist the return of autocracy.

On the economic level, we have to create the conditions that ensure the return of the Tunisian economy to its normal state, and improve the overall climate for investment, and embark on approving the necessary repairs, with extensive consultation between the Government and the economic and social players, to preserve the interests of all groups and factions. This will contribute significantly to improving the stability of the country.

On the social level, we should work altogether to provide the elements of dignity and decent livelihood for all Tunisians wherever they are, and to eliminate poverty, deprivation and inequality between various groups. This requires that we address the problem of unemployment, and particularly the unemployment of university graduates.

On the security level, even if the security conditions get improved in general, and Tunisia makes progress in confronting terrorism and protecting our borders from smuggling, a huge effort must be made in order to make a quantum leap in the fight against terrorism and in dealing with the terrorist phenomenon. This will require extending the fight in various directions and disconnecting this phenomenon from its resources wherever they may be.

Your Majesties,
Ladies and Gentlemen

We recognise that the key to achieving stability in Tunisia lies in the creation of more job opportunities for our youth and in looking more after our inland regions, especially the border areas which have suffered for decades from marginalisation and in which our people are expecting after the Revolution to achieve better living conditions. This target requires the development of infrastructures and the improvement of basic life facilities such as health, transport and education, and requires putting heavy investments and exploring the possibilities of promoting minor projects, especially because these areas have a big civilization and traditional legacy that could be a springboard for the creation of many projects, whether in agriculture or in traditional industries, if only there is proper funding and an appropriate business environment.

We are well aware of all these difficulties, and fully aware of the challenges that lie ahead. We are determined to rely on ourselves in overcoming the difficulties, and we look forward to having the support of our friends all over the world. To everyone who believes in Tunisia, we say that we will continue working for our country and will keep our bet on dialogue and consensus as a suitable approach to overcome the difficulties regardless of their size.

Thank you, and may you always be a supporter of freedom and peace.

OTHER HISTORIC DOCUMENTS OF INTEREST

United Nations Climate Change Conference Reaches Historic Agreement

DECEMBER 12, 2015

The 21st Conference of the Parties to the United Nations Framework Convention on Climate Change (COP21) and the 11th Meeting of the Parties to the 1997 Kyoto Protocol (CMP11) drew thousands of international delegates to Paris in the winter of 2015 in hopes of reaching a new global agreement on actions to address climate change. COP21 built on decades of international climate change negotiations, including a series of ongoing consultations throughout 2015, to produce a historic agreement among participating countries to significantly reduce greenhouse gas emissions by the end of the century and combat rising temperatures worldwide.

HISTORY OF THE UNFCCC

In 1992, the United Nations convened more than 170 government representatives at the Rio Earth Summit in Brazil to discuss opportunities for rethinking economic development, stopping the destruction of natural resources and reducing pollution. The Earth Summit resulted in the adoption of the UN Framework Convention on Climate Change (UNFCCC), an agreement that acknowledged the existence of human-induced climate change and assigned primary responsibility for addressing environmental issues to industrialized countries. It established a framework for stabilizing greenhouse gas emissions "at a level that would prevent dangerous anthropogenic interference with the climate system." The framework entered into force on March 21, 1994, and provided a foundation for formal consideration for climate change actions.

The first COP took place in Berlin in 1995, launching a twenty-year string of annual conferences with the primary objective of reviewing and assessing UNFCCC implementation. The process's first major accomplishment occurred at COP3 in Japan with the announcement of the Kyoto Protocol. The protocol was the result of ongoing debate among the countries involved in the Earth Summit over what commitments each country should be responsible for and the role of developed versus developing countries in advancing the goals of the UNFCCC. The resulting protocol set country-specific emissions reduction targets for developed countries for the first time in history, generally requiring about a 5 percent cut in emissions by 2012, compared to 1990 levels. Developing countries, such as China, were not given reduction targets and were in fact allowed to increase their emissions as they continued to industrialize. The protocol was a binding agreement and established a Compliance Committee to monitor and enforce implementation. It entered into force in February 2005 and was intended to cover 2008–2012. While Kyoto was an important development in global climate change negotiations, it was generally described as a weak agreement because it lacked strong enforcement mechanisms and was not ratified by some of the largest developed countries, including the United States.

The parties passed another significant milestone in 2009 at COP15/CMP5 in Denmark when all participating countries—including developed countries and some of the largest developing countries—came to a consensus around a common goal of keeping the increase in global temperatures below 2°C. This goal was influenced by research from the Intergovernmental Panel on Climate Change, which had found that an increase over 2°C would lead to serious environmental consequences, such as a greater frequency of severe climate events. Climate scientists projected that with no change in environmental policies and a continuation of current emissions levels, the world would see a 4.5–6°C temperature increase by 2100. Industrialized countries also committed to raising $100 billion per year by 2020 to help developing countries address climate change. Agreement around the 2°C was heralded as a landmark achievement, in part because it signaled that the most influential countries were finally aligned. However, others viewed COP15 as a failure because it did not result in a full and binding treaty cementing this agreement.

In 2011, during COP17 in Durban, South Africa, the UNFCCC parties agreed to the Durban Platform for Enhanced Action, which called for all countries to collaboratively develop "a protocol, another legal instrument or an agreed upon outcome with legal force" that would be adopted in 2015 and implemented beginning in 2020. The following year, the parties agreed to an extension of the Kyoto Protocol from 2013 to 2020 to cover the period between the initial protocol's expiration and the implementation of the to-be-developed legally binding document called for by COP17. This time, countries committed to cutting greenhouse gas emissions by at least 18 percent compared to 1990 levels.

COP20 in Lima marked another step toward global consensus, by establishing the foundation for a global climate agreement to be discussed further at COP21. The Lima conference also resulted in the creation of the Lima–Paris Action Agenda, which brought state and nonstate actors together to commit to accelerating collaborative climate action and supporting the Paris Agreement expected at COP21. It also encouraged nonstate actors to take their own actions and make commitments to address climate change and extended support to existing initiatives.

While not part of the official COP process, many observers also credit a joint U.S.-China plan to cut domestic greenhouse gas emissions—announced by Presidents Barack Obama and Xi Jinping in November 2014—with helping pave the way for a Paris Agreement. The announcement was considered a breakthrough in negotiations, because the United States and China had long held opposing viewpoints on needed climate change actions. Alignment between the world's two largest emitters was crucial to moving negotiations forward.

THE ROAD TO COP21/CMP11

Preparations for the 2015 conference began well before its November start date. Roughly 1,300 delegates from various countries met throughout the year in an effort to make progress toward a final agreement on which all parties would vote in December during the conference. The delegates developed an initial eighty-six-page document in February during their first meeting in Geneva, which formed the basis for all subsequent discussions, and finalized the text by their last meeting in October in Bonn, Germany.

While these delegates met, French foreign minister Laurent Fabius held two rounds of informal consultations with representatives of more than fifty ministries, seeking to reach compromises on certain measures to help keep negotiations moving forward. During their September meeting, these ministers called for a report on industrialized countries' progress toward meeting their $100 billion per year fundraising commitment. Fabius suggested in a statement that there was some disagreement among the countries over whether the $100 billion was feasible and should be maintained; the report would help prevent "endless debate" and "constant wrangling" over the numbers. In response, the Organisation for Economic Co-operation and Development and the Climate Policy Initiative published a climate finance report on October 7, which showed that developed countries had raised $62 billion in 2014. This demonstrated that the countries were making progress toward the goal of raising $100 billion by 2020, and was bolstered by a separate report from the World Resources Institute, which said the remaining gap in financing could be made up with increased funds from the World Bank, other development banks, and the private sector.

All COP parties were invited to submit Intended Nationally Determined Contributions (INDCs) before the conference. These individual roadmaps for reducing greenhouse gas emissions would form a critical component of the resulting Paris Agreement. Commitments included the European Union's pledge to cut emissions by 40 percent, compared to 1990 levels, by 2030; a U.S. promise to cut emissions by 26–28 percent, compared to 2005 levels, by 2025; and agreement from China that its emissions levels would peak by 2030. By October, 146 countries responsible for about 90 percent of global carbon emissions had submitted INDCs. The UNFCCC published a report synthesizing these commitments on October 30. According to the analysis, if these measures were implemented, the world would experience a temperature increase of roughly 3°C by 2100, suggesting the 2°C goal was reachable.

A pre-COP conference was held in Paris on November 8–10, with the goal of making additional progress on negotiations ahead of the official COP. More than 60 ministers attended.

COP21/CMP11 and the Paris Agreement

COP21/CMP11 was scheduled for November 30 to December 12, and set to take place in Paris-Le Bourget, a commune in Paris's northeastern suburbs. Led by Fabius and Environment Minister Ségolène Royal, the proceedings involved 195 countries, with an estimated 30,000 people in attendance. The UN also hosted its first "Action Week" in conjunction with the conference, bringing local governments, businesses, and banks together to discuss and showcase commitments secured through the Lima–Paris Action Agenda.

After two weeks of successful meetings, Fabius announced the adoption of the Paris Agreement on Saturday, December 12, prompting a standing ovation from the gathered delegates. Under the agreement, participating parties committed to maintaining the 2°C goal set by COP15, and even went one step further to state that countries should be aiming for a temperature increase of 1.5°C to better protect island states from the impacts of climate change, which include beach erosion and degradation of coral reefs and marine species. In 2014, the Carteret Islanders of Papua New Guinea became the first climate change refugees, and by 2015 sea level rise rendered the island entirely uninhabitable.

Furthermore, the countries agreed to set a goal of achieving carbon neutrality by the second half of the century. The agreement did not set legally binding requirements for how countries should cut emissions or how much, but rather relied on the INDCs gathered from participating countries. A key reason for this was because if the agreement included such requirements, it would have to be ratified by the U.S. Senate—a highly unlikely scenario given its vocal resistance to implementing climate change initiatives in recent years—rather than simply be approved by the executive branch.

The agreement did note the "significant gap" between which countries had made a commitment and what was needed to achieve the 2°C goal. To help address this, it instituted a legally binding system through which countries would review their INDCs every five years, beginning in 2020, with the goal of increasing their pledges to cut emissions. Participating countries would also be legally required to monitor and report on emissions levels and reductions using a universal accounting system and would meet every five years to publicly report on progress, beginning in 2023—a system dubbed "name and shame" by some observers.

Notably, the agreement did not include any significant enforcement measures. It called for the creation of a committee of experts to "facilitate implementation" and "promote compliance" with agreement, but that committee would not have authority to punish any countries that violated the agreement. This drew criticism from environmental groups and others who claimed the agreement would be too weak without a system of sanctions or other punitive measures.

The Paris Agreement also obliged industrialized countries to continue providing financing for climate initiatives in poorer countries and invited developing countries to contribute to this effort on a voluntary basis. The parties acknowledged the need to raise $100 billion in loans and donations each year, starting in 2020, to support these projects. The agreement included some discussion of whether this number should eventually increase and called for a meeting in 2025 to discuss further monetary commitments. This financial piece was not included in the legally binding portion of the Paris Agreement—a disappointing outcome for poorer countries that had made that a top priority during negotiations.

The agreement was widely viewed as a breakthrough by world leaders. President Obama characterized it as "the best chance we have to save the one planet we've got," adding, "I believe this moment can be a turning point for the world." UN secretary general Ban Ki-moon acknowledged the importance of continued collaboration to the agreement's success. "We must protect the planet that sustains us," he said. "For that we need all hands on deck." Xie Zhenhua, the senior climate change negotiator from China, noted that the agreement was "not perfect" but also described it as "fair and just, comprehensive and balanced, highly ambitious, enduring and effective." Not all welcomed the announcement, however. Thousands of demonstrators gathered in Paris to protest the agreement, arguing that it was too weak and did not go far enough.

Next Steps for Agreement Implementation

The participating countries must now individually ratify the Paris Agreement. It can only enter into force once it has been ratified by 55 countries, and those countries must represent at least 55 percent of global emissions. A signing ceremony took place on April 22, 2016, in New York City, though the agreement does ask the UN secretary general to keep the document open for signing until April 2017. COP22 will take place in Marrakech, Morocco, in November 2016.

—Linda Fecteau Grimm

Following are excerpts from the UN Framework Convention on Climate Change Paris Agreement adopted on December 12, 2015.

UN Climate Change Conference
Paris Agreement

December 12, 2015

[The UN Framework Convention on Climate Change report on adoption of the Paris Agreement has been edited to include only articles from the actual agreement.]

PARIS AGREEMENT

[Preamble text has been omitted.]

Article 1

For the purpose of this Agreement, the definitions contained in Article 1 of the Convention shall apply. In addition:

1. "Convention" means the United Nations Framework Convention on Climate Change, adopted in New York on 9 May 1992.

2. "Conference of the Parties" means the Conference of the Parties to the Convention.

3. "Party" means a Party to this Agreement.

Article 2

1. This Agreement, in enhancing the implementation of the Convention, including its objective, aims to strengthen the global response to the threat of climate change, in the context of sustainable development and efforts to eradicate poverty, including by:

    (a) Holding the increase in the global average temperature to well below 2 °C above pre-industrial levels and to pursue efforts to limit the temperature increase to 1.5 °C above pre-industrial levels, recognizing that this would significantly reduce the risks and impacts of climate change;

    (b) Increasing the ability to adapt to the adverse impacts of climate change and foster climate resilience and low greenhouse gas emissions development, in a manner that does not threaten food production;

    (c) Making finance flows consistent with a pathway towards low greenhouse gas emissions and climate-resilient development. . . .

Article 3

As nationally determined contributions to the global response to climate change, all Parties are to undertake and communicate ambitious efforts as defined in Articles 4, 7, 9, 10, 11 and 13 with the view to achieving the purpose of this Agreement as set out in Article 2. The efforts of all Parties will represent a progression over time, while recognizing the need to support developing country Parties for the effective implementation of this Agreement.

Article 4

1. In order to achieve the long-term temperature goal set out in Article 2, Parties aim to reach global peaking of greenhouse gas emissions as soon as possible, recognizing that peaking will take longer for developing country Parties, and to undertake rapid reductions thereafter in accordance with best available science, so as to achieve a balance between anthropogenic emissions by sources and removals by sinks of greenhouse gases in the second half of this century, on the basis of equity, and in the context of sustainable development and efforts to eradicate poverty.

2. Each Party shall prepare, communicate and maintain successive nationally determined contributions that it intends to achieve. Parties shall pursue domestic mitigation measures, with the aim of achieving the objectives of such contributions.

3. Each Party's successive nationally determined contribution will represent a progression beyond the Party's then current nationally determined contribution and reflect its highest possible ambition. . . .

4. Developed country Parties should continue taking the lead by undertaking economy-wide absolute emission reduction targets. Developing country Parties should continue enhancing their mitigation efforts, and are encouraged to move over time towards economy-wide emission reduction or limitation targets in the light of different national circumstances.

5. Support shall be provided to developing country Parties for the implementation of this Article . . . recognizing that enhanced support for developing country Parties will allow for higher ambition in their actions.

6. The least developed countries and small island developing States may prepare and communicate strategies, plans and actions for low greenhouse gas emissions development reflecting their special circumstances.

7. Mitigation co-benefits resulting from Parties' adaptation actions and/or economic diversification plans can contribute to mitigation outcomes under this Article.

8. In communicating their nationally determined contributions, all Parties shall provide the information necessary for clarity, transparency and understanding in accordance with decision 1/CP.21 and any relevant decisions of the Conference of the Parties. . . .

9. Each Party shall communicate a nationally determined contribution every five years . . . and be informed by the outcomes of the global stocktake referred to in Article 14.

10. The Conference of the Parties . . . shall consider common time frames for nationally determined contributions at its first session.

11. A Party may at any time adjust its existing nationally determined contribution with a view to enhancing its level of ambition. . . .

12. Nationally determined contributions communicated by Parties shall be recorded in a public registry maintained by the secretariat.

13. Parties shall account for their nationally determined contributions. In accounting for anthropogenic emissions and removals corresponding to their nationally

determined contributions, Parties shall promote environmental integrity, transparency, accuracy, completeness, comparability and consistency, and ensure the avoidance of double counting. . . .

14. In the context of their nationally determined contributions, when recognizing and implementing mitigation actions with respect to anthropogenic emissions and removals, Parties should take into account, as appropriate, existing methods and guidance under the Convention, in the light of the provisions of paragraph 13 of this Article.

15. Parties shall take into consideration in the implementation of this Agreement the concerns of Parties with economies most affected by the impacts of response measures, particularly developing country Parties.

16. Parties, including regional economic integration organizations and their member States, that have reached an agreement to act jointly under paragraph 2 of this Article shall notify the secretariat of the terms of that agreement, including the emission level allocated to each Party within the relevant time period, when they communicate their nationally determined contributions. The secretariat shall in turn inform the Parties and signatories to the Convention of the terms of that agreement.

17. Each party to such an agreement shall be responsible for its emission level as set out in the agreement referred to in paragraph 16 above in accordance with paragraphs 13 and 14 of this Article and Articles 13 and 15.

18. If Parties acting jointly do so in the framework of, and together with, a regional economic integration organization which is itself a Party to this Agreement, each member State of that regional economic integration organization individually, and together with the regional economic integration organization, shall be responsible for its emission level. . . .

19. All Parties should strive to formulate and communicate long-term low greenhouse gas emission development strategies, mindful of Article 2 taking into account their common but differentiated responsibilities and respective capabilities, in the light of different national circumstances.

[Article 5 has been omitted and discusses the need for parties to conserve and enhance, as appropriate, sinks and reservoirs of greenhouse gases.]

Article 6

1. Parties recognize that some Parties choose to pursue voluntary cooperation in the implementation of their nationally determined contributions to allow for higher ambition in their mitigation and adaptation actions and to promote sustainable development and environmental integrity.

2. Parties shall, where engaging on a voluntary basis in cooperative approaches that involve the use of internationally transferred mitigation outcomes towards nationally determined contributions, promote sustainable development and ensure environmental integrity and transparency, including in governance, and shall apply robust accounting to ensure, inter alia, the avoidance of double counting. . . .

3. The use of internationally transferred mitigation outcomes to achieve nationally determined contributions under this Agreement shall be voluntary and authorized by participating Parties.

4. A mechanism to contribute to the mitigation of greenhouse gas emissions and support sustainable development is hereby established under the authority and guidance of the Conference of the Parties. . . . It shall be supervised by a body designated by the Conference of the Parties and shall aim:

    (a) To promote the mitigation of greenhouse gas emissions while fostering sustainable development;

    (b) To incentivize and facilitate participation in the mitigation of greenhouse gas emissions by public and private entities authorized by a Party;

    (c) To contribute to the reduction of emission levels in the host Party, which will benefit from mitigation activities resulting in emission reductions that can also be used by another Party to fulfil its nationally determined contribution; and

    (d) To deliver an overall mitigation in global emissions.

5. Emission reductions resulting from the mechanism referred to in paragraph 4 of this Article shall not be used to demonstrate achievement of the host Party's nationally determined contribution if used by another Party to demonstrate achievement of its nationally determined contribution.

6. The Conference of the Parties . . . shall ensure that a share of the proceeds from activities under the mechanism referred to in paragraph 4 of this Article is used to cover administrative expenses as well as to assist developing country Parties that are particularly vulnerable to the adverse effects of climate change to meet the costs of adaptation.

7. The Conference of the Parties . . . shall adopt rules, modalities and procedures for the mechanism referred to in paragraph 4 of this Article at its first session.

8. Parties recognize the importance of integrated, holistic and balanced non-market approaches being available to Parties to assist in the implementation of their nationally determined contributions, in the context of sustainable development and poverty eradication, in a coordinated and effective manner, including through, inter alia, mitigation, adaptation, finance, technology transfer and capacity-building, as appropriate. These approaches shall aim to:

    (a) Promote mitigation and adaptation ambition;

    (b) Enhance public and private sector participation in the implementation of nationally determined contributions; and

    (c) Enable opportunities for coordination across instruments and relevant institutional arrangements. . . .

9. A framework for non-market approaches to sustainable development is hereby defined to promote the nonmarket approaches referred to in paragraph 8 of this Article.

Article 7

1. Parties hereby establish the global goal on adaptation of enhancing adaptive capacity, strengthening resilience and reducing vulnerability to climate change . . . and ensuring an adequate adaptation response in the context of the temperature goal referred to in Article 2.

2. Parties recognize that adaptation is a global challenge faced by all with local, subnational, national, regional and international dimensions, and that it is a key component of and makes a contribution to the long-term global response to climate change to protect people, livelihoods and ecosystems, taking into account the urgent and immediate needs of those developing country Parties that are particularly vulnerable to the adverse effects of climate change.

3. The adaptation efforts of developing country Parties shall be recognized. . . .

4. Parties recognize that the current need for adaptation is significant and that greater levels of mitigation can reduce the need for additional adaptation efforts, and that greater adaptation needs can involve greater adaptation costs.

5. Parties acknowledge that adaptation action should follow a country-driven, gender-responsive, participatory and fully transparent approach, taking into consideration vulnerable groups, communities and ecosystems, and should be based on and guided by the best available science and, as appropriate, traditional knowledge, knowledge of indigenous peoples and local knowledge systems, with a view to integrating adaptation into relevant socioeconomic and environmental policies and actions, where appropriate.

6. Parties recognize the importance of support for and international cooperation on adaptation efforts and the importance of taking into account the needs of developing country Parties. . . .

7. Parties should strengthen their cooperation on enhancing action on adaptation, taking into account the Cancun Adaptation Framework, including with regard to:

   (a) Sharing information, good practices, experiences and lessons learned, including, as appropriate, as these relate to science, planning, policies and implementation in relation to adaptation actions;

   (b) Strengthening institutional arrangements . . . to support the synthesis of relevant information and knowledge, and the provision of technical support and guidance to Parties;

   (c) Strengthening scientific knowledge on climate, including research, systematic observation of the climate system and early warning systems, in a manner that informs climate services and supports decision making;

   (d) Assisting developing country Parties in identifying effective adaptation practices, adaptation needs, priorities, support provided and received for adaptation actions and efforts, and challenges and gaps . . . ;

   (e) Improving the effectiveness and durability of adaptation actions.

8. United Nations specialized organizations and agencies are encouraged to support the efforts of Parties to implement the actions referred to in paragraph 7 of this Article, taking into account the provisions of paragraph 5 of this Article.

9. Each Party shall, as appropriate, engage in adaptation planning processes and the implementation of actions . . . which may include:

    (a) The implementation of adaptation actions, undertakings and/or efforts;

    (b) The process to formulate and implement national adaptation plans;

    (c) The assessment of climate change impacts and vulnerability, with a view to formulating nationally determined prioritized actions, taking into account vulnerable people, places and ecosystems;

    (d) Monitoring and evaluating and learning from adaptation plans, policies, programmes and actions; and

    (e) Building the resilience of socioeconomic and ecological systems, including through economic diversification and sustainable management of natural resources.

10. Each Party should, as appropriate, submit and update periodically an adaptation communication. . . .

11. The adaptation communication referred to in paragraph 10 of this Article shall be, as appropriate, submitted and updated periodically, as a component of or in conjunction with other communications or documents, including a national adaptation plan, a nationally determined contribution as referred to in Article 4, paragraph 2, and/or a national communication.

12. The adaptation communications referred to in paragraph 10 of this Article shall be recorded in a public registry maintained by the secretariat.

13. Continuous and enhanced international support shall be provided to developing country Parties for the implementation of paragraphs 7, 9, 10 and 11 of this Article, in accordance with the provisions of Articles 9, 10 and 11, 14. . . .

Article 8

1. Parties recognize the importance of averting, minimizing and addressing loss and damage associated with the adverse effects of climate change, including extreme weather events and slow onset events, and the role of sustainable development in reducing the risk of loss and damage.

2. The Warsaw International Mechanism for Loss and Damage associated with Climate Change Impacts shall be subject to the authority and guidance of the Conference of the Parties . . . and may be enhanced and strengthened, as determined by the Conference of the Parties. . . .

3. Parties should enhance understanding, action and support, including through the Warsaw International Mechanism, as appropriate, on a cooperative and facilitative basis with respect to loss and damage associated with the adverse effects of climate change.

4. Accordingly, areas of cooperation and facilitation to enhance understanding, action and support may include:

(a) Early warning systems;

(b) Emergency preparedness;

(c) Slow onset events;

(d) Events that may involve irreversible and permanent loss and damage;

(e) Comprehensive risk assessment and management;

(f) Risk insurance facilities, climate risk pooling and other insurance solutions;

(g) Non-economic losses;

(h) Resilience of communities, livelihoods and ecosystems.

5. The Warsaw International Mechanism shall collaborate with existing bodies and expert groups under the Agreement, as well as relevant organizations and expert bodies outside the Agreement.

Article 9

1. Developed country Parties shall provide financial resources to assist developing country Parties with respect to both mitigation and adaptation in continuation of their existing obligations under the Convention.

2. Other Parties are encouraged to provide or continue to provide such support voluntarily.

3. As part of a global effort, developed country Parties should continue to take the lead in mobilizing climate finance from a wide variety of sources, instruments and channels. . . . Such mobilization of climate finance should represent a progression beyond previous efforts.

4. The provision of scaled-up financial resources should aim to achieve a balance between adaptation and mitigation, taking into account country-driven strategies, and the priorities and needs of developing country Parties, especially those that are particularly vulnerable to the adverse effects of climate change and have significant capacity constraints. . . .

5. Developed country Parties shall biennially communicate indicative quantitative and qualitative information related to paragraphs 1 and 3 of this Article, as applicable, including, as available, projected levels of public financial resources to be provided to developing country Parties. Other Parties providing resources are encouraged to communicate biennially such information on a voluntary basis.

6. The global stocktake referred to in Article 14 shall take into account the relevant information provided by developed country Parties and/or Agreement bodies on efforts related to climate finance.

7. Developed country Parties shall provide transparent and consistent information on support for developing country Parties provided and mobilized through public interventions biennially. . . . Other Parties are encouraged to do so.

8. The Financial Mechanism of the Convention, including its operating entities, shall serve as the financial mechanism of this Agreement.

9. The institutions serving this Agreement, including the operating entities of the Financial Mechanism of the Convention, shall aim to ensure efficient access to financial resources through simplified approval procedures and enhanced readiness support for developing country Parties, in particular for the least developed countries and small island developing States, in the context of their national climate strategies and plans.

Article 10

1. Parties share a long-term vision on the importance of fully realizing technology development and transfer in order to improve resilience to climate change and to reduce greenhouse gas emissions.

2. Parties . . . shall strengthen cooperative action on technology development and transfer.

3. The Technology Mechanism established under the Convention shall serve this Agreement.

4. A technology framework is hereby established to provide overarching guidance for the work of the Technology Mechanism in promoting and facilitating enhanced action on technology development and transfer. . . .

5. Accelerating, encouraging and enabling innovation is critical for an effective, long-term global response to climate change and promoting economic growth and sustainable development. Such effort shall be . . . for collaborative approaches to research and development, and facilitating access to technology, in particular for early stages of the technology cycle, to developing country Parties.

6. Support, including financial support, shall be provided to developing country Parties . . . including for strengthening cooperative action on technology development and transfer at different stages of the technology cycle, with a view to achieving a balance between support for mitigation and adaptation. . . .

Article 11

1. Capacity-building under this Agreement should enhance the capacity and ability of developing country Parties . . . and those that are particularly vulnerable to the adverse effects of climate change, such as small island developing States, to take effective climate change action, including, inter alia, to implement adaptation and mitigation actions, and should facilitate technology development, dissemination and deployment, access to climate finance, relevant aspects of education, training and public awareness, and the transparent, timely and accurate communication of information.

2. Capacity-building should be country-driven, based on and responsive to national needs, and foster country ownership of Parties. . . .

3. All Parties should cooperate to enhance the capacity of developing country Parties to implement this Agreement. . . .

4. All Parties enhancing the capacity of developing country Parties to implement this Agreement, including through regional, bilateral and multilateral approaches, shall regularly communicate on these actions or measures on capacity-building. Developing country Parties should regularly communicate progress made on implementing capacity-building plans, policies, actions or measures to implement this Agreement.

5. Capacity-building activities shall be enhanced through appropriate institutional arrangements to support the implementation of this Agreement. . . . The Conference of the Parties . . . shall, at its first session, consider and adopt a decision on the initial institutional arrangements for capacity-building.

Article 12

Parties shall cooperate in taking measures, as appropriate, to enhance climate change education, training, public awareness, public participation and public access to information, recognizing the importance of these steps with respect to enhancing actions under this Agreement.

Article 13

1. In order to build mutual trust and confidence and to promote effective implementation, an enhanced transparency framework for action and support, with built-in flexibility which takes into account Parties' different capacities and builds upon collective experience is hereby established.

2. The transparency framework shall provide flexibility in the implementation of the provisions of this Article to those developing country Parties that need it in the light of their capacities. . . .

3. The transparency framework shall build on and enhance the transparency arrangements under the Convention, recognizing the special circumstances of the least developed countries and small island developing States, and be implemented in a facilitative, non-intrusive, non-punitive manner, respectful of national sovereignty, and avoid placing undue burden on Parties.

4. The transparency arrangements under the Convention, including national communications, biennial reports and biennial update reports, international assessment and review and international consultation and analysis, shall form part of the experience drawn upon for the development of the modalities, procedures and guidelines under paragraph 13 of this Article.

5. The purpose of the framework for transparency of action is to provide a clear understanding of climate change action in the light of the objective of the Convention as set out in its Article 2, including clarity and tracking of progress towards achieving Parties' individual nationally determined contributions under Article 4, and Parties' adaptation actions under Article 7, including good practices, priorities, needs and gaps, to inform the global stocktake under Article 14.

6. The purpose of the framework for transparency of support is to provide clarity on support provided and received by relevant individual Parties in the context of climate change actions under Articles 4, 7, 9, 10 and 11. . . .

7. Each Party shall regularly provide the following information:

   (a) A national inventory report of anthropogenic emissions by sources and removals by sinks of greenhouse gases, prepared using good practice methodologies accepted by the Intergovernmental Panel on Climate Change and agreed upon by the Conference of the Parties. . . .

   (b) Information necessary to track progress made in implementing and achieving its nationally determined contribution under Article 4.

8. Each Party should also provide information related to climate change impacts and adaptation. . . .

9. Developed country Parties shall, and other Parties that provide support should, provide information on financial, technology transfer and capacity-building support provided to developing country Parties. . . .

10. Developing country Parties should provide information on financial, technology transfer and capacity-building support needed and received. . . .

11. Information submitted by each Party under paragraphs 7 and 9 of this Article shall undergo a technical expert review, in accordance with decision 1/CP.21. . . . In addition, each Party shall participate in a facilitative, multilateral consideration of progress with respect to efforts under Article 9, and its respective implementation and achievement of its nationally determined contribution.

12. The technical expert review under this paragraph shall consist of a consideration of the Party's support provided, as relevant, and its implementation and achievement of its nationally determined contribution. The review shall also identify areas of improvement for the Party, and include a review of the consistency of the information with the modalities, procedures and guidelines referred to in paragraph 13 of this Article, taking into account the flexibility accorded to the Party under paragraph 2 of this Article. . . .

Article 14

1. The Conference of the Parties . . . shall periodically take stock of the implementation of this Agreement to assess the collective progress towards achieving the purpose of this Agreement and its long-term goals (referred to as the "global stocktake"). . . .

2. The Conference of the Parties serving as the meeting of the Parties to the Paris Agreement shall undertake its first global stocktake in 2023 and every five years thereafter unless otherwise decided by the Conference of the Parties. . . .

3. The outcome of the global stocktake shall inform Parties in updating and enhancing, in a nationally determined manner, their actions and support in accordance with the relevant provisions of this Agreement, as well as in enhancing international cooperation for climate action.

Article 15

1. A mechanism to facilitate implementation of and promote compliance with the provisions of this Agreement is hereby established.

2. The mechanism referred to in paragraph 1 of this Article shall consist of a committee that shall be expert-based and facilitative in nature and function in a manner that is transparent, non-adversarial and non-punitive. The committee shall pay particular attention to the respective national capabilities and circumstances of Parties.

3. The committee shall operate under the modalities and procedures adopted by the Conference of the Parties . . . and report annually to the Conference of the Parties. . . .

[Articles 16–19 have been omitted and present considerations for scheduling future Conferences of the Parties, selecting new Parties to the Agreement, designating a secretariat, and the functions of the Subsidiary Bodies for Scientific and Technological Advice and Implementation.]

Article 20

1. This Agreement shall be open for signature and subject to ratification, acceptance or approval by States and regional economic integration organizations that are Parties to the Convention. It shall be open for signature at the United Nations Headquarters in New York from 22 April 2016 to 21 April 2017. Thereafter, this Agreement shall be open for accession from the day following the date on which it is closed for signature. . . .

Article 21

1. This Agreement shall enter into force on the thirtieth day after the date on which at least 55 Parties to the Convention accounting in total for at least an estimated 55 percent of the total global greenhouse gas emissions have deposited their instruments of ratification, acceptance, approval or accession. . . .

2. Solely for the limited purpose of paragraph 1 of this Article, "total global greenhouse gas emissions" means the most up-to-date amount communicated on or before the date of adoption of this Agreement by the Parties to the Convention.

3. For each State or regional economic integration organization that ratifies, accepts or approves this Agreement or accedes thereto after the conditions set out in paragraph 1 of this Article for entry into force have been fulfilled, this Agreement shall enter into force on the thirtieth day after the date of deposit by such State or regional economic integration organization of its instrument of ratification, acceptance, approval or accession. . . .

[Articles 22–24 have been omitted and acknowledge that select articles apply mutatis mutandis *to the Agreement.]*

Article 25

1. Each Party shall have one vote, except as provided for paragraph 2 of this Article.

2. Regional economic integration organizations, in matters within their competence, shall exercise their right to vote with a number of votes equal to the number

of their member States that are Parties to this Agreement. Such an organization shall not exercise its right to vote if any of its member States exercises its right, and vice versa.

Article 26

The Secretary-General of the United Nations shall be the Depositary of this Agreement.

[Articles 27–29 have been omitted and outline a process for withdrawing from the Agreement and the languages in which the Agreement will be available.]

DONE at Paris this twelfth day of December two thousand and fifteen.

IN WITNESS WHEREOF, the undersigned, being duly authorized to that effect, have signed this Agreement.

SOURCE: United Nations Framework Convention on Climate Change. "Adoption of the Paris Agreement." December 12, 2015. http://unfccc.int/resource/docs/2015/cop21/eng/l09.pdf.

OTHER HISTORIC DOCUMENTS OF INTEREST

FROM PREVIOUS *HISTORIC DOCUMENTS*

- United States and China Agree to Historic Climate Change Pact, *2014*, p. 547
- Intergovernmental Panel on Climate Change Releases Report on Greenhouse Gases, *2013*, p. 460
- 2012 Doha Climate Change Conference, *2012*, p. 597

Federal Reserve Announces Interest Rate Hike

DECEMBER 16, 2015

Seven years to the day after cutting a key economic indicator—the short-term interest rate—to near zero, the Board of Governors of the Federal Reserve Bank announced that, given the economic improvement since the end of the recession, it would begin slowly increasing the short-term interest rate. Although widely expected by economic analysts, the decision to raise short-term interest rates was seen as a strong indicator of the health of the U.S. economy. Although some investors and politicians warned that increasing the short-term interest rate could have a negative impact, the Federal Reserve promised in its announcement that it would closely monitor economic indicators and pull back on its increases if the economy began to dip again.

FEDERAL RESERVE DECREASES INTEREST RATES TO HISTORIC LOWS

Despite a number of statements throughout early to mid-2008 by highly regarded financiers such as Warren Buffett, it was not until December 1 of that year that the National Bureau of Economic Research (NBER), a nonpartisan organization that dates the start and end of economic crises and officially declares recessions, announced that the United States had been in recession since December 2007. At that time, the NBER said it was making the declaration for a number of reasons, including a rapidly declining labor market, which saw 1.25 million jobs lost in the United States during the first ten months of 2008, slowing levels of personal income, and decreased retail sales and industrial production.

In response to the announcement, the Federal Open Market Committee (FOMC), an arm of the Board of Governors of the Federal Reserve, announced on December 16, 2008, that it would "establish a target range for the federal funds rate of 0 to 1/4 percent." Better known as the short-term interest rate, the target rate is what dictates the interest rate banks pay when lending to each other and when borrowing money from the federal government. The Federal Reserve had already cut the rate ten times over the fifteen months prior to its December 16 announcement, but establishing a baseline near zero was unprecedented.

Cutting the short-term interest rate was not intended to provide the American public immediate relief from deteriorating economic conditions, but the hope was that it would help slowly encourage the economy to pick up by giving banks a greater ability to increase lending at higher interest rates. The announcement gave an immediate boost to the Dow Jones industrial average and spurred the White House to call on Congress to propose new ways to restart the American economy.

Ultimately, a number of additional economic measures were implemented in an attempt to pull the United States out of recession, including the hotly debated American Recovery and Reinvestment Act and purchases made by the Federal Reserve of mortgage-related securities and long-term debt from the Treasury. On September 15, 2009, then–Federal Reserve chair Ben Bernanke announced that the recession was over, at least from a strictly economic perspective. "Even though from a technical perspective the recession is very likely over at this point, it's still going to feel like a very weak economy for some time as many people will still find that their job security and their employment status is not what they wish it was," Bernanke said.

As Economy Grows, Federal Reserve Moves to Raise Interest Rates

After the declaration of the official end of the economic crisis, economists waited for the Federal Reserve to announce that it would raise interest rates, because this was seen as a key indicator of economic momentum. The Federal Reserve declined to do so for many years over fears that a rate hike could dampen economic activity and drag down an already low inflation rate. Another part of the concern was linked to weak global markets, specifically in nations such as China, which invest heavily in the United States. During its regular meeting in September 2015, thought by many economists to be the most likely point at which the Federal Reserve would raise short-term interest rates for the first time since 2006, the group remarked that although the U.S. economy was continuing to grow and had regained a large portion of its recession losses, "recent global economic and financial developments may restrain economic activity somewhat and are likely to put further downward pressure on inflation in the near term."

On December 16, after two days of policy meetings, the Federal Reserve announced that it had gained enough confidence in global markets and the ongoing recovery in the United States to raise short-term interest rates to a range of 0.25 percent to 0.5 percent. In a statement, Federal Reserve chair Janet Yellen said the move "recognizes the considerable progress that has been made toward restoring jobs, raising incomes and easing the economic hardships that have been endured by millions of ordinary Americans." She cautioned, however, that while "the economic recovery has clearly come a long way . . . it is not yet complete."

In acknowledging that economic recovery was still ongoing, the Federal Reserve stated that it would closely monitor both domestic and global economic indicators and would cut rates again if necessary. The central banks of a number of nations that were hit by the global financial downturn had already raised their interest rates and subsequently backtracked when growth began to slow. In its announcement, the Federal Reserve said that short-term interest rates would rise an estimated 1 percentage point per year for the next three years, but that increases would only be implemented if economic growth continued. In particular, Yellen said the Federal Reserve would "monitor inflation very carefully." Abrupt action, Yellen said, "could increase the risk of pushing the economy into recession."

The markets had a tempered response to the announcement, with less than 2 percent growth seen on December 16 in the S&P 500 and Dow Jones Industrial Average. Politicians, however, quickly responded to the decision. Rep. Jeb Hensarling, R-Texas, the House Financial Services Committee chair, said that the rate cut had never worked, as evidenced by Americans "stuck in the slowest, worst-performing economic recovery of our lifetimes." Rep. John Conyers, D-Mich., echoed those remarks, saying of the rate hike that it was "unacceptable for any branch of government to take any action to slow our economy before all Americans have the opportunity to experience the jobs recovery and meaningful wage growth."

SHORT-TERM AND LONG-TERM IMPACT OF THE INTEREST RATE HIKE

The federal government would likely be the first to feel the impact of the federal rate hike, because it is the nation's largest borrower, but the U.S. economy would also take a hit. According to Moody's Analytics, a 1 percentage point increase in the short-term interest rate could stymie economic growth the next year by 0.15 percent and could decrease monthly job growth by 30,000 jobs.

The impact on Americans would likely be somewhat slower. Although the Federal Reserve has control over short-term interest rates, it does not control long-term interest rates, which are tied to ordinary purchases such as mortgages or car loans. Following the Federal Reserve announcement, economic experts predicted that long-term interest rates would grow gradually over the next two years, but that there was no need for Americans to make large purchases now. "Rates are pretty low and they're not going to change much" in the short term, said former Federal Reserve economist Dean Croushore. While this had the potential to slow the sale of cars and homes, it could also mean more interest in the pockets of anyone with a bank account, as long as banks decided to pass their increase on to account holders. Stockholders anticipated a bit more change in a shorter time period because the rate hike had the potential to further increase volatility in the stock market.

Economic analysts said they would closely watch how quickly the Federal Reserve ultimately raises rates over the next few years. The Federal Reserve predicted making four interest rate hikes in 2016; however, by the start of the year the global economic markets were still struggling, and job growth in the United States was sluggish, potentially indicating that the group would be slower to make any additional adjustments on top of the December 16 hike. Federal Reserve vice chairman Bill Dudley said in early February 2016 that "things have happened in financial markets and in the flow of economic data that may be in the process of altering the outlook for growth."

—Heather Kerrigan

Following is the text of a December 16, 2015, statement from the Board of Governors of the Federal Reserve announcing the Federal Open Market Committee's (FOMC) decision to increase short-term interest rates; and a press release from the Federal Reserve, also on December 16, 2015, regarding implementation of the FOMC's rate hike.

FOMC Announces
Interest Rate Increase

DOCUMENT

December 16, 2015

Information received since the Federal Open Market Committee met in October suggests that economic activity has been expanding at a moderate pace. Household spending and business fixed investment have been increasing at solid rates in recent months, and the housing sector has improved further; however, net exports have been soft. A range of recent labor market indicators, including ongoing job gains and declining unemployment, shows further improvement and confirms that underutilization of labor resources has diminished appreciably since early this year. Inflation has continued to run below the Committee's 2 percent longer-run objective, partly reflecting declines in energy prices and in prices of non-energy imports. Market-based measures of inflation compensation remain low; some survey-based measures of longer-term inflation expectations have edged down.

Consistent with its statutory mandate, the Committee seeks to foster maximum employment and price stability. The Committee currently expects that, with gradual adjustments in the stance of monetary policy, economic activity will continue to expand at a moderate pace and labor market indicators will continue to strengthen. Overall, taking into account domestic and international developments, the Committee sees the risks to the outlook for both economic activity and the labor market as balanced. Inflation is expected to rise to 2 percent over the medium term as the transitory effects of declines in energy and import prices dissipate and the labor market strengthens further. The Committee continues to monitor inflation developments closely.

The Committee judges that there has been considerable improvement in labor market conditions this year, and it is reasonably confident that inflation will rise, over the medium term, to its 2 percent objective. Given the economic outlook, and recognizing the time it takes for policy actions to affect future economic outcomes, the Committee decided to raise the target range for the federal funds rate to 1/4 to 1/2 percent. The stance of monetary policy remains accommodative after this increase, thereby supporting further improvement in labor market conditions and a return to 2 percent inflation.

In determining the timing and size of future adjustments to the target range for the federal funds rate, the Committee will assess realized and expected economic conditions relative to its objectives of maximum employment and 2 percent inflation. This assessment will take into account a wide range of information, including measures of labor market conditions, indicators of inflation pressures and inflation expectations, and readings on financial and international developments. In light of the current shortfall of inflation from 2 percent, the Committee will carefully monitor actual and expected progress toward its inflation goal. The Committee expects that economic conditions will evolve in a manner that will warrant only gradual increases in the federal funds rate; the federal funds rate is likely to remain, for some time, below levels that are expected to prevail in the longer run. However, the actual path of the federal funds rate will depend on the economic outlook as informed by incoming data.

The Committee is maintaining its existing policy of reinvesting principal payments from its holdings of agency debt and agency mortgage-backed securities in agency mortgage-backed securities and of rolling over maturing Treasury securities at auction, and it anticipates doing so until normalization of the level of the federal funds rate is well under way. This policy, by keeping the Committee's holdings of longer-term securities at sizable levels, should help maintain accommodative financial conditions.

Voting for the FOMC monetary policy action were: Janet L. Yellen, Chair; William C. Dudley, Vice Chairman; Lael Brainard; Charles L. Evans; Stanley Fischer; Jeffrey M. Lacker; Dennis P. Lockhart; Jerome H. Powell; Daniel K. Tarullo; and John C. Williams.

SOURCE: Board of Governors of the Federal Reserve System. "Press Release." December 16, 2015. www.federalreserve.gov/newsevents/press/monetary/20151216a.htm.

Federal Reserve Issues Decisions Regarding Interest Rate Hike

December 16, 2015

The Federal Reserve has made the following decisions to implement the monetary policy stance announced by the Federal Open Market Committee in its statement on December 16, 2015:

- The Board of Governors of the Federal Reserve System voted unanimously to raise the interest rate paid on required and excess reserve balances to 0.50 percent, effective December 17, 2015.

- As part of its policy decision, the Federal Open Market Committee voted to authorize and direct the Open Market Desk at the Federal Reserve Bank of New York, until instructed otherwise, to execute transactions in the System Open Market Account in accordance with the following domestic policy directive:[1]

"Effective December 17, 2015, the Federal Open Market Committee directs the Desk to undertake open market operations as necessary to maintain the federal funds rate in a target range of 1/4 to 1/2 percent, including: (1) overnight reverse repurchase operations (and reverse repurchase operations with maturities of more than one day when necessary to accommodate weekend, holiday, or similar trading conventions) at an offering rate of 0.25 percent, in amounts limited only by the value of Treasury securities held outright in the System Open Market Account that are available for such operations and by a per-counterparty limit of $30 billion per day; and (2) term reverse repurchase operations to the extent approved in the resolution on term RRP operations approved by the Committee at its March 17–18, 2015, meeting.

The Committee directs the Desk to continue rolling over maturing Treasury securities at auction and to continue reinvesting principal payments on all agency debt and agency mortgage-backed securities in agency mortgage-backed securities. The Committee also directs the Desk to engage in dollar roll and coupon swap transactions as necessary to facilitate settlement of the Federal Reserve's agency mortgage-backed securities transactions."

More information regarding open market operations may be found on the Federal Reserve Bank of New York's website.

- In a related action, the Board of Governors of the Federal Reserve System voted unanimously to approve a 1/4 percentage point increase in the discount rate (the primary credit rate) to 1.00 percent, effective December 17, 2015. In taking this action, the Board approved requests submitted by the Boards of Directors of the Federal Reserve Banks of Boston, Philadelphia, Cleveland, Richmond, Atlanta, Chicago, St. Louis, Kansas City, Dallas, and San Francisco.

This information will be updated as appropriate to reflect decisions of the Federal Open Market Committee or the Board of Governors regarding details of the Federal Reserve's operational tools and approach used to implement monetary policy.

SOURCE: Board of Governors of the Federal Reserve System. "Decisions Regarding Monetary Policy Implementation." December 16, 2015. www.federalreserve.gov/newsevents/press/monetary/20151216a1 .htm.

NOTE

1. This directive supersedes the resolution on the overnight reverse repurchase agreement (ON RRP) test operations approved by the Committee at its December 16–17, 2014 meeting.

OTHER HISTORIC DOCUMENTS OF INTEREST

FROM PREVIOUS *HISTORIC DOCUMENTS*

- Federal Reserve Board Chair Announces End of Recession, *2009*, p. 430
- Federal Reserve and Economists on the U.S. Financial Crisis at Year-End, *2008*, p. 557

Index